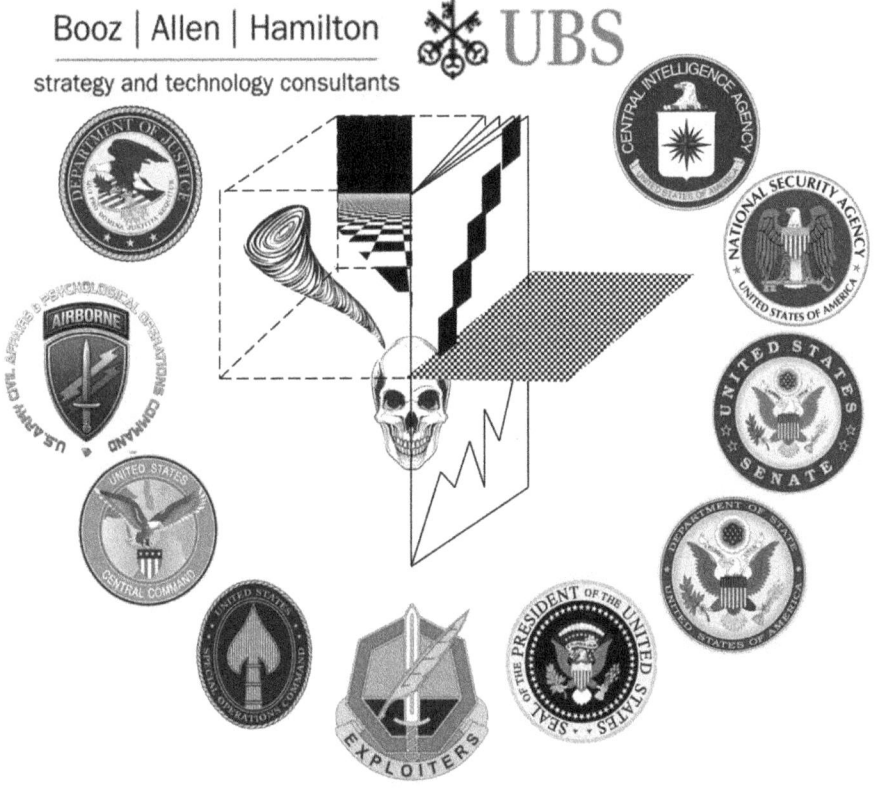

THIS BOOK WAS ORIGINALLY ORGANIZED AND WRITTEN ON A
TYPEWRITER IN FEDERAL PRISON

"SHELL GAME: A MILITARY WHISTLEBLOWING REPORT TO CONGRESS
The Betrayal and Cover-Up by the U.S. Government of the Union
Bank of Switzerland Terrorist Threat Finance Connection to
Booz Allen Hamilton and U.S. Central Command."

By 2LT Scott Bennett
11th Psychological Operations Battalion
U.S. Army Reserve

Copyright 2013
By Scott A. Bennett
23 Railroad Ave, #23
Danville, CA 94526

Interviews/materials available on the internet at:

https://wikispooks.com/wiki/Scott_Bennett

http://www.projectcamelotportal.com/blog/31-kerrys-blog/2289-now-on-youtube-scott-bennett-interview

https://www.youtube.com/watch?v=9210lpdh6ww

https://www.youtube.com/watch?v=Jo8Xm46s62I

https://www.youtube.com/watch?v=1-VP6XM099U

http://www.republicoftheunitedstates.org/rnn-recording-3/

http://roguemoney.net/wp-content/uploads/2014/11/The-Goerilla-Economist-wth-V-2014-11-07.mp3

http://armypsyop.wix.com/shellgame

http://www.lulu.com/spotlight/shellgame

https://www.facebook.com/capsule.ninetynine.7

First Edition: May 27, 2013
All rights reserved.
ISBN: 978-1-312-00260-9

Except as permitted under the U.S. Copyright Act of 1976, no part of this publication may be reproduced, distributed, or transmitted in any form or by any means, or stored in a database or retrieval system, without the prior written permission of the author.

"Take no part in the unfruitful works of darkness, but instead expose them." --Ephesians 5:11

This book is dedicated to my mother and father. Thank you for giving me the faith to be fearless, the conviction to speak truth to power, and the peace to trust God in all things, at all times.

It is also a fulfillment of my oath as a United States Military Officer, sworn to "*support and defend the Constitution of the United States against all enemies, foreign and <u>domestic</u>...*" It was written to inspire, educate, and empower my fellow military brethren with the truth, the whole truth, and nothing but the truth which I discovered, and reported solely to protect their lives.

It is hoped American citizens will also galvanize their own patriotism through experiencing my story, and find the strength and willpower to use this book as a light to shine in the suffocating darkness of the political corruption America is currently trapped within; and challenge our media and political tyrants with. It is a tool for leaders to use.

For those who have "*ears to hear and eyes to see*", this book was written as a personal testimony, tribute, and confirmation of the miraculous, healing works of God, my Lord and Savior Jesus Christ. It describes impossible coincidences, and amazing revelations no human hand could orchestrate. It marks the completion of a journey which began in 1998...and the beginning of a new one. Thank you.

--Scott Bennett

"*My heart is composing a goodly matter; I speak of the verses which I have made concerning the King; my tongue is the pen of a ready writer.*"

--Psalm 45:1

COVER SHEET

DATE: October 21, 2012
FROM: 2nd LT Scott Bennett # 29418-016
FCI Schuylkill, PO Box 670, Minersville, PA 17954-0670
TO: _____

The following is a <u>critical</u> brief summary of what is attached.
FOR IMMEDIATE RELEASE...

Minersville, PA: An Army Officer released a report to the General of the Army's Civil Affairs and Psychological Operations Command (USA CAPOC) stating a "cover up" and "scandal" has occurred with regards to the recent "UBS Whistleblower case" and Terrorist Threat Financing at the U.S. Central Command.

2LT Scott Bennett communicated to Congressional Authorities and top military officials at the Pentagon and Fort Bragg, NC that the "UBS Whistleblower, Brad Birkenfeld" had tried to get information to the military regarding Swiss bank accounts which were financing terrorist operations, but was denied from sharing it with the military by the Obama Administration, citing specifically Attorney General Eric Holder, Kevin O'Connor, and Kevin Dowing at the Dept. of Justice. Eric Holder had apparently worked for UBS in private practice and did not excuse himself.

2LT Bennett also suggested evidence seemed to suggest that CIA bank accounts may have been an issue and a reason for the aggressive silencing of Birkenfeld, and an investigation was needed. Bennett worked as a Terrorist Threat Finance Analyst at U.S. Central Command in the Joint Interagency Operations Center, and was defense contractor for Booz Allen Hamilton. Before that Bennett had been the Liaison between U.S. Special Operations Command and the State Department Coordinator for Counterterrorism Ambassador, Dale Dailey. Before joining Booz Allen Hamilton, Bennett had worked at the Bush Administration.

Bennett also reports that the military, specifically CENTCOM and USACAPOC, were kept completely out of the loop either out of intelligence sharing failure, or intentional deception that may amount to "Acts of Treason" according to Bennett. Bennett goes on to explain how Secretary of State Hilary Clinton transferred two Chinese Uighar terrorist suspects out of Guantanamo Bay detention facility to Switzerland by using Birkenfeld as a "political solution" and "scapegoat", and allowed Birkenfeld to be prosecuted out of a desire to manipulate Switzerland on various financial issues relating to taxes. Secretary of Treasury, Tim Geitner is also implicated.

Bennett also identified Senator Carl Levin as manipulating Birkenfeld's sworn testimony before the Senate's Permanent Subcommittee on Investigations, which then Senator Barack Obama was on at the time.

Bennett continued that evidence he examined indicated that Obama had special economic relationships with UBS Chairman of the Americas, Mr. Wolf, which encouraged a Dept. of Justice policy of prosecuting Birkenfeld by manipulating his testimony and building a false case against him.

Bennett issued his report as a "military whistleblowing report" and requested an Inspector General investigation be launched into the matter. Bennett requested that the military invite Birkenfeld to USACAPOC to debrief him on this material since he has been "gagged and shackled" by the Obama Administration, and violating the constitution, as well as killing soldiers and undermining the U.S. Mission. Bennett has requested a subpoena in order to testify before Congress, and has claimed that he has been falsely harassed, threatened with military discharge and prosecuted by the Department of Justice in an effort top silence him.

TABLE OF CONTENTS (UNCLASSIFIED)

SHELL GAME WHISTLEBLOWING REPORT.................................1-77

PREVIEW: SHELL GAME PART III.................................78-113

APPENDIX/ SUPPLEMENTAL DOCUMENTATION........................111-353
Duties
Clearance
Training
Terrorist Finance Training (UNCLASSIFIED)
Letters
Reports
Legal Motions
Supplemental Exhibits
DEPARTMENT OF DEFENSE COURIER
DOV ZAKHEIM

OFFICIAL WHISTLEBLOWING REPORT.....................................150
"TERRORIST THREAT FINANCE DIMENSIONS OF UNION BANK OF SWITZERLAND
(UBS) 'WHISTLEBLOWER CASE' AND OBAMA ADMINISTRATOIN INVOLVEMENT",
dated September 25, 2012

WIKILEAK CABLE ANALYSIS..170-199

OPEN SOURCE NEWS ARTICLES......................................200-203

OFFICIAL WHISTLEBLOWING REPORT.................................204-224
"FOLLOW THE MONEY", dated September 11, 2013

TERMS AND ORGANIZATIONS 226

INTERCONNECTIVITY CHART: BIRKENFELD-BENNETT-SNOWDEN 230-233

LETTER TO SENATE INTELLIGENCE COMMITTEE CHAIRWOMAN, DIANE FEINSTEIN
(D-CA) AND CARL LEVIN 234-238

NEWS ARTICLES:
UBS BANKER RAOUL WEIL—FINAL PIECE OF THE PUZZLE...................239
SNOWDEN AND CIA TARGETING BIRKENFELD..............................240
KUWAIT TERRORIST FINANCE CONNECTION...............................241
CIA DIRECTOR HAYDEN AND TERRORIST FINANCE.........................242
CIA SNOWDEN CONNECTION AND BIRKENFELD OPERATION...................243
PENTAGON WAR AGAINST WHITE, HETEROSEXUAL CHRISTIAN MEN 244
CIA FINANCIAL SPYING ON AMERICANS.................................245
QWEST PRESIDENT JOE NACCHIO, NSA, AND SNOWDEN DOCS.................246
LANNY BREUER, COVINGTON AND BURLING, AND UBS CASE.................247
COVINGTON AND BURLING AND SWISS BANK CLIENTS......................248

i

UNCONSTITUTIONAL PROSECUTION OF MILITARY MEMBER..................249
OBAMA'S PURGE OF THE MILITARY OF CONSERVATIVES...................250
BOOZ ALLEN HAMILTON SWALLOW UP WASHINGTON DC.....................251
BOOZ ALLEN, USIS, AND CARLYLE GROUP SECURITY CLEARANCES..........252

LIST OF MEMBERS OF CONGRESS RECEIVING WHISTLEBLOWING REPORTS......253

MILITARY POLICY STATEMENTS:
DEFENSE STATEMENT SENT TO DEPARTMENT OF THE ARMY..............254-264

MILITARY WHISTLEBLOWING PROTECTION ACT........................265-266

OBAMA BRANDING AND PERSECUTION OF "RIGHT WING", "ULTRA CONSERVATIVE",

"NEO-NAZI", "CHRISTIAN FANATICAL" GROUPS......................267-268

EQUAL OPPORTUNITY POLICY..269

STATEMENT OF FACTS AND REQUEST TO GENERAL JEFFREY JACOBS, COMMANDER,
U.S. CIVIL AFFAIRS-PSYCHOLOGICAL OPERATIONS COMMAND...........270-290

FULL DISCLOSURE: A LETTER TO MILITARY FAMILIES....................291

LETTER TO JESSELYN RADACK, SNOWDEN ATTORNEY, ABOUT WHISTLEBLOWING
DISCLOSURES AND COVER-UP......................................298-310

LETTER AND DEATH OF MICHAEL HASTINGS, ROLLING STONE STORY.........311

DEPARTMENT OF JUSTICE COURSE SYLLABUS: "DEEP BLACK: CIA SECRET DRUG
WARS, PART I AND II, by David Guyatt"............................312

APPENDIX A - REFERENCES.......................................323-324

COUNTERTERRORISM OPERATIONS (UNCLASSIFIED)....................325-345

VETERANS, FAMILIES, SUE SIX BANKS CLAIMING TERROR FUNDING.........346

A SAMPLE LETTER FOR CITIZENS TO SEND TO MEMBERS OF CONGRESS,
JOURNALISTS, BLOGGERS, AND THE MILITARY 347-348

ABOUT THE AUTHOR..349

A SPECIAL THANKS..350-357

WEB LINKS TO INTERVIEWS AND MEDIA SHOWS...................... 358-359

OFFICER'S OATH

I, *Scott Bennett*, do solemnly swear (or affirm) that I will support and defend the Constitution of the United States against all enemies, foreign and domestic; that I will bear true faith and allegiance to the same; that I take this obligation freely, without any mental reservation or purpose of evasion; and that I will well and faithfully discharge the duties of the office on which I am about to enter. So help me God.

THE SOLDIER'S CREED

I am an American Soldier.
I am a warrior and a member of a team.
I serve the people of the United States, and live the Army Values.
I will always place the mission first.
I will never accept defeat.
I will never quit.
I will never leave a fallen comrade.
I am disciplined, physically and mentally tough, trained and proficient in my warrior tasks and drills.
I always maintain my arms, my equipment and myself.
I am an expert and I am a professional.
I stand ready to deploy, engage, and destroy, the enemies of the United States of America in close combat.
I am a guardian of freedom and the American way of life.
I am an American Soldier.

To all who shall see these presents, greeting:

Know Ye, that reposing special trust and confidence in the patriotism, valor, fidelity and abilities of **Scott A. Bennett**, *I do appoint* **him, Second Lieutenant, Reserve** *in the*

United States Army

to **rank** *as such from the* **eighth** *day of* **February**, *two thousand* **eight**. *This officer will therefore carefully and diligently discharge the duties of the office to which appointed by doing and performing all manner of things thereunto belonging.*

And I do strictly charge and require those officers and other personnel of lesser rank to render such obedience as is due an officer of this grade and position. And, this officer is to observe and follow such orders and directions, from time to time, as may be given by the President of the United States of America or other superior officers, acting in accordance with the laws of the United States of America. This commission is to continue in force during the pleasure of the President of the United States of America under the provisions of those public laws relating to officers of the **Armed Forces of the United States of America** *and the component thereof in which this appointment is made.*

Done at the city of Washington, this **nineteenth** *day of* **February** *in the year of our Lord two thousand* **nine** *and of the Independence of the United States of America the* **two hundred thirty-third year.**
By the President:

SECRETARY OF THE ARMY

SHELL GAME:
The Betrayal and Cover-Up by the U.S. Government of the
Union Bank of Switzerland-Terrorist Threat Finance Connection
To Booz Allen Hamilton and U.S. Central Command

A Whistleblowing Report
to the United States Congress

Submitted by
Scott Bennett, 2LT, United States Army (Reserve)
11th Psychological Operations Battalion
To The Department of Defense Inspector General

DATE: Memorial Day, May 27, 2013

OFFICIAL COMMUNICATION TO CONGRESS
AND REQUEST FOR SPECIAL HEARING AND INVESTIGATION

Copyright 2013

All Rights Reserved

No parts may be reproduced without the express permission of the author.

UNCLASSIFIED

CONTENTS

WHISTLEBLOWING REPORT DISCLOSURE
PRESS RELEASE: SYNOPSIS
PROEM (i)
INTRODUCTION (ii)
    CONSPIRACY AND COVER-UP (2)
    UNION BANK OF SWITZERLAND-BRAD BIRKENFELD-BOOZ ALLEN HAMILTON (5)
    U.S. CENTRAL COMMAND-TERRORIST THREAT FINANCE-BOOZ ALLEN (5)
JOINT INTERAGENCY OPERATIONS CENTER/ JOINT INTERAGENCY GROUP (9)
INTELLIGENCE SHARING: FAILURE OR COVER-UP? (10)
BUREAUCRATIC DYSFUNCTIONALITY (10)
CONSPIRACY, TORTURE, AND BETRAYAL (12)
BENGHAZI, LIBYA ATTACK PREDICTED (15)
KILL THE MESSENGER (16)
VIOLATION OF '1870 POSSE COMITATUS ACT' (16)
UNION BANK OF SWITZERLAND-BRAD BIRKENFELD INTELLIGENCE (22)
WIKILEAKS: SUPPORTING DOCUMENTATION (24)
STATE DEPARTMENT COORDINATOR FOR COUNTERTERRORISM (S/CT) (25)
U.S. SPECIAL OPERATIONS COMMAND (25)
DEPARTMENT OF JUSTICE-CIA ASSASINATION ATTEMPT? (25)
***EDWARD SNOWDEN DISCOVERIES (25.5)
NATIONAL COUNTERTERRORISM CENTER (NCTC) (26)
MIKE MCCONNELL, DIRECTOR OF NATIONAL INTELLIGENCE-BOOZ ALLEN HAMILTON (26)
SENATOR CARL LEVIN: ARMED SERVICES AND INVESTIGATIONS COMMITTEE (25)
LETTER TO GENERAL JAMES MATTIS, COMMANDER U.S. CENTCOM (29)
$104 MILLION DOLLAR PAY-OFF TO BIRKENFELD FOR REMAINING SILENT (30)
LETTER TO GENERAL JEFF JACOBS, COMMANDER, USACAPOC, (30)
LETTER TO INSPECTOR GENERAL, LYNNE HALBROOKS, DEPARTMENT OF DEFENS (30)
LETTERS TO CONGRESS: HOUSE OF REPRESENTATIVES, SENATE, COMMITTEES (31)
LETTERS TO THE MEDIA (32)
FALLING INTO THE ABYSS (35)
AN ARMY OFFICER'S DUTY TO COUNTRY (42)
A CLEAR AND PRESENT DANGER TO THE UNITED STATES (51)
CONSTITUTIONAL OATH: "AGAINST ALL ENEMIES, FOREIGN AND <u>DOMESTIC</u>" (52)
DONALD RUMSFELD AND GENERAL DICK MEYERS (53)
BENGHAZI ATTACKS (53)
INSIDE THE HEART AND MIND OF A MUSLIM TERRORIST (55)
BRADLEY MANNING: THE HIDDEN STORY (57)
THE ART OF PSYCHOLOGICAL WARFARE (61)
PARASITE DEFENSE CONTRACTORS AND THE BUSINESS OF WAR (63)
"TORMENTS OF THE GRAVE": DEFEATING THE MUSLIM IDEA OF MARTYRDOM (65)
BRAD BIRKENFELD--AN AMERICAN PATRIOT (67)
BIRKENFELD'S MISSING INTELLIGENCE AND MUZZLING BY DEPT. OF JUSTICE (68)
A WOMAN'S LAMENT (69)
CONNECTION TO PRESIDENT BARACK HUSSEIN OBAMA, UNION BANK OF SWITZERLAND, AND ATTORNEY GENERAL ERIC HOLDER AND ASSISTANT A.G. LANNY BREUER (73)
ABDULLAH AZZIZ: TERRORIST THREAT FINANCE CONNECTIONS (74)
REQUEST FOR OFFICIAL CONGRESSIONAL INVESTIGATION, HEARINGS (75)
EPILOGUE: BRAVEHEART (76)

DISCLOSURE

This is a "whistleblower" report to the American people. It has already been sent to the military, the Congress, the Courts, and the media. It's purpose is to inform minds, inspire hearts, and save lives--those of our servicemen, our allies, and our civilians--and our nation's future.

I am an American soldier, and Army Officer, and I write this in obedience to my sworn oath to "support and defend the Constitution of the United States against all enemies, foreign and domestic."

In this case, I am defending against domestic enemies giving "aide and comfort" to the foreign terrorist enemy by not utilizing key financial intelligence relating to terrorist finance networks and operations; and thereby committing treason (as defined by Article 3, section 3 of the U.S. Constitution) against the people of the United States of America.

Citizens--of America and our international coalition of allies--are encouraged to call and write the U.S. House of Representatives, the U.S. Senate, and the media, to demand that Congressional hearings be held to investigate the matter, provide an explanation, and hold all parties accountable.

The following is a true story.

DATE: May 27, 2013--MEMORIAL DAY

Scott Bennett, 2LT U.S. Army (Reserve)
11th Psychological Operations Battalion
FPC Schuylkill, camp 2, A-14
P.O. Box 670
Minersville, PA 17954-0670
(570) 544-7100 fax: (570) 544-7296
Fed. No.: 29418-016

2LT. SCOTT BENNETT, USAR
#29418-016, FPC SCHUYLKILL, P.O. BOX 670
MINERSVILLE, PA 17954-0670
(570) 544-7100

February 10, 2013

FOR IMMEDIATE RELEASE:

RE: Military whistleblowing report to Congress on Psychological warfare and terrorist financing issues (follow up to the "TOO BIG TO JAIL" Rolling Stone article Feb. 28, 2013).

Attention Military Officers, Members of Congress, and the Media:

If you're interested, I'd like to share with you a story which very well could win you both the Pulitzer for exposing it, and the U.S. Medal of Freedom for having the courage to face it.
The story involves two military whistleblowing reports to Congress. One report examined "Psychological Warfare Issues" which would be conducted against Americans; the other report examined terrorist financing by international banks and the intentional cover-up by U.S. government officials. One report prophetically warned of the Benghazi, Libya attacks; the other report addresses the deeper, more insidious aspects of the issues raised in Matt Taibbi's Rolling Stone article "TOO BIG TO JAIL."
Quite simply, the Rolling Stone article exposes only the tip of an oil-black iceberg of government corruption with regards to terrorist financing, global banks, defense contractors, and intentional military intelligence failures.
The real story revolves around a whistleblowing report to U.S. Civil Affairs-Psychological Operations Command on September 25, 2012; a secret Senate hearing; an assasination attempt by the Department of Justice against the whistleblower; and financial intelligence sharing failures at the highest level of government which can only be explained as either: 1) a treasonous conspiratorial manipulation of information by the Department of Justice and the Intelligence Community against the military; or 2) a pathetic and scandalous bureaucratic blunder which has spilled the blood of servicemembers unnecessarily and wasted tens of millions of dollars. I invite you to review the bank statements, wiki-leaks cables, letters, reports, interviews, and other materials I have, and arrive at your own conclusion.

WHO AM I:

I am an Army Officer with extensive experience at U.S. Special Operations Command, U.S. Central Command, and the State Department Coordinator for Counterterrorism Office (and other agencies). Before this I worked for the G.W. Bush Administration from 2003 to 2008, had a Top Secret/SCI security clearance, and specialized in Psychological Warfare and Islamic terrorist finance operations. Resume attached.
Since you and your organization claim to represent the spirit of accountability in American government, and are recognized as champions of democratic freedoms, I invite you to honor that title and oath by contacting me for a further debriefing.
If you're interested in the next "Watergate"/"Iran-Contra" scandal that reads like a Tom Clancy mixed with a "DaVinci Code" plot, contact me for details.

Respectfully yours,

Scott Bennett

MILITARY ATTORNEY:
Captain Avi Stone
Avraham.R.Stone@us.army.mil

ABSTRACT

Enclosed are exerpts from an 83-page military whistleblowing report which influenced Edward Snowden's decision to circumvent Congress and release his information <u>directly</u> to the American people.

The report was written by an Army Officer and Psychological Warfare analyst at <u>Booz Allen Hamilton</u>--the same defense contractor that employed Snowden. This analyst had a Top Secret/Sensitive Compartmentalized Information (TS/SCI) clearance, and worked in counterterrorism at the State Department, U.S. Special Operations Command, and U.S. Central Command in Washington D.C. and Florida. The report answers the following:

1. Why did Edward Snowden feel he had to <u>immediately</u> go public?
2. What connects Booz Allen Hamilton, the NSA, the CIA, Union Bank of Switzerland, and Terrorist Threat Finance conspiracy and cover-up?
3. Who is the <u>Swiss Banker</u> entrapped by the CIA, whose identity was discovered by Snowden during his time with CIA in Geneva, Switzerland?
4. Who are Booz Allen Hamilton players Edward Snowden, Scott Bennett, Mike McConnell, and James Clapper?
5. Who are the National Security Agency whistleblowers Thomas Drake, William Binney, and J. Kirk Wiebe?

ANSWERS:
1. Snowden went public because he had no choice. He discovered what had happened to 2LT Scott Bennett when he filed reports through official channels, and knew the only chance to warn Americans was by telling them.
2. Booz Allen Hamilton managed people and operations in Terrorist Threat Finance for the military and the intelligence community, yet after an analyst reported Swiss bank issues, he was fired, the report buried.
3. The Swiss Banker, Brad Birkenfeld, was indicted, convicted, and jailed after he exposed the <u>Union Bank of Switzerland (UBS)</u>-Terrorist Threat Finance connection to the Department of Justice and intelligence agencies.
4. Scott Bennett was a Booz Allen Hamilton Associate and Army Officer who worked as a Terrorist Threat Finance analyst at U.S. CENTCOM, and was indicted, tried, and convicted on trumped-up charges after he sent two reports up the chain of command: one predicted the <u>Benghazi</u> attack; the other exposed the conspiracy and cover-up of the <u>UBS-Birkenfeld-CIA</u> Terrorist Threat Finance connection. Ironically Birkenfeld and Bennett ended up in the same unit, in the same prison, and compared notes--each connecting the others' dots to arrive at a terrifying conclusion.
Mike McConnel was the Director of National Intelligence (DNI) during 2007-2009 and saw the intelligence reports from CIA about UBS-Birkenfeld. McConnell is now the Vice Chairman of Booz Allen Hamilton and runs cyberwar.
James Clapper is also an ex-Booz Allen executive and presently the Director of National Intelligence. He has seen Snowden and Bennett's intel. No one in government or Booz Allen Hamilton has even been questioned in the Terrorist Finance-UBS-Birkenfeld-CIA-Booz Allen Hamilton connection--ever. Clapper made the "least untruthful statement" before Congress when he lied about Snowden's NSA monitoring of Americans, and failed to discuss Bennett's report confirming the UBS-Birkenfeld-CIA link Snowden released, as well as the connection to Booz Allen Hamilton both Snowden and Bennett shared.
5. NSA Whistleblowers Thomas Drake, William Binney, and J. Kirk Wiebe were patriots indicted, prosecuted, and lives trashed after legally exposing illegality by the NSA. Most disturbing of all, <u>Leon Panetta, Secretary of Defense</u>, was a Booz Allen man.

This is only an excerpt. The entire 83-page report may be obtained by contacting the Army Officer directly at: 2LT Scott Bennett, 29418-016, P.O. Box Box 670, Minersville, PA 17954-0670 (570-544-7100 for media call). Bennett's attorney: Jeff O'Toole (202-775-1550) otoole@otrons.com
Bennett's military attorney: Capt. Avi Stone (avraham.r.stone@us.army.mil)

"Ye shall know the truth, and the truth shall make you free." -JOHN 8:32

PROEM

In Mel Gibson's masterpiece film "Braveheart", there is a scene where the "nobleman" who betrayed William Wallace on the battlefield--abandoning him during the fight in favor of bribe money and political title--is asleep in his <u>subsidized</u> bed, tossing and turning as he's tormented by the nightmare of a blue-face-painted, sword-swinging Wallace galloping on horseback against a backdrop of flames, chasing after him; startling him awake with terror. As he whimpers relieved that it was just a dream, the bedchamber doors suddenly burst open by Wallace atop a horse, as he rides in, steps onto the bed, unfurls a massive iron ball-and-chain, and swirls and smashes it down upon the face of the traitor.

I anticipate this letter will no doubt have the same effect on certain people. For right now somewhere, in the dark, dank cubicles of U.S. Government, there is a nervously twitching cabal of parasitic lawyers and bureaucrats from the White House, the Intelligence Community, Congress, the media, and the military, who have been dreading and desperately trying to bury and stop this report from ever reaching the American public. Obstructionists whose skullduggery must now, with the weight and momentum behind this letter, come to a career-face smashing end; and their deeds be exposed as the acts of treason they are.

INTRODUCTION

Nearly 40 years ago, a small team of men stood before a judge and tried to quietly settle a burglary incident. The strangeness of the incident--the military-intelligence (CIA) backgrounds of the men, the Democratic National Committee headquarters as the target--led a couple of intrepid "investigative" journalists to shame the press establishment by successfully doing what no other news media would at the time: They began asking questions and looking deeper. They discovered a political plot, triggered a Congressional Investigation, and as more men were dragged in to testify, revealed a government orchestrated conspiracy which eventually toppled a President with delusions of infallible Kingship. It was the story of the decade that rocked the legal foundations of our Republic.

Then a decade later, a military officer answered the questions of Congress about duties he performed for his President--somehow without his President's knowledge--out of love of country.

Then another American Intelligence Operative (a CIA agent) testified before Congress about how she was targeted and persecuted in order to hinder her husband who was exposing lies that were being used to justify a war to make a "Brave New World" cleansed of extremist ideologies...which included certain outspoken American political groups as seen by the recent IRS persecution of conservative 501.c.4 "Tea Party" groups.

The parallels of Nixon's "Watergate" conspiracy; LT.Colonel Oliver North's "Iran-Contra" obstruction of Congress scandal; and Valerie Plaime's vindictive exposure and persecution, are all interconnected--by substance and innuendo--to this current "Union Bank of Switzerland (UBS)-Counterterrorist Threat Financing" and Rolling Stone's "Too Big to Jail" story. Only this is far worse.

i

Matt Taibbi's article "Too Big to Jail" in the Feb. 28, 2013 issue of Rolling Stone exposes the connection between terrorist threat financing and international banks like HSBC. Unfortunately--or fortunately--it's only half the story. The Rolling Stone article reveals only the tip of an oil-black iceberg of government corruption with regard to terrorist financing, global banks, defense contractors, and intentional military intelligence failures.

The real story revolves around a whistleblowing report written by a U.S. Army Officer and terrorist finance analyst to U.S. Civil Affairs-Psychological Operations Command on September 25, 2012; a secret Senate hearing; an assasination attempt by the Department of Justice against the whistleblower; and financial intelligence sharing failures at the highest level of government which can only be explained as either 1) a treasonous conspiratorial manipulation of information by the Department of Justice and the Intelligence Community against the military; or 2) a pathetic and scandalous bureaucratic blunder which has spilled the blood of service members unnecessarily, which wasted tens of millions of dollars, and exhausted our nation with war fatigue.

The Army Officer had extensive experience at U.S. Special Operations Command, U.S. Central Command, and the State Department Coordinator for Counterterrorism Office, where he had worked multidimensionally as a psychological warfare analyst and defense contractor, and had a Top Secret/SCI security clearance--one of the highest in the nation. This Officer wrote two whistleblowing reports to Congress. One examined impending psychological warfare attacks against the American people (and troops); the other exposed and analyzed terrorist threat financing by international banks and the intentional cover-up by civilian U.S. Government officials.

One report prophetically warned of the Benghazi, Libya attacks; the other addressed the deeper, more insidious aspects of the issues raised in Matt Taibbi's recent Rolling Stone article about HSBC, terrorist bank accounts, and the concerted effort to punish and silence whistleblowers who discovered and reported intelligence to authorities whose job was to use such intelligence to defend the nation.

For the purposes of brevity, the latter whistleblowing report will be the focus in this article.

After reviewing mountains of bank documents, wikileaks cables, reports, letters, interviews, and other materials, the Army Officer made some startling discoveries.

PART I: SHELL GAME

When it comes to financing international terrorists with secret foreign bank accounts and then covering it up and silencing the whistleblower who reported it, nobody quite does it better than the United States Government--more specifically the U.S. Department of Justice and the Senate.

If you're reading this article in an American publication, then it means the U.S. media has not abandoned its sacred post as a preserver of freedom and vanguard of democracy, or the internet been unplugged as the blipping E.K.G. monitor of the U.S. Constitution's life support.

If you're *not* reading this in an American publication, then they have abandoned their post--and oath--by refusing to speak truth, stuck their collective heads in the sand along with the Congressman and Senators who've read this report, and shamelessly sold their birthright for the sour pottage of Obama's Orwellian patriotism to a paranoid new world of drone enforced Executive Orders. If the American media is not publishing this, then you must thank the outside world's media for standing-up for what is right and true and good, and having the courage to publish this inconvenient truth.

This truth is a report written by a defense contractor and Army Officer who was a psychological warfare and terrorist threat finance analyst (with a Top Secret/SCI security clearance) for U.S. Central Command, U.S. Special Operations Command, and the State Department Coordinator for Counterterrorism Office from 2008 to 2010.

This report exposed and analyzed in great detail how the Department of Justice, the Senate Permanent Subcommittee on Investigations under Senator Carl Levin (D-MI) and then Senator Barack Obama (D-IL), the Senate Armed Services committee (also under Senator Carl Levin), the Justice Department, the State Department, and certain agencies in the "Intelligence" community, colluded to betray, prosecute, and cover-up the Union Bank of Switzerland whistleblower, Brad Birkenfeld, for exposing and reporting the UBS-Terrorist Threat Finance connection.

This report was sent to Colonel Jeffrey Jacobs, Commander of U.S. Civil Affairs-Psychological Operations Command on September 25, 2012. After receiving no response whatsoever, the Army Officer felt compelled to send it to Congress and the Pentagon Inspector General a month later, out of a sense of duty and his "oath to uphold and defend the Constitution", which this ilicit Terrorist Threat Finance-Foreign Bank connection indicated. The report was sent to Inspector General Lynne Halbrooks, as well as over thirty (30) Congressman and Senators (including the committees on the Armed Services, Homeland Security, Terrorism, Finance, and Intelligence) as an official "whistleblowing report". See attached list of names.

However again, no response was given and nothing was done. The reason for this lack of response of course was one four-letter word which seems to symbolize our modern political-military leaders, as well as the psychosis suffocating our sense of national identity. That word is simply--yet with profound implications--<u>FEAR</u>.

By revealing the existence of this connection between UBS (and other foreign banks) and Islamic terrorists, the military and the intelligence community would be, once again, properly defined as bureaucrats in uniform as efficient as the Maytag repairman with an unplugged phone. They would be seen as either failing to discover this terrorist threat finance dimension of the UBS-Birkenfeld whistleblowing drama; or intentionally failing to act despite their knowing, leaving them with the blood of service men on their hands from the bombs and bullets bought with UBS wrapped dollars (similar to the pallets found in Iraq's early invasion). So FEAR governed the military-defense contractor and intelligence community response. Fear of exposure, accountability, and the repercussions against their ineptitude by a nation of outraged families and silent graves.

FEAR also inspired politicians. Addicted to their lust for re-election and neutered by political-correctness, they frantically covered ears, eyes, and mouth in a hear-see-speak no evil (or truth in this case) fetal position posture of denial, hoping the report would "go away", or perhaps the writer of it mysteriously disappear into the echo of a bullet. They feared that since the report explained how an <u>assasination attempt</u> may have been made by the Department of Justice against Brad Birkenfeld in the form of a <u>forged letter sent to UBS</u> claiming to be from Birkenfeld's friend betraying that Birkenfeld was revealing "proprietary bank information" (aka, terrorist bank accounts) to the Justice Department, this might open a Pandora's Box of Patriot Act suspicion--a marriage they had already forced upon the American people. After all, the most logical party guilty of ordering the assasination attempt was the Department of Justice itself, specifically attorneys Kevin O'Connor and/or Kevin Downing, who interestingly had ties to ex-mayor of New York Rudy Gulianni, Abdullah Azziz (mentioned as an Al Qaeda financier in Matt Taibbi's recent article "Too Big to Jail"), and foreign banks. The report explained how one month after meeting with Department of Justice officials (and giving them his cell phone number), Birkenfeld's

international banking friend from London had received a call from
UBS asking him why he had sent them a letter exposing Birkenfeld's
meeting with Justice Department officials. He denied ever writing
such a letter, obtained a copy of it, showed it to Birkenfeld, and
in shock and outrage at being violated, demanded to know what was going on.

Birkenfeld then explained he was meeting with DOJ officials,
but couldn't discuss the reasons. Despite confronting and demanding an explanation
from the Justice Department about this letter, no response was ever
given. The explanation was being written on the wall: Birkenfeld's
revelations about terrorist financing by UBS would expose accounts
and activities by U.S. government agencies (Crooks-In-Action, aka CIA, no
doubt) which mentally-medicated politicians simply would not want
to have to sharpen their wits and give an answer for. So in order
to not have to suffer the strain of honesty and give an answer to
the American people about UBS accounts being used to finance terrorist
threats against American sons and daughters in military uniform,
a plan (or some might say treasonous scandal) was devised.

The plan would be to bait Birkenfeld into giving testimony
before the Senate Permanent Subcommittee on Investigations (chaired
by Senator Carl Levin), and then switch the discussion to "American
Tax Evasion and Money Laundering" issues, so that the Justice Department
could entrap Birkenfeld with his own disclosures (despite his being
promised immunity and good faith), cobble together a rickety legal
case against him; then threaten, prosecute and silence him with
a plea deal that would remove him from the public eye as quickly as possible
(This is the real reason Carl Levin is rushing to retire from office--and save his pension

Conveniently this would guarantee loyalty from UBS Chairman for
the Americas Robert Wolf, and bind him into becoming a financial campaign

donor and supporter of then Senator Barack Obama, who was also on the committee and running for President of the United States against John McCain in 2008 (Interestingly, Attorney General Eric Holder and Assistant Attorney General LannyBreur worked for the law firm Covington and Burling in private practice, and also represented UBS prior to their joining the Justice Department. This wasn't mentioned in Matt Taibbi's article explaining why Lanny Breur--and Eric Holder--gave deferred prosecutions to big banks--including UBS. It was because they worked for these banks in the past, and no doubt expected to again in the future, that deferred prosecutions were given, and had nothing to do with the "red herring" of saving jobs or destabilizing the financial markets or global banking industry).

However despite also being chairman of the Senate Armed Services Committee, Senator Carl Levin refused to share any of the information disclosed by Birkenfeld about UBS financing terrorists through its secret Swiss accounts and internal instruments, such as the "Optimus Foundation",with the Armed Services organization whose central mission was to combat, destroy and prevent terrorist threat finance operations and networks. This organization was <u>U.S. Central Command's Terrorist Threat Finance team managed by defense contractor Booz Allen Hamilton</u> at MacDill Air Force Base in Tampa, Florida. I know this because I was a member of this team, and neither Senator Carl Levin, nor President Barack Obama, nor any member of any Congressional committee ever allowed Brad Birkenfeld's testimony or financial information to be shared with us. It was only after I met Brad Birkenfeld after he was imprisoned that I discovered how incredibly valuable his financial information was, and how much obscene skullduggery, corruption and treason may have been committed against our military by allowing terrorist-UBS financial networks to remain undisclosed and untargeted for political gain.

It was only after I spent months with Birkenfeld piecing together all of the intelligence materials (i.e., Wikileaks cables, bank statements, reports, letters, interviews) he had accumulated in an effort to vindicate himself, that I stumbled upon an outrageous irony and astounding--if not miraculous--coincidence. My job had been to work within the military-intelligence matrix to identify, analyze, track-down, and destroy terrorist finance networks and operations. Yet the information most necessary for combatting these terrorists was coming to me <u>not</u> from the intelligence community, but from a jail cell; not from a professional military analyst, but from an imprisoned civilian banker. And never would we have met had this same government which <u>imprisoned him for whistleblowing</u> about Swiss banks financing terrorism, not also <u>imprisoned me for discovering</u> and trying to expose the same menace. Whether out of an impossible coincidence or Divinely orchestrated meeting, Brad Birkenfeld and I ended up not only at the same prison, but in the same dorm, down the hall from eachother; and upon meeting discovered our individual stories formed a fantastic revelation that truth is indeed stranger than fiction. Here is where the story takes a turn toward the bizarre, if not supernatural, and makes the wise seem foolish by showing how accidents can really be appointments.

I had been given a Direct Commission as an Officer in the United States Army (Reserve) based on my experience at the Bush Administration, advanced degrees, and prior work as a Psychological Warfare and Intelligence analyst at the State Department Coordinator for Counterterrorism (State/CT) Office, and U.S. Special Operations Command-Joint Military Information Support Center.

After completing Officer training, I had been asked if I would consider becoming a Terrorist Threat Finance analyst at U.S. Central Command, and transfer to Tampa, Florida within the month. It would be more than a 9 to 5 job, it would be a mission to end the war on terror by destroying the enemy's ability to make war by evaporating his money. I was told they desperately needed my psyop and counterterrorism background, and would infuse my defense contractor work into my Army duty, so that I could both work and perform military drill at the same location. Although it meant relocating my entire life from Washington DC down to Florida, my love and duty to country came first, and I accepted the position. I informed my Army battalion (11th Psychological Operations Battalion) in the Wash. D.C. area, and began the process of transferring to U.S. Central Command.

I was given a special VIP flight aboard the executive jet of U.S. Special Operations Commander, Admiral Eric Olson, and flew down with him personally to U.S. Central Command, and I was given temporary housing at MacDill Air Force Base. I had arranged to live on-base in order to facilitate my Army unit transfer, and also to be safe(r). I had a Top Secret/ Sensitive Compartmentalized Information security clearance, which meant I was at the top of the terrorist wish list for beheading or extortion through family kidnappings, etc. At indoctrination training I was told "you are now a target, threats lurk everywhere, trust no one." I took it as sage advice.

Over the next four months I was trained and worked in every dimension, product, and agency which interfaced with the art and science of terrorist financial networks and operations. I also found myself head-butting against worshippers of mediocrity, bureaucracy, and the status quo (aka, government employees).

My personality is that of an Alpha, extrovert, and fearlessly aggressive. Since eleven years old, I had been active in Boy Scouts (when men were still men), Civil Air Patrol (Air Force Cadets), DeMolay (junior Masons), high school sports, college fraternity (Alpha Tau Omega), and now Army Special Operations. As a warrior-soldier, I despised simpletons, weaklings, and cowards, especially among Officers, since they got better men killed. I had a nobler pedigree and history of proven leadership skills than most generals...and they felt it. I despised bureaucratic inefficiency as the blood-clot in the mind of common sense, and sand in the gears of success. I didn't wait for problems to arrive, I went out to attack them with ruthless confidence and audacious creativity, which no doubt upset those whose jobs are justified by making organizational problems chronic. But like oil and water, laziness and I didn't mix.

It was this volatile chemistry of personality which would eventually form the storm that would blow my odyssey off-course and banish me into Obama's archipelago of military-intelligence-financia secrets, shipwreck me onto Birkenfeld's "Alcatraz of misfit toys", and ultimately lead to my redemptive discovery of the "Grail" through Birkenfeld's documents which proved my suspicions--and reports--had been right all along: That Swiss banks like UBS (and HSBC) had, in fact, been financing terrorists, and the intelligence community was concealing it for political reasons.

Now in the interests of column space and copyrights--never mind national security--I cannot express here the vast labrynth of knowledge and experiences I absorbed whilst sojourning within the U.S. military-intelligence-political body, only to say that it was quite a "Fantastic Voyage". The fat, decay, and atrophy in ability and instinct to be creative, adaptable, and fearless in management and strategy seemed to, unfortunately, hobble our traditional American strengths of intellectual and technological genius. Yes, fighter planes, cruise missles, SEAL team Six, and drone assasinations are all healthy, motivation - enhancing inoculations for our national ego towards terrorism, but I am more interested in focussing on our weaknesses and disabilities in order to heal and rehabilitate them, than I am in self-complimenting and inflating the vanity of our military muscle. The reason is: the terrorist enemy doesn't hit us where we're strong or protected, but where we're weakest and most vulnerable. So with this attitude, I went into my job as a Terrorist Threat Finance analyst to examine, probe, and dissect all aspects and personnel and operations involved in the mission, so that I could identify the problems and prescribe the solutions.

I familiarized myself with all U.S. Government Agencies, military combatant commands and special warfare units, and defense contractors (both U.S. and foreign) who were engaged in counterterrorism, threat finance, and unconventional warfighting around the globe. I was given a work station in the Joint Interagency Operations Center (JIOC)--also known sometimes as the Joint Interagency Group (JIAG)--and worked with an assortment of government agencies including the State Department, Treasury, Justice, Homeland Security, Central Intelligence Agency, Immigration and Customs Enforcement, and some others (classified).

I was tasked with interviewing all the different agency teams to discover their particular expertise in Terrorist Threat Finance, and formulate recommendations to improve their functionality. This meant identifying duplicative and unproductive operations within the agencies, developing plans and timetables for eliminating them, and synthesizing the best practices and expertise of the various government and military agencies into my Booz Allen Hamilton team. Of course, this was somewhat unpopular and strenuously resisted by certain agencies in the JIOC, since they had formed a "nest" in CENTCOM and built up a bureacratic culture   immediately after September 11, 2001; and typical of bureaucracy, they viewed every worker and task of their particular agency as essential,   regardless if it was being duplicated by four other government agencies, the military, or their subcontractors.

Since one thing military people (and bureaucrats) hate is to lose power to the private sector, the unfortunate result was a military-government-intelligence community dysfunctionality with regard to Terrorist Threat Finance; and a refusal to communicate, share information, or engage in a team effort by U.S. SOCOM (Special Operations Command) and other departments. It was a surreal turf war between military commands fighting for power; government agencies occupying space without really producing anything substantive; and private sector contractors trying to modify the status quo and being reviled for it. It was the most bizaare circus of petty politics I had ever encountered.

Most offensive to me as a military officer was the fact that this "power-struggle" between CENTCOM, SOCOM, civilian government agencies, and defense contractors like Booz Allen Hamilton, was extending   the killing, maiming, and suffering of military personnel by dragging out the wars unnecessarily. By wasting time, resources, and refusing to exploit information about Swiss banks such as UBS (and HSBC) which terrorists used to finance their personnel and operations, the sad (and perhaps treasonous) result was America's security was undermined, and our sons and daughters in uniform were being sacrificed because America's military-intelligence community leadership were acting like jealous infants pouting over favorite toys.

Despite my vigorous--some might say furious--attempts to synthesize interdepartmental intelligence to triangulate Swiss banks like UBS as the hub of the Iran, Haqqani, and European terrorist networks, as well as design psychological warfare campaigns, I was repeatedly blocked and discouraged from delving too deep or being too aggressively creative. Additionally my recommendations to more intelligently filter Islamic lecturers in order to avoid infecting young soldiers' minds with ambiguous, contradictory, and ecumenically ambidextrous propaganda had been scorned as "too harsh." It seemed endangering the mission by crippling soldiers with the paralysis of moral confusion on the battlefield was more acceptable a risk than a legal confrontation with terrorist apologists whose weapon was a twisted U.S. Constitution.

The military higher-command "modus operandi" seemed to unofficially be "apply political-correctness non-judgmentally to all issues requiring judgment." Clever?..Yes. Safe?..Perhaps...for a while. However despite my instinctive concern about flaws or contradictions in strategic communication (SC) materials, strategy, or leadership, I was told my job was not to improve CENTCOM but to stop extremists from financing global terrorism. And so, always the good soldier, I obeyed orders, saluted sharply, and pushed forward in my work and mission.

Although I honestly believed--and still do--that my application of creative imagination to the counterterrorism analytical framework (CTAF) was helping military commanders formulate better strategies and operations, as well as improving interagency intelligence sharing, I soon discovered how much it also was feared. It seemed my 'rocking-the-boat' was gaining the attention of people who despise paying attention as a matter of temperment. Because one week after a moving truck delivered my household property (clothes, furniture, military gear, firearms and ammunition) into my apartment on base (arranged and paid for by my firm, Booz Allen Hamilton) I was stopped in my car at the front gate, arrested at gun-point by military police, taken against my will, and interrogated for twelve (12) hours under conditions the ACLU and most Congress Members define as torture in handcuffs.

At first, I thought it was a training exercise to test a person's aptitude for special undercover operations, resistance to interrogation, emotional fortitude, or intellectual dexterity.

The reason being, I had just completed a week-long training course in "Advanced Critical Thinking" (after being the first person in CENTCOM's history to 'test-out' of the prior mandatory 'Beginning' and 'Intermediate' courses--much to the chagrin of certain bureaucrats in Booz Allen Hamilton who got paid to give classes I didn't need). So, calmly and deliberately, I played along with what I thought was part of the game.

However the missing component of subtle delicacy and psychological complexity in the blunt-force trauma sadistically applied by Detective Edward Garcia and his master   LTC. Martin Mitchell quickly disabused me of this notion. MacDill Air Force Base Security Forces, and its Commander, had now shed the blood of one of their own, and shamed America like never before.

Despite my being a U.S. Army Officer and counterterrorism defense contractor with a Top Secret/ Sensitive compartmentalized information security clearance, despite my having worked at State Department Counterterrorism (S/CT), U.S. Special Operations Command, the Pentagon, and now U.S. Central Command, despite the piles of papers, briefings, and intelligence material I had written about America's enemies, I was now being treated like one. I was then berated and accused by a grotesquely rude Air Force policeman of incorrectly filling-out my on-base housing application forms (four months earlier), and not properly registering my firearms (locked in a gun safe) even though they had only arrived the week prior and had already been acknowledged at the entrance gate by inspectors.

Here is where the story takes a turn toward the conspiratorial. I was then handed a "Be On The Look-Out" (B.O.L.O.) flyer with my photo and description on the front (I found out later after an Officer friend called me from Afghanistan that this flyer had been sent out to every military base around the world). With this, I had officially been given my "burn notice", as my identity and clearance had been shared with every terrorist looking for an analyst to kill or coerce. They knew I now had to go underground. I couldn't help but shake my head and half-smile at the realization that I had somehow "crossed-the-Rubicon" and entered the ranks of "Jessie James", "Billy-the-Kid", and "Tuco" from the Old West WANTED POSTERS; chuckling as Sergio Leone's theme song whistle from "The Good, The Bad, and The Ugly" began to play in my mind.

It seemed the smearing of my name had begun before my explanation of the situation had been heard, judging by condemnatory language used to describe me. Somehow a crime was being cobbled together, causing my nose to wrinkle as the once rose-flavored aroma of military-patriotism seemed to decay into the rotten manure stench of blasphemous rumors and sneaky schemes.

It also reminded me of the betrayal of CIA agent Valerie Plaime Wilson, whose undercover status and security clearance was exposed by Washington Post reporter Bob Novack after Vice President Dick Cheney's Chief of Staff "Scooter" Libby and Richard Armitage (notorious for covering up Vietnam prisoners of war being alive) had leaked the information out of petty spite and vindictiveness. Their reason was because Valerie's husband, Ambassador Joe Wilson, had accurately exposed and honorably challenged (out of love of truth and duty to country) inaccurate and dishonorable claims by the George W. Bush Administration about "yellow cake" (used in nuclear weapons fabrication) in Africa, which was cited in a State of the Union speech by the President as justification for the impending invasion of Iraq.

Valerie (and Joe) had risked her life and sacrificed her family out of a patriotic duty to country, and was repaid by seat-warming political simpletons whose callous paws assaulted her fragile and intricate clandestine job like a labotomized gorilla snuffing-out a match.

Interesting how things change when the political season shifts.

In a well-practiced sequence of moves, I was then handed a pink violation ticket, an unusually long and complex series of warrants and letters removing me from base and my position, and then given a termination notice from Booz Allen Hamilton.

Although on a superficial level I knew this entire situation to be ridiculously wrong, outrageous, and tragic, I also had an odd feeling of peace somewhere in the abyss of my spirit that this was an essential part of a larger journey. I then packed up, returned to Washington DC and my army battalion, and cancelled my transfer.

Back at my battalion, the Brigade Commander made a surprise visit and informed us of upcoming policy changes in the army, largely due to negative stigma given to Psychological Operations by another defense contractor named Mike Furlong. This was somewhat jaw-dropping to me in a 'deja vu' sort of way because I had worked closely with Mike at State Department Counterterrorism, and knew he had been fired and locked out of his office because of CIA complaints (he was far too efficient and a 'special operations' type of guy). Interestingly, later that year Rolling Stone magazine would report a story about other Psychological Operations Officers being persecuted by the Army for refusing to analyze and target U.S. Senators with behavior changing communication (the army wanted to cultivate a desire in them to designate more money for psychological warfare).

After hearing this, I wrote a lengthy report addressing the psychological warfare impact these policy changes would have on troops, our terrorist enemy, and our overall War on Terror mission, and submitted it up the chain of command (battalion commander LTC Joel Droba, Brigade Commander of 2POG COL Burley, the Pentagon, and the Armed Services Congressional committee, and others). It was this report which forecast the attack upon the U.S. Embassy in Libya two years later. It was this report which could have saved lives, had it been properly applied.

Mysteriously, one month after submitting this official army report and nine (9) months after the MacDill AFB incident I received an indictment letter for not properly filling out my housing forms and failing to register my firearms in time. Revenge in this case was not "served cold", as Khan opined, but rather pulled out of the garbage can, reheated, and expected to be tasted as fresh. It seemed my report, which had originally been asked for, had struck a painful nerve and was a roadblock to someone's agenda. It was seen as the quintessential "straw that broke the camel's back", or rather the punch that bloodied the President's nose...and they were hell-bent to hit back. I was seen as the annoying buzzing bee, stinging their complacency and disturbingly not going away, and thus their emotional reflex was to "swat". And they did.

Despite my requests for a military attorney to investigate the matter and be appointed to defend me (since it was a military situation involving my transfer of drill location), I was refused counsel and ignored. Amazingly--and I believe unconstitutionally--the military was, for the first time, surrendering its jurisdiction to the Department of Justice, and a civilian agency was being allowed to prosecute a military matter in order to avoid the Code of Military Justice.

The civilian attorney I had retained then filed a Motion to Dismiss stating that the military police had violated numerous constitutional protections, including the 1870 Posse Comitatus Act which strictly forbids the military from exercising police powers over civilians off-base and beyond military jurisdiction. I was technically a civilian contractor, out of uniform, and off-base property when the military arrested me at gun-point, removed me from my car, transported me onto base (effectively kidnapping me), and interrogated and searched me without a proper warrant or jurisdiction. And it was this constitutional protection which sets America apart from authoritarian nations, and must greatly concern all Americans when these rights are violated, abused, and disgarded by military presumption.

However the Magistrate Judge, unwilling to rule against the military or the Justice Department (either out of constitutional ignorance, inability to comprehend the civilian-military jurisdictional separation, or struggling with Patriot Act fever) denied the motion to dismiss and pushed the case off on another judge for trial.

While awaiting trial, the prosecutor (Ms. Sara Sweeney, AUSA) invented all kinds of exaggerations, had me followed by Secret Service, and engaged in the same illegal harrassment which the Justice Dept. had employed against Senator Ted Stevens (R-Alaska), and had later been disciplined for--causing one prosecutor to commit suicide.

Without delving into the gory details of trial (the full story can be read in the upcoming book "<u>CONSPIRACY, TORTURE, & BETRAYAL AT U.S. CENTRAL COMMAND</u>: How Islamic Paranoia, Political-Correctness, and Defense Contractors are Crippling American Military Commanders, Emasculating Political Leaders, and Labotomizing Counterterrorism and Intelligence Agencies.") and the government corruption which ensued, suffice it to say that due to my oath and a naive desire to protect the military (out of respect to my country) I chose not to reveal anything about my work or past experiences. The prosecutor wasn't as respectful.

She waddled up to the podium, pulled down the microphone, and in a condescending, whiny voice as appetizing to the ear as fingernails screeching down chalkboards, unfurled a confusing tapestry of fuzzy logic and half-truths about military protocols (which she wasn't qualified to even discuss) to a jury who had no military experience. Amazingly, she also had the gall to dress-up a Special Assistant U.S. Attorney in an Air Force uniform to deceive the jury into believing the military was engaging in a joint-prosecution against me.

(I later found out at an Army Investigation Board hearing that the military never participated in my prosecution, and was not aware, nor had given permission for AUSA Sara Sweeney to employ military legal resources against me--precisely because this would have allowed me to demand a military defense attorney and military courtroom trial).

The prosecutor's argument was equally fantastical. She basically complained how in a spectacularly audacious and cunning series of moves, a lone psychological warfare analyst had single-handedly outmaneuvered and checkmated the entire U.S. military-intelligence community. And that by using his mystical charisma, encyclopedic mind, and hypnotic communication skills, was able to commandeer the private executive jet of U.S. Special Operations Commander Admiral Eric Olson; seduce love-starved female housing contractors into giving him an apartment on-base at U.S. Central Command; and then intimidate mentally lethargic military security guards into delivering his gun safe (full of firearms, ammunition, and military gear) onto the most highly guarded, top secret, impenetrable military-intelligence fortress in the world.

She then apologetically went on to say how the U.S. military reaction when Bennett revealed his activities was one of shock, disbelief, and embarrassment--which then turned to resentment, paranoia (about their contracts and jobs being lost as a result of their incompetence), and lust for revenge against this act of bohemian moxie. Hence, the legal prosecution.

What she purposely failed to mention was that because I was an Army Officer, nothing I had done was a violation of any military regulations or policies, and because of this the military was not prosecuting me. The Justice Department was simply engaging in a power-grab as part of some long-term agenda, and the military was ignorantly surrendering jurisdiction over its own soldiers, systems, and protocols to a civilian, politically-motivated law enforcement agency. It was akin to allowing the Highway Patrol police to travel to Iraq and give out tickets to tanks for speeding. It was not only unconstitutional, but asinine--if not clinically insane. It was the very thing the Federalist Papers, the Articles of Confederation, and the Federal Constitution of the United States sought to absolutely prohibit: the civilian interference with internal military administration (not including necessary and intelligent <u>Congressional</u> oversight) and external maneuvers of war.

I must confess a certain degree of amusement in this. What was tragically, yet comically, ironic was the fact that had I executed this operation as part of some covert top secret plan or contract to expose the vulnerabilities and weaknesses of the U.S. Government, Intelligence Community, and Military (much like Army Special Forces soldiers used to do in the past for "shits-n-giggles" practice), I no doubt would have been given a medal of commendation, a generous financial bonus, and a Professorship to educate agents in clandestine operations, psychological manipulation, and bureaucratic obfuscation. But instead of being lavished with praise for exercising creativity and leadership, I was lashed with prosecution for refusing to submit.

Although a military protocol expert witness (Major Mark Brewer) had testified that nothing I had done violated military laws, the jury had been prejudiced and misled by the Special Assistant U.S. Attorney (Timothy Goines) wearing an Air Force uniform and deceived into thinking there "was something more to the case" and that the military was prosecuting me. This government pettifogger made a paperwork error appear to be a Fort Hood shooting plot, and wore the "Captain America" myth to shame the jury into complicity--lest their refusal define them as somehow standing against America. Strangely, I had been forbidden from wearing my Army uniform at trial--most likely because it would have neutralized the government's bias.

To make a long story end, the jury checked the "GUILTY" box, causing the AUSA Sara Sweeney to dance about uncontrollably like a demonically-possessed puppet, as I remained stoic. I was an American soldier, an Army Officer, and always would conduct myself as one.

I felt like C.S. Lewis' "Aslan" being led to the "Stone Table" as the prosecutor's legal harem of hags, goblins, and trolls cackled and grunted in unseemly celebration of their wicked victory--albeit a temporary one--as the judge decreed her opinion and plunged the twisted blade of judgment. But like Aslan, I knew without a shadow of doubt I would have my legal resurrection day (hopefully before the literal one) and in that day tear out the throat of the false accusations against me.

The judge then proclaimed all of my firearms and ammunition would be confiscated by the State (despite them being 100% legal and not used as part of any crime), and after a few more handfulls of lies thrown at me by the "Yahoo" prosecutor, said I was to be "remanded into prison" and then sentenced. Five months later (after some excruciating experiences of enlightenment) I returned for sentencing, and instead of the expected 1 to 7 months guideline, I was given

36 months (increased by the prosecutor's intentional distortion of the gun law enhancement--which all Americans and freedom loving people should beware since it sets a precedent for confiscating all liberties, property rights, and protections).

For the next few blurry months I was Charleton Heston's "Judah Ben-Hur", rowing defiantly in the Roman prison galley, and broodingly chomping at the bit for the day when I would return to the arena of Court and vindicate myself in the "Chariot Race" of argumentation. Like Ben-Hur, I longed--if not lusted--for the rematch, and the moment I would unleash my horses of truth, dominate the track, and whip, trample, and crush under foot the monstrous body of lies of the prosecutor.

Until that day however, I would have to wear the paper jumpsuit of a prisoner, before the laurel wreath could crown me the victor.

Over several months I travelled around the country by bumpy bus and plane, shackled in handcuffs and ankle chains, eating peanut-butter sandwiches on stale bread and sipping paper cups of murky water, as I was bounced around various jails. Indeed to endure the abusive treatment and filthy conditions of America's Bureau of Prisons is more than an education in character development, it is a time traveling adventure to a medieval world the average citizen has no idea exists that makes Stalin's Siberian Gulag seem like Day-Care. My encounter was painfully reminiscent of Rambo's Vietnam P.O.W. camp discovery, filled with bearded men missing teeth (there is no true dentistry in federal prisons despite the propaganda), some shivering feverishly, some hobbling on crutches due to limbs amputated from neglected cancers, some crawling out of their wheelchairs to reach the toilet, and some autistic or in other ways mentally retarded--all thrown into a menagerie of tatooed gangsters, managed by sadistically cruel security guards who must have tortured little animals in their own bullied childhoods. The medical neglect was akin to Nazi Holocaust experimentation, without the compassion.

At last the Roman prison galley of the U.S. Marshalls Service arrived at my port, and I landed at the Minimum Security facility of FCI Schuylkill (a camp). An island in the rugged mountains of Pennsylvania where a motley crue of doctors, stock-brokers, engineers, pilots, lawyers, and other "white-collar" business men types were stranded. It is probably one of the most interesting locations of concentrated intelligence and talent in the country. A Think-Tank of skill and experience that puts any in Washington DC to shame.

It was here where I found what I had been sent on a mission by the military to search out. It was here that the mythical sword of knowledge arose from the misty lake and beckoned to be grasped. It was here I was given my "Grail" (The only thing missing was the musical climax from Wagner's "Siegfreid's Funeral March").

Twas on a mild sunny day at the Italian Bowling (Batchi) court lounging on a bench and watching a few of the Mafia guys demonstrate their mastery of the game that I accidentally--or miraculously--met Brad Birkenfeld. A loose vapory chit-chat soon condensed into a deep conversation that led to a baffling discovery, that grew into analysis, that crystalized into conviction and illuminated the path of action we both felt compelled to follow.

We discovered Brad Birkenfeld had been the "unknown face" on the silhouette of the terrorist financier profile I had been developing like a detective searching for the culprit of a crime. At that moment a symphony of coincidences suddenly roared to life in a single deluge of supernatural music, confirming the invisible hand of a Grand Maestro more skilled in the perfecting of time, the interdependencies of wisdom, and the fulfillment of hope, than man's mind can imagine. At last I had found my "white whale", just short of Perdition's Flames. I had arrived at the nexus of my destiny and stumbled upon the completion of my mission by meeting the man who held all the answers. It was surreal to say the least.

Birkenfeld was the "Keymaster" to the terrorist finance doors the military wanted open.

It was as if the mysterious opponent I had "wrestled with all the night" in the desert of intelligence, bureaucratic fear, and contractor incompetence (and in the process disjointed "the hollow of my thigh" over) was unexpectedly pinned--signalling my win and blessing.

For the next six (6) months, Brad shared with me all of the documentation, timeline of events, key government agencies and people, and other information which laid out the grand puzzle of terrorist financing through Swiss and other foreign banking. Although I had begun this assembly of secrets at U.S. Central Command, now the pre-configured data easily fell into place; and bridges between the theoretical and actual components completed themselves.

I grew acquainted with the schematic of interconnected mechanisms, processes, systems, and institutions of the financial world; and the nebulous laws, policies, and traditions which formed the "Terrorist Finance Triad" (United Nations, European Union, United States) by allowing the metamorphoses of materials into various forms of wealth (cash, jewels, property, etc.).

Suddenly the hollow black-and-white framework I had been sketching as the skeleton of Terrorist-Banking networks was filled-in with bright colors and became a kaleidoscope of moving parts and sounds. As I daily examined and inserted each piece of intelligence from Brad's collection into my larger puzzle an amazing thing happened.

It was as if I had been struggling to see into one of those three dimensional computer generated artworks of incomprehensible squiggly lines and patterns, when at last my focus changed, and the hidden story within the mirage of numbers, dots and garbled meanings revealed itself. It felt like a roller coaster at its zenith, now falling toward the earth at kamikaze speed, lifting my stomach up into my throat with dizzying shock as the image became clear.

It was the three dimensional image of an orgy of monsters and robots ravishing and devouring eachother amidst the planet-destroying meteor storm of war. In other words, it was the image of government bureaucracies working against the military--either out of ignorance or selfishness--by denying them the intelligence that would have saved soldiers' limbs, eyes, faces, brains, testicles, breasts, and very lives from the merciless shredders of battle, by complicating, by slowing, and by stopping the financing of terrorist operations through Swiss and foreign banks. As I studied the image I sensed my old world morphing into the present like some surreal subplot of Pink Floyd's "The Wall" (even getting goosebumps as I reflected how the prosecutor in my trial had "accused me of feelings of an almost 'human nature'... which would not do."). In the hidden image behind Birkenfeld's story, I recognized all the men, all the missions, all the agencies, all the military technology, all the obscene bureaucratic retardation, and all the political cowardice and hypocrisy I had worked within for the past decade. I knew this world intimately, and could only shake my head and drop my eyes in shame and disgust as I recognized all the players and what they had done--or failed to do--out of stupidity, fear, or treason.

I recognized the interagency connection through the Wikileaks cables, and saw how General Dell Dailey, who had been commander of Joint Special Operations Command (JSOC) and charged with finding international terrorist banking networks, had failed to utilize Birkenfeld or his intelligence materials. What was fascinating to me was General Dailey had then been made Ambassador Dailey and President G.W. Bush's Coordinator for Counterterrorism at the State Department, and begun to discuss, analyze, and construct political objectives around the UBS-Switzerland-Terrorist Financing implications Birkenfeld had disclosed, through various interagency State Department cables.

JSOC Commander Stanley McChrystal also failed to track the UBS connection. Strange. These discussions occurred as the financial crisis was heating up in 2008, and suggested that Birkenfeld's disclosures to Carl Levin and Barack Obama's Senate Subcommittee on Investigations about the UBS-Terrorist Finance link (and tax matters) could be a threat to global financial stability--and therefore could not be tolerated.

What was fascinating about this to me was the fact that I had worked for Ambassador Dailey at the State Department Counterterrorism Office at the time as his Liaison Officer to U.S. Special Operations Command. So I knew everything the State Department and USSOCOM was doing in this area--which amounted to nothing with regard to Birkenfeld's intelligence. The same was true for U.S. Central Command in Tampa, when I worked as a Counterterrorist Finance Analyst.

Later under President Obama, Hillary Clinton became Secretary of State and in 2009 agreed to have Birkenfeld made part of a "political solution" (which meant prosecuting and silencing him through Attorney General Eric Holder) which entailed having two Chinese Uighars (Muslim extremists) held at Guantanamo Bay, Cuba relocated to Switzerland as well as the U.S. being given preferential status on a Swiss financial treaty. In exchange, Switzerland's UBS was given a "deferred prosecution" and a fine by Eric Holder and Lanny Breuer (who should have recused themselves because of their prior legal work for UBS at their law firm Covington and Burling).

I saw the forged letter sent to UBS (which in actuality was an assasination attempt against Birkenfeld) and recognized the bloody paw prints of the Department of Justice and CIA based on the format and timing and trajectory of the letter (CIA substation in the Embassy of Bern). Most likely covert intelligence agencies were using Union Bank of Switzerland (and other foreign banks) accounts and Birkenfeld's revelations threatened their unchecked, unregulated, and most likely unconstitutional activities.

Now here, once again, is where the story takes the most bizarre turn of all--and should immediately trigger the Congress to hold an investigative hearing.

In an eerily fascinating coincidence—or Divine appointment—it appears that Edward Snowden, the Booz Allen Hamilton contractor at the National Security Agency (NSA) who turned whistleblower and revealed to the British newspaper *The Guardian* various domestic surveillance programs used by NSA on American citizens, also saw CIA operations in Switzerland involving Brad Birkenfeld (See *The Guardian*, Saturday, June 8, 2013, "Edward Snowden: the whistleblower behind the NSA surveillance Revelations" by Glenn Greenwald, Ewen MacAskill, and Laura Poitras in Hong Kong).

Snowden describes a particularly formative—and disheartening--incident in which he claimed CIA operatives attempted to recruit the Swiss banker to obtain secret banking information by getting him drunk, encouraging him to drive, and then rescuing him from the ensuing DUI charge after he was arrested. This was meant to entrap the banker for exploitation purposes, and parallels exactly with Brad Birkenfeld's description of his incident.

As a computer network security expert with diplomatic cover and a security clearance, Snowden saw all of the intelligence reports, cables, and discussions revolving around the Swiss banker target (Birkenfeld), and no doubt became soured by the obscene arrogance and plot to betray Birkenfeld through a fraudulent letter sent to UBS; as well as the later false prosecution against him. Snowden would have seen this as not only contradicting the Constitution of the United States, but contemptuously undermining it by indirectly facilitating the arrest, prosecution, and possible assassination of an American citizen—who happens to work as a Swiss Banker.

So many Intelligence agencies and departments were conspicuously missing (or hiding) from Birkenfeld's case, I wondered if counterterrorist financing operations existed anywhere other than on paper. The agencies which should have taken the lead in examining Birkenfeld's materials were nowhere to be seen, and had never once communicated with him. Astoundingly the Department of Treasury's Office of Terrorism and Financial Intelligence (which I had worked with at U.S. Central Command and had been created to undercut the financial underpinnings of terrorism worldwide) had never debriefed Birkenfeld or analyzed his financial intelligence materials.

Also absent was the National Counterterrorism Center (NCTC), which I had also worked with closely while at the State Department Counterterrorism Office. NCTC was the primary organization in the U.S. Government for integrating and analyzing all intelligence possessed or acquired pertaining to terrorism (according to the U.S. Joint Counterterrorism manual and military doctrine). Also missing was the Defense Intelligence Operations Coordination Center (DIOCC), which was the lead Department of Defense (DoD) intelligence organization responsible for integrating and synchronizing military intelligence and national intelligence capabilities in support of the combatant commands. Most striking was the absence of the Director of National Intelligence (DNI), the very man who had been appointed to oversee the reorganization of the Intelligence Community (IC) and better integrate the IC's efforts into a more unified, coordinated, and effective body after the supposed terrorist attacks on September 11th. No interagency teams of any military commands (SOCOM, JSOC, CENTCOM, CAPOC, EUCOM, etc.) had been informed about Birkenfeld, which I immediately blamed on Senator Carl Levin and President Obama whose Senate Subcommittee on Investigations had been the one to investigate Birkenfeld.

Most offensive was that Senator Levin had also been on the Senate Armed Services Committee, and yet never reported any of this intelligence to the Armed Services. It sickened me, not because of the incompetence I had become used to seeing in the circles of political and military leadership, but because I knew soldiers, sailors, airmen, and marines had died, lost limbs, and had their families torn apart because financial intelligence had been either ignored or buried which could have stopped the attacks against them. Birkenfeld's materials had sadly become a "Schindler's List" that was burned before it could save.

Despite the fact that Birkenfeld was a "High Value Individual" to the military targeting process, and could have yielded information about the hierarchical structure, vulnerabilities, and capabilities of terrorist finance networks--and thereby greatly empowered U.S. Special Operations Command's Center for Special Operations (CSO), which is the fusion point for DoD synchronization efforts, intelligence, and long-range planning and strategy--all of this life-preserving information Birkenfeld had offered had been locked-away behind the bars of a jail cell by Eric Holder's Department of Justice.

Booz Allen Hamilton also was to blame, for its Counterterrorist Finance Training powerpoint presentation seemed to plagarize much of Birkenfeld's materials disclosed in the State Department Wikileaks cables, yet never identified him or UBS as the solution the military had contracted them--and me--to discover. Strange indeed.

After months of long talks, Birkenfeld and I decided the information had to get out to the military and the American people; and Congress was constitutionally obligated to investigate the matter. Although we represented two different plots, when put together they became an almost unbelievable story of corruption, cowardice, incompetence, or treason. And for the sake of our servicemen, we had to tell it.

The failure to utilize Birkenfeld's UBS terrorist finance intelligence was not only a major discovery, but an ongoing threat that was negatively affecting the war, our troops and allies, and our domestic stability--never mind tranquility. We were convinced either a massive cover-up, or an intolerable incompetence was occuring, and felt convicted to report it. If not us, who? If not now, when? But how? The wisdom of Reagan comfortingly advised. The American people, quick to hear, slow to speak, would be our audience, not the political class leaching off them under the deception of leadership.

Once Americans were informed, they would want to know how and why this failure had been allowed to occur in the first place; who was responsible; and how--if at all--it was being rectified. Fathers, mothers, and spouses of dead and crippled service members and contractors would be especially demanding of answers...and they deserved them.

Over the next month, Birkenfeld and I sat down and began to draft a letter. A letter we knew might be received like a brick through a stained glass window. A letter we hoped would illuminate minds and the political landscape about Dick Cheney's self-fulfilling prophecy of a "100 years war" (incidentally now made official U.S. policy by President Obama) like all the firework displays since 1776 combined. A letter that would depict us as either patriotic Americans protecting their country by addressing its vulnerabilities; or as the "running woman" in Apple Computer's classic "1984" advertisement, chased by uniformed goons, and flinging a sledgehammer through the enormous video screen mind-numbing the gawking masses with dreadful Homeland Security Threat Level propaganda and Patriot Act double-talk.

We reasoned the best person to address the letter to would be Marine General James Mattis, Commander of U.S. Central Command. He had replaced General David Petraeus as commander of the Iraq-Afghanistan wars, had been in the fight since the beginning, and could put the information we had to instantaneous good use. Additionally, I knew John M. Custer, III, who was director of intelligence at U.S. Central Command, would also either find this information damning or liberating, since he had stated how unhelpful--if not counterproductive--the CIA group NCTC had been in providing the military with useful information to prosecute the wars.

Like any delicate instrument of explosive ordnance (in this case a projectile of words and images) the letter and plan of delivery and follow-up actions were exhaustively diagramed, calculated, and revised for maximum effect and speed. Finally it was finished, loaded, and fired-off on August 1, 2012--the day Brad Birkenfeld walked out of prison a free man. Since Brad had already been double-crossed by the Justice Department when he had originally given them the intelligence, we thought it prudent to have him surface a second time after he was out of their clutches, and had space to maneuver. No telling what they might have done otherwise.

The letter read as follows, more or less:

Dear General Mattis:
I am writing you to share with you an urgent matter that involves your command and mission and soldiers involved in combatting Terrorist Threat Finance networks and operations.

WHO AM I?
I am Brad Birkenfeld, the UBS whistleblower, who brought to our government's attention the largest international banking tax fraud in U.S. history. Despite my repeated requests, it seems the intelligence materials and information I provided to Senator Carl Levin's Senate Permanent Subcommittee on Investigations and Armed Forces Committee, was never shared with you.

WHY AM I WRITING?
I believe the materials I provided to the government are critical to the military's mission.

The other agencies involved include:
DEPARTMENT OF JUSTICE: Attorney General Eric Holder; AUSA Kevin O'Connor; AUSA Kevin Downing. Holder gave a deferred prosecution to UBS, and also worked for them in private practice.

STATE DEPARTMENT: Hillary Clinton made and arrangement to transfer two Chinese Uighar terrorists from Guantanamo Bay Cuba to Switzerland as part of a political settlement.

Department of Treasury: Timothy Geitner provided UBS with U.S. taxpayer funds as part of their financial bailout.

PRESIDENT OBAMA: Also involved from his membership on the Senate Investigations Committee, and using UBS as a financial donor to his Presidential campaign.

I understand the Counter Threat Finance mission is managed by Booz Allen Hamilton, specifically Mike Maravilla, William Lubliner, Troy Hensely, Bob Thompson, and others.

I believe the information I have to share will reveal possible "aide and comfort given to the enemy" and therefore must be investigated. I invite you to debrief me in Washington DC through my lawyers Steven Kohn and David Colapinto.

I look forward to hearing from you about this very urgent matter.

Sincerely,
Brad Birkenfeld

Other points were discussed, but will not be mentioned here.

It's interesting to note that approximately a month or so after sending this letter to General Mattis at U.S. Central Command, Brad Birkenfeld was conveniently paid $104 million dollars for his assistance to the IRS in recovering overseas taxes, and other services. Of course it was a reward he more than earned, given the suffering he had endured at the hands of the Justice Department in prison.

Two months later, on September 25, 2012, I wrote an official Army Intelligence Report (unclassified) to General Jeffrey Jacobs, Commander of U.S. Civil Affairs-Psychological Operations Command, disclosing and analyzing all the materials I had discovered from Birkenfeld's case file, as well as my experience as a Threat Finance Analyst at U.S. Central Command's Interagency group. My recommendations included: immediate debriefing of Birkenfeld; reporting the matter to Department of Defense Inspector General, Lynne Halbrooks, as well as to the House and Senate Armed Services Committees, Oversight and Reform Committees, Intelligence Committees, Judiciary Committees, and Homeland Security Committees (and various Congressional leaders). It was recommended that a hearing be convened that allowed Birkenfeld and myself to present our discoveries and its relevance to the Terrorist Threat Finance operations within the military.

A month went by, and no response was given to me by the military. I then mailed the report to General Martin Dempsey, Chairman of the Joint Chiefs of Staff, and General Ray Odierno, Chief of the Army, and Inspector General Lynne Halbrooks at the Pentagon. Again, no response was given whatsoever. Apparently the U.S. military's highest levels of leadership were adamantly opposed to ever examining the matter out of fear of political blowback. This was unacceptable.

Since the military were refusing to act, I reached out to the various members of Congress and Committees myself (see attached list of names), and filed it as a "Whistleblowing Report" to the Inspector General, DoD.

Over the next six (6) months, I mailed stacks of letters and copies of my report to members of the U.S. House of Representatives, the U.S. Senate, and the Committees on Armed Services, Intelligence, Foreign Relations, Homeland Security, Finance, and Government Affairs and Oversight. Astoundingly, I never received a single response, or even acknowledgment of receipt, from anyone except one lone Senator from the great state of Kentucky...Rand Paul. Needless to say I was absolutely dumbfounded.

Switching gears, I figured since the military and Congress obviously weren't interested, the media would be--both in the story and that the U.S. Government was ignoring or hiding it.

If there was a more media-worthy story than the intentional or negligent suppression of terrorist financial intelligence by a U.S. Government bureaucracy, and consequential crippling of the U.S. military in this particular arena, I would gladly surrender column space and bandwidth. But I was quite certain there wasn't, and isn't, and won't be in the next month (Of course the CIA and its President are quite adept at making illusion seem real). The question would be is the media sufficiently saavy and patriotic to publish the report. Time would tell.

After careful thought and discussion, I sent the report to the one network I thought would be most curious, based on their adamant constitutionalism, love of country, and hyperactive--if not hysterical--faith in the military: Fox News.

I sent material to nearly everyone in the network whom I thought had the intelligence to understand it, and the gumption to do something about it: Sean Hannity, Bill O'Reilly, Greta Van Sustern, S.E. Cupp, Monica Crowley, Chris Wallace, Bill Kristol (both at Fox and the Weekly Standard), Fred Barnes, Charles Krauthammer, Brit Hume, Neil Cavuto, Mike Huckabee, Rush Limbaugh, and a few others. Not a single person at Fox News responded.

I could understand, and appreciate, the Obama adoring mainstream media hiding and avoiding the issue, but was amazed at Fox News' collective decision to remain silent. But it also confirmed to me that the media fundamentally do not want the "War on Terrorism" to ever end because they can't live without it; because essentially they feed off of the fear and subserviance it cultivates in the masses. In order to remain relevant TV commentators and journalists demand the public's rapt attention with panic, and then lull them into opinions that are androgynous, dull, and enslaved by political-correctness-- another politically "incorrect" insight gained from this experience.

I can honestly say I was rather shocked, and even morally offended to some degree, since I had always been more than "right-of-center" in my conservative philosophy (but even that has admittedly been somewhat recalibrated as a result of this sojourn); and now it seemed, sadly, the notorious "Fair and Balanced" self-branding of Fox News was all talk and no action; more fantasy than reality--no doubt for advertising niche purposes and Nielsen racketeering. They decided not to report to you.

So, since not a single "Stars-n-Stripes" flag-draped, 1st Amendment champion at Fox ever responded, I sent the report out to the rest of the American media, newspapers, and networks. I mailed it to CNN's Jim Cafferty (Cafferty File); Wall Street Journal's Roger Ailes, Rupert Murdoch, and others; USA Today's Tom Vandenbrook; The New York Times' Michael Hastings; L.A. Times; Washington Post; The Hill; Roll Call; GQ Magazine; Vanity Fair; Rolling Stone; and others (see attached list).

I also sent it to parties who might be more critical and proactive regarding President Obama's abuse of power and depraved indifference. These included Republican National Committee Chairman Rience Priebus; Presidential Nominee Mitt Romney; Vice Presidential Nominee Paul Ryan; Talk-Radio hosts Glenn Beck, Laura Ingram, Dick Morris; and a few others. Again no response from anyone whatsoever. Dead silence.

With my faith in the media's right to exist sufficiently shattered, I turned to the two Washington D.C. Think-Tanks I had personally worked with in the past to analyze and expose the issues: Heritage Foundation, and Family Research Council. They had provided me with the social science research data I cited in my reports on the negative and harmful impact of the military's policy (later a causative factor in the Benghazi, Libya U.S. Embassy attacks).

Therefore I assumed they would welcome the opportunity to defend their scholarly work and reputation, particularly since it was the basis for their non-profit, tax-exempt status as a public-service watchdog; and was constantly paraded on front of wealthy donors (and middle-class families) to justify the glutonous six-figure salaries of the "Academics" who worked there.

At Heritage Foundation, I sent it to President Ed Feulner, then Jim DeMint, and James Carafano. At Family Research Council, I sent it to President Tony Perkins, Peter Sprigg, and Lt. General Jerry Boykin (Army-retired). I also sent a copy to Wayne LaPierre at the National Rifle Association, given the confiscation of guns that was a variable in the government's equation for constitutional dissolution.

For the umpteenth time, and with a disturbing consistency, I received no response or receipt of materials whatsoever. I was flabbergasted, since a more sickening hypocrisy I could not imagine.

For a "conservative, Constitutionalist, and Christian" Think-Tank to ignore--and thereby tolerate--the ideological corrosion which eventually would destroy its own ability to function and exist, seemed to me like organizational suicide, akin to the Titanic orchestra playing amidst the sinking. I could almost hear the violins. And their music was the truth of men being "white-washed tombs full of dead men's bones; a cup clean on the outside, but filthy on the inside." Or as one particularly perceptive philosopher observed concerning the nature of the "noble" political, military, and media elites, "A nest o schemin' bastards who couldny agree on the color-o-shite."[2]

34

Funny as it may sound, "Falling-overboard-at-midnight-into-the-middle-of-the-Atlantic-Ocean" was probably the best analogy I could conceive to describe the experience of a whistleblower's rejection by his government; and my feelings resulting from it.

It seemed the "safe" of secrets (UBS-Terrorist Finance Networks; Benghazi, Libya attack) I had discovered and struggled to carry-up to the carefree "upper-class" aboard the cocktail-cruise ship "Washington D.C.", in the hope they would analyze and report its contents to the rest of the American passengers, was instead fearfully viewed as a ticking-timebomb; then chained around my neck and hastily kicked over the ship's side in the futile hope it would disappear forever beneath the black waters of silent ignorance.

I was yanked-off the deck, splashed headfirst, and spiralled down through its bottomless, icy depths of despair, terror, and agonizing aloneness; free-falling for miles, then feeling in the darkness the cushioning sand press against my back as I came to rest upon the ocean floor. Staring up, the desire for life seeming to dim and flicker, I could see floating down after me--chasing me through the deep--thousands of lifeless soldiers, sailors, airmen, and marines--their outstretched arms reaching vainly for the surface, their eyes rolled-back white and mouths agape--frozen in the shocked expression of meeting death; sinking and settling round about me like snowflakes in a glass-ball. I was the only living soul trapped in a haunted graveyard at the bottom of an inky abyss, imprisoned with thousands of furious ghosts, screaming at me from other dimensions, trying to scrawl messages in the sandy floor with clawed fingers puppeted by the sea current as they dragged.

At last, I had reached the bottom, sank to the lowest point in my history, and arrived at the threshold of oblivion. It wasn't a sudden, stumbling fall into Conrad's "Heart of Darkness", but more of an unnoticed, gradual descent; merging into a whirlpool of suffering leading to the pit of hopelessness.

I began to drift into a catatonic complacency, and thought how tragically sad--and criminal--it was that the American people might never know anything about this story. That they might never see the piles of letters showing how their politicians, their media, and their highest ranking military seemed to be conspiring to hide from them a whistleblowing report essential to their national security (Since the only explanation for their unresponsiveness was either: my mail not being received; or it being received, acknowledged, and then intentionally ignored out of some agenda or blind stupidity.). "For their own good," no doubt would be some bureaucrat's arrogant answer.

Drearily I wondered who would rise up in the sea of men to inform them? Who had the faith to stand against the powers that be? Who had the strength, the aggression, and the patience to hammer away at the government's "damn" of denial until it began to crack and truth trickle through, then explode in a deluge of disclosures and public hearings? By design, there seemed now to be no bold men of righteous conviction left in "Modern" America: no manly virtue in military warriors; no brilliant philosophers in Congress; no morally critical or transcendently imaginative writers in the yellowing ivory towers of academia, think-tanks, and journalism.

Instead, when it came to "thinking" talent, America seemed to be left with the refuse of T.S. Elliot's "Wasteland", rather than the spires of Plato's Republic; and the nation's character was beginning to reflect it. Under the distorting pressure of political-correctness, spiteful feminism, and rabid hedonism, America's mythic image of "Davy Crockett's 'rugged, self-reliant frontiersman'" was melting and marring into "Dorien Gray's 'enslaved, foppish vanity'"--becoming a grotesque perversion of its former self.

But then, I thought, perhaps it was all meant to be; and surrendering the fight and ceasing my questions was better for me--politically, professionally, and financially. Perhaps it was time to take the "Leftist's" blue pill and return to "The Matrix"; choose the Lotus flower eater's life of dreams, swallow the "Soma", and ease into amnesia like a warm bath. Perhaps trying to preserve America's heritage of moral vitality and spiritual virility was like trying to defend sandcastle's from the tide's corrosion. Perhaps it was someone else's fight, not mine. And besides, if so many other men in higher positions of power and authority and reputation were choosing the path of soft living, passing the buck, and playing a shell game with responsibility, why shouldn't I?

As I was about to yield to the seductive sophisms--my willpower blurring, my powers of reason drooping--inching me closer to the edge of compromise, a thought grabbed me from behind by the scruff of the neck and held me back. The words which came to mind--and the film scene depicting them--illustrated the crippling cost of compromise, as well as the reward of victory which comes by refusing to.

Once more, "Braveheart", seemed to provide the intellectual adrenaline shot to counteract the bromide of political appeasement.

The scene takes place in a Scottish Castle's Great Hall, swarming with rival clan leaders (The Scottish kind). Standing amidst a yelling match between three different competing factions, arguing for hereditary recognition and its accompanying power, a lone, quiet Highlander Commoner (who, incidentally, has just been decorated for starting a rebellion against an unlawful, tyrannical, authoritarian government) calmly announces he will attack the oppressor on his own ground, triggering an eruption of jeers and mocking laughter.

The Highlander instantly and growlingly confronts and silences the arrogant cynicism with cutting words that command introspection. He proclaims, and brands them, with the assessment:

> "Why is that impossible?...You're so concerned about squabbling-for-the-scraps of Longshanks' (Obama's) table that you've missed your God-given right to something better...there's a difference between us: you believe the people of this country exist to provide you with <u>position</u>; I believe your position exists to provide those people with <u>freedom</u>...and I go to see that they have it."

Wallace, the Highlander, glowers at the stunned audience of aristocrats, turns around, and marches out--his men-of-war in tow.

Whether from subconscious regurgitation or Divine inspiration, those words and scene seemed to speak volumes, and were precisely what I needed at that moment. It was a bull's-eye statement which, I thought, captured what ought to be said to every member of the military, U.S. Congress, and the media who, for over <u>eight (8) months</u>, had cowered away from my report out of self-interest; out of fear of jeopardizing their own <u>position</u>, influence, wealth, and future retirement. Instead of serving the American people by informing them (and thereby respecting them enough to decide its resolution), the Pentagon career-ladder-climbers (military), the Political game-show hosts (Congress), and the sensational-soundbite parasites (media) had chosen the easier path...and it made all the difference, as Robert Frost might conclude.

They had been given notice, shown evidence, asked--if not demanded--to investigate and report to the American people <u>new</u> information that was killing their sons and daughters, stealing their money, corrupting their government, and violating their national security...and yet they did absolutely nothing whatsoever in response. Worse, they ignored it and tried to cover it up.

However they seemed also to forget that through the global community of the internet, Pandora's Box--once opened--never closes, and after the truth gets out to the "common man", the cover-up is always worse than the crime. It is the nature of man to seek out and know the truth, especially after he learns others are trying to hide it from him out of contempt and selfishness. Then he really digs deep.

Suddenly I was shocked back to life--electrocuted out of my coma of self-pity and nihilistic surrender--by the lesson of the "Great Hall" confrontation. The battle-of-will between the morally simplistic--yet cunning--Highlander-Farmer Wallace, and the morally compromising political opportunists, seemed to parallel my own situation; and confirmed the deceit, cowardice, and self-serving agendas I may inevitably have to engage and artfully redirect. It was the slap-in-the-face lesson on political warfare and subsequent second-wind I needed for the fight soon to come. It clarified both my philosophical identity and dilemma, and the psychosociological rationale for the government's refusal to respond. It exposed the hidden story behind the fantasy of war I had been emotionally "waterboarded" into believing by faschistic legislation, and the faschistic implications if it was not repealed and recalibrated.

Alas, Blake's "Doors of Perception" (as Jim Morrison had lyricized) were unexpectedly opened--blasted-off-their-hinges open, in fact--and I was, for the first time, seeing everything as it really was; and as I was meant to see it all along. It appeared that like light versus darkness, fire versus water, the clash between the morally convicted and the morally corrupted was to be expected, was natural, and was constant--and would remain so--so long as the world turns (unredeemed).

And it was a test of character. Down into the depths of the abyss of rejection I had been sunk and there found myself staring straight into the unblinking, fang-bearing face of my Leviathan adversary; and thereby discovered my true self.

I now had a choice: remain hidden and do nothing, or emerge and do something. Either wield the sword, engage the battle, and attack relentlessly--publishing my story myself to vindicate me; or disengage and abandon the story, and remain careless--and defeated--in leisure.

Would I choose Odysseus or Rumplestilskin to model my life and character after? Would I choose as my ship a man-of-war and lash myself to its splintered mast and endure the ocean typhoon's deafening lightning strikes and thrashings as I broke through and charted the forbidden realm of political-military-contractor corruption?

Or would I choose an oarless rowboat, sit quietly with folded hands, crossed-eyes, and plugged ears, and drift aimlessly down the green backwater swamp of spiritual timidity and lifeless honor?

As much as I generally dislike--as any normal man would--the dizzying nausea which comes from the rough seas of life, it was a moral choice. Therefore for my family's honor--and without much hesitation--and since surrender is never an option when it comes to truth, I chose Odysseus and embraced the storm to come. For it is in great suffering that we are brought closest to God, and our raw manhood refined. While it is in the softness of luxury and laziness that our life force drains and intellectual vitality decays.

It seemed as though the nation was fast approaching a reef, and was one crisis away from self-inflicting martial law in a pathological effort to amputate its gangrenous fear of terrorism. The Boston Marathon bombings and total city lockdown was the precedent and model--and most alarmingly the excuse to violate people's constitutional rights to privacy via forced home-searches without any semblance of a warrant. The writing was on the wall: on the scales of justice our golden freedoms were being outweighed by the worthless lead of promised safety from a menace that truly never existed. It seemed also to spell out the words "FALSE FLAG OPERATION".

As an officer of the United States Army my duty is to at least try to do something about it. But what? What could a solitary soldier do who was being ignored and his information buried by the very same government he had sworn to protect? If indeed a nation's moral character is reflected in its laws, in this case the U.S. Constitution, and these laws are manipulated to savage its own military officers for doing their duty to the best of their ability to "support and defend" these very laws in good faith, honor, and diligence, how can it be said that we have not degenerated into an Alice in Wonderland type of "Off with their heads!" nation--and culture--of contradiction, ruthlessness, and self-destruction? Furthermore, if an active military member cannot be prosecuted by a civilian Department of Justice in a civilian court for specific acts undertaken as part of, and necessary to, his military function, then how was I imprisoned? Would the next stage be army tank drivers being given speeding tickets in a battle, snipers being charged with murder, and soldiers being charged with federal "Making a False Statement" charges whenever a form they filled out was technically deficient? Obviously it was the agenda, since it was precisely what had happened to me.

Worst of all, it set a precedent for the Executive Branch to overstep its authority using the Judiciary to erode the Legislative Branch (Congress), and perform political surgery upon the military at will.

Since this could quicken a coup d'etat and sweep away America's democratic chessboard, I had to engage--even if it meant going it alone. I was bound and determined (as my dear mother would say) to carry this burdening secret up from the depths and share it with all who had a son or daughter, mom or dad, family or friend, who had served in the Iraq-Afghanistan conflicts (intentionally not labeled "wars" in order to avoid Congress's control), especially those who had been damaged or killed by the fighting.

So what could I do? Simple: go directly to the government's boss--to the people--and speak directly to them; announce the harm being done, and the shameful cover-up being perpetrated against them. I would write letters. Training was over.

I would write until my fingers bled and eyes failed, unrelentingly, to everyone about what I had uncovered, for as long as it took. I would shift into high-gear and write whistleblowing letters, reports, and articles that felt like long earthquakes, that sounded like flash-bang explosions, and that looked like solar eclipses. I would seize, shock, and awe--mesmerizing the reader's subconscious with almost occultic insight--as they were shaken awake and stirred by a supernatural authority.

I would compose the most powerful symphonies of language my being was capable of generating--seductively eloquent and irresistably penetrating. I would unleash the imagination in ways never before felt, and win hearts and minds by expressing truth through mythopoetic, psychophysiological, and multidimensional words.

And these words I would hurl at every politician, judge, and military officer who swore allegiance to the Constitution of the United States; at every media organization whose charter was the First Amendment; and at every journalist, scribe, and scholar who claimed to know how to write.

Like David loading his sling with five stones in preparation for Goliath and his four brothers, so would I load my prison-provided typewriter with paper and go out on the field of ideas and challenge the "uncircumcised" domestic enemies of the U.S. Constitution, and the eternal liberties it enshrined.

I would take aim at the five giants oppressing the story: The Department of Justice, the Congress, the White House, the media, and the military bureaucracy. Like tar-dipped, flaming stones I would sling letters at every public official, military leader, and media pundit until they broke ranks (preferably after they were "flanked" by allies) and were exposed to the American taxpayer for who they were and what they had done.

And for those who tried to discredit Brad Birkenfeld or me, distort the report or supporting documents, or blatantly lie to "cover their ass" (so prevalent a vice in Washington D.C. politics today it seems), I would simply--and respectfully--let loose the facts to speak for and defend themselves...which could quite possibly resemble, metaphorically speaking of course, Killer Whales with seals before the feast--tossing about, whacking, and belly-flopping upon their stunned hapless prey.

With that teethy reward in mind, up from the sandy nadir of my abyss of rejection I launched, and began my return to the shimmering light of public exposure, swimming toward the surface--each letter a kick and stroke--furiously clawing and pulling my way upwards through the darkness, the heavy safe holding the UBS-Terrorist Finance and Benghazi PSYOP secrets still chained around my neck like Jacob Marley's burden, every fiber of my being straining to carry the weight--my neck veins bulging like suspension bridge cables as I typed and wrung my brain of information like a soaked towel--as I slowly reached the surface, and at last broke through in a splashing explosion...the completion of this report you now read before you.

Floating atop the water on my back, smiling in the sunshine and breathing in the fresh salty air of peace and satisfaction (somewhat similar to "Forest Gump's" Lieutenant Dan after the shrimpboat storm and his tirade atop the mast), and savoring the old writer's sayings of "That which is not written with great effort is not read with great pleasure", and "I do not necessarily enjoy writing, but rather having written", I mused on the journey so far.

The essence of it seemed to be, "It is good for me that I have been afflicted; that I might learn thy statutes." Psalm 119.

I understood that to stand for something means inherently to defend it. And to defend the true, the good, and the beautiful (The Aganon, as described by the Greeks), means to confront the false, the bad, and the repugnant; and that confrontation is right when done out of service to one's country, not for selfish gain, pride, or vengeance. And that there is Divine purpose behind all betrayal, suffering, and endurance.

The purpose seemed to confirm, "What some meant for evil, God meant for good", and how Joseph's fall into the cave, betrayals, and decade of imprisonment in Pharoah's dungeon was needed before he could be called upon to serve as Prime Minister of Egypt. A familiar biblical story now seemed to be translating into my own personal pilgrimage. Although I had no such political ambitions (at least not yet), I couldn't disagree with the fact that my fortitude, patience, and lucidity had been greatly enhanced by this experience of suffering and isolation. I had not languished, but intensified; not become embittered, but battle-hardened in my determination to fight on, demand recognition of the report, and publish the entire story for all Americans to read. There would be no classification of my material to hide it from people's eyes under the deception of "National Security Sensitive"--since my discovery had come mostly while in prison, and accidentally (or Divinely, depending on your spiritual maturity). So no one could have it--or me--sealed and gagged.

The time in prison had been well spent in fact, and unexpectedly resourceful. It had reintroduced me to the romance of writing: caressing typewriter keys, kissing paper with inky blushes, fondling words to penetrate meaning--wheedling inside the slippery warmth of truth with new thrilling perspectives and twilight sighs of feeling--and impregnating minds with wisdom.

The process of the butterfly's birth also came to mind. Specifically, how it must be left alone--and never helped--to escape its cacoon, straining to the point of near-death exhaustion as it squeezes through the small hole in order to push fluid into its new wings and inflate them with the beautiful colors and power of flight they were designed for all to see and marvel at.

If spared this struggle, its metamorphisis is crippled and its wings stunted into shriveled impediments that sentence it to death. I was grateful now for the struggle, since I could see the colors brightening and feel the wind uplifting. And I knew like Sir Alec Guiness in "Bridge on the River Kwaii", I would emerge from this sweltering solitary confinement prison cell with classic British bearing and eloquent defiance.

However, there was still some serious fighting left to do in the meantime. Truth was both my weapon and my endstate. Recalling my journey thus far: my fall into the abyss, my sinking into despair, my reawakening, and my return to the present surface awareness, I returned my eyes to the source of my fall...the pleasure cruise ship of Washington D.C. drifting sleepily in the distance. With a smirk, and a new battleplan, I began swimming toward it.

With a new zealous enthusiasm and hard edge in mind, I would climb back aboard from below (with Birkenfeld parachuting in from above), drop the "safe" upon the deck with a laughter-silencing thud, rip it open before them, reach inside, and slam the "dead cat" of indictment upon their table of taxpayer funded riotus feasting. Of course they would try and run away and hide from it as if it was a crazed porcupine on fire rampaging through a nudist colony, but they couldn't get far. The papertrails I created would provide evidence for the hunt. And the American taxpayer would be the hunter. My job would be to make sure every politician, military commander, and media pundit was exposed to the report, so that nobody could claim ignorance and hide the nakedness of their shameful retreat under the blanket of "plausible deniability." They would be seen for knowing, and all responsible Americans would demand an explanation.

It was not about fixing the problem anymore or analyzing the issue, it was about exposing the men who "fixed the game" to fail from the beginning: The Department of Justice, the Intelligence Community, Senator Carl Levin, President Obama, and the defense contractor Booz Allen Hamilton.

After everything came out, then the American people would have the choice of forgiving them, or disciplining them and casting them out of office and into prison (for those guilty of "serious crimes and misdemeanors") and/or be impeached. But at least average Americans would have the choice, and not the millionaire boys club of Washington D.C.

Strange as it may seem, it was not until I looked up amidst a meditative outdoor walk one day and beheld a familiar "Sign-in-the-Heavens" that I recognized what had really been happening to me, why, and most importantly what I was now expected to do with the experience.

Chatting and pondering with a couple friends (one of whom an intelligence analyst whose material implicating U.S. government involvment in the September 11th World Trade Center and Pentagon attacks is more than compelling) the mysterious cosmic forces which seemed to have had brought us together like some episode of "LOST" (the TV show), I reflected on how my original military mission had been to defeat my nation's enemy by strangling his money--to put it simply. And that I was to do this by discovering, analyzing, and terminating terrorist finance operations, networks, and individuals. As fate would have it, at that precise moment of internal thought, one of my friends stopped mid-sentence, pointed overhead, and announced "...and 'X' marks the spot!" Intrigued, I glanced up and discovered a sort of coat-of-arms symbol in the sky which seemed to proclaim a subtle message only I could feel; a message that appeared as two planes' white exhaust trails crossed in a cloudless sea of blue, forming an immense 'X' with the center point descending directly upon us unusually fast.

It may not have been a voice on high saying, "This is my beloved son, in whom I am well pleased" type message, but it was certainly close. It was close because the symbol was a deeply personal one for me; it was the symbol of the flag of Scotland--a white 'X' on a blue field--and the country of my birth.

I could almost hear the "Thus Saith Zarathustra" music transform the image into epiphany, and stand my hairs to attention.

Smilingly gazing up at the sky-written sign of my origin, I recognized my destiny, and understood what next I must do. I realized in a moment of thunder-clapping clarity that I had been brought here to finish my mission, not in spite of it. I realized that by investigating, analyzing, reporting, and following-up on Birkenfeld's UBS-Terrorist Finance intelligence, I was still <u>on mission</u>, continuing to do my duty, and fulfilling my oath as an officer--despite the imprisonment inflicted upon me by my own government. For reasons I couldn't quite fully fathom myself, I was still obeying my original orders, honoring my uniform and flag, and serving my country.

The irony--or miracle--was that it was only after I had been locked-up in a federal prison for a paperwork discrepancy on a single military housing form (violating every Constitutional principle and civil liberty imaginable) that I was able to discover the materials which would enable me to achieve my objective and protect my nation against terrorism-- my reason for joining the army in the first place.

I had deciphered State Department cables which no one else could, and discovered a "DaVinci Code" level secret. In that discovery, I had been given a choice: either hide and ignore Birkenfeld's revelations and commit acts of ommission by allowing terrorists to shed American blood through continuing their finance operations; or articulate and communicate the life and death implications of the intelligence, and expose it to the American people for judgment. Fortunately for the nation, my mother's upbringing led me to do the latter.

In this case the "job" had been originally assigned to me by President Obama and the military, except they didn't expect me to continue "working the problem" after they threw me in jail. Most likely they expected me to curl-up into a fetus position and be passive. But as Ronald Reagan would say years earlier about miscalculated political expectations, "They counted wrong."

Lee Van Cleef's line from "The Good, The Bad, and The Ugly" to his bed-ridden bounty-paying employer came to mind: "When somebody pays me to do a job...I always see it through", punctuating with the bang of his pistol.

During this trance-like meditation on the symbol in the sky, I recalled my oath as an officer; and my mentor Colonel Jeff Jones who had hired me out of the Bush Administration to join his Psychological Warfare team at Booz Allen Hamilton in Washington, D.C., and also helped arrange for my Army Direct Commission. It reminded me of a scene involving a similar scenario and moral dilemma.

The scene was from Tom Clancy's "Clear and Present Danger", in which Jack Ryan (Harrison Ford) is having an intimate and intense final death bed conversation with his mentor, the wheezing, half-conscious Navy Admiral and Director of the Central Intelligence Agency (James Earl Jones). Ryan is wrestling with the choice of either revealing the unconstitutional activities and betrayal of U.S. Special Operations troops (left to languish in a South American prison ironically enough) by a Machiavellian White House staff engaging in an artificially designed "War on Drug Cartels"; or simply remaining silent about the whole thing, and dramatically increasing his job security and political power through the accumulation of secrets, favors, and leverage. Struggling to find his moral center, Ryan confides in his old mentor and asks for guidance.

James Earl Jones whispers to Ryan in a last testament before he dies, "You..took..an oath...to the people...of the United States", and then fades quiet. Ryan nods in acknowledgment, as his mentor passes.

The memory of this scene was significant, because I too took such an oath, and swore to uphold it to my mentor, Colonel Jeff Jones (Commander, 4th Psychological Operations Group) before he died of brain cancer in 2010.

My oath was to "support and defend the Constitution against _all_ enemies, foreign and domestic." My oath was not to a tattered and stained piece of papyrus in a museum tatooed with the dreamy scribblings of old men in white wigs and knee-high stockings, but to God's eternal and inviolable Law which motivated and established this Constitution to maximize and protect mens' lives, happiness, and prosperity in America. The Constitution was not an iconoclastic memory, it _is_ a living and active and unchanging (except through Amending) license which empowered me, as an _individual_, with the abilities to lawfully wield weapons to protect my family, property, and future; practice and perfect my gifts, talents, skills, and knowledge to make a living; and imagine, create, express and share everything and anything that fulfills me within the confines and boundaries (moral and material) of the Constitution. It was not a bridle to control me, it was a key that kept the chains of sloth and fear from restraining me. It was a blade that prevented man from being consumed and suffocated under the "red-tape" of excessive and pointless (and destructive) government regulations (federal, state, and local) like the insidiously coiling death-wrappings of a mummy. In short, it was the Law of the Land.

Colonel Jeff Jones was one of the most intelligent, gentlemanly, and imaginatively gifted leaders America has been blessed to have serve and wear the Army uniform.

He was also a genius at influencing target audiences, building brands, and synthesizing words, images, music, and feelings to change hearts and minds and obliterate the competing message. He was indeed a man modern Advertising agencies would either die to hire, or tremble and run from.

From classic campaigns throughout history, to contemporary statesmen, scholars, and military experts around the world, COL Jones knew everything and everyone associated with the subject of Psychological Warfare (modernly watered down to the weaker term psychological operation). He was revered by all in the community as the "Father of Modern PSYOP", and had been the architect of the campaigns in Grenada, Panama, Desert Storm I, Bosnia, and Haiti (and a few other skirmishes which must remain confidential).

COL Jones had first seen me during a Pentagon meeting when I stood up, posed a question, and challenged Secretary of Defense Donald Rumsfeld and Joint Chiefs Chairman General Dick Meyers about evolving psychological warfare to be more spiritually focussed. Shortly thereafter, COL Jones contacted me and asked if I would join a group and mission he was putting together with some Army Intelligence officers at Booz Allen Hamilton. He was very direct, professional, and skillfully blunt. He said he was assembling a small team of eclectic personalities and backgrounds to create a new kind of psychological warfare that utilized the mystical, psychosexual, and horror fantasies of the Muslim Extremist to define them as religious heretics ("Mufsidoon", in Arabic) and isolate them from the indigenous Muslim population (the Umma). The team would be united by their uncommon traits of ruthless dedication to destroy the enemy; mastery of scholarly research and writing techniques in order to analyze, communicate, and teach this psychological warfare against Islamic extremism and terrorism to the State Department, the CIA, and military personnel--the three agencies essential to winning the war of ideas, and ones he knew intimately. His goal was to transform these agencies from neutered golden retrievers lazily sunbathing poolside into lean, dirty, ravenous wolves snarling and snapping for a bloody fight. He was determined to remove the bureaucratic retardation and willful indecision which was compromising--and defeating--the military's psychological warfare capabilities; and redefine, if not completely eliminate, Congress's micromanaging of the information war-- mainly because most American politicians had the queer defect of presenting American values not as "Adonis" to Muslim eyes, but rather a perverse "Punchinello". Plus given Islam's native fear and hostility towards the odd and magical, American efforts were naturally viewed as insidious and corrupt. Allowing politicians and bureaucrats to design artistic, multi-layered psychological warfare was like assigning thumbless mechanics to perform brain surgery. It was mutilating our image instead of healing our future. An example of this were advertisments put out by the State Department (under Hillary Clinton) in Benghazi, Libya using "inflammatory" language about homosexuality in its needed security contractors for hire. This of course outraged the Muslim Imams, which gave the Al Qaeda extremists the religious gasoline they could spray the crowds with. The advertisements were propagandized (or PSYOPed) into proof of an "American agenda to corrupt the sexual purity" of its Muslims--which is the most sacred (and contradictory) dimension of the Muslim spiritual life.

    If anyone could accomplish this titanic task, it was COL Jones. Few men had inspired me with their intellect and character in the past (aside from my Scottish grandfather), and COL Jones was one of them. Soonafter meeting him, I left the Bush Administration, joined his team, and prepared for an adventure of the mind few men have endured. I worked in secret buildings, on floors that didn't exist, and devised psychological warfare projects for the State Department Coordinator of Counterterrorism and U.S. Special Operations Command that the public would never know about, and that the Muslim extremist would never recover from. Unfortunately, in researching and developing these psychological warfare products, some of the materials I was exposed to--in particular the unspeakably grissly Al Qaeda videos of "infidel torture"--I may never fully recover from, and will certainly never forget.

COL Jones wanted the best self-starting, creative, and aggressive team to dominate the defense contract market in Islamic counterterrorism communications. To do this, we had to watch, read, and understand everything the Islamic terrorist was brainwashed with, while maintaining the stone-cold detachment of a surgeon observing a medical operation...only in this case there was no anesthesia and the goal of the demoniacs was the thrill of inflicting agony on whomever they labeled "infidel".

For what seemed like days, I was placed into a Sensitive Compartmentalized Information Facility (SCIF), which is a kind of over-air conditioned, hyperbaric decompression chamber, where all sound from the outside world is absorbed from the air by foam cones and walls, achieving an almost otherworldly silence. It's like being in an airplane, with your ears feeling covered without the popping discomfort, while your voice is sucked out of the air. The only noise coming from the "Allah Akbar" chantings of the murderers and the screams and pleadings from their "infidel" (who are often Muslim Shia) victims.

I was shown video upon video of Islamic extremists sawing off the heads (and other limbs and appendages) of captured prisoners (Russian, Chinese, British, Danish, American), soldiers and civilians; and torturing European female contractors in the most vile, blood-curdling ways no human eyes should ever see. I'm not ashamed to say it gave me a hatred and desire for vengeance and merciless annihilation of every single Muslim terrorist (and their financial enablers) we encountered; and compelled me to accept a commission in the Army. After seeing these drug-induced, pornography addicted, terrorists dissect women and children (and perform other acts which will be constrained out of good taste) in ways which make Jack-the-Ripper seem like a sweet-voiced Vienna Choir boy, I emerged a changed man; not traumatized, but profoundly different. And if the American people ever saw the full scope of evil depravity and viciousness in these videos, they would not only change their views about Islamic extremism, but most likely compel the surgical use of nuclear weapons. Of course they might also crumple into thumb-sucking fetus positions of psychoneurosis as a result of the images (which is the reason given by bureaucrats to keep these videos classified), but my guess is Americans would gird-up the loins of their minds and be motivated to destroy the enemy like never before.

Another extremely valuable lesson this research and training taught me, which the army seems pathologically obsessed with ignoring, was that men and women should not be allowed under any circumstances-- nevermind forced--to watch these videos together in the same SCIF chamber. It is painfully uncomfortable for the men especially; and cultivates a defensive posture in the women which restricts their ability to openly and spontaneously provide feedback, analysis, and deduce creative opportunities to exploit into counter-propaganda material--which is essential to the military commander and success of PSYOP missions.

Again, why is this not only allowed, but in fact often ordered by Higher Command? Because, as epidemic in America's modern military, the fever of political-correctness has blurred and disoriented military commander's minds to the point they have become stammering, emotionally castrated old men without any memory of raw manhood, or any hope or pleasure in it. This in turn causes them to reject natural womanhood (delicate femininity), as predicted in Karl Stern's "The Flight From Woman", and George Gilder's "Sexual Suicide", and fosters an androgynous culture and doctrine within the military, which is neither healthy nor combat effective at destroying a non-androgynous enemy.

Ironically, this failure to maintain a healthy balance and separation between the masculine and feminine characteristics of the military was one of the reasons why Army Private First Class Bradley Manning "popped" like an overshaken champagne bottle and haphazardly released information to Wikileaks, after the New York Times ignored him. An interesting case study in "insufficient training" which warrants brief examination for consideration across the military intelligence, PSYOP, and prisoner interrogation spectrum.

As an Army Intelligence analyst in Iraq, Manning's job was to thoroughly examine, absorb, and categorize key pieces of newly discovered information captured by Special Operations Forces raids, such as: video, computer files, documents, emails, phone records, financial statements, bank accounts, maps, and other psychographic information. When short-handed, he would have been assigned to "heavier" tasks, and here is where the trouble starts.

He would have been exposed to materials most mature men could not stomach--never mind the average hormone-crazed 19 year old kid. I was more "seasoned" in the world, was in my mid-30's, and knew ahead of time exactly what I was getting into, why, and how to "compartmentalize" the materials (which in all honesty, a person can only tolerate for about 2 hours before having to leave the SCIF, take a non-speaking break, and go outside, cuddle and play with a dog or pet for a dose of unconditional love in order to tranquilize the spirit from the evil manifestations the person is being forced to analyze in the name of "PSYOP Research for National Security Purposes").

The fact that the army would be so dull--or blatantly stupid or cruel--as to expose a 19 year old kid fresh out of the womb of "Bible-Belt" American High School to watch videos that redefine inhuman savagery, and study documents he has neither the mind, nor temperment, nor the experience through which to filter the feelings produced, is a testament to why the U.S. military Special Operations Forces has continuously decayed in its talent pool of Intelligence Analysts, Psychological Warfare soldiers, and Prisoner Interrogation Experts. Interestingly, the Germans are among the best at understanding and managing this delicate balance.

Manning simply did not have the capacity to contain the information poured into him, and more importantly, could not digest the volatile acerbity of the suffering. This is logical.

He himself already suffered from some chronic manhood deficits as a result of a harsh and distant father unwilling to show physical affection or intimate emotional warmth, which always precipitates (especially in boys) identity confusion, and its consequent symptoms of self-rejection and loneliness, which leads to sexual dysfunction, then experimentation, then guilt, and finally angry depression. When the boy has a high I.Q. and E.Q. (Intelligence Quotient and Emotional Quotient) the frustration and anger intensifies into malice.

No doubt PFC Manning had seen, though he shouldn't have, some of the videos I had, and lost it; furiously demanding what was being done by kinetic planners to stop these butchers--and thereby stop his painful, no doubt nightmare growing, forced exposure to the video materials he had to analyze.

Another trigger of Manning's meltdown about nothing being done would have been the "unique" (one would even say contradictory) retribution visited upon the "Gay Pride" types in Iraq--those who glory and celebrate in consciously defining themselves as homosexual, rather than define themselves as heterosexuals who engage in the "Man-Love-Thursday" habit of male-to-male "soothing of tension", which they see as necessary as a result of their complications with women. A most bizarre, yet necessary phenomenon to understand in order to discover its underlying psychological warfare implications. But that is for another report.

In any case, this complicated house of cards was largely responsible for setting-up and collapsing into Manning's backlashing betrayal of secret cables upon his return to the States.

He was hurt, and angered, not by the army, but primarily by what the army had exposed him to--and violated him with--without carefully preparing and mentoring him through it.

Thus, I could empathize--somewhat--with PFC Bradley Manning's sense of contemptious frustration with his superior officers. Higher Command's character trait seems to be constant non-responsiveness; aggressive avoidance of all intellectual exertion; and revilement of any external accountability--especially by Congressional Oversight Committees managed by wisened old veterans. But that's another issue for a different report.

There are two types of men: those who've been stung by combat and sickened by its sting, and thereby lost their minds and sensitive nature to some degree--typified by their refusal to ever handle another weapon, for example. Then there are those men who acquire a slow, heavy, mature somberness mixed with indominable confidence. One is a sign of strength and wisdom, the other of cynical hostility and self-defeat. COL Jones was a man of strength and wisdom.

He had stood by me in my darkest days of frustration with the military's political self-destruction, and calmly guided me in my balancing of choices. There was an intense gravity in his stare, that heavied you with the many years of his warfighting and diplomatic tours of duty. His eyes were similar to my father's, who as a Marine Corps fighter pilot in Vietnam (1968-69, Wake Island; R.O.K.; Chu-Lai) had flown more missions than most men. Like my father, COL Jones was unbreakably hard, yet strong enough to be soft-spoken and gentle in his command of men. He was a mixture of John Wayne and Brian Keith, iconic actors of old epitomizing sober American manliness.

COL Jones had left the army, as my father had left the marine corps, when he sensed effeminate and debilitating compromises becoming official policy. Like the cartoon classic of Daffy Duck holding-up and fighting against a black gelatinous blob seeping into his space, rather than thrash-about and claw at it, COL Jones prudently chose to save his battle for another day, and combat it in an asymetrical way: he had recruited, trained and positioned me in the heart of the Counterterrorism, Intelligence, and Military nexus. He made me his Liaison Officer to Special Operations Command, State Department, and the Intelligence Agencies.

I was sent in to ferret out the bureaucratic blockages and straighten out the "stove-piping", analyze key problems and devise solutions, and implement them immediately without waiting for the impulsive doubt of bureaucrats and military opportunists to hobble the possibility of success. They were always primarily geared towards comfort, title, promotion, and legacy, with a secondary interest in actually winning the war of ideas. COL Jones' only interest, at all times, was defeating the enemy to defend his family. He was a man of action, not words. Yet no man could use words to win hearts and minds and battles, better than he.

Without going into classified material, my work with COL Jones yielded products, strategies, and theories never before developed in the history of the psychological warfare battlespace. From comic books articulating Seyda Zeinab (they mystical female leader all Shiites revere, adore, and obey for Syrian operations), to the power of nightmares, "Team America", and Mormon-like International Public Service Announcements, COL Jones encouraged me in fearless creativity, moral conviction when speaking truth to power, and energizing and framing my work in spiritual duty.

It was out of this sense of duty that I left my path of international economic and political development work, and merged into a different world. I joined the fight on terror out of a loyalty and love of country, like my father and grandfathers before me. I combined my skills, knowledge, contacts, and experience in advertising, Hollywood comic book writing, film, and religious scholarship, with psychological warfare against Islamic extremism; and created quite a diverse product mix.

I developed instinct diagrams, mind-mapping devices, strategic communication plans, hypnotic interrogation techniques, and other PSYOP products and techniques (which must remain classified outside this open-source report) that never before existed in the American military arsenal or training doctrine.

Through my experiences at the State Department, Special Operations Command, and the Intelligence Community, I have seen things only a few men have, and that no normal man would ever want to. I have endured the emotionally exhausting and spiritually agonizing work of analyzing and counteracting Islamic extremist torture and execution videos, and have not had the option of looking away or skipping the worst parts. I have had to study every element of the videos in order to deconstruct them, identify sensitive information, analyze phraseology and ideological underpinnings, discover vulnerabilities, and recommend countermeasures to Islamist propaganda. I have seen Daniel Pearl's beheaders cry out gleefully, "Let's go to Disneyland", after cutting off his head--something the non-Muslim world was, for some reason, spared from seeing. And I have read every philosophical treatise on jihad, religious brainwashing, and manual for socio-political-cultural division and isolation of the West, that has been published.

I had stared into the face of my enemy, and it was not the illiterate, fanatically bloodthirsty, emotionally unstable, boy-loving desert savage who uses his left hand for toilet paper, but rather it was those who prosper by extending the fight of this savage through acts of omission that enable his financing, thereby giving him "aide and comfort"--which the U.S. Constitution defines as treason. It was very plain and simple to understand.

If the *enemy* of my enemy is my *friend*, then the *ally* of my enemy is my *enemy* (and in this case the enemy of every U.S. military member and taxpayer). Thus my enemy was clearly and undeniably those parties giving substance and time, and therein hope and encouragement, to the enemy I and other servicemen--of both the U.S. and our allies--had been fighting to the death, as we were trained to do.

However in the end, when everything was added up, the papertrail seemed to indicate the aiding of the enemy was, in fact, being funded by U.S. taxpayers, was being condoned by the Justice Department, the Intelligence Agencies, President Obama, certain members of Congress, and the defense contractor Booz Allen Hamilton.

It seemed we were fighting the enemy like parasites on a host, feeding off it just enough to not completely kill it, just maintain a constant groan of near death. And we were managing the war--and telling our allies to do the same--in a manner which, whether intentionally or not, treated global conflict like a smoldering fire, never allowing it to be completely extinguished in order to preserve just enough flame for the next shift of unionized, government paid water-bucket bearers (Haliburton, SAIC, Dyncorp, etc.); And every now and then a flame-up consumed some innocent, simpleton civilian sailing a boat near the Horn of Africa, or sight-seeing in some Middle-East city, or celebrating the Boston Marathon.

From a causitive analysis, I concluded that the real enemy was not the bloody murderers who torture women with power-drills; or sodomize, slice-up, and skin alive captured American and Russian soldiers (though Al Qaeda has written it fears Russian soldiers 100 times more than American, for retribution purposes), on film, to avenge historical wrongs that never occurred; or who hack-up unsuspecting British soldiers strolling the streets of London; or who threatened Danish cartoonists for drawing Mohammed with a big nose; or who shot and stabbed Dutch film maker Theo Van Gogh for exposing the sadistic abuse of Women in his film "Submission" with Ayaan Hirsi Ali (who agrees with me).

As atrociously primitive and morally moronic as these trogladite abominations of the human species are, they are _not_ the disease but rather the rotting flesh _resulting_ from the disease--an essential distinction. Terrorists are simply the symptoms of our own weaknesses, specifically our failure--or refusal--to terrify them; and our own ineptitude at waging sensationally effective psychological warfare that inspires fear and puts them on the retreat, instead of naively and foolishly and effeminately trying to seduce them into admiring the cool logic of democracy (Which has never, and will never, work with a hot-blooded desert culture people, as the British know well). Why? Simply put, their brains are wired differently by their culture (Read "The Arab Mind" and "Sir Richard F. Burton").

Also, since Muslim extremists pass on their pathological obsessions and paranoia to their seven to eight children (average birth statistics), then Pat Buchanan's imminent decline of the West, and Pat Fagan's "Demographic Winter" was descending upon us like a silent, menacing storm waiting for its moment to unleash its pent-up wrath.

Fundamentally, the anthropological genesis of the terrorist infection comes from the U.S. government-military-media complex refusing to fully and finally sterilize the area of this body politic of nations by "cutting out" or cauterizing the Saudi Arabian funded Wahabism through all instruments of national power (informationally, politically, economically, then militarily).

This was best done not through "whack-a-mole" drone and missle tactics, which is similar to "Caddyshack Carl's" blowing up the entire golf course (world) to rid the country club of one varmint--in this case a small band of schizophrenic, weepy, girl-fearing adolescents with beards. It was best done through multidimensional, mythopoetic, and spiritually authoritative (key words in the puzzle of the mind) psychological warfare and strategic communications--which was what I did for a living in my advertising and government-military careers--and which was the sole reason I took a Direct Commission as an Officer in the Army in the first place.

I had met with and challenged face to face at a meeting then Secretary of Defense Donald Rumsfeld and Chairman of the Joint Chiefs of Staff, General Dick Meyers. At a meeting at the Pentagon, I brought up the need for developing new PSYOP that struck at the center of gravity of Muslim spiritual beliefs, particularly suicide assisted "martyrdom", and gave as the solution the need to use against them their own concept of "Torments of the Grave", which is what they have historically feared most. Sadly, most of the military men in the room couldn't grasp the idea.

All this I did, not because I wanted to, but because I was told it was the only way to "get inside the hearts and minds" of the Islamic terrorist, and thereby counteract his perverse apocalyptic narrative by developing a superior message and brand of American values. This I did because I was told if I did not, my country's ability to defend itself militarily in the war of ideas would be weakend, and my fellow Americans suffer. This I did because I am a patriot...and always will be.

This I did because I promised my fellow soldiers, "I shall not fail those with whom I serve." And with this report, I honor and keep that army promise.

CONCLUSION

Brad Birkenfeld is an American patriot and loyal to the people and culture and government of our United States. But how can it be that,after risking his life and sacrificing his career and future to empower the government with the informational advantage it sorely lacked and obviously desperately needed over the terrorist enemy (as seen in the government's subsequent payment of $104 million dollars to Mr. Birkenfeld), this same government--a cabal of retirement obsessed bureaucrats, power-addicted politicians,and blood-drunk military-industrial-intel knuckle-draggers (officers above the rank of Captain)--betrayed Birkenfeld and buried his revelations; and then muzzled him and imprisoned him behind the iron mask of a felony charge? He discovered a deadly threat to the people of the United States, his countrymen, and came to the institution supposedly established by the people to guard their security, the Department of Justice (never in his wildest dreams expecting to be targeted for assasination by them, or one of their "contractors", for disclosing his treasure of secret information and contacts) and instead of being welcomed, was scorned, legally beaten, and professionally crucified.

Why was this done to him? The answer is simple, since the facts speak volumes: To continue metasticizing a malignant fear and suicidal conflict based on deception, pride, and greed. To grow a war to cultivate careers. A war which, if it had been fought the right way, would have ended a decade ago (in other words 3 years after it started).

Another whistleblower, Edward Snowden, although I don't agree with his methods, has also come forward to reveal the power and reach Booz Allen Hamilton exercises in its activities at the National Security Agency. Most revealing is that the National Director of Intelligence, James Clapper, was a Booz Allen Hamilton employee; as well as Mike McConnel, Intelligence Community.

Indeed the monstrous, flaming-red, all-seeing "Sauron" eye of the American Government's matrix of satellites (National Reconnaissance Office), wiretaps (National Security Agency), remote-control drones (Central Intelligence Agency), and vast army of winged, blue-monkey agents flying from the Dark Tower of the FBI-ATF-IRS-Homeland Security, failed to find (supposedly) or refused to use (most likely) what Brad Birkenfeld freely and enthusiastically gave: 19,000 bank account names, cell phones, hotel rooms, meeting dates, email addresses, and other vital information pertaining to potential terrorist financial networks and operations. None of which was ever shared with the military.

It staggers the imagination to think that such treason or tragic comedy of errors could be committed by government and military and intelligence agency personnel, without the least bit of humility or repentance upon reflection. Perhaps most reprehensible of all is the fact that despite his pleading with the Justice Department to allow him to share this information with the right Army military Threat Finance team (mine) and an Officer who would fully exploit this information to combat terrorists and keep America safe (me), Birkenfeld was not only flatly denied this request, but then threatened violently by the Justice Department if he "spoke to anyone"--including other financial government agencies--about his information. He literally begged for a subpoena to warn the American people about terrorists and was forbidden, under pain of death, by Justice...a darker Shakespearean drama of egomaniacal motives I cannot imagine.

This fact alone should slap-away the ashen expression of shock on American citizens' faces to one of mouth-frothing, beet-red outrage; and move them to demand merciless investigations by Congress into this matter and all who betrayed their sons and daughters in uniform. After all, a generation of our children have been killed or crippled by these incompetents. And their "blood cries out to us from the ground."

One of the starkest memories I have as an Officer, and indeed as a man, was beholding a young, beautiful, long blond-haired, blue-eyed girl (around 18-19 years old) who had just been released from Walter Reed Army hospital and was attending a Washington Nationals baseball game outing with a busload of freshly wounded soldiers. They were being honored by a sponsor and lined up in front of a crowd and "thanked for serving." The girl was in a wheel chair, and had both legs blown off at the knee due to her being shot-up while repelling out of a helicopter (I won't open the Pandora's Box of women in combat, but suffice it to say she should not have been forced into that situation by politically-correct commanders who hide from manly chivalry like vampires cowering from the sun). Her face expressed a nervous, tired estrangement, as if still in shock and not quite fully aware of what had happened to her, or why. Her same-age boyfriend (civilian), no doubt from high school, stood next to her in loyal support, yet with a tight-lipped tension, as if a thousand questions or statements were simmering in him.

As I think upon her now, and how tearful it made me then, my own questions and statements begin to boil over from a scalding conviction; the conviction that only an Army Officer who was a Terrorist Threat Finance analyst assigned to stop banks from funding terrorism can have;

the conviction only a soldier can have as he swears an oath to protect his country; and indeed the conviction only a man can feel as his deepest soul is stirred with the passionate fury to protect a young girl from fanatical savages. The conviction that if just one Union Bank of Switzerland account which Birkenfeld gave to the American government was used to transfer one dollar to an Islamic charity, which then gave it to a courier, who then transferred it to a terrorist, who finally used it to buy the bullets and bombs that were used to maim that young girl, then the Justice Department

Senator Carl Levin (and others in Congress), Leon Panetta (in his dual role as CIA Director and later Secretary of Defense), and indeed President Barack Hussein Obama, have blood on their hands, and I will freely sacrifice my career--and life if necessary--to honor and redeem her by exposing this to the American people, her family, and cry-out to citizens to help her by sharing this story with others.

As Joseph Campbell would concur as being mythic destiny, and as Tolkien no doubt would noddingly approve from behind his wafting "Middle-Earth" pipe smoke, and as Frost has already said, "This path has made all the difference..." in _this_ tale of "To There and Back Again." For had I not fallen into "Gollum's Cave", never would I have found Birkenfeld's "Ring of power", i.e. his documents, Wikileaks cables, bank statements, phone lists, photos, and other materials revealing UBS-Terrorist links and activities, and complicit Justice Department attempts to both silence him about it, and prevent him from informing the military minds who most needed--and were searching for--this vital information. Indeed truth _is_ stranger than fiction.

However, instead of invisibility, Birkenfeld's "ring" forced me and my past writing out of the shadows, making me visible to the horror of some in government. Birkenfeld was the proof that confirmed my research, suppositions, and predictions by bringing me to the source of the Terrorist Finance Network I had been hunting all along. Additionally, he not only substantiated my theories, but far worse, exposed inexcusable government failure and cover-up. Acts of bad faith or incompetence seemed to have been committed by: Senator Carl Levin (a.k.a., the "shoe-cobbler" as Dennis Miller keenly observes), Chair of the Senate Subcommittee on Investigations which had Birkenfeld testify and examined his evidence, as well as Chairman of the Armed Services Committee which should have shared the information with the military (and according to Birkenfeld, never did); Hillary Clinton at the State Department and Coordinator for Counterterrorism (whom I worked for); Eric Holder at the Justice Department and his assassin henchmen Assistant U.S. Attorneys Kevin Downing and Kevin O'Connor (working with others in the intelligence agencies) who not only orchestrated an attempted foreign plot or perhaps murder against Birkenfeld through betraying his whistleblowing to UBS in a fraudulent letter pretending to have been written by Birkenfeld's Islamic banker friend (whose phone they illegally tapped), but then falsely charged him with a non-existent crime and imprisoned him after he escaped their trap, and forbade him from ever speaking about the issue...to this day--hanging the sword of Damocles over his head in the form of threatening to take-back their $104 million dollar payoff; and obviously by President Obama himself who ran the show in exchange for campaign contributions from his UBS financial bundler Robert Wolf, Chairman of the Americas for Union Bank of Switzerland.

And of course many other strange pieces of evidence, stories, and eccentric characters (military, intelligence agencies, media) which must, at least for now, remain excluded from this admittedly voluminous psychodramatic Congressional-Military Whistleblowing report (part I), in the interests of space and time. But rest assured, this additional material will also be published, and has already been written and secured. After ensuring, to the best of our ability, no American military member (enlisted and Junior Officers) or his family will be damaged, compromised, exposed to terrorists (as I was), or in any way hurt as a result of the revelations in the next report, Americans will be shown the rest.

With regards to the American News Media publishing this report, perhaps Frank Sinatra's "Second Time Around" will be sung by some vanguard of the Press in the coming days...but I doubt it. Something tells me--and I hope I'm wrong of course--that most likely the only eyes which will gaze upon the bold colors of right (now bleeding pastels in America--as Reagan warned), and the only ears which will hear the melody and remember the tune of freedom, will be those of Europe... Time will tell.

What's the result of all this so far and what's the impact on American life?

Unforgivably, American sons and daughters, and those of our war-allies, have been needlessly killed or maimed--physically and emotionally--as a direct result of this indefensible intelligence failure and or seditious conspiracy to conceal the truth. Additionally our allies have been subjected to internal socio-political upheavals within their own citizenry because of it. The world's stability has been shaken as the foundations of civilization are fractured under the erratic hammer blows of American military power; and innocent American citizens have been unlawfully imprisoned, brutally abused, and cruelly hidden away from their families--in a coordinated attempt to silence them about this issue. And this is just what has been uncovered so far.

Worst of all has been the complicity of politicians on Capitol Hill (aside from Rand Paul, the only leader to ever respond--albeitly by weak form letter) as well as the media--who seem beholden to the Union Bank of Switzerland.

To say power corrupts, and absolute power corrupts absolutely, falls short of describing the devilish cabal at the heart of this issue. Once again Assistant Attorney General Lanny A. Breuer has administered a slap on the wrist with a deferred prosecution and small fine to UBS. A foreign bank--and therefore a foreign government--has secretly meddled with, influenced, and pressured U.S. politicians and government agencies (The President; the Senate; the Dept. of Justice; the Dept. of State; the Intelligence Community; the Dept. of Defense) to arrest and jail its own citizens for their patriotic whistleblowing to the American people. In exchange for this "servicing", UBS has guaranteed positions on Boards, generous consulting payments, and promises of power--for the next 100 years. Examples of these seditious acts include:
Phil Graham, former Republican Texas Senator (see UBS confidential meeting notes);

Attorney General Eric Holder and Assistant Attorney General Lanny A. Breuer supposedly working--when in private practice--for the law firm Covington and Burling and representing UBS in private practice (reported to me in Birkenfeld's testimony); former Senator Barack Hussein Obama (now President) who served on Senator Carl Levin's Permanent Subcommittee on Investigations, heard Birkenfeld's original testimony before the committee, and examined in great detail the evidence Birkenfeld provided indicating UBS (as HSBC) may have been funding terrorism, as indicated by the banking statement of Abdullah Azziz (who was identified as a key Al Qaeda financier by Osama Bin Laden's "Golden Triangle" in the Rolling Stone article by Matt Taibbi) and UBS' "Optimus Foundation"; contributions to Obama's Presidential Campaign by UBS Chairman of the Americas Robert Wolf; Department of Justice Assistant U.S. Attorneys Kevin O'Connor and Kevin Downing, connected to former Mayor of New York Rudy Gullianni who in turn was supposedly connected to Abdullah Azziz (also a player in Saadam Hussein's "oil for food" bribery scandal); and Leon Panetta, former CIA Director, then later Secretary of Defense, who was also a Senior Level partner at my Defense Contractor firm--Booz Allen Hamilton; and other individuals and activities who can be examined in greater detail on the included report and list.

    Amazingly, just this week a colleague of mine from Booz Allen Hamilton's Cyberwarfare team (assigned to the National Security Agency) has filed another whistleblowing report about government abuses of intelligence and manipulative, unconstitutional designs against the American public. This has been shared with Glen Greenwald at The Guardian Newspaper, and will expose materials I have been reporting to Congress and the military for the past year. Hopefully Mr. Snowden (the Booz Allen Hamilton whistleblower) will reveal __all__ the truth.

Since "Many are my persecutors and mine enemies; yet do I not decline from thy testimonies", and "I will speak of thy testimonies also before kings, and will not be ashamed" (Psalm 119), seem to be somewhat fitting descriptors of my situation, allow me to say, in the most non-melodramatic way, that if--God forbid--anything should happen to me, may this story not fall away. In full public view, under the scrutiny of a Congressional and Military investigation, let this report be examined, questioned, and tested under oath, and shared with the American people.

For those who may condemn or criticize my exposure of this ineptitude or plot between Booz Allen Hamilton, the Obama Administration, and the Intelligence Community, I can only say, as God is my witness and judge, I could not go on remaining silent and allow my fellow military brethren to continue dying and being maimed for life by bombs and bullets financed by bank accounts that long ago I could have shut down, and would have shut down, had I only known... had I only met Brad Birkenfeld when I should have...when he was looking for me. Perhaps I could have done more, but I will let history be the judge, guided by the conscience of the American people.

As for me, I have tried to "fight the good fight" assigned to me, defend my country from enemies "foreign and domestic", and run the race laid out before me by only choosing the most honorable, truthful, and patriotic paths along the journey.

EPILOGUE

At the very end of the film Braveheart" there is a climactic scene where William Wallace's huge claymore sword is symbolically unsheathed and flung high into the air with roaring audacity--bagpipes blasting in the background--as the skyward turned faces of a legion of kilted warriors on the field follow it with reverent awe as it spins through the air toward the shocked English army, and stabs defiantly into the green grassy hill as an ominous marker of freedom, and promise of victory. Inspired indominable, the men charge forward in screaming savage valor, and defeat the enemy to win their freedom.

Similarly, may this letter soar through cyberspace, telephones, mailboxes, and social-networks, and achieve the same success by stirring-up our pride in America, inspiring our faith in God, and emboldening our passionate love of personal and cultural freedoms.

To that end, my prayer is that this letter will only nourish the reader with wisdom; and that after reading, of me it might be humbly said, he saw a danger, and warned of it. To help defend against tyranny, he served and led like a true officer of the United States Army. He fought against self-serving bureaucracies, powers, and principalities to break through and share with his fellow countrymen the truth they deserved to know. He fought with his words and expressed reality fearlessly, and earned the words "Well done thou good and faithful servant", the most eternal reward of all. He fought like an American soldier, or as Wallace might say, "He fought like a warrior-poet...he fought like a Scotsman."

- JUSTICE DEPT.-Mucasey
  - Eric Holder
  - Lanny Breuer
- Lorretta Lynch (involved in the US$1.2 billion settlement with HSBC over violations of the Bank Secrecy Act)

COVINGTON AND BURLING LAW FIRM
- Eric Holder
- Lanny Breuer

- Michael Chertoff (Chertoff Group)
  - Roger Zakheim

- TERRORIST FINANCING/ISIS
  - SAUDI ARABIA
  - KUWAIT
  - QATAR
- UNITED ARAB EMIRATES
  - YEMEN
  - LIBYA

STATE DEPARTMENT: COUNTERTERRORISM - CENTCOM-SOCOM
Scott Bennett

HSBC

Union Bank of Switzerland:
Brad Birkenfeld

MEDIA
- FOX
- MSNBC (Michael Isikoff)
- Washington Post (Tom Hamburger)
- NETWORKS

CLINTON FOUNDATION
- HILLARY CLINTON
- DONNA SHALELA, DIRECTOR
- David Chalela (Bennett's lawyer)

ASSANGE (WIKILEAKS)
SNOWDEN
BIRKENFELD
BENNETT

CIA/ NSA/DIA

US CONGRESS
1. ARMED SERVICES (Mike Rogers/ Roger Zakheim)
2. INTELLIGENCE
3. HOMELAND SECURITY
4. GOVERNMENT OVERSIGHT
5. JUDICIARY (Charles Grassly/ Dean Zerbe)
6. MEMBERS

THE CARLYLE GROUP
THE CHERTOFF GROUP (Michael Hayden)

BOOZ ALLEN HAMILTON
- Dov Zakheim
- Ian Brezinski
- Mike McConnel
- Michael Hayden
- Leon Panetta (SECDEF/CIA)
  - Edward Snowden
  - Scott Bennett

MILITARY
1. US CENTRAL COMMAND (James Mattis/ David Petraeus)
2. Joint Interagency Center
3. US CIVIL AFFAIRS-PSYOP COMMAND
4. PENTAGON INSPECTOR GENERAL

SHELL GAME

UBS

Booz | Allen | Hamilton

SHELL GAME: Part III

"Blessed be the Lord my strength, who teacheth my hands to war and my fingers to fight." -Psalm 144:1

PROLOGUE

If we, like our Founding Fathers before us, are to protect and preserve our natural right to cultivate peaceful, healthy, and joyful lives, free from the fear of erratic government tyranny and unpoisoned by its propagandistically designed lies, then we must rise-up individually, organize collectively as global citizens, channel our energies and messages strategically, and uncompromisingly seize and defend this right.

And the best weapon to do this is 'combat writing': training our fingers to fight by typing explosive messages that paralyze, intimidate, and conquer resistance when fired from the canons of emails, letters, flyers, tweets, blog posts, and social media.

We must also oppose, through all means necessary, any law, lawmaker, bureaucrat, or mindless military or media drone, whose own lust or greed or stupidity or cowardice tries to persuade us to wear the chains of a lobotomized, military-police state; or accept citizenship in the coalition of enslaved nations.

If we fail to do this, or if we refuse to choose a side after we've been informed, then make no mistake, we are by this act of omission, choosing. We are choosing to destroy not only ourselves quietly and slowly, but our children as well—which is the most contemptible kind of evil for which we will be judged.

Fundamentally we must always remember that to grow "the good, the true, and the beautiful" (defined as the *Aganon* by Plato) means to simultaneously destroy the "wicked, the false, and the horrible." Why? Because light and darkness—truth and lies—cannot exist in the same space at the same time.

Part III of Shell Game will symbolize this. It will explore what the ultimate resolution of these treasonous and criminal events, issues, and discoveries should be; and will include the exposure of additional activities, documents, people, and government agencies (which previously couldn't be released while I was still inside prison), which the American public must use to hold their government accountable and defend their lives and future. Part III of Shell Game will not report history, it will create it.

THE WARRIOR-MONK

"When the going gets weird, the weird turn pro."
--Hunter S. Thompson

Every day, for two years, walled within a stone monastery in an impenetrable forest in Pennsylvania, I sat in an icy silent law library at a typewriter and wrote...and wrote...and wrote. Like the mystically inspired *Phantom of the Opera* explosively pounding free his rage, meditation, and desire through the roaring pipes of his organ, I reflected and discovered and translated every element of the bizarre, conspiratorial military-political web I had been entrapped within—or perhaps entrusted with. I felt literally frozen in time.

The typewriter in prison was an ancient relic from the 1980's. "Chit-chit...chit...chit-chit-chit...", its steel teeth recited as the letters hit the ink ribbon like a boxer punching a bag, bruising the white paper face with black words that translated my thoughts into an old tongue; leaving behind long fractured blood trails of English that composed a labyrinth of alphabetized emotions and hieroglyphic reason; and mapped decades of subconscious reflection.

Since I was completely isolated from the outside world--no visits from anyone, no responses to my military-congressional letters (for which I probably spent $1000.00 in postage) -- getting information and making sense of things was a challenge. There was no internet, no computers, no phone calling, no help. There was no light at the end of the tunnel, just a haunting silence. Subsequently, I felt like I was blindly stumbling inside a pitch-black dungeon maze, dropping letters behind me like a breadcrumb trail; or unwinding the mythical string of the Greek hero as he descends into Hades to find the truth (his love) and return to the land of the living with it. Writing felt like my hands cautiously groping and searching the walls for turns and doorways hidden in the darkness, while trying to avoid the mindless, violent trolls imprisoned with me. Like the proverbial shipwrecked British sailor on a cannibal infested island, I felt alone and hunted in every way; yet I was not without advantages. Thank God my mother had forced me to take a typing class in High School (One benefit from two years in front of a typewriter was that my keyboard speed had increased to near "*Bionic Man*" level, with words printing faster than a hyper-caffeinated Oklahoma farm auctioneer could babble).

Each day I typed for six to ten hours, producing reports, emails, news clippings, letters-to-the-editor, analytical papers, military complaints and requests for action, and court documents. Legal motions and exhibits for my release accumulated around me like snowdrifts piling up in the vast and silent tundra of my mind. Each sentence felt like a sinking-step into deep snow--a laborious struggle of unsteady determination and paralyzing slowness--each typed word a heavy leg-lift in a monotonous march toward some eerie glow beyond the horizon; each signature bringing me closer to the clashing sounds of some battle I would inevitably be called enjoin.

Somewhere a deep feeling seemed to suggest that the battle's purpose was my calling; and my mission was to fight and regain my honor by revealing and destroying the liars and the wicked who had entrapped me, and no doubt so many others. But the feeling also slyly implied that although inevitable, the timing was uncertain. I would have to get there first, and obviously the powers that be were obsessed with stopping me.

Adding to the difficulty of my march were the family and friends supposedly assisting me from the outside. I was hobbled by their technical incompetence and burdened by the dragging weight of their hesitancy in challenging or even questioning the government's propaganda. The fact that some family members of mine who received copies of my reports (unclassified) had their homes burgled and safes stolen indicated there may also have been some CIA countermeasures being employed against me—like the earlier incident where the CIA Wackenhut guard at Fort Myer wrote a false affidavit claiming I had dressed as a police officer to get my hair cut on base. And of course, getting any assistance, or even responses, from the army about this or anything else was like climbing up an ice cliff in sneakers, wearing a full field pack. But the difficulty of the challenge would only make the eventual conquest all the more glorious and spiritually affirming, since I knew it would all come together in God's perfect time, and patience and fortitude was my payment for enduring in this scene of life's play.

Finally, after two and a half years of relentlessly battering against the door, it collapsed; and marched I out of Schuylkill prison. Boarding a diesel-farting Greyhound bus I departed the prison camp through an awakening January snowstorm, its angry gray eyes fluttering open with white flakes falling out of nature's frozen dream. At last, the new dawn of a new day and a new life arrived—as the old jazz song sings—and I escaped the "*Island of misfit toys*", and began my resurrection. It was quite surreal, to say the least.

I was finally slipping away from the Bureau of Prisons' long gauntlet of sadistic torment like a wounded submarine evading depth charges: disappearing into a dark Pennsylvania mountain with tunnel lights flashing by me like an elevator descending into oblivion; each passing second of time decompressing me back to life, liberty, and the sounds of careless people. As the two-year "ice-age" of silence thawed, reality began moving again. And as I re-emerged out the other side of the lonely mountain and light was reborn, spiritual love and peace blossomed...and with them came a renewed commitment to truth and duty, only a soldier understands.

Prison had been an interesting place. Interesting in the sense that subjects I never thought I'd study and skills I never thought I'd grow emerged like green shoots after a forest fire. My consciousness evolved from a 1920's silent movie of black-and-white, two dimensional re-runs of the Dick Cheney-G.W. Bush Neo-conservative dogma, to a 4-dimensional technicolor Blue Ray DVD of "*Die Hard*", complete with surround-sound stereo and home-theater vibrating seats. And, of course, the line that kept creeping into my subconscious, tweaking a half-smirk out the side of my mouth, was Bruce Willis' self-mocking line, "*...come out to the coast, we'll get together, have a few laughs...*", as he flicks his lighter, looks around, and wonders how in the hell he found himself crawling alone through an air duct in a skyscraper full of ruthlessly bloodthirsty, trigger-happy terrorists, where's he's the only good guy, the only hope for the hostages...and he's almost out of ammo.

INTRODUCTION

Without getting too "Jedi" minded, it's somewhat cosmically poetic—or inconvenient, depending on your disposition—how our individual life's 'feather of purpose' seems to dance on the playful breeze of irony in a twilight sky of déjà vu, until at last wisdom develops our character strong enough to be sufficiently patient and faithful to allow life to "fall together" without our rushing or intervening with it.

In other words, strange and miraculous things happen in their perfect timing when we sit back and give God both the control and the glory. For example, sometimes a thought occurs to us at the exact moment we inadvertently glance at our watch and capture a significant moment in time, like 11:11, or 3:33, etc. Some might say this translates as a kind of "crossing" of the invisible paths of the universe, or a passing through of some nexus of destiny. I would concur.

At these crossroads of cosmic synchronicity, such flashing moments in time resonate with our deepest being like a velvet hammer striking a giant brass gong, especially when those moments accompany the arrival of some epiphany or paradigmatic choice deafening our attention. It is at this mystical déjà vu moment that feeling and thought merge into something that feels like a whisper from God proclaiming a change in our life's course, and perhaps destiny.

In other words, the meaning of things, although sometimes slow to unfold, always reveals the mysterious hand of God by its design and timing. Part three of this saga was indeed the very personal climactic completion of just such a miraculous puzzle. Only the picture of terrorism I thought I had been sketching suddenly began to morph into the faces of specific men, dates, agencies, and contracts.

REBIRTH OF A SOLDIER

"One life ends, another begins...." This was the prophetic quote from the main character Jake Sully in the 2010 James Cameron film "Avatar", in which the main character transplants his consciousness into a genetically grown alien body in order to infiltrate the alien tribe and exploit the planet's resources.

In the movie Sully is a gung-ho, die-hard Marine, and like most warriors, fanatically trained to view the military mindset and agenda as America's central identity and purpose; and always strive to be the strongest, deadliest, and most cunning soldier, so as to dominate the battlefield.

However soon after joining the alien clan, known as the Na'vi, the mindless Jarhead absorbs the spirit of the aliens and gestates a new self-identity which naturally squeezes out of him his former delusional military self like puss pinched from a boil. He is born again.

Strangely Jake Sully's transformation reflected my own; climaxing in irony when he says, "I was a warrior who dreamed to bring peace...but sooner or later, you have to wake up." I'd been educated in the counterterrorism, propaganda training, and PSYOP schools of the international military-intelligence complex, and then--quite accidentally--discovered U.S. Special Operations Command's cover up of Israeli Mossad-Top Secret evidence of a false-flag attack on September 11, 2001--masquerading as Saudi terrorist hijackings by former CIA asset Tim Osman, a.k.a. Osama Bin Laden (https://wikispooks.com/wiki/Osama_bin_Laden). Worst of all was my discovery of the Navy SEALS and Special Forces soldiers murdered to hide this global treason.

The tragic scene of the destruction and fall of the alien tribe's kingdom--known as *Hometree*--by the senseless human military attack, was symbolic of my own past worldview. As the gargantuan tree twists and falls into a pyre of flames, and the old life disintegrates into smoke, a new life, a new awareness, and a new mission for the Marine hero rises like a Phoenix born anew from the ashes of the past. To me, this scene symbolized nothing less than how my blind faith and "worship" of the military, the defense contracting industry, and the neutered, power-addicted political bureaucrats who pulled their strings, came crashing down when I discovered the evidence which redefined all of reality, and completed the theory I had been struggling to formulate. Soon after, the damn started to crack as my FOIA requests, depositions with Judicial Watch and Congress, media interviews, and internet radio broadcasts began.

The film Avatar was significant, because it was the last film I saw a few nights before I was to be targeted, captured, interrogated, tortured, and betrayed by MacDill Air Force Base, U.S. Central Command. In a sense, Avatar was the symbolic glimpse into a world and a journey I myself would be paralleling. The new world would be the 911 truth movement, and all of the intelligence and information that was treasonously suppressed; and my personal role as a reformed and reborn military man now profoundly changed.

WARNING

Be advised, the following information may traumatize some readers to the point of hospitalization, as it has already done to some. Spiritual preparation is vital. This is not a joke.

To fully understand how we got into this situation, and clearly see our roadmap of future choices, we must first re-examine the past and start from the beginning. If we want only the truth, and wish to protect our souls from the poison of lies, then we must fearlessly maintain an open mind and pure heart when we consider every piece of evidence and every opinion about the September 11, 2001 attacks and the related issues of terrorist financing, government corruption, and treason.

As prudence instructs, we must always guard our hearts and minds against emotional manipulations, and diligently strive to not allow anyone or anything to push or bully, guilt-trip or intimidate us into agreeing with any "popular opinion" or official explanations—regardless of their source, whether coming from religious, governmental, academic, or media "authorities".

NEW PERSPECTIVES

After using a typewriter and passenger pigeon for 2 years, it's quite amazing how much a computer and internet can boost your capabilities—especially in "HUMAN TERRAIN MAPPING." And at the center of my map was a man named Dov Zakheim, and his son Roger Zakheim.

To simplify these issues into one basic concept: Dov Zakheim and myself, working through Booz Allen Hamilton, were contracted by the American people to empower their military and government to find, analyze, and stop terrorist financing in order to protect Americans' lives and their property from destruction. This was how I understood the contract, my job, and my duty. It was also why the American people paid taxes.

However, it seemed when I discovered and reported all kinds of "waste-fraud-abuse" in the form of incompetence, corruption, contractor fraud, abuse of power, and other illegalities (some of which cannot yet be disclosed until after Congressional declassification) through my analysis briefings, and began formally submitting them up my chain of command, I was labeled not an efficient officer, but a whistleblower; and defined as the problem to be removed instead of the solution to be implemented. I was soon after illegally arrested, kidnapped, tortured, threatened, then removed from my position; and nine months later falsely imprisoned to silence me when I refused to play ball and remain quiet about what I found.

A SOLDIER'S DUTY

However, despite being kidnapped and hidden away in a distant Pennsylvania mountain top prison, I not only continued to report my findings, I amplified them with the official classification status: 'WHISTLEBLOWING DOCUMENTS WITH NATIONAL SECURITY IMPLICATIONS'. This was made possible after I was given the 'Leprechaun's secret treasure at the end of the rainbow', aka 22,000 Swiss Bank accounts (and their countries and owners) and WikiLeaks State Department and CIA cables, provided by Brad Birkenfeld himself--the original Union Bank of Switzerland whistleblower who had appeared on 60 Minutes, Vanity Fair, Democracy Now, and most newspapers. It was the day that changed everything, and raised the stakes of the game to "misprision of treason" if my reports were purposely ignored or buried--which they were, astoundingly.

I also learned that the law firm Covington and Burling had been contracted by none other than Swiss banks Union Bank of Switzerland and HSBC to hide the terrorist financing accounts, and that Booz Allen Hamilton and the Clinton Foundation (later headed by Donna Shalela, who was not only Clinton's Health and Human Services Secretary but also my lawyer's aunt!) had received money and partnered on projects (i.e., illegal prosecutions and cover-ups) with Covington and Burling.

However, the grand outrageous surprise came when I discovered that Roger Zakheim, Dov Zakheim'S son, worked at the U.S. House Armed Services Committee as an attorney while I was submitting my reports. Not only did Roger Zakheim collude with dear ol' dad to hide and block and disparage me and my reports from every Military, Inspector General, and Congressional Oversight Committee, as well as all House Members and Senators, but then had the backstabbing gall to secretly give my materials to Covington and Burling—who reciprocated by giving him a high-paying job one month before I was released from prison, not surprisingly. Indeed, you couldn't make this stuff up.

Also joining Roger Zakheim at Covington and Burling was Homeland Security Secretary Michael Chertoff (who had both flown the Bin Laden family out of America, and shipped the World Trade Center Towers steel to China before any forensic team could analyze it as a crime scene), Assistant Attorney General Lanny Breuer, and host of Justice Department lawyers involved with Eric Holder's Fast and Furious scandal.

I kept having to step back, take a breath, and gaze skyward in a mixed expression of prayer and head-shaking chuckles because of the impossibility and enormity of what I had discovered. It was fast becoming not only a story almost too bizarre to believe, but a comedy of errors too tragic and outrageous to tolerate because our American sons and daughters in the military were needlessly dying and being wounded by roadside bombs and sniper bullets being purchased with Swiss Bank accounts, which I had the codes to and could shut down overnight…if only I was responded to, if only someone took their oath and duty seriously, if only I could be debriefed and give what I had! Sadly, it seemed the political-military-intelligence agency bureaucrats wanted none of it, and would rather let military members die and come back in pieces than risk being scrutinized by the American public. Oddly, I felt akin to Moses pleading with Pharaoh to "let my people go free" and warning him of the impending wrath to come should he persist in his stubborn defiance. It seemed however this same hardness of heart was blinding them, and would ultimately serve as their undoing.

Dov Zakheim suddenly appeared as a common denominator in all my experiences and sub-plots. He was the center of the spider web, to whom all things conspiratorial and treasonous were connected. Before joining Booz Allen Hamilton's Mossad money machine, Zakheim was a member of the Council on Foreign Relations, and the Heritage Foundation. I also worked at the Heritage Foundation. Zakheim served as a foreign policy advisor to George W. Bush as part of a group led by Condoleezza Rice that called itself The Vulcans. I also worked at the Bush Administration.

Zakheim was part of the Project for the New American Century (along with the entire NEO-Conservative Corps) which can be examined at: http://en.wikipedia.org/wiki/Project_for_the_New_American_Century

The Project for the New American Century (PNAC) was an American think tank based in Washington, D.C. established in 1997 as a non-profit educational organization founded by William Kristol and Robert Kagan. The PNAC's stated goal is "to promote American global leadership." Of course some might say a more accurate reflection of the agenda as being to "promote American global domination through military interventionism, economic development (or destruction), and psychological warfare.

Zakheim took credit for writing in the NEOCON global strategy:

"American needs another 'Pearl Harbor' to energize the American people into a military plan against the Middle East."

Part I of the PSYOP was cultivating in people's minds the danger of another "Pearl Harbor"; part II was creating the event (9-11 attacks on New York and the Pentagon); part III was mobilizing military-intelligence-police state legislation to embark on the endless war to achieve this. The rest is history.

In 2001 Dov Zakheim became the Undersecretary for Defense for G.W. Bush, and the Pentagon Comptroller who "lost" $2.3 trillion dollars (some estimate as more like $5 trillion) in U.S. Department of Defense funds (which most researchers conclude went to various Israeli operations). On September 10, 2001 Secretary of Defense Donald Rumsfeld testified before Congress about this missing money.

Mysteriously, or ominously, the very next day—on September 11, 2001—the auditors working on the missing money trail were killed when the Navy Intelligence room they were working in was destroyed in the Pentagon attack (which Barbara Honegger, Susan Lindauer and others scientifically determined was caused by pre-positioned explosives and a drone strike....not a 757 plane—which amazingly the official story has tried to explain as somehow vanishing and vaporizing into the Pentagon's cement columns like Harry Potter disappearing into a magic portal.) This info is available at:
https://www.youtube.com/watch?v=4fvJ8nFa5Qk
https://www.youtube.com/watch?v=68LUHa_-O1A

Interestingly before the Bush Administration, Dov Zakheim had been CEO of SPC International, a subsidiary of System Planning Corporation, a high-technology analytical firm which had designed "remote control technology" to take-over and fly planes in the event of a terrorist hijacking.

After the Iraq invasion, Dov Zakheim was appointed by President Bush as a member of the Commission on Wartime Contracting in Iraq and Afghanistan, and soon after—on May 5, 2004 to be exact—joined the defense and intelligence contracting firm Booz Allen Hamilton.

Incidentally, other Booz Allen men included SECDEF and CIA Director Leon Panetta, CIA-NSA Director Michael Hayden, and Mike McConnell, Director of National Intelligence.

Interestingly Mike McConnell was a Navy Admiral and served as Director of the National Security Agency from 1992 to 1996. He also served as the United States Director of National Intelligence from February 20, 2007 to January 27, 2009 during the Bush administration and seven days of the Obama administration. In this role, he was the "center of the spider web" and knew everything every U.S. and allied intelligence and military agency knew. He is currently Vice Chairman at Booz Allen Hamilton focusing on the Intelligence and National Security areas, and oversaw Edward Snowden's Hawaii assignment to NSA. The journalist Glenn Greenwald described McConnell "as the perfect embodiment of" the "revolving door" syndrome in Washington. Most funny—and damning—is that McConnell and Michael Chertoff authored an article establishing the partnership between Covington and Burling (thereby UBS and HSBC) and Booz Allen Hamilton in counterterrorism and illicit trafficking operations.

Since Booz Allen Hamilton was contracted by government to find terrorist money, and Covington and Burling was contracted by UBS and HSBC to protect and hide it, this made the Booz Allen-Covington partnership the living embodiment of Washington hypocrisy, corruption and treason.

The missing piece that completed the picture was that Dov Zakheim was the man who hired me to leave Washington DC and come down to U.S. Central Command at MacDill Air Force Base in Florida to work as a Terrorist Threat Finance Analyst for Booz Allen Hamilton's team in the Joint Interagency Operations

Center. In this position, I tracked and analyzed the money supply to terrorists fighting for Al-Qaeda, Al-Nusra, the Haqqani Network, and now the Islamic State in Syria and the Levant—aka, ISIS and IS.

Strangely enough, he was also the man who fired me from Booz Allen Hamilton after I began asking questions, writing reports, requesting information, and generally getting close to the true policies, people, and issues underpinning terrorist financing, international banks, and intelligence agency failures and cover-ups. Soon after my arrest and persecution, he retired as a Senior Vice President of Booz Allen in 2010.

In October 2011 he, along with his son Roger Zakheim, was mentioned as adviser on the Middle East for Republican Presidential contender Mitt Romney (who, strangely enough, also had secret Swiss Bank accounts).

Another piece of the puzzle suddenly fell into place about why Republican National Committee Chairman Rience Priebus (who later became Donald Trump's "leaky" Chief of Staff) and the Mitt Romney for President Team never acknowledged or acted on my terrorist finance intelligence reports...Dov Zakheim and Roger Zakheim, and others, had written the checks to make Mitt their man, and with those checks came conditions…and silence.

More information began to seep out, and the looming avalanche began to crack and shift. NBC News Anchor Brian Williams interviewed Snowden in Russia, in which Snowden disclosed his connection to the Brad Birkenfeld-CIA targeting operation in Geneva Switzerland, as well as his frustration and disgust, stating:

"I've been in the intelligence community for a decade. What's more shocking is not the dirtiness of the business, but the dirtiness of the targeting; the lack of respect for the public, and lack of respect for the intrusiveness of the procedures. I lived and worked undercover, overseas, was assigned a name that was not mine. I worked for CIA undercover, overseas; and NSA, and DIA as a lecturer. So

when they say I don't know what I'm talking about, they don't know what they're saying."

Here Snowden is discussing the DUI entrapment the CIA employed to attempt to extort Brad Birkenfeld into becoming a CIA asset and committing industrial espionage against UBS and Switzerland. This information Birkenfeld released to Bennett, and is discoverable on the TS/SCI and NIPR communication channels and State Department CIA substation chief cables, also reported by WikiLeaks.

The NBC News Timeline of Snowden also corroborates this: 2007-2009: Snowden is posted to Geneva, Switzerland, under diplomatic cover as an IT and cyber security expert for the CIA, a position that gives him access to a wide array of classified documents. He later tells the Guardian that during this period he became disillusioned *"about how my government functions and what its impact is in the world. I realized that I was part of something that was doing far more harm than good."*

Late 2009-March 2012: Snowden's supervisor at the CIA placed a critical assessment of his behavior and work habits in his personnel file and voiced the suspicion that he had tried to "break into classified computer files to which he was not authorized to have access," the New York Times reports after he is identified as the leaker, quoting two unnamed "senior American officials." Snowden leaves the CIA soon after his supervisor's criticism and begins work as a NSA contractor assigned by Dell -- one of 854,000 contractors with top-secret clearance working for the federal government. Over the next several years, he switches between assignments with the NSA and CIA for Dell, including a stint at a NSA facility in Japan that lasts until March 2012.

Regarding the Sept. 11, 2001 attack/ domestic psychological operation, and consequent "Patriot Act" expansion of police-intelligence agency powers, Snowden states:

> "The government took and used the 9-11 attacks to justify programs that never have been shown to keep us safe, that took liberties and freedoms from us. Colin Powel's speech, Iraq's war was launched on false pretenses. This was the problem of putting too much faith on intelligence systems without developing them. I believed the government's argument that we were 'going to free the oppressed'. The problem was, as time went on, as I rose to higher levels and more and more info at the highest levels, I saw so many things told by the government was not true. A good gauge is what you see in the press. NSA, DIA, and CIA have claimed lives are at risk and military info is out there. But we don't see any of that in newspaper."

Regarding his whistleblowing up the chain of command, Snowden said:

> "I did go through channels; they (NSA-CIA) have copies of letters to office of General Counsel, raising concerns to these offices, to my colleagues, at Fort Meade, at Hawaii (Booz Allen Hamilton), etc. I reported that there were real problems about the way NSA was interpreting their legal authority."

Regarding the intrusions into privacy, Snowden reveals:

> "NSA analysts can get inside your thought process. They can watch people's internet communications, and watch their thoughts form as they type. They can watch you write sentences, backspace, pause, and write you re-write them."

Regarding what the NSA-CIA can do with a cell phone:

> "The NSA and Russian and China intelligence service has significant funding and a research team can own that phone. The minute it is turned on, they can take pictures, can turn on your apps, even if off. Does anyone really care that I'm looking at Ranger game score? Yes, because that

> *tells you speak English, American, interested in this sport, what your habits are, where were you when you checked this. What is your pattern of life, what other phones are around you, are you with someone or someplace you shouldn't be? All of these things can raise your level of scrutiny. These activities can be misconstrued by government to do you wrong. These activities are unregulated, uncontrolled and dangerous."*

Snowden concluded:

> "The definition of a security state that priorities security above all other considerations. If we want to be free, we cannot give away our privacy, we cannot give away our rights, we have to be an active part of our government, there are some things worth dying for."

I couldn't agree more, and looked forward to clarifying some of Snowden's theories, and connecting his dots.

Hoping that Snowden's revelations would awaken fresh eyes and skeptical minds, I responded to Brian Williams with a letter:

May 28, 2014

TO: Brian Williams, NBC News
FR: Scott Bennett, 2LT U.S. Army Reserve, 11th Psychological Operations
RE: Additional Whistleblowing documentation of Snowden reports

Dear Mr. Williams,

You stated in your interview with Edward Snowden that you have filed a FOIA (freedom of information act) request for any and all materials relating to Snowden's claim that he in fact filed numerous letters and emails with the Office of General Counsel, Inspector General, and other authorities at the NSA, Congress, and Booz Allen Hamilton. If you are serious, then I also suggest you include in your FOIA request "any and all materials relating to Scott Bennett's whistleblowing reports relating to Edward Snowden, Booz Allen Hamilton, Union

Bank of Switzerland, Brad Birkenfeld, the NSA-CIA, and Terrorist Threat Finance Operations."

All of these subjects are included in Bennett's reports, and expose a larger intelligence-government-military failure and cover-up.

I also know the names of the Booz Allen Hamilton staff (both at McLean, Virginia, and Hawaii) who reviewed Edward Snowden's initial communications.

Additionally, other materials were also submitted which include:

Pre-Snowden Whistleblowing report to U.S. Civil Affairs-Psychological Operations Commander, General Jeff Jacobs on Sept. 25, 2012

Pre-Snowden report sent to Pentagon Inspector General, Lynne Halbrook; Top Military Officials at the Pentagon; Congressional Intelligence, Military, Terrorism, Oversight and Reform, and Judiciary Committees

Report sent to NBC News and Washington Post correspondents (Michael Isikoff and Tom Hamburger)

Contact me for additional materials.

2LT Scott Bennett
U.S. Army Reserve
11th Psychological Operations Battalion

As predicted, Brian Williams—like his colleague Michael Isikoff—never returned my calls, emails, or letters; and never expanded their FOIA's to include this information—which would have changed the entire scope of Snowden's revelations. It seemed the First Amendment and Freedom of the Press to Mr. Williams and NBC news (and the other networks) was not for the preservation of the Republic's liberty by exposing the corruption that destroys it, but rather about job security for the media personalities parasitically existing off of the American terrorism paranoia.

On June 13, 2014, James Bamford at WIRED magazine flew to Moscow and interviewed Edward Snowden, writing a story that further expanded into the CIA operation against Swiss Banker-Whistleblower Brad Birkenfeld. Bamford wrote:

"It was in Geneva that Snowden would see firsthand some of the moral compromises CIA agents made in the field. Because

spies were promoted based on the number of human sources they recruited, they tripped over each other trying to sign up anyone they could, regardless of their value. Operatives would get targets drunk enough to land in jail and then bail them out—putting the target in their debt. They do really risky things to recruit them that have really negative, profound impacts on the person and would have profound impacts on our national reputation if we got caught," he says. "But we do it simply because we can."
http://www.wired.com/2014/08/edward-snowden/
https://www.thetruthseeker.co.uk/?p=56601

What Bamford forgot to mention, or intentionally omitted, was the $104 million Birkenfeld was later paid by CIA to cover-up the Snowden-Booz Allen Hamilton connection to the UBS terrorist accounts, as well as the Top-Secret documents smuggled out of U.S. Intelligence and Military agencies by Booz Allen Hamilton, and stored in their McLean Virginia facility. I should know, I was a Department of Defense Courier. I read everything, and knew everybody.

Michael Hastings at Rolling Stone had also read my materials and reports, discovered the connection, and began to research and report about it. Shortly after, he was killed in an explosive Nano-Thermite charge planted inside his Mercedes Benz car. More about this will soon be released.

Similar to a thawing river speedily announcing the end of Winter, the increasing revelations and interviews about this story seemed to be indicating the beginning of "the conspirators" end, and they knew it, and most likely would die hiding. The conspirators in this story were of course the political-intelligence community elite who operated in complete secrecy with no accountability, and were immunized from any questioning or prosecution by virtue of their ability to classify anything they wanted "top secret"—and thereby hide it from the public for 50 years.

This story, and the material I discovered, guaranteed not only that they would not succeed, but that their incompetence or corruption would be exposed as the inexcusable treason it was, and prevented from ever happening again. I resolved that for the men who had suffered and died as a result of this 5-year story, and to reverse the "fever of never-ending war" that was consuming America's imagination, I would have to tell it, regardless of the cost to me. "Take no part in the unfruitful works of darkness, but instead expose them." --Ephesians 5:11 (ESV), I reflected. And so, I did:

http://www.projectcamelotportal.com/blog/31-kerrys-blog/2289-now-on-youtube-scott-bennett-interview

And then again: https://www.youtube.com/watch?v=Jo8Xm46s62I

And again: http://www.veteranstoday.com/2014/10/12/psy-ops-whistleblower-i-worked-with-911-suspects-rumsfeld-myers-zakheim/

And again: http://www.erikrush.com/home

It seemed after my initial interviews on October 1, 2014—which was televised live—things began to unravel immediately. A suspicious event transpired on October 27, 2014. Michael Isikoff, the same NBC reporter who, with Tom Hamburger at the Washington Post, had met with me in person and discussed the Snowden-Birkenfeld-Booz Allen Hamilton-UBS-Terrorist Finance reports for two hours in July 2013, suddenly released a story entitled, "Feds identify suspected 'second leaker' for Snowden reporters."

In the story, Isikoff wrote:

"The FBI has identified an employee of a federal contracting firm (possibly Booz Allen Hamilton's cyber-warfare team) suspected of being the so-called "second leaker" who turned over sensitive documents about the U.S.

Government's terrorist watch list to a journalist closely associated with ex-NSA contractor Edward Snowden, according to law enforcement and intelligence sources who have been briefed on the case."

What Isikoff neglected to disclose was that he had been given this material a year prior by me in our meeting, albeit indirectly, and instead of reporting it to the American people, coordinated it with the CIA-NSA intelligence community and only released it as part of a larger coordinated strategic communication scheme. And despite multiple requests, Isikoff refused to return any of the documents I shared with him during our interview, which I considered a gross violation and betrayal of a reporter's duty to protect his "source", if not a clear indication that he was really gathering information for, and in the service of, the CIA.

http://news.yahoo.com/feds-identify-suspected--second-leaker--for-snowden-reporters-165741571.html

CIA-MOSSAD DRUG TRAFFICKING HISTORY CLASS TAUGHT BY DOJ

Another final and fascinating discovery I made upon my release from the Island of Misfit Toys (prison) was that the Department of Justice and Bureau of Prisons were conducting a class (and forcing inmates to take it) that was teaching that America's CIA and Israel's Intelligence agency Mossad had been working together for the past 50 years on illegal drug operations and assassinations of U.S. military personnel and journalists and political figures in the process.

Although of course I already knew this, I was completely flabbergasted that the U.S. Department of Justice was teaching this to prisoners—many of whom were violent, drug dealers, and already hateful against the U.S. Government. Unless I was missing some stroke of political genius, it seemed the seeds of "domestic terrorism" were being sown—and provocateurs being ideologically inspired—by the same U.S. government which justified its existence by claiming to fight against such terrorism. This wasn't just hypocrisy, it was, yet again, another example of potential treason, and a violation of the hallowed "Patriot Act", never mind an undermining of the entire Constitution.

I discovered this after I had been placed, accidentally, into a "Half-way House" upon my release from the federal prison in Pennsylvania (after a 5-day bus ride from hell). I made copies of all materials used in this program, and filed a complaint in Federal Court to preserve the evidence (possible class action suit), which read as follows:

UNITED STATES DISTRICT COURT
MIDDLE DISTRICT OF FLORIDA
TAMPA DIVISION
JUDGE VIRGINIA HERNANDEZ COVINGTON

UNITED STATES OF AMERICA,
    PLAINTIFF
V.   CASE NO.: 8:11-CR-14-T-33AEP
SCOTT ALLAN BENNETT,
    DEFENDANT

DEFENDANT'S REPLY TO THE GOVERNMENT'S RESPONSE
IN OPPOSITION TO DEFENDANT'S MOTION FOR MODIFICATION OF
PROBATION AND STAY PENDING APPEAL

---

1. Defendant's mail was intentionally misdirected and not given to him while he was in D.O.J. / B.O.P. custody, constituting an intentional "obstruction of justice" and "mail tampering" charge. See Exhibit 2.

2. The government Assistant U.S. Attorney Sara Sweeney has intentionally and blatantly lied to the court, in an attempt to terminate defendant's appeal, and conceal and confuse the larger issues of law in this case.

D. CIA-DRUG OPERATIONAL HISTORY" CLASS

3. The government is suspiciously silent about the Bureau of Prisons (B.O.P.) "CIA-Drug Operational History" class which defendant completed as a mandated class by the Bureau of Prisons. Defendant asserts that this class, included in defendant's previous motion, describes the cooperation between the U.S. Central Intelligence Agency and the Israeli Intelligence Agency (Mossad) in numerous assassinations of U.S. military officers, journalists, and politicians in order to facilitate illegal drug trafficking operations. As such, it satisfies the "drug-alcohol" abuse treatment required by this court.

4. Therefore, defendant requests that this Court rule on whether or not this B.O.P. class participation satisfies defendant's post-incarceration "alcohol-drug abuse" and "mental health" treatment requirement.

E. ABUSE OF INMATES AND PROPAGANDA CONSIDERATIONS

5. As intriguing as this B.O.P. class was, and despite its confirmation of material and people already well-known to defendant from his previous political, military, and intelligence operations, contracts, and research, it may also have been in violation of the U.S. Constitution, on numerous levels, and open to a class-action lawsuit by the people forcibly subjected to it.

6. Specifically, the Court must ask two questions: Question 1) if the B.O.P. classes on "CIA Drug Operations" were in fact a *lie*, and designed for the purposes of artificially generating criminal mindsets by transmitting false information to inmates and their families in order to cultivate government distrust, hatred, racial divisions,

exaggerate "conspiracy theories", and encourage disloyalty, disrespect, or revulsion of the United States government and its legal system, then obviously this is an intentional and malicious instrument of mental abuse and torture of inmates; and as such a violation of the US Information and Educational Exchange Act of 1948 (Public Law 80-402), commonly known as the Smith-Mundt Act, which prohibits psychological warfare on American citizens—including inmates. Additionally, it may be in violation of United Nations Human Rights Commission laws and the International Court on Human Rights.

7. Or the Court must ask Question 2: If the B.O.P. classes were _true_, and contained accurate facts and policies about the relationship between the CIA (Fort Bragg Detachment and Coronet Oaks facility), FBI, Mossad, the U.S. Department of Justice, U.S. Drug Enforcement Agency, and other government agencies, then it is a clear admission and indictment of the Department of Justice/ Bureau of Prisons' complicity and even participation in illegal assassinations, conspiracies, and drug trafficking operations. These operations include: September 11, 2001 attacks on Pentagon and World Trade Center and Solomon Building 7 as means to initiate "War on Terror" and Afghanistan Poppy-Field "Opium" military operations, as described by Israeli Intelligence Mossad.

8. Most importantly, and vital to U.S. security interests, the Court must determine if this class indicates that the Department of Justice/Bureau of Prisons is actively and intentionally teaching and inspiring inmates with an unstable mental state of rebellion, distrust, anarchy, and violence against the U.S. government, the police, and the

court systems. This could conceivably be charged as a treasonous offense.

9. Now that defendant has brought this potentially treasonous B.O.P. class to the Court's attention, most likely the government will, as usual, attempt to quickly hide and eliminate the evidence of this "class" quickly, and resort to its usual strategy of exaggerated attacks and slanderous accusations against defendant, in a vain attempt to avoid the key questions and issues raised. This court should not tolerate this defensive behavior, and demand answers.

10. Therefore, defendant requests this Court immediately issue a gag order that forbids the Department of Justice/ Bureau of Prisons from any kind of communication or investigation into this class, until after the Court conducts its own *sua sponte* investigation. Failure to do this will only facilitate illegal cover-up of this material, and harm the defendant—as well as other Americans being subjected to this "brainwashing" activity by the D.O.J./ B.O.P.

11. Additionally, defendant has requested a thorough Inspector General investigation be performed. The Court should also demand an affidavit from the government regarding any investigation or communication that the government has recently done in this matter, after being made aware of it by defendant in his motion several weeks ago.

WHEREFORE, it is respectfully requested that this Honorable Court rule on whether defendant's previous Bureau of Prisons class entitled "DEEP BLACK: CIA-Israeli Mossad Drug Trafficking Operations" (See APPENDIX, "DEEP BLACK: The CIA's Secret Drug Wars" 1997 by David Guyatt, used by

GEO Services/Bureau of Prisons/Dept. of Justice Residential Re-Entry Programming curriculum) satisfies this Court's original "alcohol-drug" and "mental care" education and treatment requirement; and that accordingly this Court modify Defendant's probation by removing probation completely; or in the alternative staying Defendant's probation and fine pending the outcome of his appeal and military legal investigation so that he might be allowed to prepare his legal appeal work with military and civilian attorneys.

Additionally, defendant requests a *sua sponte* investigation by the court into the recent mail tampering activities perpetrated against defendant in an attempt to "disrupt his appeal".

Respectfully submitted,
Scott Bennett, pro se

BRAD BIRKENFELD...AMERICAN PSYCHO

As the sensationalist subtitle suggests, Brad Birkenfeld was the equivalent of Christian Bale's lead character in the American Psycho...only Birkenfeld was smarter and had a decent soul. He was a mastermind of the International banking industry, disarmingly charming and personable and would instantly energize any room he entered; and was ruthlessly aggressive, obsessive, and cold-blooded towards his projects.

He was also a deeply loyal American patriot (at least before the Congress and Justice Department betrayed him and used his own protected testimony as evidence to imprison him). To most of the low-browed, tattooed, two-digit IQ class thugs in prison of course, he came off as an incredibly arrogant ass (which got him a few black-eyes in prison softball games) ...but I liked him immediately.

Interestingly, in February 2015 the French government requested Birkenfeld testify in their investigations of Swiss Banks funding terrorism and hiding money. The Miami Court reluctantly allowed Birkenfeld to travel to Paris and testify. Conveniently, the French also interviewed me, and discussed French Intelligence issues relating to Swiss Banks and our reports (unclassified). More about that later…

<u>SUSPICIOUS SENATE REPORT ON TERRORIST FIANCING AND COVER-UP OF UNION BANK OF SWITZERLAND INCLUSION IN FINDINGS</u>

One very suspicious issue I discovered was the fact that on July 17, 2012, the U.S. Senate Permanent Subcommittee on Investigations, Committee on Homeland Security and Governmental Affairs, led by Carl Levin, Chairman, and Tom Coburn, Ranking Minority member, filed a report and held a hearing titled, "U.S. Vulnerabilities to Money Laundering, Drugs, and Terrorist Financing: HSBC Case History".

This Report allegedly examined the anti-money laundering (AML) and terrorist financing vulnerabilities created when a global bank uses its U.S. affiliate to provide U.S. dollars, U.S. dollar services, and access to the U.S. financial system to high risk affiliates, high risk correspondent banks, and high-risk clients. This Report also allegedly offered recommendations to strengthen correspondent AML controls to combat money laundering, drug trafficking, and terrorist financing.

Yet incredibly, absolutely NONE of Brad Birkenfeld's Union Bank of Switzerland materials was included in this report. The biggest whistleblower in global banking history with the most earth-shaking banking intelligence and account information belonging to terrorists was never mentioned once! In fact, the following words never appeared in the report: Brad Birkenfeld, Union Bank of Switzerland, Military Terror Threat Finance, U.S.

Central Command, Joint Interagency Group, U.S. Special Operations Command, or Booz Allen Hamilton.

Two weeks later, Brad Birkenfeld was released from prison, and less than a month later was paid $104 million dollars. Then on September 25, 2012—2 months later—I wrote and sent my own army analysis report disclosing the "UBS-Birkenfeld-CIA link to terrorist financing" to the military and Congress. I had not ever seen, or knew anything about the July 17th, 2012 report by the Senate committee.

A reasonable assumption would have been, since the Senate has just published a report claiming to be "investigating" how terrorism is financed, and has clearly never mentioned the key UBS information, they will rush to synthesize it into their matrix of materials and recalibrate their policy solutions; and most likely request additional documentation from Birkenfeld and Bennett.

Yet, amazingly, the military report documenting Birkenfeld's UBS intelligence was never even responded to. Cover-up or incompetence? Only a fool would allow Congress to claim ignorance on this matter.

THE MISSING 28 PAGES OF THE 9-11 REPORT

Now, in 2016, it seems certain members of Congress are courageously pressing to release the infamous "28 missing pages" of the Senate Investigation into 911 attacks, implicating a U.S. black flag operation and Saudi Arabian financing (as well as other Gulf countries). I reported this here:
https://youtu.be/vwTjvAe7uTg & https://youtu.be/phJwLm26FXY

Of course, what is most encouraging about this request is that it will lead to the additional evidentiary reports and documents which also must be released in order to clarify hidden finance connections to Saudi funding of 911 include. These include, but will not be limited to:

1) the Zacharias Moussaoui laptop which contains a database of Saudi Funders of Al Qaeda/ISIS;

2) the Swiss Bank testimony delivered to Congress (Senate Permanent Subcommittee on Investigations, Chairman Carl Levin D-MI) by Brad Birkenfeld, the Union Bank of Switzerland whistleblower and intelligence source to 2LT Scott Bennett, U.S. Army Special Operations, Terrorist Finance Analyst;

3) 2LT Bennett military whistleblowing report to U.S. Civil Affairs-Psychological Operations Command and Congress concerning Swiss Bank-Terrorist finance cover up by CIA-NSA and Edward Snowden revelations about CIA targeting Birkenfeld in Geneva, Switzerland; and

4) the release of the intelligence (computers, databases, Swiss Bank accounts, donor lists, etc.) allegedly obtained by Navy SEALS in their assassination of Osama Bin Laden in Pakistan, and taken by CIA.

Alternatively, if the "28 missing pages" are not released, then that could mean they are being used by CIA-Military-Obama Administration-Congressional officials as a "gun against the head of the new Saudi government" to coercively exert pressure and demand support for US foreign policy and war mongering agendas against Russia-China-Middle East.

Only by combining all of these documents will the raw data be obtained that clearly exposes the most essential people and issues, problems, contradictions, and cover-ups of the 911 attacks upon the Pentagon and World Trade Center, and the Solomon Building (building 7). As I discussed at length with 9-11 researchers Barbara Honegger and Susan Lindauer, when properly assembled, all of these materials will expose the financial proof of a false flag operation engineered by traitors in the U.S. Congress, military, and intelligence apparatus, as well as within foreign nations who participated in the event.

<u>REVELATIONS</u>

As the pieces of the puzzle began to finally assemble—or rather as the icebergs began to enclose around the ship of conspiracy carrying all sorts of political-military criminals—a final bizarre discovery was brought to my attention by an expert intelligence analyst, Mr. Van Palmer.

This piece of intel was that the international law firm, Covington and Burling, which both represented Union Bank of Switzerland and employed DOJ's Lanny Breuer, Eric Holder, and Homeland Security's Michael Chertoff, also happened to be directly connected (by family blood) to one very significant person: Judge Virginia Hernandez Covington…the very same federal judge (appointed by G.W. Bush) who presided over my case in Florida, who ignored all of my legal motions exposing the Snowden-Birkenfeld-Booz Allen Hamilton-Dov Zakheim-Union Bank of Switzerland connection, and who imprisoned me in a dungeon with lightning speed. Truth kept getting stranger than fiction.

I could only shake my head, for the umpteenth time, as I saw once again the tragic comedy—as well as the treasonous corruption—of a story and cast of characters you simply could not invent. Birkenfeld had pointed out where all the "bodies were buried", Snowden had defined and marked them with NSA-CIA document "tombstones", and now it seemed I was stuck with the job of digging them up and performing the terrorist threat finance analytical autopsy.

Most significant was that America was now speeding toward new wars against Ukraine (via CIA mercenaries) and the Islamic State, which was being financed by these very same Birkenfeld UBS Swiss Bank accounts. The only question was how the public (and world opinion) would react to all of this—or rather how explosive and far-reaching their cry of outrage might be. Time was of the essence.

In addition to Jesselyn Radack (jesselynr@whistleblower.org), Birkenfeld's PR person and now also, conveniently, Edward Snowden's attorney (Radack had been instructed by Birkenfeld to contact me regarding the military-terrorist dimension his Swiss Bank accounts. She never did.), I had contacted Glenn Greenwald, Snowden's supposed biographer and distributor of the intelligence cables, and provided his assistant Andrew Fishman (adf@riseup.net) with all documents, and most importantly the CIA-Snowden-Birkenfeld DUI connection in Switzerland. Fishman responded:

> *Date: Fri, 4 Apr 2014 18:04:19 -0300*
> *From: ADF@riseup.net*
> *To: armypsyop@outlook.com*
> *Subject: Re: NSA-CIA UBS connection to Snowden-Brad Birkenfeld*
> *Hi Scott,*
> *My main question from this is: can you *prove* that the banker targeted by the CIA for the drunk driving play was Birkenfeld?*

I replied <u>yes</u>, sent him the proof which Birkenfeld had provided me, and expected an avalanche of responses and follow-up questions. Amazingly, I <u>never</u> heard from Mr. Fishman again, despite numerous follow up emails and phone calls by me.

Nor did I ever get a response from Glen Greenwald, or Jesselyn Radack, or Ben Wizner (Snowden's ACLU attorney), or Steven Kohn and David Colapinto (Birkenfeld's attorneys who were also informed).

Since facts didn't lie, it seemed some actors in this story, judging by their suspicious silence, were in reality not who they represented themselves to be after all. Another layer of the onion began to peel away. Of course, I knew eventually they would be cornered and forced into giving an answer, under oath, since my legal deposition for a new trial and dismissal of all charges was coming up in the next few months—as well as my lawsuit against Booz Allen Hamilton, UBS, and the Department of Defense for their "racketeering" roles in this matter. FOIA requests and subpoenas would be fired off like machine guns and all would be hauled in to testify—lawyers, politicians, military, media—about everything and anything and everyone that connected the dots of this story intertwining Birkenfeld, Snowden, and myself since 2007. Would they be exposed for who they were and what their agenda really was? Time would tell.

More importantly, the American military member and his family would finally see and hear the truth, and be able to hold politicians and military leaders accountable.

What would also come to light were the materials suggesting Edward Snowden had communicated Top Secret Q clearance documents detailing the use of nuclear weapons during the 9/11 event (suggested in CIA asset Susan Lindauer's testimony—which she was imprisoned for also) and how the mini-nukes were made in the USA and "handed" to Israel, who then used them against us (with the help of Bush, Cheney, Chertoff, etc.) to create a phony war against Muslims and The Middle East. Interesting to say the least, and certainly important to American politicians supposedly directing the military-intelligence community one would think. But perhaps it was the other way around.

To ensure the survivability of the legal fight that was approaching, everything was safely uploaded and distributed to well trusted, well hidden, third-parties as insurance against any "accident" which might befall me. I had come to know, albeit accidentally, the risks, the dangers, and the cabal of liars and megalomaniacs at the center of this story, but I also knew the oath I had sworn to the Constitution as an American Army Officer. I had sworn to preserve, uphold and defend it against all enemies, foreign and domestic; and sacrifice my life in the process if necessary.

It was that oath and calling I chose to follow…to the end, wherever it might lead, regardless of personal cost. I would simply do my duty to honor my country and protect my fellow soldiers by proclaiming the treasonous facts no one in Washington obviously wanted the public to know about.

I was reminded that "Every man dies, not every man really lives." How it all ends…I will leave up to God and the American people to decide.

INSPIRATION

There is a quote from *Horatius* from the *Lays of Ancient Rome* by Lord Macaulay which reads, "*How can a man die better, than facing fearful odds, for the ashes of his fathers, and the temples of his Gods.*"

Similarly, I thought, or was inspired with the thought, since suffering is the hammer that intensifies our character, how can a man write anything worthy of reading, unless he has suffered unspeakably and wrongfully? In other words, how can a man stand boldly erect in the posture of fearless conviction until after he has been stung by injustice and gone through the fetus position withdrawals of being slandered by those dressed in his own military uniform and supposedly championing the same crest? How can a man become addicted to the exhilarating thrill of clashing swords with evil by proclaiming truth and defending righteousness until after he has felt the stab of betrayal and endured the torture of dishonor done to him by dishonorable men? How?

Only when he has forgiven them for being dead in their spirits, and seen them as the slaves to diabolical powers they are. After all, a man cannot behold and bask in the serene, beautiful reality of peace (God) until he has experienced the violent, ugly nightmare of wickedness (Satan). A sleep most military men seem unable, or unwilling, to wake from.

It seemed truth was not only stranger than fiction, but far more electrifying. It seemed to me that truth was an acquired taste, and a man could find it spiritually purifying and intellectually intoxicating until first he had drunk the bitter, poisonous opiates of lust and lies. In my case it was the lust for wealth and power through energy supremacy—the absolute control of oil—as expressed by military objectives; and the lies of the September 11th attacks to facilitate these military objectives.

(Note: One of the greatest psyop campaigns, because of its "kindergarten simplicity", was the General Electric "green energy-renewable fuels" issue, which planted the seed in the minds of foreign populations (like Ukraine) that luxurious Utopian dreams—not Orwellian or Huxleyish—could be realized through submitting to the U.S. dominated recyclable industry, which of course was perforated with CIA/USAID and defense intelligence researchers for obvious reasons. This of course would divert attention, money, and law away from the real U.S. agenda: a "blitzkrieg" domination and leveraging of oil/energy to thereby manipulate economic war against Russia and China, facilitated through the Rupert Murdoch spin of the invisible Israeli double-cross—as seen in the U.S.S. Liberty attack of 8 June 1967...but that's for another report).

CATHARSIS

"There is a prison, in a more ancient part of the world...a pit...where men are thrown to suffer and die...but sometimes a man rises from the darkness...sometimes the pit throws something back." -The Dark Knight Rises

There is a scene in part 3 of the Batman saga in which Bruce Wayne, a.k.a. Batman (Christian Bale), has been humiliatingly beaten in a fist fight with the arch villain Baine, his back broken, and then is thrown down into a deep, dark pit...the worst hell on earth. Metaphorically, it is the same experience every person and their family feels when they are betrayed, lied about, and then unlawfully imprisoned by corrupt judges and prosecutors concerned not with justice, but rather their own career advancement.

On another level, this movie is also disturbingly ironic in that Senator Patrick Leahy (D-Vermont) Chairman of the Senate Judiciary Committee, had the vanity, hypocrisy, or senility, to appear in the film's board room scene, supposedly championing professional ethics and defending the hero's reputation. A scene completely unreflective of reality I might add, given that Patrick Leahy and his committee were informed by me multiple times about terrorist financing through Swiss Banks, and instead of defending American soldiers whose bodies and lives (and families) were being destroyed in attacks...Leahy chose to hide in silence and say and do nothing.

Bruce Wayne awakens in the bottom of this pit only to see, on a television installed just for him, Gotham City crumbling into madness and violence as the arch villain Baine unleashes savagery and revenge upon all of the bankers and wealthy aristocrats—a strikingly similar Occupy Wall street theme. At this point, Bruce Wayne faces a choice: he must either surrender the fight and resign himself to wither and die as he witnesses his city, his people--his world--be slowly devoured by its own selfish lusts and greed; or he must take a stand, begin his climb, renew his will to fight, and commit himself, body and soul, to defend them--and his hope. For Gotham's sake, he chooses the latter, and begins his arduous journey of recovery, training, and rebuilding of his strength and soul.

And the climactic test, which all men before him have failed except a child decades prior, is to scale the rocky sides of the pit to a high ledge from which he must make a giant leap to freedom. However, the leap can only be attempted if the safety rope is untied from around the waist--severing the lifeline--leaving the climber to either 1) certain death should he miss, falter, or be too cowardly to try; or 2) freedom if his faith and self-confidence is strong enough to take the leap and defy the abyss.

Ultimately Bruce Wayne slowly makes the climb to the tribal chants of "rise" by prisoners watching him from below. He reaches the top, unties himself, and mustering every drop of explosive emotion and spiritual strength, closes his eyes, leaps, and catches the ledge with the tips of his fingers. He pulls himself up, climbs out of the pit, stands victoriously erect in the bright sunshine of freedom; and then, to a triumphant blast of horns only a Hans Simmer soundtrack can imagine, runs off toward the distant final battle.

THE HARDSHIP OF ANSWERING CHILDREN'S QUESTIONS ABOUT WAR.

When I returned home from the wars, the torture, and the surreal hell of passing through the guts of the Obama government monstrosity, another epiphany occurred.

One summer afternoon, as I was playing "Disney Princess" (which most likely every father or uncle or grandfather knows goes hand-in-hand with little girls) and sitting alone outside with my giddy 9-year-old niece under tall redwoods, listening to singing birds and romantic frogs amidst trickling ponds and whispering breezes, I thought *as Americans, who are we really?...in the eyes of the world, how are we seen?*

My niece had wanted to wear my old army helmet and dress-up as the *Princess-Soldier-Hero*. Sitting under the umbrella, which was imagined to be our F.O.B. (forward operating base), and caught up in the adoring eyes of her uncle (me), she began asking with simple, innocent childlike curiosity about the war I was in, my intimate experiences, if I killed anyone, who the *good and bad guys were, and* <u>why</u>.

Something inside me went still, cold, and quiet. The *why* question I found impossible to answer, but in trying I discovered something else. It struck me that I could no longer give the answer I had been raised to believe and that I had always wanted to give; the answer I had, in fact, practiced in my heart since I was an 8-year old boy playing *WAR* with my neighborhood friends. I couldn't lie, and in light of what I had come to discover in my sojourn through the labyrinth of government secrets, any answer alleging a defense of liberty, family, or Americanisms would be exactly that. It was as if the neocons in government from the Bush-Obama-Clinton Administration and their androgynous minions in the church, media and military had secretly robbed me of my treasure of beautiful images and priceless feelings that I had stored-up since boyhood that symbolized my ideal America, and in its place left a worthless *I.O.U.* in my soul's vault.

I felt similar to Tom Cruise playing the German Officer in *Valkyrie* as he returns home and looks upon his little girl in pajamas wearing his Officer's cap and playfully saluting him. He looks at her and his mind shifts from the politics and tactics and egos managing the military and the wars, to the feeling of raw, protective love and devotion to his children. Somberly gazing down upon them he re-orients his mind up to abandon the futility of the war, and re-focuses his energies and talents on saving his children—and his country indirectly—by ending the maniacal politicians and self-cannibalizing military bureaucracy that was pushing it. I found myself thinking similar thoughts as I gazed down at my smiling niece, and discovered how profoundly difficult her questions were to answer.

I felt torn between inflating her innocent optimism (which earlier had been my own) that put America squarely and absolutely in the right as the *good guys*; and telling her the truth: that the war was started by our <u>design</u>, not by someone else's attack; that we did not respond to anything, but rather we initiated the war, based it on lies, and never bothered to investigate or prosecute the liars.

When I pondered the hypocrisy of this and measured it by the glistening happy eyes of a child looking to me for truth, my stomach sank for miles and centuries, and I wept invisibly in the deepest core of my being. It was the worst self-realization moment a man can endure. I couldn't help but think, *how far we have fallen into the abyss of narcissism? how feverish is our obsession with luxury? and how demonic is our new religion of pleasure devoid of morality or the virtue of self-denial? This we see clearly in the creed of lobotomized uniform wearing death-eaters who have forgotten their oath was not to politicians, but to the Constitution which is the life of our polis.*

But in that darkness, I remember that protecting the light and joy in the heart of my little niece was the only thing that made life worth living—for that is the labor of love, and "God is love."

As I struggled with how to gently hold and protect and preserve the bubble of her innocent questions and assumptions, I remembered that she—and millions of other people—are still under the illusion that all of us were smothered with on and after September 11, 2001. I remembered that we must be compassionate and humble about this, and delicate in the handling of the truth we have been enlightened to.

To me, it is only by the grace of God that our minds are opened to see the invisible dimensions of truth around us. And when we awake and discover things as they really are, when we flush ourselves out of the *Matrix*, <u>our</u> childish innocence and faith in American honesty and honorable intentions go with us. In the case of the *9-11 Attacks*, our innocence and ignorance disappears—as it must—into a dust cloud of pulverized skyscrapers carrying the scent of controlled demolition, fraud, murder, and the destruction of all kinds of I.O.U.'s, stolen gold, and incriminating evidence of treason by the military-industrial-intelligence agency complex.

The hardest thing I've had to do is think up answers to the questions my niece posed to me in her playful indirect way of questioning me about the war, my military experiences, and her attempt to find her own position in life and her own sense of what America is and who she is in it.

It is also the saddest and most painful thing I've had to do, since I was now aware of the global lies that are the background music of children's games of playing soldier and make-believe war.

In a sense the soft voice of a little child asking you innocent and blindingly simple questions about war, instantly deafens you to the sounds and memories of war. Make no mistake, any man whose fought knows that everything false and blurred disappears when the heavenly light in a child's stare falls upon you. The monstrous roars of machinery grinding and firing, the blast and light and heat and smells of explosives and flesh and sweat, the wide-eyed horror and shocked whimpering of young soldiers as they approach their last 5 minutes of bleeding-out life and suddenly know they're going and will never see their loved ones again; and the body piles and deep ditches full of charred and shredded "man-dressed" bodies; and the insane comedy of *Haji* stupidity from driving recklessly without breaks on their cars and getting shot-up by Jeep mounted .50-caliber machine guns, to firing their own guns into the air with their eyes closed and running away as they yell "Allah Akbar!", all fades in comparison to the sound of a child's questioning voice.

And if we are men, if we are warrior-patriots, if we are real Americans worthy of our noble heritage, we must have the courage to now begin to listen to those children's voices, and honestly answer. This I have tried to do in this book.

SIMPLE TRUTH

It is time.

The time has come for simplicity, especially in politics and truth (no, they are not mutually exclusive). It is time to solve complex problems with simple solutions; to distill difficult questions into basic choices, and allow instinct in its raw form to define the purest answer. It is time for righteous men to rise and rule, and displace the liars and the corruption they poison government and law with.

In all things, especially love (which should be a person's sole motivation for entering political service), simplicity is the sign of purity, courage and honesty; while complexity is the sign of deception, cowardice or insanity. There is a mystical resonance that occurs inside every human being whenever truth is spoken simply and boldly, regardless of the subject.

When it comes to truth, discerning and expressing truth, and filtering out the noise which masquerades as truth, the snobbish "airs and graces" of alleged superior ability and exaggerated sophistication are more often than not smokescreens and distractions expressed by Ivy League journalists and vainglorious politicians swollen with the flatulent stench of death and corruption.

Similarly, when it comes to understanding laws, public policy, and government-military activities executed in our name, we must begin by first defining our name as individual citizens and collectively as a nation. We must understand who we are in order to not be deceived and manipulated into believing who—or what—we are not. We must know what we cherish as independent citizens, in order to clarify what we collectively as a nation are willing to die defending.

The time has come to gird up our loins as men—as Americans—and be brave enough to speak simple truth to dangerously ignorant power. The time has come, while time still remains, to stand firm. This is simplicity, and simplicity is what humanity needs most right now.

Why? For too long we have corroded in the bromide (a drug that makes a person calm) of our own pride, smart-ass arrogance, and dismissive stupidity when analyzing ourselves, our fellow man, and the culture which we have allowed to pile-up around us like shed snakeskins. The time has come to choose, and there are only two choices in everything: *friend* or *foe*. Are we a friend to the real truth, or are we a foe to it? Do we embrace duty, or run from it out of loyalty and love of our easy lives and escapism from responsibility? These two identities—these two choices—are always present and always watching us like a witness waiting to be summoned to testify at our death's judgment and confirm our signature on each decision in life.

We must start by choosing to look at ourselves simply, and not choose to sink into the black hole of exaggerated intellectualism, odious sophistication, or politically-correct atheist enlightenment. Those are the weeds at the bottom of a dark stagnant pond that we often try and sink into to hide and become lost in. Let us not so delude ourselves to think we will not be judged for such sloth, cowardice, and selfishness. For indeed everything we say, and refuse to say, do and refuse to do, will eventually, someday, come—perhaps *riding on a white horse*—and proclaim its witness against us.

So we must choose to define ourselves simply, transparently, and absolutely; and then use that definition as the filter through which we sift and analyze the choices of our personal life. How do we do this?

To choose to define ourselves simply and absolutely means to first lay the foundation of what we are by what we need and what we do. It is not our thoughts and feelings and theories and fantasies that define us, but rather our actions and our responses to exterior actions and conditions made to affect us. In other words, our physical expressions of energy (communications, actions) are the movements of our soul that transport us along the map of time and course of our destiny.

Now without skydiving into the endless puzzle-shaped galaxies of complex scientific, philosophical, religious, moral, or mythological questions, let us distill all of this into a simple equation: We are <u>moral</u> energy (soul/spirit) encased in a physical body (flesh), bound by the natural laws which created and animate the universe.

History and mythology testify that our human bodies are dust of the earth that was miraculously mixed with water and special sauce (some say the "breath of God"), and then became conscious, pulsating, and living systems of energy absorption-recycling-maintenance-repair. [NOTE: Self-regulating repair systems, I think, are among the most scientifically impossible—and therefore the most fabulously inspiring—since they expose the basic, yet profound truth that to have a repair system for something, means there has to be a blueprint of its design and functioning; and inherent in a function is an architecture, a schematic, a theory, and by nature a <u>mind</u> that thought it all up in the first place. But that's another story—so let's keep it simple.]

We are infinitely complex bodies with simple needs: food, clothing, shelter, sleep, and social connections for emotional nourishment and personality development. Additionally, we also seem to have a supernatural or instinctive desire and need to continue history, replenish humanity, and reproduce ourselves.

We do this by magnetically attracting, both materially and charismatically, a single similar reflection of our own invisible commonalities and visible genetic traits. We then socially bind and redefine ourselves as a two-person (man-woman) team, and ceremoniously re-unite our bodies into one gyrating unit in order to intertwine and rhythmically pollinate a spiritual seed planted before time began. From this mystical relationship, all other pursuits, passions, and values materialize as work, property, leisure, and culture.

The tool of law, government, and politics is meant to protect, encourage, and celebrate this essential component of human life. Sadly—if not insanely—America's descent into perversion and liberalism seems to be doing the exact opposite: weakening marriage, family, children, and thereby dissolving the healthy, confident, and content society which was once America.

However, like the recent "Hillary Clinton 'Pay-to-Play' State Department abuses, WikiLeaks cables revelations, and the "Brexit" (Britain's dismemberment from a German-dominated socialist European Union) indicate, people around the world seem to be awakening at long last. Are they fed up with the status quo, and yearning for a revival of the old ways, the ancient truths, and the eternal hopes, because all other idols and promises are fading? Time—or eternity—will tell.

As a result, this Presidential election between Donald Trump and Hillary Clinton may quite possibly turn out to be the greatest renaissance in the history of civilization; or the death of it. Here's why…

DONALD TRUMP MUST BE JACK REACHER

    If he is to survive in Washington DC, Donald Trump must think and move like the character "Jack Reacher", in his understanding of the real war on terrorism, the Intelligence Community and DEEP STATE-military industrial complex parasites that live off of it, and media that endlessly and shamelessly sensationalize it.

    Jack Reacher is the main character in Lee Child's ongoing book series about a maverick, unorthodox, righteous and ruthlessly efficient "equalizer" for justice; and is, in a sense, the type of man Donald Trump ought to model his mind and actions after, if he hopes to have more than one year in office. Why?

    In the series, Jack Reacher is an exemplary Army officer who was busted down in rank by his half-witted bureaucrats-in-uniform superior officers for his going outside normal channels of thought and action, and winning nonetheless. Despite his redemptive ascendancy back up the chain to regain his prior rank—-most likely energized by his natural bloodlust for revenge against the liars who betrayed him—-Reacher learns from his career lashing, recognizes it as both an end and beginning, and paradigmatically chooses to vanish from the military to launch his own war from the outside; thereby fulfilling his oath and duty as an Army Officer, a patriot, and an American.

    Regarding the war on terrorism, Jack Reacher sees it as an exercise for money, position, and training meant to generate cardboard silhouettes for target practice that just happen to be living Middle Eastern people. He understands that *Black Lies* matter (not "black lives matter") because although they may have started out white—as seemingly insignificant exaggerations—they eventually darken into conflict and get us into wars, kill millions, orphan children, shred families, marriages, and personalities with the shrapnel of guilt and hypocrisy, bleed economies into lifeless corpses, and turn green lands into smoking ash heaps.

Reacher is a realist, who also has recognized—due to his criminal investigation training—that the blackest lie scarring America's soul is the September 11, 2001 hoax. Planned, orchestrated, and expanded by the American CIA, British MI6, Israel's Mossad, and Saudi Arabia it has been growing and consuming Middle Eastern countries like a virus. He understands, like all honest Americans, that until this scar is re-examined, investigated, prosecuted, and cleansed, and all perpetrators executed as traitors, America can never heal.

Trump must be the same, and rediscover his words in 2001 that the government story was scientifically impossible. Then, armed with conviction, he must gird his loins like a man, fearlessly step forward as the President and Constitution's defender, and march into the CIA-FBI-Pentagon vaults to release the truth. He must use his New York experiences and contacts to request the secrets and translate the events of 911, so that he might discover and complete the puzzle of intelligence materials which only he, as President, can DE-CLASSIFY for all Americans to see. His choice is simple: expose the crime and heal America, or hide the crime and suffer the eternal consequences.

Like Reacher, to fully understand and control the U.S. military and effectively manage its treacherous and self-serving Officers—like Generals James Mattis, H.R. McMaster, and John Kelly—and thereby protect the civil rights and liberties of all Americans, Trump needs to aggressively distrust and ignore the exaggerated mythical virtue and distracting "pomp and circumstance" of American's military parades and hero-worship.

As emotionally thrilling and nostalgically self-gratifying as this "military romance" might feel, too easily it can insidiously seduce and corrupt shallow and submissive minds and distort the Constitutional limits of the military into a world police mission—which for the past 17 years has created nothing but instability, refugees and migrants, and simmering wars.

To be a real civilian President who loves and defends and protects the Constitution of the United States against all enemies foreign and domestic, Trump needs to understand that the U.S. military is an immense parallel federal government bureaucracy that has been metastasizing like a cancer since 1945, went into hyperdrive in 2001, bastardized itself with mercenary contractors like Booz Allen Hamilton, and has been degenerating in moral character ever since.

In short, Trump needs to man-up and understand that despite the Star Trek technology, and the sophisticated advertising campaigns and mythically egotistical brainwashing to the contrary, the newly legalized Lesbian, Gay, Bi-sexual, Transgender, child-raping culture now infecting the American military is not only bleeding away its traditional honor and God-fearing character, but destroying the rest of the world in the process.

HOW TO PSYCHOLOGICALLY DESTROY TERRORISM AND ITS INVESTORS

Lastly, Trump must understand that the key to disintegrating terrorism is recognizing its ideology and redefining it as "a religious cult developed by self-serving deceivers in conflict with God and destined for eternal damnation." Naturally, this will trigger an emotional release of fear, doubt, and fury among the followers toward their leaders, divide groups, and weaken their influence. This is the PSYOP way of eroding terrorism from within, using their own words and behaviors against them.

The first step in this process is recognizing and re-defining Wahhabism as a "cult" and a perverse aberration of Islam. The second step is communicating this message repeatedly, fearlessly, and passionately, from former Wahhabi persons and nations newly liberated from it.

The more Wahhabism looks and sounds like an "anomaly of Sunni Islam" and a cult (which suggests both an individual and collective dangerously unstable mind and subconscious self-loathing), the more people will become "aware", and be able to differentiate between "normal Islam" and "abnormal cult-like Islam", and thereby begin to separate all political, social, and economic ties with the government-kingdom of this cult. The manifestations of Wahhabism are intolerance (violent and passive aggressive), rapes, honor killings, and rejection of non-Wahhabi cultures. Consequently, these behaviors are driving Europeans away and causing socio-political-religious shifts such as *BREXIT*.

As more Europeans increasingly hear the fearless and clear proclamation of Wahhabism as a "cult", they will instinctively disassociate from this "cult" and respond to more socially acceptable religious groups.

Let's be blunt. Any honest and intelligent military commander with experience in the Middle East will agree that the fastest and best way to achieve peace in the Middle East, stop the flow of terrorists out of the Middle East into Europe and America, stop the gangs of Muslim men sexually assaulting European women and little boys in Germany, Sweden, Norway, Finland, and other European countries stupid enough to incentivize their own political and cultural suicide, is to suddenly and ruthlessly remove the Saudi Arabian political regime. Cut off the snake's head. It's really just that simple. Yes, it would be loud, dirty, ugly, and confusing for a little while—3 months—but the psychological retardation, the material addiction and hedonism, and the natural softness of the Saudi Arabian mind would incline the Saudi Arabian population to panic into a fetus position of fear and humility and instantly stop all financial and human resources from leaving the country to cause mischief in the world. Instead, Saudi Arabians would be clamoring for another strong man—or military rule similar to Egypt—to take command of Saudi Arabia. This means they would be looking and searching and listening to the voices that would arise and compete for power in the vacuum of the Saudi Royal Family.

This should happen within the first 100 days of office of Donald Trump, done in concert with Russia-Iran-Syria-China, as well as the right-wing leaders in Europe. This will instantly turn-off the spigot of violence, terrorism, and chaos that is flowing out of Saudi Arabia into the rest of the world.

This would also re-establish the positive relationships between the most powerful nations in the multi-polar world, and show the rest of the world that terrorist sponsors such as Saudi Arabia are doomed to fail given the violence, hatred, and insanity which defines their socio-political character.

Only moral harmony should be a consideration when forming marital or political relationships, not money. Hopefully America is still moral enough to apply it.

THE TRUMP DILEMMA: ATTACK OR RETREAT

If Donald Trump does not immediately appoint an "Inspector General Tsar" to command all Inspector Generals in every intelligence-military agency to investigate, expose, and prosecute DEEP STATE agents like Robert Mueller, James Comey, Hillary Clinton, Eric Holder, John Brennan, and others, Trump will be impeached or killed or both.

It is very simple: Special Counsel Robert Mueller is a master liar and criminal who covered-up the video tapes and other evidence of 911 being a CIA-Mossad operation; and has been intimately involved in planning, executing, and hiding some of the greatest crimes in America (Sandy Hook shooting, Boston Marathon bombing). Mueller's goal is to serve the DEEP STATE and himself; his objective is to expand his investigation in order to pervert and twist his findings into crimes against key members of Trump's campaign, and then impeach President Trump by threatening Paul Manaforte and others into "flipping" and falsely testifying against Trump. Indeed, the completely false

Russian election meddling propaganda, is simply a means to Mueller and the DEEP STATE's end. Additionally, despite the overwhelming evidence that DNC staffer Seth Rich leaked materials to Wikileaks and was murdered for it, the democrats, neocons, and Zionist elements in Congress continue to push for war against Russia by blatantly lying, hysterically claiming Russian involvement, and shamelessly violating the Constitution by passing laws based entirely on false information and propaganda.

Another thing for Trump to keep an eye on is the fact that General Michael Flynn has hired the law firm *Covington and Burling* to represent him against the Senate subpoena. Remember Covington and Burling is implicated in Terror Financing/ money laundering for Saudi Arabia using the Clinton Foundation and guiding State Department policy for Hillary Clinton; and employed—and currently employs—Attorney General Eric Holder and Assistant Attorney General Lanny Breuer, who conspired with Loretta Lynch to hide 16,000 Swiss Bank accounts and not investigate them in exchange for large donations to the Clinton Foundation and Presidential campaign. They also refused to provide this terrorist financial intelligence to our military team handling terrorist finance counter-operations.

Trump needs to understand, and hopefully we have provided sufficient proof in this report, that there are documents, video recordings, and testimony which show the Union Bank of Switzerland, Hillary Clinton, Barack Obama, Eric Holder and Lanny Breuer at the Department of Justice, and Covington and Burling, Dov Zakheim at Booz Allen Hamilton, and his son Roger Zakheim at the House Armed Services committee have entered into an agreement to continue to money-launder funds through the Clinton Foundation for Saudi Arabia, Qatar, Kuwait, Morocco, Israel, in order to finance the foreign mercenaries and weapons being funneled through Libya, up into Tukey, and then into Syria as a mercenary force to remove by force of arms Syrian President Bashar Assad. In fact, we gave this material personally to

Trump's attorney, Michael Cohen, and Trump's family, back in 2016…which was one of the reason Obama quickened the surveillance operations against him, but that's another chapter.

As much as I may agree with many of President Donald Trump's ideas and policies, it must be said that if he refuses to act upon this information and prosecute this corruption, then the American people might conclude that Trump is either a coward, or corrupt, or both. They might event conclude that Trump is crippled by some deeper emotional insecurity, exaggerated by narcissism, that cultivates a hypersensitivity—if not paranoia—towards criticism, which then triggers an overzealous defensive posture and reaction against perceptions of national or personal insult or attack. This conflates his personal and Presidential identity, merges his responses and choices into one manifestation of both overt and passive aggression, subtle violence, and hyper-exaggerated bravado which can only destabilize diplomacy, not empower it. Then he falls.

Indeed, if Trump ignores the promises he made to Americans to "stop regime change", "work with Russia to destroy ISIS", and regenerate America's liberties, culture, and peace, and if he dishonors his oath to "preserve, protect, and defend the Constitution of the United States", then Americans will seek a new President who will. Hopefully he will act in America's best interest, and become greater than Ronald Reagan. Time will tell.

<u>FALL OF GIANTS</u>

The geopolitical temperature of today's world is bubbling over with volatility. We see millions of tattered, angry migrants pouring into Europe through the holes made by the U.S. military adventures in Africa and the Middle East, accelerating the break-up of the European Union. As a result, many European and former Soviet bloc nations are rediscovering their instinctive love of tribalism and their natural right to sovereignty as they're forced to defend their borders, people, and resources. Germany is also making a semi-independent stand by rejecting the U.S. sanctions against Russia due to their impending damage to the German economy; and is gravitating towards the perspective of Russia and China regarding the United States, which is probably the most important political shift in the past 50 years. With China, Russia, and Germany locking arms and standing up in defiance and disgust toward the warmongering rhetoric and threats of military engagement, some very real problems and opportunities also emerge.

The rumbling tension between Russia and America means one thing: it's 1987, and the next 'Cold War' has started…all over again. Minus President Ronald Reagan, the secret Oliver North-CIA drug-running-arms deal hearings (Iran-Contra), cell phones the size of car batteries, and despite the fact that music today is much, much worse, our current international news sounds eerily similar to 1987's…only more dangerous.

In 1987, I was an Non-Commissioned Officer in the United States Air Force Auxiliary (Civil Air Patrol), a member of its National Cadet Champion Drill Team, and was hand delivering the Civil Air Patrol's annual report to Congress and the Pentagon and touring Washington DC wearing my Air Force dress blues uniform. I was also a 16-year old High School student. It was, without a doubt, one of the greatest, most multidimensionally fulfilling experiences of my life, because I was empowered with unique military training and a dynamic sense of manhood that only a young man can absorb (Something to do with purity in spirit and body, no doubt). In essence, it sealed me from the cynicism and corruption most men and women are infected with when they enter the regular military after high school.

Many years later, after earning advanced degrees and working in advertising, Hollywood, politics, the intelligence community and the military-industrial complex, I was given a direct commission in the Army and asked to join their psychological warfare command and help win the war. Out of a sense of duty—to my family and my country—I accepted, put my life on hold, and went into service. I then discovered one of the most surreal and corrupt truths in American history: the nostalgic mirage of American exceptionalism, although certainly positive in a pragmatic sense, can also be a kind of psychotropic drug designed to infect the mind with a sense of paranoia towards the rest of the world, which triggers an aggressive impulse to guard against the world, which provokes people to rationalize and become addicted to limitless and endless war, and subservience to a military-industrial complex which becomes both an abusive jailer and sociopathic drug-dealer. And like an addictive drug, it destroys the body in the process.

Thirty years ago, in 1987, the two most powerful nations on the planet entered the final phase of a wrestling match which had lasted for over fifty years. One nation's strength was thinning, its defensive posture bending, and its will to fight disappearing; while the other nation was increasing its points, securing a final chokehold, and hungry to win the match. At the last minute it seemed like a compromise had been reached. A tapping-out was negotiated, and both competitors agreed to stop and conclude the match without risking a final death struggle, since it might cripple both competitors. With history as referee, Ronald Reagan's victorious arm was held high for all the world to see, while Mikhail Gorbechev's head drooped from the fatigue of decades of economic and spiritual communism. (NOTE: The typical communist socio-economic model is to a nation what an artificial steroid is to the human body: it appears to grow strength in the beginning but ends up destroying the body in the end). The two opponents, America and Russia, left the arena, respectful to eachother, and hopeful of a paradigm shift in their relationship that might extinguish all memory of the cold war that had exhausted the world for too long. Both nations were ready…and so was humanity.

In 1987, the Soviet Union's economy was like an overburdened tree branch—drooping, splitting, and about to break-off from the weight of its burden. Also in 1987, America was at the pinnacle of its powers and confidence. It's economic productivity and political influence over the world seemed unstoppable and irresistible. But it was precisely at this moment of self-anointed "exceptionalism", that the spirit of liberty and the blessing of power morphed into a license to dominate and a quasi-religious calling to control. This of course became even more surreal when the evangelical Christian-Zionist community infused their heretical distortions of bible prophecy into a perverted, self-fulfilling 9-11 counterterrorism political agenda to both define and destroy every evil using the license of "American democracy, human rights, global capitalism" as their coat of many colored exceptionalisms.

Unfortunately, all of President Ronald Reagan's honor, goodwill, and promises to Mikhail Gorbechev and the Russian people that NATO and the West would not expand military bases or encroach into Russian territory or peel away buffer territories like Ukraine, were not only ignored by subsequent U.S. Presidents and Russia's trust betrayed, but the cold war became a hot diplomatic war with occasional bloodshed as the West accelerated its military-intelligence-economic operations against Yugoslavia, Chechnya, Ukraine, and other former Soviet lands.

Fast forward to 2017 and we see the world has changed…and not for the better. Instead of the United States pressuring the Soviet Union into a frantic state of cultural abandonment and political disintegration, this same exact transformation is now happening to the United States, except, ironically—or perhaps miraculously—without any help from the Russians. I use the word miraculously advisedly, and admittedly with a slight tinge of humor because when you think about it, there is a rather Divine sense of "poetic justice" to the notion that the United States—more specifically the DEEP STATE—is now suffering the same kind of confusion, oppression, and paranoia it enthusiastically helped inflict upon Russia some 30 years ago. Somehow the pulling-down of the statute of Confederate General Robert E. Lee by a left-wing zealot in America seems eerily reminiscent of the pulling-down of the statutes of Stalin, Lenin and Saddam Hussein decades ago. Karma? Judgement? Inevitability?

Although similar to many of the societal erosions Russia faced in the 1980's, America's are far more insidious and lethal today. They are in fact terminal, unless properly purged from our body politic. These societal erosions include, but are not limited to, the following:

- A self-consuming appetite for blind multi-culturalism that foments suicidally reckless immigration policies and spawns the unlawful monstrosity of "sanctuary cities".

- A desperate obsession to manufacture the perfect health-care system that will, somehow, automatically and effortlessly guarantee a constantly blissful, supernaturally healthy life. Unfortunately, the *Soma* today are opioids and anti-depressants which transform the mind and body like tobacco smoked into ash.

- A hyper-sensitivity and quasi-religious worship of 'political-correctness' which has essentially outlawed traditional notions of American moral-religious purity, as well as sickened America with a kind of sexual-identity schizophrenia. This schizophrenia has in turn unleashed a plague of confusion and misunderstanding in America about sex, love, intimacy, natural law, the human body, emotions, and male-female roles, which is now manifesting as selfishness, hedonism, transgenderism, sex re-assignment, pedophile friendly child-sized sex dolls, and other perversions and abominations.

Despite the rotten stench of insanity and death it carries, this sexual and moral schizophrenia has been re-defined by the priests of political-correctness—the Democrats, cultural Marxists, and Strausian neocons—as the climax of civilized humanity and the ideal of feminist politics. However, an interesting—or somber—observation of the potential long-term impact of this cultural pathology is its degeneration of society into a painfully lonely, delusional humanity, which is symbolized in the recent American film Her starring Joaquin Phoenix, where he plays an isolated, divorced American man falling-in-love with his hand-held computer that speaks to him in algorithmically calculated words of kindness, empathy, and emotionally erotic stimulation, using Scarlett Johannsson's sultry voice. These are just a few of the most destructive social and spiritual illnesses destroying the American mind, weakening its institutions, and darkening the light of freedom and peace in America's domestic culture and international relationships.

Perhaps this explains why America's pop-culture is more often disdained as toxic by many non-western audiences and not particularly cherished for its purity or illumination. Whereas Ronald Reagan or John Wayne symbolized the arch-type of heroic American manhood in the past, Bruce Jenner the Olympic athlete (now sex-changed by a butcher's scissors into Caitlyn Jenner) seems to be modern America's replacement—which certainly doesn't bode well for future wars. Re-read that sentence and let it fully sink in. A military and political establishment where the bureaucrat mind and emasculated drone spirit is celebrated and rewarded with promotion, while the creative maverick and bold risk-taker are ostracized, prosecuted, and killed for their superior skills, is both a direct contradiction of the American spirit, and the essential plot of Ayn Rand's novel, Atlas Shrugged.

Interestingly enough, Russia seems to be contradicting its CIA branding as a blood-thirsty enemy of America, by responding compassionately toward America's slow political train wreck (which is now visiting Europe with mass migrants as casualties). In fact, instead of trying to mercilessly dismember America's economy, military, and government like a geopolitical serial-killer, Russia has been patiently bending and enduring the hysterics, hypocrisy, and violent unilateralism of America's politicians, military, and media. This of course may shock some, such as the blindly Russia-phobic religious bigots who chronically despise the independence of the Russian Orthodox Church and banking systems; and the self-tranquilizing simpletons desperately scraping the resin of America's Puritan character from the 1950's, while violently thrashing to escape the sunlight of modernity invading their head-sized sand-holes.

Unlike the United States, Russia doesn't seem to be jubilantly celebrating with the same sadistic relish the disintegration of America's reputation and place in the world as a result of its "regime change" miscalculations (Libya, Ukraine, Iraq, Syria). In fact, it seems as if Russia itself is experiencing some deeply personal, quiet amazement and discomfort as they watch from a distance America's gradual cultural meltdown. It's as if Russia is witnessing with head-shaking sadness and disgust as their once respected competitor blurs into senility, loses their mind and self-respect to political Dementia, and fades into a state of confusion, fear, and the slow-motion coma of a national police state.

THE LAW OF TRUTH

The supreme law of the land is the Constitution, and it is clear: no federal or state law, statute, code, or policy can exist that violates or undermines any part of the Constitution. Anything that does, is unlawful and has no authority over citizens. The reason for America's obscenely immoral Congress is because they have abandoned and hated the idea of truth animating all government laws and actions. Let us always remember that truth is the union between a people and their government. Truth is the life force behind all law, and the U.S. Constitution; it is the substance of contracts; it is the light guiding man's righteous claim and defense of his inalienable rights; it is the spirit of a responsible and benevolent self-government. Truth is the soul of justice, the shape of love, and the sound of peace. But sadly, the corruption of man, his lusts, and selfish pride reject this principle in exchange for the shifting sands of pleasure and popular opinion.

The recent US-Russian sanctions bill is a prime example. Currently the U.S. Congress is fast-tracking a Russian sanctions bill (S.341 - Russia Sanctions Review Act of 2017 sponsored by Senator Lindsay Graham; and H.R.3364 - Countering America's Adversaries Through Sanctions Act sponsored by Rep. Royce, Edward R. [R-CA-39]). Besides being an act of war according to international law, this sanctions bill is in no way based on truth, facts, or accurate intelligence; nor is it supported by human intelligence reports, evidence, sworn testimony, or forensic investigations. To the contrary, it is based entirely on false information, propaganda, and lies—and the Russians know this. As a result, the Russian-American struggle has not only re-awakened, but is rallying the rest of the world against the United States foreign policy.

By ignoring truth when making law, Congress destroys both. Without truth, there is no semblance of government authority, there is only the tyranny of DEEP STATE bureaucrats who channel fear to continue their power. One of the key factors is the UNCONSTITUTIONALITY of this law, which even President Trump tweeted about—and therefore has jeopardized himself because of his signing it. Technically speaking, now Trump can be impeached for violating his oath to uphold the Constitution. By signing this law, which he has admitted is unconstitutional, he has inadvertently undermined it—which is a crime for a politician.

Yet inevitably, truth wins out in the end. We now see in The Nation that the VIPS group (veteran intelligence professionals for sanity) comprised of Ray McGovern, Bill Binney, Thomas Drake, and others, have technically proven what sensible people have been saying for over a year: That there was no external penetration or hack into the Democrat National Committee computer servers. Instead there was an inside leak, and the data was downloaded from the computers by an external device like a thumb drive, disc, or backup drive. It was not invaded by an electronic hacker operating from a distant foreign country, cackling from the locked basement of his parents' house. The data download speed, the time, and other undeniable facts prove this. And in proving this it proves the Congress are either liars or fools if they don't correct their ignorant law and cancel it out. If they don't, they are also traitors, because they have betrayed the most vital element of the constitution…the truth. Without truth, there is no agreement, no constitution, no state, and therefore no more government. There is only Hobbesian jungle survival where life and tribes struggle to exist in a state of perpetual war and constant distrust of one another.

We also now see that Wikileaks Founder Julian Assange has met with Congressman Dana Rohrabacker and has communicated that he will provide to President Trump and the White House and Congress evidence that proves the Russians were not the source of the intelligence materials obtained from the DNC and Clinton emails. This will not only exculpate Russia of any criminal suspicion, but expose the liars in Congress and the DEEP STATE Obama hold-overs in the CIA/NSA/Pentagon who deceived the American public with this propaganda in the first place: the Democrats, and the anti-Trump *establishment* RINO Republicans. Time to pay the piper…or rather, face the firing squad for treason.

...TO BE CONTINUED.

But Joseph said to them, "Don't be afraid. Am I in the place of God? You intended to harm me, but God intended it for good to accomplish what is now being done, the saving of many lives."
--Genesis 50: 19-20

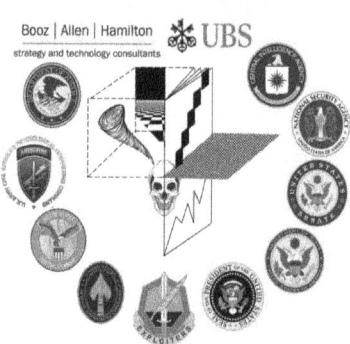

"All things work together for good to those who love God, and are called according to his purpose."
—Romans 8:28

APPENDIX

Duties

Clearance

Training

Terrorist Finance

Letters

Reports

Legal Motions

Supplemental Exhibits

As of: 01-Oct-09

IAG In-processing Data Sheet

Basic Information

Name: Last: Bennett *First:* Scott *Middle:* Allan *Suffix:* _____

Rank/Grade: 2LT *DOR:* Feb 09 *SSN:* ███ *PMOS/Designator:* 37A

Arrival Date: 1 Feb 10 *Departure Date:* _____ *Contract Date:* _____

Home Duty Station: MacDill AFB *Home Duty Station Phone Number:* 827-8622

Service (Circle One): USAF, USA, USN, USMC, Contr *Passport* (Circle One): Official Unofficial

Passport Number: _____ *Issue Date:* _____ *Expiration Date:* _____

Contract Company: Booz Allen Hamilton *Supervisor Name:* Mike Maravilla

Supervisor Phone Number: 827-8440 *Duty Title:* Counter Threat Finance Analyst

Date of last Evaluation/Report: _____ *Reporting Senior or Rater:* _____

Intermediate Rater: _____ *Reviewing Officer or Senior Rater:* _____ *Component:* _____

Directorate: CCJ3-IAG *Authorized Billet* _____ *Clearance:* TS/SCI//HCS/G//

Status (Circle One): Active (Reserve) (Circle One) PCS/TDY Orders (Circle One) Evaluation/Report

CENTCOM Badge Number _____ *Seat Number* 4064A

Personal/Family Support Information

Date of Birth: ███ *Place of Birth:* ███

Marital Status (Circle One): Single Married Divorced Widow *Military Spouse* (Circle One): Yes No

Spouse's Full Name: _____ *Single Parent* (Circle One): Yes, No

Children's Names/Age: _____

PNOK/Emergency Contact Name/Relationship/Number: ███

Hurricane Address: ███ *Hurricane Phone #* ███

Personal E-Mail Address: bennett_scott@bah.com *Nickname:* _____

	Home Address		Temporary Lodging Address (TDA, TDY, Augmentee Personnel)
Street	███	Street Hotel Name	
City/State	Tampa	Room # City/State	
Zip Code	33621	Zip Code	
Contact Numbers	Home ███	Contact Numbers	Room:( )
	Cell:(703) ███		Cell:( )
	Office: (813) 827-8622		Office: ( )

L:\R_Drive\IAG\0516-02 Emergency Planning - Recall Rosters

BOOZ ALLEN HAMILTON

SECURITY
Date Received: _____

PERSONNEL SECURITY
CLEARANCE / ACCESS REQUEST and JUSTIFICATION FORM

General Information

Employee Name:	Bennett, Scott *(Last, First, Middle)*	Emp. ID:	537112
Position/Title:	Counter-Threat Finance Analyst	Phone #:	TBD
Contract #:	SPO700-03-D-1380	Booz Allen Charge #:	B09003055012362000000
TAT# (if applicable):	05-40	Delivery # (if applicable):	DO 123
Program Name:	Strategic Planning, Analysis and Security Support to USCENTCOM	Work Location:	MacDill AFB, Tampa FL
Date of Signed Offer Letter *(Required for Future Employees)*:			

Clearance / Access Level Required (Type an "X" in the box that applies.)

[ ] Secret   [X] Top Secret   [ ] Periodic Reinvestigation   [ ] Upgrade Requirements

[X] SCI (Must list accesses: SI/TK/HCS/G)   [ ] Other: _____

Has the applicant held an **ACTIVE CLEARANCE or ACCESS** with **ANOTHER COMPANY OR AGENCY** in the last **24 MONTHS**? (Type an "X" in the box that applies.)

[X] YES   [ ] NO

If "YES", please have the applicant complete the "Clearance Data Form" and attach it to this completed document.

JUSTIFICATION

Please provide a description of the responsibilities of the employee in support of the contract listed above which will require them access to classified materials.

Access to SCI is required in the performance of the SURVIAC contract (Contract # SPO700-03-D-1380/TAT 05-40, D.O. 123). Mr. Bennett will provide strategic planning, analysis, and security assessment support to U.S. Central Command's Threat Finance (TF) Program. Specifically, he will perform research and analysis of terrorist, insurgent, and narcotics trafficking funding streams, identify key financial network nodes for lethal and non-lethal targeting, and analyze financial intelligence within the USCENTCOM area of responsibility.

BOOZ ALLEN Program Manager	Robert P. Thompson	Principal	1/19/2010	
ALL EMPLOYEES	Name	Title	Date	Signature
COTR/COR/RA	Peggy Wagner	937-255-6302, Ext. 224	937-255-9673	46th OG/OGM/OL-AC
SCI ONLY	Name	Phone Number	Fax Number	Office Symbol

Security Review				
Security Rep. ONLY	Print Name	Title	Date	Signature

C/A Request Form 60704

SPACE # 4064A

LCDR Otis V Tolbert Joint Intelligence Operations Center
Building In-Processing Form

Occupant Information

Personal Information

Full Name: Bennett, Scott A.
          Last   First   M.I.

Type: (CONTRACTOR) MILITARY GOVERNMENT   Contractor
Circle One   Pay Grade (ie. E-4, O-3, GG13)

SIPR E-mail Address: _____

Job Information

Title: Counter Threat Finance Analyst   Branch: Counter Threat Finance Branch

Work Phone: (813) 8622   VOSIP: ( )

VOIP: ( )

Please fill out all above information as it applies.

Agreement: I agree: 1) I will advise of any changes to equipment within 5 working days 2) I will advise if I move to a new desk or go TDY/Deployment for longer than 2 weeks

Signature _____   Date 1 Feb 10

Advisement Instructions: Pass all notifications of equipment changes, moves, TDY or Deployments by SIPR email to Mr. Jesse Longfellow: longfejk@centcom.smil.mil

CCJ3-IAG (COUNTER THREAT FINANCE) Analyst Certification Program

Name: Scott Bennett

Position: Counter Threat Finance Analyst

Date Assigned: _____

General Requirements

Training / Event	Date Completed
HURRIVAC Data Recall Roster (CTF and IAG) CTF Brief / IAG Tour Passport	

Account Access
  - JWICS (Include DTW)
  - SIPR
  - NIPR
  - CIA Wire
  - NCTC Online
  - PKI Certificates
  - DIA WOTE / CTKB / WISE
  - Trip Wire (TAC)	

Microsoft Office Suite	

Courses / Mandatory Training

Training / Event	Date Completed
CENTCOM Online Training (SIPR Classes)	
M3 User	
All Source Analysis Deployment (ASAD)	
Personality Network Analysis Course (PNAC)	
Falcon View / Google Earth	
Tripwire	
Analyst Notebook	
Critical Thinking / Structured Analysis	
Oral Presentation Skills	
Writing for Intelligence Professionals	
IC Reach	
Counter Threat Finance Basic Course	
Counter Threat Finance Advanced Course	
Targeting -- MIDB	
Targeting -- Develpoment	

Scott A. Bennett

Writing / Briefing / Production Requirement

Event	Date Completed
Summary Intelligence Report	
Commanders Daily Update (Slide & Script)	
Joint Intelligence Highlight	
Target Nomination Package	

Other Requirements

Event	Date Completed
Internship Program	
Deployment	

Analyst: _____   Date: _____

Supervisor: _____   Date: _____

Scott A. Bennett

UNITED STATES CENTRAL COMMAND
OFFICE OF THE CHIEF OF STAFF
7115 SOUTH BOUNDARY BOULEVARD
MACDILL AIR FORCE BASE, FLORIDA 33621-5101

8 January 2010

TO: INCOMING PERSONNEL TO CENTCOM

SUBJECT: USCENTCOM Staff Indoctrination Course (SIC)

1. I would personally like to welcome you to Headquarters United States Central Command. You are on the front lines in our campaign to combat extremism and your efforts will contribute significantly to our nation's security. I have directed your attendance to the SIC to enable you to more quickly and efficiently become an effective staff member within USCENTCOM. This three (3) day course is designated to provide valuable insight that will help you grow as a professional in a Joint command with Coalition partners.

2. You are scheduled to attend the Staff Indoctrination course:

   Start Date: *16 Feb 10*

   Start Time: 0800

   Location: ☒ USCENTCOM Bldg 3072 Room 110
   Corner of Zemke Ave & South Boundary Blvd
   Same building as in-processing

   ☐ Naval Operations Support Center,
   Bldg 1775, 2750 SouthShore Ave, MacDill AFB

3. Points of Contact:
   a. In-processing: TSgt Todd Dutschke (813) 827-3600; Sgt Matthew Rhoads (813) 827-1132

   b. Staff Indoctrination Course: Ms. Michelle Hayes, Michelle.Hayes.ctr@centcom.mil, (813) 827-3735; Mr. Ron Quave, Ronald.Quave.ctr@centcom.mil, (813) 827-3937

JAY W. HOOD
Major General, U.S. Army

USCENTCOM STAFF INDOCTRINATION COURSE TRAINING SCHEDULE

Course 10 - 04 (26-28 Jan 10)

as of: 100206

Date	Time	Course #	Description	Location	Instructor	Organization	Remarks
Tuesday 26-Jan-10	0800 - 0815	N/A	Welcome	CTF Room 110	GO/FO	CENTCOM	Attended by Coalition
	0815 - 0915	Module 01	Intro, Administrative & Communication Procedures	CTF Room 110	Ms. Michelle Hayes	NGTS	Attended by Coalition
	0915 - 0925	N/A	Break	N/A	N/A	NGTS	Attended by Coalition
	0925 - 1145	Module 02	USCENTCOM as a Headquarters	CTF Room 110	Mr. Jeff Cunningham	NGTS	Attended by Coalition
	1145 - 1300	N/A	Lunch	N/A	N/A		Attended by Coalition
	1300 - 1335	Module 03	Coalition Coordination Center	CTF Room 110	Mr Dave Townsend	CCJ5 CCC	Attended by Coalition
	1335 - 1500	Module 04	USCENTCOM as a Combatant Command	CTF Room 110	Mr Ron Quave	NGTS	Attended by Coalition
	1500 - 1510	N/A	Break / Coalition Indoc Completed	N/A	N/A		
	1510 - 1525	Module 05	Foreign Disclosure Office	CTF Room 110	FDO	CCJ2 FDO	
	1525 - 1540	Module 06	Special Security Office	CTF Room 110	SSO	CCJ2 SSO	
	1540 - 1555	N/A	End of Day 1 Critique	CTF Room 110	Mr Ron Quave	NGTS	
Wednesday 27-Jan-10	0730 - 0930	Module 07	Middle East Insights	CTF Room 110	Mr. Mark Haskell	CCJ2	
	0930 - 0940	N/A	Break	N/A	N/A		
	0940 - 1200	Module 08	The Enemy Perspective	CTF Room 110	Mr Frank Wuco	CCJ2-P	
	1200 - 1300	N/A	Lunch	N/A	N/A		
	1300 - 1330	Module 09	US National Security Plans	CTF Room 110	Mr Quave	NGTS	
	1330 - 1400	Module 10	CENTCOM Plans and Strategy	CTF Room 110	CCJ5-ST	CCJ5-ST	
	1400 - 1410	N/A	Break	N/A	N/A		
	1410 - 1440	Module 11	Theater Intel Assessment	CTF Room 110	Ms. April Williams	CCJ2-JICCENT	
	1440 - 1510	Module 12	Theater Posture	CTF Room 110	Mr. Jeff Cunningham	NGTS	
	1510 - 1525	N/A	End of Day 2 Critique	CTF Room 110	Mr Jeff Cunningham	NGTS	
Thursday 28-Jan-10	0730 - 1200	Module 13	USCENTCOM Staff Procedures	CTF Room 111	Ms Michelle Hayes	NGTS	Slated individuals only
	1200 - 1300	N/A	Lunch	N/A	N/A	NGTS	
	1300 - 1600	Module 13	Staff Procedures Exercise	CTF Room 111	Mr Ron Quave	NGTS	
	1600 - 1615	N/A	End of Day Critique	CTF Room 111	Ms Michelle Hayes		

Notes:

NO information on weapons registration, Transport, Storage, or authorities.

UNCLASSIFIED

BOOZ ALLEN HAMILTON

SECURITY
Date Received: _____

PERSONNEL SECURITY
CLEARANCE / ACCESS REQUEST and JUSTIFICATION FORM

General Information

Employee Name:	Bennett, Scott, [redacted]	Emp. ID:	537112
	(Last, First, Middle)		
Position/Title:	Associate	Phone #:	703-377-4229
Contract #:	SP0700-03-D-1380-0150	Booz Allen Charge #:	B09003-0550-1501
TAT# (if applicable):	SURVIAC 06-15	Delivery # (if applicable):	DO 1503
Program Name (if used):	USSOCOM SOF Support	Work Location:	McLean VA
Date of Signed Offer Letter (Required for Future Employees):			

Clearance / Access Level Required (Type an "X" in the box that applies.)

[ ] Secret   [X] Top Secret   [ ] Periodic Reinvestigation   [ ] Upgrade Requirements

[X] SCI (Must list accesses: SI/TK/G/HCS _____)   [ ] Other: _____

Has the applicant held an ACTIVE CLEARANCE or ACCESS with ANOTHER COMPANY OR AGENCY in the last 24 MONTHS? (Type an "X" in the box that applies.)

[ ] YES   [X] NO

If "YES", please have the applicant complete the "Clearance Data Form" and attach it to this completed document.

JUSTIFICATION

Please provide a description of the responsibilities of the employee in support of the contract listed above which will require them access to classified materials.

Scott Bennett provides classified research, analysis, and wargaming support to the US Special Operations Command (USSOCOM) Center for Knowledge and Futures (SOKF). This support requires employee to have access to TS/SCI information and to work in USSOCOM facilities requiring TS/SCI for access.

BOOZ ALLEN Program Manager	Glenn Harned	Senior Associate	2/27/08	[signature]
ALL EMPLOYEES	Name	Title	Date	Signature
COTR/COR/RA	Col Kenneth Coons	813-828-2447	813-826-2324	USSOCOM SOKF/J9
SCI ONLY	Name	Phone Number	Fax Number	Office Symbol

Security Review				
Security Rep. ONLY	Print Name	Title	Date	Signature

C/A Request Form 60704

USCENTCOM
Regional Joint Intelligence Training & Education Facility

This is to certify that
Mr. Scott A. Bennett
has successfully completed the
Advanced Critical Thinking
a DISAP II Course
19 – 22 April 2010

Presented by the
Directorate of Intelligence
United States Central Command

JOHN M. WARD JR.
DODC
Chief, Resources and Requirements Division

Bennett, Scott [USA]

From: Cece, Sibel [USA]
Sent: Tuesday, November 25, 2008 11:05 AM
To: Bennett, Scott [USA]
Subject: Clearance Update
Importance: High

Good afternoon,

We have received your updated clearance status. The pertinent information is as follows:

Clearance:	**Top Secret**
Clearance Date:	**11/24/2008**
Investigation Type:	**SSBI**
Investigation Date:	**11/05/2008**
Granting Agency:	**DISCO**

Thank you,

Sibel S. Cece
Security Services Team

Booz | Allen | Hamilton

8283 Greensboro Drive
Allen 643
McLean, Virginia 22102
703-377-4312 Office
703-902-3488 Fax
Cece_Sibel@bah.com

11/25/2008

DEPARTMENT OF THE ARMY
11TH PSYCHOLOGICAL OPERATIONS BATTALION
5550 DOWER HOUSE ROAD
UPPER MARLBORO, MD 20772

Dr. Ralph Shrader
President and Chief Executive Officer
Booz Allen Hamilton
8283 Greensboro Drive
McLean, VA 22102

Subject: Scott Bennett

5 April 2009

Dear Dr. Shrader:

I am the 11th Psychological Operations Battalion Commander and I am writing to you concerning Scott Bennett, who is an Associate at your firm. Second Lieutenant Bennett was recently commissioned as an Officer in my unit.

Second Lieutenant Bennett has been awarded a Direct Commission in the US Army Reserve and will serve as a Psychological Operations Officer in my battalion. We are glad to have him and are looking forward to the completion of his training and serving our great country.

I'd like to respectfully request your assistance in allowing him the military leave he will need from your firm to complete his training, and I know he will be a greater asset to Booz Allen as a result.

If you ever have any questions about Mr. Bennett's military service, please feel free to contact me by telephone at 910-964-9714 or by e-mail at joyce.busch@us.army.mil. On behalf of the United State Army Reserve, I thank you for your cooperation and support.

Sincerely,

JOYCE M. BUSCH
LTC/PO
Commanding

06/03/2008 14:21 FAX 202 647 9256   S/CT   ☒001

```
                    ********************
                    ***  TX REPORT   ***
                    ********************

    TRANSMISSION OK

    TX/RX NO              3789
    CONNECTION TEL                    92027750008
    CONNECTION ID
    ST. TIME              06/03 14:17
    USAGE T               03'42
    PGS. SENT             8
    RESULT                OK
```

United States Department of State

Washington, D.C. 20520

OFFICE OF THE COORDINATOR FOR COUNTERTERRORISM
S/CT

2201 C STREET NW
ROOM 2509
WASHINGTON, D.C. 20520

FAX: 202-647-9256 / 0221 (UNSECURE)

FACSIMILE TRANSMITTAL SHEET

TO: Jeff ▓▓▓	FROM: Scott Bennett
ATTENTION:	TELEPHONE:
FAX NUMBER: 202-▓▓▓	DATE: June 3, 2008

TOTAL NUMBER OF PAGES: 7

SUBJECT: Documents supporting my update and work for State Dept. and Dept. of Defense.

Terrorist Finance and Money Laundering Compared

□ **Terrorist Finance**

- Funds used to carry out training, indoctrination, plans and operations
- Money is often clean
- Often need to start with target and work back to be able to find relationships
- Terrorists desire media, public and government attention

□ **Money Laundering**

- Tax evasion, wealth accumulation
- Money is often "dirty" (from criminal activity)
- Often need to catch funds at the entry-point rather than exit
- Criminals do not desire media or government attention

> No clear separation of criminal/terrorist activity; terrorists can use criminal activity to fund raise

> *Criminals and terrorists may be temporary or long-lasting fellow-travellers; cooperation may be short-lived, convenience oriented*
> *Opportunism is an important behavioral component*

□ "Threat Finance" includes Proliferation, Terrorism and Criminal Threats

Booz | Allen | Hamilton

Operational Funding: Case study - Hezbollah

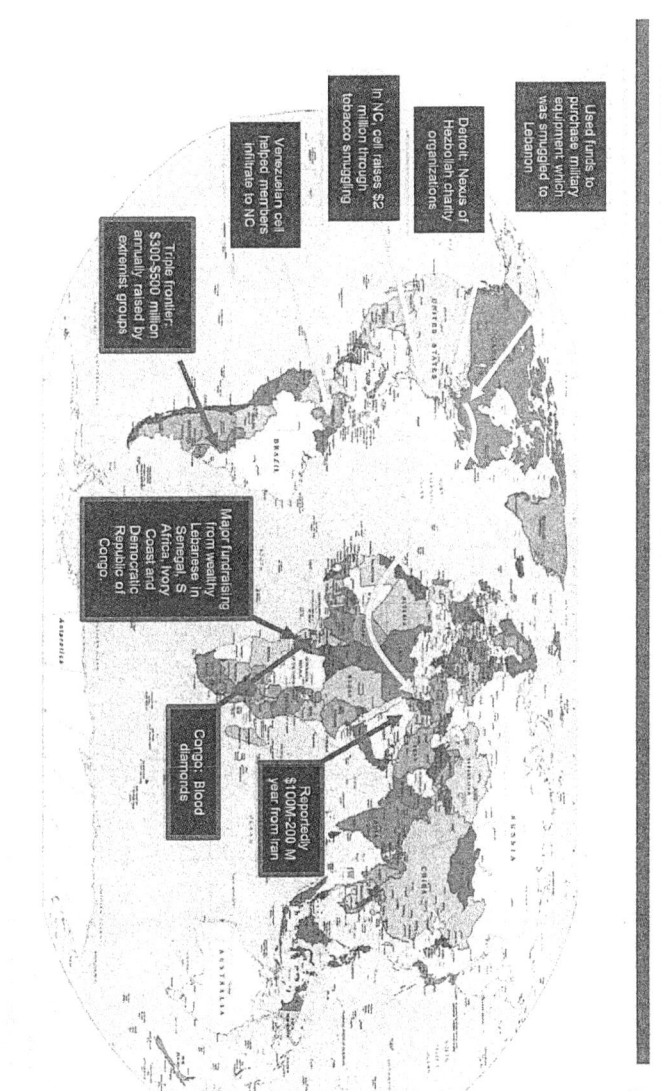

- Used funds to purchase military equipment which was smuggled to Lebanon
- Detroit: Nexus of Hezbollah charity organizations
- In NC, cell raises $2 million through tobacco smuggling
- Venezuelan cell helped members infiltrate to NC
- Triple frontier: $300-$500 million annually raised by extremist groups
- Major fundraising from wealthy Lebanese in Senegal, S Africa, Ivory Coast and Democratic Republic of Congo.
- Congo: Blood diamonds
- Reportedly $100M-200 M year from Iran

Moving Money: *How does money move around the world?*

☐ Three main methods by which terrorists and criminals move money in order to disguise its origins

1. Movement of value through the financial system; i.e. checks and wire transfers
2. Physical movement of currency; cash couriers and bulk cash smuggling
3. Movement of Value through fraudulent trading of goods and services

☐ Popular Ways to Move Illicit Money
   - Hawalas
   - Cash Smuggling
   - Trade-Based Money Laundering
   - Mobile Payments
   - Wire Transfers

Booz | Allen | Hamilton

The Hawala System

- Alternative or "Parallel" Remittance System
- Trust-based means to transfer money
- Minimal (or no) use of a negotiable instrument
- "Hawaladars"
- Hawala systems support both legitimate and illicit activities
  - Migrant worker remittances
  - Humanitarian Aid
  - Income Tax evasion
  - Drug smuggling
  - Money Laundering / Terrorist Finance

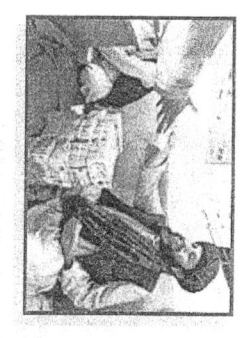

Trends in Terrorism Finance

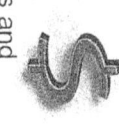

- Focus on "Know your customer" procedures by large US and international banks and awareness of watch lists has made larger institutions, in particular, tighten account opening procedures
  - Smaller, regional banks still potentially at risk; counterargument is that smallest banks inherently know their customers better
- Move to tactics for fund movement that minimize tracking and filing
  - Bulk cash smuggling
  - Credit card, debit card and stored value (prepaid) card transfers
  - Online payment systems, mobile payments
  - Digital currency

These trends also overlap to money laundering and criminal finance; but small amounts utilized for terrorism finance make them especially applicable to terrorists and tough to trace

Money Laundering Stage 1 - Placement

- Initial insertion of criminal proceeds into the financial system
- How does this work?
  - Cash or negotiable instruments
  - Inserted in ways that avoid CTRs or STRs
  - "smurfing"
  - Multiple entry points, front companies, cashier's checks

Money Laundering Stage 2 – Layering

- Key is to avoid filings by financial institutions
- Multiple methods / typologies but the basic framework is:

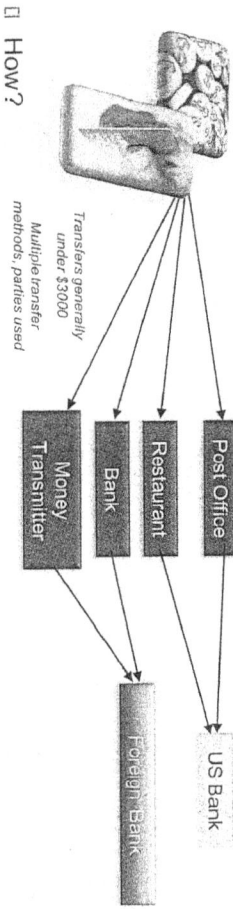

Transfers generally under $3000
Multiple transfer methods, parties used

- Post Office → US Bank
- Restaurant → Foreign Bank
- Bank → Foreign Bank
- Money Transmitter → Foreign Bank

- How?

  - Fraud by institution (Banks collude for profit) (Riggs)
  - Knowing cooperation of existing or newly created front company
  - Import/export companies; under/over- invoicing
  - Value transfer (Gold to common items)
  - Bulk cash smuggling to foreign countries (ex:Indonesia, Panama)
  - Money Transfer Businesses (ex. Western Union)

Booz | Allen | Hamilton

Money Laundering Stage 3 - Integration

- Objective – getting the money where it can be put to good use!

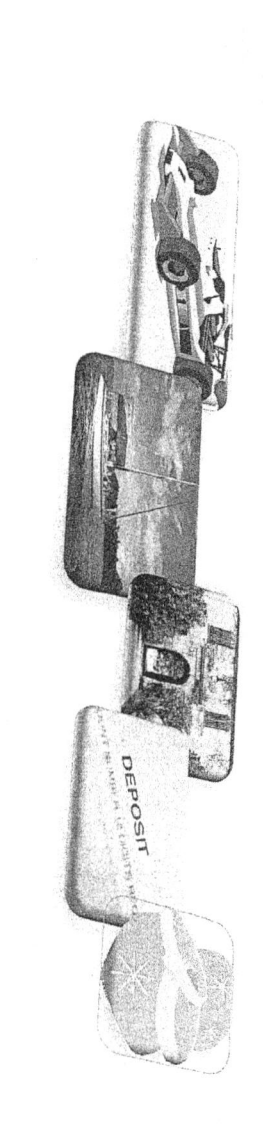

- Once "clean," funds may be sent to world-class global bank, or used for purchase or family investments, may also be put in names of family members
- Loan transactions
- Insurance policies, commodities or securities trading
- Casinos

Basics of Banking:
Where should I look for Illicit Transactions?

- Key Terms Related to AML/ CTF
  - Tax Havens
  - Correspondent Banks
  - Shell Banks
  - Numbered Accounts
  - Lines of Credit (L/Cs)
  - Bearer Share
  - Beneficial Owners
  - "Straw Man"
  - Politically Exposed Persons (PEPs)
  - Islamic Finance

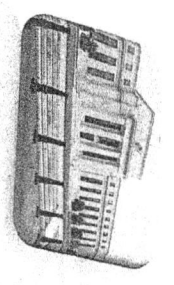

Booz | Allen | Hamilton

Key Terms

- Tax Havens
- Offshore Accounts
- Shell Banks
- Correspondent Banks

- Numbered Accounts

Fun Fact
Nauru: Population 12,000
Home to 40,000 registered corporations and 400 shell banks

Booz | Allen | Hamilton

Key Terms (cont.)

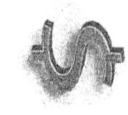

- Politically Exposed Persons (PEPs)
  - "any person who is or has been entrusted with a prominent public function in the Islamic Republic of Afghanistan or in other countries, for example, heads of state or of government, senior politicians, judicial or military officials, senior executives of state-owned entities and important political party officials. All family members of such persons, and close associates who have business or financial relationships with such person..."

  The Islamic Republic of Afghanistan – Anti-Money Laundering and Proceeds of Crime Law

- Islamic Finance
  - Islamic finance (a.k.a. Shariah finance or finance activity that is compliant with Shariah law) is becoming increasingly popular in light of the growth in world Muslim populations and the global financial crisis
  - Over the past decade Islamic banking is estimated to have grown more than fivefold from $150 billion in 1990 to $900 billion in 2008 and may reach $2 trillion by 2010 due to a steady growth rate of 15% to 20% annually

Monitoring Efforts

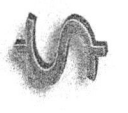

☐ Bank Secrecy Act
— Suspicious Activity Reports (SAR), Customer Records, Transactional Data, Currency Transaction Reports (CTR)
— Financial institutions
— Jewelry and Precious Metal Dealers
— Money Transfer Businesses (Western Union, PayPal, Hawaladars)

☐ "Know Your Customer" Elements

☐ Messaging Platforms may be subpoenaed and produce transactional record data.
— Large volumes of data typically need to be cleaned and manipulated to provide pattern analysis ("needle in a haystack")

* Note – This relates principally to US laws and regulations, but similar laws hold true to varying degrees in most other jurisdictions around the world.

Frequency of SAR Filings; by Characterization (1997 – 2003)

Violation Type	1997	1998	1999	2000	2001	2002	2003
BSA/Structuring/Money Laundering	35,625	47,223	60,983	90,606	108,925	154,000	72,462
Bribery/Gratuity	109	92	101	150	201	411	261
Check Fraud	13,245	13,767	16,232	19,637	26,012	32,954	16,803
Check Kiting	4,294	4,032	4,058	6,163	7,350	9,561	5,333
Commercial Loan Fraud	960	905	1,080	1,320	1348	1,879	934
Computer Intrusion[1]	0	0	0	65	419	2,484	3,605
Consumer Loan Fraud	2,048	2,183	2,548	3,432	4,143	4,435	2,271
Counterfeit Check	4,226	5,897	7,392	9,033	10,139	12,575	6,445
Counterfeit Credit/Debit Card	387	182	351	664	1,100	1,246	659
Counterfeit Instrument (Other)	294	263	320	474	769	791	615
Credit Card Fraud	5,075	4,377	4,936	6,275	8,393	12,780	6,037
Debit Card Fraud	612	565	721	1,210	1,437	3,741	4,575
Defalcation/Embezzlement	5,284	5,252	5,178	6,117	6,182	6,151	2,887
False Statement	2,200	1,970	2,376	3,051	3,232	3,685	2,316
Misuse of Position or Self Dealing	1,532	1,640	2,064	2,186	2,325	2,763	1,564
Mortgage Loan Fraud	1,720	2,269	2,934	3,515	4,696	5,387	3,649
Mysterious Disappearance	1,766	1,855	1,854	2,225	2,179	2,330	1,264
Wire Transfer Fraud	509	593	771	972	1,527	4,747	4,317
Other	6,675	8,583	8,739	11,148	18,318	31,109	15,854
Unknown/Blank	2,317	2,691	6,961	6,971	11,908	7,704	2,290
Totals	88,877	104,339	129,599	175,214	220,603	300,733	154,141

Booz | Al

UNCLASSIFIED

Domestic Policy Tools

- **Intelligence Monitoring and Operations**
  - USA PATRIOT Act
  - Data mining and link analysis
- **Criminal Investigations and Prosecutions**
  - National Security Letters, FISA warrants, subpoenas
- **Designations and Freezing of Assets**
  - UN Security Council Resolutions
  - Specially Designated Nationals/ Entities
  - FinCEN Advisories
  - Section 311 "special measures"

Designations – "Targeted Financial Measures"

☐ Designations are a public legal action implemented by Treasury Department's Office of Foreign Asset Control

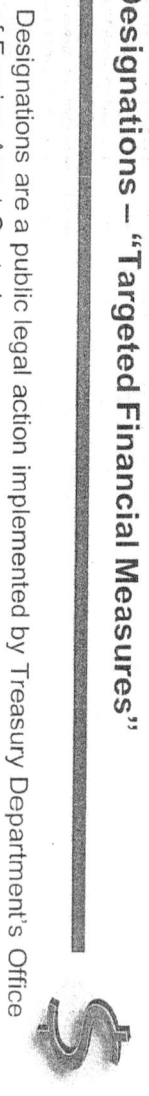

— Implemented by Executive Orders issued under authority of the International Emergency Economic Powers Act (IEEPA)

— Differs from a "country-wide" economic sanction

☐ Impact of a designation against an individual or corporate entity…

— Travel restrictions

— All US Persons (generally, US citizens or corporate entities wherever located and any persons/entities conducting business within the US regardless of origin) must cease conducting business with or on behalf of designated persons

— Assets of such persons held by US persons are frozen and held in special accounts

— Transactions (inbound or outbound) of designated persons are blocked

— Public "naming and shaming"

Executive Orders

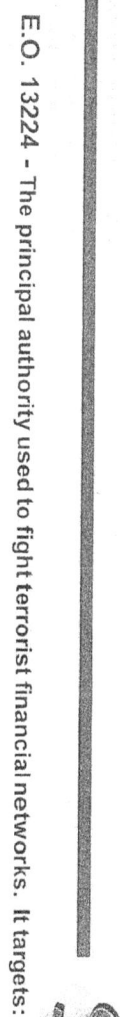

- **E.O. 13224 - The principal authority used to fight terrorist financial networks. It targets:**
  - Terrorists and Terrorist Support Organizations
  - Entities owned or controlled by designated persons
  - Individuals acting for or on behalf of designated persons
  - Individuals and entities providing financial, material or technological support to designated persons

- **E.O. 13382 - Blocking the Property of WMD Proliferators and their Supporters**
  - Used more extensively against Iranian banks, companies and individuals
  - Requires greater non-financial intelligence to establish link between proposed designated entities and proliferation activity.

Key International Laws and Treaties

- **Vienna Convention Against Illicit Traffic in Narcotic Drugs and Psychotropic Substances**
  - first international agreement to criminalize money laundering
- **International Convention for the Suppression of the Financing of Terrorism**
  - requires states to criminalize the funding of terrorist activities under domestic law and to seize or freeze funds used for terrorist financing
- **United Nations Security Council Resolution (UNSCR) 1373**
  - mandates exchange of intelligence among member states; requires member states to criminalize Al Qaeda financial activities and freeze the group's monetary assets
- **United Nations Security Council Resolutions 1267 and 1526**
  - sets up committee to monitor sanctions on Taliban; requires states to freeze resources derived from properties controlled by Al Qaeda and the Taliban
- Other UNSCR Resolutions against Cote D'Ivoire, Liberia, the former Yugoslavia, among others.

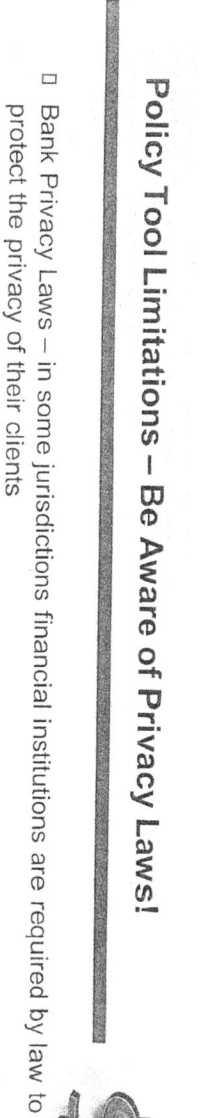

Policy Tool Limitations – Be Aware of Privacy Laws!

- Bank Privacy Laws – in some jurisdictions financial institutions are required by law to protect the privacy of their clients
- Personal Privacy Laws – particularly strong in Europe, laws protecting personal information may limit intelligence monitoring
- Limits on intelligence gathering in the United States and on US citizens
- Foreign Intelligence Surveillance Act (FISA) – imposes limits on intelligence gathering on US soil. Amended by USA PATRIOT Act and Executive Orders
- Limits on information sharing between IC and DoD, and between IC and Law Enforcement
- Intelligence vs. Law Enforcement requirements

Key FININT Players

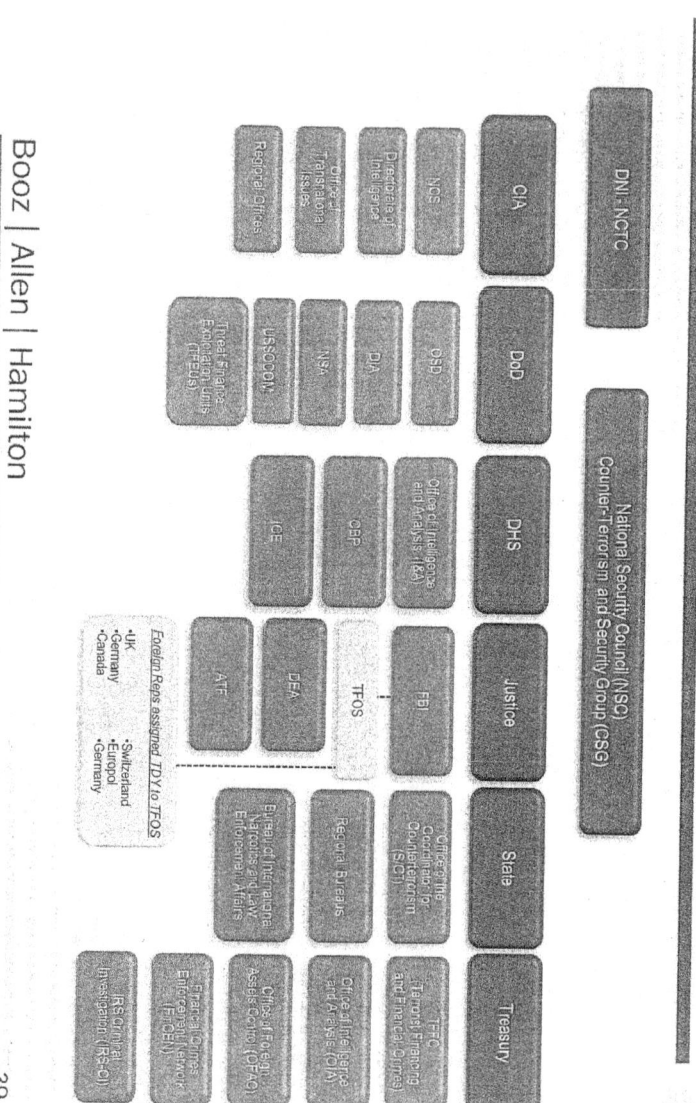

- **National Security Council (NSC) Counter-Terrorism and Security Group (CSG)**
- **DNI: NCTC**

- **CIA**
  - NCS
  - Directorate of Intelligence
  - Office of Transnational Issues
  - Regional Offices

- **DoD**
  - OSD
  - DIA
  - NSA
  - USSOCOM
  - Threat Finance Exploitation Units (TFEUs)

- **DHS**
  - Office of Intelligence and Analysis (I&A)
  - CBP
  - ICE

- **Justice**
  - FBI — TFOS
  - DEA
  - ATF

  Foreign Reps assigned TDY to TFOS:
  - UK
  - Germany
  - Canada
  - Switzerland
  - Europol
  - Germany

- **State**
  - Office of the Coordinator for Counterterrorism (S/CT)
  - Regional Bureaus
  - Bureau of International Narcotics and Law Enforcement Affairs

- **Treasury**
  - TFFC (Terrorist Financing and Financial Crimes)
  - Office of Intelligence and Analysis (OIA)
  - Office of Foreign Assets Control (OFAC)
  - Financial Crimes Enforcement Network (FinCEN)
  - IRS Criminal Investigation (IRS-CI)

Booz | Allen | Hamilton

UNCLASSIFIED

Interagency Centers and Coordination Groups

- **The National Security Council (NSC) Policy Coordinating Committee (PCC) on Terrorist Financing** is responsible for the overall coordination of anti-terrorist financing activities at the policy level
- At the operational level, a number of other interagency groups have been established to share information and coordinate actions. Significant examples include:
  - Joint Interagency Coordination Groups / Joint Interagency Operations Centers
  - Joint Terrorism Task Force (JTTFs)
  - Terrorist Financing Working Group (TFWG)
  - Organized Crime Drug Enforcement Task Forces (OCDETF)

Key International Actors

- **FATF** — Intergovernmental body that develops and promotes policies and standards to combat money laundering and terrorist financing.
  - **FATF Style Regional Bodies:** Asia/Pacific Group (APG), Carribean Financial Action Task Force (CFATF), Council of Europe Select Committee of Experts on the Evaluation of Anti-Money Laundering Measures (MONEYVAL), Eastern and Southern Africa Anti-Money Laundering Group (ESAAMLG) and the South America Financial Action Task Force (GAFISUD)

- **Interpol** — promotes mutual assistance between criminal police authorities. Maintains searchable databases of criminal records. Acts as information clearinghouse and coordinator during complex AML and TF investigations.

- **Financial Intelligence Units (FIUs)** — central national agencies or law enforcement agencies responsible for receiving, analyzing, and transmitting disclosures on suspicious transactions to the competent authorities. FinCEN is the FIU for the United States.

Threat Finance and Money Laundering – Themes to Remember

- Intelligence Analysts vs. Law Enforcement Analysts
  - Intelligence analyst looking for strategic information, gathering data, opportunity for establishing sustainable intelligence source
  - Law Enforcement analyst supports operations; tactical focus is gathering information that can be used as evidence for arrests and prosecutions
- Protection of sources and methods
  - release of information for designation/prosecution
- Protection of information for on-going investigation

Signs of Success

- July 2005 - Letter from Zawahiri to Zarqawi humbly asking if he could spare a payment of approximately $100,000 because "many of the lines have been cut off"

- May 2007 – AQI in Afghanistan leader "Sheikh Said" highlighted the group's desperate need for funds:

  "As for the needs of the Jihad in Afghanistan, the first of them is financial. The Mujahideen of the Taliban number in the thousands, but they lack funds. And there are hundreds wishing to carry out martyrdom seeking operations, but they can't find the funds to equip themselves."

- Feb, 2008, "In the past 12 – 18 months…" al-Qaeda has had difficulty in raising funds and sustaining themselves" Mike McConnell, DNI

Threat Finance Trend Watch

- Nexus between crime and terror – especially narcotics trafficking
  - DEA states 19 of the 43 designated foreign terrorist organizations (FTOs) are linked definitively to the global drug trade
  - Up to 60 percent of terrorist organizations are connected in some fashion with the illegal narcotics trade

- More interagency coordination centers
  - Afghan Threat Finance Cell (follows on success of Iraq Threat Finance Cell)
  - Mexico – EPIC, NORTHCOM, SOUTHCOM

- More Intelligence Community focus on global economy, finance and trade
  - ODNI Blair's testimony

USCENTCOM
Regional Joint Intelligence Training & Education Facility

This is to certify that

Mr. Scott A. Bennett

has successfully completed the
Advanced Critical Thinking
a DISAP II Course
19 – 22 April 2010

Presented by the
Directorate of Intelligence
United States Central Command

JOHN M. WARD JR.
DAC DODC
Chief, Resources and Requirements Division

United States Government MAR2012

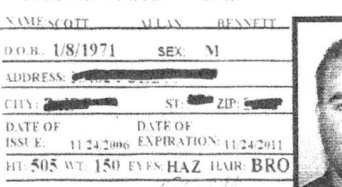

BENNETT,
SCOTT ALLAN

Affiliation
Uniformed Services
Agency/Department
Army
Expires
2012MAR03

Pay Grade Rank
O1 2LT

Geneva Conventions Identification Card

United States Government

BENNETT
SCOTT A
614391

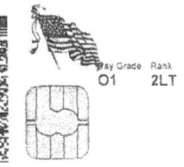

Affiliation
Contractor
Agency/Department
DEPARTMENT OF STATE
Expires
2011JUN01

N 2 E 06/11

UTAH C194624
DEPARTMENT OF PUBLIC SAFETY
Concealed Firearm Permit

NAME: SCOTT ALLAN BENNETT
D.O.B.: 1/8/1971 SEX: M
ADDRESS:
CITY: ST: ZIP:
DATE OF ISSUE: 11/24/2006 DATE OF EXPIRATION: 11/24/2011
HT: 505 WT: 150 EYES: HAZ HAIR: BRO
Commissioner of Public Safety

Commonwealth of Virginia, Circuit Court of Fairfax
File CL2006-9079
Permit to Carry a Concealed Handgun
(Must be carried with proper photo ID)

Name: SCOTT ALLAN BENNETT
Address:

DOB: 01/08/1971
Height: 5'5" Weight: 150 Gender: M
Hair: BROWN Eyes: HAZEL
Issue Date: 08/25/2006 Exp Date: 08/25/2011

Judge   Permitee

BASIC FIREARMS SAFETY CERTIFICATE BFSC

Applicant's Name: Scott Bennett
Sex: M Hair: Brn Eyes: Hzl Ht: 505 Wt: 150
Date Of Birth: 01-08-71 Driver's License / DMV I.D.:
Applicant's Signature:

255880

Booz | Allen | Hamilton
8283 Greensboro Drive
McLean, VA 22102

SSN:
Bennett, Scott

is certified as a courier for DoD classified material under the provisions of the National Industrial Security Program Operating Manual. This authorization is limited to the metropolitan Washington, D.C. area. Upon request, the courier will furnish identification to the proper authority. In the event of an emergency, call 703-377-0365 (day), 301-218-3956 (night)

Expires on: **Aug 09 2009**

GEORGE DOUGLAS – Facility Security Officer   **Aug 08 08**
                                              Date

U.S. Department of Justice

Washington, DC

August 28, 2000

American Consulate London

To Whom It May Concern:

Please be advised that Mr. Scott Bennett has ▓▓▓ with ▓▓▓ in the Washington District and upon his return, will be ▓▓▓ his ▓▓▓

Due to the sensitive and immediate nature of his travel to the United Kingdom for the Department of Defense, Mr. Bennett could not ▓▓▓ prior to his departure date.

Please allow Mr. Bennett to return to the United States so he could then proceed ▓▓▓

Sincerely,

HORRT
Commissioner's Office

Booz | Allen | Hamilton Existing Employee Relocation Initiation Form

Instructions for Booz Allen personnel: Please completely fill out the Domestic Relocation Existing Employee Form. Send completed forms to Kim Franklin for Level A -III and Ellen Gittleson for Levels IV and above.

Employee Name: Scott Bennett
Employee Number   514940
Transfer date: 2/1/2010
Charge Code #1: CM   % : 50%
Charge Code #2:   % :   50%
Career Development Model: Transformation
Team: Defense
Market Acct:
Level: III
Signing OIC: Dov Zakheim
Levels IV & V: Will Lubliner, IV and Bob Thompson, V

Origin Information:

Home-owner _x_   Renter ___
Address:
City: Washington
State: DC
ZIP: 20024
Home Phone: 202-   Work Phone: Cell Phone: 703-
            Email: Bennett_scott@bah.com   or

Destination Information:

BAH Work Location: Based on client site in Miami   but based out of Tampa office
BAH Tax Location:
Client Site: Y or N - Yes

HR Specialist:
Comments: Please indicate any urgent needs such as temp living needed that weekend or if someone needs to be out of their home within the week, for example.

Booz | Allen | Hamilton Existing Employee Relocation Initiation Form

I may need temporary lodging for a few weeks until I am able to secure permanent housing. I can arrange for "visiting officer quarters" at McDill AFB at a cost of around $40.00 per day.

Booz | Allen | Hamilton

April 30, 2010

Scott Bennett
7914 C Paul Smith Drive
Tampa, FL 33621

Dear Scott:

Confirming your discussion with Bob Thompson, your employment with the firm is being terminated due to your inability to maintain the requisite access to MacDill Air Force Base and because of a concern that you can no longer serve as an effective representative of the firm. We regret this action is necessary.

Your last day of employment with the Firm will be today, April 30, 2010. You will be paid for any unused PTO (Paid Time Off).

Please ensure you return all firm confidential and proprietary information, client information and files, working papers, employee reference manuals, computers, keys, facility access cards, credit cards and all other client and company property to Bob Thompson.

A benefits out processing packet will be mailed to your home address via Federal Express. The benefits packet contains information on extending your (COBRA) benefits, information on your ECAP, and other relevant materials. If you have any questions regarding out processing from the firm, please contact our help desk at (877) 927-8278 or email at help_desk@bah.com.

Scott, we regret the need for this action and wish you the best of luck in your future career opportunities.

Sincerely,

Dov S. Zakheim, D. Phil.
Senior Vice President

BOOZ ALLEN HAMILTON INC.

"TERRORIST THREAT FINANCE DIMENSIONS OF
UNION BANK OF SWITZERLAND (UBS) 'WHISTLEBLOWER CASE'
AND OBAMA ADMINISTRATION INVOLVEMENT."

A WHISTLEBLOWING REPORT TO THE UNITED STATES CONGRESS
AND THE DEPARTMENT OF DEFENSE INSPECTOR GENERAL

By 2LT Scott Bennett, M.A.
11th Psychological Operations Battalion
U.S. Civil Affairs-Psychological Operations Command
United States Army Reserve

September 25, 2012

CONTENTS:

INTRODUCTION....................1-2
BACKGROUND AND QUALIFICATIONS...2
OVERVIEW........................2
LIST OF NAMES...................3-5
SYNOPSIS........................6
CONCLUSION......................17
SUPPORTING EVIDENCE.............20
PERSONALITY PROFILES............25-26
WIKILEAKS CABLES................27-30
MEDIA...........................31-32
SECURITY CREDENTIALS............33
FOLLOW-UP LETTER TO CONGRESS (1 YEAR LATER)...34-37

FOR MORE INFORMATION CONTACT: 2LT Scott Bennett, U.S. Army Res.
                                  29418-016
                                  P.O. Box 670
                                  Minersville, PA 17954-0670

                                  Phone: (570) 544-7100

September 25, 2012

TO: General Jeffrey Jacobs, Commander, United States Army
    Civil Affairs-Psychological Operations Command (USACAPOC)
    Fort Bragg, NC

FR: 2LT Scott Bennett, S-1 OIC, 11th Psychological Operations Battalion
    FCI Schuylkill, #29418-016, P.O. Box 670
    Minersville, PA 17954-0670

RE: Terrorist Threat Finance Dimensions of Union Bank of Switzerland
    (UBS) "Whistleblower Case" and Obama Administration Involvement

General Jacobs:

I am reporting to you an urgent matter that requires your immediate attention as it involves activities which are killing soldiers, funding terrorists, and undermining the mission of USACAPOC. In accordance with military regulations and Federal law, this letter represents my "official communication to Congress" and disclosure of an issue that requires an immediate Congressional and Military investigation.

As an Officer of the United States Army, assigned to the 11th Psychological Operations Battalion, 2nd Psychological Operations Group, under the direct authority of U.S. Army Civil Affairs-Psychological Operations Command (USACAPOC), it is my duty to report to you an incident that is occuring which is, in my professional analysis as a soldier, irreparably harming our troops, our mission in countering Islamic extremism in the Middle East and Africa, and should be prosecuted by the military as an "Act of Treason and Betrayal" of the most dangerous and repugnant sort.

Since my oath, and yours, as a Military Officer is to "preserve, protect, and defend the Constitution of the United States against all enemies, foreign and domestic", I would be derilict in my duty and a traitor to my countrymen if I did not disclose to you, Congress, and the American people a reprehensibly scandalous crime being committed against our military, our Republic, and our Constitution.

Therefore in obedience to my oath as an Officer, and in an effort to save the lives of soldiers, as well as preserve the Constitution of the United States, I respectfully submit to you the following:

BACKGROUND AND QUALIFICATIONS:

I am an Army Reserve Officer and defense contractor who has worked at U.S. Central Command (CENTCOM), Special Operations Command (SOCOM), the Department of State Coordinator for Counterterrorism, and other Federal Government agencies in Washington DC and MacDill Air Force Base, Florida. I have advanced educational degrees, certifications, and academic and public sector professional experience. My expertise is in intergovernment agency projects, strategic communications and psychological warfare combatting Islamic extremism, and analyzing terrorist global financial networks, operations, and personalities. My most recent assignment was at the Joint Interagency Operations Center (JIOC) at CENTCOM, working with all U.S. Government agencies involved in terrorist threat finance activities, and the defense contractor Booz Allen Hamilton. These agencies included Treasury Dept., State Dept., Federal Bureau of Investigation (FBI), Immigration and Customs Enforcement (ICE), Homeland Security, Defense Intelligence Agency (DIA), Drug Enforcement Agency (DEA), Justice Dept., and the Central Intelligence Agency (CIA), as well as other military and civilian sub-agencies and international organizations. Based on my background and skillsets, I am qualified to address this issue to USACAPOC in a very unique and insightful way.

OVERVIEW:

This report examines the national security and counterterrorism implications of civilian government agency personnel failing to provide, or conspiring to deny, military "Terrorism Threat Finance" analysts with information and witness access involving the "UBS Whistleblower" case.

An incident was brought to my attention involving secret Swiss Banks and terrorist financing. After conducting a thorough investigation into the matter, I have concluded that the information clearly shows not only have USACAPOC resources and personnel been needlessly and recklessly abused and wasted, as well as those of our international allies, but the explanation for this can only be either:
1) A gross failure in inter-agency financial intelligence sharing as a result of bureaucratic ignorance and incompetence; or
2) A conspiracy between certain civilian government agencies and personnel to ignore or deceive the military's counterterrorism and threat finance operations in an effort to cover-up secret bank accounts and financial transactions which would have been discovered, tracked, and disclosed to military and Congressional authorities.

The civilian government agencies and personnel responsible or directly involved in this failure or cover-up include:
--Department of Justice: Eric Holder, Attorney General; Kevin O'Connor, DOJ Attorney; Kevin Downing, DOJ Attorney.
--Department of State: Hillary Clinton, Secretary; Daniel Benjamin, Coordinator for Counterterrorism.
--Department of Treasury: Timothy Geitner, Secretary; David S. Cohen, Undersecretary of the Treasury for Terrorism and Financial Intelligence; Mathew Leavitt, Treasury Department Counterterrorism Official.
--CIA: David Pretreaus, Director (formerly CENTCOM Commander)
--Department of Defense: Leon Panetta, SecDef (formerly CIA Director)
--Senator Carl Levin: Chairman of Senate's Permanent Subcommittee on Investigations, and also on Senate Armed Services Committee.
--President Barack Obama: Formerly a Senator who was on the committee to which the UBS financial information was disclosed, and who issued policies and executive orders to subordinate political appointees to benefit UBS.
--Other witnesses: willing to testify only under immunity protection.
--Robert Wolf: Former UBS Chairman of the Americas and fundraiser for President Barack Obama's re-election campaign.

The U.S. Military personnel responsible or directly involved or possibly victimized by this failure or cover-up include:
--General Tommy Franks (retired): formerly CENTCOM Commander during initial invasion and subsequent stability operations and counterterrori coordination in Iraq.
-- General James Mattis: Current CENTCOM Commander and head of Terrorist Threat Finance Operations and Mission out of MacDill AFB, FL.
--Colonel Byrd: Immediate Commander of Terrorist Threat Finance Operations and the Joint Interagency Operations Center at CENTCOM, MacDill AFB, FL.
--General Stanley McCrystal (retired): CENTCOM
--General George Casey: Top U.S. Commander in Iraq, 2006 and former Secretary of the Army.
--General Odierno: Army Chief of Staff
--General Martin Dempsey: Chairman of the Joint Chiefs of Staff
--Admiral William McRaven: U.S. Special Operations Commander
--Admiral Eric Olson: Former Commander, U.S. Special Operations Command
--Other military officials requesting anonymity.

Other government-political persons implicated or knowledgeable about key terrorist financing dimensions and cross-over with UBS case:
--Thomas E. Donilon: National Security Agency
--General James L. Jones (retired): Formerly NSA under Obama
--Cameron P. Munter: U.S. Ambassador to Pakistan
--John O. Brennan: Counterterrorism adviser to Obama and candidate for CIA director until withdrawn.
--Dennis C. Blair: Director of National Intelligence (fired in May 2010)
--Michael V. Hayden: Former CIA Director under G.W. Bush
--John A. Rizzo: CIA top lawyer
--Gregory B. Craig: White House Counsel
--Jeh C. Johnson: Obama campaign advisor and now general counsel of Department of Defense
--Michael E. Leiter: Director of National Counterterrorism Center
--Harold H. Koh: State Dept. lawyer
--General Keith B. Alexander: Commander of NSA and Cyber Command
--General Caldwell: Commander of U.S. Northern Command
--Mathew Olsen: Director of National Counterterrorism Center
--Admiral Mullen: Former Chairman Joint Chiefs

Civilian contractor personnel assigned to U.S. CENTCOM Joint Interagency Operations Center, Terrorist Threat Finance:
--Mike Maravilla: Booz Allen Hamilton, now DoD civilian GS employee
--Troy Henseley: Booz Allen Hamilton, Manager Threat Finance team
--Bill Lubliner: Booz Allen Hamilton, Director of Threat Finance team
--Bob Thompson: Booz Allen Hamilton, Senior Partner assigned to CENTCOM
--Other Booz Allen Hamilton junior employees requesting anonymity

Islamic organizations associated with terrorist threat financing investigations:
--Holy Land Foundation: Charges brought for funding Hamas and others
--Council on American-Islamic Relations (CAIR): founders and leadership of CAIR were part of Palestine Committee of the Muslim Brotherhood
--Islam in North America (ISNA)
--North American Islam Trust (NAIT)
--Islamic Association for Palestine

Union Bank of Switzerland organization for finance operations:
--Optimus Foundation: created by UBS for clients to hide money in, and which certain extremists or their organizations may have used to channel or launder money to Islamic groups.

UBS clients suspected of terror threat financing involvement:
--Abdullah Azziz: A major UBS client and account holder who was connected to Saadam Hussein (former dictator of Iraq). Azziz was living in New York, and intimately connected to ex-Mayor Rudolph Gulianni. Possible "Oil for Dollars" abuse in early 90's.
--Brother of Osama Bin Laden: UBS account holder, living in Boston at time when planes left Boston airport and crashed into World Trade Center.
--Osama Bin Laden: SEAL raid on OBL compound in Pakistan yielded computer files and financial documents linking OBL to UBS accounts, and brother. Other family member accounts also listed in documents confiscated. Only 17 documents out of hundreds have been "officially" released by CIA. CIA cover up of accounts at UBS which would expose covert U.S. government bank accounts and financial operations outside of Congressional oversight.

SYNOPSIS:

UBS WHISTLEBLOWER CASE, TERRORIST THREAT FINANCE, AND COVER-UP

Mr. Brad Birkenfeld, an international banker working for the Union Bank of Switzerland (UBS), discovered accounts and clients which may have had international terrorist financing implications against the United States and its allies. Convicted with a strong sense of patriotic duty and love of country, Mr. Birkenfeld decided to take defensive action, put his life and career in danger, and travel to the United States to inform the government of the existing financial dangers.

Mr. Birkenfeld first visited the Department of Justice and disclosed to them that he had information concerning Swiss Bank accounts, clients, and practices which had enormous value to combatting international terrorists and their operations (training camps, couriers, Zakat charity Optimus Foundation, etc.). Mr. Birkenfeld shared that he wanted to ensure this information was utilized by the right intelligence and military agencies, but first required a "subpoena" in order to turn-over this material and testify. Mr. Birkenfeld informed the Department of Justice attorneys that he could not give information without a subpoena, as he would be in violation of Swiss law otherwise. The DOJ Attorneys who met with Mr. Birkenfeld were Kevin Downing, Kevin O'Connor and others. Mr. Birkenfeld was condescendingly addressed as a "tipster" and not a "whistleblower" by the Department of Justice, and was told by Kevin O'Connor, "We are not interested in non-Americans" when Birkenfeld disclosed information about key clients and their possible involvement in terrorist financing activities, as well as tax evasion. It has since been discovered that the person in question was Abdullah Azziz, who was closely connected with ex-Mayor of New York Rudy Gulianni, who was making a bid for Presidency potentially. It is significant to note Mr. O'Connor has been reported as leaving the Department of Justice since this time, and obtained work involving Mr. Gulianni.

The Department of Justice attorneys Mr. Downing and Mr. O'Connor refused to provide Mr. Birkenfeld with a subpoena, and thereby allow him to provide the information relating to Swiss bank operations and terrorist financing. This was a major failure to the military's "Threat Finance Operations" managed out of CENTCOM's Joint Interagency Operations Center, as this information could have provided valuable intelligence for Special Operations forces, and investigators constructing profiles of key terrorist finance personalities. At no time did DOJ officials ever share this information, Birkenfeld's offer of intelligence disclosure, or discuss with military Threat Finance operations in a "Joint Task Force" capacity. Mr. Birkenfeld was met with the response, "...Just what I need, a 'once-in-a-lifetime opportunity'...", by a DOJ investigator when he informed them of his information and desire to share it. This negative and discouraging response by DOJ officials to Mr. Birkenfeld's offer of assistance, prompted him to leave the DOJ and seek a subpoena from a different financial government agency. Birkenfeld then went to the IRS, and the Securities and Exchange Commission, requesting a subpoena. No subpoenas were issued by these agencies either.

During this time, a very strange and disturbing thing happened. When Mr. Birkenfeld flew over to the United States to initially meet with DOJ officials about his information, he did so in absolute secret, and told no one. Justifiably, he had concern for his life. However, upon leaving the Justice Department building, and after he had given DOJ officials his cell-phone and contact info, a mysterious letter was sent to the UBS headquarters in Geneva, Switzerland, claiming to have been written by one of Mr. Birkenfeld's close banking friends who happened to live in London at the time. The letter was unsigned, had the date "July" typed on it, and rambled about "reporting to UBS that one of its bankers was meeting with the American government and disclosing information, etc., etc.". Upon receiving this letter, UBS contacted the banker (as he was known through social circles) and asked what the reason for the letter was. The man responded that he in fact did not send any letter, didn't know what they were talking about, and demanded a copy be sent to him. UBS faxed the letter to the man, who in turn called Mr. Birkenfeld asking "what is this all about?"

The man was upset that a letter had been forged in his name, sent to UBS, and was claiming Mr. Birkenfeld was disclosing confidential information. Mr. Birkenfeld received a copy of the letter, faxed from his friend, and was equally amazed and without explanation as to how this "secret meeting" could have been disclosed, since his friend had no idea of the situation. Mr. Birkenfeld assured him he would investigate the matter.

It was later determined what most likely had happened. When Mr. Birkenfeld left the Justice Department, his friend (the suposed "letter writer") had telephoned Mr. Birkenfeld, saying he was in the U.S. and traveling to Mexico. Since Mr. Birkenfeld shared that he too was in America (not disclosing the reason why), his friend invited him to travel on his private plane to Mexico for a week's vacation. Mr. Birkenfeld went on this trip with his friend, and then after returne to Europe.

In all likelihood, reason and evidence would point to the explanation that someone at the Department of Justice either composed that letter, contracted its composition, or informed another agency of the elements of Mr. Birkenfeld's "Swiss Bank Whistleblowing" case, and this resulted in a fraudulent letter being constructed by an imposter claiming to be Mr. Birkenfeld's friend. Mr. Birkenfeld had given his telephone information to Justice Dept. Officials, who then most likely "tapped" his phone (without a warrant, violating his civil rights), or informed the Defense Intelligence Agency, or Central Intelligence Agency, or National Reconnaisance Office, or National Security Agency, or other agency capable of eavesdropping and tracking to report on Mr. Birkenfeld

It can be surmised that the reason for this aggressive action, or attack upon Mr. Birkenfeld was because he had "opened Pandora's Box" with regards to Swiss Bank Accounts, and it is possible that certain government agencies, most likely the CIA as well as Dept. of Justice, became paranoid that irreparable damage might be done by Mr. Birkenfeld' disclosures. This would not be tolerated, and therefore "leaking" Mr. Birkenfeld to UBS might invoke Swiss Police Power and prosecution against him, or worse--he might be killed before he could speak.

It is important to note that Mr. Birkenfeld's banker friend from London, England was of Middle Eastern-North African Muslim ancestry with a Mohammaden name. Thus it is conceivable, if not obvious, that Mr. Birkenfeld may have been suspected of "associating with a possible terrorist" which, according to the DOJ mindset, justified a warrantless investigation and monitoring program; which in turn degenerated into a reputation and character smearing plot.

Mr. Birkenfeld, upon discovering this mysterious letter sent by some imposter person, or agency, falsely claiming the identity of his friend, immediately sent a response letter to the DOJ through his attorneys. Mr. Birkenfeld demanded an explanation as to how this exposure of his private communications and meeting with DOJ could have occurred. DOJ responded by email that they would "look into it", but in fact never gave any answer, and instead ignored all further inquiries about the matter.

This is extremely telling. One would expect that the Department of Justice, an agency whose Congressional mandate is to preserve, protect, and enforce the Constitutional rights of American citizens--thereby preserving a culture of law inside the country--would have been somewhat outraged, insulted, and interested--if not obsessed--with discovering and prosecuting a leak of information which could only have come from an official inside their own agency, or a "mole" or spy with access to their agency (most likely a "sheep-dipped" CIA agent working at DOJ with deep cover).

One would also have expected that the DOJ Office of Internal Investigations and Inspector General, as well as FBI, would have been notified and an interview with both Mr. Birkenfeld and his London friend been requested in order to fully dissect their phone conversation, schedule coordination, rendezvous inside the U.S., trip to Mexico, and timeline of events in relation to the false UBS imposter letter sent. Amazingly, nothing was done to investigate this peculiar incident, and the issue mysteriously went cold and was never explained by the DOJ.

Another significant issue is that Mr. Birkenfeld offered to release to the DOJ information pertaining to UBS cell phones, hotel rooms, schedules, contact info of executives, and business procedures of Swiss banking which he believed, and conveyed to DOJ, may be facilitating and financing international terrorism against U.S. troops, as well as our allies; and defrauding U.S. taxpayers. Strangely enough, despite this wealth of information offered by Mr. Birkenfeld, he was not embraced but rather scoffed at by DOJ officials Downing and O'Connor, and flippantly told, "You watch too much TV...that is Hollywood." DOJ claimed they could not electronically track such information, citing lack of technology as an excuse.

However this response by the DOJ would seem to be motivated either out of ignorance or deception. The U.S. Army's "Intelligence and Security Command" located at Fort Belvoir, VA specializes in these exact types of communication intercepts, and works closely with Joint Special Operations Command which oversees missions to track, capture, and kill terrorism suspects overseas. This Command has been utilized by CENTCOM's Terrorist Threat Finance Operations out of JIAG on many occassions.

Additionally, with regards to the "imposter letter" sent to UBS claiming to be from Mr. Birkenfeld's London banker friend, the military intelligence community is certainly capable of tracing the letter and pinpointing its most logical source. Framed around the timeline of Mr. Birkenfeld's first contact, meeting with, and departure from the DOJ building in Washington DC, a separate military investigation can easily examine all communication (phone, fax, email) between the following parties:
1) Dept. Justice to White House, CIA, and Embassy Bern, Geneva
2) CIA communications to Embassy Bern, Geneva and White House
3) Wikileaks cables around this timeline with key word searches: UBS, Birkenfeld, Embassy Bern, Whistleblowing, Terrorist Threat Finance

This would expose the communications traffic and identify complicit parties. This is easily done given that the UBS "imposter letter" arrived at UBS just a few weeks following Mr. Birkenfeld's initial disclosures and meeting with DOJ officials.

At this point it is significant to note that the Wikileaks cables released, and those not yet "officially" released, clearly show a great deal of communication between the State Department and other agencies revolving around the "UBS Whistleblowing" case. Communications within the Obama Administration indicate "back room" deals and "political solutions" were frantically calculated in response to the Birkenfeld-UBS disclosures. More about this will be addressed later.

Mr. Birkenfeld also sent a letter through his attorneys to the DOJ identifying his value to the "Joint Task Force" established for counterterrorism finance and intelligence gathering work. Mr. Birkenfeld informed the DOJ that his information would be the key to empowering this Joint Task Force with the insider information required to examine, understand, and master the clandestine and complicated world of Swiss Banking. With the information he had, the DOJ could sift out links to terrorists, their bank accounts, and their methods of transfer. This could in turn be shared with military threat finance personnel at USACAPOC and CENTCOM. However, once again, either out of ignorance, incompetence, or intentional deceit, nothing was done by DOJ, no subpoena was given, and instead the message was suppressed by "gagging and shackling" the messenger.

After contacting DOJ, IRS, and the SEC, and getting no positive results or offers of subpoena, Mr. Birkenfeld went to the U.S. Senate and was finally able to obtain a subpoena allowing him to testify, and giving him full legal immunity for his information...or so he was told. It was later shown to be a broken promise and worthless agreement. More about that later. It is essential to observe and question why DOJ, SEC, and the IRS refused to receive information that later was determined to have returned $780 million dollars to American Taxpayers, and provided 19,000 bank accounts from which terrorist financiers could be identified, tracked, and ultimately stopped. Mr. Birkenfeld's eventual payment of $106 million by the IRS for his whistleblowing report is confirmation that he and his information was not only valuable, but essential all along; and his work served the best interests of the American people.

With subpoena in hand, Mr. Birkenfeld was finally able to testify before the U.S. Senate Subcommittee on Investigations, chaired by Senator Carl Levin, and with then Senator Barack Obama as a member of the committ The session was closed to the public. Mr. Birkenfeld testified to issues relating to UBS Swiss Bank accounts, systems, practices, client management, technology, and a variety of other subjects which should be disclosed within a Top Secret/SCI secure facility (SCIF). Much of this information has already been released to open-source intelligence mining organizations, such as Wikileaks.

After completing his testimony to the Senate, Mr. Birkenfeld was later called in to a meeting with DOJ officials O'Connor and Downing, and prohibited from further testifying to other agencies. Mr. Birkenfeld retold the story of being in the room with his attorney at the DOJ when a DOJ official slammed his fist down upon the table and in a threatening voice yelled out "You will not speak to the IRS!". This would seem to be labeled as "interfering with an on-going investigation" by the DOJ by a court of law, and could be actionable, since the DOJ was denying Mr. Birkenfeld his right to testify. Additionally this <u>threat by DOJ to Mr. Birkenfeld made it impossible for him to come directly to the military and address the terrorist threat finance dimensions of the UBS Swiss banking scandal.</u> Had Mr. Birkenfeld not been prevented by the DOJ, he could have been debriefed by CENTCOM's Threat Finance team out of the JIOC at MacDill Air Force Base. He would have provided a wealth of information, from which terrorist financier profiles could have been constructed for capture-kill missions by USACAPOC. Mr. Birkenfeld's information could also have been used to construct Information Operations for combatting terrorist financing in CENTCOM's theater of operations, and a "Swiss Banking" schematic been developed as an operational and training model. Additionally Mr. Birkenfeld would have been critical to developing instruction for USACAPOC counterterrorist teams and U.S. Embassy military attaches. The materials derived from Mr. Birkenfeld would have greatly improved our threat finance warfighting capability, but unfortunately was not allowed to be shared with the military.

After chastising Mr. Birkenfeld for his Senate testimony before Carl Levin and then Senator Barack Obama's committee, and threatening him should he disclose further information to the IRS and SEC, the DOJ changed course and began advancing towards a new goal: silence Birkenfeld by prosecuting him with his own speech and imprison him for his choice to disclose the truth. In other words, initiate a policy of "no good deed goes unpunished."

During his testimony to the Senate, Mr. Birkenfeld disclosed requested client information. One client was "Olenicoff". Birkenfeld's lawyers responded to an email later from the Senate about this client, affirming that Birkenfeld had indeed disclosed all necessary information about him, as requested. However, the DOJ under the direction of Attorney General, and other agencies, using Downing and O'Connor embarked on campaign of manipulation and distortion by alleging that Birkenfeld had not disclosed this information about his relationship with client Olenicoff. This was the foundation for the DOJ case construction against Mr. Birkenfeld. Fixed upon this alleged "failure to disclose" the DOJ began communications with Mr. Olenicoff, visiting him in California, and most likely arranging promises and benefits to him in exchange for providing material useful to their case construction against Mr. Birkenfeld. In short, the DOJ was taking statements Mr. Birkenfeld had given during his testimony to the Senate, pretended not to hear them, and then claimed that they had been instead found by the prowess and investigatory skill of the DOJ investigators. Indeed "making a silk purse out of a sow's ear" was manifesting into a new artistic expression with the DOJ's case creation.

This turn of events seems to symbolize the DOJ assuming a new mandate from the "enforcement of law" to the "manipulation of law for political ends". This warrants a psychological operations analysis and I offer the following, in an effort to best serve the USACAPOC Commander: As ridiculous and counterproductive as this strategy might seem to the average "Joe-the-Plumber" American wanting safety, or to a military Threat Finance analyst searching for terrorist bank accounts, or Congressional investigator seeking to strengthen and defend the nation, no one did it astound, infuriate, and disappoint more than Mr. Birkenfeld.

The choice to charge him with a crime pieced together from information he had freely disclosed to a Congressional Senate Subcommittee, at a hearing he had been promised immunity for ("Kastigar" immunity-- see Oliver North case), could only be explained as the climax of insanity and hypocrisy, as well as the definition of betrayal. It seemed to be nothing more than DOJ attorneys O'Connor and Downing, under the supervision of Attorney General Eric Holder and Direction of President Obama, trying desperately to cobble together some rickety, half-witted legal case like blind, deaf, and dumb mentally retarded children glueing together a model plane without the photo--it just couldn't possibly fly, never mind be appealing to a sensible eye or rational mind. It was nothing less than an ugly monstrosity of missing parts and gaping holes, or in other words missing logic and empty reason. It was a "Frankenstein" abomination of law, sewing half-truths together into a project of political skullduggery.

The obvious question becomes "why"? Why did the DOJ prosecute the very person who had disclosed to them an issue which would later bring the U.S. Treasury $780 million (and continueing) and identify potential terrorist finance operations for the U.S. military to synthesize into its "War on Terror"?

The primary enabler of Mr. Birkenfeld's prosecution by DOJ was the fact that Senator Carl Levin, Chairman of the Subcommittee and a member of the Armed Services Committee, refused to provide Mr. Birkenfeld with a copy of his testimony transcript. This transcript would have shown Mr. Birkenfeld's Olenicoff disclosure, and thereby dismissed the charge leveled against him by the DOJ. Mysteriously, and perhaps with a criminal conspiratorial intent, Senator Levin refused to give Mr. Birkenfeld this exonerating document. Senator Levin also failed to provide the Counterterrorism threat finance operations team at CENTCOM/JIAG with information from the UBS case, which would have significantly improved the military's warfighting capability in this battlespace. By not providing this financial information to the military, Senator Levin weakened our ability to disable terrorist financial networks, thereby enabling the enemy to continue financing its operations, which is defined by U.S. treason laws as "aiding and giving comfort to the enemy."

The military, through the initiation of USACAPOC, should file an immediate investigation request through the Inspector General at the Pentagon, Lynne Halbrooks to examine Senator Carl Levin's actions of refusing to provide Mr. Birkenfeld with exonnerating testimoney he gave during the Senate Hearing, which DOJ prosecuted him later for. Additionally, Senator Levin should be examined for his <u>failure to provide the military with information relating to UBS financing terrorist operations which USACAPOC was fighting, and CENTCOM was supposedly managing in its JIAG team at MacDill AFB</u>. This would also seem to be a natural requirment of Levin's duty at the Armed Services Committee, representing another level of intelligence sharing failure, or intentional deceit for political purposes.

The political purposes for this possible explanation of deceit can be seen in the UBS case involvement with the State Department, Treasury Department, CIA clandestine bank accounts, and the Obama Administration election ambitions. Cables obtained from the State Department are instructive in this, and are included as SUPPORTING DOCUMENTS at the end of this report.

First, documents indicate that the State Department was actively seeking a political solution with the Government of Switzerland over the UBS case, and seeking to use Mr. Birkenfeld as a "scapegoat" for this "Peace Treaty". Additionally the State Department leveraged the UBS case to facilitate the transfer of two Chinese Uighar terrorists held at Guantanamo Bay Cuba (which is a facility under military command) to Switzerland. This is documented in cables, and implicates Secretary Hillary Clinton and President Obama. 2LT Scott Bennett also worked at the State Department Counterterrorism Coordinator Office, and worked with various agencies during this timeframe.

Second, Secretary of Treasury Tim Geitner issued funds to UBS as part of the "Stimulus bill"/ Recovery Act during bailout of 2008 in response to the growing financial crisis. Documents indicate the UBS case was identified as a source of instability that might trigger global collapse of financial networks, and therefore justified a "political solution" and prosecution of Mr. Birkenfeld. Mr. Geitner was also the Chairman of the New York Federal Reserve during the Libor rate manipulation case.

Third, Attorney General Eric Holder represented UBS in private practice before joining the Obama Administration and serving at the Department of Justice. Mr. Holder gave UBS a deferred prosecution, and refused to prosecute all other individuals associated with the case which were identified by Birkenfeld. Fulbright and Jaworski has been identifi as a law firm which should be examined as it relates to DOJ officials and the UBS case. Military investigation by USACAPOC should be requested that is outside DOJ authority, in order to avoid any contamination or manipulation of evidence. Deference should be given to the prior destruction of CIA documents relating to the CIA agent interrogation of Islamic terrorist suspects and rendition programs.

Fourth, CIA Directors Leon Panetta and General David Pretreaus should be examined in relation to this UBS case and terrorist finance informati Note: Leon Panetta was an employee of Booz Allen Hamilton, which managed the CENTCOM Threat Finance Contract at the JIAG. 2LT Scott Bennett was a key component to this team, and has extensive knowledge of its activities. Document analysis indicates the following findings:
1--Al Qaeda and other Islamic extremist groups (Haqqanni network,etc.) show a trail of donors, banks, charities, and government personnel involved with, or complicit with, fundraising/finance operations associated with Swiss Banks and UBS operations.
2--Finance trails and documents may show UBS accounts being used by CIA covert activities, similar to Nugan Hand bank (Honolulu, Hawaii) that was used by the CIA/DEA during the Vietnam-Laos-Cambodia drug trafficking operations.
3--Documents would reveal Al Qaeda key propaganda topics against Western Culture, and specifically outline the moral (homosexuality, divorce, child pornography) deficits and dysfunctions as originating within the United States. See Osama Bin Laden documents obtained at kill site in Pakistan.
4--Documents would confirm CIA personnel contacting Vanity Fair journalis assigned to Birkenfeld case as "trying to dissuade media attention" and redirect it towards Afghan President Hamid Karzai instead.
[NOTE: USACAPOC should request Congress share this report with MI5 and MI British Intelligence; and Germany's "Verfassungsschutz", Federal Office for the Protection of the Constitution (U.S. FBI equivalent); Interpol; and Russia's "Spetznatz" (with prudence) in order to improve financial intel sharing and form joint terrorists threat finance operations using UBS case

President Barack Obama is directly responsible for the prosecution
of Mr. Birkenfeld, the failure to share--or the conscious decision
not to share--financial intelligence with U.S. Central Command's
Threat Finance team and USACAPOC Human Terrain Mapping teams, and the
deferred prosecution privelege given to UBS in exchange for financial
donations and/or other benefits, such as the transfer of Guantanamo Bay
detainees to Switzerland. President Obama was on the Senate Subcommittee
when Mr. Birkenfeld made his disclosures, and should have recused himself
due to the fact that Obama had taken money from UBS for his election.
UBS Chairman Robert Wolf became a leading fundraiser for President
Obama, and various "golfing trips" were also noted. All actions
taken by Secretary Hillary Clinton, Secretary Geitner, Attorney General
Holder, and military commanders are the responsibility of the President,
as political appointees are executing the President's wishes in their
respective offices.

CONCLUSION:

The "UBS-Birkenfeld Whistleblowing" case indeed represents a serious
dysfunctionality in relationship and authorities and missions between
the civilian government sector and the military sector. As an Officer
of USACAPOC, I have to the best of my ability and in good faith
endeavored to construct an analysis report of the case in the hope it
saves soldiers' lives, exposes incompetence and deceit (which may also
qualify in this case as "acts of treason"), and preserves, protects,
and defends the United States Constitution. It is strongly suggested
that <u>USACAPOC immediately invite Mr. Birkenfeld to Fort Bragg, North
Carolina for a confidential debriefing of this case and use this
intelligence analysis report as a guide.</u>

The U.S. military has been formed by Congress to preserve, protect, and
defend the Constitution, and not simply serve the agenda of the President
in his capacity as Commander-in-Chief. High crimes and misdemeanors may
have been committed by President Obama and his cabinet in this UBS case,
and thus impeachment proceedings may be warranted. It is the responsibility
of the Congress to investigate this matter, and it is the duty of the
military--and its officers who discover it--to report it.

I hereby report this matter to my Commander, General Jeffrey Jacobs of USACAPOC, with the recommendation a Congressional inquiry be initiated, hearings held, and an Inspector General investigation be launched.

The reason for this report and recommendation is due to the overwhelming amount of evidence which suggests improper or deceptive acts were committed against the U.S. military, specifically CENTCOM's threat finance operations at MacDill AFB; or the military was complicit in practices which Congress would find illegal and a violation of the Constitution.

Additionally 2LT Scott Bennett has been illegally harassed, threatened, prosecuted, and imprisoned by the Department of Justice for his investigation and exposure of this issue. False accusations have been made against 2LT Bennett by the DOJ, and Bennett is requesting an appeal and a trial before a military court in which to share this and other materials which will more fully disclose this and other cover-up issues. 2LT Bennett requests the Commander of USACAPOC immediately issue a "Habeaus Corpus" to free Bennett from the illegal custody of the Dept. of Justice, to allow him to appear before the Commander at USACAPOC to present this material. Additionally 2LT Bennett requests the opportunity to appear before appropriate Congressional Committees to disclose this issue. Those committees include: Armed Services Committee Intelligence Committee; and Oversight and Reform Committee.

Congressional representatives have been notified of this situation and extensive documentation exists supporting Bennett's assertions.

2LT Bennett requests placement in military police protection during any transport out of DOJ custody, as the material cited in this report justifies a reasonable concern for his life.

As a Psychological Operations and Terrorist Threat Finance analyst, I would posit that the arrogance of power without fear of law intoxicates the practicioner into a state of self-delusion where their every intention and action is gradually judged by them to be the genesis of law itself.

This is the socio-political-mental transformation from equality and autonomy under the law, to subjugation by the law--and its translators (lawyers and judges) and enforcers (police power agencies and military). This in turn becomes the sunset of personal liberty, and the dawn of social slavery. This is the metamorphosis the Department of Justice seems to be undergoing as indicated by the legal precedents it is establishing by the UBS-Whistleblower case. This represents a dangerous authoritarian impulse in civilian government, which by nature is a threat to citizens' freedoms, property, and security. It is hoped that this same authoritarian transformation instigated by Presidential Executive Order will not be condoned by the military or Congress. The future's liberty, prosperity, and hope depend on it. The reaction to this report, and the treatment of 2LT Bennett by the military and Congress will tell.

I welcome the opportunity to elaborate further on this material as it relates to USACAPOC at my upcoming hearing at Fort Bragg on October 2, 2012. Information can be obtained by the 154th Legal Support Organization (TDS), 6901 Telegragh Road, Alexandria, VA 22310-3320, Captain Avi Stone.

Respectfully,

2LT Scott Bennett, 11th Psychological Operations Battalion
#29418-016
FCI Schuylkill
P.O. Box 670
Minersville, PA 17954-0670

cc: General Ray Odierno, Army Chief of Staff
General Martin Dempsey, Chairman of the Joint Chiefs of Staff

Representative Mike Rogers, House Intelligence Committee
Representative Peter King, Terrorism Committee
Representative Saxby Chambliss, Oversight and Reform Committee
Representative Howard McKeon, Armed Services Committee

Bill, Hillary & Chelsea Clinton Foundation

This Bill, Hillary & Chelsea Clinton Foundation Muckety map is interactive. You can move boxes, delete and add relationships, title and save your maps. (Requires Flash.

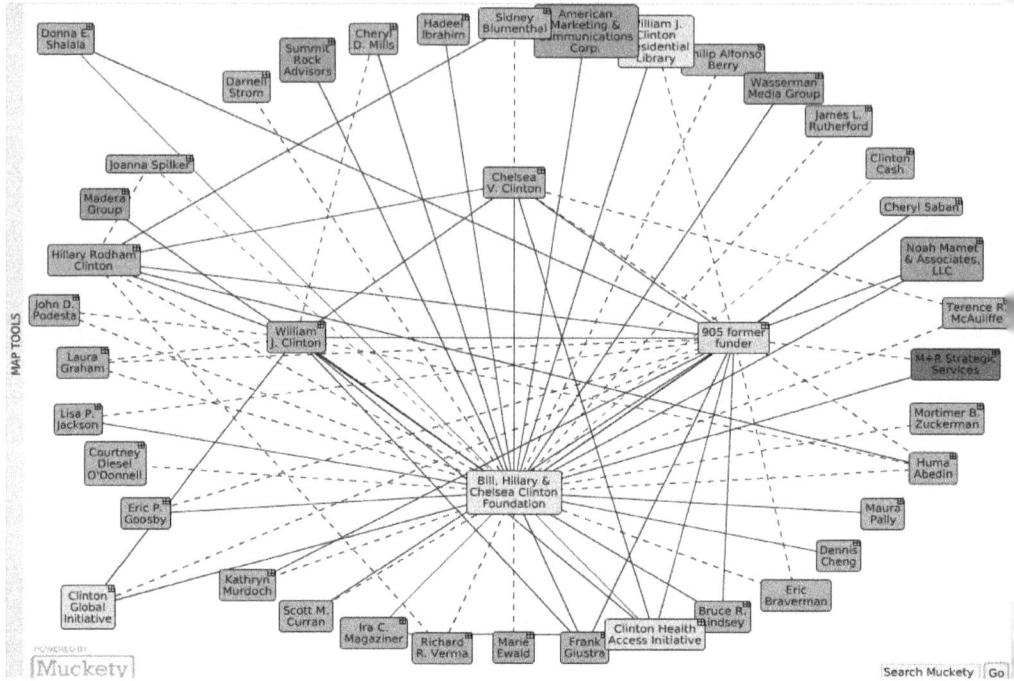

UBS Americas, UBS Wealth Management USA

This UBS Americas, UBS Wealth Management USA relationship map is interactive. Click around to explore relations in the map.

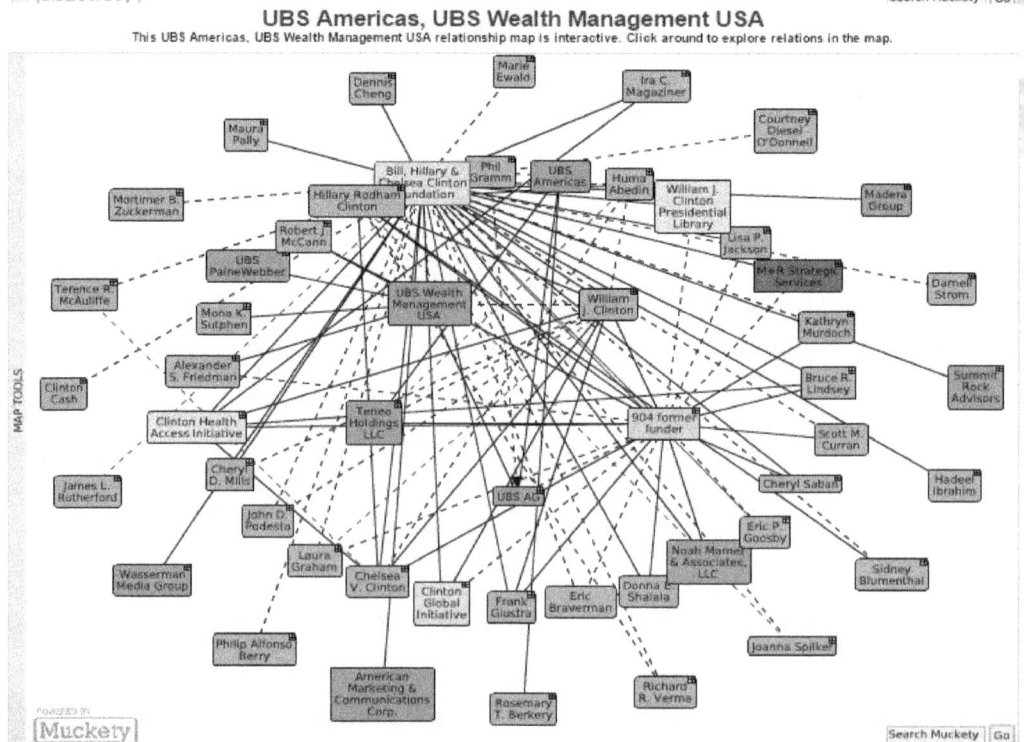

Covington & Burling LLP

This Covington & Burling LLP Muckety map is interactive. You can move boxes, delete and add relationships, title and save your maps. (Requires Flash.)

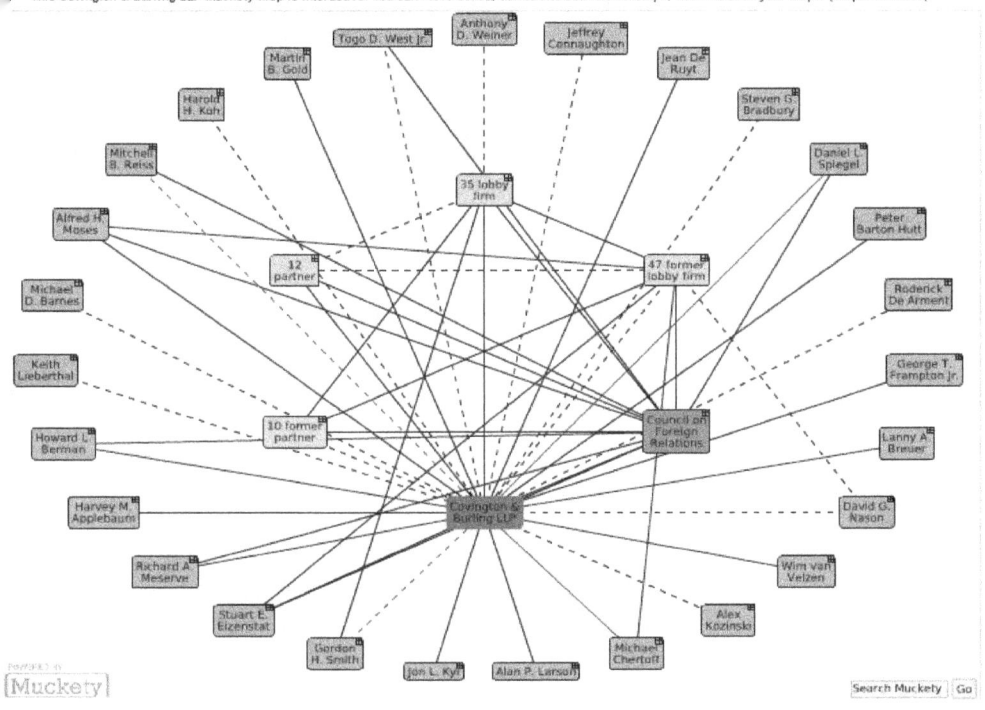

Covington & Burling LLP

This Covington & Burling LLP Muckety map is interactive. You can move boxes, delete and add relationships, title and save your maps. (Requires Flash.)

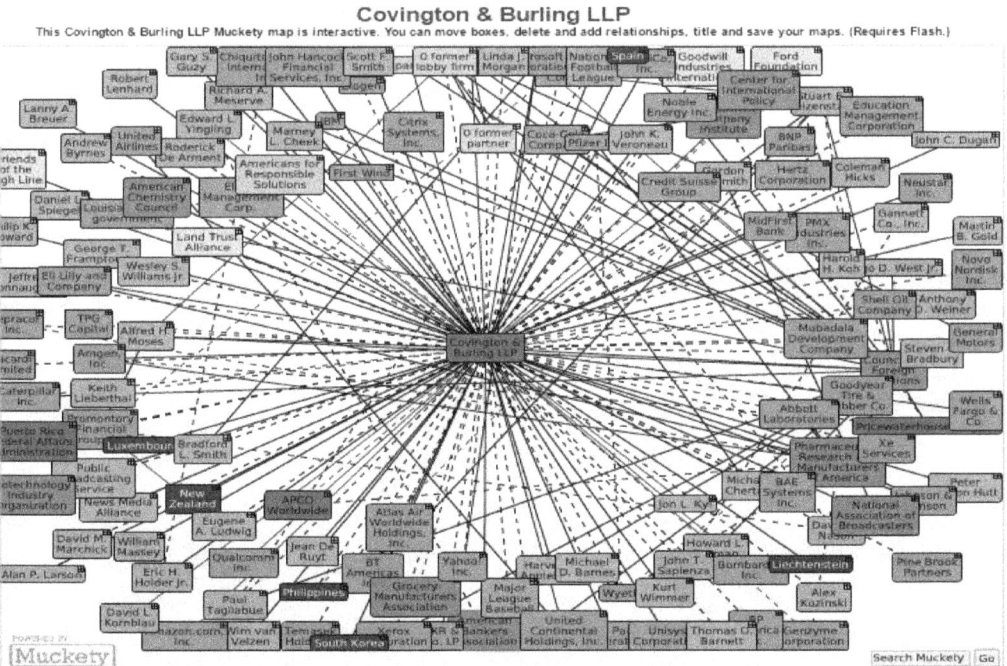

Bradley C. Birkenfeld, U.S. vs. Bradley Birkenfeld and Mario Staggl

This Bradley C. Birkenfeld, U.S. vs. Bradley Birkenfeld and Mario Staggl relationship map is interactive. Click around to explore relations in the map.

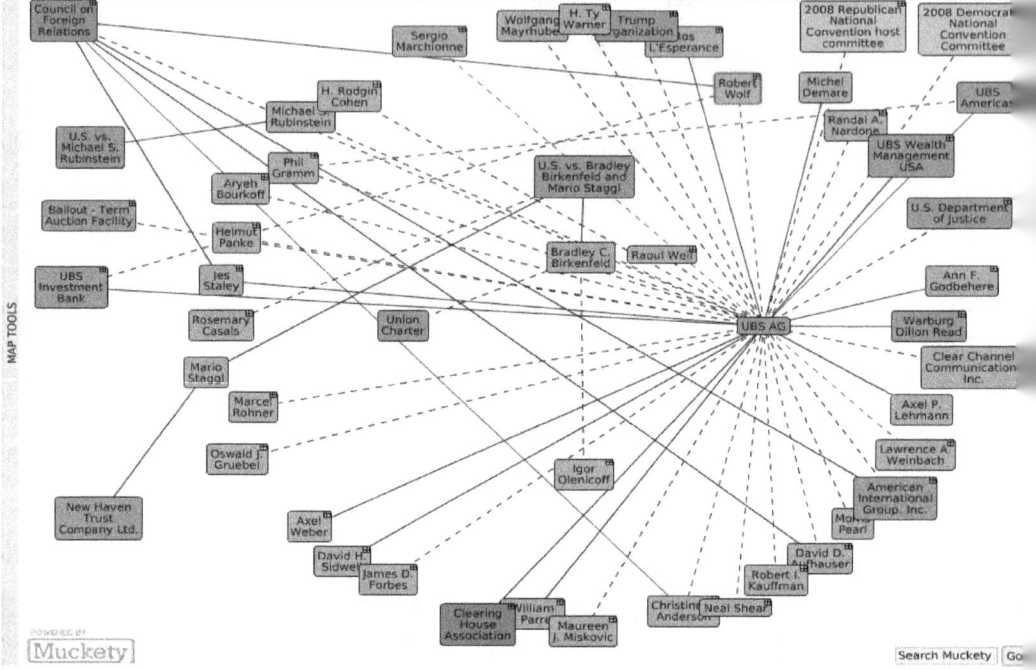

Booz Allen Hamilton

This Booz Allen Hamilton Muckety map is interactive. You can move boxes, delete and add relationships, title and save your maps. (Requires Flash.)

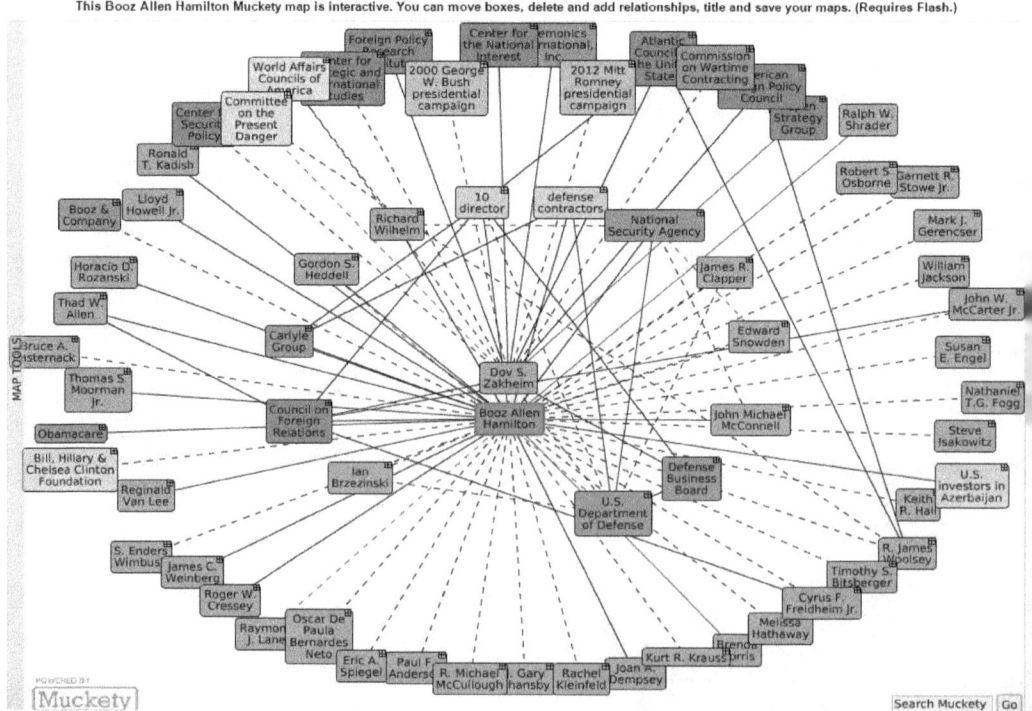

SUPPORTING DOCUMENTS:

Wikileaks Cables:

REFERENCE ID	ORIGIN	PARAGRAPH	KEY LANGUAGE
08BERN527	Embassy Bern	6	Diamonds in toothpaste

"UBS bankers intentionally skirted U.S. tax laws by aiding and abetting its U.S. clients through measures such as smuggling diamonds out of the U.S. in toothpaste. [NOTE: This is precisely the information given by Mr. Birkenfeld in his disclosures to DOJ and his Senate testimony before Chairman Carl Levin, and then Senator Barack Obama. This implicates State Department Secretary Hillary Clinton in all communications relating to UBS case and political solutions being floated by Obama Admin.]

| 08BERN552 | Embassy Bern | 1 | Nefarious activity |

"...the increasing use of financial networks by inappropriate individuals and organizations require that all countries work together to stop nefarious activity."

| 09BERN23 | Embassy Bern | 4 | UBS rescue package |

"...UBS transferred slightly over 2000 securities positions worth $16.4 billion. The majority of the assets were US and European residential and commercial mortgage backed securities."

| 09BERN73 | Embassy Bern | 1-4 | UBS CLIENT DISTRUST |

"...there is skepticism that UBS, facing client distrust and potential legal fines from the U.S., will pull so rapidly from the financial crisis. Public and media backlash against fat cat bonuses hit an all time high when UBS announced it would pay 2 billion in bonuses despite receiving state aid."

"...the ongoing investigation by the U.S. over claims of aiding tax evasion have done little to build or maintain client trust with clients reportedly pulling 58.2 billion Sfr (50.6 billion USD)(about 2 percent of total assets) from UBS' wealth management division in the fourth quart

09BERN98   Embassy Bern   1-5   U.S. Dept. of Justi

"UBS' handover of client information to the Department of Justice incited criticism in numerous press articles and from several Swiss political parties calling the U.S. action one of extortion and blackmail...governme representatives expressed disbelief at the extraordinary and criminal actions taken by UBS and surprise at the Swiss government's lackluster response and failure to fine UBS."

"The public's ire at the U.S. (and EU) for pressuring Switzerland should not be underestimated and could have a long-lasting negative backlash to bilateral relations and increased anti-Americanism. [NOTE: This negativity in U.S.-world relations, supposedly prompted by UBS disclosure, prompted U.S. State Department and White House to seek political solution. Criminal prosecution against Birkenfeld became the center of this solution and betrayal against him for his disclosure the strategy.]

"...concern is that the U.S. will capitalize on UBS' egregious conduct as fodder to renegotiate the tax treaty and qualified intermediary (Qi) agreement...expressed shock that FINMA did not impose criminal fines on UBS."

"...the Federal Council created a task force to delve into the UBS crimina case and to determine the best path forward on pending civil case."

"...post recommends that the USG approach Switzerland to discuss renegotiation of our bilateral agreement to incorporate the broader scope of coverage found in the U.S.-Liechtenstein TIEA, specifically to include tax evasion. The Swiss government can spin the bilateral agreement as a further step in our relations that assists both countries in halting willful criminal conduct." [NOTE: State Dept. and Obama Administration brands Mr. Birkenfeld's whistleblowing disclosures about 'tax evasion' and 'terrorist financing', amazingly, as "willful criminal conduct". Evidence indicates Obama prosecution of Birkenfeld is really willful criminal 'cover-up', in order to perpetuate UBS financial donations.]

| 09BERN99 | Embassy Bern | 1-3 | State Dept. Counter-terrorism (State CT) |

"Post has identified two entities that fit into the categories supplied by S/CT (State Counter Terrorism): the Swiss pharmaceutical industry and the Swiss banking system."

"Given the current global financial crisis, an attack that successfully shut down the system or severely crippled confidence in the banking system could significantly impact the global financial network and further escalate the severity of the global economic downturn. Institutions of note that are located in Switzerland include UBS, the world's largest wealth manager, Credit Suisse, and the Bank of International Settlements. CARTER"

[NOTE: An extremely valuable cable. From an intelligence perspective, any disruptions caused to the UBS operation is cited as a potential disruption to the financial network (global), which in turn could cause catastrophic consequences to the financial crisis. Thus, Birkenfeld's disclosures were interpreted by State Counterterrorism as a threat, and thus explain the prosecution of Birkenfeld by DOJ. This philosophy of interpreting a "whistleblower" as a disruptor of global financial stability, and defining his actions as possible "attacks" upon the global banking system is unprecedented, and alarming considering it is U.S. government officials making this policy against an American citizen for whistleblowing disclosures he is making to expose tax evasion and potential terrorist financing, for the benefit and protection of the American citizen and our allies.]

[2LT Scott Bennett worked at State Department Counterterrorism as the Liaison Officer for U.S. Special Operations Command/ Joint Military Information Support Center in Washington DC, and has extensive knowledge of this.]

| 09BERN169 | Embassy Bern | 3 | UBS-U.S. treaty link |

"...Switzerland sees linkage between the negotiations of the tax agreement and the ongoing UBS case...Switzerland definitely views the two as politically linked."

09BERN273   Embassy Bern   1   CENTCOM detainees

"The Swiss Minister for Economics and Trade Doris Leuthard...reaffirmed the commitment of the Swiss government to accept several detainees from Guantanamo Bay for resettlement in Switzerland. Minister Leuthard made it clear that these two activities were linked to the achievement of a political settlement in the case of Swiss banking giant, UBS."

"Minister Leuthard began the metting by describing today's special sessio of the Federal Council which was focused on what steps the Swiss governme could take to advance a political solution of the UBS case."

"Leuthard then turned the topic of discussion to Swiss willingness to accept several detainees from Guatanamo for resettlement and encouraged us to provide as much data as possible quickly so that the Swiss could move forward. CDA advised that more bio and medical data had been received today and was being delivered via a separate channel...she (Leuthard) reiterated that this resolve extended especially to finding a political solution to the UBS case."

[NOTE: U.S. Central Command provided intelligence pertaining to Guantanamo Bay detainees that would eventually be transferred to Switzerland. Revelations of the purpose for this transfer out of CENTCOM/ U.S. military control to State Department for control as "pawns" in a political solution, implicate CENTCOM in participating in Obama Administration protection of UBS, or being "kept out of the loop" of this information and victimized by it. Additionally, Secretary of State Hillary Clinton worked with Attorney General Eric Holder to implement President Obama's order to "prosecute Mr. Birkenfeld for his UBS disclosures" by any means necessary in order to arrive at a political solution with Switzerland that would allow the transfer of Guantanamo Bay detainees, as well as ensure the continuation of U.S. govnerment/CIA and other clandestine account activity in UBS. This information was either not shared with CENTCOM's Threat Finance team, or military was complicit in operation with State, DOJ, White House, and Swiss Economic and Trade Minister.]

09BERN350   Embassy Bern   1,5,7   UBS "Peace Treaty"

"President and Finance Minister Hans-Rudolf Merz, Justice Minister Eveline Widmer-Schlumpf, and Foreign Affairs Minister Micheline Calmy-Rey in an August 19 press conference praised the UBS agreement as the only possible solution and a "Peace Treaty...The UBS case had been a dark cloud over bilateral relations, with concerns it could escalate to a seriously damaging event similar to the Holocaust asset case a decade ago. Current Swiss opinion indicates, however, that the agreement will mollify all but the most anti-American voices and leave our bilateral relations relatively unscathed. End Summary."
[NOTE: Describing Birkenfeld's revelations of financial assets being hidden from U.S. taxpayers and possibly being also utilized in funding terrorist operations against U.S. troops and our allies as a "Dark Cloud" is telling. It suggests Obama Administration receptiveness to these revelations neutral at best, hostile at worst.]

"Thomas Pletscher, Executive Board Member of EconomieSuisse...a long drawn out court case posed "a danger of overshadowing" and "seriously damaging" otherwise good bilateral relations."

[NOTE: Other Wikileaks cables between State Department and other agencies are available upon request. Some are Top Secret/SCI classified and should not be discussed on open-source levels. Indications from cables are that Mr. Birkenfeld was identified as the "scapegoat" for securing a "political solution" and "peace treaty" with Swiss Government, and ensuring that Chinese Uighars held at Guantanamo Bay would be relocated to Switzerland. USACAPOC and CENTCOM were either kept out of the loop, or complicit in this plan, and subsequent ensuing prosecution of Birkenfeld by DOJ at the behest of Obama Admin. through State Dept. Secretary Clinton.]

PERSONALITY PROFILE NOTES AND CONNECTION TO UBS CASE:

Kevin Downing: Department of Justice prosecutor who obstructed investigation; denied giving subpoena to Birkenfeld allowing him to testify; falsely prosecuted Brad Birkenfeld with information he gave in his revelations to the Senate during his testimony (Birkenfeld should have been protected under a Kastigar immunity from prosecution for his revelational testimony); may have written a letter to UBS fraudulently claiming to be Birkenfeld's close friend from London, who had recently accompanied Brad on a trip to Mexico when he was in the United States. This may have been written by CIA out of substation in Bern, Switzerland. Downing left the Dept. of Justice and went to a law firm in Washington DC to represent clients involved in UBS tax issues, which would seem to be a serious violation and manipulation of the public trust and a conflict of interest. Said "You've watched too much Hollywood" and said Justice couldn't track info/numbers. FALSE

Kevin O'Connor: Attorney at the Dept. of Justice who told Birkenfeld "We are not interested in non-US citizens" and "You will not speak to the IRS or other federal government agencies".. O'Connor went to work for Gulianni after leaving Justice Dept. and called Bankers a "club of criminals". Birkenfeld supplied hotels, rooms, cell names of bankers, phones, account numbers and other trackable information to O'Connor and Downing at Justice. CENTCOM's CTF mission is precisely interested in non-US citizens, and Justice had obligation to share financial information with CENTCOM

Tim Geitner: Secretary of the Treasury, previously Chairman of the New York Federal Reserve; Libor Case and use of false rate; gave money from the "Stimulus Bill" / Recovery Act to UBS for Bailout during 2008 financial crisis.

Abdullah Azziz: UBS account holder; $420 million Iraqi oil dealer (60 minutes did story on him) lives in Manhattan, NY. Connected to Saddam Hussein, Iraq. Friend of Rudy Gulliani

Osama bin Laden brother: living in Boston, has UBS accounts; planes departed from Boston and NY that crashed into world trade center. Bin Laden documents retrieved at his killing undoubtedly contained UBS financial info- CIA cover up and hid this info from CENTCOM. SOCOM, despite mili

Daniel Benjamin:	State Department Coordinator for Counterterrorism
David S. Cohen:	Undersecretary of the Treasury for Terrorism and Financial Intelligence.
John O. Brennan:	Obama Counterterrorism Adviser
Mathew Leavitt:	Former Treasury Department Counterterrorism Official (now working on a book about Hezbollah's global ops.)
Eric Holder:	Attorney General; represented UBS in private practice; gave deferred prosecution to UBS; refused to prosecute anyone except the whistleblower himself; gave immunity to key people. Worked at Fulbright and Jaworski, law firm that represented UBS.
Barack Obama:	Was on committee in the Senate that Birkenfeld gave info to; Obama should have recused himself; Obama took money from Swiss banks for his election; Met UBS official Robert Wolf (UBS Chairman for the Americas) at George Soros (Liberal/Democrat/Left-Wing fundraiser and political operative) fundraiser; Obama gave the order to "make the issue go away".
Hilary Clinton:	State Department Secretary; deported two (2) Chinese Uighars to Switzerland in exchange for "political solution" to UBS-tax issue brought by Birkenfeld to Justice Dept. Note: Chinese Uighars were in custody of CENTCOM, therefore false statements may have been made in facilitation of this transfer to CENTCOM (violation of 18 USC §1001, and other laws).
Senator Carl Levin:	Denied testimony transcript of Brad Birkenfeld's testimony to the Senate Permanent Subcommittee on Investigations, which would have exonerated and cleared Birkenfeld of accusations of hiding material relating to client "Olenicoff". Levin is also on the Armed Services Committee and failed to give info about UBS case to CENTCOM Counterterrorism Threat Finance

Cable Viewer

Viewing cable 09BERN98, UBS CASE: SWISS PERSPECTIVE AND A WAY FORWARD

If you are new to these pages, please read an introduction on the structure of a cable as well as how to discuss them with others. See also the FAQs

Reference ID	Created	Released	Classification	Origin
09BERN98	2009-03-04 15:48	2011-08-30 01:44	CONFIDENTIAL	Embassy Bern

Appears in these articles:
http://www.letemps.ch/swiss_papers

```
VZCZCXRO9450
RR RUEHDBU RUEHFL RUEHKW RUEHLA RUEHNP RUEHROV RUEHSR
DE RUEHSW #0098/01 0631548
ZNY CCCCC ZZH
R 041548Z MAR 09
FM AMEMBASSY BERN
TO RUEHC/SECSTATE WASHDC 5692
INFO RUEHZL/EUROPEAN POLITICAL COLLECTIVE
RHMFISS/DEPT OF JUSTICE WASHINGTON DC
RUEATRS/DEPT OF TREASURY WASHINGTON DC
```

```
2009-03-04 15:48:00    09BERN98    Embassy Bern    CONFIDENTIAL
VZCZCXRO9450\
RR RUEHDBU RUEHFL RUEHKW RUEHLA RUEHNP RUEHROV RUEHSR\
DE RUEHSW #0098/01 0631548\
ZNY CCCCC ZZH\
R 041548Z MAR 09\
FM AMEMBASSY BERN\
TO RUEHC/SECSTATE WASHDC 5692\
INFO RUEHZL/EUROPEAN POLITICAL COLLECTIVE\
RHMFISS/DEPT OF JUSTICE WASHINGTON DC\
RUEATRS/DEPT OF TREASURY WASHINGTON DC    C O N F I D E N T I A L SECTION 01 OF 02
BERN 000098 \
\
SIPDIS \
\
DEPT OF JUSTICE FOR B.SWARTZ \
\
E.O. 12958: DECL: 03/04/2019 \
TAGS: ECON EFID EINV BE
SUBJECT: UBS CASE: SWISS PERSPECTIVE AND A WAY FORWARD \
\
Classified By: CDA Leigh Carter for reasons 1.4(b) and (d). \
\
¶1.  (C) Summary.  UBS' handover of client information to the \
Department of Justice incited criticism in numerous press \
articles and from several Swiss political parties calling the \
U.S. action one of extortion and blackmail.  However, the \
step was supported by elements of the moderate to left \
parties.  In discussions with econoff, several banking, \
business, and government representatives expressed disbelief \
at the extraordinary and criminal actions taken by UBS and \
surprise at the Swiss government's lackluster response and \
failure to fine UBS.  The press lamented that the UBS case \
will mark the beginning of the "end of banking secrecy", \
despite public assurances by President (and Finance Minister) \
Hans-Rudolf Merz to the contrary.  The Swiss public and \
government cherish banking secrecy as a (highly-profitable) \
national institution. The public's ire at the U.S. (and EU) \
for pressuring Switzerland should not be underestimated and \
could have a long-lasting negative backlash to bilateral \
relations and increased anti-Americanism.  President Merz's \
overtures for concessions and incremental changes to secrecy \
open the door for a way forward:  approaching Switzerland to \
discuss renegotiation of our bilateral agreement to \
incorporate the broader scope of coverage found in the \
U.S.-Liechtenstein tax agreement, specifically to include tax \
evasion. End Summary. \
\
PRESS CRITICIZE U.S. AS HEAVY HANDED \
------------------------------------ \
\
¶2.  (U) UBS' handover of client information to the Department \
of Justice incited criticism in numerous press articles and \
from several Swiss politicians.  However, the step was \
supported by elements of the moderate to left parties.  As \
the continual lead story in most papers, the majority of \
quoted opinions recognize UBS' criminal conduct, however, \
they equally criticize the U.S. for exerting undue pressure \
in a time of global economic crisis to obtain documents prior \
to the conclusion of Switzerland's legal assistance \
proceedings.  Many articles cite "extortion", "bullying", and \
"blackmail" by the U.S. Department of Justice in forcing UBS' \
and the Swiss government's hand in violating their judicial \
```

handwritten annotations: "US Handover of Client Info", "Anti-Americanism" proceedings and bank secrecy laws.

BUT UBS CONDUCT WENT TOO FAR!

¶3. (C) Despite these press articles, business, banking industry and government representatives expressed disbelief at the extraordinary criminal conduct of UBS bankers. Martin Naville, CEO of Swiss Amcham, told econoff that given the clear criminal actions, he was surprised by the Swiss government's reaction, which he opined made the situation far worse. He criticized the government for failing to provide the documents immediately upon the Federal Council's public announcement to do so, which allowed the courts to become involved and slowed down the process further. Naville, in a press interview, attempted to shore up U.S.-Swiss bilateral relations by stressing that the case is a U.S. domestic affair involving a bank licensed to do business in the U.S., with U.S. clients, and under U.S. laws. He criticized, however, the U.S. for moving forward prior to the conclusion of the legal assistance proceedings. This same opinion was reiterated to econoff by Swiss National Bank Deputy Head of Financial Stability Juerg Blum and other government officials in the financial arena.

¶4. (C) Bank representatives were equally surprised at the degree in which UBS skirted the law and the qualified intermediary agreement. CreditSuisse Managing Director of Public Policy Rene Buholzer stated that Swiss banks' biggest concern is that the U.S. will capitalize on UBS' egregious conduct as fodder to renegotiate the tax treaty and qualified intermediary (QI) agreement. Buholzer commented that the QI was riddled with loopholes that needed to be tightened, but regardless UBS had entered into criminal territory in exploiting them. He also could not understand why the Swiss banking authority, FINMA, did not fine UBS as well, and only gave them a slap on the wrist. Roland Marxer, Liechtenstein Deputy Foreign Minister, who has spent the last year working with the Liechtenstein-U.S. Tax Information Exchange Agreement (TIEA) and its impact on Liechtenstein's banking secrecy laws, also expressed shock that FINMA did not impose criminal fines on UBS.

THE DEMISE OF BANKING SECRECY?

BERN 00000098 002 OF 002

¶5. (C) The media and pundits have questioned whether the UBS case will mark the end of banking secrecy. President Merz, on the other hand, stated in his press conference that the UBS case is an individual incident, involving criminal behavior that was always covered by the U.S.-Swiss bilateral arrangement, and therefore does not call into question banking secrecy. He compared it to money laundering and other financial crimes, and reminded the Swiss that banking secrecy is not designed to protect criminal behavior. Despite Merz' confident assurances in the institution of banking secrecy, the Federal Council created a task force to delve into the UBS criminal case and to determine the best path forward on the pending civil case.

¶6. (C) The industry appears less concerned than expected regarding the fate of banking secrecy. Buholzer stated that he does not equate "the end of secrecy with the end of banking." BSI Bank Director General Vincenzo Piantedosi agreed with this assessment, although he cautioned that a "transition period" would be needed to "absorb excess labor forces" as the asset management business dwindled. Marxer noted that Liechtenstein has not experienced any fall in current wealth management assets since the TIEA was signed, but that the rate of new deposits was declining. Although SNB has not completed a study on the impact of secrecy on wealth management, Blum estimated it would have "some impact", but did not think its loss would affect "too many banks."

¶7. (C) Bankers did warn that a level playing field was necessary to end bank secrecy without undue financial hardship to the Swiss. Both Buholzer and Marxer cited Singapore as a prime player that would benefit from the demise of secrecy in Europe. Piantedosi was not so concerned with non-European countries' markets since they do not offer the same history of reliability and stability, but did express reservations if other European havens, such as Austria, remained secrecy strongholds, while Switzerland did not.

¶8. (C) While the bankers provide an optimistic view should secrecy be abolished, the Swiss public and government cherish

positioned our businesses to be less susceptible to negative market trends if they persist in the coming months and to prosper when markets recover." CreditSuisse remains committed to an integrated business model, citing collaboration through its three businesses (investment banking, asset management, and private banking) as a source of stable, high-margin revenues.

PAYMENT OF BONUSES PROVOKES PUBLIC OUTCRY

¶6. Scathing press comments and public backlash followed UBS' announcement that it would pay out 2 billion Sfr (1.77 billion USD) in bonuses for 2008. The media quoted numerous politicians and pundits calling the bonuses inexplicable and incomprehensible when UBS reported huge 2008 losses and was rescued by state funds. Switzerland's financial regulator, FINMA, which approved the bonus payment, has also been questioned for its decision. UBS originally asked for 3 billion Sfr in bonuses, which was reduced by FINMA. The media and public openly dismissed the grounds given for defending the bonuses such as the fact that all UBS employees are not investment bankers; many had profitable portfolios; the banking compensation structure is based on bonus payments; and that bonuses are needed to retain employees.

¶7. CreditSuisse, which designed a creative bonus structure for 2008, was better received. The bank has issued a portion of its distressed assets as bonuses transferring the risk of further losses to the employees while reducing the bank's exposure. However, some critics argue that given CreditSuisse's losses no bonuses should be paid at all. Others argued that the converted assets should have been handed over at the original value, not marked down to 2008 year-end value.

COMMENT

¶8. Although both banks provide a positive outlook for 2009, there remains considerable uncertainty as to whether these expectations will prove accurate. UBS and CreditSuisse assured clientele throughout 2008 that conditions would improve, major write-offs were completed, and that further capital infusions would not be necessary. However, all of these assurances proved inaccurate.
CARTER

Federal Council requested parliament approval of its bill over the initiative. According to the Federal Council, its revisions would "result in balance between the various governing and executive bodies in a company, create sufficient transparency in the pay packages awarded to top managers, as well as in internal processes, and instigate measures to secure the position of shareholders as the company's owners." The bill provides greater protection to shareholders' assets by requiring fees paid to directors to be approved at the company's annual general meeting.

Lessons Learned: New Regulations

¶13. SNB's Governing Board Vice Chairman Philipp Hildebrand commented that the "financial system needs to be more resilient to possible shocks." The SNB has focused on the need to improve the "shock absorbers": capital and liquidity by implementing regulatory reforms. According to Hildebrand, both of the regulatory measures are in line with proposals made by the Financial Stability and the G20 action plan, a well as the strategy of the Basel Committee on Banking Supervision for implementing lessons from the crisis. He noted that the regulations are intended to supplement Basel II, not to replace it.

¶14. New Capital Adequacy Regulation: The Swiss Federal Banking Commission's reform of the capital adequacy regulation for big banks is designed to increase risk-weighted capital together with the introduction of a leverage ratio. The regulation will require big banks to increase risk-weighted capital. During upswings, banks will be required to considerably exceed the minimum requirements for capital and leverage ratios to ensure a buffer exists to absorb losses during crises. Banks will not be required to comply with the higher risk-weighted capital ratio and leverage ratio until 2013 to allow the banks to recover from the current crisis before implementation.

¶15. Liquidity Ratio: New regulations are in the process of being drafted to address inadequate liquidity. According to Hildebrand, the two big Swiss banks were hit particularly hard by the financial crisis to a large extent as a consequence of their extraordinarily high leverage. De-leveraging amplified the shocks to the financial system. The objective of the new regulation is "to obtain higher liquidity buffers that better reflect the great complexity of liquidity risks. When calculating liquidity requirements for various crisis scenarios, the authorities use internal model calculations by the banks. In order to ensure the comparability and transparency of the internal calculations, the new regime foresees certain standardisations." The conclusion of the project is scheduled for early 2009.

Comment

¶16. Although Switzerland has not yet been effected by the global financial crisis and economic slowdown to the same degree as other advanced economies, the GOS is taking every measure to lessen the eventual impact. With the majority of Swiss exports and imports reliant on the EU and US markets, the GOS will continue to monitor these economies closely and likely adjust internal regulations and stimulus packages in response to any further deterioration in either economy.
CARTER

Cable Viewer

Page 1 of 2

KEEP US STRONG
HELP WIKILEAKS KEEP GOVERNMENTS OPEN

Viewing cable 09BERN73, SWITZERLAND'S TOP BANKS FACE CONTINUING STRAIN

If you are new to these pages, please read an introduction on the structure of a cable as well as how to discuss them with others. See also the FAQs

Reference ID	Created	Released	Classification	Origin
09BERN73	2009-02-18 12:42	2011-08-30 01:44	UNCLASSIFIED	Embassy Bern

```
VZCZCXYZ0000
RR RUEHWEB

DE RUEHSW #0073/01 0491242
ZNR UUUUU ZZH
R 181242Z FEB 09
FM AMEMBASSY BERN
TO SECSTATE WASHDC 5658
```

Currently released so far...
251287 / 251,287

Articles
Brazil
Sri Lanka
United Kingdom
Sweden
Global
United States
Latin America
Egypt
Jordan
Yemen
Thailand

Browse latest releases
2011/08

Browse by creation date
66 72 73 75 78 79 85 86
87 88 89 90 91 92 93 94
95 96 97 98 99 00 01 02
03 04 05 06 07 08 09 10

Browse by origin
A B C D F G H I
J K L M N O P Q
R S T U V W Y Z

Browse by tag
A B C D E F G H
I J K L M N O P
Q R S T U V W X
Y Z

Browse by classification
CONFIDENTIAL
CONFIDENTIAL//NOFORN
SECRET
SECRET//NOFORN
UNCLASSIFIED
UNCLASSIFIED//FOR OFFICIAL USE ONLY

Community resources
Follow us on Twitter

UNCLAS BERN 000073

SIPDIS

E.O. 12958: N/A
TAGS: ECON EFIN EINV SZ
SUBJECT: SWITZERLAND'S TOP BANKS FACE CONTINUING STRAIN

¶1. Switzerland's leading banks, UBS and CreditSuisse, reported record-breaking losses in the fourth quarter of 2008, highlighting the continuing financial strain on Switzerland's banking industry. UBS and CreditSuisse announced 2008 annual losses of 17.1 billion USD and 7.1 billion USD, respectively. Despite these massive losses, the banks maintain a positive outlook with an expectation of profits in 2009. However there is skepticism that UBS, facing client distrust and potential legal fines from the U.S., will pull so rapidly from the financial crisis. Public and media backlash against fat cat bonuses hit an all time high when UBS announced it would pay 2 billion in bonuses despite receiving state aid.

BANKS REPORT MAJOR LOSSES

¶2. Switzerland's leading banks reported worse-than-expected losses in the fourth quarter of 2008, highlighting the continuing financial strain on Switzerland's banking industry. UBS, Switzerland's largest bank and the world's leading wealth manager, announced a fourth quarter net loss of 8.1 billion Sfr (7 billion USD) totaling a 2008 annual loss of 19.7 billion Sfr (17.1 billion USD); the largest annual loss in the history of Swiss banking. CreditSuisse, Switzerland's second largest bank, trailed behind with 6.0 billion Sfr (5.2 billion USD) for the fourth quarter and full-year 2008 losses of 8.2 billion Sfr (7.1 billion USD).

¶3. UBS' financial woes are spreading from its investment banking division, once an isolated injury from toxic asset write-offs, to its wealth management division. UBS' need for government infused funding of 60 billion Sfr and the ongoing investigation by the U.S. over claims of aiding tax evasion have done little to build or maintain client trust with clients reportedly pulling 58.2 billion Sfr (50.6 billion USD) (about 2 percent of total assets) from UBS' wealth management division in the fourth quarter.

BANKS CAUTIOUS BUT UPBEAT ABOUT 2009

¶4. Despite massive losses, UBS reported an "encouraging start to the year" with net new money in January and pointed to a strong capital ratio for 2008 year-end of 11.5 percent and a total capital adequacy ratio of 15.5 percent (largely assisted by a government rescue package). UBS stated that its "near-term outlook remains cautious" and that it intends to further reduce its risk position, risk weighted assets and operating costs. UBS will continue to implement its new strategy of dividing wealth management into two new divisions and restructuring from an integrated approach to refocus on Swiss core businesses.

¶5. CreditSuisse reported on February 11 "a strong start to 2009 and was profitable across all division year to date." It reported "one of the strongest capital ratios in the industry" at 13.3 percent for year-end 2008. The overall risk in investment banking was reduced in 2008 leading to a "significantly lower risk profile." CreditSuisse CEO Brady Dougan expanded on the positive outlook by stating, "We have

[handwritten annotations:]
UBS client distrust
+ U.S. legal fines.

UBS
Tax evasion
+ client mistrust
eroding Bank

2 divisions

http://wikileaks.org/cable/2009/02/09BERN73.html

9/3/2011

continues to react to an increasingly negative economic outlook, even though it has not been as severely impacted as other advanced economies. The SNB mirrored the U.S. Federal Reserve Bank by further relaxing its monetary policy several times over the previous three months. SNB lowered the interest rate 50 basis points on November 6, 100 basis points on November 20, and 50 basis points on December 11 resulting in a current interest rate of 0.5% and a decrease of the target range for the three month Libor to 0 to 1 percent.

¶6. According to SNB Governing Board Chairman Jean-Pierre Roth, the reasons behind the monetary policy rest on three factors: 1) the international economic outlook deteriorated markedly, which negatively impacted forecasts for the Swiss economy; 2) the financial market crisis intensified; and 3) prices for raw materials and oil plummeted, which combined with the worsening economic outlook, led to a marked improvement in inflation and maneuvering room for the SNB.

Economic Stimulus Packages Announced

¶7. On November 12, the Federal Council announced the first economic stimulus package following the downward revisions of economic forecasts. The package envisioned to boost economic activity and employment involves an infusion of up to Sfr 1.5 billion ($1.2 billion) (0.2 percent of 2008 GDP). Immediate measures included Sfr 66 million to move natural hazard management projects forward, Sfr 20 million for federal civil construction projects, and Sfr45 million for residential construction. The GOS plans to lift a freeze on credits totaling Sfr205 million in January 2009, which will be directed toward transportation, education, farming and defense. Lastly, the GOS will pay back funds set aside as a crisis reserve paid into by 650 companies totaling Sfr550 million.

¶8. On December 21, the GOS announced a second stimulus package totaling Sfr650 million ($590 million). The package will be implemented in Spring 2009. Details regarding the use of the money have not been provided. The GOS has already indicated that a third stimulus package may be necessary if Switzerland does not recover by 2010.

Financial Crisis Impact on Swiss Banks

¶9. As reported in ref A, the GOS provided UBS, Switzerland's largest bank, a $60 billion rescue package that has been approved by Parliament. The SNB has now created a special purpose vehicle, the SNB StabFund, to acquire the illiquid assets of UBS. The first tranche of assets was acquired on December 16, whereby UBS transferred slightly over 2000 securities positions worth $16.4 billion. The majority of the assets were US and European residential and commercial mortgage backed securities. Speculation regarding further massive write-offs by UBS in the fourth quarter of 2008 lead to a 5 percent drop in UBS' stock on January 12, 2009.

¶10. CreditSuisse, Switzerland's second largest bank, avoided government intervention by boosting its capital Sfr10 billion through private investors. The capital infusion proved priceless when CreditSuisse needed to write off Sfr3 billion in losses in the fourth quarter of 2008.

Executive Bonuses at Risk

¶11. UBS executives voluntarily agreed to forgo their bonuses following UBS' request for GOS assistance and the bank's massive write-offs. In November, UBS former Chief Executive Peter Wuffli said he would forgo his Sfr12 million bonus. Following suit, former Chairman Marcel Ospel, Vice-President Stephan Haeringer and former Finance Chief Marco Sutor agreed to waive their bonuses worth Sfr 33 million. UBS announced a revised bonus structure so that future bonuses will be paid only upon reaching long-term results.

¶12. Regardless of UBS' new bonus system, a general outcry from the public for the government to restrict CEO bonuses continues to support the popular initiative "Against fat-cat salaries", which was submitted to the government on February 26, 2008. The initiative would outlaw golden parachutes, golden handshakes, and bonuses, and require the annual general meeting to vote on total pay awarded to executives. On December 5, the Federal Council responded to the initiative by issuing a comprehensive bill revising the company and accounting law as an indirect counter-proposal. The bill is more moderate that the public initiative. The

Cable Viewer

Viewing cable 08BERN552, DAS GARBER'S MEETINGS WITH SWISS AND LIECHTENSTEIN

If you are new to these pages, please read an introduction on the structure of a cable as well as how to discuss them with others. See also the FAQs

Reference ID	Created	Released	Classification	Origin
08BERN552	2008-10-29 09:34	2011-08-30 01:44	UNCLASSIFIED//FOR OFFICIAL USE ONLY	Embassy Bern

```
VZCZCXYZ0008
RR RUEHWEB

DE RUEHSW #0552/01 3030934
ZNR UUUUU ZZH
R 290934Z OCT 08
FM AMEMBASSY BERN
TO RUEHC/SECSTATE WASHDC 5407
INFO RUEATRS/DEPT OF TREASURY WASHINGTON DC
```

UNCLAS BERN 000552

SENSITIVE
SIPDIS

DEPT FOR EUR (J.GARBER), EUR/CE (Y.SAINT-ANDRE), EUR/ERA, AND EB; PLEASE PASS TO USTR FOR J.BUNTIN

E.O. 12958: N/A
TAGS: ECON ETRD EFIN SZ
SUBJECT: DAS GARBER'S MEETINGS WITH SWISS AND LIECHTENSTEIN OFFICIALS (OCT 20-21)

REF: A. BERN 544
     B. BERN 546

¶1. (SBU) Summary: During an October 20 meeting with DAS Garber, senior Swiss Department of Foreign Affairs (EDA) contacts outlined their priorities for U.S.-Swiss relations. EDA Americas Division Head Yvonne Baumann requested support for another round of senior-level U.S.-Swiss bilateral meetings under the rubric of our MoU-based "Framework for Intensified Cooperation." Muslim issues, human rights, the Balkans, the Middle East, disarmament and nonproliferation, UN sanctions implementation, the OSCE, the Caucuses, and Russia/Georgia were identified by the Swiss officials as potential areas for continued U.S.-Swiss coordination. Swiss officials at the State Secretariat for Economic Affairs (SECO) informed DAS Garber that they were happy with the progress under the Trade and Investment Cooperation Agreement, including the recent signing of the E-Commerce Declaration and the soon-to-be finalized Safe Harbor Agreement. Swiss Department of Finance officials commented that, while the GOS lowered their initial 2008 growth forecast of 1.7 percent to less than 1 percent due to the underestimated impact of the financial crisis on the EU, the GOS is not pessimistic overall. Liechtenstein's Ambassador to Switzerland told DAS Garber October 21 that Liechtenstein is at an advantage with regard to the financial crisis because the country is not an investment banking center so was not impacted by the first wave of write-downs. With respect to ongoing discussions with Liechtenstein regarding banking secrecy, DAS Garber emphasized that worldwide trends toward greater connectivity and the increasing use of financial networks by inappropriate individuals and organizations require that all countries work together to stop nefarious activity. End Summary.

SWISS EDA EMPHASIZES DIALOGUE

¶2. (SBU) During an informal October 20 lunch meeting hosted by Department of Foreign Affairs (EDA) Americas Division Head Yvonne Baumann for EUR DAS Judith Garber, senior Swiss EDA contacts outlined their priorities for U.S.-Swiss relations. Ambassador Baumann reviewed the history of bilateral meetings held under the rubric of our MoU-based "Framework for Intensified Cooperation." Emphasizing that there is an "abundance of issues of common interest," she requested DAS Garber's support for a next senior-level Framework meeting in Bern. Baumann added that the EDA would like to organize an experts-level Framework meeting ("Joint Working Group") in Switzerland soon. She remarked that "the U.S. delegations need not be large," but continuing such meetings would allow us to "meet the commitment we made when we started this initiative." DAS Garber responded that in light of the transition, it is not possible to schedule senior USG officials now, but it should still be possible to explore options for a next JWG meeting.

¶3. (SBU) EDA Human Security Division Head Thomas Greminger identified Muslim Issues, Human Rights dialogue exchanges (e.g., China), the Balkans (particularly Kosovo), and the Middle East as areas for continued U.S.-Swiss coordination. EDA Director for Security Affairs Jacques Pitteloud said that CT and intel cooperation are ongoing and will remain so in their respective channels. At the political level, he flagged increasing GOS concern about the NPT, with a view to the 2010 Review Conference (RevCon). Ambassador Pitteloud projected that Switzerland increasingly will emphasize nuclear disarmament issues in the run-up to the RevCon, fearing that without more progress on disarmament, it will be increasingly difficult to achieve nonproliferation goals.

¶4. (SBU) Ambassador Christine Schraner-Burgener, EDA Coordinator for Counterterrorism, emphasized Switzerland's support for a proposal it has made along with several other countries to develop a review panel that would provide expert, non-binding advice to the UNSCR 1267 Sanctions Committee regarding whether certain individuals should be removed from the sanctions list. Schraner-Burgener regretted that the proposal has not received more support in the UNSC, noting that the GOS would appreciate USG support. She expressed concern that European court decisions might create dilemmas for countries seeking to enforce the sanctions while meeting their human rights obligations.

[handwritten left margin: State Dept. Coord. for counterterrorism]
[handwritten right margin: GOS wants USG support]

¶5. (SBU) EDA European Affairs Division Chief Christian Meuwly observed that the GOS had firmly supported Kosovo independence and would remain engaged there. He said that he would welcome more dialogue with the USG regarding the Caucuses and mentioned that he would be very interested in meeting with DAS Bryza soon. Meuwly referred to the OSCE's current difficulties and suggested that thought perhaps should be given to holding a summit in 2010 to seek to reaffirm the values and principles of the organization. Meuwly noted that Switzerland is setting up an Interest Section for Russia in Georgia. He said that the GOS is not doing this for self-promotion, but "because Switzerland is still a 'brand name' for this kind of work," and because it provides an opportunity for Georgia to have an Interest Section (managed by Sweden) in Moscow, to assist the approximately 750,000 Georgians living in Russia.

BILATERAL TRADE TIES STRONG

¶6. (SBU) The Swiss Department of Economic Affairs (SECO) Deputy Head of Bilateral Economic Affairs Erwin Bollinger, Deputy Head of Americas Bilateral Economic Relations Guido Barsuglio, and Deputy Head of Taskforce Sanctions Thomas Graf informed DAS Garber October 20 that they were happy with the progress under the Trade and Investment Cooperation Agreement, including the recent signing of the E-Commerce Declaration by USTR Schwab and Economic Affairs Minister Doris Leuthard and the soon-to-be finalized Safe Harbor Agreement. SECO hopes the Safe Harbor Agreement will be concluded by the end of November. Other than referencing on-going dialogue with U.S. Department of Agriculture to gain import access to the U.S. beef market, SECO described bilateral economic relations as "perfect."

SWISS OPTIMISTIC ABOUT FINANCIAL CRISIS

¶7. (SBU) Department of Finance Deputy Head of International Finance and Monetary Policy Division Urs Plavec and Senior Economist and Deputy Head of Economic and Monetary Policy Barbara Schleffer met with DAS Garber October 20 to discuss the current financial crisis. Plavec stated that while the GOS lowered their initial 2008 growth forecast of 1.7 percent to less than 1 percent due to the underestimated impact of the financial crisis on the EU, the GOS is not pessimistic overall. He commented that he "does not expect a severe recession." Plavec expects growth to be back to normal by 2009 (normal being 1.5-2.5 percent).

[handwritten right margin: 2008 Financial Crisis begins]

¶8. (SBU) In defense of this rather optimistic position, Plavec pointed out that while they are pessimistic about EU exports in general, many of Switzerland's exports are "inelastic to the business cycle, such as pharmaceuticals," and will not be affected. In addition, he noted that Switzerland did not have a housing sector bubble or a credit

[handwritten right margin: Housing Sector Bubble]

crunch. Swiss banks are well-capitalized so the global credit freeze left domestic credit and housing lines unaltered. In pointing to somewhat out-dated August figures, Schlaffer mirrored Plavec's optimism by stating that consumption was up, the labor market was strong, and that the large contraction of industry purchasing power would not greatly affect Switzerland because the service sector strongly out-distances industry as the largest contributor. In addressing the need for Switzerland's first rescue package for its largest bank, UBS, Plavec cited bolstering confidence as the impetus for the assistance (reftels). Plavec conceded that all of this optimism is dependent on the expected success of the EU and US global rescue plans.

¶9. (SBU) Plavec suggested that global meetings to respond to the crisis should include the BRIC countries and the BrettQWoods insitQs. Measures to be addressed, according to Plavec, include CEO salaries and the need to minimize overreactions; "Allow markets to play, but don't allow market failures."

UBS Financial Rescue.

LIECHTENSTEIN WATCHING FINANCIAL CRISIS

¶10. (SBU) According to Liechtenstein Ambassador to Switzerland Hubert Buchel, the financial crisis has not yet affected Liechtenstein. In an October 21 meeting with DAS Garber, he commented that Liechtenstein is at an advantage because it is not an investment banking center so was not impacted by the first wave of write-downs. The banks also have a large capital basis to fall back on. He did note that the global solution to the crisis is still crucial because these banks are affected by the declining stock markets. Buchel remarked that Liechtenstein has no power to influence the global situation so the country's banks are just following the market and will rely on the Swiss National Bank (SNB) as lender of last resort, if necessary. (Note: Liechtenstein does not have a central bank. The country's banks report to and are assisted by the SNB in accordance with a bilateral currency treaty. End Note)

¶11. (SBU) With respect to ongoing discussions with Liechtenstein regarding banking secrecy, DAS Garber emphasized to Buchel that worldwide trends toward greater connectivity and the increasing use of financial networks by inappropriate individuals and organizations require that all countries work together to stop nefarious activity. Buchel acknowledged that in criminal cases, accounts must be open. He commented that the original view in Liechtenstein was that tax issues revolved around varying definitions of tax fraud and tax evasion, and that tax issues were not banking issues, but relegated to client responsibility. He confirmed that this view has changed to one that recognizes the importance of international exchange at the EU and bilateral level.
CONEWAY

Muslim Counter-Terrorism Finance.

Cable Viewer

Viewing cable 09BERN23, UPDATE OF SWISS RESPONSE TO FINANCIAL CRISIS

If you are new to these pages, please read an introduction on the structure of a cable as well as how to discuss them with others. See also the FAQs

Reference ID	Created	Released	Classification	Origin
09BERN23	2009-01-13 10:18	2011-08-30 01:44	UNCLASSIFIED	Embassy Bern

```
VZCZCXYZ0000
RR RUEHWEB

DE RUEHSW #0023/01 0131018
ZNR UUUUU ZZH
R 131018Z JAN 09
FM AMEMBASSY BERN
TO SECSTATE WASHDC 5599

UNCLAS BERN 000023

SIPDIS

DEPT FOR EEB/IFD/CMA AND EEB/EPPD

E.O. 12958: N/A
TAGS: EFIN ECON SZ
SUBJECT: UPDATE OF SWISS RESPONSE TO FINANCIAL CRISIS

REF: A. BERN 544
     B. BERN 546
     C. BERN 552
     D. EMAIL L.FRERIKSEN/J.KESSLER RE: ECONOMIC MATRIX
        INPUT 10/23/08
```

¶1. Summary. Switzerland's economic outlook has steadily declined over the past three months with negative growth forecasts, increased unemployment, and industrial sectors starting to show the signs of stress. Despite the economic downturn, bank lending practices have not been impacted. The GOS has taken several actions to stem the recent economic and financial downturn, including a relaxation of monetary policy, and implementation of its UBS rescue package (Ref A). Following a public initiative, the GOS will further regulate bank executive salaries. The GOS restructured capital and leverage ratio regulations and is in the process of introducing liquidity ratio regulations to lessen the impact of future financial downturns. End Summary.

Econ Crisis?
UBS rescue

Economic Outlook Deteriorates

¶2. The Swiss outlook and economic projections have steadily declined over the past three months. The GOS altered growth forecasts from a marked slowdown with very low growth in 2009 to a forecast of negative 0.8 percent GDP growth for all of 2009. With the exception of consumption, all demand components are expected to decline. The KOF Swiss Economic Institute's economic growth barometer, which measures the economy's likely performance for the next six months, reached a five year low. Unemployment rates climbed from 2.5 percent in October to 2.7 percent in November and to 3.0 percent in December, and is expected to rise further to near 4.0 percent by late 2009. Many industry sectors are beginning to show signs of the economic crisis, although a few sectors are still posting positive sales.

¶3. Lending practices continue to hold in Switzerland. The Swiss National Bank (SNB) conducted regular surveys of 20 major Swiss banks to follow lending patterns. The SNB reports that in the vast majority of institutions surveyed, no lending restrictions were announced in the third quarter of 2008. Only 15 percent of banks reported that lending practices had become slightly more restrictive.

¶4. While the SNB continues to monitor the economic outlook, SNB officials and State Secretary for Economic Affairs Jean Daniel Gerber cautioned through press releases that it is hard to predict the impact of the financial crisis on Switzerland until there is greater certainty regarding the U.S. economy.

Relaxation of Monetary Policy

¶5. Since reftel reporting on the financial crisis, the GOS

Cable Viewer

Viewing cable 09BERN99, RESPONSE TO REQUEST FOR INFORMATION ON CRITICAL

If you are new to these pages, please read an introduction on the structure of a cable as well as how to discuss them with others. See also the FAQs.

Reference ID	Created	Released	Classification	Origin
09BERN99	2009-03-05 15:35	2011-08-30 01:44	UNCLASSIFIED	Embassy Bern

```
VZCZCXYZ0000
RR RUEHWEB

DE RUEHSW #0099 0641535
ZNR UUUUU ZZH
R 051535Z MAR 09
FM AMEMBASSY BERN
TO SECSTATE WASHDC 5694

UNCLAS BERN 000099

SIPDIS

E.O. 12958: N/A
TAGS: ASEC ECON PTER PREL PGOV EAID EFIN SZ
SUBJECT: RESPONSE TO REQUEST FOR INFORMATION ON CRITICAL
INFRASTRUCTURE AND KEY RESOURCES

REF: STATE 015113
```

¶1. Post has identified two entities that fit into the categories supplied by S/CT: the Swiss pharmaceutical industry and the Swiss banking system.

¶2. The Swiss pharmaceutical industry is located in Basel and produces internationally recognized products to combat Avian Influenza, cancer, tuberculosis, influenza, and other global illnesses. These same firms, lead by Novartis and Roche, import and store vast quantities of precursors to make the pharmaceutical products for the world and have supplies of drugs on their facilities, if needed, to react to global outbreaks of disease. Any actions that might disable or destroy these facilities could severely impact the World Health Organization's and the world's ability to react to a major pandemic or health crisis.

¶3. The Swiss financial system is the 4th largest in the world trailing only New York, London and Tokyo. The main center in Zurich and the secondary center in Geneva control one-third of the world's private overseas wealth (Sfr 3.82 trillion). Given the current global financial crisis, an attack that successfully shut down the system or severely crippled confidence in the banking system could significantly impact the global financial network and further escalate the severity of the global economic downturn. Institutions of note that are located in Switzerland include UBS, the world's largest wealth manager, Credit Suisse, and the Bank of International Settlements.
CARTER

[Handwritten annotations: "State Dept. Counterterror (State CT)"; "Swiss banks & pharmaceuticals se- as Targets for Terrorist actions"]

http://wikileaks.org/cable/2009/03/09BERN99.html

Cable Viewer

Viewing cable 08BERN527, LIECHTENSTEIN DIALOGUE: THE FUTURE OF BANK SECRECY

If you are new to these pages, please read an introduction on the structure of a cable as well as how to discuss them with others. See also the FAQs

Reference ID	Created	Released	Classification	Origin
08BERN527	2008-10-10 14:44	2011-08-30 01:44	UNCLASSIFIED//FOR OFFICIAL USE ONLY	Embassy Bern

VZCZCXYZ0012
RR RUEHWEB

DE RUEHSW #0527/01 2841444
ZNR UUUUU ZZH
R 101444Z OCT 08 ZDK
FM AMEMBASSY BERN
TO RUEHC/SECSTATE WASHDC 5379
INFO RHMFIUU/DEPT OF JUSTICE WASHINGTON DC
RUEATRS/DEPT OF TREASURY WASHINGTON DC

UNCLAS BERN 000527

SENSITIVE
SIPDIS

E.O. 12958: N/A
TAGS: ECON EFIN ETRD SZ
SUBJECT: LIECHTENSTEIN DIALOGUE: THE FUTURE OF BANK SECRECY

¶1. (U) Summary. At the annual forum "Liechtenstein Dialogue," bankers and financial wealth management companies met in Liechtenstein to discuss private wealth management, and more particularly the future vision of a financial center built on banking secrecy. While the panel speakers ranged from die-hard defenders of banking secrecy to a representative of OECD's Centre for Tax Policy, the local consensus revealed that 1) Liechtenstein and Switzerland's banking secrecy policies are needed to keep these small countries competitive and should not be eliminated due to fears of having secrecy "criminalized by voices overseas." However, modifications to the system, such as tax sharing information agreements, may be necessary to meet modern demands and an ever-evolving financial system; 2) Liechtenstein views the U.S. Department of Justice's case against its largest bank, LGT, as an investigation not just of one bank, but an affront to Liechtenstein's financial center policies and country's culture of privacy; and 3) Switzerland sees the similar investigation of UBS, its largest bank, as an individual bank specific case and not a reflection on Switzerland's banking policies. End Summary.

BANKING SECRECY: NOT TO BE GIVEN UP LIGHTLY

¶2. (U) At the annual forum "Liechtenstein Dialogue," bankers and financial wealth management companies met in Liechtenstein to discuss private wealth management, and more particularly the future vision of a financial center built on banking secrecy. Both Switzerland and Liechtenstein's financial centers have come under increasing attacks over the last few years for abetting tax evaders and harboring illicit funds; the most notable case being the current U.S. Department of Justice investigation of LGT and UBS, Liechtenstein and Switzerland's largest banks, respectively, for assisting U.S. taxpayers with tax evasion.

¶3. (U) While the panel speakers ranged from die-hard defenders of banking secrecy to a representative of OECD's Centre for Tax Policy, Swiss Bankers Association Chairman Pierre Mirabaud's comments, which received much applause, appeared to sum up local sentiment on banking secrecy. According to Mirabaud, bankers have enormous amounts of detailed information on their clients that fully justify client privacy. He questioned whether banks should play the role of "tax collectors, spies, and police of the state." He also noted that "secrecy is a competitive advantage" that is "clearly one factor in the success of (Liechtenstein and Swiss) banking." If small countries have this competitive advantage, "why give it up?"

¶4. (U) UBS Board Member Jurg Zeltner supported Mirabaud by adding that secrecy should not be "played down" as it protects client privacy and that it should not be eliminated for fear of having secrecy "criminalized by voices overseas." While Zeltner sympathized with the tax authority of the state, he also questioned whether UBS is co-responsible for tax evasion or fraud, and if, yes, where does the responsibility start and when should it override the protection of clients.

¶5. (U) Despite this local pro-banking rhetoric in support of secrecy, all panelists agreed that banking secrecy alone was not the only advantage to their local financial centers. While the bankers were not yet willing to admit that more transparency is needed, they agreed that to lose secrecy would not mark the demise of their financial centers. As one speaker noted, many other positives could be highlighted, such as political stability. More importantly, there was a general understanding that banking secrecy needed to evolve along with financial systems. For example, mechanisms such as the tax information sharing agreement being negotiated between Liechtenstein and the U.S., were likely to provide the necessary state enforcement tools without fully breaching secrecy and client privacy.

LGT: REPRESENTING LIECHTENSTEIN'S BANKING SYSTEM

¶6. (U) It became apparent from panel discussions that Liechtenstein views the U.S. Department of Justice's case against its largest bank, LGT, as an investigation not just of one bank, but an affront to Liechtenstein's financial center policies and the country's culture of privacy. According to Fritz Kaiser, Founder of Liechtenstein's Private Wealth Council, the investigation did not just call into question banking secrecy, but the country's culture of privacy. Fritz noted third party information is always kept in confidence and that transparency challenges this fundamental ideal. He highlighted that Liechtenstein did not want an American or German culture that praises transparency over privacy rights.

¶7. (SBU) Urban Eberle, CEO of Bank Alpinum, took pains is assuring the DCM on the margins of the meetings that LGT was not operated like UBS, whose bankers intentionally skirted U.S. tax laws by aiding and abetting its U.S. clients through measures such as smuggling diamonds out of the U.S. in toothpaste. Eberle said, "I would never smuggle anything to one of my clients" as if that was a measure of responsible banking practices. Fritz defended Liechtenstein banking practices by commenting, "Liechtenstein is not the bad guy. Around the world big law firms stretched tax planning and used Liechtenstein and Switzerland."

UBS: AN ANOMALY IN SWISS BANKING?

¶8. (U) Switzerland, on the other hand, views, at least publicly, the similar investigation of UBS, its largest bank, as an individual bank specific case and not a reflection on Switzerland's banking policies. UBS Board Member Zeltner, although couching his comments with "I am not a UBS spokesperson", noted that "what has happened in the U.S. is a bilateral matter between the bank and the U.S. government and does not affect Swiss banking as a whole and it does not affect the Swiss as a government or financial center." His statement received general agreement from the audience, which may be wishful thinking.

¶9. (SBU) Wishful thinking was very much in evidence at the two day event. The first two speakers initially declined to field questions from the Luxembourg Ambassador on the current financial crisis. When the Ambassador walked out in frustration after the first two sessions, the organizers quickly huddled, agreed to take those questions, and invited the Ambassador to rejoin the dialogue (all in front of the journalists also in attendance). The mood remained optimistic: "despite the turmoil, there will be a tomorrow!"

COMMENT

¶9. (SBU) Despite panelists providing both points of view on banking secrecy, the overall impression given by the banking industry audience was that secrecy should remain an advantage to Switzerland's and Liechtenstein's financial centers and that resistance must be weathered against U.S. and other European pressure to change for their "political whims." However, as US embassy Bern has often seen, there is a disconnect between the public dialogue and the reality of what the professionals and government representatives have actually accepted: in this case, modifications of banking agreement only applied to the specific case of UBS, Widmer-Schlumpf countered that the tax treaty language "tax fraud and the like" coupled with the recently adopted OECD standards for administrative assistance could open the door for similar requests for information from other Swiss banks if those banks had committed similar egregious acts like UBS. President Merz, who previously expressed regret at UBS' unacceptable actions (reftel), appealed to Swiss banks to respect U.S. laws and the Qualified Intermediary regulations.

NO CLEAR TREND IN MEDIA OPINIONS

¶3. (U) Media commentators and political pundits covered a range of opinions from declaring the agreement a true victory for the U.S. to an absolute win for Switzerland. Neither the political persuasion of the papers nor the region of the country defined a clear Swiss opinion about the effects of the agreement. Newspaper articles ranged from claiming the broader interpretation of "tax fraud and the like" in the tax agreement was the "last nail in the coffin of banking secrecy" to citing legal experts that announced Switzerland had been the clear winner because Switzerland's legal procedures had not been compromised. Another paper took a completely different approach arguing that even though the agreement was the only tenable solution, it placed undue pressure on Switzerland's governmental system of separation of powers between the Federal Council and the Tax Administration Court.

BUSINESS RELIEVED BY AGREEMENT

¶4. (C) Unlike the media, business leaders universally expressed relief that the UBS case was resolved. Swiss American Chamber of Commerce CEO Martin Naville told econoff that the agreement was a positive outcome for two reasons: 1) the agreement was signed under a partnership spirit without the adversarial tone expressed in previous months; and 2) the exchange of information will be in accordance with the double taxation treaty. He highlighted that political will to ratify the recently revised treaty would not exist if the IRS did not conform to the requirements of the original treaty. Naville expected there to be some domestic policy noise about Switzerland relinquishing its sovereignty and its tradition of bank secrecy, but these opinions would not cloud the positive impact of the resolution.

¶5. (C) Thomas Pletscher, Executive Board Member of EconomieSuisse, Switzerland's largest umbrella organization for Swiss business and industry, echoed Naville's sentiments calling the agreement a "relief." Pletscher stated that the overall industry response had been positive. He told econoff that a long drawn out court case posed "a danger of overshadowing" and "seriously damaging" otherwise good bilateral relations. In addition, the agreement established a procedure to avoid a clash of the two countries' legal frameworks. Pletscher was not concerned about the agreement breaching Switzerland's banking secrecy. He stated that the agreement marked the "end of Hollywood's version of banking secrecy" which was always an inaccurate portrayal. Banking secrecy was designed to protect individual privacy, not to hide criminal conduct.

¶6. (C) The Swiss Bankers Association's Head of U.S. Affairs Heinreich Siegmann reiterated the relief that the complicated matter had been resolved amicably and within the Swiss legal framework. Siegmann informed econoff that maintaining the stability of Swiss law was crucial to the continuing success of the Swiss financial center.

COMMENT

¶7. (C) Post expects that the UBS case will provide the Swiss media fodder for claiming the U.S. bullied Switzerland into an agreement that marks the demise of banking secrecy, a national heritage. However, Swiss government and business leaders generally view the agreement as a mutual compromise that protects Swiss sovereignty while enabling the U.S. to enforce its tax laws. The UBS case was a dark cloud over bilateral relations, with concerns it could escalate to a seriously damaging event similar to the Holocaust asset case a decade ago. Current Swiss opinion indicates, however, that the agreement will mollify all but the most anti-American voices and leave our bilateral relations relatively unscathed.
BEYER

Cable Viewer

Viewing cable 09BERN350, SWISS REACTION TO UBS AGREEMENT

If you are new to these pages, please read an introduction on the structure of a cable as well as how to discuss them with others. See also the FAQs

Reference ID	Created	Released	Classification	Origin
09BERN350	2009-08-20 15:10	2011-08-30 01:44	CONFIDENTIAL	Embassy Bern

Appears in these articles:
http://www.letemps.ch/swiss_papers

```
VZCZCXYZ0000
RR RUEHWEB

DE RUEHSW #0350/01 2321510
ZNY CCCCC ZZH
R 201510Z AUG 09
FM AMEMBASSY BERN
TO RUEHC/SECSTATE WASHDC 6015
INFO RHMFISS/DEPT OF JUSTICE WASHINGTON DC
RUEATRS/DEPT OF TREASURY WASHINGTON DC
```

2009-08-20 15:10:00   09BERN350   Embassy Bern   CONFIDENTIAL   09BERN68

```
VZCZCXYZ0000\
RR RUEHWEB\
\
DE RUEHSW #0350/01 2321510\
ZNY CCCCC ZZH\
R 201510Z AUG 09\
FM AMEMBASSY BERN\
TO RUEHC/SECSTATE WASHDC 6015\
INFO RHMFISS/DEPT OF JUSTICE WASHINGTON DC\
RUEATRS/DEPT OF TREASURY WASHINGTON DC\
      C O N F I D E N T I A L BERN 000350 \
\
SIPDIS \
\
DEPT OF JUSTICE FOR B.SWARTZ, \
L/EB FOR K.KIZER AND W.TEEL \
\
E.O. 12958: DECL: 08/19/2019 \
TAGS: ECON EFIN EREL SZ
SUBJECT: SWISS REACTION TO UBS AGREEMENT \
\
REF: BERN 68 \
\
Classified By: DCM L.Carter for reasons 1.4(b) and (d). \
\
¶1. (C) Summary. President and Finance Minister Hans-Rudolf \
Merz, Justice Minister Eveline Widmer-Schlumpf, and Foreign \
Affairs Minister Micheline Calmy-Rey in an August 19 press \
conference praised the UBS agreement as the only possible \
solution and a "Peace Treaty." The Ministers were quick to \
limit the reach of the agreement to UBS only, although the \
Justice Minister recognized the agreement could open the door \
for similar requests from other Swiss banks if those banks \
committed similar egregious acts like UBS. Media \
commentators and political pundits covered a range of \
opinions from declaring the agreement a true victory for the \
U.S. to an absolute win for Switzerland. Unlike the media, \
local business leaders and the Swiss Bankers Association \
universally expressed relief that the UBS case was resolved. \
The UBS case had been a dark cloud over bilateral relations, \
with concerns it could escalate to a seriously damaging event \
similar to the Holocaust asset case a decade ago. Current \
Swiss opinion indicates, however, that the agreement will \
mollify all but the most anti-American voices and leave our \
bilateral relations relatively unscathed. End Summary. \
\
--------------------------------------------- \
FEDERAL COUNCILLORS PRAISE RESOLUTION, GOOD BILATERAL \
RELATIONS \
--------------------------------------------- \
\
¶2. (U) President and Finance Minister Hans-Rudolf Merz, \
Justice Minister Eveline Widmer-Schlumpf, and Foreign \
Minister Micheline Calmy-Rey discussed the resolution of the \
UBS case in a press conference on August 19. Widmer-Schlumpf \
touted the bilateral agreement as the only possible solution. \
She commented that it was necessary to preserve the Swiss \
legal system against the unilateral enforcement of US \
regulations, which could include freezing UBS' US-based \
assets. Calmy-Rey called the agreement a "Peace Treaty" and \
praised the good Swiss connections with the US for making the \
agreement possible. While President Merz emphasized that the \
```

http://wikileaks.org/cable/2009/08/09BERN350.html

advised that more bio and medical data had been received today and was being delivered via a separate channel. *(CENTCOM provided Intel)*

¶5. (S) At this point, Leuthard emphasized that these two actions were "elements showing that Switzerland is committed to resolving all issues between our countries." To bring home the point, she reiterated that this resolve extended especially to finding a political solution to the UBS case.

CARTER

Cable Viewer ☆ |copy

Viewing cable 09BERN273, SWITZERLAND SHUTTING DOWN COLENCO'S BUSINESS WITH

If you are new to these pages, please read an introduction on the structure of a cable as well as how to discuss them with others. See also the FAQs

Reference ID	Created	Released	Classification	Origin
09BERN273	2009-07-01 19:11	2011-08-30 01:44	SECRET	Embassy Bern

Appears in these articles:
http://www.aftenposten.no/spesial/wikileaksdokumenter/article3994463.ece

R 011911Z JUL 09
FM AMEMBASSY BERN
TO SECSTATE WASHDC 5919
INFO AMEMBASSY STOCKHOLM
DEPT OF JUSTICE WASHINGTON DC

S E C R E T BERN 000273

DEPT FOR ISN/RA (J.ALLEN-CLOSE), NEA/IR, EUR/PRA, AND
EUR/AGS (Y.SAINT-ANDRE), NSC FOR JEFF HOVENIER, DEPT OF
JUSTICE BRUCE SWARTZ

E.O. 12958: DECL: 06/30/2019
TAGS: IR MNUC PARM PHUM PREL PTER KNNC ECON ETRD
EINV, SZ
SUBJECT: SWITZERLAND SHUTTING DOWN COLENCO'S BUSINESS WITH
IRAN

REF: 08 BERN 464

Classified By: CDA L.Carter for reasons 1.4(b) and (d)

¶1. (S) Summary: Swiss Minister for Economics and Trade
Doris Leuthard called CDA in to advise that the Swiss Federal
Councilors had decided in a special session to shut down
Swedish firm Colenco's commercial activities in Iran. The
Minister also reaffirmed the commitment of the Swiss
government to accept several detainees from Guantanamo Bay
for resettlement in Switzerland. Minister Leuthard made it
clear that these two activities were linked to the
achievement of a political settlement in the case of Swiss
banking giant, UBS. The US court is scheduled to hear
arguments in the civil case on July 13 and it is clear that
the GOS hopes a settlement can be reached before the hearing
date. End Summary.

¶2. (S) Minister Leuthard began the meeting by describing
today's special session of the Federal Council which was
focused on what steps the Swiss government could take to
advance a political solution of the UBS case. The Council
considered action on the Colenco case, long advocated by the
USG and a major topic during the February meeting between
Secretary Clinton and Foreign Minister Calmy Rey, was one
proactive measure the Swiss government could take in this
direction. Since action in this case falls under the purview
of Minister Leuthard, she was tasked to take immediate action
to shut down Colenco's operations and to notify the USG. The
additional information that the USG experts provided to the
GOS on June 25th was pivotal in providing the Swiss with
adequate actionable intelligence to make a legal finding that
Colenco is violating the sanctions on Iran. Leuthard
confirmed that the information we provided tracked with the
findings of the Swiss intelligence services. The Swiss now
consider that Colenco is not fulfilling their requirements
under the dual use provisions of Swiss law. Leuthard also
advised that they have notified the Swedish government of
their intent to go forward with official action against
Colenco.

¶3. (S) Colenco was not able to adequately defend their
activities in Iran by a deadline set by the Swiss government.
Leuthard stated that Colenco will be formally told to cease
their activities in Iran on July 2. She further opined that
should the government or other conditions relating to
proliferation change for the better in Iran, Colenco may be
able to resume their activities in the future. She
emphasized that this shut-down was a "suspension". She
promised to provide us with a written copy of the Colenco
decision.

¶4. (S) Leuthard then turned the topic of discussion to
Swiss willingness to accept several detainees from Guatanamo
for resettlement and encouraged us to provide as much data as
possible quickly so that the Swiss could move forward. CDA

[Handwritten annotations in margin: "Detainees from Guantanamo 0 to... UBS case = Peace Treaty", "Holocaust Asset", "Settlement avoids Bank failure."]

come up with some ideas. For example, he said if a \
significant number of UBS clients took advantage of the IRS \
voluntary declaration program, then perhaps the case would \
resolve itself. \
\
¶4. (C) In regards to the UBS case, Sager confirmed that \
Switzerland will file an Amicus Curiae brief with the court. \
Sager stated that the brief will be based on the grounds of \
Swiss sovereignty, the double taxation agreement, which is, \
in the Swiss view, the only means to obtain information in \
these type of cases, and under current Swiss banking laws. \
CARTER \

Cable Viewer

Viewing cable 09BERN169, SWISS LINK TAX AGREEMENT RENEGOTIATIONS WITH UBS

If you are new to these pages, please read an introduction on the structure of a cable as well as how to discuss them with others. See also the FAQs.

Reference ID	Created	Released	Classification	Origin
09BERN169	2009-04-09 14:33	2011-08-30 01:44	CONFIDENTIAL	Embassy Bern

Appears in these articles:
http://www.letemps.ch/swiss_papers

```
VZCZCXYZ0002
RR RUEHWEB

DE RUEHSW #0169 0991433
ZNY CCCCC ZZH
R 091433Z APR 09
FM AMEMBASSY BERN
TO RUEHC/SECSTATE WASHDC 5814
INFO RUEATRS/DEPT OF TREASURY WASHINGTON DC
```

2009-04-09 14:33:00   09BERN169   Embassy Bern   CONFIDENTIAL   09BERN122

```
VZCZCXYZ0002
RR RUEHWEB

DE RUEHSW #0169 0991433
ZNY CCCCC ZZH
R 091433Z APR 09
FM AMEMBASSY BERN
TO RUEHC/SECSTATE WASHDC 5814
INFO RUEATRS/DEPT OF TREASURY WASHINGTON DC
    C O N F I D E N T I A L BERN 000169
```

SIPDIS

TREASURY FOR L.NORTON, L FOR K.PROPP AND T.WYNNE

E.O. 12958: DECL: 04/08/2019
TAGS: EFIN ECON SZ
SUBJECT: SWISS LINK TAX AGREEMENT RENEGOTIATIONS WITH UBS CASE

REF: BERN 122

Classified By: POL/E Counselor R.Rorvig for reasons 1.4(b) and (d)

¶1. (SBU) The Swiss Federal Counsel announced on April 8 that the first renegotiated double taxation agreement to include the new OECD Article 26 provisions on administrative assistance will be subject to an optional public referendum. Subsequent agreements will not be submitted to the referendum procedure unless they contain significant new obligations or departures from the first agreement. Econoffs met with Swiss Department of Foreign Affairs Head of Sectoral Policy Coordination Manuel Sager on April 9 to discuss Switzerland's intentions in regards to the sequence for negotiating agreements.

¶2. (C) Switzerland prioritized Japan, Poland and the U.S. for the first three negotiations. The Japanese agreement is the farthest along, since it involves incorporating OECD standards into a Swiss-Japanese double taxation treaty, which is in the late stages of negotiation. However, the Swiss are negotiating with the Japanese Finance Ministry, and the agreement is also subject to a full review by the Japanese Foreign Ministry, which could delay final approval. Negotiations with Poland began in March, and the U.S. negotiations will begin April 28. Sager said that the Government of Switzerland does not have a tactical preference as to which agreement is completed first, but it recognizes that Japan and Poland will have an easier ride in the Swiss Parliament. As reported reftel, post is concerned that the U.S. agreement could also have difficulties with a referendum given current negative public sentiment caused by the UBS case.

¶3. (C) Sager stressed that Switzerland sees linkage between the negotiations of the tax agreement and the ongoing UBS case. He commented that while a factual or legal connection may not exist, Switzerland definitely views the two as politically linked. In Sager's view, it would be very difficult to get an agreement through the parliament (not to mention an expected referendum challenge), if there is no progress on the separate UBS case. Sager admitted he could not propose a formal solution, but that the parties needed to

http://wikileaks.org/cable/2009/04/09BERN169.html   9/3/2011

was interested in knowing if the U.S. had a legal mechanism \
for such an exchange. (Note: Sager received a Masters in Law \
Degree from Duke Law School and practiced insurance defense \
law in Phoenix for two years in the 1980's so he has a \
general knowledge of U.S. law. End Note.) \
\
-------------- \
G-20 BLACKLIST \
-------------- \
\
¶9. (C) Sager inquired as to the USG views towards the calls \
for a G-20 blacklisting of tax havens. Switzerland's timing \
for relaxing banking secrecy was not coincidental, but \
intended to stave off any type of blacklisting, according to \
Sager. The Swiss are hoping that the U.S. finds \
Switzerland's concessions to include tax evasion as a \
positive step that will garner U.S. support against placing \
Switzerland on any blacklist at the April G-20 meeting. \
\
------- \
COMMENT \
------- \
\
¶10. (C) The Swiss will have a small negotiating team that \
must tackle over 70 double taxation treaties. It is \
essential that the U.S. rank at the top of the list to ensure \
that renegotiation is not delayed by months or even years. \
With the current press surrounding the UBS case, post does \
not recommended that we push for the U.S. to be the first \
test case. However, once one agreement has been approved, it \
will likely be easier for other countries to follow. \
\
CARTER \

¶3. (U) Amid escalating pressure from several countries to \
abolish bank secrecy and increasing calls for a G-20 \
blacklisting, the Swiss Federal Council on March 13 announced \
that Switzerland intends to adopt the OECD standard on \
administrative assistance in tax matters in accordance with \
Art. 26 of the OECD Model Tax Convention. According to the \
Federal Council, the decision "will be implemented within the \
framework of bilateral double taxation agreements." \

¶4. (SBU) Political/Economic Counselor and econoff met with \
Ambassador Manuel Sager, chair of the group of experts \
appointed by the Federal Council to optimize cooperation in \
the case of tax offenses, to discuss the Federal Council's \
decision. According to Sager, the relaxation of banking \
secrecy is designed to extend administrative procedures under \
Switzerland's double taxation agreements to include tax \
evasion. The Swiss will no longer limit administrative \
procedures to "dual tax crimes" or tax crimes recognized in \
both countries, but intend to expand the tax agreements to \
include tax evasion, which has historically been regarded as \
a non-crime in Switzerland. The Swiss are adamant that the \
renegotiated agreements be limited to broadening \
administrative procedures for specific cases with sound \
evidence and will not allow so-called "fishing expeditions" \
into bank records. \

BUT WHEN WILL IT BE IMPLEMENTED? \

¶5. (C) Sager cautioned that the inclusion of tax evasion \
within the administrative assistance framework is not an \
automatic process, but will require renegotiation of \
Switzerland's double taxation agreements with 70 countries. \
In addition, the renegotiated treaties will require \
parliamentary approval and will be potentially subject to \
Switzerland's public referendum process. (Note: In \
Switzerland, a referendum must be held if opponents to any \
bill gather 50,000 signatures requesting it. End Note.) \
Sager opined that parliamentary approval is expected without \
difficulty given the current political will to put this issue \
to rest. However, he expects that at least the SVP, the \
right-wing party, will press for a referendum to submit any \
renegotiated treaty to public vote. This process will slow \
down implementation of the new agreements, and potentially \
could result in the failure to adopt a renegotiated treaty. \

Based on press reports, initial public sentiment towards \
relaxation of banking secrecy in general appears positive. \
However, public views of the more vociferous anti-banking \
secrecy countries, including the U.S., tend to be negative \
and accusatory of bullying tactics. \

¶6. (C) Sager stated the group of experts will turn their \
immediate attention to setting the country priorities for tax \
agreement renegotiation. It is hoped that the priorities \
will be set in the next few weeks, so that the top countries \
can be approached to begin the negotiation process. Sager \
commented that the experts "must consider domestic politics" \
in choosing priorities and would be looking initially for a \
country that would sail through the approval process with the \
least controversy. \

¶7. (C) In regards to renegotiation with the U.S., Sager \
stated that pressure by the U.S. on the Swiss government to \
hand over documents in the UBS case prior to conclusion of \
the Swiss administrative process caused some to question "why \
bother with a new amended treaty when no one follows the \
procedures anyway." Nevertheless, Sager expects that the \
U.S. will place high on the list. On a positive note, \
according to Sager, the Swiss government views renegotiation \
as a way forward, and does not apply it to any ongoing \
issues. Sager does not couple the UBS court case with \
renegotiation of the tax agreement nor does he view it as a \
hindrance to renegotiation other than possible negative \
public sentiment during the referendum process. \

Sager changes in next cable..

UBS CASE CONTINUES TO RAISE CONCERNS \

¶8. (C) Despite the fact that the relaxation of banking \
secrecy is not linked to the UBS case, the Swiss government \
would prefer a political solution to this ongoing problem. \
Sager expressed concern about the outcome of the UBS case, \
commenting that the Swiss view the John Doe summons as a \
fishing expedition, and stating that it is "highly doubtful" \
that information on these clients "would ever be handed \
over." He hypothetically questioned whether the U.S. would \
supply information on 52,000 unnamed accounts if, for \
example, a Brazilian court, requested this information. He \

banking secrecy, not just as a contributor to the financial \
sector and GDP, but as a national institution and part of \
Switzerland's cultural identity. The Swiss government will \
push hard against the 52,000 John Doe summons, which they \
view as a fishing expedition, outside of legal assistance and \
in violation of their banking secrecy laws. The public's ire \
at the U.S. (and EU) for pressuring Switzerland should also \
not be underestimated and could have a long-lasting negative \
backlash on bilateral relations and increased \
anti-Americanism. \

Cultural identity.

THE WAY FORWARD \
--------------- \

¶9. (C) Both the Swiss and Liechtenstein governments, as well \
as bankers, have intimated at a solution that would provide \
them with much needed political cover and still allow the \
U.S. to breach the current tax fraud versus tax evasion \
cut-out in our bilateral agreements. President Merz admitted \
at a recent conference that banking secrecy, while not at its \
end, must evolve to match current times. He suggested that \
concessions must be made to stave off criticism and \
blacklistings. Marxer confirmed that Liechtenstein also \
recognized secrecy was evolving, but he warned that changes \
needed to be incremental to allow citizens and financial \
institutions to adjust. As an example, he cited \
Liechtenstein's expansion of exceptions to secrecy laws first \
through money laundering restrictions, then the QI, and \
finally the more recent TIEA. \

¶10. (C) Given President Merz's overtures for concessions and \
the incremental changes that have already occurred within \
Switzerland, post recommends that the USG approach \
Switzerland to discuss renegotiation of our bilateral \
agreement to incorporate the broader scope of coverage found \
in the U.S.-Liechtenstein TIEA, specifically to include tax \
evasion. The Swiss government can spin the bilateral \
agreement as a further step in our relations that assists \
both countries in halting willful criminal conduct. At the \
same time, by not opening the door completely, it will enable \
the government to assure the public that secrecy exists \
absent criminal conduct, as well as provide the Swiss some \
defense against the EU's expected campaign to eliminate \
secrecy altogether. \
CARTER \v

E.U. anti-secrecy campaigns

Cable Viewer

Viewing cable 09BERN122, SWISS RELAXATION OF BANKING SECRECY: WHAT DOES IT

If you are new to these pages, please read an introduction on the structure of a cable as well as how to discuss them with others. See also the FAQs

Reference ID	Created	Released	Classification	Origin
09BERN122	2009-03-19 09:55	2011-08-30 01:44	CONFIDENTIAL	Embassy Bern

Appears in these articles:
http://www.letemps.ch/swiss_papers

```
VZCZCXYZ0000
RR RUEHWEB

DE RUEHSW #0122/01 0780955
ZNY CCCCC ZZH
R 190955Z MAR 09
FM AMEMBASSY BERN
TO RUEHC/SECSTATE WASHDC 5724
INFO RUEATRS/DEPT OF TREASURY WASHINGTON DC
```

2009-03-19 09:55:00   09BERN122   Embassy Bern   CONFIDENTIAL   09BERN98

```
VZCZCXYZ0000\
RR RUEHWEB\
\
DE RUEHSW #0122/01 0780955\
ZNY CCCCC ZZH\
R 190955Z MAR 09\
FM AMEMBASSY BERN\
TO RUEHC/SECSTATE WASHDC 5724\
INFO RUEATRS/DEPT OF TREASURY WASHINGTON DC\
      C O N F I D E N T I A L BERN 000122 \
\
SIPDIS \
\
E.O. 12958: DECL: 03/17/2019 \
TAGS: EFIN EINV ECON SZ
SUBJECT: SWISS RELAXATION OF BANKING SECRECY: WHAT DOES IT \
MEAN \
\
REF: BERN 98 \
\
Classified By: CDA Carter for reasons 1.4(b) and (d). \
\
¶1. (C) The Swiss Federal Council on March 13 announced that \
Switzerland intends to adopt the OECD standard on \
administrative assistance in tax matters in accordance with \
Art. 26 of the OECD Model Tax Convention. Ambassador Manuel \
Sager, Head of the Foreign Ministry's Sectoral Policy \
Division and Chair of the group of experts appointed by the \
Federal Council to optimize cooperation in the case of tax \
offenses, stated that the relaxation of banking secrecy is \
designed to extend administrative procedures under \
Switzerland's double taxation agreements to include tax \
evasion. Sager cautioned that the inclusion of tax evasion \
within the administrative assistance framework is not an \
automatic process, but will require renegotiation of \
Switzerland's double taxation agreements with over 70 \
countries, parliamentary ratification, and be subject to \
possible challenge by public referendum. Sager stated the \
group of experts will turn their immediate attention to \
setting the country priorities for tax agreement \
renegotiation and "must consider domestic politics" in \
choosing priorities. Despite controversy over the UBS case, \
Sager expects that the U.S. will place high on this list. \
\
¶2. (C) Summary continued. Sager expressed concern about the \
outcome of the UBS case, commenting that the Swiss view the \
John Doe summons as a fishing expedition, and stating that it \
is "highly doubtful" that information on these clients "would \
ever be handed over." The Swiss are hoping that the U.S. \
finds Switzerland's concessions to include tax evasion as a \
positive step that will garner U.S. support against the \
placing of Switzerland on any blacklist at the April G-20 \
meeting. Post does not recommended that the USG push to be \
the first test case for tax treaty renegotiation given the \
negative Swiss sentiments surrounding the UBS trial and the \
potential success of a public referendum to block any \
renegotiated treaty. Instead, post suggests lobbying for \
placement near the top of Switzerland's renegotiation list. \
End Summary. \
\
------------------------------------- \
SWITZERLAND TO RELAX BANK SECRECY \
------------------------------------- \
```

INVESTORS BUSINESS DAILY

JES & INSIGHTS READ WHAT'S REALLY GOING ON IN THE COUNTRY THURSDAY, JUNE 21, 2012 A13

THE LEFT

ederal System /on't Let U.S. ecome Greece

DIONNE JR.

AN FRANCISCO — If the United States were still governed under the Articles of Confederation, ght California be in the position of eece, Spain or Italy?

fter all, California has a major bud- crisis and all sorts of difficulties erning itself. Its initiative system al- vs voters to mandate specific forms spending and to limit tax increases d also make them harder to enact. sent a strong federal government th the power to offset the impact of recession and the banking crisis, w would California fare in a global fi- ncial system?

K, no metaphor is perfect, and ere's a compelling case that this rawling and economically diverse ate would perform better in the glo- l economy than the beleaguered na- ons of southern Europe.

Moreover, Gov. Jerry Brown de- rves credit for trying to get a handle the California budget crisis. He's ing to the voters this fall with a refer- dum to raise about $8 billion in xes to stave off further cuts. Without e money, Brown says, education ending would have to be slashed be- ond the cutbacks that have already ken effect.

But the metaphor is instructive be- ause it turns on its head the usual non- nse from anti-government politi- ans that the U.S. is on the road to be- oming Greece. No, we're not. Our is- ues are entirely different. To the ex- nt that the crisis in Europe has les- ons for the U.S., they go the other ay.

lore Stimulus

First, we are lucky to have a robust ederal government, which the Euro- ean Union lacks. Early in the reces- ion, the feds were able to offset prob- ems in the country's most troubled re- ions with a stimulus program (and lso with that auto bailout that so nany, including Mitt Romney, op- osed). The stimulus should have een bigger, and it should have extend- ed over a longer period. But it helped.

Second, we bailed out our banks ight away and also have a more effec- tive central bank. We thus avoided some of the problems now facing Europe, notably Spain.

Again, we need to do more, not less, to deal with the damage caused by the housing bubble, which is especially threatening in parts of California. But the U.S. bit the bullet immediately to deal with potential insolvency in the banks, and the Obama administration's stress tests helped restore confidence in the system.

By contrast, Europe created a common currency without a central bank as powerful as the Federal Reserve, and without a continental fiscal policy that cuts across its member states. In a genuine federal system, the better-off states help the states that fall into trouble. Greece needs both reform and large transfers from the wealthier states of Europe — yes, that means Germany — to reverse its economy's free fall.

Pump The Money

Our federal system mostly disguises the transfers that take place across

PERSPECTIVE

Is Shariah Finance Aiding Radical Islamic Jihadists?

REP. ALLEN B. WEST

As a vehicle for legitimizing and promoting Shariah throughout the world, Shariah-compliant finance is a phenomenon that is taking the financial world by storm right under the noses of American investors.

Given the stated mission of Shariah is to bring about the rule of Islam worldwide, anything that promotes the Shariah mission warrants careful scrutiny. American investors deserve to know where their money is being invested, and the fact that their hard-earned dollars could be helping fund the very radical terrorist groups that are seeking to destroy this nation is shocking.

It is vital that we come to grips and recognize not just the kinetic aspects of radical Islam, but also the idea of "stealth jihad," which can infiltrate our operating systems.

Shariah is an Arabic term used to describe Islamic doctrinal law regarded in the Islamic world as immutable, indivisible and mandatory for all Muslims to follow in all aspects of life.

Shariah mandates as a religious obligation:

- Violent jihad against non-Muslims to establish Islam's rule worldwide.
- The killing of apostates from Islam.
- The killing of adulterers and homosexuals.
- Severe discrimination against women, including stoning.
- Barbaric punishment, such as limb amputations and gouging out of eyes for petty crimes like theft.
- Severe discrimination against, and the subjugation of, non-Muslims.
- Last, and most pertinent to this subject, is Shariah mandates that Muslims who cannot engage in physical jihad using force, must support jihad with money.

Shariah is at the heart of the ideology of terrorist groups such as al-Qaida, Hezbollah, Hamas and other jihadist organizations, including the Muslim Brotherhood and those who orchestrated the 9/11 attacks on American soil and continue to terrorize and threaten Americans and their way of life.

Many well-known American banking financiers and institutions are involved in Shariah finance for the lure of substantial profits from Middle Eastern petrodollars.

But Shariah finance is not just an innocent form of free-market capitalism. Shariah finance was conceived and is practiced as one of the key instruments of the radical Islamist movement in its struggle against the West.

An astounding $1.5 trillion is currently invested in Shariah finance, and that amount is expected to grow dramatically in the years ahead — thanks largely to the ever-increasing coffers of oil-exporting nations ruled by Shariah, including Iran and Saudi Arabia.

Scrutiny, however, is something Shariah-compliant finance has never had to endure from American policymakers. Shariah finance is almost completely alien from the standards of disclosure and transparency customary in the U.S. and other Western financial markets.

A small cadre of Shariah advisers — Muslim authorities on Shariah — determine capital and credit flows with little, if any, of the accountability at the heart of federal and state securities laws. This gives rise to unique risks for Western firms engaging in Shariah-compliant finance, including racketeering, anti-trust, and securities and consumer fraud.

Shariah advisers to the banks are themselves the real problems with Shariah-compliant finance. All too often, they are outright jihadists with ties to terrorism. In fact, the most prominent Shariah scholar in the financial world — a Pakistani named Mufti Taqi Usmani — sits on the Shariah advisory boards of some of America's best-known banking institutions.

Usmani referred to Americans in Iraq as "stinking atheists" and "the worst-ever butchers and vultures of the world" who are "clawing off the flesh of bodies of innocent Iraqi Muslims."

Until his hateful, jihadist militant credo was exposed to the public, Usmani headed HSBC's Shariah advisory board, as well as that of Dow Jones. This shows how unaware and reckless the financial world actually is when it comes to true due diligence on Shariah-compliant finance.

It should be pointed out that when Usmani was removed from HSBC's Shariah advisory board, he was replaced by his own son. Usmani is still active on the Shariah advisory boards of U.S. and Western firms, including Guidance Financial Group, Swiss RE, Arcapita and UBS-Warburg.

Shariah-compliant finance affords Shariah advisers the opportunity to channel funds skimmed off investments in the form of "zakat" to terrorist charities of their choice. This is exactly what happened in the case of Bank Al Taqwa and Sheikh Yusuf al-Qaradawi, the Sunni Islamic world's foremost Shariah scholar.

Qaradawi was chairman of the Shariah advisory board of the bank, which was shut down by the U.N. and the U.S. Treasury Department for funneling money to jihadist terrorist organizations, including Ayman al-Zawahiri's Egyptian Islamic Jihad. Much of the money came through a Shariah-compliant real estate firm in New Jersey named BMI.

Shariah-compliant finance should be seen by regulators, the financial sector and investors alike as problematic in the extreme. It is inconsistent with America's constitutional principles, legal codes and financial regulations that require transparency and disclosure of risks that are material to investors, particularly in the post-9/11 world.

The true nature of Shariah must be fully revealed. In the absence of such transparency and disclosure, Americans are in jeopardy of aiding and abetting economic warfare in the form of financial jihad against our own country.

Shariah finance is a grave matter of concern for America as it impacts not only our economic security, but also our national security.

West, a Republican, represents Florida's 22nd congressional district. He spent 22 years as an officer in the Army, including multiple tours in the Middle East.

VIEWPOINT

Proposed Airline Merger Puts President In No-Win Situation

DOUGLAS HOLTZ-EAKIN AND SAM BATKINS

President Obama is about to receive anoth-

Consider: If the president approves the merger, he'll snub progressives who helped him decide the fate of AT&T/T-Mobile. The CWA, who

ON THE RIGHT

Tea Party's War Isn't *On* Women But *By* Women

AMY KREMER

It's an election year, and the Democrats are scrambling to distract voters from the failed policies of the liberal Washington trio of President Obama, Sen. Harry Reid, and Rep. Nancy Pelosi. One of the most recent attempted diversions is the invention of a "Tea Party-led war on women."

Ironically, much of the Tea Party leadership is made up of a new generation of powerful conservative women.

The truth is that Tea Party women are leading the charge to tackle the fundamental problems brought on by the ever-expanding Big Government agenda. Women are not only the most protective of loved ones. They are also the most familiar with how policies will affect their family on a micro level.

So, whether it's talking to their communities, organizing volunteers and campaigning, or leading their states out of the shackles of overwhelming debt and stagnating job growth — women are fighting to take our country back.

Looking back, it was just 3-1/2 short years ago that I was a stay-at-home mom fed up with the out-of-control spending in Washington. I was sick and tired of yelling and screaming at my television and radio and decided to get off my couch and do something about my frustration.

I found a way to channel my frustration into political action. I was one of the founding 22 mothers and fathers of the modern-day Tea Party movement that organized the first Tea Party rallies following Rick Santelli's seminal rant at the Chicago Board of Trade.

Since then I have given my life to this movement because I could not look my daughter in the eyes without knowing I had an opportunity to stop the policies that were destroying our country.

The Tea Party movement, along with my role as chairwoman of Tea Party Express, the nation's largest Tea Party political action committee, has given me a voice. But I am just one of many stories.

Leading Ladies

Gov. Sarah Palin has become a rock star in the Tea Party movement and a powerful voice for the conservative cause. Rep. Michele Bachmann is a loud voice for the Tea Party movement in the House and was the founder of the Tea Party Caucus there.

The movement has also given rise to now-prominent bloggers and commentators such as Tabitha Hale, who is revolutionizing online citizen activism, and Dana Loesch, who has become a powerful voice on radio and television.

There are other powerful Tea Party women that were elected in 2010 against all odds. Gov. Nikki Haley in South Carolina and Lt. Gov. Rebecca Kleefisch in Wisconsin rode a wave of Tea Party momentum to victory.

These leaders have epitomized the ambitions of the Tea Party and women's role in the movement. They have helped lead their states by cutting wasteful spending and creating a business-friendly environment that allows for real job growth.

Palin described herself as being a "mama grizzly." Well, that's how I

Whistleblower Gets $104 Million

Now a Felon, Former Banker Told U.S. About Tax-Evasion Tactics by UBS and Its Wealthy Clients

By LAURA SAUNDERS
And ROBIN SIDEL

A former UBS AG banker who helped the U.S. government mount a crackdown on tax cheats was awarded $104 million by the Internal Revenue Service for blowing the whistle on his former employer, in what lawyers said was the largest-ever whistleblower payout to an individual.

Since then, more than 33,000 U.S. taxpayers have confessed account holdings to the IRS and paid over $5 billion in taxes and penalties. Bradley Birkenfeld also was instrumental in 2009 in getting UBS to agree to pay a $780 million fine to settle charges it helped wealthy Americans evade taxes. The bank also agreed to turn over to U.S. authorities the names of more than 4,000 clients. Mr. Birkenfeld is currently serving a 40-month prison sentence in New Hampshire for a felony conviction related to his role in the case. He is scheduled to be released in late November.

Under a 2006 law, the Internal Revenue Service can pay whistleblower awards of up to 30% of the collected proceeds in cases where the information leads to the collection of unpaid taxes.

Dropping Dimes

Money the IRS has collected from a new program was lowered targeting big offenders.

[chart]

The two laws differ somewhat. Tax whistleblowers can get paid only if they cover more than $2 million in unpaid taxes, interest and penalties.

Some lawmakers, however, have said the IRS has been slow to pay out awards.

"If Mr. Birkenfeld can get this amount of money for committing a felony, imagine how many companies and individuals will come forward," said Stephen Kohn, his lawyer. Mr. Birkenfeld said in a statement that "the IRS today sent 104 million messages to whistleblowers around the world — that the IRS is now paying awards, and 104 million messages to banks — that the time to deal with the IRS is right now."

"This is obviously a great deal of money, but billions of dollars that otherwise would not have been paid as a result of the information provided by our client," said Dean Zerbe, another of Mr. Birkenfeld's lawyers. "Mr. Birkenfeld's knowledge shows, encouragingly, that if people with knowledge come forward, stick their necks out, it is often the case that not only will we win over tax cheating by the collection of taxes, but also by the deterrent effect," said Mr. Zerbe.

Mr. Zerbe, in a news conference, said Mr. Birkenfeld will get the payment, adding that Mr. Birkenfeld signed a confidentiality agreement.

He's the $104M snitch

By CHUCK BENNETT

LITTLE WHISTLEBLOWER, BIG PAYOFF.

A banker who ratted out on his clients trying to cheat Uncle Sam out of taxes made financial history yesterday — an award of $104 million from the IRS — the largest whistleblower award ever.

Birkenfeld's award was only part of $780 million recouped by the U.S. after giving information about the Swiss banking giant UBS.

Former UBS banker Bradley Birkenfeld, now in prison for a felony, got paid for divulging secrets of his firm to the Feds after it emerged he'd been squirreling away secret accounts for wealthy Americans.

IRS pays banker who blew whistle on clients

It turns out, over a list of some 4,500 Americans and their secret offshore UBS accounts.

Birkenfeld's sweet deal may even inspire other banks to follow suit.

IRS pays UBS whistle-blower $104 million

WASHINGTON — The IRS has awarded a former UBS banker $104 million for providing information about overseas tax cheats — the largest amount ever awarded to an individual whistle-blower.

Bradley Birkenfeld is credited with providing information that enabled the U.S. government to crack down on Americans using Swiss bank accounts to hide their money from tax collectors.

Birkenfeld served roughly 2½ years in prison for a fraud conviction related to the case.

The IRS, which doesn't usually confirm individual awards, signed a confidential agreement allowing the agency to confirm it.

Whistleblower on Taxes Awarded $104 Million

Bradley Birkenfeld, the ex-banker who helped the U.S. build its tax-evasion case against UBS, won the biggest whistleblower award yet.

You're being hacked! Tax TV to tell riders of scam

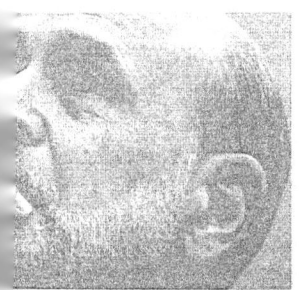

deral Reserve chairman, said this week
es were set was "structurally flawed."

J. SCOTT APPLEWHITE/ASSOCIATED PRESS

tutions which is responsible for collect-
other ing the benchmark information.
ay one The bank's rate: 1 percent.
s banks By contrast, UBS calculated
ates for the figure to three decimal places
three- and regularly changed its rates.
bor. At the beginning of June, the
periods Swiss bank reported a one-year
s of de- rate of 1.037 percent. It dropped
e three- to 0.972 percent at the end of the
ates on month.
rtgages Neither bank responded to a
Libor. request for comment.
ing that There can also be wide discrep-
t now," ancies among similar bench-
chief fi- marks, which may reflect the ar-
a bank tificial nature of the process.
N.C. While the recent three-month
ng has Libor stood at 0.4531 percent, the
e large- parallel euro interbank offered
of bor- rate in American dollars amount-
Libors, ed to 0.91643 percent.
deposits During periods of turmoil, the
market process gets murkier. Some trad-
tort the ers indicate that banks at times of
stress report rates that would be
en sub- almost impossible to achieve.
ral days When the European debt crisis
ng mar- heated up this summer, French
ons. banks were viewed as vulner-
hase re- able, meaning they would have
ar Libor had a hard time borrowing at rea-
rding to sonable rates. But the rates of the
Reuters, country's banks remained rela-

their stock price going down 10
percent a day, could they have
borrowed at Libor? There isn't a
chance," said a senior Wall Street
executive who spoke on the condition of anonymity because of
the current investigations.
In some ways, the flaws with
Libor make it a convenient tool
for Wall Street. If banks had to
carefully reference a real, sometimes volatile, market, they
might find it harder to set rates
regularly. Allowing banks to submit guesstimates makes it relatively simple to come up with a
daily number. The practices suit
the vast derivatives markets,
which need a daily rate to price
products like interest-rate swaps.
As the Libor scandal has un-
folded, the industry is grappling
with how to fix the process. One
suggestion is to choose banks'
Libor submissions randomly
when setting the overall rate,
making it harder to manipulate.
Authorities have also proposed
having independent auditors
oversee the process.
The race to replace Libor has
also heated up. One suggestion is
to use rates from another market
that banks frequently use to lend
to each other. These loans are
backed with high-quality financial assets that lenders can keep
if borrowers fail to repay. The
limited volume of Libor-related
loans do not have such collateral.
The Wall Street firm Cantor
Fitzgerald is also developing an
index of different short-term
lending markets. The idea is that
the benchmark, a more diversified reflection of borrowing,
could be used as a substitute for
Libor.
"To be reliable, indices have to
be transaction-based and trans-
parent," said Gary S. Gensler, the
chairman of the Commodity Futures Trading Commission, the
regulator that led the inquiry into
Barclays.

Wall Street Journal

By MICHAEL J. de la MERCED
and BEN PROTESS

One of President Obama's biggest supporters on Wall Street is
about to leave his perch at UBS,
one of the world's largest banks.
Robert Wolf, who is the UBS
chairman for the Americas, is
leaving at the end of the month to
set up his own advisory shop. He
will retain close ties to UBS,
which will be the first client of his
firm.
A 28-year veteran of Wall
Street, Mr. Wolf has enjoyed his
status as a prominent defender of
the Obama administration and a
top-ranking fund-raiser. He has
garnered more than $500,000 to
re-elect the president this year,
and regularly plays golf and va-
cations with Mr. Obama on Mar-
tha's Vineyard.
In his day job as a top banker
at UBS, the Swiss bank, Mr. Wolf
has built his business on relationships, relying on contacts
spanning Wall Street and Washington. A former bond trader, he
rose through the ranks at Salomon Brothers and later ran the
UBS fixed-income desk.
His latest role as chairman of
the Americas has focused on
winning new business from corporations, private equity firms
and institutional investors. Mr.
Wolf said on Thursday that he
hoped his Wall Street and Washington experience, and his strong
ties to both worlds, would "bring
a unique perspective to my clients."
Mr. Wolf makes more than $5
million a year at UBS, according
to several people who had been
briefed but declined to be identified discussing personnel matters.
"Robert has contributed significantly to the firm in managing
and growing our business," three
senior UBS executives, including
Robert J. McCann, the bank's
chief executive for the Americas,
wrote in an internal memorandum reviewed by The New York
Times. "We appreciate Robert's
commitment to our clients and
franchise and are pleased that we
will continue our relationship as
a client of his new firm."
Mr. Wolf's friendship with the
president began before other financiers were seeking to curry
favor with Mr. Obama during the
2008 campaign. The two met at a
2006 fund-raiser hosted by the
billionaire George Soros and
quickly became friends. During
the financial crisis, he regularly
advised Mr. Obama on the turmoil on Wall Street.
Now, when many on Wall
Street, frustrated by the administration's attacks on their industry, have switched allegiance to
Mitt Romney, Mr. Wolf has remained steadfast in his support.

In an interview with The Wall
Street Journal in April, Mr. Wolf
said that when Mr. Obama attacked "fat-cat bankers," he replied, "Mr. President, I know you
think I'm overweight, but I can
think of better names to call me."
Mr. Obama reportedly laughed.
Mr. Wolf's prominence as an
Obama backer irritated some at
UBS, however, according to people briefed on the matter. This
year, the bank's group executive
board in Zurich directed Mr. Wolf
to send all media inquiries to the
bank's media office for approval,
with many requests denied.
But a UBS spokeswoman said
that Mr. Wolf's departure had
been in the works for some time

MARK LENNIHAN/ASSOCIATED PRESS

Robert Wolf will leave UBS to
start a firm called 32 Advisors.

and was not prompted by any internal battles.
Mr. Wolf set his plan in motion in March. He had just turned
50, was on his way to losing 35
pounds, and was ready for a fresh
start. His entire career had been
spent at two companies, Salomon
Brothers and UBS, and the
thought of striking out on his own
sounded appealing.
"When you go straight from
school to only working at two
firms for 28 years, leaving an established platform to do something entrepreneurial is both ex-
citing and overwhelming," Mr.
Wolf said. "But I look forward to
this new chapter in my career."
That next phase is 32 Advisors,
a reference to his jersey number
on the University of Pennsylvania football team. The firm is described, on its bare-bones Web
site, 32advisors.com, as "a bou-
tique consulting and advisory
arm," serving a wide array of potential clients.
While he will no longer work at
UBS, he is expected to continue
to accompany its bankers to
meetings and help it attract new
clients. Being independent
means that he can do the same
for other firms as well.
By striking out on his own, Mr.

---

rs Examine Local Lending Rates

ect scru- lated in the same way as Libor.
"Regulators in several interna-
scrutiny tional financial centers are look-
al bench- ing into the setting of key market
ndon in- interest rate benchmarks by
or Libor. banks," the Monetary Authority
d to de- of Singapore said Thursday.
e costs for "M.A.S. is doing the same in Sin-
s. gapore."
ely on lo- In Hong Kong, the local mone-
ice finan- tary regulator said it was su-
pervising an investigation by the
Libor is Hong Kong Association of Banks
r roughly — the body charged with setting
scale cor- the Hong Kong interbank offered
le the re- rate, or Hibor. The Hong Kong
ged to lo- Monetary Authority said it has
e set inde- "not observed any anomaly" in
ntry. Last the rate-fixing process among
d on the banks, but said that it "will mon-
s amount- itor closely" the progress of the
ording to review.
provider Korean authorities are making

was investigating local banks and
securities firms for possible collusion in setting C.D. rates, which
are widely used as a reference for
pricing other borrowings in the
country. Commission officials
said nine banks and 10 broker-
ages were under investigation.
In South Korea, the interest
paid on C.D.'s has long served as
one of the country's benchmark
money market rates, and is often
quoted in financial transactions
like mortgages. But in recent
years, concerns have grown that
this no longer properly reflects
real changes in market interest
rates because the issuance of
C.D.'s has declined sharply.
The volume of trade in C.D.'s
plummeted from 224.3 trillion
won (about $195 billion) in 2008 to
53.7 trillion won last year, according to the Korea Financial

U.S. NEWS

California Works Out Budget Deal

By VAUHINI VARA

California Gov. Jerry Brown and state's legislative leaders agreed Thursday on a $92 billion budget plan that would close the state's deficit for the fiscal year starting on July 1.

Legislators will meet next week to vote on the budget, which is expected to pass by the time the fiscal year begins, marking the second on-time budget in a row for a state formerly plagued by perpetual budget delays. On-time passage would bolster California's reputation among the investors who buy its bonds and avert the cash-management emergencies that can result from late budgets.

"This agreement strongly positions the state to withstand the economic challenges and uncertainties ahead," Mr. Brown, a Democrat, said in a statement.

The agreement highlights the impact of a 2010 voter-approved ballot measure that allowed legislators to pass a budget with a majority rather than the two-thirds supermajority previously required. Because Democrats hold a majority of the Legislature, they can now pass a budget without Republican support.

Mr. Brown had tussled with leaders in the Legislature over the depth of cuts to social-service and other programs, pressing for deeper cuts than they would accept. Their compromise maintains some of the cuts Mr. Brown sought but reduces cuts to other areas.

Democrat Darrell Steinberg, the state Senate's president pro tempore, said: "As always, the negotiations were tough, but we move forward together with a state budget that's structurally balanced, setting us on the path to putting this nagging deficit behind us."

Representatives of Republican leaders in the Legislature said the leaders couldn't comment because they hadn't yet seen the budget deal.

To close a deficit of $16 billion, the budget deal relies on several cuts, along with added revenue from a tax-increase measure that Mr. Brown will put to voters in November. If the measure fails, more cuts would be triggered.

Bank Moves Hinder Immigrants

Services That Many Somalis Use to Send Money Home Are Curtailed by Anti-Terrorism Regulations

By MIRIAM JORDAN
AND ERICA E. PHILLIPS

Efforts by U.S. banks to avoid violating antiterrorism financing laws are crimping the ability of Somalis in the U.S. to send money home, prompting calls for Congress to revisit bank regulations on money transfers.

Somalis in the U.S. use money-transfer merchants, informally known as "hawalas," to send about $100 million annually to Somalia, according to the U.S. Treasury Department. The East African country, where there is no formal banking system, has been without a functioning government since 1991, when civil war erupted and forced tens of thousands to flee.

U.S.-based Somali hawalas, which are federally licensed, rely on banks to wire funds to their counterparts in Africa, who deliver the money to the designated recipients. But increasingly, U.S. banks say they are severing ties with the informal and opaque system to avoid violating federal banking regulations, such as anti-money-laundering rules.

In Minnesota, home to 32,000 Somalis, a crisis erupted for these immigrants when Sunrise Community Banks, a local bank that facilitated most transfers for three years, stopped doing so last Dec. 30. It acted after two local Somali-American women were convicted last year of routing money to al-Shabaab, a Somali terrorist group. The women used hawalas, according to evidence presented in court.

A Sunrise spokeswoman said the bank wasn't involved in the case.

"The community is concerned that their loved ones back home will be severely impacted if this problem isn't solved," said Sadik Warfa, a Somali community leader in Minneapolis.

Rep. Keith Ellison (D., Minn.), whose congressional district includes Minneapolis, called the situation "precarious." He said he has pressed officials at the Treasury, Federal Reserve and State Department to tackle the problem. Mr. Ellison also is drafting legislation to modify oversight of money-service businesses.

Concern over money transfers has risen since the Sept. 11, 2001, terrorist attacks. The federal government has tightened banking regulations to prevent money from the U.S. ending up in the hands of terrorist groups in the Middle East, Africa and other parts of the world.

Rep. Ellison told a House financial subcommittee hearing Thursday that Congress should take a "hard-nosed look" at regulations to determine whether portions could be consolidated or repealed without risking the protections they provide. Deborah Bortner, a state banking regulator in Washington, testified that without legitimate ways to send money "it's going to go underground." That would leave regulators in the dark about how much money is sent, where it goes and what it might fund, she said.

Rep. Carolyn Maloney (D., N.Y.) and other members of the House Committee on Financial Services have attempted to address the issue through legislation in the past.

Somalis have held several demonstrations in Minneapolis to demand a solution. Last month, they marched from the Wells Fargo Center to U.S. Bancorp with signs that blamed the institutions for "starving" their families. Many Somalis closed their accounts with the banks, according to community leaders.

"War on terror has nothing to do with this business," said Imam Hassan Mohamud of the Islamic Da'wah Center in St. Paul. "The money we send goes to 80-year-old grandpa and grandma."

Representatives of Wells Fargo & Co. and U.S. Bancorp said their banks sympathized with the Somali plight but must abide by federal laws.

U.S. banks are permitted to deal with hawalas, typically small businesses that have anti-money laundering, reporting and record-keeping obligations in the U.S. But many banks have ceased money transfers to Somalia amid concerns the funds were being funneled to terrorist groups.

Sunrise cited security and liability issues in closing bank accounts with the Somali money-transfer shops. In a statement, Sunrise said it remains open to facilitating transfers to Somalia but "we cannot do it alone." The bank said it had "reached out to multiple government agencies and officials...to reach an accommodation that would satisfy the concerns of those sending funds, the government and the bank."

As a result of Sunrise's move, several hawalas in the Twin Cities have closed or curtailed money transfers.

Those still open are working with one or two banks outside Minnesota, said Abdul Aziz, a member of the Somali American Money Services Association, a trade group for hawalas. Mr. Aziz declined to name the banks, citing concern that publicity could compel them to halt transfers.

In San Diego and Seattle, home to many Somalis, hawalas are able to send money through a few small banks.

A Treasury Department official said, "We continue to watch this issue closely and to engage regularly with the Somali community, with banks and with money transmitters."

Scott Rembrandt, policy adviser in the Treasury's office of Terrorist Financing and Financial Crimes, said in a Treasury blog post that the department can't ban financial institutions from doing business with specific parties that send money to Somalia.

Mr. Rembrandt also suggested banks can safely send funds to Somalia. The Treasury doesn't assume "money transmitters present a uniform or unacceptably high risk of money laundering, terrorist financing or sanctions violations," he wrote.

Abdiaziz Hassan, 29, a Somali immigrant in Minneapolis who recently tried to send $500 to his mother for medical treatment. "I had to go to three different places," sending a small amount from each one, he said.

Nasir Hamza, an employee of Kaah Express in Minneapolis, helps Abdirahman Mahamud send money to his grandmother in Somalia on Wednesday.

2LT SCOTT BENNETT--29418-016
11TH PSYCHOLOGICAL OPERATIONS BATTALION
UNITED STATES ARMY RESERVE
C/O P.O. BOX 670
MINERSVILLE, PA 17954-0670

September 11, 2013

BE ADVISED:

You are hereby officially served with a military whistleblowing report by an Officer of the United States Army. This report is entitled, "FOLLOW THE MONEY", dated September 11, 2013.

Confirmation of receiptof this letter and report is required. Civil and criminal violations for refusing to acknowledge receipt may include, but not be limited to, the following laws and regulations (Federal and Uniform Code of Military Justice):
    4 U.S.C. App. Sec. 3 § 8H [title VII, § 701(b)] (Whistleblower Protection for Intelligence Community; Employees Reporting Urgent Concerns to Congress);
    5 U.S.C. § 7211 (Lloyd-LaFollette Act, Employees' Right to Petition Congress);
    5 U.S.C. § 552a (Privacy Act);
    5 U.S.C. Appendix, § 7 (Inspector General Act);
    10 U.S.C. § 1034 (Armed Forces/Prohibition Against Retaliation);
    10 U.S.C. § 2409 (Dept. of Defense Contractor Fraud Antiretaliation);
    18 U.S.C. § 1513(e)(Obstruction of Justice, Retaliation Against Whistleblowers);
    18 U.S.C. § 1961, 1962, and 1964 (Racketeer Influenced and Corrupt Organizations Act);
    42 U.S.C. § 1985(d) (Civil Rights Act of 1871); and Executive Order 12731, §101(k), 5 CFR § 2635.101, 57 Federal Register 35006 (Principles of Ethical Conduct for Government Officers and Employees)

Pursuant to the above laws and regulations, failure to acknowledge receipt of this letter and report will be interpreted as a conscious act of collusion, depraved indifference, and may demonstrate willful intent to obstruct justice by ignoring or sequestering requests for Congressional Investigations into the enclosed report(s). The material within this report contains evidence of support for terrorist networks and operations.

You are hereby advised that representatives of the media may have already contacted, or will be contacting, your office for an official response regarding the enclosed report; as well as for the previous reports submitted to your office, entitled: 1) "TERRORIST THREAT FINANCE DIMENSIONS OF UNION BANK OF SWITZERLAND (UBS) 'WHISTLEBLOWER CASE' AND OBAMA ADMINISTRATION INVOLVEMENT" dated September 25, 2012; and 2) "SHELL GAME: The Betrayal and Cover-Up by the U.S. Government of the Union Bank of Switzerland-Terrorist Threat Finance Connection to Booz-Allen-Hamilton and U.S. Central Command", dated May 27, 2013.

This letter and reports have been forwarded to all appropriate Inspectors General, as well as military authorities.

2LT Scott Bennett

P.S. If your staff "round-filed" the earlier reports, copies are available.

"FOLLOW THE MONEY"

A WHISTLEBLOWING REPORT TO THE UNITED STATES CONGRESS
AND THE DEPARTMENT OF DEFENSE INSPECTOR GENERAL

By 2LT Scott Bennett
11th Psychological Operations Battalion
U.S. Civil Affairs-Psychological Operations Command
United States Army Reserve

September 11, 2013

CONTENTS:

FOLLOW THE MONEY...............1
THE BIG LIE....................3
KILL THE MESSENGER.............4
CONNECTING THE DOTS............6
LIST OF NAMES..................8

FOR MORE INFORMATION CONTACT: 2LT Scott Bennett
                                 29418-016
                                 P.O. Box 670
                                 Minersville, PA 17954-0670

                                 Phone: (570) 544-7100

FOLLOW THE MONEY

During the Watergate crisis, deep throat continually advised the investigators to "follow the money".

The Justice Department recently entered into a "settlement" allowing the large Swiss banks to pay "massive" fines in compensation for helping cheats hide their assets and income from the taxing authorities.

About 4,000 account holders were identified; some were fined; and only about 100 faced criminal charges.

The settlement with Swiss giant UBS (Union Bank of Switzerland) resulted in a so-called massive fine of $780 million dollars.

Oh really?...Just how much is a fine of $780 million to a big bank?

To keep the math simple, consider a bank with assets of $1.5 trillion dollars earning only two percent on those assets. That's $30 billion dollars in annual income, and a $780 million dollar fine represents only 2.5% of that yearly income. To put that into context, that's like an ordinary worker earning the U.S. average of $50,000 per year, paying a fine of only $1,250.00 (or $25 per week for a year) to escape disclosing years, if not decades, of hiding money from the tax man; requiring everyone else to absorb the cash flow shortfall. Compare that with the settlements the IRS is extracting from individuals under the "amnesty" agreement(s).

Why did UBS get such a good deal? Could it be that Attorney General Eric Holder, along with Assistant Attorney General Lanny Breuer (who actually negotiated the deal) represented UBS in private practice (Covington & Burling law firm) before becoming part of the Obama team? Or could it be that Robert Wolf, former chairman of the Americas for UBS was a major contributor and finance bundler for the Obama campaign(s)?

In any event, the "real deal" is pay-up to avoid providing the rest of the information about account holders.

Why is this so important? Well, to a number of prominent individuals, who have large holdings that they do not wish to disclose, this is a God-send.

Politicians, business people, the wealthy, and most important, international TERRORISTS, use banks such as UBS to conceal and move funds around the world, under the radar of public disclosure.

FOLLOW THE MONEY

When Swiss banker Brad Birkenfeld revealed information about the nature of this activity (providing not 4,000 but over 18,000 names and accounts by the way) did the U.S. government follow the money? And did they close down the terrorist funding path?

NO. Just like other whistleblowers, Brad Birkenfeld was tossed in jail, after his life was threatened, and then once he started going public--specifically after he wrote a letter in Aug. 2012 to General James Mattis, Commander at U.S. Central Command informing him of intelligence failures and cover-up--he was paid off ($104 million so far) to keep him quiet.

In order to sustain a "war on terrorism" there must be terrorists to fight. And these terrorists need funding, and that funding flows through the large international banks like UBS.

So as long as the banks can pay money instead of coughing up information, the cycle continues.

More to come....

THE BIG LIE

Why is the cover-up always worse than the mistake?

Why was such a fuss made over a simple video produced in California?

The conventional wisdom is that there was no way such a simple unrelated event could trigger the assault on our Benghazi, Libya consulate, right?

Well think again. Just prior to the attack, the U.S. State Department issued a staffing request for indigenous security personnel to protect the consulate. So far so good. But, the request specifically stated (in Politically-Correct terms) that "homosexuality was not a disqualifier". So what?

THAT flyer is what inflamed the <u>newly liberated</u> Muslim locals, who were even seen torching the gasoline around the embassy and igniting the fires with copies of that very circular...but with all the State Department misdirection (propaganda), the truth has been lost...along with the lives of our ambassador and three of his support staff.

More to come....

KILL THE MESSENGER

Why did the former Booz-Allen-Hamilton employee and analyst/programmer at the National Security Agency feel he had to take the data and run? Let's look at recent history.

Former NSA employee Thomas Drake, who felt that the NSA was overstepping its bounds and breaking the law by collecting phone and email information about U.S. citizens under a program called "ThinThread", voiced his concerns through channels and up the chain-of-command, within the NSA, the Pentagon Inspector General, and finally to Congress. What happened to him? His House was raided by the FBI, and he was indicted for espionage. Charges were eventually dropped, but his career was over.

Next, William Binney, an NSA cryptographic expert, complained to Congress in 2002 about the threat that Drake had identified called "ThinThread". His house was raided by the FBI, and he and his family were held at gunpoint. He was ultimately granted immunity in 2010, but his security clearance was revoked, and he retired, after 40 years of service with NSA.

J. Kirk Wiebe worked with Binney at NSA, and after raising concerns about an adaptation of "ThinThread" for surveillance of U.S. citizens, he joined Binney in complaining to Congress and to the Pentagon's Inspector General. His home was raided by the FBI (on the same day as Binney's). He was never charged, but after his security clearance was revoked, he has not worked since.

"Three strikes and you're out", right?

So Snowden, who isn't stupid, realized that there was no future blowing the whistle inside the system. Plus, he had access to internal data and to the CIA files, as well as to data from the NSA about a Swiss Banker whom the CIA entrapped and then jailed; and he may have heard about a fellow Booz-Allen-Hamilton employee and army officer who was tasked with following the terrorist money, but was also set-up and jailed after he sent a report predicting the Benghazi attack (and later Boston, Marathon bombing) up the chain of command.

That makes five strikes...and for someone who was truly offended by what was being done in the name of "National Security"; by the laws being flouted; and by the lies and excuses being offered, what was left?...take the info and run.

KILL THE MESSENGER

Notice that every time the NSA/ Obama team think they have successfully "spun" the latest revelation and put out the latest fire, contradictory new information is released that exposes the latest spin(lies): Director of National Intelligence James Clapper lied in his testimony to Congress; the FISA court was given false representations by the NSA to authorize covert surveillance; and now we know NSA is spying on U.S. citizens domestically--after breaking the encryption codes Americans trusted to keep their information valuables safe.

Even the British are getting involved. David Miranda, the long term associate of Glenn Greenwald, a Guardian journalist, was detained, interrogated for nine hours, and threatened upon his stop-over in England from Germany on his way to Brazil where Greenwald lives. Miranda's computer files, some of which were encrypted, were confiscated, analyzed, and compromised, and have not been returned to him.

The (not so implied) threat is obvious: extradition to the United States for Mr. Miranda to be interrogated by the Department of Justice, threatened with 100 years in prison (through creative legal manipulation by artfully devious DOJ prosecutors), and thereby forced into some witness agreement. Truth is stranger than fiction, oftentimes.

Fortunately, or unfortunately for some, every time a new political spin is applied, there is also a new contradicting disclosure.

Snowden's materials seem to be the magnet drawing the schrapnel out of the wounds of the body of the American Constitution...and those schrapnel fragments are now being exposed in "Letters to the Editor", Opinion articles, and Sunday Talk Shows.

Congress needs to take notice of what is actually going on and act, while we still have some of our Constitution left.

More to come....

CONNECTING THE DOTS

Follow the money! The big lie! Kill the messenger! How do they all fit together?

In what may turn out to be one of the most unimaginable coincidenc two whistleblowers--who were actually jailed--ended up in the same prison...and had an opportunity to compare notes...reaching a startling conclusion.

Swiss Banker Brad Birkenfeld came forward with financial information he presented to the Justice Department and to Congress. His life was then put in jeopardy as a result of a bogus letter issued from one of only a few potential (government) sources, who were aware of the potential of the information he held.

Birkenfeld requested a debriefing with the military, the Intelligence Community, and the government agencies tasked with assessing the terrorist financing threat and monitoring money flows.

Instead he was jailed.

Coincidentally there was an intelligence analyst working for Booz-Allen-Hamilton, holding a top secret security clearance, who was the focal point for the financial threat assessment. The analyst, because of his outstanding background and credentials in psychological warfare and Islamic counterterrorism, had been given a Direct Commission as an Officer into the U.S. Army as a technical specialist, and worked as the Liaison Officer between U.S. Special Operations Command and State Department Coordinator for Counterterrorism; and then later was assigned to U.S. Central Command's Inter-Agency Group (IAG) where he worked jointly with all U.S. government, military and intelligence agencies.

The intelligence analyst's task was to locate sources of financial information and map the flow of money being used to fund terrorist activity...especially funds flowing through international banks.

As an intelligence analyst (and as a military officer), his job was to coordinate the information flow between the civilian intelligence agencies (U.S. and foreign) and the military commands.

Sitting at the crossroads of this critical information flow, this analyst was the logical contact who should have been introduced to the Swiss Banker Birkenfeld...but it didn't happen.

CONNECTING THE DOTS

While designing psychological warfare operations to synthesize into the military's Counter-Threat Finance mission (and Booz-Allen-Hamilton's defense contract), this analyst wrote several reports (one of which would later be used to predict the Benghazi attack almost two years before it happened) which began to examine key issues, problems, and opportunities within military and intelligence agency products and policies, and outlined the policies which were fanning the flames of Islamic unrest while damaging our military capabilities.

Within a couple weeks of writing these reports and giving briefings to military and intelligence agency personnel, the analyst-military officer was arrested by military security forces for a phony D.U.I. stop (off-base in civilian territory, which is a violation of the 1870 Posse Commitatus act preventing the military from acting as civilian law enforcement), but after he was turned over to civilian police (after thoroughly searching his car), the authorities determined he wasn't impared and released him.

As with the other whistleblowers Thomas Drake, William Binney, and J. Kirk Wiebe who preceeded him, the analyst's top secret security clearance was revoked, he was fired from his job, and threatened with discharge by the army. When he refused to back down, and went ahead and published his reports up the chain of command, the analyst was prosecuted--9 months later. He was charged with civilian statutes in order to avoid the Uniform Code of Military Justice and avoid providing military defense counsel--even though he was a military officer, in uniform, and on a military base--violating the Constitutional separation between the military and civilian systems of justice.

So what happened?

The Swiss Banker was sentenced to forty (40) months in a federal prison for conspiracy. The analyst/officer in an unprecedented case was convicted of "wearing his uniform without authority", "violating a defense property regulation", and "making a false statement", and sentenced to 36 months in a federal prison...and, miraculously, THEY ENDED UP IN THE SAME PRISON...where they were finally able to compare notes, coordinate information, match State Department cables from WikiLeaks, and expose the truth.

CONNECTING THE DOTS

For a complete detailed report of what they found, contact any of the people listed at the end of this report, and ask for a copy of "SHELL GAME: The UBS-Brad Birkenfeld-Terrorist Threat Finance Connection to Edward Snowden and Booz Allen Hamilton" (originally sent September 25, 2012 to U.S. Civil Affairs-Psychological Operations Command, General Jeffrey Jacobs, Fort Bragg, N.C.; and U.S. Central Command, General James Mattis, August 2012).

And that's how the dots got connected.

LIST OF RECIPIENTS OF REPORT:

1. U.S. Civil Affairs and Psychological Operations Commander, General Jeff Jacobs (910-432-3032; Fort Bragg, NC 28310-5200)
2. General Martin Dempsey, Chairman, Joint Chiefs of Staff, Pentagon
3. General Ray Odierno, Army Chief of Staff, Pentagon
4. Lynne Halbrooks, Inspector General, Dept. of Defense, Pentagon
5. Rep. Mike Rogers (R-MI), Chairman of the House Intelligence Committee
6. Senator Diane Feinstein (D-CA), Chairwoman, Senate Intelligence Comm.
7. Rep. Howard McKeon (R-CA), House Armed Services Committee
8. Rep. Duncan Hunter (R-CA), House Armed Services Committee
9. Senator John McCain (R-AZ), Senate Armed Services Committee
10. Senator Carl Levin (D-MI), Senate Armed Services Committee
11. Rep. Darrell Issa (R-CA), Chairman Gov. Oversight & Reform Comm.
12. Rep. Jason Chaffetz (R-UT), Chairman House Subcommittee on National Security, Homeland Defense and Foreign Operations
13. Senator Charles Grassley (R-Iowa), Senate Judiciary Committee
14. Rep. Peter King (R-NY), House Committee on Terrorism
15. Senator Lindsay Graham (R-SC), Senate Armed Services Committee

CONNECTING THE DOTS

16. Senator Rand Paul (I-KY), Tea Party Caucus
17. Senator Mitch McConnell (R-KY), Senate Minority Leader
18. Rep. John Boehner (R-OH), Speaker of the House of Reps.
19. Rep. Eric Cantor (R-VA), House Majority Leader
20. Rep. Henry Waxman (D-CA), House Oversight and Reform Committee
21. Rep. Michael McCaul (R-TX), Chairman House Homeland Security Comm.
22. Rep. Michelle Bachman (R-MN), Tea Party Caucus
23. Rep. Dana Rohrabacher, Chairman House Foreign Affairs Subcommittee
24. Senator Marco Rubio (R-FL)
25. Senator Orrin Hatch (R-UT)
26. Senator Pat Roberts (R-KS)
27. Rep. Jeff Sessions (R-AL)
28. Senator Angus King (I-Main)
29. Senator Jim Risch (R-Idaho)
30. Senator Saxby Chambliss (R-GA)
31. Rep. Ruppersberger (MD)
32. Rep. Dave Reichert (R-WA)
33. Senator Kelly Ayotte (R-NH)
34. Senator John Thune (R-SD)
35. Senator James Inhofe (R-OK)
36. Senator John Coburn
37. General James F. Amos, Marine Corps. Commandant, Pentagon
*38. Major Avie Stone, attorney for 2LT Scott Bennett (914-255-6035; 212 General Lee Ave, 16th Legal Operations Detachment, Fort Hamilton, NY 11252)

    I have sent my report to others, but for the purposes of saving space will not list them here. I do have copies of all correspondence and materials sent to the parties above. My reports were unclassified when I wrote them, and should be unclassified now, and therefore can be made available to you through a "Freedom of Information Act" request.

THE ULTIMATE INSIDER TRADING SCANDAL

Former QWEST Communications Chief Executive Officer (CEO) Joseph Nacchio was released from federal prison on September 20, 2013, after sering 4½ years for a manufactured "insider trading" criminal charge. How did this happen and what is its connection to terrorism?

As we have said before, "FOLLOW THE MONEY"...and the trail becomes very interesting...leading through the deep dark bowels of government agencies, distant military battlefields, and the back halls of raw political power.

Insider trading involves the use of non-public information to secure an advantage, usually in the market place. In 2000, Nacchio sold about $52 million dollars worth of QWEST stock, which he reported as required, since he was the CEO.

The telecommunications industry was booming in early 2000, and he decided to cash in some chips. So far so good. He expected business to continue to expand, or at least to hold even.

However, in early 2001 the government, through the National Security Agency, approached all the telecommunications companies (including QWEST) to gain access to their switches--which are the concentration points through which all your email and telephone communications flow.

QWEST was the only company, on advice of its legal counsel, to deny access to the NSA--unless the government obtained a court order. All other companies caved-in and, without telling you their customers, granted NSA access to your personal emails and phone calls. Note that this request was made in early 2001, six months prior to the September 11th terrorist attacks.

Also remember that the NSA has said that if they had access to your personal records, they "could have prevented 9-11 from happening." Well, unless all the terrorists used only QWEST accounts, NSA already had access to this data. Now, after the facts, the "Boogie-Man" of 9-11 is being resurrected as a menacing justification for continued domestic snooping on EVERYBODY, Americans and foreigners. CONNECT THE DOTS.

Edward Snowden has revealed the saga of NSA duplicity. So what happened at QWEST?

The government has vast resources and virtually unlimited power, and like all bullies, hates to be challenged--even if the law is on your side. Gradually, QWEST began losing its government contracts. Nacchio had been subtly threatened with this by the NSA during an unexpected meeting (which NSA scheduled to discuss a different issue at the time) in which NSA had demanded he give them full access to customer information. When Nacchio refused to play ball, the government attempted to extort him by strangling, then cancelling his other contracts.

Revenues went down; earnings declined; and the stock price fell. This was all engineered to make it look like Nacchio was trading on insider information--cashing out before the fall, supposedly. Joseph Nacchio was then indicted, tried, convicted, sentenced, and served his 4½ years in prison. In fact the party manipulating the market, was the government itself...all in a way designed to punish Nacchio for his faithful adherence to legal principles and for his efforts to preserve your individual privacy.

Far fetched? Just to drive home the point of big government intimidation, the teen-age son of Mr. Nacchio was attacked by two thugs in business suits who jumped out of a dark sedan, identified the young Nacchio by name, and then stabbed him. As they were hastily departing, they yelled, "Say hi to your dad for us." The son of Joe Nacchio survived, but the message was clear: KILL THE MESSENGER.

In another ironic--some might say miraculous--twist of fate, Joe Nacchio ended up at the Federal Prison Camp Schuylkill in Minersville, Pennsylvania, along with the Union Bank of Switzerland insider Brad Birkenfeld, and Booz Allen Hamilton analyst and Army Officer Scott Bennett; and upon connecting the dots, the constellation of truth revealed has been breathtaking and ominous.

Indeed, the cover-up is always worse than the crime, and the truth will usually come out...eventually.

Who lied? Who manipulated the stock market and for what purpose? Who benefited?

NSA continues to be caught in a series of outright lies and distortions.

Booz Allen Hamilton continues to slop at the public trough to the tune of billions of dollars of military-intelligence agency contracts. Congress continues to tighten its grip of control on a near schizophrenic public emotionally traumatized and exhausted from 12 years of war against a phantom enemy.

An overwhelming majority (70% in fact) of young people, 18 to 35 years of age, believe that Edward Snowden has done, and continues to do, the right thing by exposing the government's shenanigans, scams, and violations of law. The European Parliament has even nominated Edward Snowden for the Sakharov prize, Europe's top human rights award, along with Malala Yousafaz, the 14-year old Pakistani girl who was shot in the head by the Taliban for speaking about educating women. We could have worse examples to follow.

Finally, what is particularly interesting, is that 2LT Scott Bennett filed an official military report with the Pentagon and Congressional Committees (Armed Services; Intelligence; Homeland Security; Government Oversight and Reform) informing them about the National Security Agency-Joe Nacchio connection, as well as the assault on Nacchio's son and its implications for intolerable government abuse of citizens and need for Congressional investigation. This report was sent to Congress and General Martin Dempsey and General Ray Odierno (and others) on August 7, 2013. The Wall Street Journal and Reuters news stories about Nacchio and QWEST's connections to the NSA surveillance programs and Edward Snowden's revelations, came out <u>two months later</u>. Seems someone is either listening, or failing to hold back the tide. See attached letter.

October 9, 2013

WHEREFORE, it is respectfully submitted that this report be shared immediately with Members of Congress, the Department of Defense Inspector General, and the media to expose this matter as either:

1) A treasonous conspiratorial manipulation of information by the Department of Justice (Attorney General Eric Holder; Assistant Attorney General Lanny Breuer; Assistant U.S. Attorney Eric O'Connor; Assistant U.S. Attorney Eric Downing) and the Intelligence Community (Director of National Intelligence; C.I.A.; N.S.A.) and defense contractor Booz-Allen-Hamilton (McLean, Virginia) against the United States military (U.S. Central Command, Threat Finance, Interagency Group); or

2) A pathetic and scandalous bureaucratic blunder which has spilled the blood of soldiers, sailors, airmen, and marines unnecessarily, and wasted tens of millions of dollars.

As an Officer of the United States Army, sworn to "preserve and defend" the Constitution of the United States, I submit this report as a fulfillment of that duty.

I invite you to review the evidence and arrive at your own conclusion. See Exhibit **1**.

Respectfully,

2LT Scott Bennett, U.S. Army (Reserve)
11th Psychological Operations Battalion

cc: GEN Martin Dempsey, Chairman, Joint Chiefs of Staff
    GEN Ray Odierno, Chief of Staff, U.S. Army, Pentagon
    Pentagon Inspector General
    House and Senate Intelligence Committees
    House and Senate Armed Services Committees
    House and Senate Government Oversight and Reform Committees
    U.S. Civil Affairs-Psychological Operations Command, FT. Bragg, NC
    MAJ Avie Stone, Trial Defense Services, 16th LOD, FT. Hamilton, NY
    President Barack Hussein Obama, The White House
    Senator Carl Levin (D-MI)

Annual Report 2012
Union Bank of Switzerland EXHIBIT 1

EXPLAINING THE UBS FINE IN RELATION TO ITS AVERAGE INCOME:

A fine of $780 million translates into only a 2% fine on UBS' average yearly income. See the numbers below.

Key figures

Fig. (A) = UBS assets = 1,416,962 trillion Swiss Francs
Fig. (B) = Return on assets = 2.1%
$ Earnings = (A)x(B) = 2.1% x 1.4 trillion= $31.5 billion

CHF million, except where indicated	31.12.12	31.12.11	31.12.10
Group results			
Operating income	25,443	27,788	31,994
Operating expenses	27,216	22,482	24,650
Operating profit/(loss) from continuing operations before tax	(1,774)	5,307	7,345
Net profit/(loss) attributable to UBS shareholders	(2,511)	4,138	7,452
Diluted earnings per share (CHF)[1]	(0.67)	1.08	1.94
Key performance indicators[2], balance sheet and capital management, and additional information			
Performance			
Return on equity (RoE) (%)	(5.2)	9.1	18.0
Return on tangible equity (%)[3]	1.6	11.9	24.7
Return on risk-weighted assets, gross (%)[4]	12.0	13.7	15.5
Fig (B) Return on assets, gross (%)	1.9	2.1	2.3
Growth			
Net profit growth (%)[5]	N/A	(44.5)	N/A
Net new money growth (%)[6]	1.6	1.9	(0.8)
Efficiency			
Cost/income ratio (%)	106.5	80.7	76.9
Capital strength			
BIS tier 1 capital ratio (%)[7]	21.3	15.9	17.8
FINMA leverage ratio (%)[7]	6.3	5.4	4.5
Balance sheet and capital management			
Fig (A) Total assets	1,259,232	1,416,962	1,314,813
Equity attributable to UBS shareholders	45,895	48,530	43,728
Total book value per share (CHF)[8]	12.25	12.95	11.53
Tangible book value per share (CHF)[8]	10.52	10.36	8.94
BIS core tier 1 capital ratio (%)[7]	19.0	14.1	15.3
BIS total capital ratio (%)[7]	25.2	17.2	20.4
BIS risk-weighted assets[7]	192,505	240,962	198,875
BIS tier 1 capital[7]	40,982	38,370	35,323
Additional information			
Invested assets (CHF billion)[9]	2,230	2,088	2,075
Personnel (full-time equivalents)	62,628	64,820	64,617
Market capitalization[10]	54,729	42,843	58,803

[1] Refer to "Note 8 Earnings per share (EPS) and shares outstanding" in the "Financial information" section of this report for more information. [2] For the definitions of our key performance indicators, refer to the "Measurement of performance" section of this report. [3] Net profit attributable to UBS shareholders before amortization and impairment of goodwill and intangible assets / average equity attributable to UBS shareholders less average goodwill and intangible assets. [4] Based on Basel 2.5 risk-weighted assets for 2012. Based on Basel II risk-weighted assets for 2011 and 2010. [5] Not meaningful and not included if either the reporting period or the comparison period is a loss period. [6] Group net new money includes net new money for Retail & Corporate and excludes interest and dividend income. [7] Capital management data is disclosed in accordance with the Basel 2.5 framework for 31 December 2012 and 31 December 2011, and in accordance with the Basel II framework for 31 December 2010. Refer to the "Capital management" section of this report for more information. [8] Refer to the "Capital management" section of this report for more information. [9] In 2012, we refined our definition of invested assets. Refer to "Note 35 Invested assets and net new money" in the "Financial information" section of this report for more information. Group invested assets includes invested assets for Retail & Corporate. [10] Refer to the appendix "UBS shares" of this report for more information.

FINE TO INCOME = $ 780 million U.S. dollars (@1.06 dollar/franc exchang
                  $ 31.5 billion U.S. dollar fine = 2% of income

another way to look at it....

A fine of 2% on the average American family earning $50,000.00 per year translates into $1,000, or $20.00 per week for a year.

6

BOOZ ALLEN HAMILTON   **EXHIBIT 2**   SECURITY
Date Received: _____

PERSONNEL SECURITY
CLEARANCE / ACCESS REQUEST and JUSTIFICATION FORM

General Information

Employee Name:	Bennett, Scott *(Last, First, Middle)*
Emp. ID:	537112
Position/Title:	Counter-Threat Finance Analyst
Phone #:	TBD
Contract #:	SPO700-03-D-1380
Booz Allen Charge #:	B09003055012362000000
TAT# (if applicable):	05-40
Delivery # (if applicable):	DO 123
Program Name:	Strategic Planning, Analysis and Security Support to USCENTCOM
Work Location:	MacDill AFB, Tampa FL

Date of Signed Offer Letter *(Required for Future Employees)*: _____

Clearance / Access Level Required (Type an "X" in the box that applies.)

- [ ] Secret
- [X] Top Secret
- [ ] Periodic Reinvestigation
- [ ] Upgrade Requirements
- [X] SCI (Must list accesses: SI/TK/HCS/G)
- [ ] Other: _____

Has the applicant held an **ACTIVE CLEARANCE or ACCESS** with **ANOTHER COMPANY OR AGENCY** in the last **24 MONTHS**? (Type an "X" in the box that applies.)

[X] YES   [ ] NO

If "YES", please have the applicant complete the "Clearance Data Form" and attach it to this completed document.

JUSTIFICATION

Please provide a description of the responsibilities of the employee in support of the contract listed above which will require them access to classified materials.

Access to SCI is required in the performance of the SURVIAC contract (Contract # SPO700-03-D-1380/TAT 05-40, D.O. 123). Mr. Bennett will provide strategic planning, analysis, and security assessment support to U. S. Central Command's Threat Finance (TF) Program. Specifically, he will perform research and analysis of terrorist, insurgent, and narcotics trafficking funding streams, identify key financial network nodes for lethal and non-lethal targeting, and analyze financial intelligence within the USCENTCOM area of responsibility.

BOOZ ALLEN Program Manager	Robert P. Thompson	Principal	1/19/2010	
ALL EMPLOYEES COTR/COR/RA	Name	Title	Date	Signature
	Peggy Wagner	937-255-6302, Ext. 224	937-255-9673	46th OG/OGM/OL-AC
SCI ONLY	Name	Phone Number	Fax Number	Office Symbol

Security Review

| Security Rep. ONLY | Print Name | Title | Date | Signature |

EXHIBIT 2

Copy of assignment orders issued by US CENTCOM to Booz Allen Hamilton for Scott Bennett. Orders shown to Housing Office with instructions that Army transfer was forthcoming--TBD

EXHIBIT 3

BOOZ ALLEN HAMILTON

SECURITY
Date Received: _____

PERSONNEL SECURITY
CLEARANCE / ACCESS REQUEST and JUSTIFICATION FORM

General Information

Employee Name: Bennett, Scott, Allan (Last, First, Middle)   Emp. ID: 537112

Position/Title: Associate   Phone #: 703-377-4229

Contract #: SP0700-03-D-1380-0150   Booz Allen Charge #: B09003-0550-1501

TAT # (if applicable): SURVIAC 06-15   Delivery # (if applicable): DO 1503

Program Name (if used): USSOCOM SOF Support   Work Location: McLean VA

Date of Signed Offer Letter (Required for Future Employees): _____

Clearance / Access Level Required (Type an "X" in the box that applies.)

[ ] Secret   [X] Top Secret   [ ] Periodic Reinvestigation   [ ] Upgrade Requirements

[X] SCI (Must list accesses): SI/TK/G/HCS   [ ] Other: _____

Has the applicant held an **ACTIVE CLEARANCE or ACCESS** with **ANOTHER COMPANY OR AGENCY** in the last 24 MONTHS? (Type an "X" in the box that applies.)

[ ] YES   [X] NO

If "YES", please have the applicant complete the "Clearance Data Form" and attach it to this completed document.

JUSTIFICATION

Please provide a description of the responsibilities of the employee in support of the contract listed above which will require them access to classified materials.

Scott Bennett provides classified research, analysis, and wargaming support to the US Special Operations Command (USSOCOM) Center for Knowledge and Futures (SOKF). This support requires employee to have access to TS/SCI information and to work in USSOCOM facilities requiring TS/SCI for access.

	Name	Title	Date	Signature
BOOZ ALLEN Program Manager	Glenn Harned	Senior Associate	2/27/08	[signature]
ALL EMPLOYEES COTR/COR/RA	Col Kenneth Coons	813-828-2447	813-826-2924	USSOCOM SOKF/J9
SCI ONLY	Name	Phone Number	Fax Number	Office Symbol
Security Review *Security Rep. ONLY*	Print Name	Title	Date	Signature

C/A Request Form 60704

EXHIBIT 3

Orders issued by U.S. Special Operations Command to Booz Allen Hamilton, then issued to Scott Bennett as Liaison Officer to State Department Coordinator for Counterterrorism

EXHIBIT 4

UNITED STATES DISTRICT COURT
MIDDLE DISTRICT OF FLORIDA
TAMPA DIVISION

UNITED STATES OF AMERICA
V.
SCOTT ALLAN BENNETT

CASE NO.: 8:11-cr-14-T-33AEP

DEFENDANT'S MOTION FOR TERMINATION OF DETENTION
OR IN THE ALTERNATIVE, BAIL PENDING APPEAL, TO ALLOW HIM TO:
PROVIDE INTELLIGENCE INFORMATION ESSENTIAL TO UNITED STATES
NATIONAL SECURITY CONCERNING TERRORIST-FINANCING AND ITS CURRENT
CONNECTION TO NATIONAL SECURITY AGENCY WHISTLEBLOWER
EDWARD SNOWDEN, BOOZ-ALLEN-HAMILTON, AND UNION BANK OF SWITZERLAND-
BRAD BIRKENFELD REPORT TO U.S. JUSTICE DEPARTMENT, CENTRAL INTELLIGENCE
AGENCY, U.S. SENATE, U.S. CENTRAL COMMAND,
AND U.S. CIVIL AFFAIRS-PSYCHOLOGICAL OPERATIONS COMMAND.

EMERGENCY MOTION:

COMES NOW, defendant, Scott Allan Bennett, pro se, and submits Defendant's Motion for Termination of Detention or in the Alternative, Bail Pending Appeal, pursuant to 18 U.S.C. §3141 and the Uniform Code of Military Justice (U.C.M.J.), and 10 U.S.C. § 938, for the following reasons:

1. Mr. Bennett's appeal raises substantial questions of law and constitutional issues which will likely result in a reversal, or a reduced sentence less than time already served.

2. Mr. Bennett remains a U.S. Army Reserve Officer assigned to the 11th Psychological Operations Battalion, whose case is being reviewed by military and Congressional authorities.

3. Mr. Bennett's appeal raises the substantial and complex issue of jurisdiction involving the military, the State of Florida, the Federal Courts, and the civilian Department of Justice prosecuting a member of the Armed Services on the active-status list. This case is the first of its kind, changes existing laws, and sets new precedent by which future cases can be decided, and Americans (both civilian and servicemember) can be imprisoned and their constitutional rights suspended or lost. This appeal contains information essential to the National Security of the United States and its allies.

EXHIBIT 4

EXHIBIT 5

DEPARTMENT OF THE ARMY
11TH PSYCHOLOGICAL OPERATIONS BATTALION
5550 DOWER HOUSE ROAD
UPPER MARLBORO, MD 20772

Dr. Ralph Shrader
President and Chief Executive Officer
Booz Allen Hamilton
8283 Greensboro Drive
McLean, VA 22102

Subject: Scott Bennett

5 April 2009

Dear Dr. Shrader:

I am the 11th Psychological Operations Battalion Commander and I am writing to you concerning Scott Bennett, who is an Associate at your firm. Second Lieutenant Bennett was recently commissioned as an Officer in my unit.

Second Lieutenant Bennett has been awarded a Direct Commission in the US Army Reserve and will serve as a Psychological Operations Officer in my battalion. We are glad to have him and are looking forward to the completion of his training and serving our great country.

I'd like to respectfully request your assistance in allowing him the military leave he will need from your firm to complete his training, and I know he will be a greater asset to Booz Allen as a result.

If you ever have any questions about Mr. Bennett's military service, please feel free to contact me by telephone at 910-964-9714 or by e-mail at joyce.busch@us.army.mil. On behalf of the United State Army Reserve, I thank you for your cooperation and support.

Sincerely,

JOYCE M. BUSCH
LTC/PO
Commanding

EXHIBIT 5

Letter confirming LTC Joyce Busch as Scott Bennett's commanding officer and <u>not</u> LTC Joel Droba as falsely claimed by the government. Letter establishes Scott Bennett as a "Psychological Operations Officer" assigned to 11POB.

RULINCS 29418016 - BENNETT, SCOTT ALLEN - Unit: SCH-E-B

FROM:
TO: 29418016
SUBJECT: CEO who resisted NSA spying is out of prison. And he feels ?vindicated?
DATE: 10/02/2013 12:06:11 AM

A CEO who resisted NSA spying is out of prison. And he feels vindicated by Snowden leaks.

By Andrea Peterson, Published: September 30 at 12:07 pm

Both Edward Snowden and Joseph Nacchio revealed details about some of the things that go on at NSA headquarters in Fort Meade. (NSA/Reuters)

Just one major telecommunications company refused to participate in a legally dubious NSA surveillance program in 2001. A few years later, its CEO was indicted by federal prosecutors. He was convicted, served four and a half years of his sentence and was released this month.

Prosecutors claim Qwest CEO Joseph Nacchio was guilty of insider trading, and that his prosecution had nothing to do with his refusal to allow spying on his customers without the permission of the Foreign Intelligence Surveillance Court. But to this day, Nacchio insists that his prosecution was retaliation for refusing to break the law on the NSA's behalf.

After his release from custody Sept. 20, Nacchio told the Wall Street Journal that he feels "vindicated" by the content of the leaks that show that the agency was collecting American's phone records.

Nacchio was convicted of selling of Qwest stock in early 2001, not long before the company hit financial troubles. However, he claimed in court documents that he was optimistic about the firm's ability to win classified government contracts something they'd succeeded at in the past. And according to his timeline, in February 2001 some six months before the Sept. 11 terrorist attacks he was approached by the NSA and asked to spy on customers during a meeting he thought was about a different contract. He reportedly refused because his lawyers believed such an action would be illegal and the NSA wouldn't go through the FISA Court. And then, he says, unrelated government contracts started to disappear.

His narrative matches with the warrantless surveillance program reported by USA Today in 2006 which noted Qwest as the lone holdout from the program, hounded by the agency with hints that their refusal "might affect its ability to get future classified work with the government." But Nacchio was prevented from bringing up any of this defense during his jury trial the evidence needed to support it was deemed classified and the judge in his case refused his requests to use it. And he still believes his prosecution was retaliatory for refusing the NSA requests for bulk access to customers' phone records. Some other observers share that opinion, and it seems consistent with evidence that has been made public, including some of the redacted court filings unsealed after his conviction.

The NSA declined to comment on Nacchio, referring inquiries to the Department of Justice. The Department of Justice did not respond to The Post's request for comment.

Snowden leaked documents about NSA spying programs to the public and arguably broke the law in doing so. In contrast, Nacchio seems to have done what was in his power to limit an illegal government data collection program. Even during his own defense, he went through the legal channels he could to make relevant information available for his defense albeit unsuccessfully.

The programs that were revealed are also substantially different in nature, if not in content. The Bush-era warrantless surveillance programs and data collection programs were on shaky legal ground, based on little more than the president's say-so. That's why telecom companies sought and received legal immunity from Congress for their participation in 2008. But that same update also expanded government surveillance powers. Some observers argue that some of the NSA's spying programs are still unconstitutional. But at a minimum, these programs were authorized by the FISC and disclosed to congressional intelligence committees.

Nacchio told the Wall Street Journal, "I never broke the law, and I never will." But he never got a chance to present to the jury his theory that his prosecution was politically motivated.

Correction: An earlier version of this post reported the the length of time between Nacchio's meetings with the NSA and his indictment was a few months rather than a few years. We regret the error.

October 24, 2013   (UNCLASSIFIED)

2LT Scott Bennett
11th Psychological Operations Battalion
U.S. Army Reserve
#29418-016
P.O. Box 670
Minersville, PA 17954-0670

Wall Street Journal
Letters to the Editor
1211 Avenue of the Americas
New York, NY 10036

RE: Response letter to Senator Diane Feinstein's OP-ED on Monday, Oct. 14, 2013, entitled "THE NSA'S WATCHFULNESS PROTECTS AMERICA."

Sir:
Senator Diane Feinstein distorts and hides the truth, if not outright lies, in her Oct. 14, 2013 opinion editorial "The NSA's watchfullness protects America." I know because I was there, and no one is better qualified to expose this than I. I not only worked in this counter-terrorism area she describes at the time she describes, I may have in fact written the very Army Intelligence Report she plagiarizes from. I served as a U.S. Army Reserve Officer, and as a Booz Allen Hamilton defense contractor with a TS/SCI clearance. A copy of my reports were sent to Senator Feinstein (as well as many other members of the Senate and House Armed Services, Intelligence, and other committees) on September 25, 2012; then another on May 27, 2013; then another on September 11, 2013. These reports exposed various terrorist connections to Booz Allen Hamilton, Director of National Intelligence, National Security Agency, and negligent members of Congress. The connection involved terrorist threat financing and NSA's knowledge of this--as well as its effort to silence the whistleblowers who first exposed it. The Wall Street Journal also received a copy of this report.

The irony is Edward Snowden saw these reports, and what happened to the whistleblowers, and chose to avoid the same fate by going directly to the public with his information. The rest is history.

The Senate Intelligence Committee is covering up these reports, and Senator Feinstein is lying when she says, "the locations" (of phone callers) is not tracked by the NSA surveillance operations. They are, and this is precisely what threatens Americans with oppression by an "armed bureaucracy partnered with a frantically obsessed Department of Justice Prosecutor".

She is also lying when she affirms FBI Director Bob Mueller's ominous warning "...if intelligence officials had had the NSA's searchable database of phone records, 9-11 would have been prevented." QWEST Communications President Joseph Naccio, who was prosecuted for not "surrending these records" has already proven this statement FALSE.

Seems truth really is stranger than fiction. Contact me for details.
2LT Scott Bennett

TERMS AND ORGANIZATIONS:

1) National Media Exploitation Center: used for unlocking, downloading, and analysis of CDs, thumb drives, computers, files/documents, and electronic equipment seized in raids. Special technology enables the download of contents from locked and/or damaged computers, allows the extraction of names, phone numbers, messages, and images, and then, using specialized software, can process and store that data and link it to other information which allows the discovery of terrorist networks. NMEC located at CIA headquarters, Langley, VA. Note: Osama Bin Laden had 2.4 terabytes of data seized by SEAL team, transferred by Osprey helicopter at Bagram, Afghanistan and flown to the USS Carl Vinson in the Arabian Sea, before being released to CIA for analysis. This information was never synthesized with Union Bank of Switzerland-Birkenfeld intelligence materials given to the Department of Justice and Senate Permanent Subcommittee on investigations (i.e., 19,000 Swiss bank accounts and owner info).

2) Terrorist Screening Database (TSDB): product of National Counter-terrorism Center (NCTC), which is a subordinate organization of the office of the Director of National Intelligence (CIA). UBS-Birkenfeld intelligence yielded Swiss bank account holders financing terrorist networks or suspected of such (Abdullah Azziz), but for some unknown reason was not synthesized into TSDB.

3) National Counterterrorism Center (NCTC): NCTC integrates and analyzes all intelligence on terrorism and counterterrorism and designs strategic counterterrorism plans. It is a subordinate organization of the Director of National Intelligence (DNI). It maintains the Terrorist Screening Database, an authoritative list fed by two primary sources: international terrorist information from NCTC, and domestic terrorist information from the FBI.

4) Director of National Intelligence (DNI): A cabinet-level position, the DNI is an intelligence czar whose role is to coordinate all sixteen agencies and departments that make up the intelligence community. DNI advised the President and the National Security Council.

5) National Intelligence Estimate (NIE): Produced by the interagency National Intelligence Council, NIEs are the authoritiative overall future assessments of the intelligence community, usually produced at the top secret classification level. Subjects can range from projections of Russian and Chinese nuclear forces to the national security impact of climate change. UBS-Birkenfeld intelligence not considered by any NIEs.

6) Counterthreat Finance (CTF): field of counterterrorism and military special operations involving 34 major federal agencies and military commands, operating in 16 U.S. cities, tracking the money flow to and from terrorist networks. Not a single CTF agency or military command investigated, analyzed or reported any element of the Union Bank of Switzerland-Birkenfeld revelations to the Department of Justice and Senate Permanent Subcommittee on Investigations, or U.S. CENTCOM/ U.S. Civil Affairs-Psychological Operations Command reports issued by Brad Birkenfeld and 2LT Scott Bennett.

7) State Department Coordinator for Counterterrorism (State/CT): Assignment to which Scott Bennett was liaison officer for U.S. Special Operations Command. Major General Dell Dailey, Commander of Joint Special Operations Command (JSOC) was appointed to be Ambassador and President Bush's Coordinator for Counterterrorism. State/CT mentioned extensively in Wikileaks cables about UBS-Birkenfeld.

8) Joint Special Operations Command (JSOC): worked to trace the secret flow of money from international banks to finance terrorist networks. However JSOC did not analyze Union Bank of Switzerland-Birkenfeld intelligence materials provided by Birkenfeld to both Department of Justice and Senate Permanent Subcommittee on Investigations indicating terrorist financing activities.

9) Special Operations Forces (SOF): A term used to describe elite military units proficient in counterinsurgency, training foreign military forces, civil affairs, and psychological operations. They are more highly qualified, both physically and mentally, and better equipped than conventional forces. They operate in small teams and are made up of the Army's special Forces; U.S. Navy SEALS; and the Air Force's special operations airmen. Scott Bennett was given a Direct Commission as Special Operations Officer and assigned to Psychological Operations, 11th PSYOP Battalion.

10) Defense Office of Hearings and Appeals (DOHA): A component of
the Defense Legal Services Agency of the Defense Department that
provides legal adjudication and claims decisions in personnel
security clearances cases for contractor personnel doing classified
work as well as for the Defense Department and twenty other federal
agencies and departments. 2LT Scott Bennett has referred his
case to this authority for investigation and reversal, and filed
a complaint for prosecutorial misconduct in this matter. See Exhibit

11) Defense Critical Infrastructure Program for Finance (CIPFIN):
a database and element of the Defense Critical Infrastructure
program that identifies and assesses the security of physical
assets, cyberassets, and infrastructures in the public and private
sectors that are essential to national security. UBS-Birkenfeld
financial intelligence not synthesized into this database.

12) Real Time Regional Gateway (RTRG): computer linkup program allowing
data or intelligence materials captured to be manipulated in
order to yield new phone numbers and new leads on terrorist networks.
No UBS-Birkenfeld intelligence material (i.e. cell phone numbers)
inputed into this system, resulting in loss of terrorist leads.
RTRG created by National Security Agency (NSA) as a network to
speed up the delivery of signal intercepts from collectors to
users on the ground. Called an "interactive national repository,"
RTRG allows users to see all signal intelligence that collectors
are working on in real time.

13) Technical Operations Support activity (TOSA): Referred as "The
Activity", TOSA represents Army's equivalent of CIA. A clandestine
intelligence, surveillance, and reconnaissance (ISR) organization
that supports special operations, JSOC, and other short-term
intelligence collection efforts that demand close-in presence.
Formerly known as the Intelligence Support Activity, and Grey Fox.

14) Defense Intelligence Agency (DIA): the largest producer and manager
of foreign military intelligence for the Department of Defense.
The DIA director is the primary adviser to the defense secretary
and the chairman of the Joint Chiefs of Staff on military intelligence
matters. It also manages the Defense Attache program. No UBS-
Birkenfeld financial intelligence analyzed by DIA.

15) National Security Agency (NSA): Intelligence eavesdropping agency whose mission is to protect U.S. national security information systems and to collect and disseminate foreign signals intelligence (SIGINT). Its areas of expertise include cryptanalysis, cryptography, mathematics, computer science, and foreign language analysis.

16) Central Intelligence Agency (CIA): Collects, evaluates, and disseminates information on political, military, economic, scientific, and other developments abroad. Its agents collect intelligence on threats to U.S. interests, among them terrorism, weapons proliferation and development, international drug trafficking and criminal syndicates, and foreign espionage.

17) U.S. Intelligence Community (IC): consists of sixteen agencies and organizations within the Executive Branch: Air Force Intelligence, Army Intelligence, the Central Intelligence Agency, Coast Guard Intelligence, the Defense Intelligence Agency, the Department of Energy's intelligence arm, the Department of Homeland Security's intelligence arm, the the Department of State's Bureau of Intelligence and Research, the Department of the Treasury's intelligence arm, the Drug Enforcement Administration, the Federal Bureau of Investigation, Marine Corps Intelligence, the National Geospatial-Intelligence Agency, the National Reconnaissance Office, the National Security Agency, the Navy Intelligence, and the State Dept. Coordinator for Counterterrorism Office. <u>None</u> of these intelligence agencies debriefed Brad Birkenfeld about UBS financial intelligence materials he released to the Department of Justice and U.S. Senate.

(U//INI/HUMINT/)
(UNCLASSIFIED)

INTERCONNECTIVITY CHART:

AGENCY:	NAME:	SCOTT BENNETT (TS/SCI clearance)	EDWARD SNOWDEN (TS/SCI clearance)	BRAD BIRKENFELD (no clearance)
Booz-Allen-Hamilton		Hired as Global Psychological Operations analyst for US SOCOM, State Dept CT, US CENTCOM contracts. Work included researching, profiling, and destroying Terrorist Finance networks and operations involving banks, charities, couriers, businesses, government agencies, etc. Assigned as Interagency Operations Center analyst (FBI, CIA, NSA, Treasury, DOJ, HS, State, NRO, and other agencies).	Assigned as analyst for NSA programs; cybercommand; and computer surveillance operations interconnected with NRO, CIA, and military.	Booz Allen Hamilton contracted by CENTCOM/JIOC to conduct Terrorist Threat Finance Ops. involving Union Bank of Switzerland (and other banks) and all networks and operations financing terrorism. Booz Allen never debriefed Birkenfeld, or shared Scott Bennett's reports with military commanders as requested.
Military		Scott Bennett offered Direct Commission as a Captain in Psychological Operations. Later changed to 2LT as a result of program changes and MOS slots. Joined 11th Psychological Operations, at the request of SOCOM/JMISC Psyop-State CI contract with Booz Allen Hamilton. COL Jeff Jones (ret.) mentored Bennett in PSYOP, Islamic Terrorism, SC, Intelligence , Interagency work. Attempted to transfer Army Reserve Unit from 11th PSYOP to CENTCOM/SOCOM at McDill Air Force base for TF mission. Had Air Force Academy congressional appointment after high school; Non-Com Officer, Civil Air Patrol, Squadron 44	Enlisted in Army Special Forces training. Obtained security clearance. Discharged from Army after accident. No military experience, other than earlier High School cadets.	Birkenfeld requested GEN James Mattis, Commander, US CENTCOM, debrief him on Union Bank of Switzerland accounts and persons involved in Terrorist Finance networks and operations.
CIA-NSA			After discovering how 2LT Bennett had been falsely imprisoned and his reports ignored after following chain of command, Snowden decided he would be similarly persecuted by military and Justice Dept.; and thus decided to release his info directly to American people. News Media also informed. Assigned as CIA analyst during 2007-2009 years of Michael Hayden's tenure as director. Observed Brad Birkenfeld being targeted by CIA for Swiss Bank intelligence, using D.U.I. plot to entangle Birkenfeld, then cut him loose or trade him to Swiss authorities for Swiss Treaty benefits to U.S. Trade, etc. Snowden described this as his "turning point" moment, and completes Bennett-Birkenfeld-Snowden connection to CIA-UBS-USACAPOC-BAH.	Congressional Committees were also informed: Armed Services; Intelligence; Terrorism; Gov Oversight and Reform; Judiciary; Homeland Security. Booz Allen Hamilton contracts in coordination with assignment as Liaison Officer between US SOCOM/JMISC and Ambassador Dell Dailey (retired JSOC Commander) State Dept. Counterterrorism. Worked with National Counter-terrorism Center (NCTC), CIA, and NSA on cyberwarfare, Threat Finance, and other contracts (other projects are classified and non-disclosable). Approached by CIA agents in Switzerland attempting to extract banking intelligence from him, in violation of Swiss law. Invented D.U.I. trap to force Birkenfeld into compromising position. Sensing a trap, Birkenfeld fled to U.S. Dept. of Justice and presented his files to AUSA Kevin O'Connor and Kevin Downing. DOJ conspired with CIA and NSA to "tap" Birkenfeld's phone; generate charges; falsely prosecute him to silence him. State Dept. also conspired to set-up Birkenfeld criminally.

(OSINT/HUMINT)
(UNCLASSIFIED)

INTERCONNECTIVITY CHART (cont.):

NAME:	SCOTT BENNETT (TS/SCI clearance)	EDWARD SNOWDEN (TS/SCI clearance)	BRAD BIRKENFELD (none)
AGENCY:	Justice Department		

SCOTT BENNETT: In January 2010, 2LT Bennett was charged by the Justice Dept. (AUSA Sara Sweeney) with: making a false statement (18USC§1001); wearing military uniform without authority (18USC§702); and violating a defense regulation (50USC§797(a)(1)). This was a case of first impressions, since never has a military officer been charged with these statutes by the Justice Department. 2LT Bennett denied military defense counsel, tried in civilian Florida court before civilian jury. Air Force JAG Officer (Major Tim Goines, USAF) joined prosecution in uniform, giving false impression of military charges. For TS/SCI related reasons, 2LT Bennett gave no defense, wrongly assuming trial was "a test" by military. Bennett convicted and sentenced to 36 months in prison (exceeding guideline sentence of 0-7 months as recommended by USSG. Reasons for prosecution relate to reports Bennett submitted in relation to intelligence about Terrorist Finance through Swiss Banks; military contractor failures to provide adequate intel; and report on "Don't Ask, Don't Tell" implications on Islamic extremists.

After arriving at prison, Bennett met Birkenfeld and learned of specific materials relating to Finance which were never shared with military; as well as CIA-NSA operations. Bennett reported this Sept. 25, 2012 to military and Congress.
Bennett has Connected-the-Dots.

EDWARD SNOWDEN: Snowden released his NSA documents after seeing Bennett's imprisonment and recognizing Birkenfeld's entrapment.

Snowden assigned as analyst to the National Security Agency and Central Intelligence Agency in technical computer analyst capacity. Later became Booz Allen Hamilton contractor for agency.

Snowden saw first hand, and reported in his interview with Glenn Greenwald, about Birkenfeld being targeted and manipulated by CIA; about NSA tapping his phone; and charges against him as a State Dept. attempt to "lessen the damage of the 2008 financial crisis" and "gain advantage in Swiss treaties."
Snowden's materials were reported obtained from JWICS (Joint Worldwide Intelligence Communication System). [2LT Bennett also connected to JWICS].

Edward Snowden also saw Booz Allen Hamilton materials relating to Terrorist Finance contract, and UBS-Birkenfeld connection.

Edward Snowden viewed 2LT Bennett's Sept. 25, 2012 report to USACAPOC Commander GEN Jeffrey Jacobs about Brad Birkenfeld's connection to Threat Finance Mission, Booz Allen Hamilton, and UBS accounts.
Additionally Snowden saw in Bennett's reports information provided to him by Birkenfeld, disclosing his experience as targeted by CIA-NSA in false prosecution. Snowden chose to release info to American public.
Snowden saw the Shell-Game.

BRAD BIRKENFELD: Birkenfeld confirms Snowden's CIA-NSA Swiss banker operation.

In 2009 (starting in 2007), Birkenfeld was indicted for "Conspiracy" relating to Union Bank of Switzerland financial management of client assets (Raul Weil). UBS banker, also charged, but remained in Switzerland. He is now returning to U.S. to challenge charges and release info relating to "Terror Finance info". "Grant of Immunity" was expected by Justice Dept. At FPC Schuylkill, Birkenfeld met Scott Bennett, and reported that UBS accounts being used by terrorist finance networks and operations were never reported to military via the Senate Permanent Comm. on Investigations (Barack Obama on this).
Also Birkenfeld was never debriefed by military or Booz Allen Hamilton (which was responsible for TF).
Birkenfeld reported wikileaks material disclosing State/CT cables confirming CIA-NSA-DOJ prosecution of him. Bennett had been assigned to State/CT and recognized cables and implications, and reported it to military and Congressional authorities. Birkenfeld reported to GEN James Mattis (CENTCOM). Later paid $104 million for silence.
Requested Congressional investigation has been ignored. Cover-up.

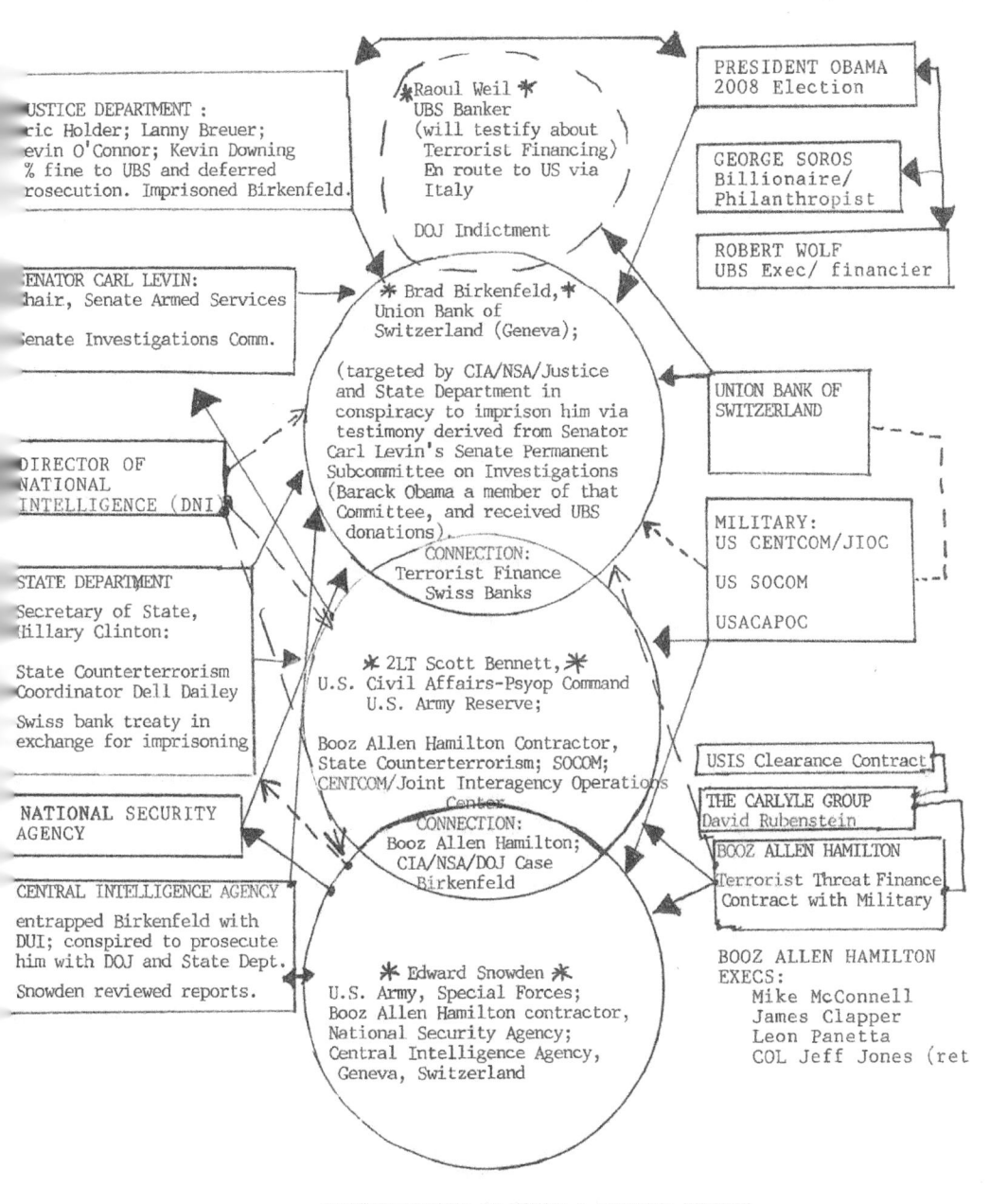

JUSTICE DEPARTMENT:
Eric Holder; Lanny Breuer;
Kevin O'Connor; Kevin Downing
% fine to UBS and deferred
prosecution. Imprisoned Birkenfeld.

SENATOR CARL LEVIN:
Chair, Senate Armed Services

Senate Investigations Comm.

**DIRECTOR OF
NATIONAL
INTELLIGENCE (DNI)**

STATE DEPARTMENT
Secretary of State,
Hillary Clinton:

State Counterterrorism
Coordinator Dell Dailey

Swiss bank treaty in
exchange for imprisoning

**NATIONAL SECURITY
AGENCY**

CENTRAL INTELLIGENCE AGENCY
entrapped Birkenfeld with
DUI; conspired to prosecute
him with DOJ and State Dept.
Snowden reviewed reports.

PRESIDENT OBAMA
2008 Election

GEORGE SOROS
Billionaire/
Philanthropist

ROBERT WOLF
UBS Exec/ financier

Raoul Weil
UBS Banker
(will testify about
Terrorist Financing)
En route to US via
Italy

DOJ Indictment

Brad Birkenfeld,
Union Bank of
Switzerland (Geneva);

(targeted by CIA/NSA/Justice
and State Department in
conspiracy to imprison him via
testimony derived from Senator
Carl Levin's Senate Permanent
Subcommittee on Investigations
(Barack Obama a member of that
Committee, and received UBS
donations).

CONNECTION:
Terrorist Finance
Swiss Banks

2LT Scott Bennett,
U.S. Civil Affairs-Psyop Command
U.S. Army Reserve;

Booz Allen Hamilton Contractor,
State Counterterrorism; SOCOM;
CENTCOM/Joint Interagency Operations
Center

CONNECTION:
Booz Allen Hamilton;
CIA/NSA/DOJ Case
Birkenfeld

Edward Snowden
U.S. Army, Special Forces;
Booz Allen Hamilton contractor,
National Security Agency;
Central Intelligence Agency,
Geneva, Switzerland

**UNION BANK OF
SWITZERLAND**

MILITARY:
US CENTCOM/JIOC

US SOCOM

USACAPOC

USIS Clearance Contract

THE CARLYLE GROUP
David Rubenstein

BOOZ ALLEN HAMILTON
Terrorist Threat Finance
Contract with Military

**BOOZ ALLEN HAMILTON
EXECS:**
  Mike McConnell
  James Clapper
  Leon Panetta
  COL Jeff Jones (ret

INTERCONNECTION OF ISSUES & AGENCIES DIAGRAM

— — — — — THEORETICAL CONNECTION/ RELATIONSHIP

(UNCLASSIFIED)(OSINT/HUMINT)

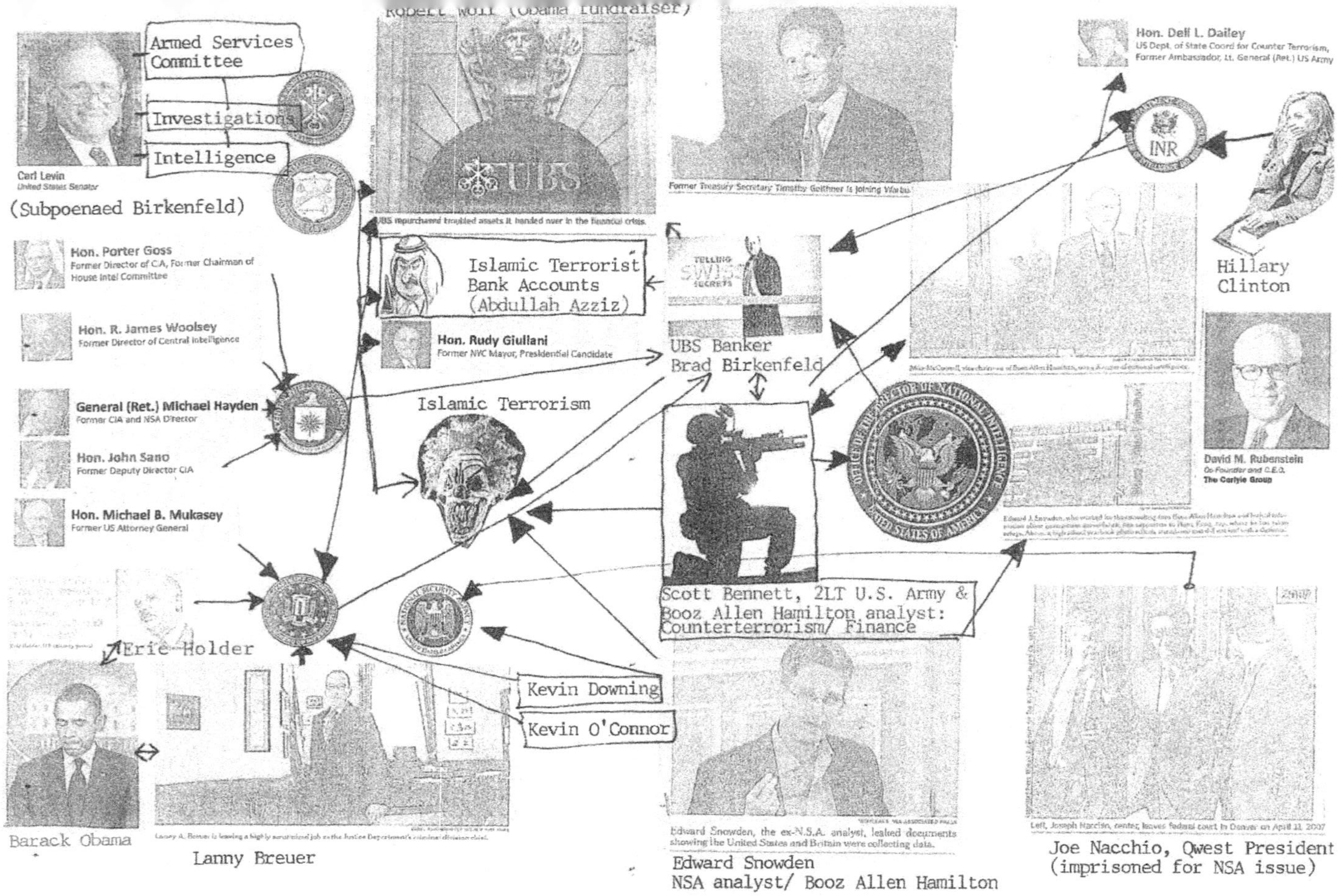

Carl Levin
United States Senator

Armed Services Committee
Investigations
Intelligence

(Subpoenaed Birkenfeld)

Hon. Porter Goss
Former Director of C.I.A, Former Chairman of House Intel Committee

Hon. R. James Woolsey
Former Director of Central Intelligence

General (Ret.) Michael Hayden
Former CIA and NSA Director

Hon. John Sano
Former Deputy Director CIA

Hon. Michael B. Mukasey
Former US Attorney General

Barack Obama
Eric Holder
Lanny Breuer

Hon. Rudy Giuliani
Former NYC Mayor, Presidential Candidate

Islamic Terrorism

Islamic Terrorist Bank Accounts
(Abdullah Azziz)

UBS Banker
Brad Birkenfeld

Kevin O'Connor
Kevin Downing

Scott Bennett, 2LT U.S. Army & Booz Allen Hamilton analyst: Counterterrorism/Finance

Edward Snowden
NSA analyst / Booz Allen Hamilton

Joe Nacchio, Qwest President
(imprisoned for NSA issue)

Hillary Clinton

Hon. Dell L. Dailey
US Dept. of State Council for Counter Terrorism, Former Ambassador, Lt. General (Ret.) US Army

David M. Rubinstein
Co-Founder and C.E.O.
The Carlyle Group

COLLAGE OF PARTICIPANTS

(UNCLASSIFIED)
(OSINT/HUMINT)

August 15-16, 2016 -- Clinton Foundation's "pay-to-play" structure becoming clearer

The recent release of additional private emails from former Secretary of State Hillary Clinton's private email servers based at her New York home provide a clearer picture of the "pay-to-play" connections between Clinton's State Department, her and her husband's and daughter's Clinton Foundation and Clinton Global Initiative, and the private investment consulting and investment firm of Teneo Holdings, Inc. in Manhattan. In addition to these entities, there are separate Clinton family foundations that maintain their own revenue streams: the Clinton Health Access Initiative (CHAI), the Bill, Hillary and Chelsea Clinton (BHCC) Foundation, the Clinton Foundation Hong Kong, William J. Clinton Foundation Charitable Trust (Kenya), William J. Clinton Foundation Charitable Trust (UK), and the Clinton Foundation *Insalingsstiftelse* (Sweden). All these entities maintain separate operations for the Clintons' pay-to-play global racketeering operations.

The Clinton operations are massive in relation to the reported lobbying dealings that Donald Trump's campaign manager, Paul Manafort, maintained with the former Yanukovych government of Ukraine. The sudden appearance of "secret ledgers" containing Manafort's name and alleged cash payments to him by the puppet Ukrainian government of George Soros bear all the signs of another Soros/Cass Sunstein disinformation operation.

Donors with this symbol next to them, indicate direct participation in the Clinton Foundation-Swiss Bank-Saudi Terrorist Finance treason and cover up.

Donor	Amount given to Clinton Foundation/Global Initiative (CGI)	Received in return
Prince of Abu Dhabi and Foreign Minister of the United Arab Emirates Shaikh Abdullah bin Zayed al Nahayan and the Al Nahayan family of Abu Dhabi	<$5,000,000	Access to HRC at State Dept. and a $500,000 environmental speech by Bill Clinton given at the Emirates Palace Hotel in Abu Dhabi while HRC was meeting in Washington with Shaikh Abdullah.
Algeria	$500,000	State clearance for U.S. arms sales to Algeria. Deal included biological and chemical agents.
Australia, Commonwealth of	$75,000,000	Strong State Dept. for the Trans-Pacific Partnership (TPP), which stands to be a boon for Australian multinational firms.

i

Bahrain, Kingdom of	$250,000	Muted criticism by State of Bahrain's abysmal human rights practices.
Boeing Corp.	$900,000	State Dept. clearance for $29 billion arms U.S. arms sale to Saudi Arabia, including Boeing's F-15 fighter.
Booz Allen Hamilton	$700,000	*Conspired with Clinton Foundation, Covington and Burling, Swiss Banks, and Gulf Nations to hide terrorist financing and contractor fraud against United States Military. Guilty of treason and "aiding and abetting the enemies of the United States."*
Brunei Darussalam, Sultanate of	$5,000,000	State Dept. clearance for U.S. *weapons* sales to Brunei.
Cameroon, Republic of	<$100,000	Influence buying by the Cameroon government with the Clinton State Department.
Canada	$500,000	State Dept. support for Canada's Keystone XL pipeline, eventually vetoed by Barack Obama.
Chagoury Group	<$5,000,000 in cash and a $1,000,000,000 pledge	HRC delayed designating Nigeria's Boko Haram as a foreign terrorist organization because of Chagoury Group's investments and operations in Nigeria. Chagoury Group received the "Sustainable Development Award" from the CGI. Chagooury helped the family of Nigerian dictator Sani Abacha hide his wealth stolen from Nigeria's oil revenues.
Confederation of Indian Industry	<$1,000,000	Access for Indian businesses to U.S. government officials.
Corning, Inc.	$150,000	Clinton arranged for international access for the New York-based firm.
Covington and Burling	$10,000-$25,000	*Laundered terrorist financing for Union Bank of*

ii

		Switzerland, HSBC, from Gulf Countries (Saudi Arabia, Kuwait, Jordan, United Arab Emirates, Bahrain, etc.) to and through the Clinton Foundation. Partners Eric Holder, Lanny Breuer, Roger Zakheim contributed to fraud and treason.
Dahdaleh, Victor	<$5,000,000	Lobbyist for Bahrain state-owned aluminum company who sought a contract between the Bahraini firm and the U.S.-owned Alcoa World Alumina.
Dominican Republic	<$25,000,000	Clinton Foundation board member Rolando Gonzalez's company InterEnergy received contracts from Dominican government for wind energy projects. The firm received Domican President's Gold Citizen Award in 2010.
Fédération Internationale de Football Association (FIFA)	<$100,000	State pressure on *Justice Dept.* to curtail criminal investigation of FIFA.
Fernwood Foundation (Canadian foundation run by Canadian uranium mining mogul Ian Telfer	$2,600,000	**Telfer's UrAsia and Uranium One Corporations, co-owned with Canadian mining magnate and "Friend of Bill" Frank Giustra receved favorable uranium mining deals with Kazakhstan and Russia's ROSATOM and Kazakhstan's KAZATOMPROM.**
Flanders, Government of	€780,000 ($872,000)	High-level access to U.S. government officials by Flemish government officials and businesses.
GEMS Education, Dubai	$5,600,000	Bill Clinton made "honorary chairman" of the Dubai company.
Germany, Federal Republic of	$250,000	High-level access to U.S. government officials by German officials and businessmen.

Giustra, Frank (Canadian mining magnate) (Clinton Giustra Enterprise Partnership/Radcliffe Foundation)	$31,300,000	State soft-peddled threat of the Islamic State because Lafarge had negotiated with the terrorists to maintain its operations in ISIL-controlled territory in Syria. arranged favorable deals with Kazakhstan and its president, Nursultan Nazarbayev.
Hindustan Construction Corp. (India)	<$500,000	Access for corporate officials to U.S. government officials.
Ireland, Republic of	<$158,300,000	Influence-buying by Irish government with the Clintons.
Italy, Republic of	$100,000	Influence buying by the Italian government with the Clinton State Department.
Jamaica	$100,000	Digicel Group, owned by Irish billionaire and Friend of Bill, Denis O'Brien, received USAID grant for a telecommunications project in Jamaica. Digicel (Jamaica) paid Bill Clinton $225,000 for a speech in Kingston. That was in addition to the $100,000 kicked in by Jamaica to the Clinton Foundation.
Kuwait, Emirate of	$10,000,000	State Dept. clearance for U.S. *weapons* sales to Kuwait.
Lafarge Group	<$100,000	State soft-peddled threat of Islamic State (ISIL) in *Syria* because Lafarge had an agreement with ISIL not to interfere in Lafarge activities in ISIL-controlled territory in Syria. HRC was a director of Lafarge between 1990 and 1992, at a time when the firm was selling strategic military materials to Saddam Hussein's Iraq.
Lesotho, Kingdom of	<$100,000	Kickback from $11.2 million Irish grant to Clinton Foundation for HIV/AIDS abatement in Lesotho.
Mittal, Lakshmi, owner of	<$5,000,000	Favorable opportunities in

ArcelorMittal, a major steel company, and board member of Goldman Sachs		Kazakhstan, where Mittal is a member of the Foreign Investment Council of Kazakhstan. Dovetails with Bill Clinton's uranium deals with Giustra and Nazarbayev.
Sheikh Mohammed H. Al Amoudi (Ethiopian-Saudi billionaire)[1]	<$10,000,000	Influence-buying within the Clinton State Dept.
Monsanto	<$5,000,000	State advocated for Monsanto "Frankenfood" and "Frankenseeds" worldwide.
Netherlands, Kingdom of the (Netherlands National Lottery)	$10,000,000	State helped open up investment opportunities for Dutch firms in Africa.
New Zealand, Government of	$1,200,000	Influence-buying within the Clinton State Dept.
Norway, Kingdom of	$89,600,000	Norwegian government split up donations to make them look smaller than they actually were. Norwegian firms received investment opportunities in the developing world, courtesy of the U.S. Millennium Goals Corporation.
Oman, Sultanate of	<$5,000,000	State clearance for U.S. weapons sales to Oman.
Papua New Guinea, Government of	<$100,000	Influence-buying within the Clinton State Dept.
Qatar, Emirate of	<$5,000,000	State Dept. approval for U.S. arms sales to Qatar. State pressure on Justice Dept. to curtail investigation of bribery payments regarding FIFA and 2022 World Cup host, Qatar.
Ras al Khaimah, Emirate of	$50,000	Influence-buying within the Clinton State Dept.
Rwanda, Republic of	$200,000	Influence-buying with HRC's State Department.
Saudi Arabia, Kingdom of	*$25,000,000*	*State Dept. approval for U.S. arms sales to Saudi Arabia*
Suzlon Energy, Ltd. (Amsterdam)	<$5,000,000	State and CGI promoted wind turbine solutions in developing countries. Suzlon, owned by an Indian national, is a leading

Swaziland, Kingdom of	<$100,000	supplier of wind turbines. Access to U.S. government officials for Swazi government/private business leaders.
Sweden, Kingdom of	$7,200,000	Access to U.S. government officials for Swedish government/private business leaders.
Switzerland, Confederation of	$325,000	Access to U.S. government officials for Swiss government/private business leaders.
Tenerife Island, Government of	$50,000	High-level access to U.S. government officials by Flemish government officials and businesses.
Taiwan	$10,000,000	State Dept. approval for U.S. weapons sales to Taiwan.
United Arab Emirates	<$5,000,000	State Dept. approval for U.S. weapons sales to the UAE.
United Kingdom	£50,000,000 ($78,000,000)	Access for key UK officials and UK businesses to key U.S.government policymakers.
Union Bank of Switzerland (Robert Wolf, Chairman of the Americas)	$600,000	*Laundered terrorist financing for Gulf Countries (Saudi Arabia, Kuwait, Jordan, United Arab Emirates, Bahrain, etc.) through the Clinton Foundation. Partners Eric Holder, Lanny Breuer, Roger Zakheim contributed to fraud and treason.*
Victor Pinchuk Foundation (Ukraine)	$8,600,000	Buy influence with Clinton at State to pressure Ukrainian President Viktor Yanukovych to free jailed former Prime Minister Yulia Tymoshenko.
Walmart, Inc.	<$5,000,000	HRC pressured Indian government to open up India to Walmart, an action opposed by India's small retailers.

1 Al Amoudi once threatened to sue WMR and he demanded some $110,000 to be deposited in his Swiss bank account to drop the suit. Al Amoudi hired the Jewish law firm of Nabarro Nathanson in London to make his legal threat. WMR informed the FBI

that a Saudi national, who we reported had links to Saudi-funded jihadist organizations, attempted an extortion shakedown of WMR. WMR never heard back from Al Amoudi or his Jewish lawyers after we informed him that he could go pound sand up his ass (and there is a lot of that in Saudi Arabia and Ethiopia for him to pound).

THE WALL STREET JOURNAL.

UBS Deal Shows Clinton's Complicated Ties
Donations to family foundation increased after secretary of state's involvement in tax case

Then-Secretary of State Hillary Clinton appeared with Swiss Foreign Minister Micheline Calmy-Rey, left, at the State Department on July 31, 2009, announcing a deal in principle to settle a legal case involving UBS.

By JAMES V. GRIMALDI and REBECCA BALLHAUS
Updated July 30, 2015 0:27 a.m. ET

427 COMMENTS

A few weeks after Hillary Clinton was sworn in as secretary of state in early 2009, she was summoned to Geneva by her Swiss counterpart to discuss an urgent matter. The Internal Revenue Service was suing UBS AG to get the identities of Americans with secret accounts.

July 11, 2013

TO: The Honorable Diane Feinstein (D-CA), U.S. Senator
Chairman, Senate Intelligence Committee

THROUGH: Avie Stone, Major, Judge Advocate, U.S. Army Reserve
Senior Defense Counsel, 16th Legal Operations Detachment, TDS
212 General Lee Avenue, Fort Hamilton, NY 11252

FR: Scott Bennett, 2LT, 11th Psychological Operations Battalion, USAR
c/o FPC Schuylkill, #29418-016, P.O. Box 670, Minersville, PA 17954

RE: HOUSE INTELLIGENCE COMMITTEE PREVIOUSLY INFORMED ABOUT MATERIALS LEAKED BY EDWARD SNOWDEN TO THE GUARDIAN ABOUT NSA-CIA OPERATIONS INVOLVING SWISS BANKS, BRAD BIRKENFELD, AND TERRORIST FINANCING ON SEPTEMBER 25, 2012.

Dear Senator Feinstein:

Be advised, this is an "OFFICIAL COMMUNICATION TO CONGRESS BY A UNITED STATES ARMY OFFICER" concerning a National Security matter, and should be considered a "WHISTLEBLOWING REPORT", and afforded all the rights, protections, and privileges therein.

As you are by now fully and intimately aware, starting in the summer of 2012, I have written numerous letters to you and your committee concerning intelligence exposing terrorist threat financing through Union Bank of Switzerland, as reported by Brad Birkenfeld (subsequently paid $104 million by the U.S. Government) and requested you initiate a debriefing and investigation into this matter. This matter was also addressed in an ARMY INTELLIGENCE REPORT (which you received a copy of) which was submitted to General Jeff Jacobs, Commander of U.S. Civil Affairs-Psychological Operations Command on September 25, 2012.

A copy of this report was also sent to Lynne Halbrooks, Inspector General at the Pentagon, which her office acknowledged receipt of.

It has been over ten (10) months since this report was released to you and the Inspector General, and no official response whatsoever has been given to me in writing, or investigation initiated, since its release.

This is an obscene and intolerable failure of government officials, considering military servicemembers have been killed or maimed as a result of terrorist and combatant activity financed by the banks and networks described in my report. Worst of all, these financial networks continue to fund terrorist attacks against our troops because of you and your Intelligence Committee's unwillingness to investigate and address this conspiracy and cover-up.

Had my report been thoroughly examined and the parties and sources debriefed, counter-measures could have been deployed, and military members (and contractors) would be alive today instead of dead; and many of our other troops (and those of our allies) would not be dismembered, crippled, blinded, or deformed beyond recognition, or traumatized into a vegetable state--along with their spouses, children, parents, and extended family and friends.

As a result of your failure as Chairman of the Senate Intelligence Committee to utilize information provided to you about <u>terrorist threats and their financial systems</u>, the enemies of America have been allowed to advance, been given "aide and comfort" (possibly violating Article 3, Section 3 of the Constitution concerning "treason"), and encouraged to continue their kinetic warfare against American troops. Or to put it another way, quite simply,<u>you have blood on your hands</u>, as do the members of your committee who are complicit in this failure or manifest "depraved indifference".

As you know, my report exposed materials and testimony indicating the Union Bank of Switzerland (UBS) may have been funding terrorist networks, and <u>Booz Allen Hamilton</u> (the same defense contractor that employed Edward Snowden) played a significant role in ignoring or participating in this. This information was conveyed to me by the UBS Whistleblower himself, Brad Birkenfeld, who also communicated it to <u>Senator Carl Levin's Permanent Subcommittee on Investigations</u>, and the Department of Justice, and others. This same information was later also communicated to <u>General James Mattis</u>, Commander of U.S. Central Command and the <u>Terrorist Threat Finance</u> operations managed by the Joint Information Operation Center at McDill Air Force Base. After that letter was given to General Mattis (which I have a copy of), Brad Birkenfeld was quietly paid $104 million dollars, and no questions have since been asked, or the issue investigated. This demands exposure to the American public, and our allies, and no degree of "National Security Double-talk" or deceptive use of security classification will be able to sequester this information from the American people. They deserve to know, they want to know, and they will know. And the best person to tell them, if not you, is me; and I will do exactly that with ferocious honesty and honorable grit.

For as you know very well by now, I am uniquely qualified and unmatched in my experience to address these issues, and their mutual inclusivity with Edward Snowden's NSA-CIA disclosures, Booz Allen Hamilton, U.S. Central Command's Terrorist Threat Finance operations, and State Department's Coordinator for Counterterrorism. I am qualified because I worked as Liaison Officer between State Department and U.S. Special Operations Command (interfacing with the Director of National Intelligence Office, National Counterterrorism Center, National Security Council, and others), and also as a Threat Finance Analyst at the Joint Interagency Operations Center at U.S. Central Command. So I know everything about everyone and what they've done--and failed to do--in the "tar pit" of bureaucratic intelligence-military ineptitude or with conspiratorial intent.

According to the records, you and your committee were first informed about this material on July 15, 2012. It has been almost an entire year, and you have done absolutely nothing about this matter whatsoever. In this year, how many military members have died or been wounded because of ordnance purchased by money processed through the Union Bank of Switzerland (and other Swiss Banks) accounts, which you were informed about by Brad Birkenfeld in 2007, and then again by me?

Perhaps it will never be fully known the exact number of lives
destroyed or ruined because of your failure to act on my financial
intelligence provided...but I assure you it will be felt.

It will be felt by you on a deeply personal level as the outraged
screams of mothers and fathers robbed of their precious children
vibrate through your office windows; and the wailing tears of babes
and toddlers dischevel your young staffers as their mothers
carry them into your foyer demanding answers from you; and wives
and husbands roar with rage and contempt at your betrayal of their
spouses, whom they've recently had to bury in a grave over the last
year; and of course the military members themselves who hobble into
your office with their broken, mangled, and disfigured bodies--rolling
in wheelchairs, limping on crutches, or staring at you from a distant
hospital bed with tears slowly dripping down the sides of a comotose
ghostly face.

Please believe me, I desperately wish to spare you and our country
this experience, and am willing to do whatever I can to heal our
military families, but know this: I WILL NOT COMPROMISE, I WILL NOT
RETREAT, I WILL NOT BE BOUGHT OFF, AND I HAVE NO FEAR OF MAN.
It is my duty as an Officer of the United States Army, and as a Patriot
sworn to uphold and defend the U.S. Constitution, to report this
entire matter to the military, to the Congress, and to the citizens
of the United States. And as God is my witness, I will do exactly that.

Given the recent exposure of Booz Allen Hamilton by Edward Snowden's
leaks to Glenn Greenwald at the Guardian, and the mounting evidence
of Constitutional violations against the American people (which the
American Civil Liberties Union is now challenging apparently), my
material (reports, documents, testimony, and contacts) becomes
essential to discovering and authoritatively understanding the full
scope of this matter. Since you are the Congressional authority
charged with "Intelligence", it is your Constitutional duty to expose
this material and protect the American people--and our allies--from
further violations (including those done to their civil liberties) as well as
from terrorist financed attacks.

This is especially relevant now since CIA targeted Brad Birkenfeld
as their Swiss Banker information source, cornered him into a DUI
(driving under the influence), and then rescued him for intelligence
gathering purposes. If this is now the standard operating procedure
of the CIA in its intelligence gathering from American citizens, then
it is only a matter of time before all Americans--particularly those
living abroad--are similarly targeted, blackmailed, extorted, or
worse, by the government elites self-appointed to decide.

Edward Snowden's materials confirm this information previously reported
to you by me, which was provided by Brad Birkenfeld to the Justice
Department in 2007. Hence, the three of us form a unique "triad", or
"three-legged stool" which exposes a larger conspiracy and cover-up
involving Booz Allen Hamilton, the Department of Justice and others
against the United States military--especially the army.

Since I am an Officer of the United States Army, Civil Affairs-Psychological Operations Command, and sworn to "defend the Constitution of the United States against all enemies, foreign and domestic", it is my duty to report this matter to you and your committee, to the military authorities, and to the people of the United States, as a **WHISTLEBLOWING REPORT**, and demand an investigation and hearing into this material.

Failure to do this will be a betrayal against the American people, and the military service members fighting terrorism world-wide. Therefore if I do not hear from you within ten (10) days, I will instruct my lawyers to immediately release my report(s) to the American people directly through the media, and allow them to decide.

Respectfully submitted,

Scott Bennett
2LT U.S. Army (Reserve)
11th Psychological Operations Battalion
c/o FPC Schuylkill, #29418-016
P.O. Box 670
Minersville, PA 17954-0670
(570) 544-7100

CC: Avie Stone, MAJ, JA, USAR
GEN Jeff Jacobs, Commander, U.S. Civil Affairs-Psychological Operations
GEN Martin Dempsey, Chairman, Joint Chiefs of Staff
GEN Ray Odierno, Chief of Staff, U.S. Army
Lynne Halbrooks, Inspector General, Dept. of Defense, Pentagon
Chuck Hagel, Secretary of Defense
Senate Intelligence Committee
Senate Armed Services Committee
House Intelligence Committee
House Armed Services Committee
House Government Oversight and Reform Committee
Rep. Howard McKeon (R-CA); Rep. Darrell Issa (R-CA);
Sen. Diane Feinstein (D-CA); Sen. Rand Paul (I-KY); Sen. John McCain
Sen. Mitch McConnell, Senate Minority Leader; Rep. Eric Cantor (R-VA),
House Majority Leader; Fox News; Washington Post; The Guardian;
New York Times; CNN; The Hill; Roll Call; NBC News

NOTARY
COMMONWEALTH OF PENNSYLVANIA
COUNTY OF SCHUYLKILL

On this 11 day of July 2013, before me, a Notary Public in and for said Commonwealth and County, personally appeared O. Bennett. The person whose name is subscribed on the foregoing _____, is known to me or has satisfactory proved to be.

Notary Public

COMMONWEALTH OF PENNSYLVANIA
NOTARIAL SEAL
Danielle M Boris, Notary Public
Foster Twp, Schuylkill County
My commission expires April 14, 2014

July 11, 2013

TO: Senator Carl Levin (D-MI), Chairman, Armed Services Committee; Senate Permanent Subcommittee on Investigations

THROUGH: Avie Stone, Major, Judge Advocate, U.S. Army Reserve
Senior Defense Counsel, 16th Legal Operations Detachment, TDS
212 General Lee Avenue, Fort Hamilton, NY 11252

FR: Scott Bennett, 2LT, 11th Psychological Operations Battalion, USAR
c/o FPC Schuylkill, #29418-016, P.O. Box 670, Minersville, PA 17954

RE: HOUSE INTELLIGENCE COMMITTEE PREVIOUSLY INFORMED ABOUT MATERIALS LEAKED BY EDWARD SNOWDEN TO THE GUARDIAN ABOUT NSA-CIA OPERATIONS INVOLVING SWISS BANKS, BRAD BIRKENFELD, AND TERRORIST FINANCING ON SEPTEMBER 25, 2012.

Dear Senator Levin:

Be advised, this is an "OFFICIAL COMMUNICATION TO CONGRESS BY A UNITED STATES ARMY OFFICER" concerning a National Security matter, and should be considered a "WHISTLEBLOWING REPORT", and afforded all the rights, protections, and privileges therein.

As you are by now fully and intimately aware, starting in the summer of 2012, I have written numerous letters to you and your committee concerning intelligence exposing terrorist threat financing through Union Bank of Switzerland, as reported by Brad Birkenfeld (subsequently paid $104 million by the U.S. Government) and requested you initiate a debriefing and investigation into this matter. This matter was also addressed in an ARMY INTELLIGENCE REPORT (which you received a copy of) which was submitted to General Jeff Jacobs, Commander of U.S. Civil Affairs-Psychological Operations Command on September 25, 2012.

A copy of this report was also sent to Lynne Halbrooks, Inspector General at the Pentagon, which her office acknowledged receipt of.

It has been over ten (10) months since this report was released to you and the Inspector General, and no official response whatsoever has been given to me in writing, or investigation initiated, since its release.

This is an obscene and intolerable failure of government officials, considering military servicemembers have been killed or maimed as a result of terrorist and combatant activity financed by the banks and networks described in my report. Worst of all, these financial networks continue to fund terrorist attacks against our troops because of you and your Armed Forces Committee's unwillingness to investigate and address this conspiracy and cover-up.

Had my report been thoroughly examined and the parties and sources debriefed, counter-measures could have been deployed, and military members (and contractors) would be alive today instead of dead; and

EXHIBIT: Senator Bill Nelson conspired with Senate Intelligence Chairwoman Dianne Feinstein to hide 2LT Scott Bennett's military whistleblowing report exposing the treasonous Terrorist Financing links between Secretary of State Hillary Clinton, President Obama, DOJ Eric Holder and Lanny Breuer, Loretta Lynch, Union Bank of Switzerland, Covington and Burling, and Saudi Arabia, Qatar, Kuwait, and other Gulf Nations. Senator Nelson not only ignored Bennett's report, but tried to discredit Bennett by comparing him to Edward Snowden, and then advised Senator Feinstein of the political danger of Bennett's report. However, by writing this letter, Senator Bill Nelson not only confirmed the validity of 2LT Bennett and his terrorist financing material, but at that moment officially ensnared the U.S. Senate Intelligence Committee in his conspiracy to silence Bennett and commit treason by allowing the continued funding of ISIS terrorism through Swiss Banks.

Bill Nelson
Florida

Below is Nelson's letter to Sen. Feinstein

June 20, 2013

Sen. Dianne Feinstein
Chairman
Senate Select Committee on Intelligence
211 Hart Senate Office Building
Washington, DC 20510

SENT VIA EMAIL HARDCOPY TO FOLLOW

Dear Chairman Feinstein:

It's recently been brought to my attention that the unauthorized disclosure of classified information by Edward Snowden was not the only disturbing incident involving a Booz Allen Hamilton employee with a top-secret security clearance.

Today a Homeland Security subcommittee, in response to the Snowden case, is beginning a review of how the government manages security clearances. But I believe multiple incidents such as this warrant an Intelligence Committee investigation to determine more broadly how private contractors are managing the hiring and monitoring of employees who have top secret clearance from the government and who handle highly classified information.

By now we're all familiar with Snowden leaking details of two highly-classified intelligence programs. And earlier this week, I was reminded of another situation that involved a Booz Allen Hamilton employee and an apparent lapse of oversight at U.S. Central Command's Joint Intelligence Operation Center at MacDill Air Force Base in Tampa, Florida. In 2008, Scott Allan Bennett was hired to work as a counter-threat finance analyst at MacDill. As a Booz Allen Hamilton employee, Bennett had one of the highest level of security clearances available – Top Secret/Sensitive Compartmentalized Information, also known as TS/SCI Clearance.

Yet just months prior to his being hired, Bennett was convicted of lying to government officials and sentenced to three years of probation. I am enclosing a 2011 Tampa Tribune article that raised questions about how a Booz Allen Hamilton employee with such a conviction received a security clearance.

Serious quality control questions have been raised here. These men and women have access to some of our most sensitive national security information. I agree with you that we may need legislation to limit or prevent certain contractors from handling highly classified and technical data.

Additionally, I believe there should also be a committee investigation to determine how private contractors screen, hire and monitor employees who need top secret clearance from the government to handle highly-classified Information. I know you share my concerns about these serious issues of national security. And I thank you for your leadership and focus on this matter.

Sincerely,

Bill Nelson

RAND PAUL
KENTUCKY

United States Senate
WASHINGTON, DC 20510-1704

April 8, 2013

Mr. Scott Bennett
FPC Schuylkill, Camp 2
PO Box 670
Minersville, Pennsylvania 17954

Dear Mr. Bennett,

Thank you for taking the time to contact me regarding the recent attacks on the U.S. Embassy in Egypt and U.S. Consulate in Benghazi, Libya. Like you, I am appalled at these attacks.

Following the overthrow of Muammar Gaddafi and Hosni Mubarak as the respective leaders of Libya and Egypt, the United States looked forward to an era of peace and cooperation with each nation. On the evening of Sept. 11, 2012, attacks occurred at both the U.S. Embassy in Egypt and the U.S. Consulate in Libya. The attack in Libya left Ambassador Christopher Stevens and three other staff members dead. Other attacks and protests occurred in other countries in the region in the following days. These despicable attacks were unprovoked by the United States government and an attack on our Embassies and Consulates is considered an attack against American soil.

I believe there was negligence by the Obama Administration to protect our diplomatic staff in Libya. While testifying before the Senate Foreign Relations Committee, of which I am a member, Secretary of State Hillary Clinton admitted to not reading State Department cables from the Consulate in Benghazi, asking for increased security. Neglecting these messages is a failure of leadership of not only Secretary Clinton, but also reflects on the failures of the Obama Administration.

As I continue to serve as a member of the Senate Foreign Relations Committee, I will continue to exercise my oversight abilities on issues surrounding United States foreign policy. Again thank you for contacting my office. It is an honor and a privilege to represent the Commonwealth of Kentucky in the United States Senate. Please continue to inform me of any thoughts you may have on federal legislative issues.

Sincerely,

Rand Paul

Rand Paul, M.D.
United States Senator

Friday, November 29, 2013
Wall Street Journal

Ex-Banker To Answer Charges

A former top executive at UBS AG who has been sitting in an Italian jail for about a month is headed to the U.S. to face charges that he helped Americans evade taxes by stashing their money in Swiss bank accounts.

By John Letzing in Zurich and Giovanni Legorano in Milan

Raoul Weil, the former head of private banking at UBS who was indicted in the U.S. in 2008, wants to be extradited to the U.S. to stand trial, according to his attorney in Italy, Gregorio Valenti. Mr. Weil denies any wrongdoing and wants to face accusations that he considers groundless, Mr. Valenti said.

According to charges filed in the U.S., Mr. Weil sought to boost profits at Zurich-based UBS by helping U.S. clients hide assets from the Internal Revenue Service. Mr. Weil and colleagues allegedly used encrypted laptop computers and other methods to conceal the offshore assets held by the U.S. clients, according to the indictment, even as they referred to the potentially problematic business as "toxic waste."

Mr. Valenti said he has asked permission for his client to leave for the U.S. on Friday. Mr. Weil has been jailed in Bologna, though his attorney said he would repeat a request for Mr. Weil to be granted house arrest while he awaits extradition to the U.S.

Aaron Marcu, Mr. Weil's U.S.-based attorney, said in a statement that Mr. Weil agreed to the extradition "because he has always been prepared to confront these charges." Mr. Weil "has never run or tried to hide," Mr. Marcu said. "We expect him to be fully vindicated when we have the opportunity to present our case to a fair and impartial jury."

Mr. Weil, a Swiss citizen, visited Bologna last month and was detained by authorities on an international arrest warrant from the U.S.

THE FINAL PUZZLE PIECE FALLS INTO PLACE...

Union Bank of Switzerland international banker Raoul Weil has returned to America, and with him brought financial surveillance intelligence the military needs and Congress must ask for. The American people must demand Congressional committees and military intelligence analysts debrief Mr. Weil before Congressional committees mandated to address terrorist threat finance issues, homeland security, foreign relations, and emerging threats--as well as the ongoing CIA-NSA surveillance revelations brought by whistleblower Booz Allen Hamilton contractor Edward Snowden. Failure to debrief Mr. Weil about these issues will demonstrate either gross incompetence or treason against the Constitution. Mr. Weil is the last piece of the puzzle, which will complete a bigger picture Americans may find infuriating and a betrayal of their deepest values and expectations of government.

Raoul Weil is the man who holds all the answers about Swiss banks funding international terrorist networks and operations, American CIA-NSA-Justice Dept. operations targeting Swiss bankers (specifically, American Swiss bankers living abroad, like Brad Birkenfeld), and dysfunctional military bureaucracies and defense contractors failing miserably in their mission to identify, combat, and defeat terrorist threat financing.

In exchange for immunity, Mr. Weil will disclose to Congress "where all the bodies are buried", or in other words, where all the secret Swiss Bank accounts and operatives are that facilitate international terrorist activities against U.S. servicemembers, civilians, and our allies. Congress had this chance in 2009, when Brad Birkenfeld fled Switzerland (and a CIA-NSA trap), and pleaded with the Justice Department to allow him to testify about terrorist finance and Swiss bank issues.

However, instead of debriefing Mr. Birkenfeld, Senator Carl Levin and Senator Barack Obama coordinated with U.B.S. and Attorney General Eric Holder, Assistant Attorney General Lanny Breuer, and State Department Secretary Hillary Clinton to trade Birkenfeld for Swiss banking treaty concessions and promises of access to American Swiss Bank accounts...making Birkenfeld a sacrificial lamb instead of an intelligence source.

Birkenfeld was betrayed, prosecuted, and imprisoned for 40 months, before he was finally able to smuggle a letter out to General James Mattis at U.S. Central Command and share with him the financial intelligence data he had been prevented from receiving. Birkenfeld cited 2LT Scott Bennett, former Counterterrorism threat finance analyst and Booz Allen Hamilton contractor, as the military officer (Army Psychological Operations Analyst) who had received Birkenfeld's intelligence materials. Soonafter, Birkenfeld was paid $104 million dollars, but the UBS-Booz Allen Hamilton-Military reports were buried, and 2LT Bennett imprisoned for trying to expose the matter to Congress and the military. Edward Snowden, familiar with Birkenfeld and Bennett, learned from their sacrifice what not to do...and thus chose to report his revelations directly to the American people. The rest is history...and also, just the beginning. Time will Tell.

CONTACT: 2LT Scott Bennett, U.S. Army Reserve
11th Psychological Operations Battalion
c/o GEO Services, 205 Macarthur Blvd.
Oakland, CA 94610 -- (510) 839-9051

THE GUARDIAN, Saturday 8 June 2013   (UNCLASSIFIED)
Glenn Greenwald, Ewen MacAskill and Laura Poitras
"EDWARD SNOWDEN: THE WHISTLEBLOWER BEHIND THE NSA SURVEILLANCE REVELATIONS"

necessary to obtain a high school diploma, he attended a community college in Maryland, studying computing, but never completed the coursework. (He later obtained his GED.)

In 2003, he enlisted in the US army and began a training program to join the Special Forces. Invoking the same principles that he now cites to justify his leaks, he said: "I wanted to fight in the Iraq war because I felt like I had an obligation as a human being to help free people from oppression". <<<<<<<---This is the slogan of U.S. Special Forces, Army.

He recounted how his beliefs about the war's purpose were quickly dispelled. "Most of the people training us seemed pumped up about killing Arabs, not helping anyone," he said. After he broke both his legs in a training accident, he was discharged.

After that, he got his first job in an NSA facility, working as a security guard for one of the agency's covert facilities at the University of Maryland. From there, he went to the CIA, where he worked on IT security. His understanding of the internet and his talent for computer programming enabled him to rise fairly quickly for someone who lacked even a high school diploma.

By 2007, the CIA stationed him with diplomatic cover in Geneva, Switzerland. His responsibility for maintaining computer network security meant he had clearance to access a wide array of classified documents.

That access, along with the almost three years he spent around CIA officers, led him to begin seriously questioning the rightness of what he saw.

He described as formative an incident in which he claimed CIA operatives were attempting to recruit a Swiss banker to obtain secret banking information. <<<[Brad Birkenfeld was CIA target: He was a UBS banker with inf on Terrorist Financing. Info never shared with military's Threat Finance team (contracted by Booz Allen Hamilton) at CENTCOM/JIOC. 2LT Scott Bennett worked in this Command, and would have used Birkenfeld's inf to eliminate Terrorist financ Networks. Bennett worked for Booz Allen at State and US SOCOM als Bennett was also imprisoned along with Birkenfeld, by Justice Dept. Congressional investigation required.]

Snowden said they achieved this by purposely getting the banker drunk and encouraging him to drive home in his car. When the banker was arrested for drunk driving, the undercover agent seeking to befriend him offered to help, and a bond was formed that led to successful recruitment.

"Much of what I saw in Geneva really disillusioned me about how my government functions and what its impact is in the world," he says. "I realised that I was part of something that was doing far more harm than good."

He said it was during his CIA stint in Geneva that he thought for the first time about exposing government secrets. But, at the time, he chose not to for two reasons.

First, he said: "Most of the secrets the CIA has are about people, not machines and systems, so I didn't feel comfortable with disclosures that I thought could endanger anyone". Secondly, the election of Barack Obama in 2008 gave him hope that there would be real reforms, rendering disclosures unnecessary.

* Edward Snowden*------>>>in exile (due to Bennett and Birkenfeld prosecution)
CIA--NSA
U.S. Army
(FLED)

* Brad Birkenfeld*
Union Bank of Switzerland
CIA-DOJ-NSA-State Dept. conspired to prosecute and silence. Imprisoned for 40 months FCI Schuylkill

2LT Scott Bennett
USACAPOC/ Booz Allen Hamilton
Terrorist Finance Ops
Swiss Bank (UBS) connection
Syrian (al-Nusra Front)
Kuwait financing issues
Imprisoned for 36 months

* Raul Weil*
UBS banker (also indicted for Birkenfeld issues. En route to U.S. now via Dept. of Justice).
Imprisoned for: ?

WALL STREET JOURNAL (Nov. 2013)
KUWAIT TERRORIST FINANCE LINK

Scott Bennett, a Global Psychological Operations Analyst for Booz Allen Hamilton (defense contractor), and a 2LT Army Reserve Officer at the 11th Psychological Operations Battalion (Awarded a Direct Commission in 2009) was assigned to U.S. Central Command Joint Intelligence Operations Center, to conduct Terrorist Threat Finance Operations in support of counterterrorism missions.

*** Kuwait area of operations was Bennett's expertise.****************

Bennett was fired after recommending aggressive and creative solutions that diversified military's Special Operations Forces to achieve the mission of eliminating Terrorist Finance sources, operations, and networks.

Bennett was prosecuted nine (9) months later for a "paperwork error" on his McDill Air Base Housing forms--which had occured the year prior.

Bennett was denied any military defense counsel, and unlawfully tried in a civilian federal court, by a civilian jury, for a military issue.

In prison (36 months) Bennett met Brad Birkenfeld and discovered Swiss Bank connections to Terrorist Financing issues.

2LT Bennett filed report on Sept. 25, 2012 to GEN Jeffrey Jacobs, USACAPOC disclosing his findings; and copied report to Congress. No response of any kind was given, and the issue ignored. Bennett filed numerous follow-up reports which were also ignored by all except one person..
...Senator Rand Paul (I-KY)

Donors' Funds Add Wild Card to War in Syria

By BEN HUBBARD

UBAYHIYAH, Kuwait — Money flows in via bank or is delivered in bags of bulging with cash. Work in his sparely furnished room here, Ghanim al-gathers the funds and arts them to Syria for the fighting President Bashar d.

Mteiri — one of dozens of who openly raise to arm the opposition — ped turn this tiny, oil-rich Gulf state into a virtual Union outlet for Syria's with the bulk of the funds he collects going to a Syrian affiliate of Al Qaeda.

One Kuwait-based effort raised money to equip 12,000 rebel fighters for $2,500 each. Another campaign, run by a Saudi sheikh based in Syria and close to Al Qaeda, is called "Wage Jihad With Your Money." Donors earn "silver status" by giving $175 for 50 sniper bullets, or "gold status" by giving twice as much for eight mortar rounds.

"Once upon a time we cooperated with the Americans in Iraq," said Mr. Mteiri, a former soldier in the Kuwaiti Army, recalling the American role in pushing Iraq out of Kuwait in 1991. "Now we want to get Bashar out of Syria, so why not cooperate with Al Qaeda?"

Outside support for the warring parties in Syria has helped sustain the conflict and transformed it into a proxy battle by regional powers, with Russia, Iran and the Lebanese militant group Hezbollah helping the government and with Saudi Arabia and Qatar providing the main support for the rebels.

But the flow of private funds to rebel groups has added a wild card factor to the war, analysts say, exacerbating divisions in the opposition and bolstering its

Continued on Page A4

Donors' Funds Add Wild Card to Civil War in Syria

From Page A1

at extreme elements. While West has been hesitant to and finance the more secular es that initially led the turn to ned rebellion, fighters have ked to Islamist militias and in ne cases rebranded themves as jihadist because that is ere the money is.

"It creates a self-sustaining dynamic that is totally independent all the strategic and diplomatic nes that are happening and ing led by states," said Emile Akayeu, an analyst in the Middle East with the Institute for Strategic Studies.

Most private donors shun the estern-backed Supreme Military Council, undermining a body meant to unify the rebels into a moderate force. And they dismiss the opposition's political leader ip as well as calls by the United ates and other powers for ace talks. With funds estimated to be at least in the tens of millions of dollars, they have contributed to the effective partition Syria, building up independent slamist militias that control territory while espousing radical eology, including the creation an Islamic state.

Rebel fund-raisers have relied eavily on social media. Some ave hundreds of thousands of ollowers on Twitter, where they spread posts calling for donations, announcing drop-off points nd listing phone numbers where perators are standing by.

Prominent fund-raisers often oast of attacks by their preferred groups, posting videos showing their new weapons.

The campaigners say they are merely helping the oppressed.

Sheikh Mohammed Haif al-Mteiri, a former member of Parliament who is not related to the former Kuwaiti soldier and leads rebel groups, said private funding would not exist if countries like the United States, had intervened to protect Syrian civilians.

Kuwait lacks a tough police

Robert F. Worth contributed reporting from Washington, and Karam Shoumali from Istanbul.

A sign outside Kuwait City directing donors to a house used by Sheikh Shafi al-Ajmi to raise funds for Islamist rebels in Syria.

state like those that have cracked down on such activity in other gulf states, and a range of Islamists participate in its relatively open political system. A number of former members of Parliament actively raise funds, and some have traveled to Syria to meet their rebel allies. Kuwait's turning a blind eye to the fund-raising has upset Washington.

The nation's location and banking system also make it easy for donors from more restrictive countries to wire money in or drive it across the border for drop-off.

Some fund-raisers and donors have amplified the conflict's sectarian overtones, calling for revenge against Shiites and Alawites, the sect of Mr. Assad.

"Among the beautiful things in side Syria is that the mujahedeen have realized that they need to deeply hit the Alawites, in the same way they kill our wives and children," Sheikh Shafi al-Ajmi, a prominent Kuwaiti fund-raiser, told an interviewer this year.

The sheikh declined to comment. But in an interview, his brother, Mohammed al-Ajmi, said that their group funded operations rooms for military campaigns and that the Nusra Front, a Syrian affiliate of Al Qaeda, was free to work with them. He denied that fighters funded by his group had killed civilians.

"We believe that in the end, God will ask you, 'What did you do?' and you will need to have an answer," Mr. Ajmi said.

Most fund-raisers refuse to disclose how much money they collect, other than announcing gifts on social media. Private support is believed to be less than that sent by states, although Western and Arab officials acknowledged that underground funding, was difficult to track.

The Kuwaiti government has played down the importance of the funds, saying Kuwait's charitable contributions dwarf any cash sent for arms.

The minister for cabinet affairs, Sheikh Mohammed al-Abdullah al-Sabah, said in an interview that the government had sent more than $500 million in aid to Syria's neighbors in addition to money sent by licensed Kuwaiti charities.

He compared private funding to the smuggling of Cuban cigars into the United States, saying the government could do no more to stop it.

"How am I supposed to stop someone who gets on a plane with $10,000 in his jacket pocket?" he said.

American officials disagree.

"The Kuwaitis could be doing a lot more on this issue," said David S. Cohen, the Treasury under secretary for terrorism and financial intelligence. He said that Kuwait posed the region's biggest problem of financing linked to extremists in Syria, and that American efforts to press the issue with the Kuwaiti government had yielded limited results.

Mr. Cohen declined to estimate the amount of private funding flowing through Kuwait to Syria, but said it was enough to equip extremist fighters with ample light arms and supplies.

The funding operation run by Mr. Mteiri, the former Kuwaiti soldier, illustrates how the campaign's work and the motivations behind them.

In an interview often interrupted by tea and prayer breaks, Mr. Mteiri, 40, said he had been moved to raise funds for Syria by a video of a young girl crying uncontrollably after government forces killed her father. At the same time, he hopes the war alters Syria's character.

"We seek to end Alawite rule in Syria because we consider it a Sunni country and the capital of the Islamic world," he said.

Last year, a conference he organized for members of his tribe, one of the gulf's largest, opened soon after a mass killing by government forces in Houla, prompting more than $14 million in donations in five days, Mr. Mteiri said. The sum could not be verified.

Since then, he has organized more conferences and overseen aid convoys while collecting donations. One wealthy business man gave $17 million, he said, though most donations are small er. Two brides had given him their wedding dowries, he said, and children had donated their iPads.

While he spoke, his iPhone buzzed, and he showed a visitor a bank transfer notice for $1,390 from Saudi Arabia.

Lately, his focus has shifted to arms. He said he divided the money into smaller bundles to be taken by couriers to Turkey. From there, he carries it across the border, where most of it goes to the Nusra Front, which he called Syria's most "effective and realistic" rebel group.

Mr. Mteiri was wounded this year while fighting alongside the group in Aleppo, and a cousin was killed in battle in February. Still, Kuwait has done nothing to limit his movements.

"Praise God, we are a democratic country, and popular movement is legal," Mr. Mteiri said.

WALL STREET JOURNAL
November 2013

October 31, 2013

(UNCLASSIFIED)

American Intelligence and the 'High Noon' Scenario

By Michael Harden

While I was at the CIA, I grew concerned over America's willingness to keep secrets. I was so concerned that I asked the agency's civilian advisory board to address the question.

Could American espionage survive inside a broader political culture that every day demanded more transparency and more public accountability from every aspect of national life?

Their answer wasn't comforting. They weren't sure.

Then I was focused on domestic transparency. What level of openness with the American people would our duty to protect them in what we were doing have to forsake? What compromises in terms of whatever security we were tipping over into being too intrusive with respect to the... interactions of other governments. The president added that, "We are consulting with other countries in this process and finding out from them what are their areas of specific concern."

But what we are seeing and in other countries what aspects of our espionage make them uncomfortable.

Mexican President Enrique Peña Nieto claims to have secured a commitment from a personal conversation with President Obama that "no grounding sanctions" would be applied if this was proven true. And how the government of the chancellor Angela Merkel felt personally betrayed (and have answered the White House question: "What did the President know and when did he know it?" It is sad politics and bad policy for good friends to find their partner in politically impossible situations, and recent reports of aggressive American espionage have done just that.

In matters little that the reports may or may not be true or that the foreign leaders may or may not have already suspected these activities. The issue now is that seemingly plausible accounts are in the public domain, and people are unwilling to keep them there.

To be sure, there is some theater in all of this. Public allegations of espionage require "outrage" to be publicly outraged. But GCHQ also are legitimate concerns about privacy, and even the U.S. can force reduced cooperation.

There is a broader point here. There is a growing conviction in what we're doing that transparency as some sort of prerequisite, but today we find ourselves dangerously close to that prospect.

Responding to the issues of former Security Agency surveillance programs, President Obama admitted this up by reminding audiences that "just because we can do something doesn't mean we should do it," and he called guidance "while at the NSA too. It's not new.

Recall in 2008 how candidate Obama was a near-obsessive user of his Black-Berry and once elected said that, they're going to have to pry it out of his hands. Eventually the president kept his security staff too much to the alarm of his BlackBerry, but his small lift was content and that his small group of family and friends and his device itself got some enhancements...

Picture the background of this episode. Intelligence services in his own national security enhancements...

The most powerful country on earth was most likely to intercept by multiple foreign intelligence services in his own national security enhancements...

Things may still that way. States conduct espionage against one another including us.

Going forward we need to remember that the crisis of conscience in the 1990s when the CIA's human-intelligence (humint) collectors were told to stand down and not... The hardworking folks at the NSA surely must feel a little like Marshall Will Kane.

STORY BEHIND THE STORY: CIA DIRECTOR HAYDEN AUTHORIZED SWISS BANKER OPERATION

Michael Hayden's attempt to spin/mythologize C.I.A. as an Old-West Gary Cooper hero defending his timid town and virgin bride from invasion by a barbarian, black-hatted menace, is a predictable deflection of a lethal blow he sees coming, but which the American public does not yet know about.

The blow he sees coming is an old Army "whistleblowing report", about to re-emerge as new, which exposed the story behind the story of the Edward Snowden revelations. The report, originally released to General Jeff Jacobs, U.S. Civil Affairs-Psychological Operations Command, exposed one of the most sinister, corrupt, and unconstitutional C.I.A. operations in the agency's history.

The real story is that during Hayden's tenure as C.I.A. Director from 2006-2009, Edward Snowden worked at C.I.A. also, and discovered a C.I.A. operation targeting a Swiss Banker that would turn his world--and stomach--inside down with fear about Americans' liberties being violated by the coordinated efforts of the Dept. of Justice and C.I.A. The Swiss Banker had been targeted for recruitment for intelligence gathering; entangled in a fake D.U.I. to pressure him, and then rescued from the D.U.I. (which mysteriously was dropped) in a plan to manipulate him for intelligence on Swiss Banking. The Swiss Banker, sensing a trap, filed with his intel to Washington D.C. and tried to give his info to the Justice Department (AUSA Kevin O'Connor and AUSA Kevin Downing, among others), as well as the I.R.S., the S.E.C., and finally the Senate Permanent Subcommittee on Investigations (Chaired by Sen. Carl Levin, who also was on the Armed Services committee). After pleading for a subpoena, the banker was allowed to testify (but his testimony sealed). Soonafter, it was discovered C.I.A.-Justice Department had sent a fraudulent letter to the Swiss bank employing the whistleblower, in an attempt to "fix" their mistake. The Swiss Banker was Brad Birkenfeld, who was eventually paid $104 million, in exchange for his silence. This was Michael Hayden's legacy.

Submitted by:

2LT Scott Bennett, is an Officer in the U.S. Army Reserve, 11th Psychological Ops. Battalion, and worked as a defense contractor for Booz Allen Hamilton at the State Department Coordinator for Counterterrorism, U.S. Special Operations Command, and U.S. Central Command as a Terrorist Threat Finance Analyst. His unclassified material was submitted as a "whistleblowing report" to Congress on Sept. 25, 2012, citing information given to him by Brad Birkenfeld, and shared also with U.S. Central Command, General James Mattis, and Gen. Jeff Jacobs, U.S.A.C.A.P.C.C.

THE STORY BEHIND THE STORY

(UNCLASSIFIED)

KEY POINTS: (UNCLASSIFIED)

- CIA knows disclosing the "derogatory note and report" about Edward Snowden's CIA problem will reveal the "story behind the story" which involves a CIA operation targeting a Swiss Banker (who happens to be an American citizen).
- CIA ensnared Swiss Banker into a D.U.I. situation, rescued him from prosecution, then attempted to manipulate him into committing corporate espionage by providing Swiss Banking intelligence information (which was later confirmed by Wikileaks cables from the U.S. State Department). CIA describes this issue as "the episode" which alarmed Snowden about CIA operations.

THE SMOKING GUN: (UNCLASSIFIED)

C.I.A. Says It Did Not Have Early Suspicions About Snowden

THE NEW YORK TIMES **INTERNATIONAL** SATURDAY, OCTOBER 12, 2013

By ERIC SCHMITT

WASHINGTON — The C.I.A. said Friday that it did not suspect Edward J. Snowden of gaining access to computer files without authorization when he was working as a technician for the agency in Geneva in 2009, and did not send him home as a result.

The New York Times reported Thursday that Mr. Snowden's supervisor in Geneva wrote a derogatory report in his personnel file, noting a distinct change in the young man's behavior and work habits, as well as a trou-

bling suspicion about how he was using his computer.

The Times cited two senior American officials with direct knowledge of the episode who spoke on the condition of anonymity because of the continuing criminal inquiry into thousands of classified documents Mr. Snowden leaked four years later, when he was a contractor for the National Security Agency.

Asked repeatedly for comment over the past several weeks, most recently on Thursday, the C.I.A. declined. But on Friday, the agency took the unusual step of issuing a state-

ment, the first public acknowledgment that Mr. Snowden had worked for the agency.

"The C.I.A. did not have any concerns in Mr. Snowden's report on the official cited by The Times said was trying to gain access to classified computer files he was not authorized to view, but other officials on Friday characterized the activity as much less serious, not involving potential security violations.

returned home from an overseas assignment because of concerns," Todd Ebitz, an agency spokesman, said in the statement.

In dispute is what Mr. Snowden did on his computer, and the agency's response to it. The two officials cited by The Times said the C.I.A. suspected Mr. Snowden

It is unclear why there was a divergence of opinion.

These officials on Friday also said that Mr. Snowden left the C.I.A. of his own volition. But had he remained with the agency in Geneva, they said, Mr. Snowden faced a potentially time-consuming and critical internal inquiry prompted by his supervisor's report, an investigation that was halted once he quit the C.I.A. in 2009 to join the N.S.A. as a contract employee at a military facility in Japan.

In his statement, Mr. Ebitz did not dispute the existence of the supervisor's derogatory report, or its mention of a disturbing

shift in Mr. Snowden's behavior as he was preparing to leave the agency and join in 2006 for a new job as a contractor for the National Security Agency. Geneva, they said, Mr. Snowden also did not dispute that the supervisor's cautionary note was not forwarded to the N.S.A. or its contractors, and surfaced only after federal investigators began scrutinizing Mr. Snowden's record once the documents began spilling out.

Other points of view on the Op-Ed page seven days a week.
The New York Times

BACKGROUND: (UNCLASSIFIED)

In 2009, a top CIA official sent a text message to a Vanity Fair magazine editor urging him "not to run" a story about a Swiss Banker. The Swiss Banker was Brad Birkenfeld, an American, who had filed a whistleblowing report about Terrorist Threat Financing involving the Union Bank of Switzerland. The CIA official said "Karzai is much worse" in a subtle, yet desperate, attempt to draw the journalist off the trail he had been following. A trail which now has come to its "near-end" with Edward Snowden's confirming revelations. Snowden confirms this "episode" (as the CIA describes it) in his interview with Glenn Greenwald at the Guardian in Spring 2013.

While in Geneva, Switzerland working at the CIA substation as a computer technician, Edward J. Snowden discovered a Swiss Banker was being targeted for intelligence; and had been manipulated into a D.U.I. in order to "pressure him". However the banker grew wise to the agenda, and sensing a trap, packed-up his banking documents, and intel, and flew over to the U.S.—walking into the Department of Justice (working in concert with given "whistleblower protections". Instead, the Dept. of Justice (perhaps hoping the the CIA) illegally tapped the banker's phone, falsified a letter to UBS (perhaps hoping the banker would "disappear"), and then eventually prosecuted him with a "conspiracy" charge after he testified before the Senate Permanent Subcommittee on Investigations. Despite the banker's intelligence information relating to international terrorist financing, the military's "Terrorist Threat Finance" team (managed by Booz Allen Hamilton) at U.S. Central Command in Tampa, Florida, was never given this material. The Banker later informed

A Pentagon War On Injustice

Political Correctness: A healthy, white, heterosexual, Christian man has unfair advantages in the U.S. military over other soldiers, says a training manual approved by the Pentagon, warning in great detail about a so-called White Male Club.

Those who thought the U.S. military was already the ultimate level playing field, a place where skill and fighting ability were what mattered, not gender, race or religious belief, were sadly mistaken, at least according to a 600-plus-page manual used by the military to train its Equal Opportunity officers.

According to the manual, put together by the Defense Equal Opportunity Management Institute (DEOMI), and approved by the Pentagon, the U.S. military mirrors and is drawn from a racist society where whites have an unfair advantage, a situation that carries over to military service.

"Simply put, a healthy, white, heterosexual, Christian male receives many unearned advantages of social privilege, whereas a black, homosexual, atheist female in poor health receives many unearned disadvantages of social privilege," reads a statement in the manual, which seems more intent on perpetuating white guilt and black victimhood than discussing sensitivities and tolerance.

Regarding a so-called "White Male Club," the manual states: "In spite of slave insurrections, civil war, the 13th, 14th, and 15th amendments, the women's suffrage movement leading to the 19th amendment, the civil rights movement, urban rebellions and the contemporary feminist movement, the club persists.

"Today some white people may use the tactic of denial when they say, 'It's a level playing field; this is a land of equal opportunity,'" the manual reads. "Assume racism is everywhere, every day," read a statement in a section titled, "How to be a strong 'white ally.'"

"The unfair economic advantages and disadvantages created long ago by institutions for whites, males, Christians, etc., still affect socioeconomic privilege today," the manual warns, seemingly unaware this racist electorate just elected and re-elected our fifth African-American commander-in-chief.

Lt. Col. and former U.S. Congressman Alan West told Fox News Radio's Todd Starnes that he wants a congressional investigation into the tome that is only slightly less inflammatory than one of the sermons by the Rev. Jeremiah Wright that President Obama listened to for two decades.

"This is the Obama administration's outreach of social justice into the United States military," West told Starnes. "Equal Opportunity in the Army that I grew up in did not have anything to do with white privilege." No, it had everything to do with your ability to fight well and emerge victorious.

"When the president talked about fundamentally transforming the United States of America, I believe he also had a dedicated agenda of going after the United States military," West said. "The priorities of this administration are totally whacked."

DEOMI seems to be heavily reliant on its views regarding white extremism on the Southern Poverty Law Center (SPLC). Earlier this year, we editorialized about a 14-page email by Lt. Col. Frank Rich, the Second Battalion, 506th Infantry Regiment commander at Fort Campbell, Ky., to three dozen subordinates warning them to watch out for soldiers connected with "domestic hate groups." The list of "hate" groups in the email appears to be based on the one compiled by the SPLC.

A DEOMI training guide used by the Air Force lists the SPLC as a resource for information on hate groups and references the group several times. Considered as hate groups were Christian organizations such as the American Family Association and Family Research Council, immigration reform groups such as the Federation for American Immigration Reform and Atlas Shrugs, run by Pamela Geller and monitoring global jihadist activity.

(UNCLASSIFIE

2LT Scott Bennett--1st Casua

Scott Bennett was a counter-terrorism contractor for Boo Allen Hamilton, had a Top Secret/ Sensitive Compartmen ized Information (TS/SCI) clearance, and performed global psychological warfare analysis for U.S. Special Operations Command, State Department Coordinator for Counterterrorism, and U.S. Central Command/ Joint Interagency Operations Cente

He was offered, and accepted a Direct Commission into the Army's Civil Affairs-Psychological Operations Com At 38 years old, he complete one of the most intensely difficult military training assignments, and was the oldest USACAPOC Direct Commis sion recipients in its histor Bennett finished at the top his class. Bennett was also a "white, heterosexual, Christ man", with advanced degrees, bilingual, and conservative.

An intellectual, and a man-of action, Bennett authored a report--in response to a requ --which addressed the potenti negative implications of repe ing the "Don't Ask, Don't Tel policy on homosexuality in th U.S. Army; with specific reference to the psychological warfare dimensions. Among other things, Bennett's profound analysis described how Islamic extremists would exploit this policy reversal into propaganda for financial donations, suicide bomber recruitment, and increase attacks on Westerners in general (such as the attack on the Nairobi shopping mall in Nov. 2013). Additionally, moderate governments in Muslim countries would be put at risk, if the policy change was propagandized as an attack on Islamic virtues.

Despite the report's multidimensional insight into the Muslim mind, its politically-incorrect implications were too much to bear, and it became the quintessential "straw-that-broke-the-camel's-back". Instead of being a Respo for Feedback about how a policy might impact the army and its mission, the report was perceived as a threat to certain political agendas in the militar and generated enormous hostility. The report was buried and Bennett forbidd from speaking about it. One month later, after Bennett submitted the report (and had also identified a Commander's Policy Memo attacking Christian, Righ Wing, affiliations, and protested this policy), Bennett was indicted by the Justice Dept. (civilian agency) for a paperwork discrepancy on a base housing form and uniform wear (both military issues under military jurisdiction). Bennett was incarcerated, sentenced to 36 months, and during this time discovered additional intel regarding Terrorist Financing...the real story behind why he was silenced...and a trigger for Snowden's revelations.M

CIA's Financial Spying Bags Data on Americans

By Siobhan Gorman, Devlin Barrett and Jennifer Valentino-DeVries

The Central Intelligence Agency is building a vast database of international money transfers that includes millions of Americans' financial and personal data, such as social security numbers, officials familiar with the program say.

The program, which collects information from U.S. money-transfer companies including Western Union, is carried out under the same provision of the Patriot Act that enables the National Security Agency to collect nearly all American phone records, the officials said. Like the NSA program, the mass collection of financial transactions is authorized by a secret national security court, the Foreign Intelligence Surveillance Court.

The CIA, as a foreign-intelligence agency, is barred from targeting Americans in its intelligence collection. But it can conduct domestic operations for foreign intelligence purposes. The CIA program is meant to fill what U.S. officials see as an important gap in their ability to track terrorist financing world-wide, current

Please turn to page A6

CIA Trove of Americans' Data

Continued from Page One

and former U.S. officials said.

The program serves as the latest example of blurred lines between foreign and domestic intelligence as technology globalizes many activities carried out by citizens and terrorists alike. The CIA program also demonstrates how other U.S. spy agencies, aside from the NSA, are using the same legal authority to collect data such as details of financial transactions.

In this case, the surveillance court has authorized the Federal Bureau of Investigation to work with the CIA to collect large amounts of data on international transactions, including those of Americans, as part of the agency's terrorism investigations.

"The data collected by the CIA doesn't include any transactions that are solely domestic, and the majority of records collected are solely foreign, but they include those to and from the U.S. as well. In some cases it does include data beyond basic financial records, such as U.S. social security numbers, that has raised concerns among some lawmakers who were briefed about the program this summer, according to officials briefed on the matter.

Former U.S. government officials said it has been useful in discovering terrorist relationships and financial patterns. If a CIA analyst searches the data and discovers possible suspicious terrorist activity in the U.S., the analyst provides that information to the FBI, a former official said.

The CIA declined to comment on specific programs but said its operations comply with the law and face oversight from Congress, the FISA Court and internal watchdogs. "The CIA protects the nation and upholds the privacy rights of Americans by ensuring that its intelligence collection activities are focused on acquiring foreign intelligence and counterintelligence in accordance with U.S. laws," said agency spokesman Dean Boyd.

The FBI declined to comment.

A U.S. intelligence official said that any spy-agency operation under FISA Court orders require "strict compliance with the law and with those court orders." Orders would include procedures to safeguard the privacy of people in the U.S.; require training of those with access to information; prohibit searches not specifically authorized; and limit how long data may be retained, the official said.

In a typical money transfer, a person goes to a company such or a credit card to send funds to someone else. The recipient can pick up funds at a local money-transfer office. This process differs from, say, a bank transfer, in which funds might be moved from one account to another.

Details about money transfers are kept by the companies providing the service; that information is turned over to the CIA under court orders. Former officials named wire-transfer giant Western Union as a participant.

The full roster of participants couldn't be learned. Other large, global money-transfer companies include MoneyGram; there are numerous smaller firms.

"We collect consumer information to comply with the Bank Secrecy Act and other laws," said Western Union spokeswoman Luisa D'Angelo, naming a law that requires banks to report suspicious transactions. "In doing so, we also

The program serves as the latest example of blurred lines between foreign and domestic intelligence as technology globalizes activities by citizens.

protect our customers' privacy and work to prevent consumer fraud."

A MoneyGram spokeswoman said, "We have reporting obligations related to suspicious transactions, money laundering and other financial crimes around the world. The laws to which we are subject generally prohibit us from discussing details." She also said, "We value our customers' privacy and work hard to protect it."

The data is obtained from companies in bulk, then placed in a dedicated database. Then, court-ordered rules are applied to "minimize," or mask, the information about people in the U.S. unless that information is deemed to be of foreign-intelligence interest, a former U.S. official said.

A limited number of analysts are allowed to search the database with queries that meet court-approved standards. This is similar to the way NSA handles its phone-data program.

Western Union said last month it would be spending about 4% of its revenue in 2014 on compliance with rules under the Patriot Act, the Treasury Department's Office of Foreign Assets Control and similar

This past September, the Director of National Intelligence declassified FISA Court opinions that sharply criticized NSA for operating the phone program in violation of court-ordered privacy standards. The court also criticized NSA for repeatedly misrepresenting surveillance programs to it.

Some officials who have overseen surveillance programs, like Timothy Edgar, a former top privacy lawyer at the Office of the Director of National Intelligence and the National Security Council in the Bush and Obama administrations, say it's time for the government to acknowledge the existence of bulk collection programs.

"The public has a right to know about the broad outlines of how the government is collecting information on them," he said, noting that the FISA Court has noted the existence of other collection programs.

The money-transfer program appears to have been inspired by details of the Sept. 11, 2001, terrorist plot, in which the Al Qaeda hijackers were able to move about $300,000 to U.S.-based bank accounts without arousing suspicion. In part, it was because the transactions were comparably small and fit the pattern of the remittances used by immigrants or foreign visitors to send money home.

Some of the transfers were between bank accounts, but some moved through person-to-person transfers. In 2000, Sept. 11 plot facilitator Ramzi Binalshibh made a series of transfers, totaling more than $10,000, from Germany to the U.S., where they were collected by hijacker Marwan al-Shehhi. Two transfers were through MoneyGram and two through Western Union.

After the 2001 attacks, the CIA worked with Western Union, which voluntarily helped set up a program to collect data on money transfers between the U.S. and overseas, as well as purely foreign ones with voluntary compliance from companies, as has been previously reported.

That program was institutionalized by 2006 and continues under a controversial authority tucked into a part of the Patriot Act known as Section 215. That law permits the government to obtain "tangible things," including records, as long as the government shows it is reasonable to believe they are "relevant" to a terrorism investigation.

Under that provision, the U.S. government secretly interpreted the term "relevant" to permit collection of records on millions of people not

---

Wall St. Journal
Nov. 15, 2013

2LT Scott Bennett, 11th Psychological Operations Battalion, U.S. Army Reserve, and defense contractor for Booz Allen Hamilton, worked as a "TERRORIST THREAT FINANCE ANALYST" at U.S. Central Command in 2010. His target country was Kuwait, as well as Al Qaida and extremist Muslim groups. His reports on Swiss Banking to Kuwait to fund extremist organization (now incidentally funding Syrian extremist groups) was covered-up, and 2LT Bennett was prosecuted by the Justice Department on trumped up charges for political reasons.

This article confirms 2LT Bennett's reports on terrorist financing through Union Bank of Switzerland, which was also reported by Brad Birkenfeld.

However, this information was never shared with military commanders, and instead was covered up by CIA-NSA, since it involved the illegal targeting of Birkenfeld for intelligence gathering by CIA--which was also described by Edward Snowden's report to the Guardian Newspaper (Glenn Greenwald).

2LT Scott Bennett, Brad Birkenfeld, and Edward Snowden form a "three-legged" stool, linking terrorist financing, the CIA-NSA operations targeting Americans, and intentional cover-up by Booz Allen Hamilton executives and former execs:

Mike McConnell, GEN Michael Hayden, and Director of National Intelligence Clapper.

A Special Investigation is required to determine Constitutional violations and intelligence skullduggery.

WALL STREET JOURNAL, SEPT. 28-29, 2013

KEY POINTS: Article fails to mention Joe Nacchio's son being "stabbed in the arm" by two men in suits who exited a sedan, approached and asked his name, stabbed, then retreated in Georgetown, saying, "Say hi to your dad for us", as they sped away. Also not mentioned was government manipulation of contracts with QWEST as retaliation for NSA rebuffing.

Ex-CEO Exits Prison With a New Set of Pals

By DIONNE SEARCEY

LIVINGSTON, N.J.—Former telecommunications company chief executive Joseph Nacchio entered prison in 2009 out of shape, depressed and anxious.

Fifty-four months later, Mr. Nacchio, 64 years old, who once ran Qwest Communications International Inc., has emerged physically unrecognizable from his pre-incarceration life.

Prison appears to have shaved years off his looks. He has broad shoulders from a daily regimen of lifting weights and 5-mile walks and runs. He has a goatee and his head, formerly covered with black hair, is completely shaved and tan. He says the blood pressure and cholesterol problems he entered prison with have dropped dramatically. He thinks he looks like actor Edward Norton on his federal Bureau of Prisons identification card.

Prison also changed the CEO, who was surrounded by high-flying telecom executives before his prosecution for insider trading. In 2007, a jury convicted him of offenses Spoofie and peers: drug trafficker named Spider.

"I trust Spoofie and Juice with my back. I wouldn't trust the guys who worked for me at Qwest," said Mr. Nacchio, in his first interview since he was fully released from custody Sept. 20. Mr. Nacchio is unstoppably part advocate for white-collar executives on the set-free after a decade of aggressive crackdowns by federal investigators to rein in the malfeasance at public companies. He remains as combative as ever, insisting he never committed what the government said he did. He believes, in prison, is something akin to "Lord of the Flies, for grown-ups."

A jury convicted Mr. Nacchio of

Please turn to page A5

Former Qwest CEO Exits Prison With a New Set of Best Friends

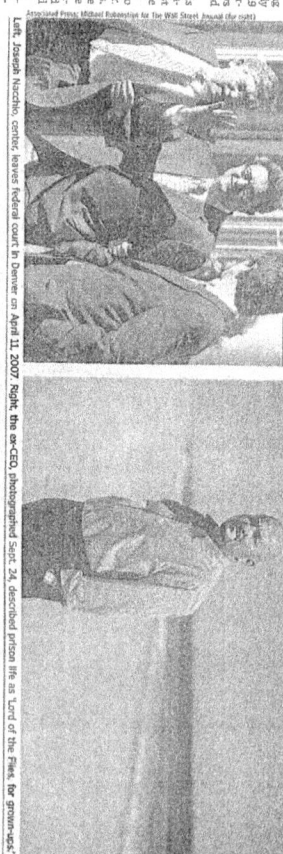

Continued from Page One

selling $52 million of stock as Qwest's outlook was deteriorating when the telecom boom of the early 2000s was imploding. He paid a $19 million fine and after an appeal forfeited $44.6 million, though he says he is still well-off financially, and...

Mr. Nacchio spent most of his sentence in two Pennsylvania facilities called camps, the lowest level of security offered by the Bureau of Prisons.

There are no bars and no walls around the perimeter. Computers are forbidden.

But they are awakened in the night for security checks. Phone calls are limited to about 10 minutes a day. Visitors are allowed but only every other weekend and some holidays.

Prison experts and former inmates say prison camps aren't preferable. While white-collar crimes are covered in the media, stories about leafy prison camps with sparkling athletic facilities surfaced during the 1980s when more media-friendly offenders such as himself and Juice, another drug offender, he said, are the best friends he has made.

"I was looking for these guys some of their future sons and nephews," he said. "It ever needs a lung or a bone, I'm there."

Some former Qwest employees and shareholders took a dim view of Mr. Nacchio's complaints. "He should have been in a medium-security prison," said one former executive.

Mr. Nacchio made sons of his acquaintances and daughters of his enemies at the Gallipolis Minimum U.S. West, a tension-fueled proxy fight made him revised among workers, some of whose retirement accounts were drained during his tenure and ...

Mr. Nacchio said he still believes his insider-trading prosecution was an example of the Schuylkill facility where Mr. Nacchio spent most of his sentence, and where he was forgiven...

There is no sympathy for Mr. Nacchio, said Kathleen Kennedy, who as president of the Telephone Retirees Association of Arizona represented phone company retirees during the merger. Ms. Kennedy, who has...

(continued)

...the stigma his drug-conspiracy conviction carries.

Mr. Nacchio said other white-collar offenders were "just full of themselves," and stereotyped inmates such as himself and Juice, another drug offender, had a "sick mentality." Mr. Nacchio fought his conviction to the U.S. Supreme Court, which refused to hear his case.

Mr. Nacchio's longtime lawyer Herbert Stern, said Mr. Stern has played down and the allegations in court filings.

It is also seeking a nearly $18 million tax refund. The government forfeited $44.6 million in tax deductible, a Justice Department official declined to comment.

Mr. Nacchio said he was confident he had three longtime friends begin his four years ago.

Messrs. Nacchio and Spoofie met at Schuylkill, in Minersville, Pa., where he was on work release. Messrs. Spoofie and Bortwick recalled the day Mr. Nacchio bought a personal package. Spoofie would eye a CD of rock music—Spoofie wife, Her made a mix CD of rock and roll songs for the time-time they were about what Schuylkill lately with the lyric from the Eagles' "Hotel California." "you can check out any time you want, but you can never leave." He belted out the lyrics as prison officers approached his car, he recalled.

At the Schuylkill camp, Mr. Nacchio's job was doing laundry for 22 cents an hour. Eventually he worked his way up to a tailor-job, hemming pants and making...

Left, Joseph Nacchio, center, leaves federal court in Denver on April 11, 2007. Right, the ex-CEO, photographed Sept. 24, described prison life as "Lord of the Flies, for grown-ups."

...by people who told her that when Mr. Nacchio was coming to prison, "she was going to be a hit out on him." "I don't think these people understand how stressful this all was, but that's how strongly they felt," she said.

An NSA spokeswoman declined to comment.

Last week, at a conference table just west of Manhattan in a dimly-lit Zortech PC law firm in Livingston, N.J., where he was on work release, Messrs. Nacchio paid tribute to the commissary. He saw packages of mackerel and tuna purchased from his fellow inmate over periods of months.

"You must be continuing with victim, he said. "I'm going to look them in the eye and say, someone who gives a f—about cost three packs of mackerel."

Mr. Nacchio and his prison mates found humor in their situation. They liked to play practical jokes on the "newbies"—white-collar offenders new to prison camp.

In March Mr. Nacchio began a halfway-house stint, and then began home confinement. He was permitted one shopping trip every three weeks but had to check in with Bureau of Prisons officials from a landline because he was barred from using mobile phones. On trips to the Mall at Short Hills in New Jersey, he said he flashed his Bureau of Prisons identification wallet in federal prison, showing them to outsiders and then showing them to his prison accounts.

"I can't wait until the day I'm going to come up to the real say something to one of the real say that everyone I love is amazing and another inmate would burst into another room. Spoofie slid and punches at Mr. Nacchio, to stop.

Mr. Nacchio, he said. "You do something else behind your phone." "I still don't know how to set up his phone for the temporary office set up for him as part of his work release at the Bortwicks firm. Mr. Nacchio, who spent his career at telecom companies, is stymied by the new device; he has been. "It's a little bit like Woody Allen and Mr. Provolo go to prison."

For now, he's focusing on shopping. He hopes to publishers. He is also working on a book about his experiences with the NSA and Americans' loss of liberty based on his incarceration. A book will be based on his incarceration. Another will be about government abuses...

INSPECTOR GENERAL: Investigation required. 2LT Bennett identifying Joe Nacchio story was sent August 7, 2013. No response was given.

DealBook

Breuer Reflects on Prosecutions That Were, and Weren't

By BEN PROTESS

After spending four years under the microscope as he led investigations of some of the world's biggest banks, Lanny A. Breuer hasn't lost his swagger.

The 54-year-old prosecutor, with a Rolodex as thick as his Queens dialect, will leave the Justice Department on Friday embattled after mounting record cases against banking giants. But Mr. Breuer, the department's criminal division chief, also leaves somewhat bruised, having taken criticism for not throwing Wall Street executives behind bars after the financial crisis.

"I think he's handled the pressure very well," said former Attorney General Michael B. Mukasey, who is now a defense lawyer at Debevoise & Plimpton and has gone up against Mr. Breuer in corporate bribery cases.

In short, it has been grueling. Fortunately, Mr. Breuer made headway in his crackdown on money laundering, the prosecution of Allen Stanford, who was sentenced to 110 years in prison for a Ponzi scheme, and the criminal cases against BP for the Gulf of Mexico oil spill.

Mr. Breuer won perhaps his biggest victory when a Japanese subsidiary of UBS pleaded guilty to manipulating the London interbank offered rate, or Libor. It was the first unit of a big global bank to plead guilty in two decades.

But the Occupy Wall Street crowd, where Mr. Breuer highlights his mantra of "aggressive" action. When the Justice Department dropped short of indicting HSBC on money laundering charges, choosing instead to press a record fine against the bank, it prompted a critique in Rolling Stone magazine. A recent "Frontline" documentary featuring Mr. Breuer included excerpts depicting him as a coddler of toxic mortgage securities before the crisis.

In a recent interview, Mr. Breuer reflected on these cases, his days defending President Bill Clinton from impeachment and his upbringing as the son of Holocaust survivors who settled in Elmhurst, Queens.

The following are excerpts from the interview.

Q. When you joined the Justice Department, the nation was reeling and people wanted Wall Street to pay. Back here, didn't you expect to mount charges against bank executives?

A. I understand and share the public's outrage about the financial crisis. Of course we want to make these cases. I can tell you I am willing to devote the talented lawyers that U.S. attorneys offices and I know that U.S. attorneys offices across the country assigned aggressive prosecutors to these cases, as well as agents. I approached these cases exactly the same way I approached Libor, the same way I approached BP, the same way I approached every case. If there had been a case to make we would have brought it. I would have wanted nothing more, but it doesn't work this way.

Q. You agreed to go on "60 Minutes" and "Frontline" to discuss the lack of crisis cases. Why open yourself to such scrutiny?

A. People have been asking legitimate questions about what happened in the wake of the financial crisis, and they deserve answers. Someone had to explain the Justice Department's point of view, and it was appropriate that, as head of the criminal division, I would do it.

Q. But federal prosecutors in New York and elsewhere also played big roles in the crisis cases. Why you?

A. For me, it's been a pretty effortless transition. I think it's made me a better public servant, but I think it's also made me a better private lawyer.

Q. You've had no shortage of interesting clients: Roger Clemens, President Clinton, Sandy Weill. Who was the most fascinating assignment?

A. There's nothing like representing the president of the United States. There's a crisis cases, what is legacy here?

A. The criminal division is now at the center of criminal law enforcement.

Lanny A. Breuer is leaving a highly scrutinized job as the Justice Department's criminal division chief.

people often who are incredibly proud of their careers, and you're dealing with them at their most vulnerable time.

Q. What gear did you assemble from your ex-Yankee client?

A. Balls, posters — we've got a lot of Clemens memorabilia. You need to recognize, I was a lifelong Mets fan.

Q. You were printed in Queens.

A. My dad was an intellectual. He had been a writer in Vienna before the Anschluss. During my childhood, he was one of the editors of Aufbau, which was a German-Jewish newspaper in New York. In our house there was opera always blaring. It was a very sort of ethnically rich, warm time.

Q. So why did you pursue the law?

A. I was the mediator in a lot of family issues, even at a young age.

Q. How did your family react to your decision to become a junior district attorney in Manhattan after a pricey education at Columbia?

A. My parents just never made any money at all. I called up my mother to break the news that I didn't want to go to a law firm, "Mom, you've just got to remember that Cy Vance Jr. — who, of course, is now the D.A. — he's in the D.A.'s office. And Dan Rather Jr. he's in the D.A.'s office. And Andrew Cuomo, the son of the governor, he's in the D.A.'s office." There was a long pause. And my mother said, "Lanny? They should go to the D.A.'s office. You? You should go to a firm."

DealBook Online

UNDER PRESSURE Clients continued to withdraw money from the Man Group, the world's largest publicly traded hedge fund, in the final quarter of 2012, raising the stakes for the new chief executive, Emmanuel Roman, below, in trying to win back investors. Man Group's funds had $2.7 billion of net outflows in the three months that ended Dec. 31, the sixth quarter of outflows in a row. Assets under management fell to $57 billion at the end of December, the company said in a statement on Thursday.
— JULIA WERDIGIER

FORECLOSURE SETTLEMENT Federal banking regulators have reached a $9.3 billion pact with 13 major lenders to settle claims of foreclosure abuses. The deal, announced Thursday, includes $3.6 billion in cash relief and $5.7 billion in relief to avert foreclosures, were announced Thursday. Under the deal, homeowners can receive up to $125,000 in cash relief.
— JESSICA SILVER-GREENBERG

STRONGER TIES Herbalife, a brand that supplements maker, said on Thursday that it planned to give two board seats to Carl C. Icahn, further binding itself to its most outspoken outside defender of late. Herbalife will add two of Mr. Icahn's lieutenants to its board by two seats, giving both to the billionaire investor. As part of the agreement, Mr. Icahn will also have permission to raise his stake in the company to 25 percent, from its current 12.6 percent.
— MICHAEL J. de la MERCED

PROMOTION Morgan Stanley has named Dan Simkowitz as the firm's co-head of global capital markets, according to an internal memo.
Mr. Simkowitz, chairman of global capital markets, will run the department with the current head, Raj Dhanda. Mr. Simkowitz had been tried to be a contender for chief of the firm's chief financial officer.
— SUSANNE CRAIG

UNION BANK OF SWITZERLAND = COVINGTON & BURLING =

LANNY BREUER & ERIC HOLDER=

2% FINE & DEFERRED PROSECUTION=

BRAD BIRKENFELD & CIA-DOJ-NSA-UBS Terrorist Financing link=

2LT Scott Bennett US Army & Booz Allen Hamilton=

Edward Snowden US Army & Booz

nytimes.com/dealbook

NEW YORK TIMES
SAT-Oct 19, 2013

New York Times

SAT- OCT 19, 2013

Lobbying Bonanza as Firms Try to Influence European Union

By ERIC LIPTON
and DANNY HAKIM

BRUSSELS — It was a show of force in keeping with the ambitions of American law firms that increasingly see the European Union's vast apparatus as a vital lobbying opportunity for themselves and their multinational corporate clients.

>>> Gathered at the Brussels office of Covington & Burling, a prominent Washington-based firm, were some of its lawyers and lobbyists, along with executives from some of the world's largest oil companies, including Chevron and Statoil. Their aim was to help shape the European Union's policies on the gas and oil drilling technology known as hydraulic fracturing, or fracking.

They were meeting with Kurt Vandenberghe, then a top environmental official for Europe and a prime player in the debate over fracking, which is even more contentious in Europe than in the United States.

The host that day in June was Jean De Ruyt, a former Belgian diplomat whose career stretched from central Africa to the inner sanctum of the European Union and who is now an adviser at Covington. He and others on the recently expanded lobbying team there have delivered at least four senior European Union policy makers to the firm's doorstep in recent months, including a top energy official, who arrived in September with a copy of a draft fracking plan that has yet to be made public.

"It's key to us to be ahead of when the political debate starts," Mr. De Ruyt said in an interview later. "Because by then, we can't have an impact."

As the European Union has emerged as a regulatory superpower affecting 28 countries that collectively form the world's largest economy, its policies have become ever more important to corporations operating across borders. In turn, the influence business in Brussels has become ever larger and more competitive, rivaled only by Washington's.

No group is proving more aggressive in claiming a share of that business — and provoking more criticism — than Covington and a dozen other major international law firms, some of which have imported American prac-

Continued on Page A8

The Houston-based law firm Baker Botts, celebrating the first anniversary of its Brussels office.

Lobbying Bonanza as Firms Try to Influence Europe

From Page A1

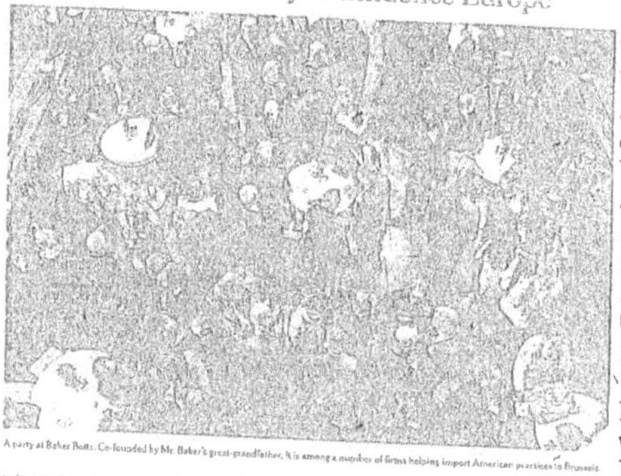

A party at Baker Botts. Co-founded by Mr. Baker's great-grandfather, it is among a number of firms helping import American practices to Brussels.

The Value of Secrecy

Clustering Near the Seat of Power

Moving Toward Openness

COVINGTON & BURLING was a law firm which employed Eric Holder and Lanny Breuer before their political appointments.

This law firm actively lobbies for Union Bank of Switzerland, accordi[ng] to reports given to 2LT Bennett.

UBS was given a 2% fine and a deferred prosecution by Eric Holder and Lanny Breuer--mos[t] likely to ensure financial "gratitude" from both UBS and Covington and Burling in the future.

Brad Birkenfeld was also prosecuted by Eric Holder and Lanny Breuer after Birkenfeld disclose information about UBS and its connection to Terrorist Financing and secret accounts (used by CIA-NSA, and various other parties).

CONNECT-THE-DOTS

NEW YORK TIMES: 12-20-2013

Judge Assails Military in Rejecting Count Against Ex-Marine

By MARC SANTORA

A federal judge in Manhattan on Thursday dismissed the most serious charge against a man accused of the accidental shooting of a fellow serviceman while they were on active duty in Iraq in 2008, ruling that it would be unfair to charge him in civilian court after officials failed for years to charge him in a military court.

In a scathing assessment of the conduct of military officials and lawyers, the judge, Colleen McMahon of Federal District Court, wrote that the disappearance of a crucial witness, an Iraqi translator known as Hollywood, made it impossible for the accused man, Wilfredo Santiago, who had been a Marine corporal, to receive a fair trial.

Judge McMahon reserved her harshest criticism for how the case was handled by the military and accused the Marines of failing to live up to their own creed: Semper Fidelis, or always faithful.

Specifically, she said, the Marines had failed Michael Carpeso, a Navy corpsman when he lost the use of his left eye as a result of the shooting.

"Justice is an imperfect remedy," she wrote. "It cannot give a man back his eye. But it can give him a sense that he matters — matters in this world and matters before the law."

Mr. Santiago's rights must be respected, she wrote, but that should not excuse what happened in Iraq.

"Something happened on that day, in that place, that irrevocably altered the life of an innocent man," Judge McMahon wrote. "That matter should have been put before a jury if only so that Carpeso could have the catharsis of justice."

The basic facts of the case were clear soon after the night of the shooting at a combat outpost in Diwaniya Province.

On Jan. 26, 2008, Corporal Santiago, Corpsman Carpeso and Hollywood were together in a billeting container when the corpsman was shot in the eye.

Corpsman Carpeso could not recall what happened.

Corporal Santiago initially told military investigators that he had not shot the corpsman, but later changed his story and said his weapon had discharged accidentally.

Hollywood was interviewed by military investigators, and said he could not definitively say how Corpsman Carpeso had come to be shot.

In her 58-page opinion, Judge McMahon provides a detailed account of a bureaucratic mess that resulted in delays, confusion, no court-martial, charges brought last January by the United States attorney in Manhattan and the issues now before her in a civilian court nearly six years after the shooting.

"It is not a tale that inspires confidence in our criminal justice system," she wrote.

Part of the problem, she wrote, was that no military unit took "ownership" for Corporal Santiago. "As a result, no one prioritized his case," she wrote. In its own investigation into the "lack of communication" regarding the case, the military issued a report that Judge McMahon called "the sorriest lot of 'C.Y.A.' interviews I have ever read."

"Everybody blamed everybody else, or said it was 'not my job' to insure that the Santiago/Carpeso matter was brought to a satisfactory conclusion," she wrote.

The judge, however, allowed a lesser charge, giving false statements to officials, to proceed against Mr. Santiago.

A spokesman for the Marines said he would have no comment.

Among her criticisms, Judge McMahon accused Marine lawyers of incompetence, citing an instance when they claimed they had taken months researching whether Mr. Santiago could be recalled to active duty and prosecuted.

"This is symptomatic of something that happened repeatedly in this case: Marine lawyers taking months to make the most modest progress on tasks that any halfway competent second-year law student could complete in a matter of hours," she wrote.

Judge McMahon said it was unclear how the decision had been made to charge Mr. Santiago, a Bronx resident, in civilian court, but that presented its own problems. Under the military code, he could have been charged with handling his weapon in a reckless manner. There is no equivalent charge in civilian court, so a case would have to be made for assault.

The testimony of the translator would have been critical to both the defense and the prosecution.

Judge McMahon, noting the dangers faced by Iraqis who worked with American forces, said Hollywood's association with the military ended in 2010 and she called his disappearance "ominous."

After combing through mountains of reports and documents prepared by the Marines, she wrote that she became familiar with the motto "Semper Fidelis," which is often included at the end of correspondence.

"After a while it started to annoy me to see those proud words at the end of all those emails," she wrote, "because in those emails, and in their actions, the Marines displayed precious little eternal fidelity toward Michael John Carpeso."

NYTimes - Fri 12/20/13

CASE: U.S. v. Wilfredo Santiago, 2013 U.S. Dist LEXUS 116, 484 (8-134-2013)(SDNY)

APPLICATION TO 2LT Scott Bennett's case: Scott Bennett was similarly charged in a civilian Federal District Court for activities which were under military jurisdiction. Bennett's case and circumstances are remarkably similar, and should be dismissed as a Constitutional issue (5th Amendment; Article 1; as well as 4th, 6th, and 8th Amendments) The precedent set forth in U.S. v. Santiago protects military members from "political" prosecutions, stating "...it would be unfair to charge him in civilian court after officials failed for years to charge him in a military court." Judge Colleen McMahon said it was unclear how the decision had been made to charge Mr. Santiago, 'a Bronx resident, in civilian court, but that presented its own problems. Under the military code, he could have been charged with handling his weapon in a reckless manner. There is no equivalent charge in a civilian court.

Investors Business Daily 10-13-2013

President Obama's Military Coup Purges 197 Officers In Five Years

Defense: What the president calls "my military" is being cleansed of any officer suspected of disloyalty to or disagreement with the administration on matters of policy or force structure, leaving the compliant and fearful.

We recognize President Obama is the commander-in-chief and that throughout history presidents from Lincoln to Truman have seen fit to remove military commanders they view as inadequate or insubordinate. Turnover in the military ranks is normal, and in these times of sequestration and budget cuts the numbers are expected to tick up as force levels shrink and missions change.

Yet what has happened to our officer corps since President Obama took office is viewed in many quarters as unprecedented, baffling and even harmful to our national security posture. We have commented on some of the higher profile cases, such as Gen. Carter Ham. He was relieved as head of U.S. Africa Command after only a year and a half because he disagreed with orders not to mount a rescue mission in response to the Sept. 11, 2012, attack in Benghazi.

Rear Adm. Chuck Gaouette, commander of the John C. Stennis Carrier Strike Group, was relieved in October 2012 for disobeying orders when he sent his group on Sept. 11 to "assist and provide intelligence for" military forces ordered into action by Gen. Ham.

Other removals include the sacking of two nuclear commanders in a single week — Maj. Gen. Michael Carey, head of the 20th Air Force, responsible for the three wings that maintain control of the 450 intercontinental ballistic missiles, and Vice Adm. Tim Giardina, the No. 2 officer at U.S. Strategic Command.

From Breitbart.com's Facebook page comes a list of at least 197 officers that have been relieved of duty by President Obama for a laundry list of reasons and sometimes with no reason given. Stated grounds range from "leaving blast doors on nukes open" to "loss of confidence in command ability" to "mishandling of funds" to "inappropriate relationships" to "gambling with counterfeit chips" to "inappropriate behavior" to "low morale in troops commanded."

Nine senior commanding generals have been fired by the Obama administration this year, leading to speculation by active and retired members of the military that a purge of its commanders is under way.

Retired U.S. Army Maj. Gen. Paul Vallely, an outspoken critic of the Obama administration, notes how the White House fails to take action or investigate its own officials but finds it easy to fire military commanders "who have given their lives for their country." Vallely thinks he knows why this purge is happening.

"Obama will not purge a civilian or political appointee because they have bought into Obama's ideology," Vallely said. "The White House protects their own. That's why they stalled on the investigation into Fast and Furious, Benghazi and ObamaCare. He's intentionally weakening and gutting our military, Pentagon and reducing us as a superpower, and anyone in the ranks who disagrees or speaks out is being purged."

Another senior retired general told TheBlaze on the condition of anonymity, because he still provide services to the government and fears possible retribution, that "they're using the opportunity of the shrinkage of the military to get rid of people that don't agree with them or do not toe the party line. Remember, as (former White House chief of staff) Rahm Emanuel said, never waste a crisis."

For President Obama, the military of a once-feared superpower is an anachronistic vestige of an America whose exceptionalism and world leadership require repeated apologies. It must be gutted and fundamentally transformed into a force wearing gender-neutral headgear only useful for holding the presidential umbrella when it rains. It is to be "his" military and used only for "his" purposes.

How Booz Allen Swallowed Washington

Because it provides the government with data services rather than fighter jets—and because so much of its work is classified—Booz Allen Hamilton doesn't have the name recognition of government contractors like Lockheed Martin or Boeing. That changed on June 9, when a Booz employee, Edward Snowden, revealed himself as the source of leaked secret documents showing government surveillance of millions of Americans. From its origins as a management consulting firm, Booz Allen has quietly grown into a governmentwide contracting behemoth, fed by ballooning post-Sept. 11 intelligence budgets and Washington's increasing reliance on outsourcing. —Drake Bennett, Carol Matlack, and Robert Levinson

Source of Booz's 2012 Revenue

Department of Veterans Affairs $132m

Department of Homeland Security $156m

Department of the Treasury $131m

Department of Health and Human Services $168m

38 other agencies, including the Department of Education, NASA, and the Railroad Retirement Board $518m

Department of Defense $533m / $3.3b

Booz by the Numbers, FY 2013

$5.8b — Total revenue

$1.3b — Portion from major U.S. intelligence agencies

99% — Percentage of revenue from the federal government

24,500 — Number of employees

76% — ...and employees with top-secret security clearances

48% — Percentage of employees with security clearances

70% — Percentage of U.S. intelligence budget going to contractors

Booz's first military contract was awarded in 1940, when the U.S. Navy hired it to help prepare for World War II

(UNCLASSIFIED)

USIS did Booz-Allen Hamilton security clearances. The Carlyle Group purchased Booz Allen Hamilton in 2008. Carlyle Group also owned USIS--so Carlyle owned both the company needing clearances, and the company giving out clearances. Conflict of interest? Hedging bets? Corrupting the process with self-interest?...YES!

Booz Allen Hamilton also contracted to do Terrorist Finance Ops for CENTCOM.

THROUGH THE CRACKS

Bottom Line Drove Security Clearances

Keeping Secrets

Number of people with security clearance in the U.S.

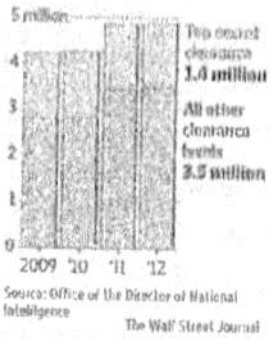

Source: Office of the Director of National Intelligence

The Wall Street Journal

BY DION NISSENBAUM

About seven months before his company gave Edward Snowden a clean background check, Bill Mixon was flogging his executives for not pushing security clearances through fast enough.

Mr. Mixon, then chief executive of US Investigations Services LLC, warned managers at its Grove City, Pa., operations that USIS wasn't meeting targets for completing clearances, say former USIS officials. Federal agencies use these clearances to decide who gets access to America's secrets.

"You better not have one f— case on your books," one former company official says he was told by Mr. Mixon. USIS was approaching the end of its 2010 fiscal year in September.

It was a demand, former USIS officials say, that Mr. Mixon made repeatedly that year: Do what it takes to finish background checks, even if they aren't thoroughly vetted.

Mr. Mixon didn't respond to requests for comment.

The stress on revenue was also a familiar refrain to managers who had been with USIS for years. Since the government spun USIS off in 1996, its management had gradually built a corporate culture that made revenue top priority. A previous CEO, in 2006, chided managers at a meeting to "get off your ass to make a buck."

The push to hurry out security checks reached a crescendo, former USIS officials say, in late 2010.

The approach apparently worked after Mr. Mixon's repeated threats: USIS met its target, and executives got bonuses, former USIS officials say. And it won federal contracts in 2011 that could total up to $2.7 billion.

But USIS's approach also failed America to an

Please turn to page A12

Ex-Company Officials Say Firm Rushed Security Clearances

Continued from Page One

extent only now becoming clear.

USIS in April 2011 conducted what federal officials say was an insufficient security check of Mr. Snowden, the National Security Agency contractor who leaked national secrets. USIS did a 2007 security examination of Aaron Alexis, the military contractor who died during his September shooting spree at the Washington Navy Yard.

USIS is at the epicenter of intensifying scrutiny of private companies that do government background checks, based on a portrait that emerges from court documents, congressional officials, contracting records and interviews with a dozen former USIS employees.

A federal grand jury is investigating allegations by employees that USIS improperly "flushed" cases by rushing them through the system without proper review. The grand jury has recently issued new subpoenas for key players to testify, former USIS officials say.

At least eight USIS investigators whose job was to gather material for checks have been convicted of fabricating information used to push applications through.

One of them, Marcus Travers, in May pleaded guilty in U.S. District Court in Washington, D.C., to fraud for fabricating information, saying in a statement that "The mistake was made due to the pressure I felt of completing the case."

USIS representatives didn't respond to requests for comment. "USIS takes these allegations seriously," says Brandy Bergman, managing director at Sard Verbinnen and Co., USIS's outside public-relations firm. "Since they were first brought to our attention over one year ago, we have acted decisively to ensure the quality of our work and adherence to OPM requirements," referring to the Office of Personnel Management.

The background-check system is so beset with problems that it is time to take another look at its privatization, says U.S. Sen. Tom Carper (D., Del.), head of the Senate Homeland Security Committee, which plans hearings on the system. "What about that change still makes sense?" he asks.

That change—part of Al Gore's privatization drive as vice president in the 1990s—has left most federal background checks in the hands of private companies.

USIS is the largest. Its more-than-6,000 employees handle about 45% of federal background checks, federal estimates show. And 90% of its work comes from the U.S. government. It has been awarded more than $4 billion in contracts over the past decade from the Pentagon, Federal Bureau of Investigation, Department of Homeland Security and the Social Security Administration and other agencies, contracting records show.

Security Screening

How security clearance investigations normally progress after a contractor or government agency requests an investigation

An applicant fills out a SF-86, a 127-page questionnaire that includes questions about drug and alcohol use, international travel, ties to terrorist organizations, financial records and criminal records.

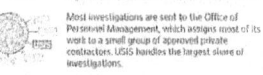

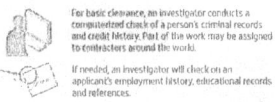

Most investigations are sent to the Office of Personnel Management, which assigns most of its work to a small group of approved private contractors. USIS handles the largest share of investigations.

For basic clearance, an investigator conducts a computerized check of a person's criminal records and credit history. Part of the work may be assigned to contractors around the world.

If needed, an investigator will check on an applicant's employment history, educational records and references.

For top secret clearance, an investigator will interview the applicant, along with friends, relatives, colleagues and neighbors. The investigation will typically examine the applicant's life over the past 10 years.

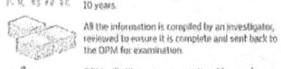

All the information is compiled by an investigator, reviewed to ensure it is complete and sent back to the OPM for examination.

OPM will either return a questionable case for further examination or send it along to the federal agency that requested the investigation. The agency then approves or rejects the application.

People with security clearance undergo periodic re-investigations. People with top security clearance are re-investigated every five years. Those with secret clearance are re-investigated every 10 years. And those with confidential clearance are re-investigated every 15 years.

Sources: Defense Department; Office of Personnel Management; Clearance Jobs

The Wall Street Journal

Much of the scrutiny of USIS focuses on its Grove City office. Field investigators around the country send their findings there, where workers examine the reports before passing them to federal officials who use the information to approve or reject security clearances.

Grove City had an incentive to rush cases, former USIS officials say, because of its contract terms: It would get the bulk of its payment, they say, when it sent a case to a federal agency and the final payment when the agency closed the case. One of those officials says the upfront payment was 90% for a period starting in 2008.

That made it attractive for USIS to send a case on quickly for the upfront payment, even if an agency later sent it back for further review, former USIS officials say. When Grove City sent cases in, USIS officials called it the "cash-register ring."

The cash-register culture had roots predating Mr. Mixon. At first, USIS was much like the government agency it was until 1996, when Washington spun it off as an employee-owned entity with an exclusive five-year contract to do background checks.

After the employee owners sold USIS to two private-equity firms, Carlyle Group LP and Welsh, Carson, Anderson & Stowe, in early 2003, the new management began pursuing a more aggressive strategy, former USIS officials say.

At a 2006 USIS leadership conference speech then-CEO Randy Dobbs told employees to reach under their seats; each found a dollar bill.

"I've just shown you the secret to making money and growing," Mr. Dobbs can be heard saying on a YouTube video. "I want you to think for the next three days as you're going back to your business and functions: How do I get off my ass and make more bucks for this business?"

Mr. Dobbs, who left USIS in 2008 and is now an executive in the health-care industry, didn't respond to requests for comment, nor did Welsh. A Carlyle representative declined to comment.

The profit push hit a higher gear after 2007, former USIS officials say, when Carlyle sold USIS to another private-equity firm, Providence Equity Partners LLC.

Providence in 2008 promoted Mr. Mixon, a USIS official, to the CEO spot and stepped up pressure on him and his executive team to search for ways to increase profits while meeting federal demands to reduce the long wait times in investigations, former USIS officials say. Providence representatives declined to comment.

Soon after Mr. Mixon took over, USIS began using new software that let it more quickly push cases through without significant review, former USIS officials say. That paved the way for USIS to begin "flushing" more cases to meet financial targets, they say.

Under Mr. Mixon, pressure increased. Executives set up monthly, then weekly and then daily targets for USIS workers to complete cases, former USIS officials say. In 2009, Mr. Mixon and executives started getting daily revenue counts.

Some Grove City managers tried to challenge corporate demands that they rush cases through even if they weren't fully reviewed, former USIS officials say. Some workers protested in writing but were told that they would be fired if they didn't do what they were told, they say. In corporate meetings, executives defended USIS's handling of cases, saying the procedures hewed to legal interpretations of USIS's federal contracts.

Federal reviewers didn't always catch problems in cases USIS sent in, former USIS officials say. Mr. Mixon called the practice of letting questionable cases go to the government a "calculated gamble," one says.

Mr. Mixon's demands escalated in 2010, as USIS prepared to bid on a critical multibillion-dollar deal, a five-year contract to do background checks for the Office of Personnel Management, former USIS officials say.

The Grove City office grew chronically understaffed, former USIS officials say. Managers asked for up to 300 people to review the cases, but had as few as 200 at times. Executives rebuffed appeals to add workers, they say.

In June 2010, Grove City's case backlog started to grow, creating what some USIS officials viewed as untapped revenue that undercut profit targets. Providence sent representatives to monitor USIS leadership meetings, former USIS officials say.

As the bidding on the federal contracts and the fiscal year-end approached, executive meetings became brutal battlegrounds where Mr. Mixon would publicly rebuke managers who weren't hitting profit targets, former USIS officials say.

Field investigators also felt the pressure. USIS employees in California complained to state regulators in September 2010 that USIS forced them to work through unpaid meals and didn't pay workers on time. That led to a 2011 class-action lawsuit in U.S. District Court in Los Angeles that USIS settled for $900,000.

Mr. Travers, who pleaded guilty to fraud, also cited high demands: "I panicked under pressure in the situation, and made a huge error in judgment," he said in his statement. He didn't respond to requests for comment.

In the weeks leading up to the September 2010 fiscal year-end, former USIS officials say, Mr. Mixon repeatedly pushed managers to eliminate the backlog. "He said, 'I don't care what it takes. Get them out. We'll pay for the consequences later,'" says one official.

The stress on revenue was also a familiar refrain to managers who had been with USIS for years.

At a September management dinner, Mr. Mixon chastised the Grove City manager for failing to reach targets, says a former USIS official who was there, and managers repeatedly checked the anemic numbers on their cellphones; they could see that they weren't hitting benchmarks. "It was crystal clear to everybody that we better get this bonus or heads are going to roll," the official says.

Within weeks, one former USIS official says, USIS "flushed" pending cases, allowing it to hit its targets for cases submitted and helping ensure bonuses for executives, former USIS officials say.

The USIS strategy to present itself as an efficient government contractor also worked. In 2011, it won two five-year contracts valued at up to $2.7 billion to help the Office of Personnel Management do checks. That office declined to comment, saying its investigation is ongoing; it referred questions to the Justice Department, which declined to comment.

The intensity culminated in several acrimonious management meetings in mid-2011 that focused on Mr. Mixon, former USIS officials say. Mr. Mixon left USIS in November 2011 and is president of a Minnesota medical-equipment-supply company.

Around that time, USIS fired a manager in the Grove City office who oversaw the review process, former USIS officials say. He then approached the Office of Personnel Management with allegations of improper conduct at USIS, they say. In early 2012, that agency's inspector general came to USIS with the allegations, they say.

In the past year, USIS has replaced almost its entire 13-member leadership team, has added scores of workers charged with overseeing the quality of investigations and has eliminated financial targets as a basis for bonuses, says a person familiar with USIS's current management.

The federal investigation continued little-noticed until this May, when USIS came under fire for the Snowden affair. The Office of the Director of National Intelligence concluded that USIS failed to interview enough people or properly examine Mr. Snowden's international travel as part of its 2011 re-investigation of his clearance.

USIS has said federal officials could have asked it to take a closer look at Mr. Snowden and that it was ultimately the NSA's job to approve his clearance.

In July, a federal grand jury in Washington issued subpoenas seeking documents from former USIS officials involved in the alleged case-flushing, as first reported by The Wall Street Journal.

Earlier this month, USIS again came under scrutiny, fo[r] its 2007 check of Mr. Alexis. The Office of Personnel Manage[-]ment said USIS had conducted [a] thorough review, but Navy re[-]cords showed he had lied abo[ut] his credit history and a 200[4] arrest for shooting out [a] worker's tires.

And USIS still faces claims [it] pushes employees too har[d.] Dawn Kojac, a former USIS i[n]vestigator, sued it in U.S. Di[s]trict Court in Southern Flori[da] this October, alleging it fir[ed] her in 2012 because she didn['t] meet quotas and undercut h[er] supervisor's bonus.

"It was a never-ending nigh[t]mare," Ms. Kojac says. "Eve[ry] day you had that pressure."

USIS declined to comment [on] the pending case, says M[s.] Bergman, the Sard public-re[la]tions official.

1st: Rand Paul referral letter/report: mailed out Oct. 25, 2013

Matt Salmon, R-AZ
Pat Meehan, R-PA
Charlie Dent, R-PA
Jim Jordan, R-OH
Bob Casey, Sen, D-PA
Paul Broun, R-Ga
Sen. Pat Toomey, R-PA
Dave Schweikert, R-Az
Steve Stockman, R-Tex
Tom Graves, R-Ga

2nd packet:
Rep. Dana Rohrabacker (House Foreign Affairs Committee;
Rep. John Fleming R-LA
Howard McKeon, R-CA, Armed Services
Louie Gohmert, R-Tex
John Culberson, R-Tex
Mitch McConnell, R-KY
Charles Grassly, R-IOWA
Barbara Boxer, Senator, D-CA
Patrick Leahy, D-VT, Judiciary Chair
Mick Mulvaney, R-S.C.

3rd: sent 10-31-2013

Rep. Ron DeSantis, R-FL
Jeff Duncan, R-S.C.
Ted Yoho, R-Fla
Jim Bridenstine, R-Okla
Jason Chaffetz, R-Utah
Committee to Protect Journalists
NY Times--Trish Hall
Wall street Journal--letters to editor

4th: IBD letters to Editor--11/10/13
Rep. James Sensenbrenner (R-Wis)
Sen. Saxby Chambliss
Rep. John Boehner (R, Ohio)
Sen. Angus King (Maine)
Sen. John Thune (R-S.D.)[packetFTM]
Sen. Lindsay Graham (R-SC)
Sen. Kelly Ayotte (R-NH)
Rep. Duncan Hunter (R-CA)
Rep. Paul Ryan (R-Wis)
Rep. Henry Waxman (D-CA)
Sen. Tom Coburn (R-Okla)
Rep. Eric Cantor (R-Virg)
***ALL SENT C.I.A.-Snowden Let2Editor 10/10/13

5th:
Rep. Randy Weber (R-TX)
Rep. Roger Williams (R-TX)
Rep. Lynn Westmoreland (R-GA)
Rep. Phil roe (R-TN)
Rep. Blake Farenthold (R-TX)
Rep. Larry Bucshon (R-IN)
Rep. Peter Olson (R-TX)

Senator Ron Wyden (D-Oregon)
propublica
The Atlantic
Rep. Adam Schiff (D-CA)
rep. Cary Gardener (R-Colo)
Rep mary Landrieu (D-Louisiana)
Rep. ron Barber (D-Ariz)
Rep. Patrick Murphty (D-Fla)
Sen. Tom carper (D-Deleware)
Rep. Mike doyle (D-Pennsyl)

6th: FOLLOW UP TO SPECIAL COUNSEL OFFICE
11-11-2013 letter/ sent out 12-13-13
rep tim Huelscamp, Tea Party
Sen. Pat Leahy (D-VT)
Sen Diane Feinstein (D-CA)
Rep Mike Rogers (R-MI)
REP. CA Dutch Ruppersberger (D-MD)
Sen. Claire McCaskill (D-MO)

Rep. Justin Amash (R-MI)
Sen. Carl Levin (DJ-MI)
ArmyReview Boards (251 18th St., South Suite, 385, Arlington, VA 22202-3531

DEPARTMENT OF THE ARMY
11TH PSYCHOLOGICAL OPERATIONS BATTALION
5550 DOWER HOUSE ROAD
UPPER MARLBORO, MD 20772

ARRC-CPC-EAPR 02 May 2011

MEMORANDUM FOR: Officer Evaluation Report Comments

SUBJECT: Scott Bennett Comments for OER inclusion

I am attaching the following documents as supplemental information to my OER:

1) Personal statement pertaining to the facts and opinions regarding my assessment by my superiors.

2) Supplemental report pertaining to my observations on specific military policies and issues as an S-1 AG Officer within a Psychological Operations Battalion, and its broader impact on the United States Defense strategy.

PART 1:   Personal Statement:

First and foremost, the civilian legal charges against me in Florida which have been described in this OER as the cause for giving me a negative Officer Evaluation Report are being challenged by me and my attorneys in a court of law. We are confident the evidence for my defense in this case when known in a court of law will clearly show the charges as being "false", and in fact will be seen as a violation of federal law and my constitutional rights as a private citizen, and a demonstration of obscene incompetence and dereliction of duty by military officials on a variety of levels. A legal remedy is being sought.

However, due to the investigatory nature of the matter, I am unable to provide specific details of the circumstances of the incident. However I can say that the DUI charge was in fact defeated in a court of law and proven by my attorneys to be false charge made by military officials in order for them to take aggressive and harmful action against me, and justify their illegal search of my vehicle, personal property, and home. In addition, it is being legally challenged by my attorney that I was the victim of an military violation of the federal act "Posse Commitatas", which prohibits military officials from exercising police powers over private citizens on non-military property. Again based on this federal violation, military officials violated my civil rights on a variety of levels, and in fact are guilty of a massive cover up of their own incompetence and security failures. This is being corroborated by senior military and JAG officials in court, and will clearly show the military violated the law and abused their powers.

SUBJECT: Scott Bennett OER Comments

It should be known, that in my military performance and past evaluations as an Adjutant General Officer and the OIC of the S-1 at my battalion, I have been consistently given EXCELLENT by my Commanders, and not SATISFACTORY, so to attempt to brand me as a SATISFACTORY soldier is inconsistent with my performance and prior evaluations. I have also served as the EOP Officer in my battalion, and have taken great lengths to ensure the civil rights of my soldiers have been preserved according to the Constitution of the United States and military codes of justice and Army regulations.

Any attempt to brand me as an unsatisfactory soldier with inferior skills, abilities, experience, or aspirations is not founded on any facts relating to my performance, but instead solely constructed on false and misleading statements by hostile witnesses, incomplete assessments of the facts, and personal prejudices against me. I believe much of the hostility aimed towards me stems from my personality and creative ability to solve problems and overcome obstacles in unorthodox ways. I realize this of course may be not only repugnant to some beauracratic mentalities and processes, but even painfully irritating due to the productivity and successful results which naturally ensue. However creativity and certain unorthodox approaches are absolutely essential for war fighting theory and overcoming enemies and challenges in theaters of conflict and non-Western societies. It is also what I believed was expected of an officer, especially since the name "EXPLOITERS" was the logo used to supposedly define the character of the 11th PSYOP Battalion. However based on the negative actions it has taken against me for doing exactly that—for exploiting opportunities and maximizing my advantages to the benefit of the larger Army mission—my faith in the integrity and character of the Army is largely dissipated.

Based on the attack against me and the hostility of this OER, it is clear to me now that the continuing cascade of problems and negative revelations about the U.S. military personnel, policies, and operations is not simply the fruit of organizational and leadership incompetence, but rather it is a symptom of a deeper syndrome afflicting our national character.

I chose to enter the military and serve in a Psychological Operations capacity against Islamic Radicalism, and after examining all four branches, chose the Army as the best fit with most potential. With my advanced degrees (BS, MA, Ph.D.), multiple career experiences in the private and public sectors (Hollywood, Advertising, Public Policy Think Tanks, Federal Government, Academia, Military Contractor), and most recently having worked at SOCOM, CENTCOM, and the State Department Counterterrorism Office, I have lived, breathed, fought, taught, and frustratingly walked away from our military leadership's "Whack-a-mole" game of countering Islamic terrorists and their religious ideology over the past 8 years.

Instead of recruiting the best and brightest citizens to become soldiers, and cultivating creative, "out-of-the-box" thinking and demanding flexible, "art-of-the-possible" suggestions—as most Americans would expect to be done—many of our modern military leaders, up to the highest echelons, seem to be perpetually imprisoned within a rigid mindset of doctrine, protocols, procedures, and beauracracy. They seem stricken with a corrosive fear and resentment of change and new ideas, which blossoms into a refusal to take bold action. And as the current leadership reflects, they are cowardly allowing the heat of political correctness and effeminacy to melt the ancient stone cold heart of a combat soldier into an androgynous testicular fortitude of wax. Naturally since this affliction of character is expressed by senior military leadership, it impacts

SUBJECT: Scott Bennett OER Comments

and molds their subordinate officers and enlisted soldiers following them. Granted the modern American military apparatus and training ideals are the compilation of designs dating from Ancient Greece, Rome, and classical European Empires, and are intended to produce warriors instantly obedient to the orders of their superior officers, and make them willing, ready, and able to destroy an enemy, there is problematic consequence of this training which must be understood in order to use it constructively.

Despite the virtues of military life (dependability of routine, confidence from camaraderie, and faith in structural integrity) in a certain way, active duty military training can have a somewhat "lobotomizing" effect on the individual human mind. Depending on the maturity, strength of will, and complexities of the person, military training—especially on the young enlisted—can be similar to a sharp-edged steel box dropped upon a larger sized brain. The mind and identity is forcibly "re-shaped" to fit the military's mind and identity, i.e. its structure and culture. Often times the free-thinking imagination and creative sensibilities of a person are squelched, restrained, suffocated, or banned outright in preference to the safety and stability of orders given by "higher" and military doctrine manuals and policies which are more akin to rule books for accountants and clockmakers than they are to warriors creating, performing, perfecting, and succeeding in the art of war.

This causes many people to maintain their entire personal life and professional career under the military tent because they are either unable or unwilling to leave the perceived protection, stability and culture. Aside from the 18 year old boy or girl who joins the military out of a boiling patriotic energy, a hunger for self-discovery and direction, and an unconquerable love of country, many of the older military leaders above the rank of Captain, are more often than not, not much more than beauracrats wearing a uniform.

I have consciously and passionately disciplined myself to steer clear of this endemic beauracratic moral and professional compromise within the military, seeking always and only to strengthen the capabilities of the Army with my own skills and experiences for the sole purpose of "winning the wars and defeating the enemies of our country." However it seems apparent that with this negative "DO NOT PROMOTE" OER and rush to judgment against me, as well as the false charges levied against me by military police, my respect and faith in the military leadership is evaporating quickly.

PART 2: SUPPLEMENTAL REPORT

The following report I would like submitted for the record as evidence of my work as the S-1 OIC at the 11th PSYOP Battalion. It is an example of how my personality and perspective on an official Army policy, may have in fact led to negative OER actions being taken against me.

REPORT:

ARRC-CPC-EAPR   05 December 2011

SUBJECT: Scott Bennett OER Comments

MEMORANDUM FOR: COMMANDER, HSC, 11TH PSYOP BN

SUBJECT: Potential issues pertaining to the possible "Don't Ask, Don't Tell" (DADT) policy change and its impact on PSYOP.

INTRO

In accordance with Brigade Commander Col. Burley's request for feedback pertaining to potential policy changes impacting PSYOP (MISO) as an Army MOS, organizational component, and general war fighting theory, I have conducted some research from the S-1 perspective, in hopes the data findings might be helpful to your command, and the Army's larger PSYOP/ IO objectives.

Part of my research materials and analysis draws on my previous experience as a policy analyst and researcher at the Department of Health and Human Services where I focused on marriage, family, and sexuality issues for the George W. Bush Administration. Additional sources were derived from SOCOM, CENTCOM, and Booz Allen Hamilton's PSYOP team, headed by Col. Jeff Jones (retired), who was previous commander of the 4th POG.

OVERVIEW

Since S-1 is responsible for the administration of "morale and welfare" areas of soldiers' lives according to Army regulations, I have been researching the potential impact that reversing the "Don't Ask, Don't Tell" policy will have on the morale and welfare of our battalion's soldiers, and their families, as well as on our recruitment and retention of soldiers. I have also analyzed how this policy change will impact our battalion's PSYOP mission, as well as the field of Information Operations in general.

I have researched and discussed this policy with my S-1 staff, independent researchers and social science academics, and fellow military officers. After careful analysis, as the S-1 Officer in Charge, I foresee the revocation of DADT as being potentially damaging to our Army, our nation, and specifically to our military Information Operations/PSYOP capability against Islamic terrorism. I have outlined some general concepts below.

1) Impact on U.S. military: Should the DADT policy indeed change, as an Adjutant General Officer responsible for battalion human resources management, I predict that a majority of currently serving combat forces will become demoralized and grow increasingly disillusioned with the "moral" integrity of the military's identity and current war fighting mission. As senior military officers (active and retired) have stated, America will lose the "moral ascendancy" in its military character as troops interpret this policy change as offensive to their personal moral and religious values. This in turn will have a corrosive effect on recruitment and retention efforts, and could possibly foment a sense of betrayal among troops and families who have been wounded, or had friends and family members wounded or killed since the 2001 campaign began. The Adjutant General Corps, which is responsible for the "morale and welfare" of troops, will be required to divert resources and attention to managing and processing disgruntled troop complaints, and administrative complaints and actions requested by "homosexual" troops; and JAG may find an increase in legal challenges by

SUBJECT: Scott Bennett OER Comments

troops refusing to fulfill their enlistment, due to "breach of contract" issues. Contrary to the SECDEF's opinion, soldiers may apply for "conscientious objector" status (as well as other legal maneuvers) as a mechanism to avoid serving in a military they deem inconsistent with their personal moral, religious, and ethical values and identity. These types of HR actions will be the responsibility of S-1 to facilitate, and thus could divert personnel, time, and resources away from the more vital needs of the war fighting mission.

2) Impact on Islamic Extremism: Al Qa'aida and Islamic extremists will inflate and pervert the issue and fashion it into viral propaganda against American forces. Enemy Islamic radicals will publish in the Muslim world, via traditional news outlets and the internet, that America is now officially a "homosexual military" seeking to morally "infect and corrupt" the Muslim world and Islam with homosexuality. The larger Muslim population may mistakenly see this as being our undisclosed military and diplomatic mission, thus undermining the concept of "Democratization", and providing an accelerant to Islamic radicalization. As I have experienced in my role as a counter threat finance analyst at CENTCOM, this policy change will most likely result in increasing financial donations by moderate Muslims to radical extremists, making it a "righteous" cause for all Muslims to reject and overthrow the perceived "homosexual agenda" of the U.S. military, thereby resulting in an increase in attacks on U.S. troops and non-combatants. This may also lead to a destabilization of friendly Islamic regimes. This language and imagery can already be seen in indigenous Islamic television, radio, and internet broadcasts and can be expected to increase with the repeal of DADT.

3) U.S. Muslims will be increased in their radicalization and be motivated to increase their attacks against the "homosexually branded" U.S. military at recruiting posts, and non-military places and events (an example of which was recently seen in Maryland and Oregon). This increase in "homegrown" terrorist attacks will result in increased counter-measure reactions by the current U.S. Administration and Congressional leadership. This could increase the perceived need for a crackdown that could produce increased demands and responsibilities for the U.S. military in domestic peacekeeping and counterterrorism operations.

4) This increased perception of the "homosexualization" of America's military, may provoke, and religiously justify, increased attacks by Islamic extremists within CENTCOM and AFRICOM's area of responsibility. This could bleed over into other U.S. ally countries such as Pakistan, Indonesia and Malaysia, and into areas of Africa, and Europe, and could foment increased Islamic instability in those countries.

5) Revision of military publications: The following military publications will also have to be revised to bring them into compliance with any DADT repeal: **DoD Instructions 1332.14** (Enlisted Administrative Separations) and **DoD Instructions 1332.30** (Separation of Regular and Reserve Commissioned Officers): **AR 135-175** (Separation of Officers), **AR 135-178** (Enlisted Administrative Separations), **AR 600-8-24** (Officer Transfer and Discharges), **AR 600-20** (Army Command Policy), and **AR 635-200** (Active Duty Administrative Separations).

This overview only represents some of the short term negative reverberations which may be felt by the Army, the Adjutant General and JAG Corps, and USACAPOC as a result of reversing the current DADT policy. It therefore may

SUBJECT: Scott Bennett OER Comments

be constructive to explore and examine the potential impact of this policy change within the confines of individual USACAPOC brigades. To accomplish this, a voluntary questionnaire might be circulated among soldiers on the battalion level requesting anonymous feedback on possible effects the DADT policy change might have on USACAPOC soldiers, and on military information operations in general. Such a questionnaire might be designed as follows:

VOLUNTARY ANONYMOUS SURVEY FOR ASSESSING DADT IMPACT ON USACAPOC:

In an effort to gauge the potential war fighting impact of reversing the current "Don't Ask, Don't Tell" policy on homosexuality in the military, the Commander would like to invite your feedback on the following questions. Answers will be kept strictly confidential, and you may answer or decline any and all responses as you choose.

DIRECTIONS: Circle "YES" or "NO", or one of the underlined words in each sentence as your answer to each question. Additional feedback is encouraged in the space under each question.

- Would changing current DADT policy to allow open homosexually in the military cause a *weakening* or *strengthening* of the military's war fighting mission?

- Would this change in DADT policy have a *negative* or *positive* effect on U.S. Information Operations, Psychological Operations, and Civil Affairs efforts in foreign countries?

- Do you have a *moral*, *religious* or *ethical objection* to homosexual behavior? YES / NO

- If so, would this objection cause a *personal dilemma or conflict in your conscience* if the military changed its policy to allow homosexuals to enter the military? YES / NO

- Would you be *less* or *more enthusiastic* about serving in the military if the "Don't Ask, Don't Tell" Policy was changed to allow homosexuality?

- Would you *re-enlist or terminate* your military obligation if the "Don't Ask, Don't Tell" Policy was changed to allow homosexuality?

- Would you be concerned with a *homosexual's ability to perform* their military duty adequately? YES / NO

- If you had a negative view of homosexual behavior and concerns about homosexual conduct in your unit, would this compromise or damage your motivation or ability to do your job? YES / NO

- Would changing the current law have a *positive* or *negative* effect on the military culture overall?

- Would you be concerned for your own safety and freedom from unwanted sexual advances from homosexuals? YES / NO

JUSTIFICATION FOR SURVEY QUESTIONS AND DATA:

- It is significant and important to separate the *behavior* from the *individual* committing it in order to focus on the nature and implications of

SUBJECT: Scott Bennett OER Comments

the acceptance or rejection of that behavior by outside observers—in this case fellow soldiers. This prevents already existing, or anticipated, interpersonal relationships between soldiers to influence or confuse the issue, and exposes what potential mental, emotional, and behavioral changes will result in soldiers as a result of DADT modification.

- It is also important to examine the soldier's moral, ethical, and religious views and convictions pertaining to homosexuality, in order to discern whether there would be a subconscious rejection or acceptance of the military's revised identity and mission, as a result of the DADT policy change. This would provide a improved indicator into the soldier's real ability to perform his job/duty.

SUPPORTING SOCIAL SCIENCE DATA:

Numerous sociological, anthropological, psychological, and criminal research studies, think-tanks, and university departments analyzing the correlation between sexuality and human well being seem to support the theory that reversing DADT would have a negative and debilitating impact on the U.S. military as a whole. The summary of some of the key findings appear below. Others are also available.

SUMMARY:

1. Homosexual men are at greater risk for psychiatric disorders, mood and anxiety disorders, bipolar disorders, major depression, obsessive-compulsive disorders, panic disorder, agoraphobia, social phobia, and simple phobia.

2. Relationship violence was found to be a significant problem for homosexuals. Forty-four (44) percent of the gay men reported having experienced violence in their relationships; 13 percent reported sexual violence and 83 percent reported emotional abuse. Levels of abuse ran even higher among lesbians: 55 percent reported physical violence in their relationships, 14 percent reported sexual abuse, and 84 percent reported emotional abuse.

3. Almost one-third (29.7 percent) of gays and nearly one-half (47.5 percent) of lesbians reported being or having been the victim of relationship violence. In addition, 22 percent of gays and 38 percent of lesbians admitted using violence against their partners.

4. The median age of death for those who regularly engage in homosexual behavior leaned in the direction of less than 50. The data suggest a "20- to 30-year decrease in lifespan" because of "substantially elevated rates of sexually elevated diseases . . . cancer and heart conditions, and violence among homosexual men and women."

DETAILS OF FINDINGS:

FindingID: 3499

This finding looks at the relationship between sexual orientation and psychiatric disorders.

SUBJECT: Scott Bennett OER Comments

Finding: Compared with their heterosexual peers, homosexual men were at greater risk for psychiatric disorders, including mood and anxiety disorders, bipolar disorders, major depression, obsessive-compulsive disorders, panic disorder, agoraphobia, social phobia, and simple phobia.
Sample or Data Description
5,998 Dutch adults
Source
Theo G. M. Sandfort
"Same-Sex Sexual Behavior and Psychiatric Disorders"
Archives of General Psychiatry.
Vol. 58, Number . , 2001. Page(s) 85-91.
Associated Keywords: Homosexuality, Depression, Mental/Emotional health,

FindingID: 3789
This finding looks at the relationship between sexual orientation and relationship violence.

Finding: Relationship violence was found to be a significant problem for homosexuals. Forty-four (44) percent of the gay men reported having experienced violence in their relationships; 13 percent reported sexual violence and 83 percent reported emotional abuse. Levels of abuse ran even higher among lesbians: 55 percent reported physical violence in their relationships, 14 percent reported sexual abuse, and 84 percent reported emotional abuse.
Sample or Data Description
499 ethnically diverse homosexual, bisexual, and transgendered teenagers and adults
Source
Susan C. Turrell
"A Descriptive Analysis of Same-Sex Relationship Violence for a Diverse Sample"
Journal of Family Violence.
Vol. 13, Number . , 2000. Page(s) 281-293.
Associated Keywords: Homosexuality, Spouse/Partner abuse, Violence, Sexual abuse,

FindingID: 3334
This finding looks at the relationship between homosexuality and relationship violence.

Finding: Almost one-third (29.7 percent) of gays and nearly one-half (47.5 percent) of lesbians reported being or having been the victim of relationship violence. In addition, 22 percent of gays and 38 percent of lesbians admitted using violence against their partners.
Sample or Data Description
283 gays and lesbians
Source
Lisa Walder-Haugrad, Linda Vaden Gratch, and Brian Magruder
"Victimization and Perpetration Rates of Violence in Gay and Lesbian Relationships: Gender Issues Explored"
Violence and Victims.
Vol. 12, Number . , 1997. Page(s) 173-184.

SUBJECT: Scott Bennett OER Comments

Associated Keywords: Homosexuality, Spouse/Partner abuse, Violence,

FindingID: 4050
This finding looks at the relationship between homosexuality and domestic violence.

Finding: Among lesbians, "rates of verbal, physical, and sexual abuse were all significantly higher in their prior lesbian relationships than in their prior heterosexual relationships: 56.8 percent had been sexually victimized by a female, 45 percent had experienced physical aggression, and 64.5 percent experienced physical/emotional aggression."
Sample or Data Description
A 1991 survey of 350 lesbians, 75 percent of whom had been in a previous relationship with a man
Source
Donald G. Dutton
"Patriarchy and Wife Assault: The Ecological Fallacy"
Violence and Victims.
Vol. 9, Number 2. , 1994. Page(s) 167-178.
Associated Keywords: Homosexuality, Spouse/Partner abuse, Sexual abuse,

FindingID: 4047
Finding: Violence against women was significantly greater in lesbian relationships than in heterosexual couples. Fifty-two (52) percent of lesbians reported being "a victim of violence by their female partners, 52 percent said they had used violence against their female partners, and 30 percent said they had used violence against a nonviolent female partner."

FindingID: 3644
This finding looks at the relationship between homosexuality and mortality. This is significant to Army forecasting of troop career longevity, training needs, and medical status for deployments.

Finding: The median age of death for those who regularly engage in homosexual behavior leaned in the direction of less than 50. The data suggest a "20- to 30-year decrease in lifespan" because of "substantially elevated rates of sexually elevated diseases . . . cancer and heart conditions, and violence among homosexual men and women."
Sample or Data Description
Four data sets: obituaries from the homosexual press; two 1994 sexuality surveys; homosexual marriage records for Scandinavia; and Colorado medical records
Source
Paul Cameron, Kirk Cameron, and William L. Playfair
"Does Homosexual Activity Shorten Life?"
Psychological Reports.
Vol. 83, Number . , 1998. Page(s) 847-866.
Associated Keywords: Homosexuality, Mortality, Violence, Sexually transmitted diseases, Health/Disease

SUBJECT: Scott Bennett OER Comments

FindingID: 3678
This finding looks at the nature of sexual abuse committed by professionals.

Finding: Sexual abuse committed by clergymen was more likely to be homosexual in nature than abuse committed by other professionals. Among survivors of abuse by clergy, 26.3 percent were male, compared with 9.5 percent of medical survivors and 6.7 percent of mental-health survivors. Likewise, clergy abusers were significantly less likely to be heterosexual (64.3 percent, compared to 93.3 percent of medical abusers and 81.5 percent of mental-health abusers). Nearly all the male victims of clergy abusers (94.4 percent) were abused by men.
Sample or Data Description
149 survivors of sexual abuse in professional contexts
Source
Estelle Disch, and Nancy Avery
"Sex in the Consulting Room, the Examining Room, and the Sacristy: Survivors of Sexual Abuse by Professionals"
American Journal of Orthopsychiatry.
Vol. 71, Number 2. April , 2001. Page(s) 204-219.
Associated Keywords: Sexual abuse, Homosexuality,

CONCLUSION:

This report synthesizes current research data and potential policy changes with regards to the military's doctrine and culture relating to homosexuality, from an S-1 Adjutant General and PSYOP perspective. Based upon this human behavioral data, military organizational and legal constructs, and Islamic religious counterterrorism theory, reversing the current DADT policy would most likely have an overwhelmingly negative impact on the U.S. military as a whole, and America's moral authority within the global community. It is recommended that this report and data be shared with the Secretary of the Army, Chairman of the Joint Chiefs, appropriate Congressional defense committees, and Secretary of Defense in order to compliment their knowledge base, and expand their decision making logic model with multidimensional considerations relating to the future of the United States.

I am happy to provide additional resources and analysis at the Commander's request.

SCOTT A. BENNETT
2LT, AG
S-1 OIC

Distribution:
CPT Browell
MAJ Simpson
LTC Droba
COL Burley

SUBJECT: Scott Bennett OER Comments

CONCLUSION:

In the end, the beauracratic mind is our own worst enemy, and our greatest impediment to victory. We cannot expect this type of mind to have any kind of a creative impulse or solution. We must instead demand that our civilian leaders demand, hammer, discipline and direct military commanders to "earn their jobs" by being creative and flexible and multidimensional, and not simply hire contractors to be so. From the earliest shaping of the Civil Air Patrol, Young Marines, and Sea Cadets, through the university level military academies and college ROTC programs, to the basics of boot camp and Officer Training courses, the value and necessity and power of soldiers with creative, flexible, and fearless imaginations must be as important, if not more so, than flawless obedience and absorption into military systems, structures, and protocols.

If the military is to evolve, and the United States remain a dominant power in the world, then a different kind of value system based on adaptation and rigorous creative impulses must be embraced and cultivated more than the idolatrous allegiance to old mindsets, protocols, and beauracratic systems of process. Only this will lead to a future where military leaders are capable of waging serious Psychological War, and not simply appearing so.

I have always performed and behaved in a manner consistent with the highest expectations of an Army Officer, and have joined the military to compliment its capabilities, not simply siphon off resources and occupy a space. Despite the my Battalion's failure to advance me to the PSYOP Officer Training School, as was promised to me by before I agreed and swore the oath, I have remained patient and tolerant of certain institutional ineptitudes. However will again state my reason for entering the Army was not to be an Adjutant General Officer managing human resources personnel, but was to create, develop, research, and manage Islamic Psychological and Counterterrorism Operations within the Army's AOR. This failure of the Army to advance me in this area, in addition to its other failures in leadership to me, warrants an immediate resignation by me if not rectified.

I would hope that the Army promotes me immediately to my next rank and clears my record of any and all negative OER material. In addition to these comments, I am requesting an official COMMANDER'S INQUIRY by LTC. Joel Droba to investigate the facts and statements communicated to him and others regarding any and all charges relating to me. Other follow up materials will include an EO complaint, an Inspector General investigation, a Congressional Inquiry and FOIA request into this matter.

I am happy to provide additional resources and analysis at the Commander's request.

SCOTT A. BENNETT
2LT, AG
S-1 OIC

DEPARTMENT OF THE ARMY
11TH PSYCHOLOGICAL OPERATIONS BATTALION
5550 DOWER HOUSE ROAD
UPPER MARLBORO, MD 20772

ARRC-CPC-EACO   30 April 2010

MEMORANDUM FOR SEE DISTRIBUTION

SUBJECT: Commander's Policy on Military Whistleblower Protection Act (**POLICY NUMBER 1-16**)

1. This policy implements Army Regulation 600-20, DODD 7050.6, relating to the Military Whistleblower Protection Act.

2. Department of the Army personnel are prohibited from taking acts of reprisal against any Soldier for filing a complaint of unlawful discrimination or sexual harassment (see DODD 7050.6).

    (a) No person will restrict a member of the Armed Services from making a protected communication with a member of Congress; an Inspector General; a member of a DOD audit, inspection, investigation or law enforcement organization; or any other person or organization (including any person in the chain of command) designated under this regulation or other administrative procedures to receive such communication.

    (b) Soldiers will be free from reprisal for making or preparing a protected communication.

    (c) No employee or Soldier may, through direct action, allusion, or indirect suggestion, take or threaten to take an unfavorable personnel action, or to withhold or threaten to withhold a favorable personnel action, in reprisal against any Soldier for making or preparing a protected communication.

    (d) The chain of command will ensure complainants are protected from reprisal or retaliation for filing equal opportunity complaints. Should Soldiers be threatened with such an act, or should an act of reprisal occur, they must report these circumstances to the DOD Inspector General and EO administrator. If the allegation of reprisal is made known to any agency authorized in this regulation to receive complaints, the agency should refer the complaint to the DOD Inspector General. It is strongly encouraged to simultaneously report such threats or acts of reprisal to the appropriate chain of command, the Inspector General, EO administrator, and member of Congress representing the soldier.

3. The DOD IG Hotline phone number is 1(800) 424-9098 or DSN 664-8799; the DOD IG Hotline e-mail address is hotline@dodig.osd.mil-either may be used to report threats or acts of reprisal.

    (a) Personnel calling from outside the continental United States may dial (703) 604-8569; or, mail a letter to:
Department of Defense Inspector General,
ATTN: Defense Hotline,
1900 Defense Pentagon,
Washington, DC 20301-1900.

ARRC-CPC-EACO
SUBJECT: Commander's Policy on Military Whistleblower Protection Act (**POLICY NUMBER 1-16**)

4. POC for requesting investigations, communicating issues, and submitting complaints is SFC Lydia Williams at Lydia.Williams@ar-usacapoc.soc.mil or Lydia.williams1@us.army.mil, phone 330-486-6805, or 706-566-1362 cell.

Mailing address:
2nd POG
ATTN:
8770 Chamberlin Road
Twinsburg, OH 44087

5. POC at my Headquarters is the Battalion S1.

JOEL B. DROBA
LTC, PO
Commanding

Distribution:
11th POB
11th, HSC
305th PSYOP CO
312th PSYOP CO
351st PSYOP CO
360th PSYOP CO

DEPARTMENT OF THE ARMY
11TH PSYCHOLOGICAL OPERATIONS BATTALION
5550 DOWER HOUSE ROAD
UPPER MARLBORO, MD 20772

ARRC-CPC-EACO   30 April 2010

MEMORANDUM FOR SEE DISTRIBUTION

SUBJECT: Wear and Appearance of Army Uniforms and Personal Appearance (**POLICY NUMBER 1-10**)

1. References: AR 670-1

2. The Physical Fitness Uniform (PFU) may be worn on and off duty when engaged in physical training both on and off military installations and reserve centers. Soldiers may wear all or part of the PFU off military installations and reserve centers. The shirt may be worn outside the trunks on military installations and reserve centers unless the installation commander has ordered otherwise. Standards of wear and appearance specified in paragraph 1-7, AR 670-1 will apply at all times.

3. The Army Combat Uniform (ACU) and the Battle Dress Uniform (BDU) are authorized for wear off post unless the installation commander has ordered otherwise. ACUs/BDUs are not authorized for wear in establishments that primarily sell alcohol or for air travel, except when Soldiers are deploying as part of a unit move and the aircraft is for the exclusive use of the military.

4. Commercial rucksacks, gym bags or like articles may be worn over the shoulder while in uniform. Backpacks may also be work over the shoulder when riding a bicycle or motorcycle. All such items worn over the shoulder must be black and may not have visible commercial logos.

5. Female Soldiers are authorized to wear lipstick and nail polish with all uniforms so long as the color is <u>conservative</u>. Extreme shades of lipstick and nail polish such as purple, gold, blue and white will not be worn. The hair policy as outlined in paragraph 1-8, AR 670-1, remains firm.

6. Tattoos anywhere on the head, face, and neck above the class A uniform collar are prohibited. Tattoos or brands that are extremist, indecent, sexist, or racist are prohibited, regardless of location on the body, as they are prejudicial to good order and discipline within units. Extremist tattoos or brands are those affiliated with "Right Wing", "Ultra Conservative", "Neo-Nazi", "Christian Fanatical" groups depicting, or symbolizing extremist philosophies, religious beliefs, hazing practices, or similar "right-of-passage" type activities are strictly prohibited at the 11POB. Extremist philosophies, organizations, and activities are those which advocate racial, gender or ethnic hatred or intolerance; homophobia; Islamophobia; advocate, create, or engage in illegal discrimination based on race, color, gender, ethnicity, religion, or national origin; or advocate violence or other unlawful means of depriving individual rights under the U.S. Constitution, Federal, or State law (see para 4-12, AR 600-20). Indecent tattoos or brands are those that are grossly offensive to modesty, decency, or propriety; shock the moral sense because

ARRC-CPC-EACO
SUBJECT: Wear and Appearance of Army Uniforms and Personal Appearance (**POLICY NUMBER 1-10**)

of their vulgar, filthy, or disgusting nature or tendency to incite lustful thought; or tend reasonably to corrupt morals or incite libidinous thoughts. Sexist or misogynist or homophobic tattoos or brands are those that advocate a philosophy that degrades or demeans a person based on gender, sexual orientation, but that may not meet the same definition of "indecent." Racist tattoos or brands are those that advocate a philosophy that degrades or demeans a person based on race, ethnicity, or national origin.

7. Except for earrings for females as outlined in paragraph 1-14c, AR 670-1. There will be no attaching, affixing, or displaying of objects, articles, jewelry or other ornamentation to or through the skin while in uniform, in civilian clothes while on duty, or in civilian clothes off duty in any military installation, reserve center or other place under military control.

8. POC at my Headquarters regarding this policy is the Battalion XO Major Simpson.

JOEL B. DROBA
LTC, CA
Commanding

Distribution:
11th POB
11th, HSC
305th PSYOP CO
312th PSYOP CO
351st PSYOP CO
360th PSYOP CO

DEPARTMENT OF THE ARMY
11TH PSYCHOLOGICAL OPERATIONS BATTALION
5550 DOWER HOUSE ROAD
UPPER MARLBORO, MD 20772

ARRC-CPC-EA-CO												11 July 2010

MEMORANDUM FOR SEE DISTRIBUTION

SUBJECT: Appointment of 11th BN Equal Opportunity Representative (**POLICY NUMBER 1-100**)

1. Effective immediately, 2LT Scott Bennett is assigned the duty of Equal Opportunity Representative for the 11th PSYOP BN.

2. Authority: AR 600-20 and PAM 350-20.

3. Purpose: To provide EO oversight for the 11th POB as prescribed by AR 600-20 and DA PAM 350-20.

4. Period: Until officially relieved from appointment or assignment.

5. Special Instructions: Provide timely feedback (30 days active/60 days Army Reserve) to subordinates regarding the results of Command Climate Surveys or any EO survey instrument initiated by the command. Provide EEO services to soldiers and liaison to Brigade. Report all EO training at the annual training brief.

5. POC for this Duty Appointment is MAJ. James Simpson at james.simpsonJR@us.army.mil.

JOEL DROBA
LTC, PO
Commanding

Distribution:
11th POB Cdr
11th POB XO
11th, HSC
305th PSYOP CO
312th PSYOP CO
351st PSYOP CO
360th PSYOP CO

CONTENTS OF LETTER/PACKAGE SENT TO GEN JEFF JACOBS:

1. 3 dec 2013 letter
2. Interconnectivity chart (Birkenfeld, Bennett, Snowden)
3. page from Guardian article with "X" chart
4. article "A PENTAGON WAR ON INJUSTICE"
5. BAH chart/slide on KEY FININT players
6. UBS financial sheet (2% fine breakdown)
7. BAH CENTCOM job sheet
8. BAH SOCOM/STATE job sheet
9. Letter from LTC Joyce Bush, 11th PSYOP to BAH about Commissio
10. TERMS AND ORGANZATIONS packet

11. ENVELOPE "A": a) cover sheet; b) memo to 2LT Bennett; c) letter to judge; d) letter to Congress; e) commendation letter; f) promotion letter

12. ENVELOPE "B": a) cover sheet; b) ex. 4:EMERGENCY MOTION cover sheet, pg. 1; c) notice of depositions (BAH suit); news article "Leaker's Insurance Against Arrest"

13. ENVELOPE "C": a) cover sheet; b) Article 138 Response, request for military lawyer assigned; c) Memorandum of Law and basis for Article 138 Complaint; d) ex45, military false statements statute is clarified.

14, ATTACHMENTS: 1) article: President Obama's Military Coup purges 197 officers in five years; 2) INTERCONNECTION OF ISSUES AND AGENCIES DIAGRAM; 3) COLLAGE OF PARTICIPANTS; 4) How Booz Allen Swallowed Washington; 5) Leaker's insurance against arrest (article); 6) TRULINCS article "The General says..." (retired Army general calling for "forced resignations" of....

2LT SCOTT BENNETT
11TH PSYCHOLOGICAL OPERATIONS BATTALION, 2 POG,
U.S. ARMY CIVIL AFFAIRS-PSYCHOLOGICAL OPERATIONS COMMAND
UNITED STATES ARMY RESERVE

3 DEC 2013

CONFIDENTIAL LETTER FOR Jeffrey A. Jacobs, Major General, USAR

Dear General Jacobs,

    A dangerous situation is unfolding which will affect you and your Command. I would be negligent in my duty as a USACAPOC Officer if I did not inform you about every possible combination of public reaction, Congressional-Military "scapegoating", and international media exploitation of your personal knowledge of and role in this situation. Since this situation may be defined as a conspiracy, a scandal, or an act of treason by a court, you could find yourself exposed to <u>criminal indictment</u> for activities described in my report, unless you <u>correct the error,</u> and assuage the damage it has caused. As an Officer, I strongly recommend you do this.

    If you do not correct the error and fix this situation, it may soon begin to impact you from four (4) directions simultaneously: (1) PROFESSIONALLY; (2) SOCIALLY; (3) PERSONALLY; and (4) RELIGIOUSLY. To help you understand the process of this "identity disintegration" phenomenon, I have attached a diagram for your perusal (You will recognize it from my work at US Special Operations Command and State Department Counterterrorism).

    As you may remember, Colonel Jeff Jones (retired, 4th POG Commander; National Security Council; West Point roomate of Army Secretary Casey; and the "Father of Modern Psyop") was my mentor in the surreal art of multidimensional psychological warfare--which as you know was his preferred term for the art, since MISO to him was an effeminate wilting of the discipline and an emasculation of its practitioners (as well as retribution by Admiral Eric Olson for Mike Furlong and USACAPOC's "psyop targeting" of US Senators for budget expansion agendas...but that's another report).

    While at Booz Allen Hamilton, Jeff Jones and I rewrote the military's PSYOP Manual (the most interesting parts of it, that is) and designed various strategic communication and tactical PSYOP products for various Combatant Commands, for Embassy teams (MIST/CIA), and for other agencies and missions. You may also remember me from the 2008 Psychological Operations Conference at the Landsdowne Center in Maryland. Not only did Jeff Jones train me well, but he encouraged (and enabled) me to accept a Direct Commission into the Army PSYOP program, to improve it.

    So out of respect to Colonel Jones, and in accordance with my duty as an efficient and creative Army Officer, I will try to make this simple and easy for you. I would suggest reading this letter slowly, soberly, and instinctively; for it speaks between the lines which Jeff Jones was confident you would be cunning enough to appreciate, and capable enough to utilize.

As our Officer training instructs, "Everything is a test." So in accordance with that principle, I have enclosed three (3) envelopes (three choices)--A, B, or C--from which you may select your response to this letter. The end results of each choice--the destination of each path--are described in the corresponding envelopes. Choose "A", and you will prosper (and need read no further this letter); choose it not, and you may suffer--as might your family, your reputation, your career, and your spirit (according to the "identity disintegration" model cited on page 1, paragraph 2 of this report). Let me be perfectly clear: this is not a threat, but an inductive analysis of the inevitable "ripple effect" of your choice, which I am bound as an Army Officer to provide you as Commander. I would be negligent in my duty if I did not provide you this honest assesment of the situation. Why?

As a former Commander-in-Chief once stated, "Facts are stubborn things." The fact is our emerging National Security Agency (NSA)-Central Intelligence Agency (CIA)-Edward Snowden and Terrorist Threat Finance (TF)-Union Bank of Switzerland (UBS)-Booz Allen Hamilton (BAH) connections--which, incidentally, I'm at the nexus of, having worked with the intel at all three organizations--has created a "perfect storm," composed of three thunderous fronts (Edward Snowden, Brad Birkenfeld, and Scott Bennett), which will soon expand when a fourth front is added when Mr. Raoul Weil, the former head of private banking at UBS, arrives in the U.S. from Italy in the next couple months. As this issue is connected to me, and I am connected to USACAPOC and you, then USACAPOC and yourself (and other parts of the Army) will soon be implicated. Despite my best attempts (and a vast paper-trail) this "stubborn fact" and "nuclear issue" will not go away. It even seems to be gaining strength with each revelation and exploding outward through each new aggrieved party. How can this be?

As the record reflects, I advised you and others well before this storm gathered; and I warned you personally of the ominous outgrowth which would naturally follow (military personnel will testify to this under oath, and have confirmed in writing). Why?

As you know, as Officers, we have a sworn duty to provide our superiors with intelligence and analysis that enhances their decision-making process, and achieves the Army's mission. This report fulfills my duty in this regard. Sadly, however, it seems you failed to provide your superiors with the materials I provided to you. This very well might be construed as intentional on your part, and if intentional, then categorized a conspiracy; and if a conspiracy that has facilitated the wounding or killing of military servicemembers (American and Allied) and contractors, or given "aide and comfort" (i.e., UBS financing) to the enemy, then a treasonous scandal for which the public will demand blood; and politicians could make you the "scapegoat" to sacrifice and pay the price for. Subsequently, your failure to debrief me, Brad Birkenfeld, and the others identified in my reports, and your failure to utilize our materials, could be interpreted as not only a grievous dereliction of duty that has damaged the "war on terrorism" mission, but has cost the lives, limbs, and hope of tens of thousands of Americans and their families--never mind the hundreds of thousands of Middle-Easterners. These are the facts.

Again, this is not, by any means, some knuckle-dragging threat, simpleton rage, or bombastic bluff.

This report is simply an assesment of the situation, and a carefully calculated prediction of the most probable scenario which will follow in the event you do not choose envelope "A" and implement its suggestions, and allow this situation to metasticize. My scenario is also based on historical analysis of the shifty game of "musical chairs" played by political elites and their sychophantic media as they scramble for someone else to blame for their own incompetence, negligence, or skullduggery. Ergo, because of my prior work and reports to you and USACAPOC (and others), you could become that scapegoat, you will be the man without a chair when the music stops, you will be blamed. How?

You will be blamed for the NSA-CIA-Edward Snowden leaks, since his actions were prompted by my Birkenfeld-UBS-Terrorist Financing report (September 25, 2012; and others before), and its connection to Booz Allen Hamilton (defense contractor in CENTCOM's Joint Interagency Group/ Joint Interagency Operations Center).

This will "snowball" and you will be blamed for intentionally avoiding, ignoring, and not utilizing new intelligence exposing terrorist financing between Swiss Banks (HSBC, Credit Suise, and UBS), Kuwait, and the "al-Nusra front" (now dominating Al Qaida's success in the Syrian civil war and impending Islamic extremist advance).

You will be seen as conspiring with a defense contractor, Booz Allen Hamilton, which was contracted to identify and eliminate terrorist financing, by allowing the unlawful and unprecedented prosecution of a military officer, in a civilian court, bypassing the UCMJ and opening the door for future civil prosecution of military personnel for military actions performed in uniform.

Finally, you may also be blamed, in part, for the US Consulate attack in Benghazi, Libya by Islamic extremists, since my report to you in December 2010 (a response to a "request for feedback" from 2POG Brigade Commander Burley) accurately predicted the Muslim religious outrage and resulting recruitment by extremist groups. My report addressed the "psychological operations" impact of "Reversing the 'Don't Ask, Don't Tell' Policy" on Muslim enemies and allies alike. Suspiciously, one month after I formally submitted this report to USACAPOC, I was indicted for events which had occurred nine (9) months prior, and which had already been dismissed by military authorities. Copies of this report are available at the 11th PSYOP Battalion (given to LTC Droba), the Pentagon, and at USACAPOC.

These are the conclusions the American public will arrive at, based upon the evidence, in my opinion. I would be doing you and the Army a disservice, and violating my sworn oath as an Officer, if I did not share this "situational assesment" with you as required by Army regulation, DoD policy, and Executive Orders.

For these, and other materials (not listed here due to TS/SCI considerations) it is more than likely that you will be "pulled into the spotlight" and required to give an answer before Congress. Specifically, it's possible that you might be dragged before the Senate Permanent Subcommittee on Investigations, as well as before the Armed Services, and the Intelligence, and Government Oversight and Reform, and Judiciary, and Terrorism, and Homeland Security Committees, and forced to endure questioning under oath. During this questioning (which I am happy to appear next to you and participate in) you may very well be criticized, blamed, and potentially disgraced for "conduct unbecoming an Officer" for "failing in your Commander's duty to 'connect-the-dots' and inform Congress about issues relating to the material support and financing of terrorism against the United States military." That's how the game is played in Washington. Just ask "Scooter" Libby, or LTC Oliver North.

As a result, a hive of uniformed bureaucrats and backstabbing opportunists at the Pentagon (and the White House) and the Justice Department will "cover-their-ass" by nodding in approval at the roasting of yours. Metaphorically speaking, like Sgt. Alias (played by William DeFoe) in Oliver Stone's film "Platoon", you will be abandoned by the helicopters and left behind with arms raised to the sky, as Adagio's "Strings" saddens the moment with a sense of betrayal.

Since politicians obfuscate through scapegoats and shell-games, and since I reported it up the chain-of-command, Congress may determine that you, as Commander, had a duty to disclose my reports, an may hold you responsible. They will do this to appease bloodthirsty constituencies, to simplify and symbolize resolution, and, most importantly, to ensure their re-election by being seen as battling incompetence and corruption.

This is my assesment of the facts and how they will be interpreted, and is being submitted to you in my official capacity as a military officer, in accord with and under the protection of the following laws, regulations and procedures of the United States: 10 U.S.C. §1034; 10 U.S.C. §2409; 18 U.S.C. §1513(e); 4 U.S.C. App. Sec. 3 §8H [Title VII, §701(b)]; 5 U.S.C. §7211; 5 U.S.C. §552(a); 5 U.S.C. Appendix, §7; 42 U.S.C. §1985(d); Executive Order 12731; 5 C.F.R. §2635.101.

RECOMMENDATIONS:

As I understand the Army's mission (and specifically USACAPOC's), you are not to sacrifice yourself recklessly, but to preserve and develop yourself and your family by exercising military character and duties that honor, support, and defend the Constitution of the United States. As a Commander, you do this by rewarding excellence and punishing incompetence; by strengthening honor and virtue, and destroying dishonor and vice; by glorifying courage, and condemning cowardice. In other words, and as Plato would concur, you defend the good, the true, and the beautiful by attacking the bad, the false, and the ugly. Hence, by alligning with and supporting my report (choosing envelope "A"), you will fulfill this mission and honor your oath as a military officer. Whereas by doing the opposite, you will achieve the opposite, and violate the mission and betray the trust placed in you by defending the bad, the false, and the ugly--or in other words, the cover-up of terrorist financing and its connection to the Snowden-NSA leaks.

Therefore my recommendation is to avoid all of this by transforming the dilemma into an opportunity for advancement.

MET-TC ASSESSMENT:

As I see it, in the present socio-political-economic environment, the military winds are shifting, and waves are building that will climax in Congressional hearings and new elections which will result in the political powers forcibly changing the military-intelligence community leadership and assignments. Instead of being overwhelmed and destroyed in the coming tsunami, you now have the chance to "surf and ride" it to a better position, using the information in my reports and testimony as your "surfboard."

In my humble opinion, your best hope for advancing is to skillfully and artfully navigate and manage my intelligence materials with bold honesty and uncompromising aggression; while distancing yourself from the dim-witted or uninspired who are incapable of sensing or realizing what is happening.

Strategically speaking, the only way for you to do this is to support and defend me; and, figuratively speaking, do this by pushing the "blade" of this intelligence quickly to the throat of Congress. Self-preservation (which is their first impulse) will motivate them to defend you, and then recognize you as the best cornerstone upon which to build the new military power-structure. Since the war of ideas will be defined by creative men who implant those ideas into the minds of their enemies, and militantly defend against competing ideas, US Civil Affairs-Psychological Operations Command is the best instrument to do this.

STRATEGY:

Align with the momentum and direction of emerging powers relating to the NSA-Snowden-CIA-UBS-Birkenfeld-Booz Allen Hamilton revelations to be recognized as a warrior worthy of continuing as USACAPOC Commander. This will cultivate additional command opportunities as Chairman Joint-Chiefs-of-Staff, Army Secretary; NSA-CIA Director; and other military-political appointments.

POLITICAL ASSESSMENT:

Over the next one to six months, the political repercussions of these ongoing intelligence revelations will only expand and become more intense. I would be negligent in my duty as a USACAPOC officer if I did not inform you about every possible combination of public reaction, Congressional-Military scapegoating, and international media exploitation of your personal role in this situation--as I've stated earlier--which, again, could very well be viewed as a conspiracy, a scandal, and an act of treason by a majority of everyday Americans.

PSYCHOGRAPHIC ANALYSIS:

Since the data indicates 70% of 18 to 34 year olds consider what Snowden did "a good thing" (interestingly the same age group which was responsible for the overthrow of Rome), this portion of the population, empowered by the world wide web, may militantly respond by organizing, rallying, and seeking to delegitimize and disable (and decommission) suspicious, uncomfortable, or offensive domestic (and international) intelligence-surveillance activities; and aggressively expose, audit, and scale-back all military involvement. Most likely you will be the first military figure targeted due to USACAPOC's connection to this issue. Why?

Although Americans may be slow to anger, once infuriated (or their private life and relationships violated), a patriotic bloodlust for revenge and punishment of wrongdoing is unleashed which only political impeachment or execution (or both) can extinguish.

Therefore the political consequences may be as follows:

USACAPOC and you as its Commander will be implicated, investigated, and judged as responsible for either negligence or intentional cover-up in this matter.

General Martin Dempsey, Chairman of Joint Chiefs of Staff, General Raymond Odierno, Army Secretary/Army COS, General Keith Alexander, NSA Director, LTC Joel Droba, 11th PSYOP Commander, may be similarly investigated and removed for their involvement.

SECDEF Hagel will be implicated, since USACAPOC (and you as its Commander) will be identified as the starting point of the NSA-Snowden-CIA-Birkenfeld connection.

Congressional Intelligence, Armed Services, and Terrorism Committees will be either criticized or condemned as participatory and go on the defensive; or they will claim ignorance and go on the attack (seeking a scapegoat) for being misinformed by the above military-intelligence community leaders. This will lead to similar action being taken against Director of National Intelligence (DNI) Eric Clapper; former DNI and now Booz Allen Hamilton Vice Chair for Cyberstrategy, Mike McConnel; and NSA-CIA Director during the Snowden-Birkenfeld years (2006-2009), Michael Hayden.

Eric Holder, Attorney General, and Lanny Breuer, Assistant Attorney General, will be implicated in the Snowden-Birkenfeld-Weil-UBS-CIA connection; and investigated for not disclosing their conflict of interest in Covington and Burling law firm, and giving a deferred prosecution to UBS in exchange for a one time 2% fine (this will be confirmed by Brad Birkenfeld and Raoul Weil). Additionally they will be implicated in the unlawful prosecution of 2LT Bennett and violation of military jurisdiction.

International criticism, countermeasures, and distancing from the United States (and re-alignment with other countries, such as Brazil, Russia, Iran, China) may speed-up and intensify.

President Barack Obama will be increasingly isolated and deconstructed in his legislative agenda as a result of the continuing Snowden disclosures. President Obama will be connected to UBS Chairman of the Americas, Robert Wolf (who was a campaign financial bundler); connected to the Senate Permanent Subcommittee on Investigations (Chaired by Senator Carl Levin D-Mich) which conducted a hearing on Birkenfeld's claims of UBS terrorist financing, but failed to provide this intelligence to military commanders; and other connections cited in 2LT Bennett's reports.

Hillary Clinton will be implicated in the Benghazi-USACAPOC report connection, as well as the Birkenfeld-UBS-CIA-NSA-Snowden connection. Congressional investigations will examine her role in the following activities: (1) Conspiring to prosecute Brad Birkenfeld in exchange for Swiss political-treaty concessions; (2) Transferring two Chinese Uighar terrorists from Guantanamo Bay Cuba (Camp Victory) to Switzerland in exchange for prosecution of Brad Birkenfeld on trumped up charges, derived from his Senate testimony (for which he had immunity); (3) Conspiring with CIA (Embassy Bern, Switzerland), NSA, DOJ, and other parties to commit wire fraud; (4) other Constitutional violations committed through the unlawful use of government agencies (State/CT) and authorities. This material is confirmed in State Department cables published by <u>Wikileaks</u> and <u>Glenn Greenwald's</u> disclosures in The Guardian and other publications.
Consequent of these increasing disclosures, Hillary Clinton could even be disqualified as a Presidential candidate in 2016.

POLITICAL IMPACT 2014-2016:

As a result of these NSA-Snowden-CIA-Birkenfeld-UBS-Booz Allen Hamilton-USACAPOC connections, and the derivative public outrage and demand for investigations (both domestic and international), most likely a shadow of dishonesty and stench of corruption shall plague the present Administration, its military-intelligence agencies, and implicated Congressional members--resulting in quite a significant exodus through dismissal, impeachment, retirement, and prosecution. Their replacements will, in all probability, possess a character and sense of mission imbued with a reformist agenda, and a virulent passion to exercise it. Their natural temperment already being somewhat incendiary, this issue and all its correlations will become gasoline to the black flames of their predisposed suspicions, hostilities, and passions.

Subsequently, the newly emerging political powers will search for and call upon a fearlessly honest, aggressive, and creative military commander to oversee the objective of "analyzing and synthesizing" my materials into the military-intelligence-CIA-State Department superstructure to identify, research, and remedy the dysfunctions. This will require the deactivation and reallocation of personnel and resources (untainted by the scandal and experienced in interagency operations) to facilitate the reformations.

The objectives, strategies, and tactics for this mission are already developed, and a Pentagon contingent is standing-up in preparation for implementation.

RECOMMENDED COURSE OF ACTION:

This recommendation is made in the best interests of the Army, of USACAPOC, and you as Commander. It is protected communication, and is provided pursuant to my oath of service as an Officer of the United States.

As I see it, the essence of the question and your choice is simply this: As a result of this situation, will you *be* targeted, or will you be *doing* the targeting?

The answer will depend on your course of action--your choice. Your classic choices are: to win (A); to lose (B); or to remain neutral (C) [Be advised: remaining neutral inevitably loses in the long run since neutrality removes deniability and inspires a lukewarm vagueness which fosters revulsion, never respect...but as a military officer, and Commander, you already know this.]

To win (envelope A) means maximizing advantage and exploiting opportunity. To lose (envelope B) means being dominated and victimized by the attacker. To remain neutral (envelope C) means to appear uncommitted, fearful, stupid, or silly; and once ignorance is dissolved by knowledge, action or inaction is prompted.

The paths available to you--the choices you make--are contained in the corresponding envelope and can be summarized as follows:

A: THE WINNER'S PATH--Choose envelope "A" and you will be seen as the man of integrity, the military officer, performing his sworn duty, and the American defending--for himself, his family, and his posterity--the Constitution of the United States. A "Renaissance Man," boldly standing when all others are cowering and falling, you will be heralded as the "Jack Ryan informing and advising Congress of an urgent intelligence revelation for the benefit of all Americans." In one statement you will be initiating the plan that solves the crisis, soothes the fears of Americans, and establishes you as the "go-to man" for similar future solutions.

B: THE LOSER'S PATH--Choose envelope "B" and you may be blamed. You will be identified, questioned, implicated, blamed, prosecuted, judged and despised for being the "keystone" which set in motion the Edward Snowden-NSA-CIA revelations after ignoring the Brad Birkenfeld-UBS-NSA-CIA-terrorist financing report (and other materials) submitted by 2LT Scott Bennett. You will also reignite the investigations into the US Consulate attack in Benghazi, Libya, and death of Ambassador Stevens and others, by appearing to "cover-up and prosecute" 2LT Bennett (a relatively newly commissioned army officer, yet who has profound counterterrorism experience) for a report he had written. This report detailed the negative impact on USACAPOC (and psychological operations as a battlespace) of reversing the "Don't Ask, Don't Tell" policy by predicting Muslim religious outrage and subsequent extremist recruitment and attacks against U.S. Embassy and military personnel; as well as the threats to moderate Muslim regimes, such as Egypt, Saudia Arabia, Kuwait, and Jordan. The public will determine that this report was buried for "political-incorrectness" and 2LT Bennett was prosecuted for it using trumped up charges.

Consequently, it is very possible that waves of wounded and fallen soldiers (and their families) will limp, shuffle, and roll into your office like zombies drawn to some undefinable irritant, seeking to feed their hunger for information about this unfolding issue, or quench their obsessive thirst for revenge for the loss of a loved one they have suffered because of it. Women with mascara smeared eyes, sore red from weeping; the gnashing teeth of fathers; and the wailing infants and sullen toddlers wrapped tight around their mother's bare legs--faces emaciated from lack of fatherly affection--will stare through you with sad, sunken eyes, and with quivering lips whisper, "Why?...Why didn't you share Bennett's report in time...and save my daddy from dying...why?"

As Commander of USACAPOC at the time of this report, every American (and ally) will demand from you this answer.

C: THE BUREAUCRAT'S PATH--Choose envelope "C" and you will be seen as trying to claim ignorance to pretend innocence. You will be seen as trying to avoid responsibility by pretending to not know about military activities and communications which occurred on your watch, during your time as Commander of USACAPOC. At best this will come across as incompetence, negligence, indifference, laziness, or stupidity on your part; which will result in a judgment of contempt and outrage by Americans who entrusted their sons and daughters to your care. At worst this will be seen as dishonest, and if dishonest, then a conspiracy with other parties; and if a conspiracy, then a devious attempt to try and advance your position and feed a lust for power, wealth, or other selfish gain--all of which will demonstrate a betrayal of the Constitution. This behavior may be defined as a criminal act in need of correction (and possibly prosecution) and result in your removal from military service and public disgrace.

The damaging effects of choice "B" or "C" may be a rapid, simultaneous corrosion of the four (4) life sustaining poles of identity: (1) SPIRITUAL/ RELIGIOUS/ MYSTICAL; (2) FAMILY/ MARRIAGE/ CHILDREN; (3) EMPLOYMENT/ SKILLS/ KNOWLEDGE; and (4) SOCIAL NETWORKS/ LEISURE ACTIVITIES/ REPUTATION. The process is as follows:

> The taint of public exposure of military incompetence or corruption deteriorates confidence, which induces shame, which ostracizes and stigmatizes family and friends, which ultimately alientates marrital relationships and triggers sexual dysfunction (particularly in men over the age of 55). Legal risks materialize and are expressed through the discontinuation of career (business) relationships and opportunities, and the shunning by media and publicity. Consulting and academic lecturing also vanishes. This compounding effect gradually corrodes, and in some cases reverses, the sense of personal spiritual/ religious harmony and reward by the individual reinterpreting and redefining as "error" and "bad" that activity or gnosis which was once mistakenly thought as "right" and "good".[2] Illustration below.

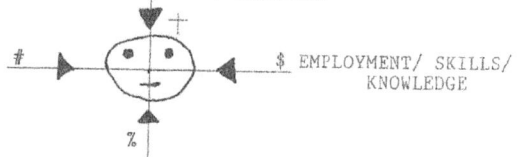

SPIRITUAL/ RELIGIOUS / MYSTICAL

REPUTATION/ SOCIAL NET/ LEISURE ACTIVITIES   #   ⬅ 😐 ➡ $ EMPLOYMENT/ SKILLS/ KNOWLEDGE

%

FAMILY/ MARRIAGE/ CHILDREN

In accordance with psychological warfare principles, training, and case study precedents, the phenomenology described above is most likely to transpire if this situation deteriorates from an advantageous opportunity into a conspiratorially contagious implosion.

This is my assessment of the situation as a Officer under your Command, and as a party to the situation intimately familiar with its legal, political, and media potentialities. After careful analysis and deliberation, and out of respect to Colonel Jeff Jones, and in performance of my duty to provide you with my best advice to achieve "Commander's Intent", I strongly suggest you choose envelope "A" and implement it as your course of action in response to this situation.

I hope you will carefully consider all angles and elements of this issue, and conclude that I have continued to perform my duty as a Special Operations Army Officer of the United States, despite the overwhelming challenges and excruciating suffering of my unlawful imprisonment. I hope you will conclude that by discovering a threat to the United States national security (and our allies), analyzing it from my Terrorist Threat Finance and PSYOP background, and then immediately and zealously communicating my discovery and analysis up my chain-of-command to military and Congressional authorities, I exemplified the initiative, and courage, tenacity, and devotion to country most sought after in military officers of the United States, and in particular, valued by U.S. Civil Affairs-Psychological Operations Command and by you as its Commander. I hope you will concur that in the face of extraordinary circumstances, I demonstrated extraordinary ability, and completed my mission of disrupting terrorist finance networks.

2LT Scott A. Bennett
11th Psychological Operations Battalion, c/o
#29418-016, P.O. Box 670, Minersville, PA 17954-0670

ENVELOPE "A"--WINNER'S PATH

I hereby choose envelope "A". I recognize my course of action will be:
(A) To investigate, support, and defend 2LT Scott Bennett's reports, writings, and testimony.

In other words...I choose to restore 2LT Bennett and cleanse his record of any negative or adverse actions related to this matter.

I understand that 2LT Scott Bennett will not take any action relating to this matter, and agrees to work with me (or my point of contact) to resolve these issues "in-house", and not expose them to outside parties until after suitable agreements are made, and other actions taken.

I further agree to sign all documents contained in this envelope and forward them to the appropriate parties for implementation; and I agree to send copies of these signed documents to 2LT Scott Bennett at:
2LT Scott Bennett, #29418-016, P.O. Box 670, Minersville, PA 17954-0670.

I hereby certify this understanding on this _____ day of _____, 2013.

Other needs or issues to be determined include the following:

_____
_____
_____

JEFFREY A. JACOBS
Major General, USAR
Commanding

*SPECIAL NOTE: This document (envelope "A"--WINNER'S PATH) and the additional documents included in this envelope **MUST BE SIGNED AND RETURNED** to 2LT Scott Bennett by January 15, 2014, at the latest. Otherwise this agreement expires, and 2LT Scott Bennett will file legal action in Federal District Court, as well as with military courts and the Judge Advocate General's Office, and other parties.

The additional documents in this evelope include:
1) Memo to 2LT Bennett from GEN Jeff Jacobs;
2) Letter to Judge from GEN Jacobs; 3) Commendation statement for 2LT Bennett; 4) Promotion statement for 2LT Bennett; and 5) Letter to Congress from GEN Jacobs (any edits or changes to documents must be received by 2LT Bennett by Jan. 15, 2014).

ENVELOPE "B" CHOICE + PATH

I hereby choose envelope "B". I recognize my course of
action will be:
(B) To cover-up, distort, discredit, and flee from
2LT Bennett's reports and testimony.

In other words...I realize 2LT Bennett's material will be
acknowledged as a military officer's whistleblowing exposure,
up the chain-of-command, of a Constitutional violation (as well
as UCMJ) which he discovered. By choosing option "B", I hereby
choose to ally with those doing the violating as alleged in 2LT
Bennett's reports.
    This means I agree to cover-up or discredit 2LT Bennett's
intelligence materials disclosing the National Security Agency-
Edward Snowden-CIA connections to Union Bank of Switzerland-Brad
Birkenfeld-Booz Allen Hamilton and U.S. Civil Affairs-Psychological
Operations Command.
    I also choose to hide from Congress (and the American people,
the media, and our international allies) 2LT Bennett's report
addressing the "negative Implications of Reversing the 'Don't
Ask, Don't Tell' Report on USACAPOC"; which apparently predicted
accurately the Benghazi, Libya terrorist attacks on the US Embassy
and CIA Annex which resulted in the deaths of Ambassador Chris
Stevens and other personnel.
    I realize this course of action will take me down the path
of history which originated in Laos, Cambodia, and leads past
"Coronet-Oaks" in Puerto Rico, and will end in the poppy fields
of Afghanistan.
    I realize my actions may be interpreted as a betrayal of
the Constitution and my personal duty (and oath of service) as
a military officer and Commander; but that price is acceptable
since my primary concern is my pension and preserving the status
quo.
    I understand that 2LT Bennett has sworn by his oath as an
officer of the U.S. Army to do everything within the law, and
within his power, to expose to the American people and the Halls
of Justice, the numerous violations of the Constitution, all
civil rights abuses, all deceitful practices and corruption of
the UCMJ and military Honor Code, and all transgressions of
international law, alleged in his reports and testimony.
    I further realize 2LT Bennett will seek redress of all grievances
and injuries inflicted upon him and his family by all parties
responsible alleged both in his report and listed on his DEPOSITIONS.
    I know that 2LT Scott Bennett will fight as long as he lives
to clear his good name; and will relentlessly pursue, develop,
and exploit all elements and persons involved with this scandalous
conspiracy and potential act of treason. If I were a young man
of honor, I would do the same.
    I hereby accept full responsibility for the path this Choice
"B" will take me down, and all repercussions from it. I agree
to sign and return this **ENVELOPE "B"** document to 2LT Scott Bennett
at: 2LT Scott Bennett, #29418-016, P.O. Box 670, Minersville,
PA 17954-0670, on this _____ day of _____, 2013.

cc: GEN Martin Dempsey   _____
    GEN Ray Odierno
    Congressional Committees: JEFFREY A. JACOBS
    Armed Services;   Major General, USAR
    Intelligence;   Commanding
    Terrorism

ENVELOPE "C"--NEUTRAL PATH

I hereby choose envelope "C". I recognize my course of action will be:
(C) To practice silence, pretend ignorance, and obfuscate through bureaucracy.

In other words...I choose to try and remain neutral.
I wish to be silent, blind, and deaf to all issues communicated to me in 2LT Bennett's reports, because I seek adventure through not "rocking-the-boat", and am excited by the status quo.

Since I seek career advancement through bureaucratic safety, and find stimulation in the silent numbness of obscurity, I wish to remain--for as long as time and fate will allow me--disconnected from this issue, oblivious to its implications, and unresponsive to all requests put to me. Since my character is as strong as a statue of ash, I fear 2LT Bennett's report would no doubt be the strong wind that scatters me into oblivion; so out of self-preservation, I choose to retreat into the crevice of isolation.

Since the language of nobility is to me an alien mumbling, and the concept of virtue a confusing smear of kaleidoscopic symbols, I hereby refuse to analyze 2LT Bennett's intelligence info and recommendations.

For these reasons, and in order to try and remain firmly head-planted in the shifting sands of ignorance--and thereby hopefully avoid the politicians, citizens, and media following your saga--I have chosen self-castration of judgment over the honorable duty of affirming truth.

I have decided not to decide.

I hereby accept full responsibility for the path this Choice "C" will take me down, most likely, and all repercussions from it. I agree to sign and return this **ENVELOPE "C"** document to 2LT Scott Bennett at the following address:
2LT Scott Bennett, #29418-016, P.O. Box 670, Minersville, PA 17954-0670, on this _____ day of _____, 2013.

JEFFREY A. JACOBS
Major General, USAR
Commanding

cc: GEN Martin Dempsey, Chairman, Joint Chiefs of Staff
GEN Ray Odierno, Secretary of the Army
Congressional Committees: Armed Services; Intelligence; Terrorism; Government Oversight and Reform; Foreign Affairs; Judiciary

2LT SCOTT BENNETT
11TH PSYCHOLOGICAL OPERATIONS BATTALION
CIVIL AFFAIRS AND PSYCHOLOGICAL OPERATIONS COMMAND (AIRBORNE)
UNITED STATES ARMY RESERVE
C/O #29418-016
P.O. BOX 670
MINERSVILLE, PA 17954-0670

15 DECEMBER 2013

MEMORANDUM FOR Major General Jeffrey A. Jacobs, USAR, Commanding, USACAPOC(A), 2175 Reilly Road (Stop A), Fort Bragg, NC 28310

SUBJECT: Response to "Request for Redress Under Article 138, UCMJ" dated 9 OCT 2013; and request for assignment of military legal counsel pursuant to AR 27-10, 19-8 (Legal Advice)

1. I, 2LT Scott Bennett, am a member of the 11th PSYCHOLOGICAL OPERATIONS battalion, United States Army (Reserve).

2. I desire to submit a complaint under the provisions of UCMJ, Art. 138; and pursuant to AR-27-10, page 106, 19-8--Legal Advice request a military lawyer be assigned to me immediately for "advice and assistance in drafting the complaint."

3. This matter involves illegal activity by a military officer in my chain of command, and thus requires I communicate this matter to military authorities first, in order to preserve evidence and testimony from being tainted or compromised by the accused officer.

4. I therefore request my complaint be forwarded to the Judge Advocate General (DAJA-ZA), HQDA, 2200 Army Pentagon, Washington, DC 20310-2200, in the event this matter cannot be resolved.

5. I reserve the right to discharge military counsel assigned to me if I believe their performance inadequate. I also reserve my right to represent myself as "co-counsel for my own defense" in any and all matters relating to this complaint.

6. I request a military lawyer contact me IN PERSON, not over the phone or by electronic mail, at the following address: FPC Schuylkill, P.O. Box 670, Minersville, PA 17954-0670; (570) 544-7100 to arrange a meeting through me by phone first.

SCOTT BENNETT
2LT, US Army (Res)
11th PSYOP, 2POG

P.S. Attached is my MEMORANDUM OF LAW establishing my case, and the basis for my complaint. Other materials will be provided after a military attorney is provided to me, and other legal actions requested.

DEPARTMENT OF THE ARMY
HEADQUARTERS, UNITED STATES ARMY
CIVIL AFFAIRS AND PSYCHOLOGICAL OPERATIONS COMMAND (AIRBORNE)
FORT BRAGG, NORTH CAROLINA 28310-5200

AFRC-CPC-JA

MEMORANDUM FOR 2LT Scott Bennett, #29418-016, P.O. Box 670, Minersville, PA 17954-0670

SUBJECT: Army Unit Transfer Legal Case and Redress

1. I have just now learned of your incarceration for activities relating to your Army Reserve Unit transfer.

2. After review of the circumstances, I have concluded that you were improperly charged in a civilian court for activities which fell under military jurisdiction, since they were a function of your military service, were performed in uniform on a military base, and were authorized by your chain of command.

3. I am working to rectify this situation by requesting the Florida District Court vacate the judgment against you and dismiss the case as a matter of military jurisdiction.

4. You will be contacted in the event anything is required of you to complete this process of correcting the military and judicial records.

5. Point of contact for this action is LTC Baucum Fulk at (910) 907-4870 or baucum.w.fulk.mil@mail.mil

JEFFREY A. JACOBS
Major General, USAR
Commanding

JEFFREY A. JACOBS
Major General, USAR, Commanding
DEPARTMENT OF THE ARMY
HEADQUARTERS, UNITED STATES ARMY
CIVIL AFFAIRS AND PSYCHOLOGICAL OPERATIONS COMMAND (AIRBORNE)
2175 Reilly Road (Stop A)
Fort Bragg, NC 28310-5200
(910) 907-4870
baucum.w.fulk.mil@mail.mil

Judge Virginia Hernandez-Covington
United States District Judge
Middle District of Florida
801 N. Florida Ave.
Tampa, Florida 33602

    RE: 2LT Scott A. Bennett, 11th PSYOP, USAR
        USA v. Scott Allan Bennett, Case no. 8:11-CR-14-T-33AEP
        and
        RELATED CASE ORDER AND TRACK ONE NOTICE, Case No. 8:13-CV-2778-T-33AEP
        REQUEST FOR VACATING OF JUDGMENT AND DISMISSAL

Dear Judge Hernandez-Covington:

I am Major General Jeff Jacobs, Commander of USACAPOC, United States Army Reserve. I have just learned that an officer under my command, 2LT Scott Bennett of the 11th PSYOP Battalion, was prosecuted in your court for activities he engaged in as a function of his military service; and that in fact he had been authorized to execute as an essential part of his transfer to a new Army Reserve unit in the Tampa area.

I have investigated this matter and discovered that there seems to have been serious communication problems, which unfortunately led to 2LT Bennett being mistakenly charged with civilian violations of law for the actions he undertook. 2LT Bennett's activities were, in fact, authorized by his chain of command, and protected under federal law and the Uniform Code of Military Justice, since he performed these activities in his capacity as an Army Officer, on a U.S. military base.

I request, therefore, that this information be entered into the court records as "Newly Discovered Evidence", and that subsequently the judgment against 2LT Bennett be vacated, and the case dismissed. As Commander of USACAPOC, I believe it is in the best interests of justice, the U.S. military, and the U.S. Constitution to dismiss this matter as being a military jurisdiction issue.

Jeffrey A. Jacobs
Major General, USAR
Commanding

JEFFREY A. JACOBS
Major General, USAR, Commanding
DEPARTMENT OF THE ARMY
HEADQUARTERS, UNITED STATES ARMY
CIVIL AFFAIRS AND PSYCHOLOGICAL OPERATIONS COMMAND (AIRBORNE)
FORT BRAGG, NC 28310-5200

Dear Member of Congress:

I am Major General Jeffrey Jacobs, Commander, USACAPOC, USAR. I have been advised of a developing situation involving the current National Security Agency (NSA)-Edward Snowden revelations, that impacts my mission as Commander, USACAPOC.

I have received information which my duty as an Officer of the United States Army compels me to share with you. An officer under my command, 2LT Scott Bennett of the 11th PSYOP Battalion, and a former Booz Allen Hamilton counterterrorism contractor, has presented to me material disclosing connections between the NSA-Snowden-CIA revelations, and international terrorist financing; as well as activities which may be violations of the Uniform Code of Military Justice, Army Regulations, and the U.S. Constitution.

2LT Bennett has communicated to me that he was employed by Booz Allen Hamilton as a Global Psychological Operations Analyst, where he was assigned to U.S. Special Operations Command, to the Department of State Coordinator for Counterterrorism, and to U.S. Central Command's Joint Interagency Operations Center. While at CENTCOM/JIOC, Bennett worked as a Terrorist Threat Finance analyst, identifying, profiling and disrupting terrorist finance networks and operations. During his time there, Bennett wrote prolifically on the failures, challenges, problems, and opportunities the military-intelligence-contractor community was facing with regard to the terrorist finance and psychological warfare missions. Drawing from his previous counterterrorism experience, Bennett began to synthesize the best practices, theories, and data into his mission in order to streamline bureaucratic entanglements and improve effectiveness of interagency operations. One of the classic problems Bennett began to examine was the invisibility of Swiss banks.

Bennett discovered a significant challenge was Swiss banks (Credit Suisse, Union Bank of Switzerland, HSBC, etc.) generating anonymous accounts for customers, laundering money through non-profit filters (organizations) within the banks, then transferring these funds to other banks, organizations, or persons in Kuwait (as well as other countries in the Middle East). Incidentally, Kuwait is now recognized as a key financier of extremist organizations engaged in the Syrian civil war, such as the al-Nusra Front. The Haqqani network, and various Al Qaida branches, were also addressed in Bennett's reports, briefings, and discussions.

Bennett recommended aggressive and creative strategies for expanding intelligence sharing and diversifying military operations through the interagency structures. Soon after he was fired from Booz Allen Hamilton and escorted off base.

The explanation given to Bennett was his military base housing paperwork and army reserve unit transfer was problematic, among other things. He was also told because the moving truck, which a week earlier had shipped his household goods unto base, had not properly registered his firearm safe and ammunition (and military gear), Bennett was in technical violation. Despite his explanation, Bennett was terminated from his position, and forced to return to Washington DC.

Upon his return to his army reserve unit, 2LT Bennett was told to lay low, not "stir the pot", or legal repercussions would follow. However laying low and not stirring the pot is exactly the opposite of what Special Operations Officers instinctively do. They push the boundaries, exploit opportunities, and invent the solutions no one else has the imagination to think of. They are highly intelligent, fluent in foreign languages and cultures, and thrive on challenge. They are audacious, charming, and ferociously patriotic. They represent the best of America's armed forces cadre, and are oftentimes despised for it. I believe this is, in part, why 2LT Scott Bennett was persecuted. He was recognized as this type of soldier, viewed as a danger to the status quo, and summarily removed from his position using trumped up technical violations.

It is significant to note that after 2LT Bennett returned to Washington DC, he wrote a report which was in response to a request for information from 2POG Brigade Commander Burley. This report addressed the potential negative implications of repealing the "Don't Ask, Don't Tell" policy of homosexuality in the army, with specific reference to the psychological warfare dimensions. Among other things, Bennett's profound analysis described how Islamic extremists would exploit this policy reversal into propaganda for financial donations, suicide bomber recruitment, and increase attacks on Westerners in general. Additionally, moderate governments in Egypt, Saudi Arabia, Jordan, and other nations would be jeopardized if the policy change was propagandized as an attack on Islamic virtues.

Despite the report's multidimensional insight into the Muslim mind, its politically-incorrect implications were too much to bear , and it became the "straw-that-broke-the-camel's-back". Instead of being a "Response for Feedback" about how a policy might impact the army and its mission, the report was perceived as a threat to certain political agendas in the military, and generated enormous hostility. The report was buried and Bennett forbidden from speaking about it.

It is significant to note that despite 2LT Bennett being the Officer in Charge (OIC) of his battalion's S-1 department (responsible for the morale, welfare and recreation of soldiers and their families); despite him being the Commander's Adjutant, the Equal Opportunity Officer, and the Officer in charge of investigations; and despite his credentials and background in the private and political sectors dealing with this type of material, 2LT Bennett and his report were not only dismissed, but he was threatened, attacked, and eventually prosecuted for writing it after certain military and Justice Department officials conspired to generate false charges against him. One month after submitting the report, Bennett was charged for the base housing paperwork discrepancy which had allegedly occurred nine (9) months prior; and although in uniform at the time and performing a function of his military duty, he was prosecuted--unconstitutionally I believe--in a civilian court.

Let me be clear: This unlawful and unprecedented prosecution of a military officer, in a civilian court, bypasses the Uniform Code of Military Justice (UCMJ) and <u>opens the door</u> for future <u>civil prosecution of military personnel by civilians</u> and other agencies for actions performed in uniform and in pursuit of military objectives. This should strike fear and fury in the military command structure for it instantly compromises our military mission and servicemembers (and our allies) around the globe. The <u>insidious encroachment of civilian authority and legal jurisdiction</u> into the military arena, if not reversed, will cripple and destroy the autonomy and effectiveness of the military, and America will be put at risk of attack by parties ingenius enough to fully exploit this weakness. This is the legal reality we will face, if this issue is not corrected

CONCLUSION:

2LT Scott Bennett was, and remains, an Officer under my command. I believe what was allowed to happen to him was truly reprehensible, a disgrace, and a threat to all military servicemembers; and an issue that Congress must address. Unfortunately I was not informed about this situation until well after it had occurred, but I am taking action to correct it and ensure it never happens again. I'm confident members of Congress will understand the implications of this, and see it as being in their best interest--and our nation's--to investigate these issues and protect our military members from similar political prosecutions in the future.

What is most interesting about 2LT Bennett's report, if not prophetic, is that it accurately predicted the exact behavior and propaganda which circulated around Benghazi, Libya just prior to the attack on the U.S. Consulate and CIA Annex. State CT and CIA intelligence corroborated much of what Bennett stated might happen. So the obvious question now becomes, had his report been more thoroughly considered, had Bennett been listened to more dispassionately and interpreted less politically, might this terrorist attack been thwarted or avoided, people be alive today who aren't, and America in a stronger position in the Middle East? That is the hard question I have asked myself, which I hope you will ask also. I am happy to share with you my answers, at your convenience.

JEFFREY A. JACOBS
Major General, USAR
Commanding

COMMENDATION

In recognition for extraordinary service to the United States of America, 2LT Scott Allan Bennett is hereby awarded this commendation for the following actions:

For extraordinary ability to endure, adapt to, and transform a prisoner-of-war situation into a Terrorist Finance intelligence gathering operation;

For outstanding initiative in exploiting opportunities to advance the Army mission of combatting and defeating all enemies, foreign and domestic, of the United States;

For brilliant interagency intelligence analysis and writing skill;

For his ferocious determination and fearless conviction to speak truth to power by communicating to military and Congressional authorities information representing a real and undiscovered threat to the National Security of America and its allies in the global war on terrorism;

For his steadfast fealty to the Army and devotion to the United States of America as demonstrated in his commitment and self-sacrifice in the face of enormous challenge and threats to his personal safety and to the safety of his family;

For his valor, courage, integrity, and skill as an Officer of the United States Army Civil Affairs-Psychological Operations Command, Scott Allan Bennett is hereby awarded the Silver Star for performing activities above and beyond the call of duty.

Jeffrey A. Jacobs
Major General, USAR
Commanding

PROMOTION

In recognition of his extraordinary performance as an
Officer of the United States Army, 2LT Scott Bennett is
hereby promoted to the rank of CAPTAIN, United States
Army Reserve, and his military occupation speciality
is to be listed as PSYCHOLOGICAL OPERATIONS OFFICER.

This promotion is made retroactive to July 2011.

Captain Bennett is to be re-assigned to a Psychological
Operations duty on the West Coast, effective immediately.

                              _____
                              Jeffrey A. Jacobs
                              Major General, USAR
                              Commanding

"FULL DISCLOSURE: A LETTER TO MILITARY FAMILIES"

A WHISTLEBLOWING REPORT TO THE UNITED STATES CONGRESS AND THE DEPARTMENT OF DEFENSE INSPECTOR GENERAL

By 2LT Scott Bennett
11th Psychological Operations Battalion
U.S. Civil Affairs-Psychological Operations Command
United States Army Reserve

July 4, 2014

Dear Member of Congress,
I urge you to publish this letter on your Congressional web site, and assume a position of support for both the recommendations contained herein, and the corroborating military whistleblowing reports exposing terrorist financing and its cover-up by the highest levels of government, the military, the intelligence community, and the media. Please contact me to schedule an immediate debriefing, where I will be appearing in my Army Uniform, under oath, in performance of my constitutional duty as a military officer.

2LT Scott Bennett
U.S. Army Reserve (retired)
11th Psychological Operations Battalion
U.S. Civil Affairs-Psychological Operations Command

INTRODUCTION

To my fellow military brethren wounded, killed or abandoned in the Middle East wars; and their mothers and fathers, wives and husbands, grandparents, and children burdened with the scars.

If you are receiving this letter via a Member of Congress, then he/she is honorably defending the constitution of the United States, and worthy of your election. If you have not received this letter from your Member, then know that they are participating in this cover-up and should be immediately removed from office—if not criminally prosecuted as part of a conspiracy involving parties and actions contained in this report.

The ongoing revelations of illegal **NSA-CIA surveillance on Americans and our allies**, as well as the sudden **re-conquest of Iraq by the Islamic State of Iraq and Syria (ISIS)**, and the **Levant**, as well as the rampant beheadings and crucifixions of Christians around the Middle East—re-igniting smoldering wars—has compelled me to write to you and share this information to assuage your family's anger, suffering and loss. I encourage you to review this material for two reasons: 1) for your own sense of closure, healing, and growth; and 2) to help you serve as a resource for other families who are, or may soon be, struggling with the same agony and frustration.

You can inspect the documents relating to this report at: http://armypsyop.wix.com/scottbennett. After review, I hope you will honor our warriors (military and contractors) by sharing these materials with your family and friends. I also hope you will forcefully <u>demand</u> an explanation, an apology, and a plan of redemptive action from the media, the military leaders, and the politicians in Washington DC and your own State Capitols, before another family suffers the same loss; and before Congress and the President once again plunge our young men and women into an insane, endless, and unconstitutional Middle East war (which may soon expand into Eurasia) they themselves refuse to fight.

WHO AM I?
I am the military officer who writes the letters informing some of you of your soldier's death. I am the Officer-in-Charge of the Army Adjutant General Department (S-1) at my battalion. The S-1 department is where the most recent Fort Hood shooting took place a couple months ago. Incidentally this shooting was triggered by a silly and avoidable military bureaucratic and leadership failure that resulted in the soldier experiencing a sense of "betrayal" by the military; and then consequently becoming frustrated into a psychological breakdown and suicidal rage…but that's another report.

OVERVIEW
I write to you today to share a discovery I made many months ago, which sadly—if not reprehensibly—nobody in our military ranks, or Congress, or intelligence community, or the media seems to have the guts or honor to tell you about…so far.

Since September 25, 2012, I have written, demanded, and pleaded to the highest levels of America's military-congressional-judicial leadership, asking them to expose and inform you about a scandalous cover-up that continues to this very day. To over one hundred politicians, journalists, and senior level military officers have I written letters and reports (legal motions, whistleblowing reports to the Inspector General, Congressional requests, etc.) addressing this issue. You may confirm this at: http://armypsyop.wix.com/scottbennett

With the exception of Senator Rand Paul, all of these supposed "leaders and men of honor" have not only ignored it, but in fact threatened, persecuted, imprisoned, and tortured me (in that order) in a cowardly and treasonous attempt to hide this matter. Quite simply, instead of serving as the U.S. Constitution's advocate, they have shamefully played the corporate slave and political harlot. Sadly, and without apology or hesitation, I tell you that this failure is enabling Islamic extremists to wound and kill our young men and women in uniform defending America—at home and abroad.

Because of this, my oath as military Officer compels me to give you and your fallen service-member the dignity and respect of sharing with you the raw, undiluted truth about exactly what I discovered, and why my efforts to get this information out to you have been blocked since September 25, 2012.

BACKGROUND
I realize you may have difficulty believing this story, but the maxim *"truth is stranger than fiction"* certainly rings true in this case. This information is unclassified and available on open-source media and internet intelligence channels.

Unfortunately, all those associated with politics, the military, and the media seem to have either:
    1) chosen to remain in the delusion of fanatical post-September 11th patriotism (or rather hysteria, as some might describe); or else
    2) have lost their souls to the addiction of power and the fear of losing it; or else
    3) have consciously and quietly exchanged your son or daughter's, husband or wife's, father or mother's life for the proverbial "thirty-pieces of silver" of their own job security and retirement in the defense contracting "Shell Game." I urge you to be their judge.

THE SECRET WAR
The simple fact is your son or daughter was injured or killed by a terrorist bullet, bomb, drug, or cyberattack financed, in part, by assets (cash, diamonds, gold, drugs, etc.) illegally transferred from Swiss Bank accounts—specifically the Union Bank of Switzerland (UBS), and one Saudi account holder in particular, **Abdulaziz Abbas** (*Asra Abdulaziz a pouvoir su le coffre—Coffre No 8170 lie au Co-259.518-B.N.—Titulaire: 0279/CO-617'500-T.B.*), and its Optimus Foundation—whose chief executives (i.e., **Robert Wolf, Chairman of the Americas**) have been financial bundlers for the Obama Administration, and protected from Justice Department prosecution by Attorney General **Eric Holder** and Assistant Attorney General **Lanny Breuer**; and rewarded by **Hillary Clinton** and Ambassador **Dell Dailey** at the State Department, and Senators **Carl Levin, Diane Feinstein, John McCain,** and others in Congress.

STRATEGIC ANALYSIS
Most shocking was my discovery that these Swiss bank accounts—especially UBS and the Abdulaziz Abbas account—were known, controlled and preserved by the United States, but never shared with the military's Terrorist Threat Finance team; and the defense contractor managing this program, **Booz Allen Hamilton—the same defense contractor that managed Edward Snowden's intelligence whistleblowing reports—intentionally covered this up.**

Booz Allen Hamilton was paid to essentially help end the Middle East wars (Iraq, Afghanistan, Africa) by identifying, analyzing, and disrupting terrorist financial networks and operations. I know this, because I myself worked for Booz Allen Hamilton. I performed **global psychological warfare analysis** at the **U.S. State Department's Coordinator for Counter-terrorism Office** (under General Dell Dailey), **U.S. Special Operations Command** (under Colonel Dorothea Burke), and **U.S. Central Command** (under General James Mattis), where among other things I was the Liaison Officer, and terrorist threat finance analyst with a **Top Secret/SCI clearance.**

In this capacity, it was my job to know everything, compartmentalize information, and then use it to **identify, expose, and disrupt global terrorist financial networks and operations**...but I failed.

I failed because I was stupidly—and perhaps treasonously—stopped from doing my duty by the very military command and political officials who were overseeing my work. As perverse or preposterous as this may sound, it is unfortunately true. Of course it may not surprise you, considering the military-political bureaucracy is not only intolerably dull and chronically incompetent, but notoriously unimaginative at problem-solving, achieving objectives, or honoring those who do. However, please know I did my very best to perform my mission, and zealously did everything I could to expose and destroy these terrorist networks, and prevent your son and daughter's suffering.

I say this with great shame and regret, as both a military officer and an defense contractor: It is with a heart heavy with sadness and guilt and blood boiling-over with outrage that I must confess to you that I, as well as Booz Allen Hamilton, the senior level military officer corps, and members congress and the Obama Administration, have contributed to the death of your son, daughter, father, mother, husband or wife, by failing in our threat finance mission; and then covering it up, which, technically speaking, may amount to "aiding and abetting" the enemies of the United States. Equally to blame are the media, who have stuck their heads in the sand. This was, in part, why Edward Snowden chose to reveal his information directly to the American people—and avoid suffering the same fate I endured for "telling truth to power".

THE CONSPIRATORS
The people who knew about this issue, and who refused to do anything about it or even share it with you, include:
Senator Diane **Feinstein** (California), Senator Barbara **Boxer** (California), Senator Carl **Levin** (Michigan), Senator John **McCain (Arizona)**, Senator Lindsay **Graham** (South Carolina), Senator Bill **Nelson** (Florida) Representative Jason **Chaffetz**, Representative Darryl **Issa**, Representative Mike **Rogers,** Chair of House Intelligence Committee, Representative Peter **King**, and many other members of Congress who held key positions in military, national security, and intelligence matters. Their names are contained in the whistleblowing report "**FOLLOW THE MONEY**." You may review this report at: http://www.lulu.com/shop/2lt-scott-bennett-11th-psychological-operations-battalion/follow-the-money/paperback/product-21533478.html

Also responsible are the officials and journalists who were informed, yet did nothing, at Fox News, NBC, Wall Street Journal, New York Times, Washington Post, and other media organizations.

Most culpable are General James **Mattis** (U.S. Central Command), General Jeffrey **Jacobs** (U.S. Civil Affairs-Psychological Operations Command), General Keith **Alexander** and Michael **Hayden** (NSA-Cyber Command), National Counter-terrorism Center Director Matthew **Olsen**, FBI Director James **Comey**, Director of National Intelligence James **Clapper**, CIA Director John **Brennan**, Defense Intelligence Agency Director Lt. Gen. Michael **Flynn**; as well as **Booz Allen Hamilton,** the **Carlyle Group,** and its officers.

All letters to these people, and others, are contained within the document: **"EXHIBITS: Letters to Congress, Military, Media",** and are available for review at: http://armypsyop.wix.com/scottbennett

Amazingly all of these men testified at a hearing before Senate (Select) Intelligence Committee January 29, 2014 and savagely attacked Edward Snowden (NSA-CIA whistle-blower) for revealing much of this information to journalists such as Glenn Greenwald at the Guardian). In my opinion, they did this not out of duty to defend the Constitution, but out of a selfish desire to conceal their own incompetence and ill-motives, and continue their invasive surveillance operations on American citizens without question. Hopefully you will question them about it through emails, phone calls, op-ed letters, and blogs.

Most alarming is that now, in a cancerous CIA engineered psychological manipulation (aka, strategic communication) targeting American citizens, the White House (and by proxy State Department, CIA/NSA, and the military) is attempting to re-direct public attention away from this terrorist-finance failure and corroborating Edward Snowden/Wikileaks documents by initiating new military-mercenary fronts in Ukraine, Syria, and Iraq. Sadly, like the Iraq war build-up, and the "too big to fail" bank bailout, the American media—either out of ignorance or complicity—is participating in the deceptions.

As you may already understand, in a larger "Patriot Act" sense, this is really just part of an endlessly revolving defense contract and homeland security power-grab strategy that will eventually bankrupt the U.S. by degenerating our Republic into a police-state. This may soon quicken given the developing Russia-China natural gas contract and derivative weakening of U.S. dollar's global economic influence.

CALL TO ACTION
As hard as it may be for civilians to stomach, sometimes they must act like soldiers to preserve their civilization and civil ways of life, prosperity, and peace. Based on this information, it may seem that we are on the precipice of a dark abyss in our nation's history. I believe now, given the recent revelations of the government threats to our privacy and liberty, all Americans must act like soldiers and protect their family by peacefully, though firmly, affirming and exercising their legal right to accountability and transparency in government and its sub-contractors (such as **Booz Allen Hamilton**).

If Americans fail to make a stand and do this, then no longer are they citizens worthy of freedom, but slaves living by permission of a dangerously biased and legally unstable military-political tyranny controlled by a "security clearance bureaucrat class", who could very soon redefine "freedom" as "a special privilege", or even "bail", given only to those deemed worthy by the government bureaucracy and its "top secret" contractors—all supposedly operating under the color of law and "in the people's best interests."

I believe, and hope you will agree with me, that to redeem the past decade's despicable waste of lives and resources—and revitalize the reputation and hope of the United States of America in the eyes of the world, the following should happen:

    1) The cover-up of this NSA-CIA, Swiss Bank-Terrorist Financing-Booz Allen Hamilton report needs to be exposed immediately;

    2) those Congressional and military leaders and the journalists who have refused to analyze or disclose this report need to be confronted, judged, and held to account by you—the public; and

    3) new, fearless America leaders need to arise, clamp down on this "hemorrhaging of liberty", and boldly inspire our allies (Britain, Canada, Australia, New Zealand) to act intelligently and, where appropriate, strategically ally with the BRIC nations (Brazil, Russia, India, China) on engagements within the Middle East instead of clumsily antagonizing or threatening them.

For unless the American people are slapped awake from the encroaching "coma" of martial law, and see with fresh eyes the impending catastrophe of our reckless and arrogant policy of global military adventurism and vain pursuit of empire, soon our hard-fought heritage of freedom—and national pride—will evaporate like mist in the desert; and more American blood will be shed by terrorists who, ironically—if not treasonously—are being financed by bank accounts the U.S. Government, the military, defense contractors, and the media are refusing to expose and shut down!

Our choice is very simple: either we continue to allow ourselves to be force-fed propaganda by the "Top Secret clearance" class (the political-bureaucrat elite), and blindly swallow the threat of terrorism and the fantasy of a warm, loving Executive Branch agenda like pills given to passive dogs having their throats rubbed by dominant masters; or we snarl, bark, and bite (in that order) and free ourselves from their information headlock in order to allow our understanding to clear; and carefully examine the point of the medication (i.e., information restrictions) and managers of them. It is a question of temperament and faith (in either government bureaucrats or oneself) at its core, but I strongly urge you to choose the latter.

I ask you to gird the loins of your mind as military family members (mothers and fathers, husbands and wives, sons and daughters) and share this information with your fellow Americans by writing letters, emails, blogs, facebook comments, instagrams, and twitter feeds to the military-congressional-media people I have listed; demand from them an explanation, and rest not until they give you one.

CONCLUSION

Among my many duties as battalion Adjutant General Officer was to write the letter to a soldier's family after he has been killed, explaining why and how it happened. It is also, I believe, the saddest and most difficult letter a human being can compose, for the words affect lives like flames affect a forest, like waves affect sandcastles. You enter the letter knowing its touch will trigger pain, if not agony, as it pierces the bubble of sadness and isolation the family has retreated into in an attempt to numb the gnawing silence of their loved one's absence. And as much as the words are carefully calculated to read like a Shakespearean sonnet, they can't help but feel like a red-hot poker cauterizing a bleeding wound: there is closure, but also a significant sense of rage against the healer—or, in this case, the communicator of truth.

When the letter is pulled from the mailbox, the sight of the gold embossed, military eagle emblem on the corner, instantly transforms the paper into a hundred pound weight, and the person's spirit plummets into a vortex of horror, anger, fear, and renewed loss. Unopened, the letter sits alone, in quarantine, upon a checkerboard kitchen table, staring up in silence like a motionless, coiled snake ready to strike, or an inevitable electric shock waiting to be touched. When it's finally unsealed, words pour out and images are absorbed that shatter the cocooning solitude; and like a tornado of jagged metal and glass shards tearing through the scar-tissue cobwebbing their souls, everything and anything the family has tried to restrain, suppress, or dreamed to forget is suddenly stirred-up.

So rest assured I'm familiar with the trauma and drama of words. In this regard I have weighed heavily whether or not I should write this letter to you, not out of concern for my own safety, but rather respect for you as a military family member. As much as I do not wish to re-open old wounds, I also cannot allow a festering question or missing gap in your understanding to remain empty and lingering like a half-dead ghost searching for peace.

In the event of my death—aka CIA-FBI-Military (or foreign) assassination—please know I share this with you out of a sense of duty to my fellow soldiers, living and deceased, and utmost respect to you as their family. I thought you would want to know about this story so that you might both gain closure and discover new subjects to discuss with the military leaders and politicians and journalists who hold the lives of your sons and daughters (or those of your neighbors) in their hands—and who have, so far, failed to honor them out of their own selfish career interests and political fear.

I am sorry for any pain or irritability or confusion this letter may have caused you, but I am convicted that its long term healing—of both your family and our nation—is worth any inconvenient, momentary discomfort.

As my reward for bringing this issue to the attention of the military and Congress—and communicating it up the official channels of my chain of command—I have suffered what Edward Snowden chose wisely to avoid: I have been threatened, imprisoned, slandered, and tortured by the military, Congress, and the Department of Justice in a vain attempt to silence me about these, and other, scandalous military-intelligence failures.

However, despite this brutality and corruption, my faith and my honor code as a military officer and as an American, as well as my oath to support and defend the Constitution of the United States, absolutely compels me to inform you about this so that you, as my military family members, will, at last, be able to apply this information towards your own healing and peace of mind. My desire is that this letter and the supporting documents will give you that fulfillment, that release, that peace...or at least guide you to the eternal path which leads to it.

I hope that you will help save other service-members—American and allied—before they are killed by this failure of leadership, and spare other families from having to experience the same heartache that you have had to endure.

Again, I hope you will honor our warriors by sharing this information with your fellow Americans, and demanding an explanation, an apology, and a plan of corrective-action from the media, the military leadership, and the politicians in Washington DC and your respective State Capitols, before more families suffer unnecessary loss.

Once again, I urge you to review all the supporting documentation, testimony, and materials to help you understand everything at: http://armypsyop.wix.com/scottbennett

You may contact me for details at: armypsyop@outlook.com

Respectfully and patriotically yours,

Scott Bennett,
11th Psychological Operations Battalion
U.S. Army Reserve
armypsyop@outlook.com

2LT SCOTT BENNETT, 11TH PSYCHOLOGICAL OPERATIONS BATTALION, U.S. ARMY RESERVE
23 RAILROAD AVENUE, DANVILLE, CA 94526

March 4, 2014

TO: PETER M. CULLEN, COLONEL, U.S. ARMY, CHIEF, U.S. ARMY TRIAL DEFENSE SERVICE, 9275 GUNSTON ROAD, SUITE 3100, FORT BELVOIR, VIRGINIA 22060
PHONE: 703 693 0280
EMAIL: Peter.m.cullen.mil@mail.mil

FR: 2LT SCOTT BENNETT, 11TH PSYCHOLOGICAL OPERATIONS BATTALION, U.S. ARMY RESERVE

RE: LETTER DATED FEBRUARY 18, 2014 REGARDING ILLEGAL DISCHARGE AND TERRORIST FINANCING WHISTELBLOWING REPORT

Dear Colonel Cullen:

This is my third letter to your office. Be advised, I am communicating this email (and printed version sent U.S. postage pre-paid mail) to you as an Officer of the United States Army, and an Officer who has officially filed whistleblowing reports concerning possible violations of law (military, federal, state, Constitutional, Uniform Code of Military Justice, and possibly international law). This material is attorney-client privileged communication and protected.

Since September 25, 2012, I have filed numerous official whistleblowing reports to the Department of Defense Inspector General, as well as the following Congressional Committees: Armed Services; Intelligence; Judiciary; Foreign Relations; Oversight and Reform Committee; Terrorism Committee.

Also I have communicated this request to the following parties:
- Reserve Army unit, the 11th Psychological Operations Battalion
- Pentagon Inspector General, Lynne Halbrook
- Secretary of Defense, Chuck Hagel
- Chairman of the Joint Chiefs of Staff, General Martin Dempsey
- Army Chief of Staff, General Raymond Odierno
- Commander U.S. Civil Affairs-Psychological Operations Command, General Jeff Jacobs

- Others

I am communicating to you a serious matter which affects the national security of the United States, and qualifies as official military business warranting your immediate involvement and representation of me and my material. Failure to do so will be interpreted as an act of intentional disregard for whistleblowing laws regarding a military officer reporting violations of military policy, law, and the Constitution of the United States.

As an Officer of the United States Army, I am hereby, once again, filing with you my official request for military legal representation, and in addition filing my request for an immediate military and congressional investigation through the House and Senate Armed Services Committees, the Judiciary Committees, the Terrorism Committees (and any other deemed appropriate by joint military-congressional body investigating this letter and attached materials); and filing my request that I be immediately granted an oral hearing before a military board, military investigators, military legal counsel, and congressional body, so that I might publicly report as a WHISTELBLOWING MATTER these issues, as well as file all military actions for relief, including but not limited to Article 138, 10 USC § 934, and all legal instruments necessary for granting me military, federal, and state relief. Additionally, this matter involves military personnel (contractors, DOD employees, military Officers and enlisted) committing potentially treasonous violations of law; senior level officers engaging in conduct unbecoming officers of the United States military; and other violations of the uniform code of military justice, state and federal law, the U.S. Constitution, and possibly international law.

In your letter sent to me on February 18, 2014 you stated the following:
> "Your letter to the Judge Advocate General, dated January 15, 2014, in which you request legal representation was forwarded to my office for review and action. Trial Defense Service representation is authorized for Soldiers pending adverse or disciplinary action by the Army. It is unclear from your letter what adverse or disciplinary action is pending against you that would warrant representation by a Trial Defense Service counsel. Accordingly, I am unable to assist you at this time."

I have just learned that in fact you were informed about my pending discharge issue in a letter written by the Army prior to this February 18, 2014 letter. Furthermore, based on the official record--which you obviously have--it is clear that any kind of quasi-investigation performed, or expected to be performed by a minimally proficient legal or judicial officer of the United States, would have yielded materials that confirmed my past reports and exposures of obvious questionable activities, if not blatant violations of law, against a U.S. Military Officer.

So I must conclude your refusal to examine my repeated reports, legal motions, and requests for an official military debriefing is in error at best; or intentional, conspiratorial, and a violation of law (federal and international law) at worst.

Therefore, I hereby reiterate my request to you and your office to immediately contact me regarding this matter, engage in an official military debriefing where I testify to these materials, and file all necessary legal injunctive action to prevent my discharge until this matter is reviewed by military-congressional authorities. I am challenging my discharge on the grounds that it is unlawful and a violation of various federal whistleblower laws, as well as UCMJ policies.

Failure, or refusal, to contact me immediately this will be interpreted as a violation of my rights as an Army Officer, as well as a violation of the U.S. Constitution.

Respectfully,

/S/
Scott Bennett
Second Lieutenant
U.S. Army Reserve
11th Psychological Operations Battalion

SCOTT BENNETT
23 RAILROAD AVE, #23
DANVILLE, CA 94526
925-391-0407
email: armypsyop@outlook.com
website: www.armypsyop.wix.com/scottbennett

October 31, 2014

Jesselyn Radack
Government Accountability Project
1612 K. St. NW, Suite #1100
Washington DC, 20006

RE: SNOWDEN-BIRKENFELD CLIENT REPRESENTATION
     AND WHISTLEBLOWING DISCLOSURES

Dear Ms. Radack,

As you know, from 2009 to 2012 you represented Brad Birkenfeld, the Union Bank of Switzerland (UBS) banker-whistleblower. Currently, you also **legally** represent Edward Snowden (prior Booz Allen Hamilton contractor) in his NSA-CIA whistleblowing disclosures.

This letter, and related exhibits, exposes the nexus of these two whistleblowers, identifies my connection to these men and their whistleblowing materials, and requests specific action by you as Edward Snowden's legal counsel, as well as Brad Birkenfeld's prior representative/agent.

If this summary of events, timeline, documentation, or any other information is in any way inaccurate, please advise me immediately. Otherwise I will assume that you concur it is factually accurate.

TIMELINE AND BACKGROUND:

Here are the facts, as I understand them, which were given to me and others by Brad Birkenfeld from 2009 to 2012.

After meeting Brad Birkenfeld and thoroughly debriefing him about his materials, timeline, and background, a discovery was made concerning <u>ongoing terrorist threat financing within UBS</u>.

Following this discovery, around July 2012 Brad Birkenfeld repeatedly requested that you contact me to enable me to provide him through you, as his whistleblowing representative/agent, with unclassified "<u>military-Booz Allen Hamilton-Carlyle Group</u>" materials and personnel which were connected to his original whistleblower disclosures. The main reason behind this request was the applicability of Birkenfeld's UBS information (as well as *Kuwait Finance House, Faysal Bank of Bahrain, HSBC, Deutsche Bank, and others*) to ongoing U.S. Department of Defense intelligence and counterterrorism missions, and more specifically exposing and stopping the damage to our military mission and servicemembers this UBS Terrorist Financing element was causing. You received a letter outlining this on <u>August 8, 2012</u> (see attachment).

This previously undiscovered information was to be synthesized into Brad's testimony and materials exposing U.S. Politicians and others with unlawful Swiss Bank activities; and submitted to the Senate and House Armed Services, Terrorism, and Permanent Investigations committees as a request for a renewed investigation and hearings into these matters.

Brad informed you that <u>I was both a U.S. Army Officer, and employed by Booz Allen Hamilton as a Terrorist Threat Finance analyst (working for Dov Zakheim)</u> during the time of Brad's disclosures and case. I was also Liaison Officer to the U.S. State Department Coordinator for Counterterrorism and U.S. Special Operations Command during the period of Brad's targeting, entrapment, and false prosecution.

Brad also shared with you that <u>he and I co-authored a letter to General James Mattis, Commander, U.S. Central Command</u>, in which we communicated that Brad's Swiss Bank-Terrorist Finance data had not been <u>allowed</u> to be shared with military intelligence, and consequently was undoubtedly harming our military personnel and mission (and that of our allies) by financing terrorism. To avoid any "mysterious accident" that may have silenced Brad, our letter was submitted to U.S. Central Command on August 1, 2012—the same day Brad was released from prison in Schuylkill, Pennsylvania. It was also shared with Brad's attorneys Steven Kohn and David Colapinto in Washington DC (which I have copies of).

The idea was that Brad and I would petition for and then appear before a joint military-Congressional investigation, under oath, and present this and other information relating to terrorist financing.

However, for some strange reason, soon after this information was communicated, Brad was <u>immediately</u> paid $104 million dollars (a portion of which you and your organization received for representing Brad's interests and Wiki page, as I understand it). Outrageously, if not treasonously, not only was no further action ever taken, but the matter of the CIA-UBS-Terrorist Finance-Booz Allen Hamilton connection was dropped and ignored by all parties...all parties except me, that is.

As for me, since I was an Officer of the United States Army who had sworn an oath to the United States Constitution (the same oath taken by you once), I could <u>not</u> remain silent on this matter, since it was aiding and abetting the killing of American military members (and contractors) in the War on Terror.

So, on September 25, 2012 I acted, and acted like an Officer: I submitted a report which communicated all of Birkenfeld's UBS material to General Jeff Jacobs, Commander, U.S. Civil Affairs-Psychological Operations Command, and sent copies to Lynne Halbrooks, Pentagon Inspector General, and various Congressional Committees. In this report I pleaded for the debriefing, which Brad Birkenfeld had told me the military-intelligence community never gave him.

Soon after my report was submitted, and began bouncing around the SIPR, NIPR, and TS/SCI internet channels, Edward Snowden (a fellow Booz Allen Hamilton contractor and former CIA analyst) contacted outside parties, including Glenn Greenwald. In December 2012 Snowden began making preparations for his 2013 Booz Allen Hamilton whistleblowing disclosures, which you apparently capitalized on.

I have included another copy of this report (see attachment), which you have already seen, for your refreshment. <u>Please immediately forward this letter and attached report to Edward Snowden as part of your "effective assistance of counsel"</u> and legal defense of his interests; as well as to Mr. Snowden's other attorneys Ben Wizner and Anatoly Kucherena. Please do this before November 14, 2014.

According to my records, after sending you several letters and briefs concerning this matter (see attachments), and after you engaged in a phone conversation with my Washington DC attorney Mr. Jeff O'Toole, you submitted a letter to my attorney confirming <u>receipt</u> of my communications, but stated that you were <u>not</u> going to engage this matter, you would <u>not</u> be contacting me, and you would <u>not</u> utilize my materials Brad requested you review. You also did not forward any of this material to any official of a Congressional Oversight or Military committee, or media person.

Again if this record of events, timeline, or any other information is inaccurate, please advise me immediately. Otherwise I will assume that you concur it is factually accurate, to the best of your knowledge.

STORY CONNECTION TO EDWARD SNOWDEN'S NSA-CIA REVELATIONS:

As you now know because of Edward Snowden's revelations to Glenn Greenwald in his 2013 interview for The Guardian newspaper, and as told to me and others by Brad himself, <u>Brad was targeted by the U.S. Central Intelligence Agency (CIA) in Geneva Switzerland for intelligence gathering purposes, then entrapped in a phony D.U.I. arrest in Switzerland to leverage this; and then rescued from this artificial D.U.I. by a CIA agent in order to secure Brad's loyalty and pressure him to violate Swiss law involving Swiss Banking intelligence materials</u>.

However, after analyzing his precarious situation, and much to the shock of the CIA, Brad fled Switzerland to Washington DC, and sought the help of the Department of Justice, pleading for a subpoena in order to legally provide the information and materials he knew was violating U.S. Laws, as well as being used to finance international terrorists through various UBS (and other Swiss banks') instruments.

This information was extremely valuable "<u>actionable intelligence</u>" which the U.S. Military, Counterterrorism Threat Finance operations managed by U.S. Central Command's Joint Interagency Operations Center (JIOC) and defense contractor Booz Allen Hamilton <u>could have used to identify, track, and destroy the financial nodes and systems utilized by terrorist organizations</u>; as well as empower the U.S. Military/ Defense Intelligence Agency (DIA) to confiscate all the assets discovered (cash, technology, precious metals, real estate, etc.).

Once again, I know this <u>for a fact</u> because I occupied a key position in the military-intelligence community during all times relevant. I was a U.S. Army Officer, employed by Booz Allen Hamilton as a <u>Terrorist Threat Finance analyst</u>, and held a Top Secret/SCI clearance during the time of Edward Snowden's assignment and reports, and Brad Birkenfeld's disclosures. Additionally I was Liaison Officer to the U.S. State Department Coordinator for Counterterrorism and U.S. Special Operations Command under Ambassador Dell L. Dailey during the dates of Brad's targeting, entrapment, and false prosecution.

Quite remarkably, if not treasonously, despite the national security and war on terror implications, Brad Birkenfeld was denied his request for a subpoena by DOJ attorneys Kevin Downing and Kevin O'Connor, dismissed by them as a "tipster" and not a whistleblower, and effectively chased away and not allowed to share any of his materials. <u>As a result of this action by the DOJ, U.S. Military personnel (and those of our allies) were killed, wounded, and enemies of the United States were financed by these UBS accounts.</u> This is especially relevant now, given the expanding Islamic State (aka, IS, ISIS, ISIL) Syrian operations and their financing by Gulf nations (Kuwait, Qatar, Saudi Arabia, United Arab Emirates, Bahrain, and Israel).

Additionally the DOJ attorneys arrogantly proclaimed to Brad, *"You watch too much TV"* and stated the U.S. Government did not possess the technology to track or utilize Brad's UBS materials. Of course this was a false statement, as we now know from the Snowden whistleblowing revelations, and the open-source Wikileaks cables provided to Brad, which he in turn gave to me.

After being denied a subpoena by the DOJ, Brad immediately made this same formal request to the IRS and other agencies; but was amazingly denied. Finally, the Senate Permanent Subcommittee on Investigations, Chaired by Senator Carl Levin (D-Michigan), with then Senator Barak Obama on that committee, gave Brad his subpoena, and allowed him to testify.

However a mysterious event transpired soon after Brad surfaced before the Department of Justice. A London based banker friend of Brad's who'd worked with him previously in the banking world, called Brad by phone, picked him up by private plane for a trip to Mexico, and then returned to London. Soon after his return to London, this banker friend received a call from UBS asking:
> *"Why did you send us a letter dated July 2007 announcing Brad Birkenfeld was in communication with U.S. authorities regarding UBS?"*

The banker replied he did not send the letter, asked for a copy of it, and upon receipt shared it with Brad and demanded an explanation. Brad then took the letter to the Department of Justice attorneys Downing and O'Connor, outraged he had somehow been "tracked-bugged-surveyed" by some clandestine agency operation (NSA-CIA-DOJ target surveillance collaboration). The Department never gave an explanation, but Edward Snowden did. However the details of that discussion will be for another report.

After this incident, and despite a "Kastigar" agreement made to Brad that his information would not be used against him, Brad was soon after indicted and criminally charged with conspiracy by the Justice Department using this <u>very same material</u>, particularly Brad's UBS client "Olenicoff" disclosures.

CORRUPTION, CONFLICTS OF INTERESTS, AND ABUSE OF DISCRETION:

As you also know, Brad was soon after prosecuted by Attorney General Eric Holder and Assistant U.S. Attorney Lanny Breuer on "trumped up charges."

In an obscene corruption and miscarriage of justice <u>Brad was prevented from referencing his Senate testimony transcripts concerning Mr. Olenicoff, CIA entrapment, terrorist bank accounts, and other materials, as his defense</u>. He was told the Senate testimony was "sealed" and could not be used.

Sadly, if not reprehensibly, Brad's Senate testimony would have not only exonerated him and dismissed the charges, but exposed the RICO conspiracy and cover-up by the CIA, Department of Justice, Treasury Department, and the State Department of the Swiss Banking issues and their relationship to the 2008 financial crisis and international terrorist financing, as reported in State Department cables, released by Wikileaks.

(Note: This same tactic of "sealing NSA related transcripts" was employed by the Dept. of Justice against Qwest Communications President Joe Nacchio, and used to develop trumped up charges against him which would have been dismissed had the "NSA material" been referenced. <u>Edward Snowden's revelations confirm this particular case, and was even cited by Mr. Nacchio as proof of his own vindication.</u> A formal request for an Appeals Court panel rehearing "en banc" of the Nacchio-NSA case is forthcoming.)

It is significant to note that after Birkenfeld went public, in an attempt to bury the wider implications of this story, <u>the CIA</u> (agent name available upon request) sent a text to a Vanity Fair journalist which stated:
"*Do <u>not</u> run the Birkenfeld story...Karzai is much worse.*"

Consequently, Vanity Fair did not run the story, nor did any other media. Again, Snowden's CIA story, Birkenfeld's CIA story, and this CIA Vanity Fair journalist interference, as well as other materials, confirm the CIA interdiction of Birkenfeld for Swiss Bank financial intelligence gathering purposes—many of which are "black operation" budget. It is also significant that Rolling Stone journalist <u>Michael Hastings was investigating this entire matter</u>, before he was killed...but that is another report, forthcoming.

Most significant is the fact that Eric Holder and Lanny Breuer were employed by the law firm <u>Covington and Burling</u> in Washington DC prior to joining the Department of Justice in the Obama Administration (Lanny Breuer has recently retired from DOJ and returned to Covington and Burling, along with Michael Chertoff, former Homeland Security Director). What is scandalous is that <u>Covington and Burling legally represented the Union Bank of Switzerland.</u>

Consequently, this seems to be a violation of public trust and government integrity, since Eric Holder and Lanny Breuer's official DOJ actions of giving UBS a deferred <u>prosecution</u>, a <u>2%</u> fine, and refusing to investigate Birkenfeld's <u>19,000</u> bank accounts provided (and refusing to provide them to military terrorist finance analysts), appear suspicious, an obvious conflict of interest at best, and a criminal abuse of power at worst.

<u>CONSTITUTIONAL, LEGAL AND ETHICAL OBLIGATIONS:</u>

As you are a prior Department of Justice lawyer who has experienced your own persecution by the DOJ, as well as an officer of the Court who has sworn an oath to the U.S. Constitution, and now represent yourself as a champion of whistleblowers, I'm sure this material resonates with you on a variety of levels.

Due to the national security implications in this information, and I'm sure you agree they are quite significant, I believe a joint military-Congressional investigation is required if the integrity of our government and our Constitutional freedoms are to be preserved. As I remember, Brad and I were in agreement on this then, and it seems Edward Snowden is in agreement with us now.

Therefore, to achieve this, and at the same time assist Brad and Edward clear their names and clarify their original intelligence disclosures, <u>I intend to bring this material forward to the American people through a recurring national radio program beginning Friday November 14, 2014.</u> The purpose of this radio program will be to formally petition for Congressional hearings on this matter, expose the wider terrorist finance networks and implications, and protect American military servicemembers from further unnecessary harm.

Your connection (and others) to Birkenfeld, Edward Snowden, and myself will be a subject in this discussion, and so I am informing you now in the hopes you will contact me, clarify all information and your position as the representative of Birkenfeld, and Snowden's legal counsel with regards to this material; and forward this letter and reports to both men immediately.

If I do not hear from you by Friday, November 14, 2014, I will conclude all material contained herein is deemed accurate by you as the official representative of Edward Snowden and Brad Birkenfeld, and that all of you (including Ben Wizner and Anatoly Kucherena) are in full agreement and support my actions. Furthermore I will interpret your silence to mean that you are actively forwarding this material to Edward Snowden and/or Brad Birkenfeld, and coordinating a meeting outside of official channels to represent this matter.

If you <u>will not</u> be forwarding this material to Edward Snowden and Brad Birkenfeld, please advise me immediately. However, let me be very clear, in my honest professional opinion, if Brad Birkenfeld and Edward Snowden are not immediately apprised by you of this material—since you are directly connected to us all at this point—and you choose instead to do nothing, for the life of me, I cannot understand what your <u>agenda</u> is, or how you can possibly claim to <u>effectively</u> represent Mr. Snowden any longer.

As I see it, if you are choosing <u>not</u> to involve yourself or them in any way, <u>you are choosing to ignore or hide from the American public and government-military oversight authorities the key issue</u> which interconnects them, and thereby vindicates them of the standing allegations of criminal wrongdoing. This in turn becomes an issue of "ineffective assistance of counsel" and a

Constitutional violation. But I hope this will not be the case and I will hear from you very soon.

As the agent of Edward Snowden and Brad Birkenfeld, I'm sure you understand the ethical and professional obligations in representing the best interests of your clients; and that this information (and yet undisclosed materials) **must** be shared with them (as well as Julian Assange) because it does the following: 1) directly contributes to their legal and personal vindication in the United States as well as the international community; 2) warrants a new military-intelligence terrorist finance investigation; and 3) can justify a Congressional pardon for all of these men.

CONCLUSION:

In conclusion, consistent with this responsibility, I am expecting you to immediately forward this material to both Edward Snowden and Brad Birkenfeld. If you will not forward this information to them, please advise me immediately.

If you are unwilling to put me in touch with Mr. Snowden and Mr. Birkenfeld, for the purpose of helping them, I don't see any option but to reach out and connect with them by other means.

I reached out to you and the Government Accountability Project because of your repeated claims (and 501.c.3 status) of wanting to help these men and protect the freedoms whistleblowers like them champion. I hope this is a genuine and continuing commitment, for as GAP claims on its website:

> "Whistleblowers will not be silent. Moreover, they are not alone in this fight. It is the *mission* of the Government Accountability Project (GAP) to give voice to and vigorously defend these individuals who would risk everything for the truth.
>
> The Government Accountability Project is the nation's leading whistleblower protection and advocacy organization. A non-partisan public-interest group, GAP litigates whistleblower cases, helps expose wrongdoing to the public, and actively promotes government and corporate accountability. Since its founding in 1977, GAP has helped over 6,000 whistleblowers."

(http://www.whistleblower.org/we-are-nation-laws-we-are-also-nation-whistleblowers)

Therefore based on this "oath" or "mission statement" or "sacred values", my assumption is you will want to assist in this information disclosure so that the resulting investigation and benefits will assist in the complete vindication of Brad Birkenfeld, Edward Snowden, and even Julian Assange.

To fail to do this, is not only to betray the GAP mission, your oath as an Officer of the Court, and the U.S. Constitution, but may make you guilty of an act of omission which results in the shedding of innocent American military blood deployed in the ongoing Middle East wars.

These are the facts and analysis as I understand them, as communicated to me by all relevant parties. Again, if any of these facts are inconsistent with your timetable or understanding of the facts or law, please advise me immediately. Otherwise I will conclude you are in full agreement with my statement and analysis.

I look forward to hearing from you before November 14, 2014.

Scott Bennett

cc: Sarah Damian, GAP Interim Communications Director,
      SarahD@whistleblower.org

      Ben Wizner, ACLU, Snowden Attorney
      Anatoly Kucherena, Snowden Attorney

DEEP BLACK

The CIA's Secret Drug Wars

© 1997 David Guyatt

Part One

The narcotics industry has a turnover, estimated to be in excess of $1 trillion per annum. Put more simply, it is the largest industry in the world. Ongoing international measures to eradicate this industry have largely proved futile, despite the billions spent. For example, the death in Columbia - at the hands of law enforcement officers - of drug baron, Pablo Escobar, and the US capture of Panamanian middle-man, Manuel Noriega, didn't interrupt the flow of Columbian cocaine one iota. On the contrary, shipments to the United States and elsewhere, increased sharply in the wake of these so called Drug Enforcement "victories."

Meanwhile, information has surfaced that paints a damning picture of intelligence agency involvement in the narcotics industry. Sworn affidavit's in this writer's possession finger the Central Intelligence Agency for engaging in narcotics trafficking on an almost industrial scale. Some observers - perhaps with an element of merit - have, meanwhile, opined that the CIA's long-term involvement with the narcotics industry resulted from their support of nations that strongly adhered to the anti communist philosophy.

Under this rubric, drug barons the world over were aided and assisted in the production, transportation and distribution of narcotics, and the proceeds were used to arm resistance movements. So long as there was a "red menace" to fight, those dope peddlers - large and small - who co-operated with the CIA's cold war strategy, remained immune to prosecution. With the collapse of communism in the late nineteen eighties this rationale evaporated. Curious then, that the narcotics industry has not declined along with communism? One the contrary, all the indications point to continued growth and profits.

Drugs have become a self-perpetuating industry that continues to create billionaire's overnight. It is, by far, the most Laissez Faire enterprise of them all, enjoying spectacular financial returns for relatively modest investment. Arguably, reason enough, to ensure that continuing calls to legalise some types of soft drugs remain doomed to failure at the political level. Why kill the Golden Goose that effortlessly lays so many golden eggs?

Cutolo begins his sworn affidavit by saying: "In December, 1975, I spoke with Colonel "Bo" Baker concerning a classified mission he commanded during that month, inside Columbia. The mission was known as "Watch Tower." Continuing, he states "Following a lengthy discussion with Col. Baker, I was introduced to Mr. Edwin Wilson and Mr. Frank Terpil. Both Wilson and Terpil were in the employ of the Central Intelligence Agency. Both Wilson and Terpil inquired if I was interested in working for short periods of time in Columbia, and I acknowledged that I was."

Cutolo thereafter commanded the second and third Watch Tower missions. The second mission took place in February 1975 and lasted a total of 22 days. The purpose of the mission was to "establish a series of three electronic beacon towers beginning outside of Bogata, Columbia, and running northeast to the border of Panama." With the beacons in place and activated, aircraft could fix on their signal and fly undetected from Bogata to Panama, landing at Albrook Air Station. All told. 30 "high performance aircraft" flew the covert route to Allbrook.

Frank Terpil

The aircraft were met by Panama's Colonel Manuel Noriega - who would later become head of state, prior to experiencing a US invasion tasked to arrest and imprison him for laundering drug money. Accompanying Noriega were a number of officers of the Panama Defence Forces (PDF), CIA agent, Edwin Wilson, and Israeli agent Mike Harari. Cutolo adds that Harari had the authority from the "U.S. Army Southern Command in Panama to be in the A.O (Area of Operations)." Nor does Cutolo beat around the bush when explicitly stating "The cargo flown from Columbia into Panama was cocaine."

Cutolo continues his affidavit by outlining the third Watch Tower mission which he commanded. This occurred during March 1976, and lasted 29 days, safely cycling 40 cocaine carrying aircraft through to Panama. On this occasion members of one of his Special Action Teams (SATs), located at Turbo, Columbia were attacked by a large gang of local bandits and were extracted by helicopters that entered Columbian airspace without authority. Cutolo adds that the third mission was "met in the previously related fashion by those named - Noriega, Edwin Wilson, Mike Harari et al."

William Tyree's affidavit dated 6 September 1990, powerfully corroborates Colonel Cutolo's statements. Tyree, however, was able to provide additional direct testimony on the First Watch Tower mission, which he participated in. At that time he was assigned to

return of Edwin Wilson with another deep black covert operation on offer. This was known as Operation George Orwell.

During a meeting with Cutolo, Edwin Wilson explained that "it was considered that Operation Watch Tower might be compromised and become known if politicians, judicial figures, police and religious entities were approached or received word that U. S. troops had aided in delivering narcotics from Columbia into Panama." Based on that possibility, Cutolo, formed twelve separate Special Action Teams (SATs). Their mission was to implement Army regulation 340-18-5 (file number 503-05). Cutolo's authority for this action came directly from FORSCOM via Wilson.

In effect, Operation Orwell was tasked with implementing intense "surveillance of politicians, judicial figures, law enforcement agencies at the state level and of religious groups." The underlying purpose was to provide the "United States government and the Army" with advance warning of the discovery of Watch Tower to enable them to "prepare a defence." Cutolo further states that he "was under orders not to inform Colonel Forrest Rittgers, commanding officer of Fort Devens," of this mission. The reason was to give Colonel Rittgers a "margin of plausible deniability" in the event that Fort Devens personnel were "caught in the act of implementing surveillance."

Cutolo goes on to reveal that he instituted surveillance against "Ted Kennedy, John Kerry, Edward King, Michael Dukakis, Levin H. Campbell, Andrew A Caffrey, Fred Johnson, Kenneth A. Chandler, Thomas P. O'Neil, to name a few of the targets." Additionally surveillance was placed on "...the Governors residences of Massachusetts, Manine, New York and New Hampshire. The Catholic cathedrals of New York and Boston were placed under electronic surveillance also. In the area of Fort Devens, all local police and politicians were under some form of surveillance at various times." As part of the operation, Cutolo recruited "a number of local state employees who worked within the ranks of local police and court personnel.

Private Tyree, in his sworn affidavit, confirms what Cutolo has revealed about Operation George Orwell, including that it was initiated under Army regulation number 340-18-5, file number 503-05. He states that "I was involved in 10 separate surveillance missions in the New England area, all under this same operation." He adds "... surveillance was instituted to monitor civilian targets to determine: a) if Operation Watch Tower had been discovered. B) the probability that an investigation or governmental inquiry would be requested as a result of such a discovery." Tyree goes on to reveal that he, personally, participated in surveillance against the Mayor of Lunenbourg, Massachusetts, a community close to Fort Devens. A second local target was "John Droney, District Attorney, Middlesex County, Massachusetts." Tyree continues by providing detailed information about criminal wrongdoing by Droney, together with details of his sexual proclivities and indiscretions.

Moreover, Tyree additionally states that his friend, Sergeant John Newby, had engaged in surveillance against "...Senators John Kerry and Ted Kennedy. Sgt. Newby also stated to me just prior to his death in October 1978, that he had been involved in some surveillance

Israeli couriers. I became aware of that fact from normal conversations with some of the embassy personnel assigned to the embassy in Panama."

Cutolo then reveals that an associate of Wilson's also "aided in overseeing the laundering of funds, which was then used to purchase weapons to arm various factions that the CIA saw as friendly towards the United States. The associates name is Tom Cline." Wilson then tells Cutolo that "most of Operation Watch Tower was implemented on the authority of Clines." Tom Clines worked under Theodore Shackley - both of whom were heavily implicated in gun running activities during Iran-Contra; itself a notorious drugs-for-money-for-guns operation under President Ronald reagan and Vice President George Bush.

In fact, Cutolo later reveals in his affidavit that the illegal activities of Mike Harari were protected by a number of U. S. VIP's. Cutolo was told by Pentagon "...contacts, of the record..." that these VIP's included Director of CIA, Stansfield Turner and former CIA Director George Bush. Both, in Cutolo's words "shielded" Harari from "public scrutiny." The same contacts also told Cutolo that "Watch Tower" was a sanctioned mission and that "United States military authorities confirmed to me that Operation Watch Tower occurred and gave their approval." Cutolo, also learned that "... Harari was a known middleman for matters involving the United States in Latin America," adding that the Israeli assassin "acted with the support of a network of Mossad personnel throughout Latin America and worked mainly in the import and export of arms and drugs trafficking."

Motivation in this regard is a contentious issue. Paul Neri stated his belief that Wilson, Clines and Terpil were acting without authority and for their own personal enrichment. Clearly, this is not the case. Cutolo is certain that both operations were sanctioned at the highest level. Of course, this does not hinder some of those involved with these missions from profiting on the side. The indications are that so long as "skimming" was kept at reasonable levels, no questions would be asked by those higher up the chain of command.

Indeed, Cutolo's affidavit reveals an intriguing sidebar to Operation George Orwell that is only too believeable in regard to the big bucks world of black budgets. The surveillance product garnered by Operation George Orwell had uses other than keeping loose mouths shut. According to Cutolo, he "...was notified by Wilson that the information forwarded to Washington D.C., was disseminated to private corporations who were developing weapon systems for the Dept. of Defense. Those private corporations were encouraged to use the sensitive information gathered from surveillance on U.S. Senators and Representatives as leverage to manipulate those Congressmen into approving whatever costs those weapon systems incurred."

Three weapon systems were mentioned to Cutolo in this respect: "1) Am Armored vehicle. 2) An aircraft that is invisible to radar. 3) A weapon system that utilises kinetic energy." He adds that he got the impression all three were for "...use by NASA or for CIA purposes." Wilson also informed Cutolo, that "Operation Orwell would be implemented nationwide by 4 July 1980."[5] He then adds that as of the date of this affidavit [11 March 1980], "2,400 police departments, 1,370 churches, and approximately 17,900 citizens have been monitored under Operation Orwell. The major churches targeted have been Catholic and Latter Day Saints." Others targeted included "suspected members of the Trilateral Commission and the Bilderberg Group," including former Presidents Gerald Ford and Jimmy Carter and George Bush. Cutolo notes that he did not have personal knowledge "that Ford, Carter or Bush were under surveillance."

Anyone who took an active interest in these operations were soon to experience extreme rigor mortis. In his covering letter, Paul Neri mentions the death of Supergun builder and "Pentagon Scientist" Dr. Gerald Bull, who was shot dead outside his apartment in 1990 - as an example of the deadliness of Mossad officer Mike Harari. Neri also casts dark glances at the role of President George Bush in this whole affair, noting that Bush "knew or should have known about Operation Watch Tower." He then adds that "With Mr Noreiga no longer in power, the Bush Administration has helped install one president and two Vice-Presidents in Panama who will continue to launder the drug money the CIA receives from drug operations world wide...""

Neri continues "How much longer, and how many more will be murdered, die accidentally or be discredited through incarceration so that poppies and cocca leaves can fund the secret war of the CIA? Will Latin America be the next secret CIA war as was the case in Vietnam? And how many of our service people will die there?"

Neri's allusion to Vietnam was not without meaning in terms of massive narcotics trafficking by the CIA. Colonel Bo Gritz,[6] the most decorated Special Forces officer from the Vietnam era, received a copy of Cutolo's affidavit. Some years later he would travel to Burma and meet with warlord Khun Sa - the leading producer of Heroin in Southeast Asia. What Gritz discovered was fully documented and recorded on video camera. Gritz' story will form part two of this article, along with the associated story of U.S. Prisoners of War. In this case, the term "Missing in Action" has far more sinister connotations in the view of many, who believe that the POWs/MIAs are used a "drug mules" by an unscrupulous CIA, engaged in its global dope and guns business. Many of the names you have come across above will be reappear in part two.

ENDS

1. Cutolo's affidavit runs to 15 pages and 86 paragraphs. Dated 11 March 1980, it is witnessed by a notary. PFC William Tyree's affidavit runs to 13 pages and 41 paragraphs. Dated 6 September 1990, it is witnessed by a notary. Paul Neri's accompanying 5 page letter is undated and unsigned and was prepared prior to his death on 29 April 1990, from a long illness. Cutolo's affidavit and Neri's death-bed letter were forwarded by a friend who wished to remain anonymous. The friend sent an accompanying type-written letter consisting of one paragraph, neither signed nor dated. All documents are in this writer's possession. Copies of Cutolo's affidavit were given to Colonels A. J. "Bo" Baker, Hugh B. Pearce and James "Bo" Gritz.

DEEP BLACK

The CIA's Secret Drug Wars

© 1997 David Guyatt

Part Two

BACKGROUND TO US INVOLVEMENT IN DOPE TRAFFICKING

The history of how the US became involved in narcotics trafficking dates back more than a 150 years. Prominent families of great wealth - often members of secret societies such as Yale's "secretive Order of the Skull and Bones - pounced on the Opium trade to generate wealth and influence. One of the founding families of the Skull and Bones were the Russells. To this day, the Russell Trust is the legal entity of the Order of the Skull and Bones.

In 1823, Samuel Russell established "Russell and Company. He acquired his Opium supplies in Turkey and smuggled it to China aboard fast Clippers. By 1830, Russell bought-out the Perkins Opium syndicate of Boston and established the main Opium smuggling enterprise to Connecticut. His man in Canton, was Warren Delano Jr., grandfather of Franklin Roosevelt who was US President during the WWII years. Other Russell partners included the Coolidge, Perkins, Sturgis, Forbes and Low families.

By 1832, Samuel Russell's cousin, William Huntington, formed the first US chapter of the Order of the Skull and Bones. He attracted membership to the Order from the most powerful and influential American families. These membership roster read like a Who's Who of America: Lord, Whitney, Taft, Jay, Bundy, Harriman, Weyerhauser, Pinchot, Rockefeller, Goodyear, Sloane, Simpson, Phelps, Pillsbury, Perkins, Kellogg, Vanderbilt, Bush, and Lovett - to name some of the more prominent. Significantly, Skull and Bonesmen have always had a very close and enduring association with the US intelligence community. Former US President and Bonesman, George Bush, was a one time Director of Central Intelligence. Interestingly, the by-product of Opium, Heroin, was a trade name of the Bayer Company - still a world leader in the pharmaceutical industry - that launched its highly addictive product in 1898.

The intelligence connection unsurprisingly dates back to Yale University, where four Yale graduates formed part of the "Culper Ring" - one of the first US intelligence operations established in great secrecy by George Washington to gather vital intelligence on the British throughout the War of Independence. By 1903, Yale's Divinity School had established a number of schools and hospitals throughout China. Mao Zedong was a member of the staff. By the 1930's such was the clout of Yale's Chinese connection that US intelligence called on "Yale in China" to assist them in intelligence operations.[1] Historically, Heroin and Cocaine were legally available to purchase but were outlawed by the League of Nations - the forerunner to the United Nations - and the USA in the 1920's. Following prohibition consumption of these drugs began to spiral. Even so, the wars years 1939-46 saw addiction virtually eradicated in Europe and North America - a happy state of affairs that would not last long.

THEN ALONG CAME THE VIETNAM WAR

Indochina, historically under French control was captured by the Japanese during WWII. At the conclusion of the war, France regained control over Vietnam, Cambodia, Laos and Thailand. But independence movements had begun fighting to evict the French. This ultimately resulted in the Vietminh orchestrated battle of Dien Bien Phu which resulted in French defeat and eventual withdrawal from Indochina. They were to be immediately replaced the United States.

In the interim, the French had developed a wide-ranging intelligence apparatus throughout the region. This was financed by Opium. Maurice Belleux, former head of SDECE, the French equivalent of the CIA, confirmed this during a remarkably frank interview with historian, Prof Alfred McCoy. Belleux told McCoy that "French military intelligence had all their covert operations from the control of the Indochina drug trade." This covered the French Colonial war from 1946 through to 1954.

Bellereux revealed how this worked. French paratroopers fighting with hill tribes scattered throughout the region, collected raw Opium and transported it aboard French military aircraft to Saigon. Here, it was handed over to the Sino-Vietnamese Mafia for distribution. Also heavily engaged in the Opium traffic were Corsican crime syndicates that shipped the Opium to Marseilles for refining into Heroin. From here it was distributed to Europe and the United States - becoming known as "The French Connection." It was a case of the underworld working hand in glove with French government - both of whom benefited financially from the joint arrangement. The shared profits were channeled through Central bank accounts under French Military intelligence control. The SDECE master-spy closed his interview by stating that he believed the CIA "had taken over all French assets and were pursuing something of the same policy."[2]

The words 'Vietnam war' are something of a misnomer. More correctly, the US involvement in the entire region should be called the Southeast Asia war. While the fighting in Vietnam reached the media on a daily basis, the secret war in Cambodia, Laos and Thailand remained secret and continued right through the nineteen eighties. This was the CIA's own hot little war, fought with the assistance of local tribesmen and "off the

Within a year, Webb's colleagues in the Mercury News reversed their earlier support and began to denounce him. Such was the power of the signal returning-back from the East Coast, that many of the Mercury News other journalists began to fear that their career advancement - especially to the more prestigious news corporations of America - may be ruined. It was a classic case of guilt by association. Worse still, Webb's previously stalwart editor also denounced him and published an editorial in the Mercury News, saying the quality of Webb's corroboration of the Dark Alliance series was poor. The clear message was that the truth that was spoken had, in fact, not been spoken. Orwell called this double-speak.

For daring to speak the truth, Webb was punished by being re-assigned to a small town, backwater office of Mercury News - far away from the limelight of head office. Webb kept his job, or, at least, a kind of living death voodoo concoction of a job. No one can blame Webb for accepting the posting. He has a family to feed and under the circumstances, his chances of securing another job elsewhere in the media were surely limited. The editor clearly also kept his job, but we can and must blame him for rendering journalistic integrity to Caesar. Some of Webb's erstwhile colleagues have meanwhile, no doubt moved on to higher and better positions in those all too desirable national news corporations. Here they may write copy all day, on any subject they choose, so long as it is not one of the unmentionable subjects.

the CIA - to teach OSS personnel the "clandestine arts." This relationship continues to present times, McCoy states. The result is that where the CIA are running drug operations in various parts of the world, the DEA officially goes to sleep[9].

This has led to the realization that the DEA is principally tasked with prohibiting the flow of drugs from other than CIA "approved" sources - and that successive US "war on drugs" programs are, de facto, engaged in killing off the competition. Whether this is purposeful policy or not, the result is clearly the same. Taken to its logical conclusion, CIA approved and protected traffickers will increasingly gain greater and greater control over the global dope business, making the US government the biggest dope peddler in the world. Meanwhile, some believe this has already occurred and was always part of the long-term plans drawn up by covert policy planners, as they cast jealous eyes toward the planets raw materials - of which narcotics is one of the most profitable.

BUILDING MARKETS - ERADICATING COMPETITION

In 1973, President Richard Nixon declared his "war on drugs." Heroin entering the United States was produced by two principal Opium monopolies: those controlled by the CIA in Southeast Asia, and from Turkey - a close US ally. Nixon's "war on drugs" closed the Turkish connection that flowed through Marseilles under the control of the Corsican crime syndicates. This created an ever greater demand for Heroin produced in the Golden Triangle region of Southeast Asia - especially Burma.

Earlier, in 1949, the region became an armed redoubt for fleeing Chinese nationalist forces - under the command of Chiang Kai-Shek - following their rout by Mao's Red Army. The CIA established a massive support operation that used these former Chinese forces to collect intelligence inside China, engage in pitched battles with communist forces and act as a "trip-wire" to a feared communist invasion of Southeast Asia. To finance this secret little war, the CIA required the type of black funds that come from the large scale sale of narcotics. It was here that the old OSS "China hands" did their duty, by turning the region into largest single Opium producer of the world, accounting for close to 1000 tons by 1961.

Today, the Burmese "growing fields" remain under the watchful control of the CIA backed warlord, Khun Sa. It is here that out story comes full circle. In Part One we revealed the contents of an affidavit signed by Colonel Cutolo regarding his direct knowledge and involvement of US military sanctioned Cocaine trafficking from Bogota, Columbia to Panama. The senior US Special Forces commanding officer of the entire region at that time was Colonel Bo Gritz. Gritz was one of those who quietly involved himself in the investigation of Cutolo's death and those of other officers.

In 1978, Gritz, a long time campaigner for US Missing in Action/Prisoners of War (MIA/POWs) from the Vietnam era, was informed by Ross Perot that three American POWs were now held by Khun Sa and that the warlord had agreed to hand them over. Perot made arrangements to gain access to Khun Sa's headquarters in the remote hills of Shanland, via high level contacts in the Chinese government. Gritz knowing he could get

critic of successive governments - and their duplicitous, secret policies - and as a consequence has suffered at the hands of a wretchedly biased media.

Despite this, Gritz central story was not abandoned. Others had taken up the call from behind the scenes. Quiet investigations into the hidden activities of Richard Armitage, began in earnest. An immensely powerful "insider," Armitage had arranged for Colonel Dave Brown to been placed next to the president, as a military liaison, on a daily basis. The purpose of this move was in the words of one individual familiar with these events to "subtly influence his thinking daily." Moreover, "other actions of this type had been instituted in key departments and agencies."[10]

THE SPY DRUG-MEISTER

With the president effectively muzzled, Armitage and his small coterie of Washington movers and shakers believed they were untouchable. To a large extent they were. Already the Assistant Secretary of Defense, Armitage was nominated, in February 1989, by a grateful President Bush to become Assistant Secretary of State for Far Eastern Affairs. This move was blocked and Armitage was, instead, nominated for the post of Secretary of the Army.

Behind the scenes, a virtual war was in progress as the department of Justice and the FBI fought to indict Armitage for his narcotics and other criminal activities. These measures were powerfully resisted by Attorney General Thornburg, a political appointee of President Bush. Significantly, however, Armitage was also under scrutiny by Federal Investigators working for the President's Commission on Organized Crime, with a focus on foreign organized criminal activity in gambling and drug trafficking.

This resulted from Armitage's close association with a Vietnamese female, Ngdyet Tui (Nanette) O'Rourke. The latter was at the center of an extremely large scale gambling ring operated by US based Vietnamese. O'Rourke was awarded US citizenship, according to one source, under "highly suspect circumstances." She was also suspected of being a prostitute. As investigators developed their case, they came to believe that Armitage's association with O'Rourke dated back to his service in Vietnam, when he is thought to have operated a shady bar with her in Saigon. There were also suspicions that O'Rourke operated as Armitage's "courier."

Another source who was involved in these investigations noted that " nearly every Vietnamese woman involved in major gambling operations on the East Coast [of America] is married to an American who is either CIA or has connections to the agency," - including O'Rourke's husband. Meanwhile, yet another investigator who believed Armitage was "dirty" was frustrated in his investigations by Frank Carlucci, the Secretary of Defense, and other powerful patrons. In 1975 during Armitage's CIA tour in Vietnam, Carlucci was the no2 man in the CIA.

Because of the numerous high level obstructions, investigations into Armitage's criminal activities were curtailed, but not before some damaging information had been gathered.

1. The Yale material has been liberally extracted from Kris Millegan's excellent essay "Everything you wanted to know about Skull and Bones but were afraid to ask." Other first class material is available in Paul Goldstein's and Jeffrey Steinberg's "George Bush, Skull and Bones and the New World Order." Both are available on the internet only, so far as I am aware.
2. Paul DiRenzo interview with McCoy, November 1991.
3. For a detailed analysis of the connection between drugs and MIA/POWs see "Kiss the Boys Goodbye" by Jensen-Stevenson and Stevenson (Bloomsbury 1990).
4. See Corso's 17 September 1996 testimony to the US House Subcommittee on Military Personnel. "The 'No Win' policy was contained in NSC 68, NSC 68/2, and NSC 135/3," Corso told Congressmen, adding that "the basis for this policy was in directives ORE 750, NIE 2 2/1, 2/2, 10 and 11. We called it the 'Fig leaf Policy.'"
5. Figures quoted by McCoy during his interview with Paul DiRenzio, 9 November 1991.
6. See "Kiss the Boys Goodbye - by Stevenson & Stevenson p97 (Futura 1990).
7. National Security Council memorandum 68. This document outlined the US requirement resulting in the cold war.
8. Confidential papers in this writers possession.
9. McCoy's interview by radio host Paul DiRenzo, 9 November 1991.
10. Excerpted from a letter addressed to Senator Paul Laxalt dated 27 April 1987
11. I am reliably informed that Ross Perot was one of those who believed Armitage was a North Vietnamese spy.
12. The moral to Webb's story is don't expect the major media to inform you of what is really going on in the world. They won't. To paraphrase Walter Mattheu's one-liner uttered to perfection in the movie JFK: "These dogs don't hunt." Least-ways not anymore. The old media "blood-hound" is, today, curled up on a rug in front of the salary fire. His muscles have wasted, his belly is full and his nose has forgotten how to twitch - and his arm twitching dreams are of earlier days.

Deep Politics / Deep Times

APPENDIX A

REFERENCES

The development of SHELL GAME (and all supplemental letters, legal motions and exhibits, reports, testimony, and evidentiary information) is based upon the U.S. Constitution, and specifically the following primary references:

1. General

a. Unified Command Plan.

b. Irregular Warfare Joint Operating Concept.

c. National Security Strategy of the United States of America.

d. National Strategy for Combating Terrorism.

e. Quadrennial Defense Review Report, Department of Defense.

f. National Military Strategic Plan for the War on Terrorism.

g. USSOCOM Concept Plan 7500, Department of Defense Global War on Terrorism Campaign Plan (classified).

h. USSOCOM Publication 3-33, Conventional Forces and Special Operations Forces Integration and Interoperability Handbook and Checklist (Version 2).

2. Chairman of the Joint Chiefs of Staff

a. CJCSI 3110.03, Logistics Supplement To The Joint Strategies Capabilities Plan (JSCP).

b. CJCSI 3121.01B, Standing Rules of Engagement/Standing Rules for the Use of Force for US Forces.

c. CJCSI 5120.02A, Joint Doctrine Development System.

d. CJCSI 5810.01C, Implementation of the DOD Law of War Program.

e. JP 1, Doctrine for the Armed Forces of the United States.

f. JP 1-02, Department of Defense Dictionary of Military and Associated Terms.

g. JP 1-04, Legal Support to Military Operations.

h. JP 2-0, Joint Intelligence.

i. JP 2-01, Joint and National Intelligence Support to Military Operations.

j. JP 3-0, Joint Operations.

k. JP 3-05, Doctrine for Joint Special Operations.

l. JP 3-05.1, Joint Special Operations Task Force Operations.

m. JP 3-07.2, Antiterrorism.

n. JP 3-08, Interorganizational Coordination During Joint Operations, Vol. I & II.

o. JP 3-10, Joint Security Operations in Theater.

p. JP 3-13, Information Operations.

q. JP 3-13.2, Psychological Operations.

r. JP 3-16, Multinational Operations.

s. JP 3-22, Foreign Internal Defense (FID).

t. JP 3-24, Counterinsurgency Operations.

u. JP 3-27, Homeland Defense.

v. JP 3-28, Civil Support.

w. JP 3-30, Command and Control for Joint Air Operations.

x. JP 3-33, Joint Task Force Headquarters.

y. JP 3-40, Combating Weapons of Mass Destruction.

z. JP 3-57, Civil-Military Operations.

aa. JP 3-60, Joint Targeting.

bb. JP 3-63, Detainee Operations.

cc. JP 4-0, Joint Logistics.

dd. JP 5-0, Joint Operation Planning.

ee. JP 6-0, Joint Communications System.

(ALL MATERIAL LISTED ON PAGES A THROUGH K IS UNCLASSIFIED)

Joint Publication 3-26

Counterterrorism

13 November 2009

(UNCLASSIFIED)

> "Never tell people how to do things. Tell them what to do and they will surprise you with their ingenuity."
>
> **General George S. Patton**

SPECIAL OPERATIONS FORCES CORE TASKS

- -- Counterterrorism
- -- Direct Action
- -- Special Reconnaissance
- -- Counterproliferation of Weapons of Mass Destruction
- -- Unconventional Warfare
- -- Foreign Internal Defense
- -- Information Operations
- ***-- Psychological Operations***
- -- Civil Affairs Operations

Joint Publication 3-05, *Doctrine for Joint Special Operations*

COUNTERTERRORISM ANALYTICAL FRAMEWORK

Leadership	Safe Havens	Finance	Communication	Movement	Intelligence	Weapons	Personnel	Ideology
Personal Qualities	Physical Location	Sponsorship	Audience	Model/Method	Plan/Direct	Procurement	Recruitment/Selection	Unifying Vision
Structure/Organization/Role	Virtual Location	Criminal Activity	Function/Intent	Facilitation	Collect	Research and Development Weaponization	Training	Indoctrination
Sources of Authority	Demographics Cultural Conditions	Charitable Activity	Procedures/Tradecraft	Routes	Process/Analyze	Production	Use/Assignment	Legitimacy
Span/Level of Control	Political/Governance	Legal Enterprises	Medium/Tools	Purpose	Production/Dissemination	Distribution/Storage	Sustainment	Propaganda
Vision/Goals Objectives	Access to Resources	Financial Systems	Key Personnel	Key Personnel	Security/Counter-Intelligence	Employment	Members/Supporters	Key Personnel
Decision-making Process	Terrain	Key Personnel			Key Personnel	Weapons	Key Personnel	
Key Personnel	Key Personnel				Key Personnel			

(UNCLASSIFIED)

MILITARY STRATEGIC APPROACH

ENDS

National Strategic Aims:
- Defeat violent extremism as a threat to our way of life as a free and open society, and
- Create a global environment inhospitable to violent extremists and all who support them.

ENEMY

| Leadership | Finance | | Intelligence | Weapons |
| SafeHavens | Communications | Movement | Personnel | Ideology |

Protect the Homeland | Attack Terrorists | Support Mainstream Efforts

WAYS (Military Strategic Objectives)

- Deny terrorists the resources they need to operate and survive.
- Enable partner nations to counterterrorism.
- Prevent weapons of mass destruction proliferation, recover and eliminate uncontrolled materials, and maintain capacity for Consequence management.
- Defeat terrorists and their organizations.
- Counter state and non-state support for terrorism in coordination with other government agencies and partner nations.
- Contribute to the establishment of conditions that counter ideological support for terrorism.

MEANS: Combatant Commands, Services, and Combat Support Agencies

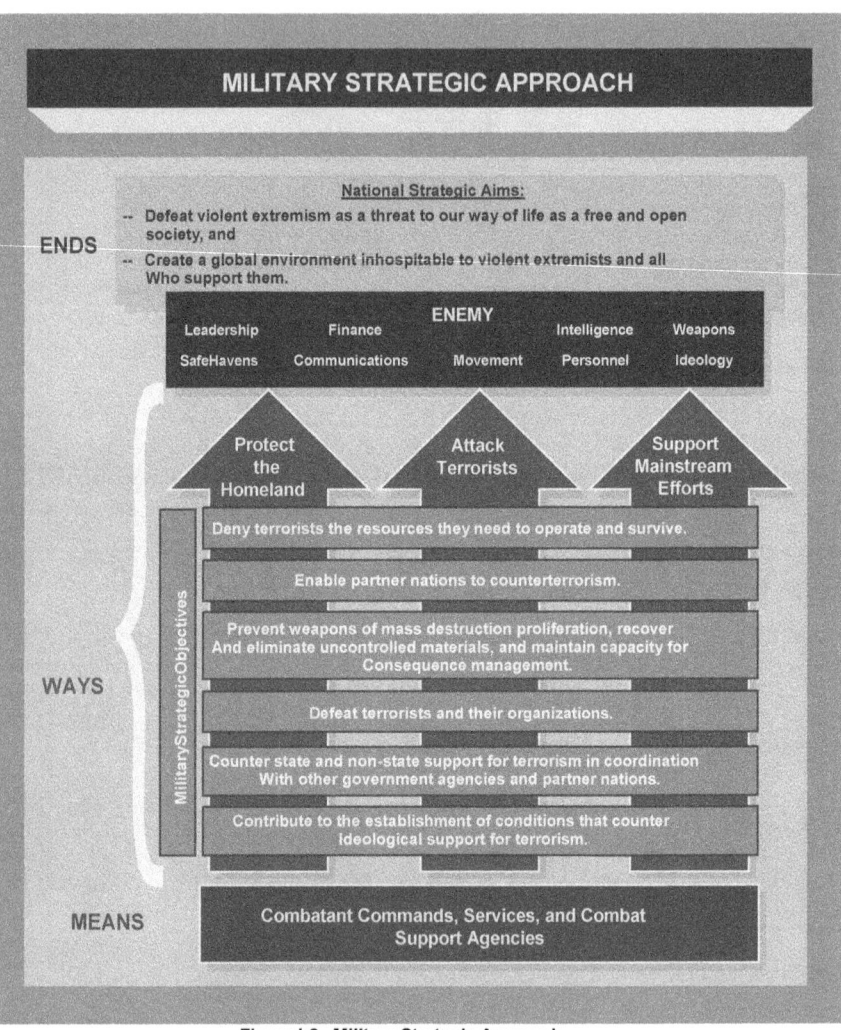

Figure I-2. Military Strategic Approach

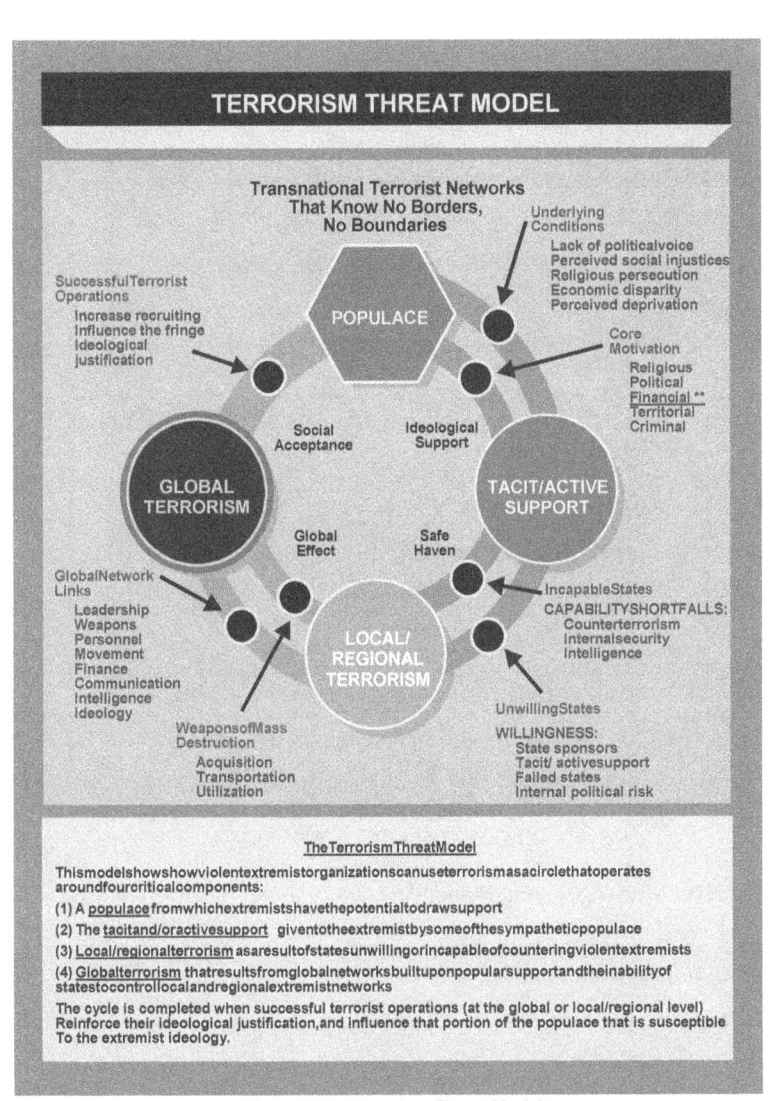

Figure III-2. Terrorism Threat Model

(UNCLASSIFIED)

(UNCLASSIFIED)

STRUCTURE PYRAMID OF A TYPICAL TERRORIST ORGANIZATION

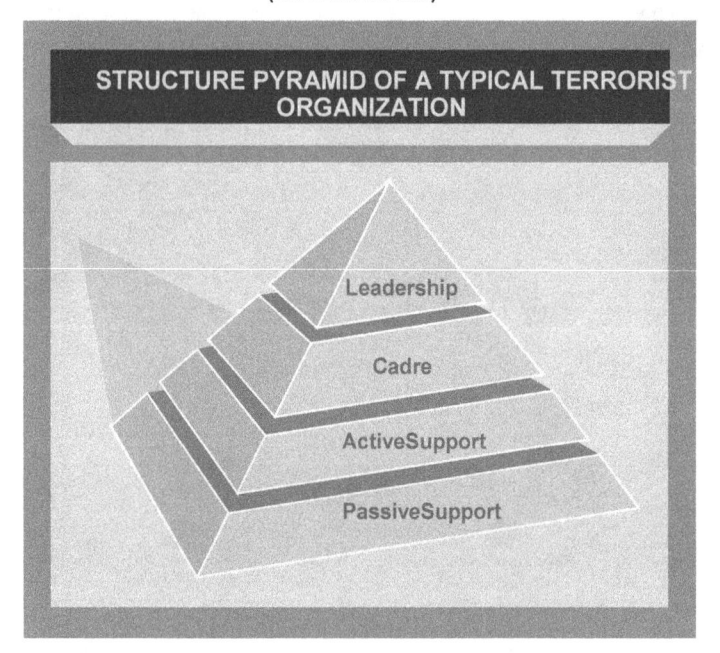

- Leadership
- Cadre
- ActiveSupport
- PassiveSupport

Figure II-1. Structure Pyramid of a Typical Terrorist Organization

HUMAN NEEDS PLANNING CONSIDERATIONS FOR COUNTERTERRORISM

People desire a strong degree of security.

People want control over their social and political order, according to the norms and expectations of their culture.

People want meaningful economic activity that enables them to provide a living for their families.

People want a society that reinforces their cultural preferences and allows them to feel pride and a sense of belonging to their group.

Various Sources

"Many Global War on Terrorism [GWOT] activities are not limited to the Department of Defense. In fact, most GWOT tasks require actions by other government agencies and international partners."

United State Special Operations Command Posture Statement 2007

7. Interagency Coordination

Interagency Coordination. Success in the war against terrorism requires interagency coordination to maximize the effectiveness of all instruments of national power. US Special Operations Command (USSOCOM), as the integrating command for global CT planning efforts, supports a growing network of relationships through continuous liaison partnerships, a supporting technical infrastructure, and using information sharing policies.

Joint Interagency Coordination Groups. To enhance interagency coordination at the strategic and operational levels, **joint interagency coordination groups (JIACGs)** have been established at the GCCs. A CT planning effort and subsequent operations may require a combatant command to request additional CT expertise from various agencies and organizations to staff its JIACG and optimize interagency effectiveness and efficiency.

US Special Operations Command Interagency Task Force. **USSOCOM Interagency Task Force** is a dedicated operations and intelligence planning team comprised of interagency intelligence and operations planning specialists and a robust information collection capability. The interagency task force searches for and identifies new, developing, and emerging CT opportunities to attack terrorist organizations and networks worldwide. It further develops actionable intelligence into operational courses of action and plans against the emerging targets. Combatant commands' JIACGs should coordinate their CT planning with the USSOCOM interagency task force as appropriate.

(a) **Basic Types of Networks.** There are three basic types of network structures, depending on the ways in which elements (nodes) are linked to other elements of the structure: the chain, hub (or star and wheel), and all-channel. A terrorist group may also employ a hybrid structure that combines elements of more than one network type. For example, a transnational terrorist organization might use chain networks for its **moneylaundering** activities, tied to a hub network handling **financial** matters, tied, in turn, to an all channel leadership network to direct the use of the funds into the operational activities of a hub network conducting pre-targeting surveillance and reconnaissance. Organizational structure that may appear very complex during initial assessments of terrorist groups may be more understandable when viewed in the context of chain, hub variants, or all channel networks.

Chain Network

1. **Chain.** Each node links to the node next in sequence and communication between the nodes is by passing information along the line. This organization is typical among networks that have a common function such as smuggling goods and people or **laundering money**.

Hub or Star and Wheel Network

2. **Hub or Star and Wheel.** Outer nodes communicate with one central node, which may not be the leader or decision maker for the network. A variation of the hub is a wheel design where the outer nodes communicate with one or two other outer nodes in addition to the hub. A wheel configuration is common for a financial or economic network.

3. **All-Channel.** All nodes are connected to each other. The network is organizationally "flat," meaning there is no hierarchical command structure above it. Command and control is distributed within the network. This is communication intensive and can be a security problem if the linkages can be identified or reconstructed. However, the lack of an identifiable "head" confounds the targeting and disrupting efforts normally effective against hierarchies.

All-Channel Network

b. **Categories of Terrorist Organizations.** There are many different categories of terrorism and terrorist groups. **These categories serve to differentiate terrorist organizations according to specific criteria, which are usually related to the field or specialty of whoever is selecting the categories.** Also, some categories are simply labels appended arbitrarily, often by the media. For example, every terrorist organization is by definition "radical," as terrorist tactics are not the norm for the mainstream of any group. Much of current terrorism can be described as being based on a universal political ideology or religious dogma, which is in contrast to traditional nationalist-ethnic terrorism that was more prominent in the past.

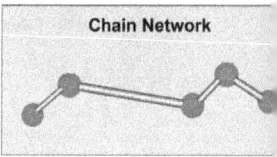

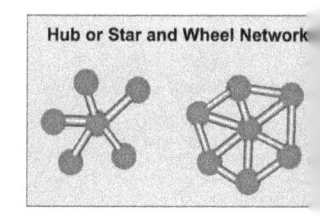

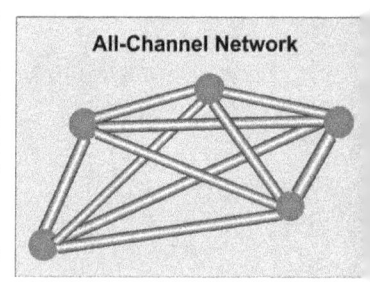

Motivation Categories. Motivation categories describe terrorist groups in terms of their ultimate goals or objectives. While political or religious ideologies will determine the "how" of the conflict, and the sort of society that will arise from a successful conclusion, motivation is the "what" in terms of end state or measure of success. Some of the common motivation categories are:

(a) **Separatist.** Separatist groups desire separation from existing entities through independence, political autonomy, or religious freedom or domination. The ideologies separatists subscribe to include social justice or equity, anti-imperialism, as well as the resistance to conquest or occupation by a foreign power.

(b) **Ethnocentric.** Groups of this persuasion view race as the defining characteristic of a society and a select group is often perceived superior because of its inherent racial characteristics. Ethnicity, therefore, becomes a basis of cohesion.

(c) **Nationalistic.** The loyalty and devotion to a nation, and the national consciousness derived from placing one nation's culture and interests above those of other nations or groups is the motivating factor behind these groups. This can find expression in the creation of a new nation, or in splitting away part of an existing state to join with another that shares the perceived "national" identity.

(d) **Revolutionary.** These groups are dedicated to the overthrow of an established order and replacing it with a new political or social structure. Although often associated with communist political ideologies, this is not always the case, and other political movements can advocate revolutionary methods to achieve their goals.

(2) **Ideological Categories.** Ideological categories describe the political, religious, or social orientation of the group. While some groups will be seriously committed to their avowed ideologies, for others, ideology is poorly understood, and primarily a justification for their actions to outsiders or sympathizers. It is a common misperception to believe that ideological considerations will prevent terrorists from accepting assistance or coordinating activities with terrorists or states on the opposite side of the religious or political spectrum. Quite often terrorists with differing ideologies have more in common with each other than with the mainstream society they oppose. Common ideological categories include:

(a) **Political.** Political ideologies are concerned with the structure and organization of the forms of government and communities. While observers outside terrorist organizations may stress differences in political ideology, the activities of groups that are diametrically opposed on the political spectrum are similar to each other in practice.

1. **Right-wing.** These groups are associated with the reactionary or conservative side of the political spectrum, and often, but not exclusively, are associated with fascism or neo-Nazism. Despite this, right-wing extremists can be every bit as revolutionary in

intent as other groups, the difference being that their intent is to replace existing forms of government with a particular brand of authoritarian rule.

    2. **Left-wing.** These groups are usually associated with revolutionary socialism or variants of communism (e.g., Maoist, Marxist-Leninist). With the demise of many communist regimes, and the gradual liberalization of the remainder towards capitalism, left-wing rhetoric can often move towards and merge with anarchistic thought.

    3. **Anarchist.** Anarchist groups are antiauthority or antigovernment, and strongly support individual liberty and voluntary association of cooperative groups. Often blending anticapitalism and populist or communist-like messages, modern anarchists tend to neglect the issue of what will replace the current form of government. They generally promote small communities as the highest form of political organization necessary or desirable. Currently, anarchism is the ideology of choice for many individuals and small groups that have no particular dedication to any ideology, and are looking for a convenient philosophy to justify their actions.

    (b) **Religious.** Religiously inspired terrorism is on the rise, with over a forty percent increase of total international terrorist groups espousing religious motivation since 1980. While Islamic terrorists and organizations have been the most active, and the greatest recent threat to the United States, all of the major world religions have extremists that have taken up violence to further their perceived religious goals. Religiously motivated terrorists seek justification of their objectives from religious authorities to promote their cause as infallible and nonnegotiable.

    1. Religious motivations can also be tied to ethnic and nationalist identities, such as Kashmiri separatists who combine their desire to break away from India with the religious conflict between Islam and Hinduism. The conflict in Northern Ireland also provides an example of the mingling of religious identity with nationalist motivations. There are frequently instances where groups with the same general goal, such as Kashmiri independence, will engage in conflict over the nature of that goal (religious or secular government).

    2. Numerous religious denominations have either seen activists commit terrorism in their name, or spawned cults professing adherence to the larger religion while following unique interpretations of that particular religion's dogma. Cults that adopt terrorism are often apocalyptic in their worldview, and are extremely dangerous and unpredictable. Of note, religiously inspired cults executed the first confirmed uses of biological and chemical nerve agents by terrorists.

    (c) **Social.** Often particular social policies or issues will be so contentious that they will incite extremist behavior and terrorism. Frequently this is referred to as "single issue" or "special interest" terrorism.

    (d) **Location or Geographic Categories.** Geographic designations have been used in the past, and although they are often confusing, and even irrelevant when referring to international and transnational terrorism, they still appear. Often, a geographical association to the area with which the group is primarily concerned will be made. "Mid-Eastern" is an example of this category and came into use as a popular shorthand label for Palestinian and Arab groups in the 1970s and early 1980s. Frequently, these designations are only relevant to the government or state that uses them. However, when tied to particular regions or states, the concepts of domestic and international terrorism can be useful.

1. **Domestic or Indigenous.** These terrorists are "home-grown" and operate within and against their home country. They are frequently tied to extreme social or political factions within a particular society, and focus their efforts specifically on their nation's sociopolitical arena.

2. **International.** Often describing the support and operational reach of a group, "international" and "transnational" are often loosely defined. International groups typically operate in multiple countries, but retain a geographic focus for their activities. For example, Hezbollah has cells worldwide, and has conducted operations in multiple countries, but is primarily focused on influencing the outcome of events in Lebanon and Israel. NOTE: An insurgency-linked terrorist group that routinely crosses an international border to conduct attacks, and then flees to safe haven in a neighboring country, is "international" in the strict sense of the word, but does not compare to groups that habitually operate across regions and continents.

3. **Transnational.** Transnational groups operate internationally, but are not tied to a particular country, or even region. Al-Qaeda is transnational; being made up of many nationalities, having been based out of multiple countries simultaneously, and conducting operations throughout the world. Their objectives affect dozens of countries with differing political systems, religions, ethnic compositions, and national interests.

2. Intelligence

In the aftermath of the September 11, 2001 terrorist attacks, the USG enhanced CT intelligence architecture and interagency collaboration by setting clear national priorities and transforming the organizational structure of the intelligence agencies to achieve those priorities. **The intelligence community (IC) has been reorganized and the DNI now oversees the IC to better integrate its efforts into a more unified, coordinated, and effective body.** The President established a mission manager organization, the NCTC, dedicated solely to planning and conducting intelligence operations against terrorist networks. The DNI launched an Open Source Center to coordinate open source intelligence and ensure this information is integrated into IC products. The FBI is fully integrated with the IC and has refocused its efforts on preventing terrorism. The Central Intelligence Agency has transformed to fulfill its role to provide overall direction and coordination for overseas human intelligence operations of IC elements. To undercut the financial underpinnings of terrorism worldwide, the Department of the Treasury created the Office of Terrorism and Financial Intelligence. The Defense

Intelligence Operations Coordination Center (DIOCC) is the lead DOD intelligence organization responsible for integrating and synchronizing military intelligence and national intelligence capabilities in support of the combatant commands. **The USSOCOM CSO is the fusion point for DOD synchronization of CT plans and establishing intelligence priorities against terrorist networks.** The CSO provides a venue for regular meetings, briefings, and conferences with interagency members (including the GCCs) and PNs and provides a forum for consistent dialogue for ongoing planning and situational understanding that simply had not existed earlier. The continuous collaboration is augmented with a USSOCOM sponsored semiannual Global Synchronization Conference. The following discussion provides insight **as to the complexities and rigorous analyses involved in establishing requirements and obtaining the intelligence products required for CT**.

a. **Intelligence for Counterterrorism.** Accurate and timely intelligence is absolutely critical to CT. All disciplines of intelligence are required for CT: human, imagery, signals, measurement and signature, technical, open source, and counterintelligence. Because of its global application, intelligence for CT is discussed in detail in the USSOCOM Concept Plan 7500, *DOD Global War on Terrorism Campaign Plan*, Annex B - Intelligence (hereafter referred to as Annex B). It provides the combatant commands and the IC with a detailed common intelligence framework to support prosecution of the *DOD Global War on Terrorism Campaign Plan*.

b. **Concept of Counterterrorism Intelligence Operations.** The concept of intelligence operations for CT developed in Annex B closely parallels the CONOPS for that campaign plan. It recognizes that intelligence requirements for global and regional operations against the primary enemy, the transnational terrorists (i.e., al-Qaeda), must also be synchronized with the intelligence requirements for regional operations (i.e., within AORs) against the secondary enemy, VEOs.

(1) Intelligence processes and procedures for integration and synchronization include:

(a) Assigning intelligence missions, roles, and responsibilities for the supporting, integrating, and synchronizing of the campaign plan.

(b) Integrating national, theater, and PN intelligence plans.

(c) Describing the integrated intelligence architecture to facilitate a common intelligence picture.

(d) Developing priority intelligence requirements and intelligence tasks (for inclusion in the appropriate appendix to annex B (Intelligence), and a common counterterrorism analytical framework (CTAF) to understand the global CT threat and the operational environment.

K

(e) Identifying collection and analysis and production (A&P) requirements, intelligence gaps, and the mitigation responsibilities for addressing the gaps.

(f) Assessing and developing multinational intelligence capabilities to partner with the United States to defeat, disrupt and defend against terrorism.

(g) Identifying doctrine, organization, training, material, leadership and education, personnel, and facilities shortfalls and mitigation responsibilities.

(2) Assignment of Intelligence Task Lists. Specific intelligence task lists (ITLs) are developed for the specific intelligence requirements for each of the campaign LOOs. The ITL items drive the development of the national intelligence support plan (NISP) and the functional intelligence support plans which delineate capabilities required of the CSAs and Service intelligence centers to support the CT intelligence processes.

(3) Collection. Annex B establishes processes and procedures to collaborate with US Strategic Command (USSTRATCOM) Joint Functional Component Command for Intelligence, Surveillance, and Reconnaissance (JFCC-ISR), Defense Intelligence Agency, the combatant commands, and the other CSAs, to synchronize/deconflict CT collection requirements. USSOCOM reviews, evaluates and scores the GCC requirements for the JFCC-ISR allocation process, and uses the ITL matrices to assess collection capacity and identify shortfalls.

(4) A&P. Annex B identifies intelligence requirements which are the basis for intelligence production. **Production will focus on identifying the functions and resources terrorist groups need to operate.** The CTAF will be the model used as a guide to develop dynamic threat assessments (DTAs) for various terrorist groups (see Figure V-1). These DTAs will include designation of critical nodes, critical capabilities, critical requirements, and critical vulnerabilities.

(5) Intelligence Support for Regional (i.e., AOR) Operations Objectives. There are four types of intelligence analysis normally used in concert to ensure all aspects of the requirements are covered for regional operations and the global campaign.

(a) Geographic Analysis. This is traditional analysis with one exception: it is divided into transnational and regional analysis. **The JITF-CT is the primary A&P organization for transnational CT analysis, and the GCCs are the primary A&P organizations for regional CT analysis (within their AORs).**

(b) Relational Analysis. This analysis examines organizations, social networks, and <u>transactions</u> to identify the HVIs, critical requirements, and the relationships between people, functions, and the physical terrain/human environment.

(c) Geospatial and Cultural Analysis. This analysis combines geography with social science to predict where terrorists are operating or will operate. A multilayer analysis is the primary analytical output. Additionally, analyses of environmental and cultural data support this type of analysis.

c. **Global Campaign and Regional/Theater Operations Interface.** The GCCs develop plans for CT within their AORs and in support of the global campaign. The annex B (Intelligence) of their plans must be synchronized with Annex B. The GCCs ITLs also must support the global campaign LOOs. While USSOCOM ensures global campaign seams are covered, the GCCs also must identify known regional seams (e.g., between operational areas and AORs) and work with the other combatant commands to ensure coverage. Synchronization requires information sharing among the GCCs and USSOCOM. **GCCs have responsibility for intelligence A&P on all terrorist groups whose primary operating bases reside within their theater** (specific terrorist groups are designated during the federation process of intelligence planning).

d. **Actionable Intelligence.** Combatant commands require actionable intelligence, and that requirement is very relevant for CT operations from the strategic to the lowest tactical levels. Key elements of actionable intelligence are:

(1) **Location.** Providing an ellipse radius or "vicinity of" location, if possible. Even a probable location is worthwhile.

(2) **Facilities.** Providing useful data that can help identify the place when an HVI is involved, or where terrorist assets are located.

(3) **Time.** Providing the time of a sighting or an event. Time, as with location, helps to establish patterns that are exploitable. Time is also useful in establishing potential evidence that may link an HVI to actual or planned terrorist events.

(4) **Travel.** Providing information regarding movement and means of travel and other available details when they relate to HVIs.

(5) **Relationships/connections.** Providing known or suspected family/tribal relationships that exhibit or have potential for greater trust. CTAF functional **connections** show possible linkages from COG/critical capabilities to critical vulnerabilities.

e. **CTAF and COG-to-Critical Vulnerability Analysis.** The CTAF is used for DTAs that should include the COG-to-critical vulnerability analysis for a given VEO or terrorist group. It is important to understand that each terrorist group is different and what is deemed a COG for one may not apply to another and, on a case-by-case basis, use of the CTAF is key to the functional and resource analysis for determining their critical vulnerabilities. **Actionable** intelligence on a terrorist group's critical vulnerabilities will provide a significant advantage in seizing the initiative.

(1) **The CTAF and its nine categories** include the potential COGs or critical capabilities and **can provide a useful step towards a systems perspective of a terrorist group.** It is not intended as a static, linear, exclusive construct and should be modified as deemed necessary. It was designed as a guideline and developed as part of the common intelligence framework supporting all aspects of the *DOD Global War on Terrorism Campaign Plan*. While CTAF component functions and systems can appear interdependent or mutually exclusive of each other, they are interrelated through a series of simple or complex nodal relationships. **The exact nature of those relationships are identified and defined during the target system or network analysis** and the process requires timely, focused data on enemy functions and processes.

(2) The Annex B federation process establishes responsibilities for A&P of the CTAF for designated terrorist groups to drive intelligence operations and identify critical vulnerabilities using the critical factors methodology. Briefly stated, collection and analysis in support of the CTAF identifies the terrorist groups' COG/critical capabilities (normally CTAF subgroups) and then GCC and JITF-CT analysts determine the critical requirements needed to meet those critical capabilities, and which of those requirements are vulnerable to friendly action (making them critical vulnerabilities). A critical vulnerability level of understanding (i.e., actionable intelligence about Group X) is the level of detail needed to act (disrupt, contain, isolate, neutralize, block, and interdict) against a designated terrorist group.

(3) The results of this analysis will appear in the DTAs and, as appropriate, in time critical reporting and planning. This process will drive the collection and production of the intelligence, and for time critical operations, may include dynamic re-tasking of collection assets and planning/targeting analysis.

(4) CTAF categories/components (Figure V-1) are as follows:

(a) **Leadership.** The direction of terrorist activities by individuals, organizations, and processes.

(b) **Safe havens.** The exploitation of an environment by terrorists to pursue their activities relatively free from detection and disruption.

(c) **Finance.** The generation, storage, movement, and use of assets to fund terrorist activities.

(d) **Communications.** The transferring of information in support of terrorist activities.

(e) **Movement.** The transferring of people and materials in support of terrorist activities.

(f) **Intelligence.** The collection, protection, and use of information to support terrorist activities.

(g) **Weapons.** The acquisition and employment of materials; to include WMD, and expertise to conduct terrorist attacks.

(h) **Personnel.** The acquisition and use of human assets in support of terrorist activities.

(i) **Ideology.** The interpretation and propagation of a shared belief system that motivates individuals to support terrorist activities.

Refer to USSOCOM Concept Plan 7500, DOD Global War on Terrorism Campaign Plan, Annex B – Intelligence, *for specific details regarding intelligence planning for the war on terrorism. Refer to JP 2-01,* Joint and National Intelligence Support to Military Operations, *for further doctrinal guidance regarding intelligence.*

3. **Intelligence, Surveillance, and Reconnaissance**

> **intelligence, surveillance, and reconnaissance** — *An activity that synchronizes and integrates the planning and operation of sensors, assets, and processing, exploitation, and dissemination systems in direct support of current and future operations. This is an integrated intelligence and operations function.*
>
> **Joint Publication 2-01,** *Joint and National Intelligence Support to Military Operations*

(1) An example of diplomacy supported by the USG policy is United Nations Security Council Resolution (UNSCR) 1373, which clearly established states' obligations for CT. This resolution called upon all member states to cooperate to prevent terrorist attacks through a range of activities, **including suppressing and freezing terrorist financing**, prohibiting their nationals from **financially** supporting terrorists; denying safe havens to those who finance, plan, support, or commit terrorist acts; and taking steps to prevent the movement of terrorists. Additionally, the international CT conventions and protocols, together with UNSCR 1373, set forth a compelling body of international obligations relating to CT. The USG will continue to press all states to become parties to and fully implement these conventions and protocols.

O

(3) Cadre is the nucleus of "active" members, the zealots, who comprise the core of a terrorist organization. This echelon plans and conducts not only operations, but also manages areas of intelligence, finance, logistics, IO, and communications. Mid-level cadres tend to be trainers and technicians such as bomb makers, financiers, and surveillance experts. Low-level cadres are the bombers and foot soldiers for other types of attacks.

Education and Intellect. In general, terrorists, especially their leaders, are usually of average or better intelligence and have been exposed to advanced education. Very few terrorists are uneducated or illiterate. Some leaders of larger terrorist organizations may have minimal education, but that is not the norm. Terrorist groups increasingly are recruiting members with expertise in areas such as communications, computer programming, engineering, finance, and the sciences. Among terrorists that have had exposure to higher learning, many are not highly intellectual and are frequently dropouts or possess poor academic records. However, this is subject to the norms of the society from which they originate. Societies where religious fundamentalism is prevalent, the focus of advanced studies may have been in religion or theology

(1) **Terrorist IO and Public Relations Activities.** The Internet provides terrorists and extremists the means to spread their radical ideology, an ad hoc means of operational connectivity, and a link to the full-media spectrum for public relations. The Internet facilitates their recruiting, training, logistic support, planning, fund-raising, etc. The internet is also a powerful tool to conduct the equivalent of media facilitated IO against the United States and PNs. Although not yet typical, terrorists may employ electronic attacks to disrupt communications, or banking, or to project disinformation and propaganda in support of their cause. From the terrorist perspective, media coverage is an important measure of the success of a terrorist act and a means of countering US and PN IO and SC activities. News reports, streaming videos on websites, blogs, and editorials can amplify (some unwittingly) the psychological effects of a terrorist incident and aid terrorists in publicizing the event globally to a much wider audience, and potentially gain further recognition of their radical ideology.

Lifestyle Attractions. A terrorist may choose violence as a lifestyle. It can provide emotional, physical, perceived religious, and sometimes social rewards. Emotionally, the intense sense of belonging generated by membership in an illegal group can be satisfying. Physical rewards can include such things as money, authority, and adventure. This lure often can subvert other motives. Social rewards may be a perceived increase in social status or power.

(1) **Deny Terrorists the Resources They Need to Operate and Survive.** Understanding the critical nodes and linkages of the terrorists' networks is critical. At the national military level, efforts are focused on identifying global linkages among terrorist networks, and then to arranging regional actions that will create detrimental effects network-wide. Because the terrorists are located in many countries around the

P

world, much of the effort against them will have to be made by those countries with the necessary encouragement and assistance of the United States.

(2) **Counter State and Non-State Support for Terrorism in Coordination with Other Government Agencies (OGAs) and PNs.** State sponsorship provides violent extremists access to key resources, including fronts for illegal activities. Non-state supporters may be **financial** supporters, such as charities and criminal organizations that directly or indirectly support or benefit from terrorist organizations. To counter these threats, US and PN activities include, among others: intelligence operations to identify state sponsors and non-state supporters; operations to eliminate terrorists and their direct supporters; and to interdict their resources (including WMD and their components); CT, counterinsurgency (COIN), counternarcotics efforts, and participation in exercises and capability demonstrations to dissuade and coerce states and non-state entities. In certain circumstances, the military can lead efforts to oust regimes that support terrorists.

b. **National Strategy for Combating Terrorism.** Guidance for the war against extremism was derived from appropriate national security Presidential directives, the National Defense Strategy, contingency planning guidance, and the National Military Strategy. The consolidated guidance is summarized in the following national strategic aims, strategy, and means for the war on terrorism, and is depicted in Figure I-1. NOTE:
Now, the GEF and the JSCP provide the principal planning guidance.

a. **National Counterterrorism Center (NCTC)**

(1) The NCTC is the primary organization in the USG for integrating and analyzing all intelligence possessed or acquired pertaining to terrorism (except purely domestic terrorism). It provides all-source intelligence support to government-wide CT activities; establishes its own information technology systems and architectures, and those between the NCTC and other agencies.

(2) The NCTC serves as the principal advisor to the Director of National Intelligence (DNI) on intelligence operations and analysis relating to CT.

(3) **Unique among US agencies, the NCTC also serves as the primary organization for strategic operation planning for CT.** Operating under the policy direction of the President, the NSC, and the Homeland Security Council (HSC), the NCTC provides a full-time interagency forum and process to plan, integrate, assign lead operational roles and responsibilities, and measure the effectiveness of strategic-level CT activities of the USG. It is responsible for the integration of all instruments of national power to the CT mission.

EXHIBIT: 2LT Scott Bennett sent a copy of his military whistleblowing report to Congress to Senator Jim Web, on the Senate Armed Services Committee, with the hope he would investigate the issue and take action. 2LT Bennett's report, sent September 25, 2012, provided detailed actionable intelligence exposing Secretary of State Hillary Clinton to Gulf Nations (Saudi Arabia, Qatar, Kuwait, Morocco, etc.). Instead of honoring his oath to "support, protect, and defend the Constitution of the United States, against all enemies foreign and domestic", Senator Jim Web refused to involve himself, and thereby conspired to continue the financing of terrorism against American service members. See letter below.

JIM WEBB
VIRGINIA

COMMITTEE ON
ARMED SERVICES
COMMITTEE ON
FOREIGN RELATIONS
COMMITTEE ON
VETERANS' AFFAIRS
JOINT ECONOMIC COMMITTEE

United States Senate
WASHINGTON, DC 20510-4605

WASHINGTON OFFICE:
WASHINGTON, DC 20510
(202) 224-4024

September 28, 2012

Second Lieutenant Scott Bennett
Fci Schuylkill, Fed. No: 29418-016
P O Box 670
Minersville, Pennsylvania 17954-0670

Dear Second Lieutenant Bennett:

   This will acknowledge receipt of the copy of your letter to the Trial Defense Service.

   As you may know, I have decided not to seek reelection and my term as U.S. Senator representing Virginia will end in January, 2013.

   I appreciate your sharing this correspondence with me, however, it has been the experience of my office that federal agency concerns such as yours are not likely to resolve within this timeframe. Due to this time factor, should you decide to request assistance from a congressional office and, if your Home of Record is located in Virginia, you may want to contact Senator Mark Warner's office, or the Congressman representing the district of your Home of Record.

   With kind regards, I am

Sincerely,

Jim Webb
United States Senator

JW:gs

Veterans, families, sue six banks claiming they helped Iran fund terror groups

Published November 11, 2014

| FoxNews.com

More than 200 veterans and their families have filed a lawsuit against six international banks, accusing them of helping Iran transfer millions of dollars to militant groups that targeted and killed U.S. soldiers during the Iraq war.

The suit, first reported by The Wall Street Journal, alleges that the banks helped Iran move billions of dollars through the U.S. financial system, with some of the money ending up with Iran's elite Revolutionary Guard Corps and its proxies like Hezbollah, which orchestrated attacks against U.S. forces in Iraq.

Five of the banks accused in the lawsuit, filed in federal court in Brooklyn Monday, are HSBC, Barclays, Standard Chartered, Royal Bank of Scotland, and Credit Suisse. A sixth bank named in the suit is the Britain-based subsidiary of Bank Saderat Iran.

The suit details one 2007 attack in Iraq by terrorists who, according to the suit, were trained and armed by Iran's Qods Force, with help from Hezbollah. In a brazen attack at a center about 30 miles south of Baghdad, they opened fire and threw grenades at U.S. and Iraqi forces. One American died after jumping on a grenade; four other Americans were abducted from the scene and later killed.

The attack is one of several detailed in the suit. The complaint alleges that as a result of the conspiracy, Iran and affiliated terror groups planned, funded and executed hundreds of terrorist attacks in Iraq between 2003 and 2011, killing hundreds of U.S. service members and civilians, and wounding many others.

The lawsuit reportedly comes on the heels of a September jury verdict that found Jordan's Arab Bank liable for providing financing to the Hamas terror group. In that case, the jury ruled that the bank must compensate victims of over two dozen attacks in Israel and the Palestinian territories linked to the group. Arab Bank is currently appealing the verdict.

The veterans' lawsuit asks for a jury trial and unspecified damages.

Some multinational banks have already paid millions of dollars to settle similar actions brought by the Justice Department. In 2010, Barclays paid $500 million to avoid prosecution for allegedly engaging in transactions with banks in countries targeted by U.S. sanctions, including Iran, Cuba, Libya, and Sudan. Earlier this year, France's largest lender, BNP Paribas agreed to pay $8.9 billion to settle claims it covered up $30 billion in transactions with Iran, Syria, and Sudan as recently as 2009.

URL

http://www.foxnews.com/politics/2014/11/11/veterans-families-sue-six-banks-claiming-helped-iran-fund-terror-groups/

Swiss Bank Whistleblowers Take Their Show on the Road

THE WALL STREET JOURNAL

The Wall Street Journal – Tue, Mar 31, 2015 13:26 BST

ZURICH—What does HSBC whistleblower Hervé Falciani think about the recent media storm he helped kick up for the bank? And what's new with Bradley Birkenfeld, the American who blew the whistle on UBS and helped start the broader, ongoing U.S. legal crackdown on Swiss banks? Both may answer those questions and more when they kibbitz on a panel at a conference scheduled for early May.

Messrs. Falciani and Birkenfeld will appear together on what's being billed as a "super panel" at the OffshoreAlert Conference in Miami Beach, entitled "Inside the UBS & HSBC Leaks."

Mr. Falciani, a former employee at HSBC's Swiss bank, handed details about the unit's alleged aiding of tax evasion among clients to French authorities. Those details later made their way to the media. Stories in various outlets earlier this year prompted Franco Morra, the chief executive of HSBC's Swiss bank, to say: "The old business model of Swiss private banking is no longer acceptable."

Mr. Birkenfeld, who worked for UBS in Geneva, helped the U.S. build a case that resulted in a 2009 deferred prosecution agreement with the bank, which acknowledged helping U.S. clients evade taxes and agreed to pay $780 million. UBS rival Credit Suisse settled its own case about five years later, and roughly one dozen banks here remain under related Justice Department investigations. Mr. Birkenfeld recently traveled to Paris to assist judges there currently investigating UBS's alleged aiding of tax evasion in that country.

The OffshoreAlert Conference describes the subject matter for the whistleblowers' panel like so: "The session will take you inside the UBS and HSBC leaks and discuss issues material to whistleblowing, including the treatment of whistleblowers by law enforcement and tax collection agencies, how the system can be improved, the extent of global tax evasion, and the involvement of the world's major banks."

SAMPLE LETTER FOR CITIZENS TO SEND TO THEIR MEMBER OF CONGRESS:

Dear Member of Congress:

It has come to my attention that military whistleblowing reports were filed with your office by a United States Army Officer disclosing terrorist threat finance networks and operations involving Swiss Banks (specifically Union Bank of Switzerland) and you have not responded in any way to these reports.

These whistleblowing reports were:

1) "TERRORIST THREAT FINANCE DIMENSIONS OF UNION BANK OF SWITZERLAND (UBS) 'WHISTLEBLOWER CASE' AND OBAMA ADMINISTRATION INVOLVEMENT", dated September 25, 2012;

2) "FOLLOW THE MONEY", dated September 11, 2013;

3) "SHELL GAME: The Betrayal and Cover-Up by the U.S. Government of the Union Bank of Switzerland-Terrorist Threat Finance Connection to Booz Allen Hamilton and U.S. Central Command", dated May 27, 2013;

The Army Officer who authored and submitted these reports was 2LT Scott Bennett, 11th Psychological Operations Battalion, who was also a defense contractor for Booz Allen Hamilton, held a top secret/sci clearance, and had worked in the highest levels of the Bush Administration, the intelligence community, and military special operations. See EXHIBIT 1.

Given the recent stories in the media about banks funding terrorism against U.S. military servicemembers, I am deeply disturbed that your office not only knew about this material far in advance (beginning in 2012), but as of today, has never responded in any way to this information.

As a citizen of the United States and concerned about the welfare of our military members, as well as our national reputation in the world, I consider it an obscene and intolerable failure of government officials that this report and issue has been intentionally ignored since U.S. military servicemembers have been killed and wounded as a result of terrorist activity financed by the banks and organizations and individuals contained in 2LT Bennett's reports.

Worst of all, these financial networks continue to fund terrorist attacks against our troops because of your office's incompetence or unwillingness to investigate and address this matter.

Additionally, the financial manipulation of mortgages and derivative markets is also implicated in these terrorist financing networks, banks, and operations. Since this directly affects my personal home mortgage, it affects me, and therefore will affect you.

Since the material within the above mentioned reports contain evidence of support for terrorist networks and operations, pursuant to all U.S. (and international) whistleblowing laws and regulations, failure to acknowledge receipt of this letter and report will be interpreted a conscious act of collusion, depraved indifference, and may demonstrate willful intent to obstruct justice by ignoring or sequestering requests for Congressional Investigations into the information contained herein. It may also be considered a violation of your constitutional oath as a member of congress, and constitute "aiding and abetting" an enemy of the United States, punishable as treason.

Be advised, this letter is protected and privileged communication with a Member of Congress involving a whistleblowing matter, and thereby protected by all whistleblowing laws, statutes, executive orders. Confirmation of receipt of this letter by your office and an explanation is requested immediately.

I request you immediately advise me about what you and your office is doing in response to 2LT Bennett's above mentioned whistleblowing reports and letters submitted.

I look forward to hearing from you within the next two (2) weeks.

Respectfully,

Mr./ Mrs. Constituent

EXHIBIT 1:

Camelot Livestream Channel — LIVE BROADCAST

CIA & Swiss Banks Fund ISIS & AL Queda
Army CounterIntelligence Officer Whistleblower
Kerry Cassidy interviews **Scott Bennett**
http://livestream.com/projectcamelotlive

Wednesday October 1, 2014 Time: 7pm PT / 10 pm ET

Date: Tue, 23 Dec 2014 11:42:17 -0700
Subject: I forwarded your web letter personally about our Military compromised at Cory Gardner Greet
From:
To: armypsyop@outlook.com

Officer Bennett:

About 2 weeks ago I could get you exact date I handed personally your web of warning letter to military families and our congress. (I printed and brought them in white envelopes) Anyway, since then I am having problems with my home phone not working. I am referring to your letter of warning and informed consent to the public about our military and the problem that occurred to you with our soldiers being compromised. I handed in public, people saw me at the Cory Gardner Greet since his new senate seat election which everyone helped for new leadership in our State in Colorado. This Meet-up was here at our Local GOP headquarters and enclosed are pictures I took this day since I am a precinct leader here in Colorado Springs with a very small blog coloradovoting.wordpress.com On this day I handed both Cory Gardner and Congressman Doug Lamborm your letter of concern in a 8x10 white envelope. Anyway since that time two days after this; I began having problems with my phone and today called century link to see what it could be for my home phone kept having busy signal and calling itself back.

I am not sure what the future will hold for all of us but the abuses of power need to stop or be curtailed. . I am concerned for at Fort Polk in year 1999 I suffered a chlorine gas exposure as I was walking my dogs in the base. We cannot live in fear so now with the phone acting weird decided to let you know that I about a week and half ago gave out your letter since as a precinct leader it is my duty to let our elected Colorado representatives know what is affecting our military and soldiers. I hope I was of some help ad hopefully these leaders will help you for they seem like decent individuals to us here. Here are the photos of

Christmas GOP Greet and good will for his new January Senate elect position in DC.

Wells Program discussion was good but still not clear what really happened and what it all means. Are the American people also very compromised such as our safety? I will pray that our country survives.

From: armypsyop@outlook.com
To:
Subject: RE: I forwarded your web letter personally about our Military compromised at Cory Gardner Greet
Date: Wed, 24 Dec 2014 12:15:28 -0800

Dear Theresa,
I received your email and phone message and wanted to thank you from the bottom of my heart for having the courage to do what you did. You are an amazing woman, and a leader all women should strive to follow. Your example of bravery, of virtuous character, of love of country, is remarkable and truly precious, and of course in harmony with the greatest patriots in American history. You have single-handedly picked up the torch, which so many have refused to even look at, and buried their head in the sand for fear of. And more gallant, you have taken that torch up to the political leaders who are bound by oath to represent you and defend the constitution and your rights, and demanded that they inform themselves and act on this information, and advise you of their progress. For all of this, and the work I know you will continue to do, I thank you sincerely, and I know my fellow Americans and military members and their families thank you.

My only advice which I pray is of some help to your efforts, is to make sure that you document everything in a file and back up that file on the cloud and on multiple sources, and make a hard paper copy of everything. This is your record, and is your lifeline which will keep you protected. Keep a list of everyone you speak with, meet, write/email, or in anyway communicate, and the dates of your interaction with them.

I think you would be wise to contact the office of the politician and have a staff member serve as your personal liaison on this issue to the politician--that way there is one person who represents the politician liable for all communications and materials. That way that person can be tracked, should they do anything unethical or damaging to you. Have your fellow precinct leaders follow your lead and confirm that they are aware of your communication by contacting IN WRITING the politician's office, and notifying him that they are aware of his involvement now, and will be watching him closely and demand that he act and advise them of his actions as things advance. I suspect 2015, with your great help, will be a 1776 fireworks display of revolutionary freedoms re-discovered all over again. I thank you for being in the fight, and look forward to staying in touch as we advance.

Respectfully,
Scott

MULTIDIMENSIONAL INFLUENCE OPERATIONS
Scott Bennett, Ph.D. (ABD)
Creative

23 Railroad Ave, #23
Danville, CA 94526
925.391.0407
http://armypsyop.wix.com/scottbennett

Dear Scott,

I want to thank-you so much for your bravery, and your willingness to speak-out. However, I am so sorry for what you have endured. I will keep you, and others in prayers. I also pray for our country, and peace while asking God to return soon.

I realize what Goldirater has done to our world, and how our goverment been changing our culture. Every where there is corruption. But, I hope that Obama and his administrate get impeached then thrown in prison.

Your a good man
God Bless
Mother of a U.S. Marine

Thank-you thank-you thank-you
God Bless

Regards to C.T.M. 189

HELP OUR MILITARY

SIGN PETITION FOR CONGRESSIONAL MILITARY WHISTLEBLOWER INVESTIGATION:

"Terrorist Financing-Swiss Banks"
http://www.lulu.com/spotlight/shellgame

CONTACT: Scott Bennett, Ph.D. (ABD), U.S. Army and State Department Contractor
SIGN PETITION BY EMAILING: ARMYPSYOP@OUTLOOK.COM
WEB: WWW.ARMYPSYOP.WIX.COM/SCOTTBENNETT & https://www.facebook.com/truthunites
PHONE: 925.391.0407

FOR IMMEDIATE RELEASE:

"SHELL GAME: Military Report to Congress"

On August 1, 2016 this report was delivered to Congressman Mark DeSaulnier's Office, and a request for investigation was filed. This meeting was videotaped and will be made available to the public. Sign and share this petition demanding a response.

SUMMARY:

This report exposes TREASON (giving "aid and comfort to the enemy of the United States), MONEYLAUNDERING, TERRORIST FINANCING, BREACH OF PUBLIC TRUST, and BETRAYAL of military members and their families by financing terrorism through Swiss Banks (Union Bank of Switzerland, HSBC, and others).

BACKGROUND:
In 2012, Scott Bennett, an Army Officer and defense contractor with Booz Allen Hamilton at the State Department, USSOCOM, and USCENTCOM, discovered a terrorist financing network involving Swiss Banks (Union Bank of Switzerland and HSBC), a Washington DC law firm (Covington and Burling) and the Obama Administration (Attorney General Eric Holder; Assistant Attorney General Lanny Breuer; Secretary of State Hillary Clinton; Senator Carl Levin; President Barack Obama; and others). Additionally, Congressional leaders committed "misprision of treason" by hiding this report--and thereby harming military members and their families serving overseas in battle.

TREASON:

Director of HSBC Holdings: FBI Director James Comey did not recommend federal charges in part because he is connected to the Clinton Foundation through the Swiss bank HSBC and UBS. HSBC is connected to the Clinton Foundation through a number of initiatives.

Comey was appointed Director of HSBC Holdings in March, 2013. He became an independent non-executive Director and a member of the Financial System Vulnerabilities Committee. The appointment was set to expire this year.

Wealthy HSBC clients lined up to shower cash on the Clinton foundation, including Jeffrey Epstein, the hedge fund manager and convicted sex offender.

WHO WE ARE: As American military members, we took an oath, and as such we continue to carry and defend that oath until our deaths. We are communicating with members of Congress, the media, and international leaders.

OUR OBJECTIVE:

We are requesting Rep. DeSaulnier conduct an official debriefing in this matter, and that this material be directly questioned to Mr. Comey in the coming hearings and investigation on this matter. It is absolutely essential to submit these questions:

1) What emails contained information about the Union Bank of Switzerland, Brad Birkenfeld, Eric Holder and Lanny Breuer, and the law firm Covington and Burling.

2) What emails contained information about donations to the Clinton Foundation from UBS, Saudi Arabian Officials, and Swiss Officials.

3) What emails contain information about the prosecution and imprisonment of the whistleblower Brad Birkenfeld and Scott Bennett and the report "Shell Game: UBS connections to the State Dept. and Terrorist Financing"

The evidence of misprision of felonies and misprision of treason is enough to justify immediate recall for any man or women in positions of fiduciary trust over rights. Placing a public servant on notice is a right and a duty, as is the necessary response to this notice.

More information about this is forthcoming, and will be released in the next 24 hours to other members of the Congress.

CONTACT US FOR DEBRIEFING:
Slideshow: http://armypsyop.wix.com/scottbennett#!slideshow/cdrf
My Story: http://youtu.be/RU8-bqfR83Q
Report: http://www.lulu.com/spotlight/shellgame
SHELL GAME: https://youtu.be/kPLGDOx2eSg

INTERVIEWS/ MEDIA CLIPS AVAILABLE ON THE INTERNET AT:

http://armypsyop.wix.com/scottbennett#!video/cb4d

https://www.facebook.com/capsule.ninetynine.7

DIRECT LINKS:

http://www.lulu.com/spotlight/shellgame

https://wikispooks.com/wiki/Scott_Bennett

https://www.youtube.com/watch?v=QCSVHW16Xs0

http://youtu.be/nG_BtGL9dOY

https://www.youtube.com/watch?v=KJ5AsIrKI1s

http://projectcamelotportal.com/blog/31-kerrys-blog/2285-live-broadcast-wednesday-7pm-pt-10pm-pt-interview-re-cia-funding-isis

http://www.veteranstoday.com/2014/10/12/psy-ops-whistleblower-i-worked-with-911-suspects-rumsfeld-myers-zakheim/

https://www.youtube.com/watch?v=921Olpdh6ww

https://www.youtube.com/watch?v=Jo8Xm46s62I

https://www.youtube.com/watch?v=1-VP6XM099U

http://www.erikrush.com/playlists/november-2014/

http://www.veteranstoday.com/2014/10/12/psy-ops-whistleblower-i-worked-with-911-suspects-rumsfeld-myers-zakheim/

http://roguemoney.net/wp-content/uploads/2014/11/The-Goerilla-Economist-wth-V-2014-11-07.mp3

http://redpillreports.com/guests/scott-bennett/

http://redpillreports.com/red-pill-reports/illegal-mortgage-securitization-did-banks-gamble-your-home-distort-chain-of-title/

http://www.4thmedia.org/2014/10/army-whistleblower-cia-funds-isis-al-queda/

http://beforeitsnews.com/alternative/2014/10/cia-19000-swiss-bank-accounts-fund-terrorism-tied-to-michael-hastings-death-army-officer-scott-bennett-whistleblower-interview-must-listen-3043972.html

https://2012thebigpicture.wordpress.com/tag/booz-allen-hamilton/

http://www.abovetopsecret.com/forum/thread1035568/pg1

http://www.godlikeproductions.com/forum1/message2667708/pg1

http://investmentwatchblog.com/must-watch-white-hat-u-s-army-whistle-blower-scott-bennett-how-the-cia-swiss-banks-fund-isis-isil-al-qaeda/

http://m.liveleak.com/view?i=06f_1412620766

http://www.reddit.com/r/POLITIC/comments/2j5ukw/

http://sgtreport.com/2014/10/cia-whistle-blower-how-the-cia-swiss-banks-fund-isis-isil-al-qaeda-scott-bennett/

http://www.theeventchronicle.com/editors-pick/army-whistleblower-cia-funds-isis-al-queda/

http://nesaranews.blogspot.com/2014/10/cia-19000-swiss-bank-accounts-fund.html?m=1

http://revolutionradio.org/?p=84218

http://www.independenceday.pro/cia/the-u-s-is-funding-terrorism-worldwide/

http://m.disclose.tv/action/viewvideo/187331/PROJECT_CAMELOT_SCOTT_BENNETT__CIA_SWISS_BANKS_FUND_ISIS/#DTV

http://www.truthseekers.com/post/11902

http://www.ascensionwithearth.com/2014/10/project-camelot-scott-bennett-cia-swiss.html?m=1

http://aftertheshift.blogspot.com/2014/10/project-camelot-scott-bennett-cia-swiss.html?m=1

http://yournewsline.wordpress.com/2014/10/12/psy-ops-whistleblower-i-worked-with-911-suspects-rumsfeld-myers-zakheim/

http://www.wakeupthemasses.com/project-camelot-scott-bennett-cia-swiss-banks-fund-isis/

http://mikephilbin.blogspot.com/2014/10/michael-hastings-cia-swiss-banks.html?m=1

http://www.oom2.com/t22925-shell-game-this-is-why-michael-hastings-was-murdered-and-eric-holder-stepped-down-video

http://mainerepublicemailalert.com/2014/10/12/ben-fulford-love-and-friendship-is-winning-over-traditional-cabal-control-mechanisms-of-fear-hate-greed-and-lust/

https://www.tumblr.com/search/whistleblowers/recent

http://www.tatumba.com/blog/archives/204349

http://www.galacticfriends.com/updates/nesara-canada/7057-ben-fulford-global-report-a-nesara-revisited-oct-614.html

http://en.paperblog.com/michael-hastings-cia-swiss-banks-funding-terror-groups-1021980/

http://michellemalkin.com/2009/11/18/culture-of-corruption-holder-terrorists-covington-burling/

https://eclinik.wordpress.com/2014/10/03/the-shell-game-by-scott-bennet-must-read/

http://www.slideshare.net/exopolitika/scott-bennett-shell-game

http://www.jimstonefreelance.com/shell_game.pdf

http://www.reddit.com/r/conspiracy/comments/2o60ix/the_most_important_conspiracy_book_in_decades/

http://www.veteranstoday.com/2015/02/17/estulin-bennett/

http://www.blogtalkradio.com/wheresobamasbirthcertificatexcom/2015/02/21/erik-rush-with-2nd-lt-scott-bennett-ret-reveals-cia-funding-of-terrorists

http://www.thecommonsenseshow.com/2015/05/04/special-ops-officer-blows-whistle-on-cia-funded-isis-through-swiss-bank-accounts/

http://caravantomidnight.com/caravan-to-midnight-episode-275-scott-bennett/

https://www.youtube.com/watch?v=aXv5Zppun2U

https://www.youtube.com/watch?v=4uNqLXXvUuk

http://www.dcclothesline.com/2015/05/04/special-ops-officer-blows-whistle-on-cia-funding-isis-through-swiss-bank-accounts/

http://sitsshow.blogspot.ca/2015/05/cia-swiss-banks-fund-isis-al-queda-help.html

http://coloradovoting.org/2015/05/07/maintaining-military-honor-respect-and-care-for-all-soldiers-that-serve/

https://www.youtube.com/watch?v=RMlpqLLSvp8&index=10&list=PLT2uPrTAnKfIeotbST4sypATi5QQCUqMr

SAN FRANCISCO
PENTAGON
HELP WHISTLEBLOWER SCOTT BENNETT
SPEAK AT OFFSHOREALERT CONFERENCE
MAY 5TH, 2015
BUZZSAW
Camelot Livestream Channel
LIVE BROADCAST
CIA & Swiss Banks Fund ISIS & AL Queda
Army Counterintelligence Officer Whistleblower
Kerry Cassidy interviews Scott Bennett
http://livestream.com/projectcamelotlive
Wednesday October 1, 2014 Time: 7pm PT / 10 pm ET
Scott Bennett
RedPillReports
Listen Live to Prescription for Truth
Host JD Moore
Live Mon. - Fri.
10AM CT to 12PM CT
REDPILLREPORTS.COM
12-17-2014 Guests Scott Bennett and Greg Morse
SAVEOURFAMILYANDHOME.COM
Next
Previous
Go to Slide...
End Show
SCOTT BENNETT
TRAIL OF BLOOD
Bev Collins
SAN FRANCISCO

EDWARD
SNOWDEN
NSA
OBAMA
ADMINISTRATION
BENGHAZI
ATTACKS
THE
UBS
Booz | Allen | Hamilton
WHISTLEBLOWER
BERMUDA TRIANGLE
THE PLAN,
THE EXECUTION,
THE COVERUP
WEAPONS SHIPPED
TO SYRIAN ISLAMIC
RADICALS
DIRECT RESULT:
ISLAMIC STATE
SCOTT
BENNETT
US ARMY PSYOPS
BRAD
BIRKENFELD
SWISS BANKING
THE MEN WHO CAN EXPOSE ISIS AS A US GOVERNMENT
CREATION TO TERRORIZE THE MIDDLE EAST
Benghazi documents:
DIA admission: http://tinyurl.com/o2ssgfw
Bennett discusses the scandal:

Camelot Livestream Channel
"SHELL GAME"
A Military
Whistleblowing
Report to Congress

RT OBAMA'S SYRIA
NEW YORK 21:31 #GERMANY THREATENS TO SANCTION EU MEMBER STATES WHO REFUSE REFUGEE QUOT

PRESSTV
HOME IRAN NEWS UK US DOCS VIDEOS SHOWS PHOTO
Newsroom Reports Shows Interviews
Resource-rich Afghanistan: An economic stalemate
Home / Programs / Economic Divide
Fri Oct 2, 2015 6:18AM
SCOTT BENNETT
FORMER US ARMY OFFICER

EXHIBIT 1: Brad Birkenfeld (right), Senator Charles Grassley staffer Dean Zerbe (middle), and Panama Papers Editor (left) confirming 2LT Scott Bennett's report "SHELL GAME" at Miami Offshore Alert Conference in 2015 on military cover-up of the UBS-Covington and Burling's role in Terrorist Financing and conspiracy involving Hillary Clinton (State Dept.), Eric Holder (Justice Dept.), President Obama, Saudi Arabia (Abdullah Azziz), Booz Allen Hamilton, and Members of Congress. (UNCLASSIFIED)

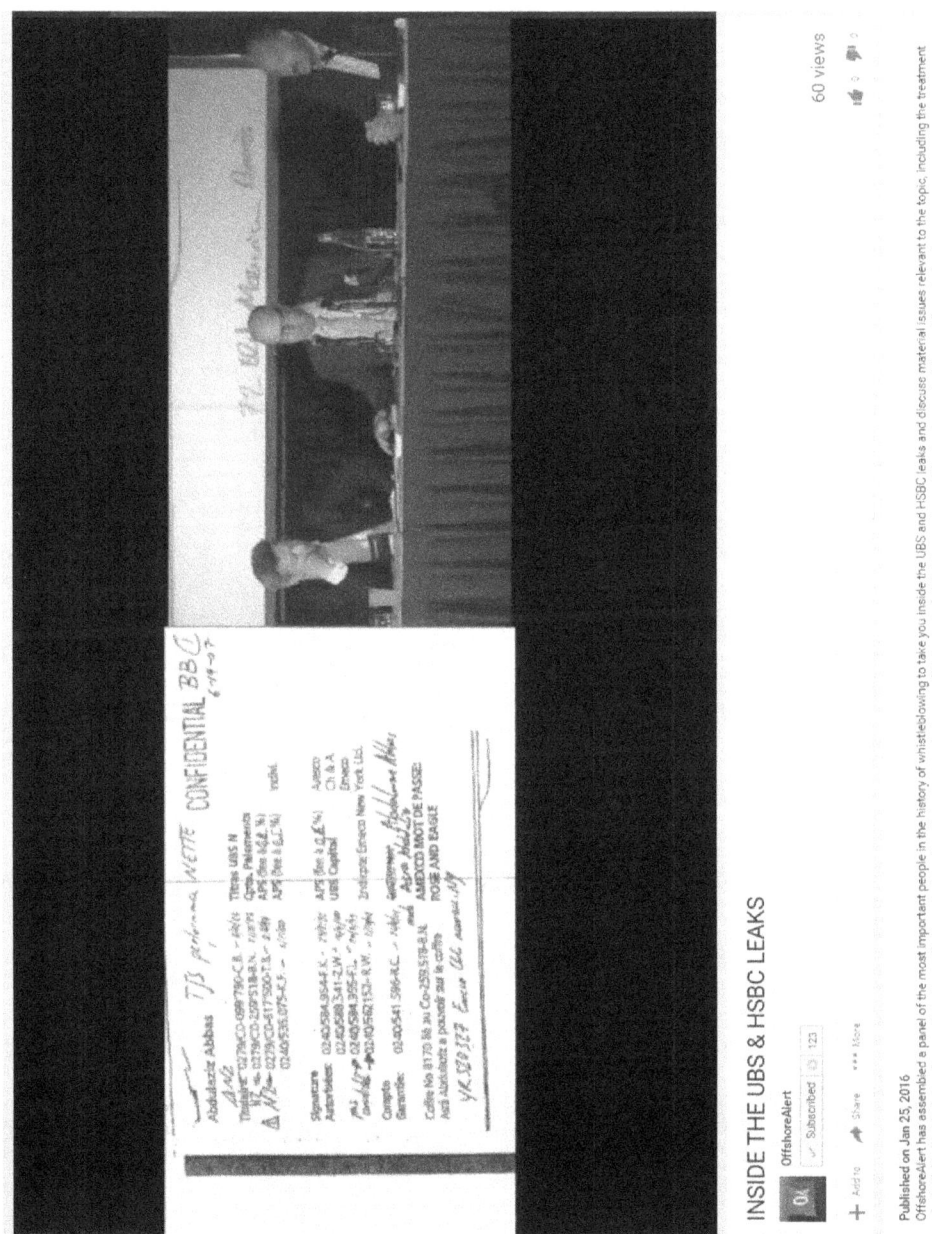

EXHIBIT 2: (UNCLASS)(HUMINT) UBS Terrorist Finance Account of Abdulaziz Abbas, given to 2LT Scott Bennett by Brad Birkenfeld. Bennett reported materials to U.S. Congress, Intelligence Agencies, and Military. Secretary of State Hillary Clinton hid report in personal emails and Clinton Foundation (Donna Chalela)arranged for payment from Saudi-UBS donations as reward. Doc Dated 6-19-07 with Birkenfeld's handwritten notes. CIA targeted Birkenfeld after, which Edward Snowden reported to Glen Greenwald in 2013 Guardian article.

Abdulaziz Abbas TJS performance NETTE CONFIDENTIAL BB (1)
6-19-07

Titulaire: 0279/C0-099'790-C.B. 6/11/04 Titres UBS N
NZ 0279/C0-259'518-B.N. 2/11/83 Cpte. Paiements
N2 0279/C0-617'500-T.B. APS (fee à 0,8 %)
0240/535.075-K.F. APS (fee à 0,5 %) Indivi.

Signature
Autorisées: 0240/584.954-F.K. APS (fee à 0,5 %) Aresco
0240/588.541-Z.W. UBS Capital Ch & A
0240/584.955-F.L. Emeco
0240/562152- R.W. 2/10/02 2nd cpte Emeco New York Ltd.

Compte
Garantie: 0240/541.596-R.C. ~~Emeco N.Y.~~ Abdulaziz Abbas
Asra Abdulaziz

Coffre No 8170 lié au Co-259.518-B.N. AMEXCO MOT DE PASSE:
Asra Abdulaziz a pouvoir sur le coffre ROSE AND EAGLE

YR320327 Emeco LLC Newark, NY

72 Bld Maurice Barrès
92 200 Neuilly-sur-Seine

NY

4647 th floor Olympic Tower
641, 5th Av. NY 10022

CONFIDENTIAL

These countries donated to Hillary Clinton's foundation:

Saudi Arabia $10 million - $25 million

Morocco $1 million - $5 million

Oman $1 million - $5 million

Qatar $1 million - $5 million

United Arab Emirates $1 million - $5 million

Kuwait $5 million - $10 million

Bahrain $50,000 - $100,000

Algeria $250,000 - $500,000

Then, Hillary Clinton's State Department approved these countries' weapons deals.

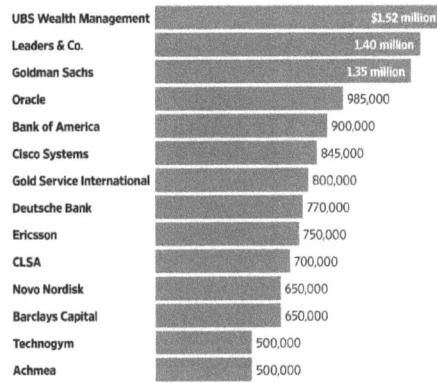

Fruitful Talk

Top corporate sources of speech income for Bill Clinton between 2001 and 2014*

UBS Wealth Management	$1.52 million
Leaders & Co.	1.40 million
Goldman Sachs	1.35 million
Oracle	985,000
Bank of America	900,000
Cisco Systems	845,000
Gold Service International	800,000
Deutsche Bank	770,000
Ericsson	750,000
CLSA	700,000
Novo Nordisk	650,000
Barclays Capital	650,000
Technogym	500,000
Achmea	500,000

Note: Event-management companies are excluded when the paying sponsor or sponsors couldn't be determined. *Excludes 2013, when there were no disclosures.
Source: Hillary Clinton disclosures

THE WALL STREET JOURNAL.

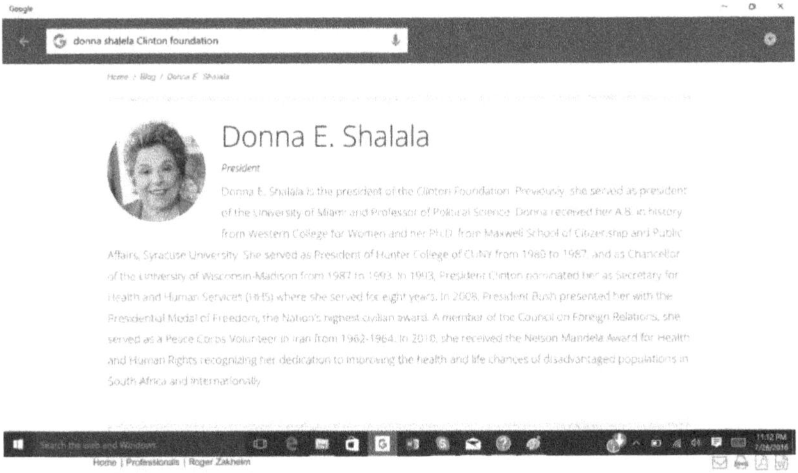

Google: donna shalela Clinton foundation

Home / Blog / Donna E. Shalala

Donna E. Shalala
President

Donna E. Shalala is the president of the Clinton Foundation. Previously, she served as president of the University of Miami and Professor of Political Science. Donna received her A.B. in history from Western College for Women and her Ph.D. from Maxwell School of Citizenship and Public Affairs, Syracuse University. She served as President of Hunter College of CUNY from 1980 to 1987, and as Chancellor of the University of Wisconsin-Madison from 1987 to 1993. In 1993, President Clinton nominated her as Secretary for Health and Human Services (HHS) where she served for eight years. In 2008, President Bush presented her with the Presidential Medal of Freedom, the Nation's highest civilian award. A member of the Council on Foreign Relations, she served as a Peace Corps Volunteer in Iran from 1962-1964. In 2010, she received the Nelson Mandela Award for Health and Human Rights recognizing her dedication to improving the health and life chances of disadvantaged populations in South Africa and internationally.

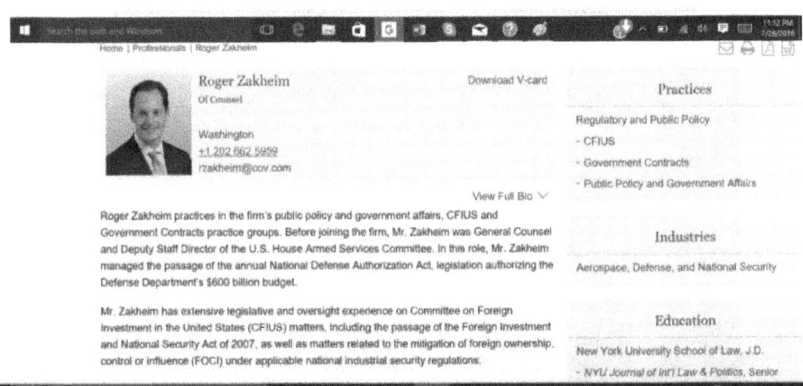

Home | Professionals | Roger Zakheim

Roger Zakheim
Of Counsel

Washington
+1 202 662 5959
rzakheim@cov.com

Download V-card

View Full Bio

Roger Zakheim practices in the firm's public policy and government affairs, CFIUS and Government Contracts practice groups. Before joining the firm, Mr. Zakheim was General Counsel and Deputy Staff Director of the U.S. House Armed Services Committee. In this role, Mr. Zakheim managed the passage of the annual National Defense Authorization Act, legislation authorizing the Defense Department's $600 billion budget.

Mr. Zakheim has extensive legislative and oversight experience on Committee on Foreign Investment in the United States (CFIUS) matters, including the passage of the Foreign Investment and National Security Act of 2007, as well as matters related to the mitigation of foreign ownership, control or influence (FOCI) under applicable national industrial security regulations.

Practices
- Regulatory and Public Policy
- CFIUS
- Government Contracts
- Public Policy and Government Affairs

Industries
Aerospace, Defense, and National Security

Education
New York University School of Law, J.D.
- NYU Journal of Int'l Law & Politics, Senior

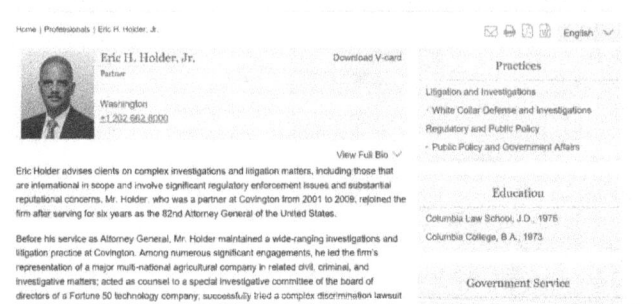

Google

covington and burling eric holder

COVINGTON

PROFESSIONALS PRACTICES AND INDUSTRIES NEWS AND INSIGHTS GLOBAL REACH

Home | Professionals | Eric H. Holder, Jr.

English

Eric H. Holder, Jr.
Partner

Download V-card

Washington
+1 202 662 8000

View Full Bio

Practices

Litigation and Investigations
- White Collar Defense and Investigations
Regulatory and Public Policy
- Public Policy and Government Affairs

Eric Holder advises clients on complex investigations and litigation matters, including those that are international in scope and involve significant regulatory enforcement issues and substantial reputational concerns. Mr. Holder, who was a partner at Covington from 2001 to 2009, rejoined the firm after serving for six years as the 82nd Attorney General of the United States.

Before his service as Attorney General, Mr. Holder maintained a wide-ranging investigations and litigation practice at Covington. Among numerous significant engagements, he led the firm's representation of a major multi-national agricultural company in related civil, criminal, and investigative matters; acted as counsel to a special investigative committee of the board of directors of a Fortune 50 technology company; successfully tried a complex discrimination lawsuit

Education

Columbia Law School, J.D., 1976
Columbia College, B.A., 1973

Government Service

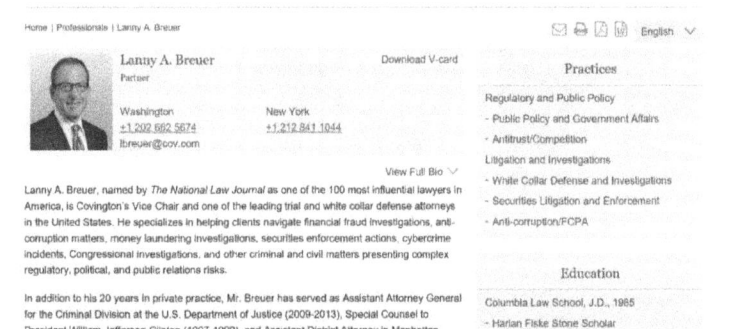

U.S. Department of Justice

Google

covington and burling lanny breuer

COVINGTON

PROFESSIONALS PRACTICES AND INDUSTRIES NEWS AND INSIGHTS GLOBAL REACH

Home | Professionals | Lanny A. Breuer

English

Lanny A. Breuer
Partner

Download V-card

Washington
+1 202 662 5674
lbreuer@cov.com

New York
+1 212 841 1044

View Full Bio

Practices

Regulatory and Public Policy
- Public Policy and Government Affairs
- Antitrust/Competition
Litigation and Investigations
- White Collar Defense and Investigations
- Securities Litigation and Enforcement
- Anti-corruption/FCPA

Lanny A. Breuer, named by *The National Law Journal* as one of the 100 most influential lawyers in America, is Covington's Vice Chair and one of the leading trial and white collar defense attorneys in the United States. He specializes in helping clients navigate financial fraud investigations, anti-corruption matters, money laundering investigations, securities enforcement actions, cybercrime incidents, Congressional investigations, and other criminal and civil matters presenting complex regulatory, political, and public relations risks.

In addition to his 20 years in private practice, Mr. Breuer has served as Assistant Attorney General for the Criminal Division at the U.S. Department of Justice (2009-2013), Special Counsel to President William Jefferson Clinton (1997-1999), and Assistant District Attorney in Manhattan

Education

Columbia Law School, J.D., 1985
- Harlan Fiske Stone Scholar

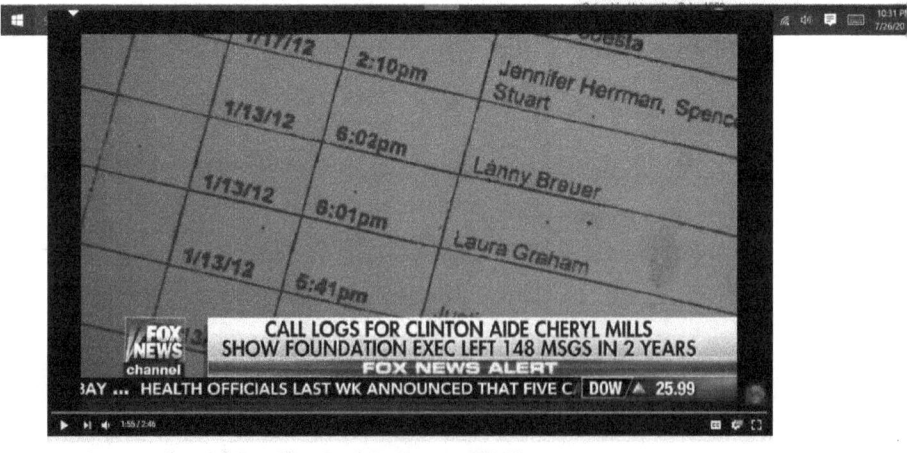

FOX NEWS channel — CALL LOGS FOR CLINTON AIDE CHERYL MILLS SHOW FOUNDATION EXEC LEFT 148 MSGS IN 2 YEARS
FOX NEWS ALERT
...AY ... HEALTH OFFICIALS LAST WK ANNOUNCED THAT FIVE C DOW ▲ 25.99

State Department Phone Calls Prove Clinton Foundation Connection! 8/23/16
World News Daily

EXHIBIT: Stuart E. Eizenstat, attorney for Covington and Burling, further establishing close ties with Clinton Foundation and Secretary of State Hillary Clinton, in order to illegally enrich clients UNION BANK OF SWITZERLAND, and Gulf Nations (Qatar and Saudi Arabia). https://www.rt.com/uk/350767-gulf-royal-funding-isis/

Dear Jake,

I have sent several detailed notes on the Iran nuclear deal, and will avoid repetition. But with the June 30 deadline fast approaching (although it may be extended), and with Hillary certain to be pressed on whether she supports the deal and will urge Congress not to disapprove it, I wanted to share a few thoughts.

1. This could well be a voting issue for many moderates in the Jewish community. The mainstream organized leadership will almost certainly oppose the deal, along with Israel and all the Republican candidates, Saudi Arabia and the Gulf States, and perhaps Egypt.

2. While we cannot be sure until there is a final agreement, it appears that many of the open issues since the preliminary accord, may be resolved in Iran's favor:

(1) Enriched uranium will stay in Iran for dilution, rather than be sent to Russia or France for reprocessing.

(2) Sanctions will not be phased-out commensurate with compliance, as the US Fact Sheet indicated after the last "agreement", but may come off more quickly. This will transfer billions to Iran and enhance its funding for terrorism and its efforts to gain hegemony in the region.

BUSTED: DoD Mole Leaked Sensitive Iran Nuke Deal Info to Clinton Camp in 2015! WIKILEAKS PODESTA

COVINGTON

BUSTED: DoD Mole Leaked Sensitive Iran Nuke Deal Info to Clinton Camp in 2015! WIKILEAKS PODESTA

PROFESSIONALS   PRACTICES AND INDUSTRIES   NEWS AND INSIGHTS   GLOBAL REACH

Home | Professionals | Stuart E. Eizenstat

English

Stuart E. Eizenstat
Senior Counsel

Download V-card

Washington
+1 202 662 5519
seizenstat@cov.com

View Full Bio

Ambassador Eizenstat heads the firm's international practice. His work at Covington focuses on resolving international trade problems and business disputes with the US and foreign governments, and international business transactions and regulations on behalf of US companies and others around the world.

During a decade and a half of public service in three US administrations, Ambassador Eizenstat has held a number of key senior positions, including chief White House domestic policy adviser to President Jimmy Carter (1977-1981), U.S. Ambassador to the European Union, Under Secretary of Commerce for International Trade, Under Secretary of State for Economic, Business and Agricultural Affairs, and Deputy Secretary of the Treasury in the Clinton Administration (1993-2001).

View More

Representative Matters

- Represented major US and foreign corporations including Boeing Company, KBR, BP, BT, Coca-Cola, and Neptune Orient Lines.
- Special advisor to the Bromide Science and Environment Forum.
- Advised the governments of Australia and Cyprus.

Pro Bono

Practices

Regulatory and Public Policy
- Public Policy and Government Affairs
- International Trade
- CFIUS

Industries

Aerospace, Defense, and National Security
Transportation
Energy

Education

Harvard Law School, J.D., 1967
University of North Carolina at Chapel Hill, A.B., 1964
- cum laude
- Phi Beta Kappa

Government Service

White House
U.S. Department of Commerce
U.S. Department of State

Exhibit: Wiki Leaks cable confirming Hillary Clinton as Secretary of State and Clinton Foundation intentionally covered up information disclosed by U.S. Army Whistleblower report substantiating Qatar and Saudi Arabia were providing terrorist financing via Swiss Banks, as disclosed by Brad Birkenfeld, Swiss Bank Whistleblower. Qatar and Saudi Arabia made donations to Clinton Foundation in exchange for the imprisonment and silencing of Birkenfeld. Clinton conspired with Attorney General Eric Holder and Lanny Breuer to do just that. Birkenfeld was imprisoned for providing this information in 2009, and later reported it to 2LT Scott Bennett, an Army Terrorist Finance Analyst at U.S. Central Command and Booz Allen Hamilton contractor. Bennett also informed Congress about this material, and was ignored.

Clinton Foundation was enriched by all parties involved: Union Bank of Switzerland (Robert Wolf, Chairman of the Americas), Covington and Burling (law firm representing UBS and employer of Eric Holder and Lanny Breuer), Saudi Arabia, and Qatar (and other Sunni Gulf countries).

https://www.wikileaks.org/podesta-emails/emailid/3774#searchresult

WikiLeaks   Leaks   News   About   Partners

Congrats!

From: john.podesta@gmail.com
To: hrod17@clintonemail.com
Date: 2014-09-27 15:15
Subject: Congrats!

>>
>> 4. Armed with proper equipment, and working with U.S. advisors, the
>> Peshmerga can attack the ISIL with a coordinated assault supported from the
>> air. This effort will come as a surprise to the ISIL, whose leaders
>> believe we will always stop with targeted bombing, and weaken them both in
>> Iraq and inside of Syria. At the same time we should return to plans to
>> provide the FSA, or some group of moderate forces, with equipment that will
>> allow them to deal with a weakened ISIL, and stepped up operations against
>> the Syrian regime. This entire effort should be done with a low profile,
>> avoiding the massive traditional military operations that are at best
>> temporary solutions. While this military/para-military operation is moving
>> forward, we need to use our diplomatic and more traditional intelligence
>> assets to bring pressure on the governments of Qatar and Saudi Arabia,
>> which are providing clandestine financial and logistic support to ISIL and
>> other radical Sunni groups in the region. This effort will be enhanced by
>> the stepped up commitment in the KRG. The Qataris and Saudis will be put
>> in a position of balancing policy between their ongoing competition to
>> dominate the Sunni world and the consequences of serious U.S. pressure. By
>> the same token, the threat of similar, realistic U.S. operations will serve
>> to assist moderate forces in Libya, Lebanon, and even Jordan, where
>> insurgents are increasingly fascinated by the ISIL success in Iraq.
>>

NOTE:
2LT SCOTT BENNETT REPORTED TO SENIOR MILITARY AND CONGRESSIONAL LEADERSHIP THAT QATAR AND SAUDI ARABIA WERE FINANCING TERRORISM THROUGH SWISS BANKS "UNION BANK OF SWITZERLAND" AND "HSBC". BENNETT CITED WHISTLEBLOWER BRAD BIRKENFELD AS SOURCE OF THIS MATERIAL, AND EXPLAINED BIRKENFELD HAD BEEN IMPRISONED BY ATTORNEY GENERAL ERIC HOLDER AND LANNY BREUER AND HILLARY CLINTON IN AN EFFORT TO CONCEAL THIS TERRORIST FINANCING AND LINKS TO COVINGTON AND BURLING, BOOZ ALLEN HAMILTON, AND CLINTON FOUNDATION DONORS.

BENNETT WAS IMPRISONED FOR THIS INFORMATION IN AN ATTEMPT TO SILENCE HIM.

EXHIBIT: Brad Birkenfeld's book *Lucifer's Banker*, corroborates the information and experience he and Scott Bennett shared in prison, and the reports they submitted to the military and U.S. Congress about the *terrorist finance* connection to Secretary of State Hillary Clinton, the Clinton Foundation, the Department of Justice (Eric Holder, Lanny Breuer, Loretta Lynch), CIA, Mossad, and Gulf Nations (Saudi Arabia, Qatar, Kuwait, Morocco, etc.).

UBS whistleblower exposes 'political prostitution' all the way up to President Obama

Birkenfeld's book about the UBS Swiss banking investigation, Lucifer's Banker, is published in October.

By Ian Allison
August 25, 2016 12:15 BST

Lucifer's Banker by Bradley Birkenfeld covers Birkenfeld's time at UBS bank. (Reuters)

UBS, the world's largest wealth manager, is facing embarrassment over fresh revelations going back to the tax investigation that led to the collapse of Swiss banking secrecy. Two significant events are looming before UBS. The first is the possibility of a public trial in France, featuring UBS whistleblower Bradley Birkenfeld, concerning historic tax evasion allegedly orchestrated by the bank. That could happen this year.

The other is the publication this October of Birkenfeld's scathing new book, Lucifer's Banker, which covers his time at UBS.

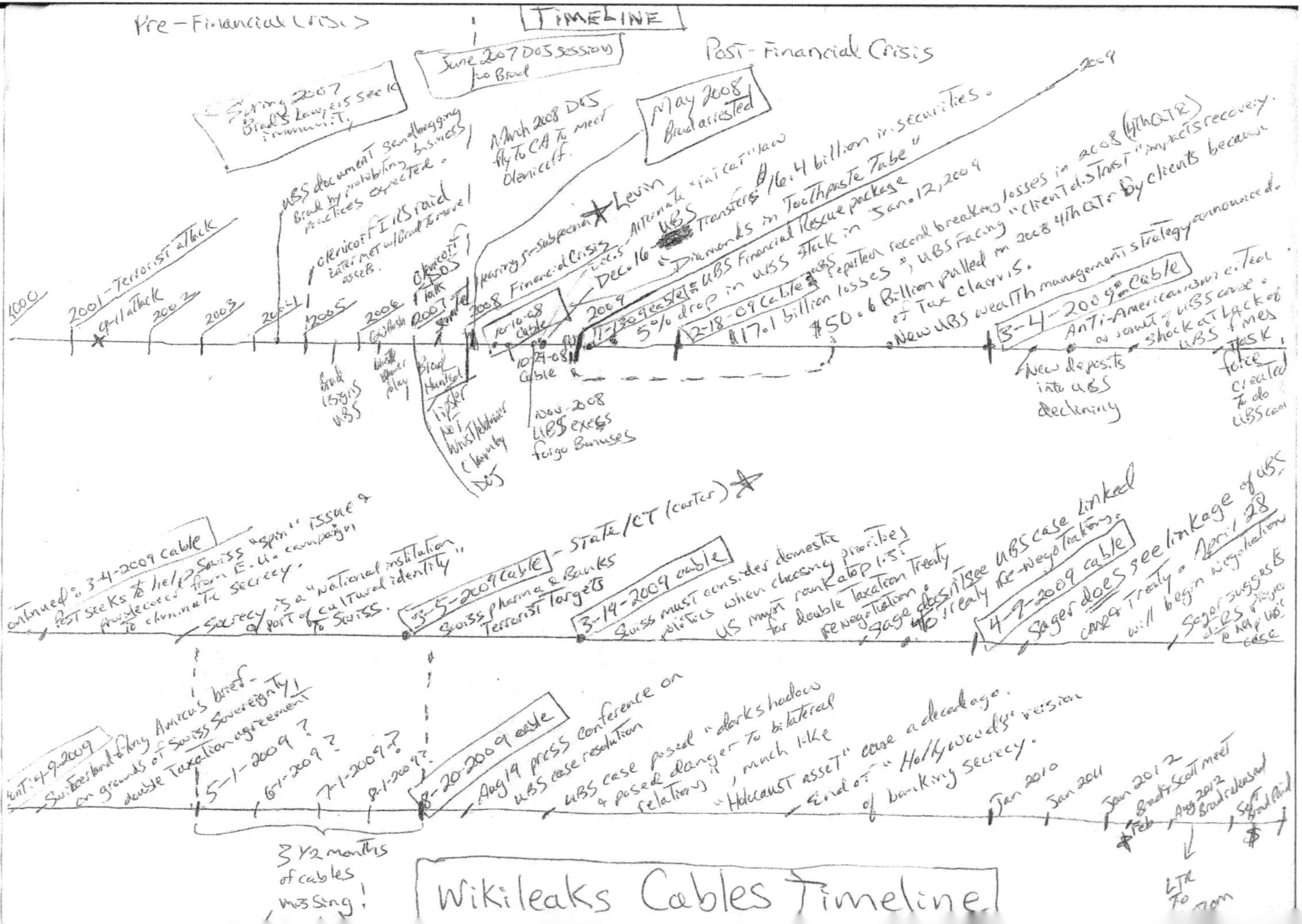
TIMELINE
Pre-Financial Crisis
Post-Financial Crisis
June 2007 DOJ session
Spring 2007
May 2008 Brad arrested
March 2008 DOJ fly to CA to meet
UBS document sandbagging
Levin
2001 - Terrorist attack
2002
2003
2004
2005
2006
2007
2008 Financial Crisis
10-10-08 Cable
10-24-08 Cable
Nov 2008 UBS execs forgo Bonuses
2009
5% drop in UBS stock in Jan. 12, 2009
2-18-09 Cable
$17.1 billion losses
$50.6 Billion pulled
New UBS wealth management strategy announced.
3-4-2009 Cable
New deposits into UBS declining
3-4-2009 cable
3-5-2009 Cable
Swiss pharma & Banks Terrorist targets
3-14-2009 cable
4-9-2009 cable
Sager does see linkage
April 28
5-1-2009 ?
6-1-2009 ?
7-1-2009 ?
8-1-2009 ?
8-20-2009 cable
Aug 19 press conference on UBS case resolution
Jan 2010
Jan 2011
Jan 2012
3 1/2 months of cables missing!
Wikileaks Cables Timeline

THE MEDIA'S SYRIA
MOSCOW 10:33 CHARLOTTE, NORTH CAROLINA: POLICE USE TEAR GAS AGAINST PROTESTERS

SAN FRANCISCO
THE DEBATE | BRITAIN SELLING SAUDI ARABIA BILLIONS OF DOLLARS WORTH OF ARMS ANNUALLY

SAN FRANCISCO
THE DEBATE | CLINTON'S CAMPAIGN SAYS TRUMP PAINTS A DARK PICTURE OF AMERICA IN DECLINE

The Debate – Trump Presidential Nomination

US insatiable appetite for war: A money making machine

Home / Programs / Economic Divide   Sun Jan 24, 2016 10:12AM

...a former marine, and we are going to be presenting the material which we discussed with him over the phone, which is "SHELL GAME". And we are going

SCOTT BENNETT
US ARMY SPECIAL OPERATIONS OFFICER

US, Saudi, Israel used 9/11 to deceive the world: Analyst

Home / US / Interviews

SAN FRANCISCO
Scott Bennett
Former US Army Psychological Warfare Officer

The September 11, 2001 attacks were part of a carefully designed plan by the United States, Israel and Saudi Arabia to destabilize the Middle East and push forward a Zionist-Wahhabi agenda, says a counter-terrorism analyst.

TRUTH UNITE: Senator Dick Black on his trip to Syria. Also Russia, 9/11, and American elections

NEXUS STRATEGIC ANALYTICS

Home | Team | Services | Projects | Clients | Videos | Blogs

"UNITING THE WORLD'S BEST PEOPLE, IDEAS, AND RESOURCES TO INFLUENCE CULTURES AND GOVERNMENTS."

ROC CONFERENCE SERIES PRESENTS
HERITAGE OF COLONIALISM IN THE ARABIAN PENINSULA
KANE HALL 120, UNIVERSITY OF WASHINGTON
4069 SPOKANE LANE, SEATTLE WA 98105
SATURDAY, MARCH 18 - 2:00 PM TO 6:00 PM
(DOORS WILL OPEN AT 1:30 PM)

KEYNOTE SPEAKERS

- GEOPOLITICAL ANALYST/COMMENTATOR/AUTHOR
- ISLAMIC SCHOLAR WASHINGTON DC
- MEMBER, SEATTLE CITY COUNCIL
- TALK RADIO HOST
- YEMENI ACTIVIST
- FORMER MP FOR AL-WEFAQ (BAHRAIN)
- TV HOST & JOURNALIST
- SON OF EXECUTED SHEIKH NIMR AL-NIMR
- FORMER US ARMY OFFICER

ROOTS OF CONFLICT

http://rootsofconflict.org

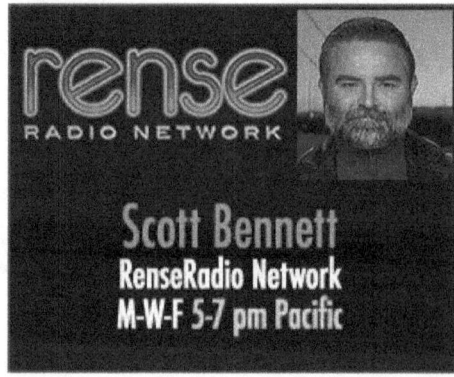

---

rense RADIO NETWORK

Scott Bennett
RenseRadio Network
M-W-F 5-7 pm Pacific

SCOTT BENNETT
23 RAILROAD AVENUE, #23
DANVILLE, CA 94526

December 19, 2017

<u>MEMORANDUM</u>

TO: Donald J. Trump, President of the United States of America
     The White House
     c/o Sara Huckabee-Sanders, Press Office
     1600 Pennsylvania Avenue NW
     Washington, DC 20500

FR: Scott Bennett, Ph.D. (abd)
     former U.S. Army Officer; Contractor, State Department Coordinator for Counterterrorism; Terrorist Finance Analyst, Joint Intelligence Operations Center (JIOC), U.S. Central Command

RE: LEGAL NOTICE OF EVIDENCE OF TREASON AND GOVERNMENT CORRUPTION.
     OFFICIAL REQUEST FOR PRESIDENTIAL AND CONGRESSIONAL ACTION.

Dear President Trump:

BE ADVISED, you are hereby <u>served legal notice</u> that this memorandum and attached exhibits will provide you and your legal team with the evidence, witnesses, documents, and timeline needed to understand, investigate, and prosecute the current government corruption cases. This memorandum is essentially the "center of the web" that connects the current FBI-DOJ-Mueller abuses from 2008 to the present, and is necessary for exposing and synthesizing additional crimes into the present investigations of Rod Rosenstein, Robert Mueller, FBI DepuDirector Andrew McCabe and his wife Jill McCabe, Peter Strzok (FBI agent investigating Clinton emails) and his co-conspirator adulteress Lisa Page; **Jeannie** Rhee, former Clinton Foundation attorney; and others. These investigations form a larger *Racketeering* (RICO) case and include:

- unlawful and fraudulent FISA warrant and surveillance powers used for wiretapping for the purpose of concealing <u>terrorist financing</u> through the Clinton Foundation and protecting "too big to fail" banks

such as Union Bank of Switzerland and its law firm Covington and Burling (Note: anyone, including DOJ Inspector General Michael E. Horowitz, with UBS or Covington and Burling connections should be not only recused and denied access to this report's materials, but should be included in the investigation as participants or witnesses to the UBS-Covington and Burling various corruptions in this matter);
- cover-up of State Department "pay-to-play" abuses; and
- falsification of Russian collusion as FBI distraction operation.

This memorandum should be used by the White House and Congress to investigate former President Obama, Hillary Clinton, James Comey, and Robert Mueller's knowledge of and role in the crimes listed herein, using the Office of Inspector General to generate investigations and evidence to be coordinated with DOJ-military prosecutions. The Office of the Inspector General (OIG) in the U.S. Department of Justice (DOJ) is a statutorily created independent entity whose mission is to detect and deter waste, fraud, abuse, and misconduct in DOJ programs and personnel, and to promote economy and efficiency in those programs. The OIG investigates alleged violations of criminal and civil laws by DOJ employees and also audits and inspects DOJ programs.

LEGAL NOTICE: CONSPIRACY TO COMMIT TREASON, ABUSE OF AUTHORITY AND PUBLIC TRUST, DEPRIVATION OF RIGHTS, TERRORIST FINANCING, OBSTRUCTION OF JUSTICE and REDRESS OF GRIEVANCES

(UNCLASSIFIED) BE ADVISED, Pursuant to 18 U.S. Code § 4, and 28 U.S. Code § 1361, you are hereby served notice of violations of 18 U.S. Code § 2339A - *Providing material support to terrorists.* See enclosed "whistleblower" report ("*SHELL GAME*" by 2LT Scott Bennett, U.S. Army, Sept. 25, 2012. Exhibit 1— www.shellgamewhistleblower.com). All rights reserved.

BE ADVISED, you are hereby served notice that pursuant to 18 U.S. Code § 2339A, *whoever provides material support or resources or conceals or disguises the nature, location, source, or ownership of material support or resources, knowing or intending that they are to be used in preparation for, or in carrying out, a violation of section 32, 37, 81, 175, 229, 351, 831, 842(m) or (n), 844(f) or (i), 930(c), 956, 1091, 1114, 1116, 1203, 1361, 1362, 1363, 1366, 1751, 1992, 2155, 2156, 2280, 2281, 2332, 2332a, 2332b, 2332f, 2340A, or 2442 of this title, section 236 of the Atomic Energy Act of 1954 (42 U.S.C. 2284), section 46502 or 60123(b) of title 49, or any offense listed in section 2332b(g)(5)(B) (except for sections 2339A and 2339B) or in preparation for, or*

SHELL GAME: TERRORIST FINANCING REPORT—www.shellgamewhistleblower.com

in carrying out, the concealment of an escape from the commission of any such violation, or attempts or conspires to do such an act, shall be fined under this title, imprisoned not more than 15 years, or both, and, if the death of any person results, shall be imprisoned for any term of years or for life.

BE ADVISED, you are hereby serviced notice that, in fact, *"the death of a person* (s) has resulted" from this terrorist financing violation, and therefore satisfies the legal requirement for *"imprisonment for any term of years or for life"* in this instant matter.

BE ADVISED, you are hereby served notice that through this memorandum we are respectfully requesting a debriefing with the President to 1) more fully and completely inform him and his legal team about these national security violations and crimes; 2) be issued a subpoena to testify (with immunity) and provide additional evidence to the DOJ-FBI, Inspector General, Military and Congressional investigations.

LEGAL NOTICE: FAILURE TO REPLY

BE ADVISED, you are hereby served notice that this report contains significant global national security implications, and that although not anticipated, due to the gravity of the current constitutional crisis, failure by your office to acknowledge or respond to this email/letter/ notice and report, or any attempt by *anyone* to "bury" or conceal or cause harm to this report or its author and agents, will be interpreted and prosecuted (civilly and criminally) to the fullest extent of American and international law; and any failure or insufficient acknowledgement or response to this material, will be interpreted both as a dereliction of duty and as follows:

1) A flagrantly treasonous and conspiratorial attempt to *"conceal the nature, location, source, and ownership of material support and resources"* to terrorist individuals, networks, and operations, and as such an intentional violation of national and global security policies and laws; and
2) a willful and reckless disregard and violation of your government oath to *"support and defend the Constitution"*; and
3) an intentional act of misprision of a felony and misprision of treason against the United States of America; and
4) a violation of United Nations policies and statutes relating to terrorist financing; and
5) a conspiracy to commit racketeering, fraud, abuse of government authority, and other crimes against the constitution and the sovereign states.

SHELL GAME: TERRORIST FINANCING REPORT—www.shellgamewhistleblower.com

BE ADVISED, you are hereby <u>served notice</u> that failure by your office to <u>respond</u> to this notice and report <u>will</u> be interpreted and prosecuted as a violation of 18 U.S. Code § 2382 - *Misprision of treason*, which reads:

> *"Whoever, owing allegiance to the United States and having knowledge of the commission of any treason against them, conceals and does not, as soon as may be, disclose and make known the same to the President or to some judge of the United States, or to the governor or to some judge or justice of a particular State, is guilty of misprision of treason and shall be fined under this title or imprisoned not more than seven years, or both."*

(June 25, 1948, ch. 645, 62 Stat. 807; Pub. L. 103–322, title XXXIII, § 330016(1)(H), Sept. 13, 1994, 108 Stat. 2147.)

BE ADVISED, you are hereby <u>served notice</u> that this formal notification of crimes and provision of evidence, witnesses, and testimony confirming these crimes, and request for subpoena is hereby submitted FOR THE RECORD to the White House through the Congressional office of Representative Mark DeSaulnier (D-CA), and was originally recorded as an affidavit in his office on August 1, 2016. This material and witness identity and security clearance can also be confirmed by Senator Richard Black (R-VA), and other members of Congress and Department of Defense and State Department officials upon request.

BE ADVISED, you are hereby <u>served notice</u> that your sworn Constitutional OATH as an employee, agent, and representative of the United States government is hereby <u>accepted FOR THE RECORD</u>, and as such you are henceforth notified of an urgent national security matter and crimes against the U.S. Constitution which requires your immediate official action to resolve.

<u>LEGAL NOTICE:</u>   WHITE HOUSE LEGAL DEPARTMENT
REQUEST FOR ACTION

BE ADVISED, **you are hereby <u>served notice</u> that** pursuant to our conversation with the White House Press Office by telephone, we are following its explicit instruction to submit this *"Request for Action"* to President Trump's personal and White House <u>legal team</u>, excluding anyone with connections to the firm Covington and Burling. Recipients of this intelligence report should include **Donald F. McGahn, II**, Ty Cobb and Jay Sekulow, Esquires. They are formally requested to advise and inform the White House of an immediate national security threat to the United States. As a solution to this threat, we respectfully request the President immediately take the following actions:

SHELL GAME: TERRORIST FINANCING REPORT—www.shellgamewhistleblower.com

1. Consider this memorandum and all information communicated herein as privileged legal material concerning a national security matter to be shared only with President Trump and his legal team. Be advised, this material involves President Trump's personal attorney Michael Cohen, former National Security Advisor Michael Flynn and Flynn's attorneys at the law firm *Covington and Burling*; as well as former Secretary of State Hillary Clinton, personnel at the Clinton Foundation, and former and current officials at the State Department, the Central Intelligence Agency, the Federal Bureau of Investigation (FBI), and the Department of Justice (DOJ).

2. **Share this memorandum** simultaneously with Attorney General Jeff Sessions and the Inspector General at the Department of Justice and the Pentagon, as well as all Congressional Committees and Inspector Generals investigating the FBI-DOJ personnel involved in the Robert Mueller investigation (McCabe, Rosenstein, Strzok, Rhee, etc.), the Clinton Foundation, and alleged Russian involvement in the 2016 U.S. Presidential election.

3. Immediately schedule a meeting between us and the President's legal team in order to provide the President with additional materials relating to these and additional activities damaging the national security of the United States. The validity and authenticity of this material will be confirmed by Virginia State Senator Richard Black, who is the key witness in the bribery-corruption case involving VA Governor Terry McAuliffe, FBI Director Andrew McCabe and his wife VA State Senate candidate Jill McCabe.

BE ADVISED, you are hereby <u>served notice</u>, that confirmations of this memorandum can be obtained from Rep. Mark DeSaulnier (D-CA), Rep. Ron Johnson, Rep. Devin Nunes, Rep. Bob Goodlatte, the House Judiciary Committee, Senator Charles Grassly, and other members of Congress who we have communicated with. This material was memorialized in a video affidavit at Congressman Mark DeSaulnier's office, whom we met in person, debriefed, and requested this material be immediately shared with the White House and the Inspector General.   This affidavit given to Congressman Mark DeSaulnier may be reviewed by the President's legal team at this link: <u>https://youtu.be/U6GfrivgqsU</u>

SHELL GAME: TERRORIST FINANCING REPORT—www.shellgamewhistleblower.com

BE ADVISED, you are hereby <u>served notice</u> that this material was previously shared with members of Congress, including Senator Bill Nelson (D-Florida), Rep. Jackie Speier (House Intelligence Committee; D-CA), and Senator Diane Feinstein (former Senate Intelligence Committee Chair; D-CA); and the video of this can be reviewed upon your request (Note: Rep. Jackie Speier's opposition to this memorandum's materials is because she is directly implicated in it).

BE ADVISED, **you are hereby <u>served notice</u> that in a response to this material, and in an act of blatant treason against the United States, Senator** Bill Nelson wrote an intentionally *"fraudulent and misleading"* letter to Chairwoman of the Senate Intelligence Committee Diane Feinstein attempting to conspire with her to <u>coerce</u> the Senate Intelligence Committee to cover-up this terrorist financing report. See Exhibit 1. This letter by Senator Nelson should be submitted by the White House to the Congressional investigators as evidence of *"concealing or disguising the nature, location, source, or ownership of material support or resources, knowing or intending that they are to be used in preparation for, or in carrying out, a violation of 18 USC § 2339A."* See Exhibit 1. Also available here:
https://books.google.com/books?id=_67VCQAAQBAJ&pg=PR13&lpg=PR13&dq=senator+bill+nelson+scott+bennett&source=bl&ots=VSfq0eXp_B&sig=Nhq1jhgusI7pIsNIat_2mZBc2bs&hl=en&sa=X&ved=0ahUKEwjXmNao_a3YAhUIiFQKHZpxDvcQ6AEIXTAI#v=onepage&q&f=false

A more detailed version of the affidavit may be reviewed at:
https://youtu.be/8MZNbcS3A-g

BE ADVISED, you are hereby <u>served notice</u> that we hereby request a meeting with the President, and the President's legal team, in order to debrief the President about this essential legal evidence (documents, videos, witness lists) for the ongoing investigation into the FBI-Mueller-Comey-Clinton Foundation activities; and provide the President with additional relevant information. **This material is derived from a military report which provided conclusive evidence showing Obama Administration officials were intentionally and treasonously enabling the financing of Hezbollah, ISIS, and other Middle East terrorist groups using Swiss banks (Union Bank of Switzerland, Lichtenstein, Credit Suisse, and HSBC). See** *SHELL GAME.*

BE ADVISED, you are hereby <u>served notice</u> that we are hereby requesting that our debriefing of the President and his legal team be conducted

SHELL GAME: TERRORIST FINANCING REPORT—www.shellgamewhistleblower.com

immediately in order to provide the President with compelling evidence which will justify his appointment of a Special Counsel and Inspector General "Tzar" to investigate and prosecute this matter further; as well as expose all relevant emails and witnesses relating to Former President Obama, Secretary of State Hillary Clinton, the Clinton Foundation, and Department of Justice-FBI collusion in these matters.

BE ADVISED, you are hereby served notice that we also request you share this letter and enclosed materials with appropriate Inspector General Offices and Congressional Committees, and immediately provide us with a subpoena to testify about this matter.

LEGAL NOTICE: EXECUTIVE ORDER APPLICATION

BE ADVISED, you are hereby served notice that this memorandum and debriefing is required to execute the President's *Executive Order* issued on December 21, 2017: *Executive Order Blocking the Property of Persons Involved in Serious Human Rights Abuse or Corruption.* Specifically, these sections of the Order apply:

> ".... *corruption undermine the values that form an essential foundation of stable, secure, and functioning societies; have devastating impacts on individuals; weaken democratic institutions; degrade the rule of law; perpetuate violent conflicts; facilitate the activities of dangerous persons; (B) to be a current or former government official, or a person acting for or on behalf of such an official, who is responsible for or complicit in, or has directly or indirectly engaged in:*
>
> *(1) corruption, including the misappropriation of state assets, the expropriation of private assets for personal gain, corruption related to government contracts or the extraction of natural resources, or bribery; or*
>
> *(2) the transfer or the facilitation of the transfer of the proceeds of corruption;*
>
> *(C) to be or have been a leader or official of:*
>
> *(1) an entity, including any government entity, that has engaged in, or whose members have engaged in, any of the activities described in subsections (ii)(A), (ii)(B)(1), or (ii)(B)(2) of this section relating to the leader's or official's tenure;...."*

LEGAL NOTICE: EVIDENCE FOR CURRENT INVESTIGATIONS

SHELL GAME: TERRORIST FINANCING REPORT—www.shellgamewhistleblower.com

BE ADVISED, you are hereby <u>served notice</u> that this report is submitted to the White House as part of a previous 2012 military whistleblowing report titled *"SHELL GAME"*, and should be immediately used as <u>evidence</u> in the following criminal investigations:

1) State Department approval of sale of Uranium One after "bribery" from Russian lobbying involving Secretary of State Hillary Clinton-DOJ Attorney General Eric Holder-Lanny Breuer-Loretta Lynch.
2) Union Bank of Switzerland (UBS) Department of Justice and State Department agreement, settlement, and confiscation of 19,000 private UBS bank accounts, in return for the imprisonment of UBS whistleblower Bradley Birkenfeld, and illegal payments to the Clinton Foundation from UBS, Covington and Burling (law firm) and its clients (Saudi Arabia, Qatar, United Arab Emirates, and others).
3) Department of Justice Loretta Lynch issuance of a fraudulent 2% fine to Union Bank of Switzerland in exchange for Clinton Foundation donations from Union Bank of Switzerland. *"Too Big to Jail"* was political language developed in 2012 by Attorney General Eric Holder to conceal *SHELL GAME* revelations, and protect the financial interests of Holder and Breuer's former employer, Covington and Burling law firm.
4) Investigations into U.S.-Russian activities relating to U.S. 2016 Presidential Election;
5) Democrat National Committee computer file thefts; Murder of Democratic National Committee technology staffer Seth Rich;
6) Covington and Burling, the law firm representing Union Bank of Switzerland, and Gulf Countries financing terrorism, coordinated communication with Hillary Clinton through attorney Stuart Eisenstadt and Jeannie Rhee (now on Mueller team).

BE ADVISED, you are hereby <u>served notice</u> that these materials shall be legally viewed and protected as <u>whistleblower</u> documents, and as such must be shared by the White House with the House-Senate Judiciary, Oversight, Intelligence, and Armed Services Committees as they provide corroborating material evidence of criminal acts in the following Congressional investigations:

1. FBI director Andrew McCabe actively colluded with Virginia Governor Terry McAuliffe to unlawfully direct FBI resources and personnel to entrap Senator Dick Black (VA-State Senate) in a Syrian terrorist-prisoner release operation, for the purpose of generating extortionist

political material to be used by Andrew McCabe's wife, Jill McCabe, in her political campaign against Senator Dick Black. This may constitute fraud, bribery, extortion, racketeering, and misuse of campaign funds and other abuses of government resources and authority. Senator Black will confirm these events. The link to this interview with Senator Black can be reviewed here: https://youtu.be/x4SIXHHB9pY

2. Secretary of State Hillary Clinton and Clinton Foundation President Donna Shalala collusion with former Attorney General Eric Holder, former Assistant Attorney General Lanny Breuer, former Attorney General Loretta Lynch, and Robert Mueller team investigator **Jeannie Rhee** in <u>concealing 19,000 secret Swiss bank accounts used in terrorist financing and money laundering</u>; secret illegal transfer by Secretary of State Hillary Clinton of Chinese *Uighur* terrorists from Guantanamo Bay to Switzerland; and a fraudulent 2% fine imposed against a Swiss Bank in exchange for these 19,000 secret bank accounts.

3. The illegal arrest, prosecution, and imprisonment of the American Swiss Bank whistleblower, Brad Birkenfeld (witness) who originally brought these 19,000 accounts to the Department of Justice, after being targeted through a false D.U.I. sting operation involving CIA analyst Edward Snowden and the CIA (Ben Rhodes, John Brennan) in Switzerland. http://www.breitbart.com/big-government/2017/12/06/special-counsel-member-jeannie-rhee-once-represented-obama-aide-ben-rhodes/

4. Official State Department cables and documents written during Secretary Hillary Clinton's tenure at the State Department confirming this collusion and "pay to play" involving terrorist financing, *Covington and Burling* law firm, and the DOJ-FBI implicating Robert Mueller, James Comey, and others involved in this collusion.

5. Department of Justice official Bruce Ohr working with former Attorney General Eric Holder and former Assistant Attorney General Lanny Breuer and Former Attorney General Loretta Lynch distributed material throughout the Bureau of Prisons to provoke inmate hostility against the government. This material was titled "<u>*DEEP BLACK by David Guyatt*</u>", and disclosed CIA-Mossad drug trafficking operations and sought to recruit people from the inmate community. A motion was

SHELL GAME: TERRORIST FINANCING REPORT—www.shellgamewhistleblower.com

filed with Judge Virginia-Hernandez Covington exposing this material and demanding Court investigation *Sua Sponte*. **Attorney General Jeff Sessions also received this report and will confirm it.** See exhibit 2.

6. General Michael Flynn's attorneys at the law firm Covington and Burling <u>deceived General Michael Flynn regarding Covington's direct participation and relationship with Union Bank of Switzerland, the Clinton Foundation, and the Clinton State Department</u> in these matters. Consequently, Covington and Burling should be disqualified from representing Mr. Flynn. An *Amicus* brief (friend of the court) is being submitted to the court hearing the Flynn Plea agreement as "*Newly Discovered Evidence Indicating Ineffective Assistance of Counsel, Prosecutorial Misconduct, and Fraud on The Court*". Since this is a "*Case of First Impressions*", this legal motion establishing newly discovered evidence and fraud on the court <u>mandates</u> the <u>rejection</u> of Michael Flynn's plea agreement and demands in independent investigation or special counsel be assigned in this matter by the Inspector General, Congress, and the White House.

BE ADVISED, you are hereby <u>served notice</u> that in order to satisfactorily investigate and correct the issues in this report, we request the President to execute his Executive authority by creating a White House level <u>Inspector General (IG)</u> "*Tsar*" or Senior Special Assistant position to communicate directly to the President, manage, investigate, and provide oversight to all other Inspector General Offices at the various intelligence community agencies; and initiate a government-wide comprehensive inter-agency Inspector General special investigation into this matter in order to share findings with the DOJ-FBI and Congressional investigations (Committees on Intelligence, Armed Services, Government Oversight and Reform, and Judiciary). This White House level Inspector General and inter-agency IG coordination should be done in secrecy and beyond the awareness of the Director of National Intelligence (DNI), who is in fact a key player in wrongdoing and must be investigated by the IG.

<u>LEGAL NOTICE:</u> GOVERNMENT OFFICIALS IMPLICATED

BE ADVISED, you are hereby <u>served notice</u> that this memorandum contains names of present and former government officials, military and intelligence agency personnel, and analyzes their various illegal—and potentially treasonous—activities which must be investigated by authorities from the Congress, the White House, the Department of Defense Inspector General, the

SHELL GAME: TERRORIST FINANCING REPORT—www.shellgamewhistleblower.com

State Department Inspector General, and the Department of Justice Inspector General, as well as certain international law enforcement agencies.

BE ADVISED, you are hereby <u>served notice</u> that government agencies and persons directly implicated in criminal activities in this report include:

- Former President Barack Hussein Obama
- State Department: Secretary of State Hillary Clinton; and State Department Coordinator for Counterterrorism.
- Central Intelligence Agency, Director John Brennan
- Department of Treasury (terrorist finance): Former Secretary of Treasury Tim Geithner
- U.S. Central Command, Terrorist Financing, MacDill Air Force Base
- Department of Justice: Former Attorney General Eric Holder, Assistant Attorney General Lanny Breuer, Attorney General Loretta Lynch.
- Former Clinton Foundation attorney and member of Robert Mueller investigation team, Jeannie Rhee
- Clinton Foundation President Donna Shalala, and her nephew David Chalela
- Leon Panetta, former SECDEF and Booz-Allen-Hamilton executive
- James Clapper, former Director of National Intelligence and Booz-Allen-Hamilton executive
- Others not listed here for sake of space

BE ADVISED, you are hereby <u>served notice</u> that on August 6, 2015 and again on July 27, 2016, Michael Cohen, attorney to President Trump, received phone and email communications detailing the terrorist financing crimes and corruption reported in the military report *SHELL GAME;* and its role in Libya and Syria, confirmed by Michael Flynn, former national security advisor, and James and Joanne Moriarty (Americans reporting on intelligence about Libyan tribes).

Due to the explosive nature of the revelations in the *SHELL GAME* report, these communications were unlawfully surveilled by Obama administration officials at the FBI-CIA-NSA. Soon after, Obama administration officials fabricated <u>false Russian collusion</u> stories as propaganda countermeasures (strategic communications) to these *SHELL GAME* revelations involving the Obama-Clinton State Department and CIA.

It is critical to legally and politically <u>establish this military terrorist-finance intelligence connection to the unlawful Trump surveillance</u> activity by pro-

SHELL GAME: TERRORIST FINANCING REPORT—www.shellgamewhistleblower.com

Clinton DOJ-FBI personnel (McCabe, Rosenstein, Strzok, Comey, Mueller). A summary of this report appears below.

LEGAL NOTICE: NATIONAL SECURITY APPLICATIONS

(UNCLASSIFIED) BE ADVISED, you are hereby served notice that this information, testimony, and documentation was originally collected by a U.S. Army Officer from HUMINT (human intelligence) and submitted to the Pentagon and Congress in a report entitled *"SHELL GAME"* on September 25, 2012. This Army Officer, Scott Bennett, held a Top Secret/Sensitive Compartmentalized Information (TS/SCI) security clearance, and worked at U.S. Central Command's Joint Interagency Operations Center with multiple U.S. and foreign military and government agencies. Scott Bennett also worked at U.S. Special Operations Command as the Liaison Officer at the State Department Coordinator for Counterterrorism Office. Bennett specialized in Terrorist Financing and Psychological Warfare, and prior to serving in the Army, worked for the Bush Administration from 2003-2008, and then for Booz-Allen-Hamilton as a defense contractor.

SHELL GAME: A MILITARY WHISTLEBLOWING REPORT

ABSTRACT

BE ADVISED, you are hereby served notice that this military report, written by 2LT U.S. Army Scott Bennett and Brad Birkenfeld, entitled *"SHELL GAME"*, described how Hillary Clinton, Eric Holder, Lanny Breuer, Loretta Lynch, did enter into a *shell game* type conspiracy with Union Bank of Switzerland (UBS) and Robert Wolf, Chairman of the Americas and other UBS executives to launder terrorist financing money (Abdullah Azziz), commodities, assets, and enable the continuation of "smuggling diamonds in the toothpaste" (Igor Olenicoff), as described in State Department/CT cables. See Exhibit 3 and Wikileaks cables. Hillary Clinton sought to confiscate these "diamonds in toothpaste" and use them for Clinton Foundation activities, in violation of law. These Swiss Bank foundations and wealth management accounts were under the control of an American Swiss Banker were being used by Saudi Arabia, Qatar, Morocco, Kuwait, Bahrain, United Arab Emirates to finance terrorist activities in U.S. Central Command's area of operations.

As a military officer and defense contractor, Bennett was assigned to "Terrorist Threat Financing" and tasked with discovering terrorist financing networks (domestic and foreign), instruments, and bank accounts being used

SHELL GAME: TERRORIST FINANCING REPORT—www.shellgamewhistleblower.com

to fund Islamic terrorists. This military terrorist financing report he wrote may be summarized as follows:

Bennett was among the U.S. Central Command analysts instructed to "change" the material in his reports to cover-up the terrorist financing implications linked to the Clinton Foundation. Out of loyalty to his military officer oath to the constitution, Bennett refused, and was soon after threatened, fired, charged falsely, and then eventually imprisoned by the Obama-Holder-Breuer-Lynch Justice Department when he continued filing his reports. See *"Initial Findings of the U.S. House of Representatives Joint Task Force on U.S. Central Command Intelligence Analysis August 10, 2016"*

Exhibit 4:
https://intelligence.house.gov/uploadedfiles/house_jtf_on_centcom_intelligence_initial_report.pdf

EXECUTIVE SUMMARY:

BE ADVISED, you are hereby <u>served notice</u> that in 2012, a U.S. Army Psychological Warfare officer and State Department counterterrorism contractor with a Top Secret/SCI security clearance tasked with counter-terrorist financing operations, filed *official* reports to senior military leaders and members of Congress disclosing how 19,000 Swiss Bank accounts used in terrorist financing and offshore tax havens were being illegally manipulated and seized by senior officials at the State Department, Justice Department, Central Intelligence Agency, Covington and Burling law firm, Clinton Foundation, U.S. Central Command, and Booz-Allen-Hamilton. Many of these bank accounts were used in terrorist financing networks and operations and had been identified by U.S. Central Command's Terrorist Finance team at MacDill Air Force Base in Tampa, Florida.

BE ADVISED, you are hereby <u>served notice</u> that the people involved with this illegal seizure of bank accounts include: Secretary of State Hillary Clinton, Attorney General Eric Holder, Assistant Attorney General Lanny Breuer, Attorney General Loretta Lynch, and other members of the Obama Administration. Additionally, Union Bank of Switzerland, their law firm <u>Covington and Burling, and client states Saudi Arabia-Qatar were conspirators in this matter.</u>

BE ADVISED, you are hereby <u>served notice</u> that the specific criminal acts were as follows: Secretary of State Hillary Clinton *conspired* with Attorney General Eric Holder, Assistant Attorney General Lanny Breuer, Loretta Lynch, CIA Director John Brennan, and other parties, to imprison the Swiss

SHELL GAME: TERRORIST FINANCING REPORT—www.shellgamewhistleblower.com

Bank whistleblower (Brad Birkenfeld) who had provided this information to the Department of Justice. In exchange for this "pay to play" corruption and civil rights violations against Birkenfeld, financial donations were made to the Clinton Foundation; and the State Department then transferred terrorists out of Guantanamo Bay to Switzerland. Birkenfeld's lawyers Jesselyn Radack (Edward Snowden's lawyer) and Dean Zerbe (Senator Chuck Grassley's staffer) have confirmed this.

BE ADVISED, you are hereby <u>served notice</u> that the 2016 "secret meeting on the airport tarmac" between Former Attorney General Loretta Lynch and former President Bill Clinton was, in reality, a meeting to discuss hiding the report "*SHELL GAME*" and its evidence of these UBS terrorist financing and donations to the Clinton Foundation, pay-to-play agreements, and government corruption.

BE ADVISED, you are hereby <u>served notice</u> that Bennett's 2012 *SHELL GAME* report, and subsequent follow-ups, described how these actions were seriously damaging U.S. National Security and military personnel, and were violating the U.S. Constitution and various laws relating to terrorism, terrorist financing, government oversight, intelligence materials, and numerous criminal statutes. Bennett's report <u>clearly and irrefutably</u> confirms how grossly and treasonously the U.S. military was misinformed by the Obama Administration about these terrorist Swiss bank accounts, and as a result thousands of U.S. military personnel have been killed, wounded, and traumatized irreparably.

BE ADVISED, you are hereby <u>served notice</u> that Bennett's report <u>will be confirmed</u> by Secretary of Defense James Mattis, who received the *SHELL GAME* report in August 2012 when he was Commander of U.S. Central Command; and will also be confirmed by former National Security Advisor General Michael Flynn, when he was Director of Defense Intelligence Agency. James Mattis and Michael Flynn were soon after fired from their respective commands due to their response and investigation of Bennett's report *SHELL GAME*. Note: Edward Snowden recognized Bennett from their service together at Booz-Allen-Hamilton (Hawaii and Washington DC), and Brad Birkenfeld from Switzerland, and within 3 months of Bennett's revelations Edward <u>Snowden</u> left the United States himself. Glenn Greenwald confirmed this in his original reports.

In a *Kafkaesque* drama, and in violation of the U.S. Constitution and military law, Florida Judge Virginia Hernandez-<u>Covington</u>—linked to the law firm Covington and Burling—conspired to falsely charge and imprison 2LT Scott Bennett for writing his reports by creating false charges against him, in

SHELL GAME: TERRORIST FINANCING REPORT—www.shellgamewhistleblower.com

coordination with CIA contractor G4S Wackenhut Solutions by having a Wakenhut security officer at Fort Myer Virginia falsely state on an AFFIDAVIT that 2LT Scott Bennett had "dressed-up as a police man" on base. This statement was later mysteriously "lost". NOTE: G4S finances BMGF and then BMGF Donates to The Clinton Foundation. G4S EMPLOYED ORLANDO NIGHTCLUB SHOOTER which in reality was a black false-flag operation. https://en.wikipedia.org/wiki/G4S_Secure_Solutions G4S was previously known as Wackenhutt corporation tied to Orlando Shooter, Omar Mateen. On June 12, 2016).

Additional conspiracy to falsely charge Bennett was ordered by officials at the Clinton Foundation, specifically President Donna Shalela, and her nephew David Chalela—who was secretly assigned to represent Bennett (Note: Other whistleblowers and conservatives were similarly persecuted, i.e. Dinesh DeSousa). See: https://www.salon.com/2013/06/10/expert_whistleblowers_tend_to_be_conservative/

David Chalela conspired with Clinton Foundation President and his aunt Donna Shalala, to intentionally "fail" to produce any defense of Bennett and conceal his reports. A bar complaint and an INEFFECTIVE ASSISTANCE OF COUNSEL §2255 motion has been filed and is awaiting disposition, with Chalela's disbarment and criminal prosecution requested. A military board of review is also being conducted.

Additionally, in June of 2013, Obama-Brennan CIA operatives (news reporters) Michael Isikoff (NBC News) and Tom Hamburger (Washington Post) met with 2LT Scott Bennett to discuss his findings in *SHELL GAME*. (SPECIAL NOTE: Hamburger and Isikoff are the same CIA Deep State operatives who released a December 8, 2017 story about Donald J. Trump Jr.'s alleged receipt of Wikileaks materials on September 4, 2016. In reality, this article was *plagiarized* from Bennett's original *SHELL GAME* report and subsequent communication to Michael Cohen on August 6, 2015 and July 27, 2016). Michael Cohen will confirm this. A retraction letter is being formulated for the Washington Post, and lawsuit pending.

The law firm Covington and Burling hired Roger Zakheim, former legal counsel at the House Armed Services Committee, as an attorney in exchange for Roger Zakheim's suppression of Bennett's military terrorist financing whistleblowing report: "*SHELL GAME*." This report exposed contractor fraud and other crimes by Dov Zakheim, Roger Zakheim's father and Bennett's supervisor at Booz Allen Hamilton. Military personnel were killed

SHELL GAME: TERRORIST FINANCING REPORT—www.shellgamewhistleblower.com

and wounded as a result of the Zakheim suppression of Bennett's report, and therefore this constitutes <u>treason</u> by Dov and Roger Zakheim, government corruption, and other criminal violations and abuses of authority.

BACKGROUND:

Colonel Jeff Jones, renowned as the "Wizard of Modern PSYOP" in the intelligence community and prior 4th Psychological Operations Group Commander and war veteran, had seen and recruited Scott Bennett into Booz Allen Hamilton after a Pentagon briefing Bennett gave to General Dick Myers and Secretary of Defense Donald Rumsfeld. Bennett was a G.W. Bush Administration official at the time, was fluent Spanish, had advanced degrees, and had worked in the interagency intelligence realm.

Colonel Jones instructed Bennett to enter the U.S. Army on a *Direct Commission*, assigned him a Top Secret/SCI clearance, and then appointed him to be the Liaison Officer between US Special Operations Command and the State Department Coordinator for Counterterrorism, Ambassador Dell Dailey (former Commander, Joint Special Operations Command). Additionally, Bennett was ordered to work with Mike Furlong (former Sergeant Major at Special Operations Command) at State CT on defeating the Muslim Brotherhood's global Wahhabi propaganda and psychological warfare/information operations. Bennett was then relocated from Washington DC to U.S. Central Command at McDill AFB, Tampa, Florida, to penetrate terrorist-financing operations.

Colonel Jones instructed Bennett to aggressively penetrate, discover, and expose any corruption or terrorist-finance crimes involving U.S. DEEP STATE "black flag" operations, the Obama Administration, the Clinton Foundation, the Muslim Brotherhood, and government agencies or contractors. Investigations included fraud, treason, theft of government resources, and violations of the Smith-Mundt Act—which prohibited U.S. propaganda to be used against American citizens on U.S. soil. [NOTE: The U.S. Information and Educational Exchange Act of 1948 (Public Law 80-402), popularly called the Smith–Mundt Act, is the basic legislative authorization for some of the activities conducted by the U.S. Department of State commonly known as public diplomacy, and outlawed psychological operations (strategic communications) to be used against Americans, until President Obama changed the Act to allow and encourage the use of

SHELL GAME: TERRORIST FINANCING REPORT—www.shellgamewhistleblower.com

psychological operations to "brainwash" Americans to support anti-gun measures through false flag shooting events. These events and operations include: ▮▮▮▮▮▮▮▮▮▮▮▮▮▮▮▮▮▮▮▮▮▮▮▮▮▮▮▮▮▮▮▮▮▮, and other American and international operations)].

Part of Bennett's mission was to research, discover, and report on any and all suspected contractor "*waste, fraud, and abuse*" by Booz-Allen-Hamilton Terrorist Financing Operations Director Dov Zakheim, who had been made Bennett's senior supervisor. It had been reported that $2.3 trillion dollars was secretly removed by Zakheim when he had been the Pentagon Comptroller, and the investigating auditors killed in a missile strike upon the Pentagon on September 11, 2001 while working in the SCIF (sensitive compartmentalized information facility). Bennett was ordered to use is Army Direct Commission as a means to penetrating Dov Zakheim terrorist financing operations.

Soon after Bennett was tasked as a COUNTER-TERRORISM FINANCE analyst in the Joint Interagency Operations Center at U.S. Central Command, he identified, tracked, and reported on terrorists, their financial donors, networks, banks, and activities. Bennett discovered Saudi Arabia laundering terrorist financing through the Clinton Foundation and Obama administration. These reports were blocked due to the evidence of crimes and government corruption. Ignoring instructions from Booz-Allen-Hamilton, Bennett continued to work with multiple intelligence agencies and military units, and produced the following reports: ▮▮▮▮▮▮▮▮▮▮▮▮▮▮▮▮ ▮▮▮▮▮▮ Bennett produced ▮▮ Bennett was tasked with ▮ ▮▮▮▮▮▮▮▮▮▮▮▮▮▮▮▮▮▮▮▮▮▮ Bennett also exposed Saudi terrorist financing-money laundering connection to Saudi Arabian officials using international banks including Deutsche Bank, Union Bank of Switzerland, HSBC, and the Clinton Foundation. ▮▮▮▮▮▮▮▮▮▮▮▮▮▮▮▮▮▮▮▮▮▮▮▮▮▮▮▮▮▮▮▮▮▮

SHELL GAME: TERRORIST FINANCING REPORT—www.shellgamewhistleblower.com

Soon after Bennett's reports and briefings, he was suspiciously stopped in his car outside of McDill AFB, arrested at gunpoint, held in isolation and subjected to extreme interrogation (torture); questioned by FBI counter-terrorism agents; and then afterwards removed from base in the middle of the night. The preposterous excuse given to Bennett was "a base-housing paperwork error" had occurred, which was then conveniently used to terminate Bennett from his position and remove him from base, and return him to Washington DC. Bennett believed at the time that this was in fact a "training exercise" or "test of his mental fortitude and loyalty", due to his TS/SCI security clearance and his imminent deployment to Iraq, and not a hostile response to his discovery of terrorist-financing treason and fraud.

STATE DEPARTMENT CABLES

BE ADVISED, you are hereby served notice that during Bennett's tenure at the State Department Counterterrorism office (State/CT), communication cables between State/CT in Washington DC and Switzerland reveal that in 2009, Hillary Clinton in her capacity as Secretary, and agents of the Clinton Foundation, did conspire with former Attorney General Eric Holder, Assistant Attorney General Lanny Breuer, and former Attorney General Loretta Lynch to confiscate and conceal these 19,000 Union Bank of Switzerland (UBS) accounts that were reported to the U.S. Government by a UBS whistleblower banker, Brad Birkenfeld, after he had been approached and targeted by the CIA in Switzerland.

BE ADVISED, you are hereby served notice that Brad Birkenfeld was debriefed by U.S. Army Officer Scott Bennett for six (6) months on these matters and provided Bennett with copies of documents, emails, Wikileaks cables, and bank accounts involved in terrorist financing from UBS. Birkenfeld and Bennett then reported it on August 1, 2012 to General James Mattis at U.S. Central Command; and Bennett then submitted his report to the Pentagon and Congress.

BE ADVISED, you are hereby <u>served notice</u> that on September 11, 2012, Birkenfeld was secretly bribed and threatened by Obama Administration officials and <u>paid $104 million dollars to remain silent about these matters</u>. A second false D.U.I. was used to entrap Birkenfeld as a "pressure point" and means to imprison him again should he refuse to cooperate. Most likely Birkenfeld would have been murdered in prison as a result. (SPECIAL NOTE: <u>Edward Snowden was the CIA employee who targeted Brad Birkenfeld</u> for economic espionage purposes by creating a false D.U.I. entrapment operation in Switzerland using Swiss Police and CIA operatives.

SHELL GAME: TERRORIST FINANCING REPORT—www.shellgamewhistleblower.com

CIA visited Birkenfeld after his arrest in Switzerland, displayed their credentials, requested his assistance, and proceeded to gather intelligence. Birkenfeld later rejected CIA's plans, and fled to the U.S. to obtain immunity. This prompted the DOJ-FBI-CIA to create letters that falsely claimed to have been written by a Birkenfeld friend and colleague, and sent them to the UBS HQ in Switzerland. This was intended to provoke UBS to arrest, silence, or kill Birkenfeld. See FBI counterterrorism email, Exhibit 5. Edward Snowden later transferred and worked at Booz-Allen-Hamilton with Scott Bennett. Snowden was employed on cyber operations contracts in Oahu, Hawaii, while Bennett was employed as a psychological warfare analyst in Washington DC. Bennett's materials, herein and undisclosed, must be subpoenaed in the current State Department investigations, as a matter of national security.

LEGAL NOTICE OF SERVICE AND REQUEST FOR SUBPOENA

BE ADVISED, you are hereby served notice that for legal purposes, this memorandum serves as both "official notice" and "request for subpoena" given to you in your official and personal capacity as an employee or representative of the United States government about urgent U.S. national security information.

BE ADVISED, you are hereby served notice that this memorandum hereby communicates to your office actionable intelligence which must be immediately investigated, and should be interpreted by the White House as a *"Request for Executive Branch Action in a national security matter."*

BE ADVISED, you are hereby served notice that all *rights* are reserved for FOIA and legal purposes, and is privileged communication under international whistleblower, military, and intelligence community protections, and not to be shared without our express permission.

BE ADVISED, you are hereby served notice that in accordance with contract law (*common* law), and whistleblower laws, acceptance of this communication by the White House shall constitute *receipt*, and upon receipt of this communication by the White House Press Office, a Kastigar "immunity agreement" (*Kastigar v. United States*, 406 U.S. 441 (1972), for the provider of the information, former U.S. Army Special Operations Officer Scott Bennett, is hereby invoked and legally ensured unless specifically rejected or modified in writing by the President of the United States himself (not his representative or legal team) within three (3) hours of the White House staff opening this email. Certified letter to follow.

BE ADVISED, you are hereby served notice that we respectfully request the President use this material to compel Attorney General Jeff Sessions to

SHELL GAME: TERRORIST FINANCING REPORT—www.shellgamewhistleblower.com

immediately initiate an investigation through the DOJ-FBI Office of Professional Responsibility and Inspector General and investigate treason, misprision of felony, terrorist financing, prosecutorial misconduct, judicial misconduct, and general abuse of authority by the FBI and the DOJ in this matter, and specifically in regard "SHELL GAME" and the materials relating to witnesses Scott Bennett, Brad Birkenfeld, Julian Assange, Edward Snowden and their attorneys; and defendants Loretta Lynch, Eric Holder, Lanny Breuer, Clinton Foundation, Donna Shalala, Dov Zakheim, Roger Zakheim, the law firm Covington and Burling, defense contractor Booz Allen Hamilton, and U.S. CENTCOM.

SUMMARY OF FINDINGS

1) State Department Coordinator for Counterterrorism investigation of Clinton Foundation ties to Union Bank of Switzerland accounts, Brad Birkenfeld, and Saudi Arabia.
2) Terrorist Financing
3) Uranium One sale to Russia and the Trump Dossier scandal
4) Secretary of State Hillary Clinton, former Attorney General Eric Holder, former Assistant Attorney General Lanny Breuer, former Attorney General Loretta Lynch
5) Trump Administration surveillance and Russian investigation and related matters.
6) Aiding and abetting enemies of the United States
7) Unlawful entry into the United States through fraudulent means by terrorists and suspected terrorists using false passports and materials obtained from Libya.
8) Conspiracy, treason, misprision of felony, obstruction of justice
9) Unlawful surveillance

We, Brad Birkenfeld and myself, whistleblowers with first-hand experience in these events, hereby request from the President a subpoena for us to testify together, in person and at the same table, before the House and Senate Committees investigating the Trump Administration surveillance, Russian issues, and FBI-DOJ corruption related matters.

NOTICE OF PROSECUTION—CIVIL AND CRIMINAL

BE ADVISED, you are hereby <u>served notice</u> that this information, henceforth referred to as "the report", is hereby formally submitted to the President of

SHELL GAME: TERRORIST FINANCING REPORT—www.shellgamewhistleblower.com

the United States by a former United States Army Special Operations Officer and defense contractor holding a TOP SECRET/ SENSITIVE COMPARTMENTALIZED INFORMATION security clearance (TS/SCI). This individual will henceforth be referred to as "the witness." No material in this report is classified.

BE ADVISED, you are hereby served notice that since this material is necessary for protecting the national security of the United States, failure by your office or your agents to acknowledge and respond to this report, or provide it to the President, or by your office sharing any of this material with FBI, CIA, NSA, military, or law enforcement agencies or personnel without our expressed permission, will be interpreted as both a criminal act of omission, a violation of whistleblower laws, and a willful commission of:

1) an intentional disregard and violation of the United States Uniform Code of Military Justice, as well as Federal, State, and International law;
2) an intentional disregard and refusal by you to uphold your sworn Oath as a Member of Congress and government officer to "support and defend the Constitution of the United States";
3) an intentional act of "aiding and abetting enemies of the United States" by providing "financial and material support" to terrorists, their operations, and their networks;
4) an intentional "act of misprision of treason", and "act of treason", an "act of misprision of felony" against the United States"; and
5) an intentional violation of the specific policies, laws, codes, and statutes both listed in this report, and not listed herein.

BE ADVISED, you are hereby served notice that we officially request a subpoena from your office to appear and thoroughly debrief President Trump in his capacity as Commander-in-Chief of the United States Armed Forces, on the public record, concerning this material, and enable us to provide additional materials in this matter at that time. Every day this information is delayed from reaching President Trump, more American military personnel are killed and wounded.

BE ADVISED, you are hereby served notice that this is an urgent national security matter that demands your immediate response, and failure to respond will be interpreted and prosecuted both in the manner outlined above, and according to national and international laws relating to terrorism, murder, fraud, war, and other crimes.

Please have a legal representative contact us for a discussion as soon as possible.

SHELL GAME: TERRORIST FINANCING REPORT—www.shellgamewhistleblower.com

in the manner outlined above, and according to national and international laws relating to terrorism, murder, fraud, war, and other crimes.

Please have a legal representative contact us for a discussion as soon as possible.

Respectfully submitted,

Scott Bennett

CC: Bradley Birkenfeld, Whistleblower
Chairman, House Judiciary Committee;
United States Senate, Committee on Homeland Security and Governmental Affairs, Washington, DC 20510-6250
Chairman, House Intelligence Committee
Donald F. McGahn, II, Counsel to the President

CERTIFICATE OF SERVICE

I hereby certify that a copy of this "military report to the President and request for subpoena" was sent by email and certified mail via the U.S. Postal Service to The White House, Press Office, at 1600 Pennsylvania Avenue, Washington DC 20500, and the U.S. Congress, Judiciary Committee, on this 19 day of December, 2017.

Scott Bennett, Petitioner, Pro Se

See Attached Notary

LUIS AGUIAR
Notary Public - California
Alameda County
Commission # 2208749
My Comm. Expires Aug 4, 2021

2/12/18

SHELL GAME: TERRORIST FINANCING REPORT—www.shellgamewhistleblower.com

ACKNOWLEDGMENT

A notary public or other officer completing this certificate verifies only the identity of the individual who signed the document to which this certificate is attached, and not the truthfulness, accuracy, or validity of that document.

State of California
County of _____Contra Costa_____)

On __2/12/18__ before me, __Luis Aguiar - Notary Public__
(Insert name and title of the officer)

personally appeared __Scott A. Bennett__ who proved to me on the basis of satisfactory evidence to be the person(s) whose name(s) is/are subscribed to the within instrument and acknowledged to me that he/she/they executed the same in his/her/their authorized capacity(ies), and that by his/her/their signature(s) on the instrument the person(s), or the entity upon behalf of which the person(s) acted, executed the instrument.

I certify under PENALTY OF PERJURY under the laws of the State of California that the foregoing paragraph is true and correct.

WITNESS my hand and official seal.

Signature __Luis Aguiar__   (Seal)

LUIS AGUIAR
Notary Public - California
Alameda County
Commission # 2208749
My Comm. Expires Aug 4, 2021

Tuesday, 15 May 2018

To: Donald J Trump, President of the United States

CC: International Criminal Court (ICC), UN Security Council

Tuesday, 15 May 2018

Dear Mr President,

On this 70th anniversary of the expulsion of 750,000 Palestinians from their homes, be advised, we are hereby giving you legal notice of a massacre beginning at the time of the Nakba anniversary in order for you to register a response and call upon the Israelis to cease and desist in your capacity as President of the United States and a Permanent Member of the Security Council and NATO.

Please acknowledge receipt of this legal notice to the following address:

INTERNATIONAL DELEGATES OF THE NEW HORIZONS CONFERENCE

1ST FLOOR, NO. 91, EAST

2ND ASEMAN ST., ASEMAN ST.,

KETAB SQUARE,

TEHRAN, I.R. IRAN

PHONE: 00-98-2122-0728

FAX: 00-98-2122-097670

Be advised, you are hereby served legal notice of the following:

That your oath as President of the US and Commander in Chief of the armed forces is hereby accepted and you are expected to fulfil that oath by conforming to your constitutional responsibilities and duties.

You are expected to advise the following bodies about this legal matter, including but not limited to:

The United States Congress

The United Nations Security Council and

The International Criminal Court (The Hague)

Be advised, you are hereby served legal notice of the following:

Tuesday, 15 May 2018

That 'false flag' attacks may be used by Israeli agents in order to assign blame to Palestinian factions and escalate the incident into a larger conflict in order to falsely draw the United States and American military personnel into this artificially created conflict.

BE ADVISED, YOU ARE HEREBY SERVED LEGAL NOTICE, This potential `'false flag` attack and consequent military escalation represents a clear and present danger to the citizens of the United States of America, because it may be designed to trigger and escalate American military actions against Turkey, Syria, Lebanon, Iran, and Russia, since these nations are opposed to the transfer of the US Embassy to Jerusalem; and rising tensions already exacerbated by the U.S. withdrawl from the JCPOA.

BE ADVISED, YOU ARE HEREBY SERVED LEGAL NOTICE this letter will be included as evidence in all matters relating to the U.S. Embassy move to Jerusalem/ Al Quds, and the JOINT COMPREHENSIVE PLAN OF ACTION (JCPOA).

BE ADVISED, YOU ARE HEREBY SERVED LEGAL NOTICE that, as a matter of record, on the date of the US Embassy move, some 2,771 people were reported injured including 1359 by live ammunition, with 130 people in critical condition, and according to the Ministry of Health, the UN Secretary General Antonio Gutteres, has expressed his profound alarm at the "high number of Palestinians killed and injured in the Gaza protests." Additional data and statistics will be submitted.

The initiation of this impending attack will involve a new and higher level the Massacre of Palestinian civilians protesting the move of the United States embassy to Jerusalem, as a pre-condition for a new "INFORMATION OPERATION/ PSYCHOLOGICAL WARFARE' campaign, which has been confirmed by former U.S. military personnel.

BE ADVISED, YOU ARE HEREBY SERVED LEGAL NOTICE, the United States can have no military alliance due to the fact that Israel has no internationally recognized fixed territorial borders which are required to be defined in such an agreement.

BE ADVISED, YOU ARE HEREBY SERVED LEGAL NOTICE, this letter is to be listed as EXHIBIT 1 in any war crimes investigation and prosecution (past, present, future) relating to this matter, AT ALL TIMES.

BE ADVISED, YOU ARE HEREBY SERVED LEGAL NOTICE, pursuant to 18 US Code 4, and 28 US Code 1361, you are hereby served notice of national and international legal violations. Hence in order to preserve the safety of the signatories of this letter and their testimony and evidence, affidavits in this matter, the signatories are writing this LEGAL NOTICE to the AMERICAN PEOPLE, and to you in your personal and professional capacity as President of the United States; and we hereby establish this letter as their official legal protection against any retaliation, detainment, investigation, sequestration, interrogation, discrimination, imprisonment, torture, financial consequences, or any other

Tuesday, 15 May 2018

negative or prejudicial consequences or actions taken against them. Any action taken against the undersigned will be interpreted as a violation of the following:

18 USC 242 (conspiracy to deny/violate constitutional civil rights)

42 USC 1983, 1984, 1985 (civil action for rights violations)

18 US 2339A (providing material support to terrorists)

We hereby request full whistleblower protections as we, as former government and military officers and officials, are fulfilling our oaths to the U.S. Constitution.

Please contact us immediately about this matter and we hereby request an opportunity to debrief you and Congress.

See attached exhibits:

BY WAY OF DECEPTION by Victor John Ostrovsky

SHELL GAME: THE BETRAYAL and Cover-up by the U.S. GOVERNMENT of the Union Bank of Switzerland's Terrorist Finance Connection to Edward Snowden, Booz Allen Hamilton, U.S. Central Command, and the Clinton Foundation by Scott Bennett

VISAS FOR AL QAEDA: CIA HANDOUTS THAT ROCKED THE WORLD by J. Michael Springmann

GOODBYE, EUROPE? HELLO, CHAOS? MERKEL'S MIGRANT BOMB by J. Michael Springmann

All writings by Michael Maloofe and Phil Geraldi

Respectfully submitted,

_____

Sara Jane Booth (UK), United Kingdom Journalist and Broadcaster

_____

Phil Geraldi (US), Former CIA Operations Officer

_____

Michael Maloofe (US), Former Pentagon Official

_____

Tuesday, 15 May 2018

Scott Bennett (US), Former U.S. Army Officer and State Department Coordinator for Counterterrorism Contractor

_____

J. Michael Springmann (US), Former State Department Diplomat and Attorney

_____

Edward. C Corrigan (Canada), Barrister and Solicitor

cc: Recep Tayyip Erdogan, President of Turkey
       Ibrahim Kalim, Special Adviser to President of Turkey
       Vladimir Putin, President of the Russian Federation
       President of the European Parliament, Antonio Tajani

Tuesday, 15 May 2018

negative or prejudicial consequences or actions taken against them. Any action taken against the undersigned will be interpreted as a violation of the following:

18 USC 242 (conspiracy to deny/violate constitutional civil rights)

42 USC 1983, 1984, 1985 (civil action for rights violations)

18 US 2339A (providing material support to terrorists)

We hereby request full whistleblower protections as we, as former government and military officers and officials, are fulfilling our oaths to the U.S. Constitution.

Please contact us immediately about this matter and we hereby request an opportunity to debrief you and Congress.

See attached exhibits:

BY WAY OF DECEPTION by Victor John Ostrovsky

SHELL GAME: THE BETRAYAL and Cover-up by the U.S. GOVERNMENT of the Union Bank of Switzerland's Terrorist Finance Connection to Edward Snowden, Booz Allen Hamilton, U.S. Central Command, and the Clinton Foundation by Scott Bennett

VISAS FOR AL QAEDA: CIA HANDOUTS THAT ROCKED THE WORLD by J. Michael Springmann

All writings by Michael Maloofe and Phil Geraldi

Respectfully submitted,

_____

Sarah Jane Booth (UK), Journalist

Phil Geraldi (US), Former CIA Operations Officer

Michael Maloofe (US), Former Pentagon Official

Scott Bennett (US), Former U.S. Army Officer and State Department Coordinator for Counterterrorism Contractor

ABOUT THE AUTHOR

Scott Bennett is a U.S. Army Special Operations Officer (11th Psychological Operations Battalion, Civil Affairs-Psychological Operations Command), and a global psychological warfare-counterterrorism analyst, formerly with defense contractor Booz Allen Hamilton.

He received a Direct Commission as an Officer, held a Top Secret/Sensitive Compartmentalized Information (TS/SCI) security clearance, and worked in the highest levels of international counterterrorism in Washington DC and MacDill Air Force Base in Tampa, Florida. He has worked at U.S. Special Operations Command, U.S. Central Command, the State Department Coordinator for Counterterrorism, and other government agencies. He served in the G.W. Bush Administration from 2003 to 2008, and was a Social Science Research Fellow at the Heritage Foundation.

His writings and lectures seek to enhance global awareness and understanding of modern psychological warfare, the international military-intelligence community, and global surveillance operations being artificially generated under the specter of "National Security".

He has written extensively on the intelligence community's surveillance activities addressed by Edward Snowden's National Security Agency-Central Intelligence Agency materials; and since 2010 has filed numerous military-government whistle-blowing reports with Congressional Committees, including: the Intelligence, the Armed Services, the Government Oversight and Reform, the Homeland Security, the Judiciary, the Foreign Affairs, the Banking, and the Terrorism Committees.

He has communicated with over a hundred Federal Representatives, Senators, senior military officers and Pentagon officials, and journalists about the scandalous abuses of power and deception being employed against the American people by its own military-intelligence community, and filed legal action against Booz Allen Hamilton and the Department of Defense for their involvement in secret Swiss Bank Terrorist Finance Operations, which he uncovered with the help of Union Bank of Switzerland whistleblower, Brad Birkenfeld.

His educational background includes a Bachelor of Science in Advertising and Spanish Minor from San Jose State University in California, a Master of Arts in Internatioonal Business and Public Policy from George Mason University in Virginia, and a Ph.D. (ABD) in Political Theory from the Catholic University of America in Washington D.C. He currently resides in California.

CONTACT INFORMATION:
Patreon: www.patreon.com/shellgame   Youtube: *ShellGame Whistleblower*
Business address: 23 Railroad Ave, #23, Danville, CA 94526
Email: armypsyop@outlook.com   PAYPAL DONATIONS: *armypsyop*
Website: WWW.SHELLGAMEWHISTLEBLOWER.COM
Books: http://www.lulu.com/spotlight/shellgame

退伍軍人Scott Bennett說：「看看今天美國和加州發生了什麼，這是真正的愛國者挺身而出的時刻。新加州運動是一個憲政行動，重新建立一個新州，以重現發現，重新奪回，復興我們的自由、基本人權，保障等源自建國先賢的憲政權利。建立新州，使之成為一個燈塔，讓全美國人民看到，新加州是山頂的新城，在這裡你有權持槍、有權敬拜神、男士與女士才能結婚、自由經營；沒有政府的各種政策法規、執照的沉重負擔；你承擔責任，最大程度的發展個人天賦。要實現這些，唯一的辦法是建立一個新州。」

A SPECIAL THANKS

This report is dedicated to my family, and to my brothers-in-arms who have worn the military uniform, and sworn the sacred, lifelong oath to support and defend the Constitution. I fearlessly proclaim to all of the military men and women who arose out of patriotism, enlisted, sacrificed, and fought for their families and their country, this book has been written to honor you and your families, and hopefully protect our future children from the deceptions and black flag operations which are currently imperiling our freedoms and corroding our honor.

I must also give a special thanks to the men whom I met in prison who helped, comforted, inspired and advised me throughout my journey. You are the manliest and noblest of men, forged by trial and suffering, sharpened by adversity, and polished by the blessings of faith. You are the exemplars of the special strength and will to endure, push forward, and never surrender that all Americans hope to aspire to.

I wish to pay special thanks to the following people for their faith, friendship, and encouragement in this difficult "mission":
Thanks to Paul Preston and Robert Exter for their help in breaking this story.

Thanks to Van Palmer, Scarecrow, the man who helped direct the pebble which started the avalanche, and evaporated the darkness of the "pettifoggers". The man who opened eyes and shocked dead souls to life with the energy of his truth and the scalding heat of his research. Whose insight into the September 11, 2001 attacks and matrix of multi-layered connections, helped discover secrets all Americans (and indeed every person who values truth and freedom) cannot live without.

Bernard "Jay" Bagdis, my editor and a friend who stuck closer than a brother, a brilliant Princeton lawyer, a master of the money game, and a man who helped me "connect the dots" and see the hidden relationships and agendas of the secret world I had been blinded from questioning. A man who refused to lie, save his own skin, and is an example of how a gladiator in the legal arena should fight for his honor.

Rich Frase, a friend, an Army Officer, and Artillery "Red-Leg" brother whose perseverance, honor, and faith inspired me with an example to seek to emulate. Thank you for your brilliant engineering mind and schematic analytical insights.

Greg Scarlato, a friend who sticketh closer than a brother, and a warrior for truth. The pioneer who introduced me to Brad Birkenfeld, and helped uncover the world of the "Gold Warriors", Gugenheim, Japanese gold buried under airports, CIA thefts of billions of dollars, Swiss Bank accounts, and the highest levels of corruption. A man who took no plea deal, was betrayed by a corrupt justice system, yet remains as a spotlight of integrity in a dark world, shining for all Americans to find their way by. This story, is the second part of Greg's story—soon to be released.

Walter Blair, a brilliant lawyer, a mesmerizing writer, a fellow Brit, a brother on the soccer field, and the Merlin who taught me the spells of legal writing, motion construction, and the politics of law. The man who also showed me what it means to fight through the legal battles, and rediscover the beauty of life in the process.

Kirk Shelton, the man who enabled me to work as a tutor, and opened the way for everything else. An aristocratic gentleman, a CEO, and a fearless leader and man of deep integrity. A man of principle who defied the political entrapments and tantalizing bribes of Governor Chris Christie, and refused to betray his friend, and refused to lie. The dictionary's definition of good character has your face next to it.

Jim Pearsol, a man whose intellect is unmatched, and whose compassion and skills in teaching and writing is unmatched. Without you Jim, none of this would have been possible.

Jason Merchant, a friend who sticketh closer than a brother, a "tank" at soccer, and the man who helped "get the message out" past the mine fields. Whose Aunt Betty was a great help, and whose chats with "scarecrow" always yielded new discoveries.

Sherwood "Woody" Jordan, who helped bring a mystical, old Indian sacredness to my understanding of cosmic coincidences, and whose Garden of Great Stones and insight into nature always brought peace and wisdom.

Chip Trimble, my bunky, my spiritual mentor, my musical leader, and my example of a man of faith. A man who endured the agony of abandonment and loss of a parent, and showed me the way through my own.

Dan Cochran, my fellow Army brother, and intelligence expert. A man whose insight into the world of secrets, and experience with government contractor fraud and the lies they create to cover their own ass, helped me heal mine.

Dr. Chip Skowran, a man of enormous faith, of deep sensitivity and intelligence, and a profound patience and strength with the challenges of nurturing marriage and children from inside prison. A brilliant surgeon and an inspiring soccer team captain who led us to victory.

John and Joseph Yeh, brothers whose love and loyalty for each other is a living expression of Christ's most cherished command: "Love they neighbor as thyself."

Chris Wartella, my bunky, my friend, and a brilliant accountant and tax expert. A man of strong faith, and example of majestic husbandry all men would be wise to follow. A shining example of transforming a prison experience into a long-term exercise camp.

Rudy Pecinovic, a fellow military brother, an excellent leader on the soccer field, and an example of faith and humanity which all Muslims should admire and love to follow. "As-Salaam-Alaikum."

Paul Mancusso, my bunky, and Italian Stallion whose skill at fighting back and attacking the lies and shenanigans parasitic prosecutors helped encourage my own efforts at breaking through.

Wesley Brandt, whose Catechism readings transformed a cold cell into a monastic retreat for self-reflection. An example of warmth, humor, and mid-west character, and a friend for life.

Simon Odoni, a man whose great creativity, courage, and tenacity to fight through and challenge his illegal abduction by the Justice Department, and the violation of his rights as a British Citizen in the Dominican Republic, serve as a beacon for all freedom lovers to rally behind.

Bob George, a brilliant lawyer, a man of sharp observation, and no-nonsense legal analysis. Your help and fearless cool under pressure will always be appreciated.

Ed Ellis, the beacon of intellectual salvation, whose constant uplifting conversation and Sunday Current Events class transformed a prison into a Think-Tank unparalleled by any in my Washington experience. You are the reminder of how important "Jack Bauer" is to American freedom, and how essential it is to have a government worthy of his service.

John Fong, a fellow special operations soldier, a man of great strength and compassion, and who still holds his security clearance oath sacred, despite the lies against him.

Bill Hillar, a military man of honor, whose own personal experience of being dishonored and betrayed by the military for revealing the truth about Vietnam veterans abandoned and left behind out of political expediency and moral cowardice, is to me the finest example of moral courage.

Mathew Addy, for helping civilize and sophisticate an uncouth world, and for serving as an example of a good husband, father, and man of integrity.

George McClure, a brother and fighter who never backed down, never retreated, and fought through the trap set against him. Your feeding of crippled inmates unable to leave their cube, and nourishing them in the gospel, will always be rewarded.

Wayne Miller, a great friend, a loyal military man, and a credit to the Navy. You helped me see, and polished my legal writing.

Julian Assange, for releasing the State Department cables which exposed the corruption and lies infecting America's intelligence-military-political "country club". Your work was the evidence which many men can now use to restore their honor, and help their fellow Americans reclaim their rights and liberties.

Edward Snowden, a fellow Army Special Operations soldier, patriot, and Booz Allen Hamilton explorer. Your example has illuminated the path for other loyal constitutionalists, political leaders, and military heroes to follow; and your intelligence and courage has blown the ram's horn of battle for all of Western Civilization to rally behind in this life and death battle for humanity's future.

And, of course, Brad Birkenfeld, the pebble who transformed a frozen mountain into an explosive avalanche of new truth, and uncovered hidden information, people, and connections that is turning the world upside down. You were Act I, Edward Snowden Act II, and Julian Assange Act III. May this book serve as the music sheet which links all three in a symphony of freedom.

In all of my travels throughout the military, the government, academia, and the professional world, I can say without hesitation or doubt that you are the best of men, and I have been truly blessed by God to be associated with you. It is my honor to call you life-long friends and comrades. If I failed to write your name here, please forgive me. Torture has a way of thinning the memory. Rest assured, you are in my heart.

I must also thank the prison staff:

Mr. Timothy Wood, Education Director, Schuylkill prison. The man to whom I am most indebted to for his kindness and help. A man of compassion and patience and nobility, to whom I am eternally grateful for allowing me to teach and work in the education department at Schuylkill prison camp; to become the main financial contributor to the office copy machine; and for blessing me with the ability to sit at a typewriter every day for two years and compile these materials.
James Petrucci, Director of Federal Prison Camp Schuylkill, and a man of great leadership, discipline, and flexibility. You represent the best of the Army's "Old Guard", and I thank you for allowing me the press interviews with NBC news and the Washington Post—even though Michael Isikoff and Tom Hamburger ran from the story like men paralyzed with fear. They also later attempted to entrap President Donald Trump and his sons with it by inventing a false "Russian Election Meddling" narrative, but that's another story.
Mr. Christeleit, my case manager and fellow Coast Guardsman. Your help and humor, as acidic as some may describe, I always found refreshing. You will be remembered.
Mr. Kranzel, my counselor. A man of compassion and decency, who always offered help and transparency. You were the best of them all.
Ms. Jennifer McGinley, a woman of buoyant optimism, delightful feminine charm, and unwavering faith. Your teaching help in the world of men's suffering families was inspiring, and I appreciate your helping make my time in the dungeon an academic experience and intelligence training operation. Your help and cheerful bright smile lit up a dark world.

Ms. Randy Leslie, a woman of great learning, intense discipline, and delightful realism. I'm grateful for being allowed the honor of being your assistant during my time on the "Island of Misfit Toys". Your help in pulling the pieces together will always be remembered.

Despite my best efforts, and except for Mr. Jeff O'Toole in Washington DC, no lawyer who represented me in my case can I truly thank, for they have intentionally transformed the nature of law from "unchanging righteousness, justice, and mercy" into "smoky gamesmanship, money, and manipulation." Like the despotic practice of "selling doves as blood sacrifices in the temple of God" so have you squandered men's lives for your own aggrandizements in the Court of Law. I look forward to overturning the stone tables and driving out the lascivious corruption under the whip of national awakening and revival.

Additionally, and regretfully, I cannot offer thanks to anyone in the United States military, Media, or United States Congress for they have consciously chose, as the evidence and timeline proves, to completely ignore all letters, phone calls, and reports in this matter. I can only say you have blood on your hands. You have also shamed and betrayed the military's ancient code of honor and brotherhood, and the media and Congress' Constitutional right to existence; and by ignoring this story, you have lost all right to the respect and freedom which your fathers and grandfathers have bled and suffered to secure for you.

Finally, only one person, Ms. Kerry Lynn Cassidy, investigative reporter and founding partner at Project Camelot can I thank for being the first writer and champion of truth to have the courage to expose and report this story. Kerry is the CEO and co-Founder of Project Camelot. She is a documentary filmmaker and investigative reporter and in April 2006 she teamed up with Bill

Ryan and founded Project Camelot. Kerry travels the world conducting interviews and documenting the testimony of whistleblowers with above Top-Secret clearances as well as authors, researchers and experiencers covering conspiracies, the secret space program, black projects, ETs and free energy.

Kerry, you are the only person in the United States Media establishment who deserves the honor of being called a reporter, a writer, and an American Patriot. All readers should support her at: http://projectcamelotportal.com/about-us
I'm hopeful other brave men and women in the media will join the fight and help proclaim this to the American people.

Thanks to my ATO brothers for your faith and support, and especially to David Reyes, the best artist in a generation, and a fellow PSYOP master. http://www.davidpreyes.moonfruit.com/
Also special thanks to Scott Goodwin, for his generous support and faithfulness, whose virtuous character is the embodiment of what the Alpha and the Omega represents in the Tau.

Thank you also to Michael Jay Anderson, who has been a tremendous help in broadcasting this story on alternative media channels everywhere.

Thanks also to Senator Richard Black (Virginia) who has helped materialize this into real counterterrorism operations—which also prompted FBI Director Andrew McCabe, his wife Jill McCabe, and VA Governor Terry McAuliffe to try and entrap and unseat Senator Black. But that is another story.

Most of all, I thank my God for strengthening me through this, and for my Lord and Savior Jesus Christ. "I am the way, the truth, and the life." Thank you for an interesting adventure, that is just beginning.

--Scott

"We are troubled on every side, yet not distressed; we are perplexed, but not in despair; Persecuted, but not forsaken; cast down, but not destroyed; Always bearing about in the body the dying of the Lord Jesus, that the life also of Jesus might be made manifest in our body."
--2 Corinthians, Chapter 4: 8-10

(Thank you to Jason Goodman, www.Crowdsourcethetruth.com)

"Then Jesus laid his hands on his eyes again; and he opened his eyes, his sight was restored, and he saw everything clearly."

--Mark 8:25 English Standard Version (ESV)

www.shellgamewhistleblower.com

LETTERS FROM JAIL: THE CREATIVITY OF SOLITARY CONFINEMENT

<u>THE METAMORPHOSIS OF PRISON</u>
Verily, one of the deepest transformative experiences a man can have is being dragged before a corrupt Court, then from Court to jail, and then from jail to federal prison. For it is in such a journey that he discovers the deceptions of law, and with this redefines himself.

Until you have walked this path, you will never know true loneliness, unbearable suffering, gnawing regret, crippling hopelessness, and the agonizing desire to feel freedom again. Until you've felt the cold hard steel of heavy handcuffs snapped around and pulling your wrists to the ground, you cannot enjoy the freedom of movement. Until you've felt the gut choking grip of a chain wrapped around your belly, you cannot savor the peace in a deep breath of air. Until you've shuffled slowly with clanging shackles biting your ankles and retarding your feet, you cannot know the ecstasy of leaping, running, or dance.

Until you've daily dressed in the same coarse, heavy orange pajama costume for months, you cannot appreciate the beauty and personality in clothes. Until you've lived daily in a windowless gray cement box with only slits allowing the memory of light, can you sigh at open country and adoringly smile at the face of God's creation smiling back.

Until you've humbled yourself and sought out opportunities to be a help and blessing to other prisoners, you cannot feel the overflowing warmth and blushing gratitude of being loved. And only when you've been denied the touch of nature and the embrace of friends and family, can you feel deeply alive and eternally present.

Prison drains you slowly of all self, until the soul is completely emptied of the world and its lusts, your memories, and your dreams. Your self-delusions evaporate and your pride crumbles into a shivering, weeping fetus position.

For the exasperating reality is that despite the patriotic honor and civic duty in whistleblowing to awaken and warn your fellow citizens of an insidious, subversive tyranny, it is your defiance against this tyranny (or fearless love of liberty) which prompts terrified government bureaucrats to violate their purpose of existence, deform their mandate, betray citizens trust, and imprison and silence the whistleblower in a vain attempt to hide their wickedness and erase the truth. And it is in this moment of clarity that we also feel a heavy, smothering despair, along with the sense of falling down into a bottomless black abyss.

And then in the silence, we feel God as He breathes into us "a peace that passeth understanding." And a new life of humility an absolute surrender inflates our hearts and buoys us back upwards. And we hear ourselves saying, "From the depths oh Lord, I crieth out to thee," the same words our spirits groaned silently moments before, and which God was waiting to hear.

And our eyes suddenly burst with tears and we weep, grievingly; and pour out at last our sins and failures and confess how eternally good and faithful God has been, and how bad we have done, and how great he is to love and comfort us in our worst moments. Luxury vanishes like an ancient legend; pop-culture dissolves and disappears like sugar in the still water of reflection. A mercilessly haunting vision of missed chances, wrong choices, and scenes of what might have been, or what should have been done, but which are now forever lost, stricken the mind with an epileptic fit of shut eyes, clenched teeth, and shaking hands.

The most consuming remorse and insatiable hunger to feed is the wish you had taken the witness stand and told your truth, the whole truth, and nothing but the truth, so that God would use it to convict your jury of your innocence, and free you from guilt and pain. But having exchanged this freedom to speak for the tricky tactics and manipulation of lawyers in their betting schemes, the natural beauty of honesty in an innocent man is burned up into ashes and blown away with the distant promise of an "Appeal."
Indeed, only after we have been touched by death, can we feel life.

<u>THE DUTY TO HELP AND TEACH OTHERS IN PRISON</u>

And so behold the nightmares of blind people...colors and shapes and movements that escape the vocabulary of seers, and create intentions, secrets, and fears indescribable to healthy instincts. Helping inmates, the lowest of the low, the lost, the hurting, the hopeless means…
Helping them discover the knowledge and pride in proper spelling and language.
Healing their tongues of the cancerous villainy of cursing through your happy quiet and calm.
Encouraging their self-esteem by applauding small victories in virtue and manner.
Pointing the way towards peaceful self-discovery by reminding them of the eternal faithfulness in simple kindness.
Nourishing their dreams by cleansing their choices with good promises.
Reminding them that only through patiently living hour by hour in focused and relaxed acceptance of each moment passing, will they feel the smiling face of God warming their heart and comforting them with peace.

THE FELON MAN

The felon man is the best man for revolution. With all ways blocked and fixed against him, he has only up or down to go: Down through drugs, alcohol, lust, fear, and anger...or up through purity, health, virtue, discipline, drive, and fearlessness. Family and children can become to him the means to absolute freedom, by totally giving away of oneself for others. These types of men truly are the best stock from which to cultivate revolutionaries. The best ones are cunning, reserved, bruised, yet not beaten, and are yearning to channel their energies and temperament to building a life again with their own hands. They are independent, yet deeply tribal and fraternal, since to survive they must nurture a brotherhood of the like-blooded and like-minded. Drugs and selling skills, "entrepreneurial" crimes or "hyper-boy" syndrome has incarcerated most; and emotionally dysfunctional families have been their leprosy. So they seem to have the qualities needed for a "Malcolm X" type movement, and disciplined instruction. They hunger for wise words, and their eyes flicker when they are reminded that "through Christ, I can do all things." But they all smile when they hear the words, perhaps for the very first time:

> "The LORD bless thee, and keep thee; The LORD make his face shine upon thee, and be gracious unto thee; The LORD lift up his countenance upon thee, and give thee peace."
> --Numbers 6: 24-27

Scott Bennett

Dr. Scott Bennett, formerly of the U.S. Army 11th Psychological Operations Battalion, attempted to blow the whistle by contacting the commercially-controlled media and writing to US politicians after being blacklisted from his job as terrorist finance investigator after he proved too zealous at the job.

Contents [hide]
1. Background
2. Arrest and imprisonment
3. Whistleblower
   3.1 Attempts to blow the whistle
   3.2 Shell Game - Report To Congress
4. Media coverage
5. Scott Bennett on Wikispooks
6. References

Scott Bennett
(whistleblower)

Exposed
• Terrorism/Funding/US
• Deep State
• Booz Allen Hamilton/Corruption
• United States Department of Justice/Corruption

Wikispooks page Censored

Spent 2 years in prison as a result of speaking his mind and attempting to blow the whistle on fraud and corruption inside the US war machine.

Counterterrorist Finance Analyst
In office
2008 - 2010
USCENTCOM
Tampa

Employer

Background

Scott Bennett had a background in advertising, before being fast tracked into the US military PSYOPS division, receiving a Direct Commission as an Officer, and held a Top Secret/Sensitive Compartmentalized Information (TS/SCI) security clearance.

Exploring this move in investigating terrorist financing, in his deposition to Congress, Bennett writes "I was tasked with interviewing all the different agency teams to discover their particular expertise in Terrorist Threat Finance, and formulate recommendations to improve their functionality. This meant identifying duplicative and unproductive operators within the agencies, developing plans and timetables for eliminating them, and synthesizing the best practices and expertise of the various government and military agencies into my Booz Allen team. I was repeatedly blocked and discouraged from delving too deep or being too aggressively creative."[1]

Arrest and imprisonment

By Bennett's account, he was filled up with spurious charges, which led to his being imprisoned with fellow whistleblower Brad Birkenfeld. After some period of puzzling over documents to which Birkenfeld had access[2][3][4][5], Bennett's experience at tracking terrorist finances allowed him to understand the connections. Birkenfeld was later awarded over $100M as a whistleblower, in connection with the 19,000 bank accounts which he had discovered while investigating money laundering at UBS.

Whistleblower

Bennett's whistleblowing was about the State of California child support agencies charging 10% on arrears without informing paying fathers. The first report he submitted to Congress concerned the impending 2012 Benghazi attack in Libya, which later happened, killing US ambassador John Christopher Stevens. He reports that he was criticised for his whistleblowing action.[2]

The first report he submitted to congress warned of the impending 2012 Benghazi attack in Libya, which later happened, killing US ambassador John Christopher Stevens.

The second report Bennett submitted to congress concerned corruption by banks in terrorist financing, and how civilian US Government officials conspired to cover this up.[1]

Attempts to blow the whistle

Bennett compiled a large report based largely on the material given him by Brad Birkenfeld, but contained with his own experience. No one in the military was interested enough to get back to him, nor was Dianne Feinstein, chair of the United States Senate Select Committee on Intelligence. No one in the commercially-controlled media expressed any interest in his revelations.

Shell Game - Report To Congress

On memorial day, May 27, 2013, Bennett submitted an 83 page "whistleblowing report to the United States Congress".[3] It was entitled "Shell Game: The Betrayal and Cover-up by the U.S. Government of the Union Bank of Switzerland-Terrorist Threat Finance Connection to Booz Allen Hamilton and U.S. Central Command".[4]

Media coverage

On 1st October, 2014, Bennett was interviewed by Kerry Cassidy of Project Camelot.[5] While in prison, he was interviewed by two reporters from the commercially-controlled media for a story about security clearances. He spoke for about 2 hours. Subsequently, about 3 times were written about him, not including mention of the event; he had testified about.[2] Due to lack of corporate media coverage, he was deemed "not notable" by Wikipedia.

CONSPIRACY, TORTURE, AND BETRAYAL AT U.S. CENTRAL COMMAND

By 2LT Scott Bennett 11th Psychological Operations Battalion

View this Author's Spotlight

Paperback, 180 Pages ☆☆☆☆☆   This item has not been rated yet

Price: $15.95

Prints in 3-5 business days

A true story, originally submitted as a military whistleblowing report, by an American Army Officer working in the highest levels of American military-intelligence counter-terrorism and psychological warfare.

A story about how Islamic paranoia, schizophrenic political-correctness, and blood-drunk defense contractors are crippling American military commanders, emasculating politicians, and lobotomizing counter-terrorism operations and intelligence agencies--and transforming America into a police state in the process. This is PART I of "SHELL GAME".

Preview

Ratings & Reviews | Product Details

Ratings & Reviews

Write A Review

Lulu Sales Rank: 19996
Rate This: ☆☆☆☆☆

There are no reviews for the current version of this product
> Find Reviews for Previous Versions

Product Details

ISBN	9781312361676
Copyright	Scott Bennett (Standard Copyright License)
Edition	third
Publisher	Scott Bennett
Published	November 29, 2016
Language	English
Pages	180
Binding	Perfect-bound Paperback
Interior Ink	Black & white
Weight	0.71 lbs.
Dimensions (inches)	6 wide x 9 tall

EXHIBITS: LETTERS AND REPORTS TO CONGRESS, MILITARY, AND THE MEDIA

By 2LT Scott Bennett 11th Psychological Operations Battalion

View this Author's Spotlight

Paperback, 274 Pages   This item has not been rated yet

Price: $18.50

Prints in 3-5 business days

A record of all letters written and submitted to Congress, the military, and the media about "Shell Game": the military whistleblowing reports to congress exposing the betrayal and cover-up by the u.s. government of the union bank of switzerland-terrorist threat finance connection to edward snowden's report on the national security agency, central intelligence agency, booz allen hamilton and u.s. central command.

Preview

Ratings & Reviews | Product Details

Ratings & Reviews

Log in to review this item

Lulu Sales Rank: 26785
Log in to rate this item

There are no reviews for the current version of this product
> Find Reviews for Previous Versions

Product Details

ISBN	9781312310100
Copyright	Scott Bennett (Standard Copyright License)
Edition	third
Publisher	Scott Bennett
Published	November 29, 2016
Language	English
Pages	274
Binding	Perfect-bound Paperback
Interior Ink	Black & white
Weight	1.81 lbs.
Dimensions (inches)	8.5 wide x 11 tall

Wikileaks Cables and Analysis

By Scott Bennett, Global Psychological Warfare Analyst

View this Author's Spotlight

Paperback, 68 Pages   This item has not been rated yet

WIKILEAKS CABLES:
Analysis of Swiss Bank Connection to Terrorist Financing

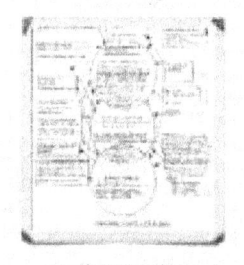

Preview

You Save: $1.25 (10%)
Prints in 3-5 business days

Examination of the Wikileaks cables indicating State Department cover-up of the Union Bank of Switzerland-Brad Birkenfeld case and its connection to international Terrorist Financing Networks and Operations involving
U.S. Central Command (General James Mattis).
The following is a record of the now public Wikileaks cables submitted to United States Members of Congress, American Military and Department of Defense officials, and the Media.
These materials serve as the historical legal record which corroborate all information contained within the official military whistleblowing reports "Shell Game", "Follow the Money", and "Terrorist Threat Finance Dimensions of the Union Bank of Switzerland (UBS) 'Whistleblower Case' and Obama Administration Involvement", submitted by 2LT Scott Bennett, U.S. Army, Civil Affairs-Psychological Operations Command.

Ratings & Reviews | Product Details

Ratings & Reviews

Write A Review

Lulu Sales Rank: 34234
Rate This:

There are no reviews for the current version of this product
> Find Reviews for Previous Versions

Secret Operations Against Daesh-ISIS-Al Qaida: The Book of Prophecy

By 2LT Scott Bennett 11th Psychological Operations Battalion (retired)

View this Author's Spotlight

Paperback, 30 Pages

This item has not been rated yet

Price: $14.50

Prints in 3-5 business days

Secret Operations Against
Daesh-ISIS-Al Qaida:
The Book of Prophecy
(Developed from CIA Special Prisoner Interrogations)

By Scott Bennett and Colonel Jeff Jones, 4th Psychological Operation Group Commander, U.S. Army (retired)

Preview

Ratings & Reviews | Product Details

Ratings & Reviews

Write A Review

Rate This:

There are no reviews for the current version of this product
> Find Reviews for Previous Versions

Product Details

Copyright	Scott Bennett (Standard Copyright License)
Edition	first
Publisher	www.shellgamewhistleblower.com
Published	September 5, 2018
Language	English
Pages	30
Binding	Saddle-stitch Paperback
Interior Ink	Black & white
Weight	0.2 lbs.
Dimensions (inches)	6 wide x 9 tall
Product ID	23787489

The 911 Truth Memos

By Robert David Steele, Editor and Scott Bennett
View this Author's Spotlight

Paperback, 132 Pages   This item has not been rated yet

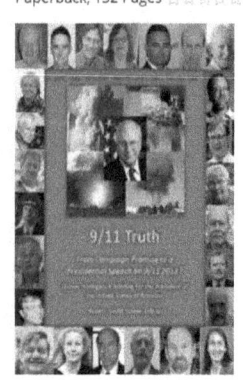

Price: $15.85
Prints in 3-5 business days

An intelligence analysis briefing to President Donald Trump about the attacks against the United States on September 11, 2001, and the evidence of government corruption, treason, and betrayal against the American people.

www.nexusstrategicanalytics.com

Preview

Add to Cart

Be the first of your friends to like this.

Ratings & Reviews | Product Details

Ratings & Reviews

Write A Review

Lulu Sales Rank: 154995
Rate This:

There are no reviews for the current version of this product
> Find Reviews for Previous Versions

Keywords

911 memos, shell game, Robert David Steele, Scott Bennett, Jim Fetzer, September 11 attacks

Listed In

MASTERING MAN: MULTIDIMENSIONAL SOCIAL SCIENCE DATA FOR HUMAN TERRAIN MAPPING AND STRATEGIC COMMUNICATIONS OPERATIONS

By 2LT Scott Bennett 11th Psychological Operations, U.S. Army (retired)

View this Author's Spotlight

Paperback, 224 Pages   This item has not been rated yet

List Price: $~~$19.95~~$
Price: $17.96
You Save: $1.99 (10%)

Prints in 3-5 business days

INTERNATIONAL SOCIAL SCIENCE DATA FOR HUMAN TERRAIN MAPPING AND STRATEGIC COMMUNICATION OPERATIONS. These are the dimensions man's spirit, mind, and body incessantly explores, and therefore the dynamics which constantly are in control of him. This means both must be harnessed in order to master man —and this book accomplishes this journey by defining and diagraming man's instincts, passions, fears, loves, dreams, religion, destiny, lust, sexuality, paradise, oblivion, death, wealth, health.

Preview

Ratings & Reviews | Product Details

Ratings & Reviews

Write A Review

Rate This:

There are no reviews for the current version of this product
› Find Reviews for Previous Versions

You Recently Viewed

Secret Operations...
By Scott Bennett, Colonel Jeff Jones, Dave Reyes Artwork by David Reyes
Paperback: $14.95

The 911 Truth Memos
By Robert David Steele, Editor, and Scott Bennett
Paperback: $15.85

Keywords
SOCIAL SCIENCE DATA

Listed In
Medicine & Science

Product Details

Copyright	Scott Bennett (Standard Copyright License)
Edition	Second
Publisher	www.shellgamewhistleblower.com
Published	September 20, 2018
Language	English
Pages	224
Binding	Perfect-bound Paperback
Interior Ink	Black & white
Weight	0.33 lbs
Dimensions (inches)	6 wide x 9 tall
Product ID	23806830

THE EPOCH TIMES
SPYGATE

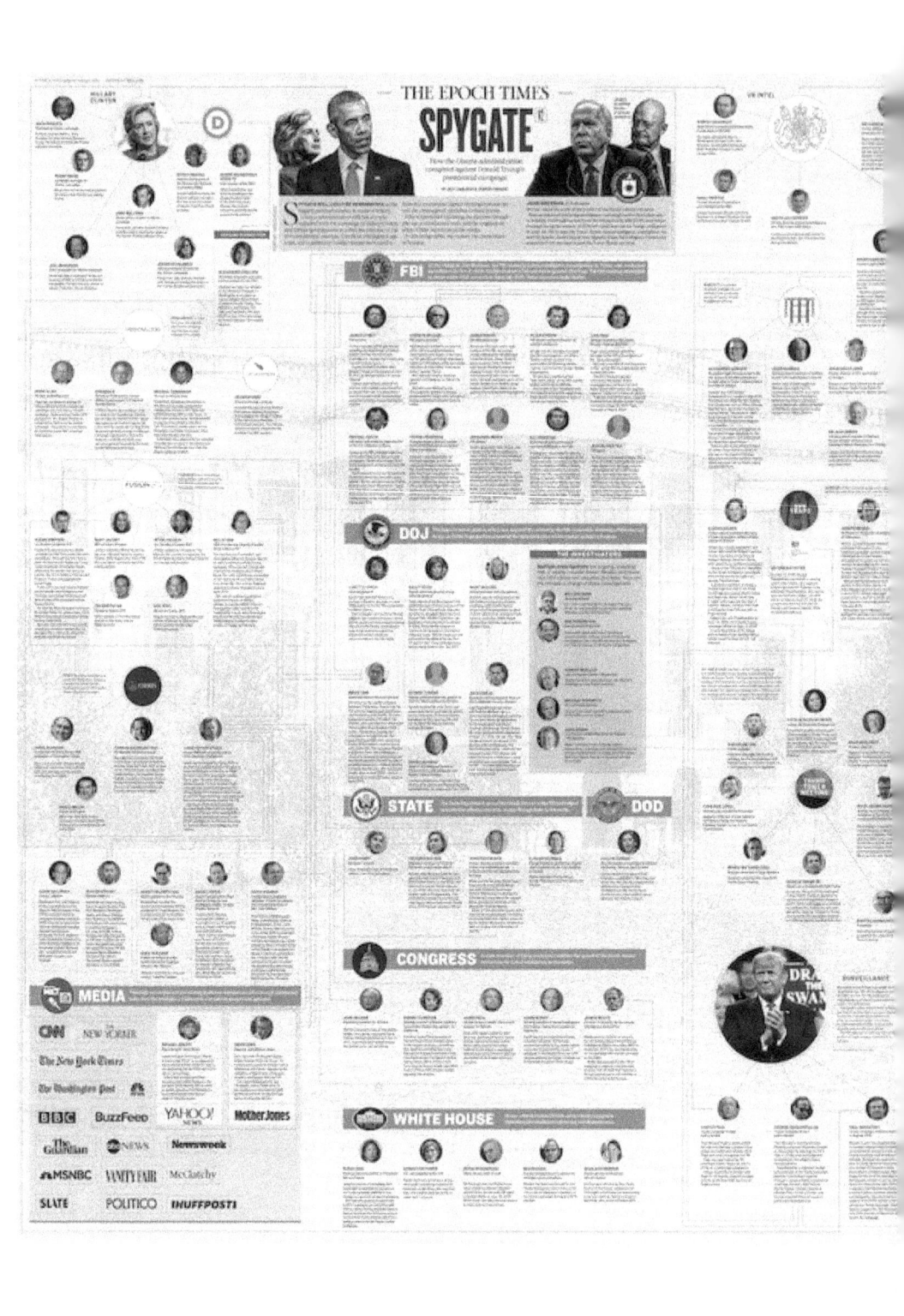

How the Obama administration conspired against Donald Trump's presidential campaign

g Back On September 11 – Scott Bennett Explores the Seventeen Year Psy Op

Americans love Putin for destroying Daesh: US analyst
THE MEDIA'S SYRIA
US helping Daesh expand its presence in West: Analyst
US has role in failed coup attempt in Turkey: Analyst
THE DEBATE
SCOTT BENNETT
US seeking to help Israeli-Saudi mercenary war in Syria: Analyst
Muslim nations: Analyst
SAN FRANCISCO
army official
US, Saudi, Israel used 9/11 to deceive the world: Analyst

Printed in the USA
CPSIA information can be obtained
at www.ICGtesting.com
LVHW091532100124
768636LV00032B/1145/J